David Remnick

Reporting

David Remnick is the editor of *The New Yorker*.
He is the author of several books, including *King
of the World* and *Lenin's Tomb*, for which he won
the Pulitzer Prize in 1994. He lives in New York
City with his wife and three children.

Reporting

WRITINGS FROM *The New Yorker*

David Remnick

Vintage Books
A Division of Random House, Inc.
New York

For Natasha, Noah, Alex, and Esther

The Library of Congress has cataloged the Knopf edition as follows:
Remnick, David.
Reporting : writings from the New Yorker / David Remnick.— 1st ed.
p. cm.
I. Title.
AC8.R453 2006
081—dc22
2005044709

Vintage ISBN: 978-0-307-27575-2

Book design by Iris Weinstein

www.vintagebooks.com

Contents

Preface

My first regular reporting job was on the night-police beat in Washington writing anonymous squibs about the catastrophes of others. A typical start, in other words. On my first night—the shift began at six and ended at two or three in the morning—I drove to D.C. police headquarters on Indiana Avenue to check out the "press room." With visions of cigar smoke, poker games, snapping typewriters, and some William Powell–type reporters making wised-up remarks about "the desk" swirling unaccountably in my mind, I found the right door, opened it, and switched on the light. The bare fluorescent tubes overhead flickered, then buzzed into being. There were a couple of gray metal desks shoved into a corner, and, on one of them, a heavyset man still wearing a hat was fast asleep, wheezing a shrill fugue from under his pea-green raincoat. Finally, stirred by the light, he rose to his feet, squinted at me, and then fumbled around for a while in a shopping bag. He retrieved two cans and shoved them in his pockets.

"Hello," he said, stepping smartly across the linoleum. "I'm the night guy for *The Washington Times*. You must be the latest *Post*-ie." He reached into his jacket and pulled out a Schlitz. "Wanna beer?"

And so I began my time in the employ of Katharine Graham, Benjamin C. Bradlee, and the Washington Post Company. On all counts, I was lucky and knew it. I was living in a small apartment in Adams-Morgan and working for a paper that still enjoyed the residual glamour of its Watergate exploits. My friendly rival from the *Times* was in the employ of the Reverend Sun Myung Moon and lived in his car—a vintage Cadillac hearse—where he spent his leisure hours reading police procedurals. My job, which I did at first with great enthusiasm, was to make a cycle of hourly telephone calls to the various city and county police departments, fire stations, and emergency rooms in the *Post*'s readership area and ask if there were any "crimes, fires, or accidents that I should know about." There often were. At the time, Washington was miserably governed, racially divided, and in the midst of the crack epidemic. The city was a perennial contender for the country's murder capital and some of the surrounding suburbs were also making a fair showing. In the event of mayhem, I was under orders either to stop by the crime scene for the details or, if it was too late, gather them by telephone. Invariably, the night editor, after being informed of the grisly facts, would say, "Two graphs. Slug it 'slay.' " His inflection was mordant but practiced, self-conscious; even on the city desk post-modernism was well under way. The literary form that embodied his instruction was as precise as a villanelle. Typically: "A Northwest man, aged 25, was shot and killed last night on the 1300 block of Florida Avenue. Police sources said they believed narcotics were involved." If there was room to fill out the drama with regional color, the streets were described either as "garbage-strewn and drug-infested" or "quiet and tree-lined."

At the *Post*, I was the opposite of a specialist. The beats to which nearly everyone aspired were on the National staff: the White House, the State Department, the Pentagon, the Hill. For the most part, I was on the margins. For the Sports department, I covered a fledgling (now deceased) football team called the Federals and, because no one any longer cared, the three-quarters-dead world of boxing. For Style, the main features department, my subjects ranged from the funeral of a Gypsy king (whose floral arrangements were dyed and constructed in the shape of a pack of Marlboros, a Glock, and a guitar) to the disappearance, and likely murder, of Shergar, the Irish racehorse. In this extended apprenticeship, I wrote for nearly every section of the paper *except* National, and when I eventually volunteered for the paper's Moscow bureau, I was sent abroad with the firm understanding that there had not been more volunteers (it is cold in Russia and the food is heavy) and that I was, in a two-person bureau, the number two.

Whatever I may have learned in that time, I cannot pretend to have developed unerring instincts—or even particularly sharp ones. By the summer of 1991, my wife, who was working for *The New York Times,* and I were packing up our apartment on Kutuzovsky Prospekt. Our term in Moscow was up. To be sure, the political atmosphere that summer was overheated: there were liberation movements on the rise from the Baltic states to Central Asia; the Communist Party was fracturing; there was a cornered-animal sense of endangerment within the KGB; there were even rumors of a coup d'état, the overthrow of Mikhail Gorbachev. One afternoon, as a kind of going-away present, Aleksandr Yakovlev, who had been Gorbachev's most trusted and liberal-minded adviser, gave me an interview and let it be known that he, too, expected a full-blown putsch. It was practically inevitable, he said. And yet there seemed no reason to over-react. Rumors of apocalypse in Moscow were a constant—if you took them all seriously you'd go out of your mind—and so a couple of days after the *Post* published my story on the Yakovlev interview, we said our goodbyes. We left Moscow. Which was a mistake. Twelve hours later, back in New York, with a television tuned to CNN, my wife and I watched a column of tanks rumbling past our apartment building. The coup had begun. The next morning I took a flight back to Sheremetyevo Airport, and then sheepishly hitched a ride to the barricades, where the anti-coup protesters were already feeling confident enough to be sticking long-stemmed carnations into the barrels of the army's machine guns. The KGB had lost the power to intimidate and the confidence to fire—at least for the moment. Two days later, the coup was finished; by Christmas, so was the Soviet Union.

Flying *away* from the scene of the crime is a journalistic felony that can be forgiven with time only if you remind yourself that even the most observant can see only hints of a large event as it is happening. Take George Orwell, every reporter's hero. As a soldier in the Spanish Civil War—a soldier who went to war as both a political idealist and a self-conscious writer—Orwell could not always discern the shape of the conflict, the factional politics in Barcelona and Madrid, the movement of troops, the involvement of foreign powers. Certainly not when he was living in a trench. It was dark and miserable there and he was blinkered, ignorant of nearly everything outside of the hole in which he lived. He could record the feel of *his* war, the cold, the rain, the filth, the lack of fuel, the lice, what it was like to be shot at, and what it was like to look down the barrel of your own rifle at another human being and fire. The political analysis, the considered judgments—they could be filled in later.

The pieces collected here—all written for *The New Yorker,* where I have worked since 1992—attempt to see someone up close, if only for a moment in time: Aleksandr Solzhenitsyn as he packed his bags to return to Russia, Václav Havel as he prepared to end his magical career as President and leave Prague Castle. Some of my favorite Profile writers, including the magazine's two great Joes, Liebling and Mitchell, often wrote about people who were distinctly unfamous and were free with their time. The results of that work, the human, emotional material, often ran as deep as the best fiction. My subjects here tend to be more elusive. They are figures in the public arena, people who are in the midst of a crisis, passing out of one, or anticipating one on the horizon. They are, with some exceptions, people obsessed with altering the history of their era or recording it. Their time was usually limited and sometimes grudgingly provided. They had reputations to protect, public and private agendas to consider, sometimes even a machinery of public relations to keep reporters at bay. The hope, as well as the vanity, is that eventually even public figures will let down their guard, they will be themselves, they will cross the line. Generally speaking, they do what they can to make sure that does not happen.

Part I

The Wilderness Campaign: Al Gore

"Hey, Dwayne? . . . Dwayne?"
"Yes, Mr. Vice-President?"
"Could I have some more coffee?"
"Yes, Mr. Vice-President. Coming . . ."
"Thanks, Dwayne."

It was ten in the morning in Nashville, a quiet weekday, with most of the neighbors off to work, and Albert Gore, Jr., sat at the head of his dining-room table eating breakfast. His plate was crowded with scrambled eggs, bacon, toast. His pond-size mug had, in a flash, been refilled by Dwayne Kemp, his cook, a skilled and graceful man who had been employed by the Gores when, as his boss often puts it, "we were still working in the White House." Freshly showered and shaved, Gore was wearing a midnight-blue shirt and gray wool trousers. In the months after losing the battle for Florida's electoral votes and conceding the Presidency to George W. Bush, on December 13, 2000, Gore seemed to let himself go, dropping out of sight, traveling around Spain, Italy, and

Greece for six weeks with his wife, Tipper. He wore dark glasses and a baseball cap tugged down low. He grew a mountain-man beard and gained weight. When he began appearing in public again, mainly in classrooms, he took to introducing himself by saying, "Hi, I'm Al Gore. I used to be the next President of the United States." People looked at this rather bulky and hirsute man—a politician who had only recently won 50,999,897 votes for the Presidency, more than any Democrat in history, more than any candidate in history except Ronald Reagan in 1984, and more than half a million more votes than the man who assumed the office—and did not know quite what to feel or how to behave, and so they cooperated in his elaborate self-deprecations. They laughed at his jokes, as if to help him erase what everyone understood to be a disappointment of historic proportions—"the heartbreak of a life-time," as Karenna, the eldest of his four children, put it.

"You know the old saying," Gore told one audience after another. "You win some, you lose some—and then there's that little-known third category."

Gore has since dispensed with the beard but not the weight. He is still thick around the middle. He eats quickly and thoroughly, and with a determined relish, precisely like a man who no longer has to care that he might look heavy on *Larry King Live*. "You want some eggs?" he asked. "Dwayne's the best."

This has been the first election season in a generation in which Al Gore has not pursued national office. He ran for President in 1988, when he was thirty-nine; for Vice-President, on Bill Clinton's ticket, in 1992 and 1996; and then again for President in 2000. Having decided that a rematch against Bush would be too divisive (or, perhaps, too difficult), Gore has made an effort not to brood on the sidelines. Instead, he used words like "liberated" and "free" with a determined conviction to describe his inner condition. He was free of the burden, free of the pressure, free of the camera's eye. At home in Nashville, the phone barely rang. There were no advance people at the door, no aides at his shoulder. He could say what he wanted and it hardly made a ripple in the media. If he felt like calling George Bush a "moral coward," if he felt like comparing Guantánamo and Abu Ghraib to islands in an "American gulag" or the President's media operatives to "digital Brown Shirts," well, he just went ahead and did it. No worries, no hesitation. True, at noon at the Belcourt Theatre, he was to deliver a speech to a group called the Music Row Democrats, but the only cameras were likely to be local. He jokingly outlined the speech on a small notepad with just two words: "war" and "economy."

When Al and Tipper Gore had recovered from the initial shock of the

2000 election, they spent $2.3 million on the house they live in now: a hundred-year-old colonial on Lynwood Boulevard, in the Belle Meade section of Nashville. They still own a place in Arlington, Virginia—a house that was built by Tipper's grandfather—and a ninety-acre cattle farm in the Gore family seat of Carthage, Tennessee; but Arlington was perilously close to Washington, and Carthage was too remote for a full-time residence, especially for Tipper. Belle Meade, which resembles Buckhead, in Atlanta, or Mountain Brook, near Birmingham, is a prosperous redoubt for businessmen and country-music stars; it encompasses a neighborhood of broad, sloping lawns, and houses with magnolia trees and "estate" driveways up front and glassy modern additions and swimming pools out back. Chet Atkins used to be a neighbor; Leon Russell still is. Some of the features of the house, which the couple expanded with the help of an architect, are distinctly Gore-ish: Tipper's full drum set, in the living room (complete with congas); Al's grip-and-grin photographs with the Clintons and world leaders, along the walls. There are fewer books and more televisions than you might expect. When the architect was designing the rear addition to the house, Gore asked him to curve the walls inward in two places in order to save several trees. "The trees weren't anything special, nothing rare or anything," he said. "I just couldn't bear to bring 'em down." In the backyard, around the patio and the extra-long pool, where Al and Tipper do laps, Gore also installed an anti-bug system that sprays a fine mist of ground chrysanthemums from various discreet sources: a tree trunk, a patio wall. "The mosquitoes just hate it," he said. Other features of the house are less environmentally correct. A 2004 black Cadillac, which Gore drives, was parked in the driveway. A '65 Mustang—a Valentine's Day gift from Al to Tipper—was parked in the garage.

Gore finished his eggs. He walked to a covered patio on the side of the house and settled into a soft chair. Dwayne brought his coffee cup and refilled it.

Gore has hardly been a recluse since deciding, in late 2002, not to run again. In the past year, he has delivered a series of speeches in New York and Washington sharply criticizing the Bush Administration, but he has answered few questions. "It's better that way for a while," he said. He has given speeches for money all around the world. And he is teaching courses, mainly about the intersection of community and the American family, at Middle Tennessee State University, in Murfreesboro, and Fisk University, in Nashville.

"We've got about forty hours of lectures and classes on tape," Gore said, deadpan. "Now's your chance to watch them."

Gore is beginning to make serious money. He is a board member for Apple and a senior adviser to Google, which just went through its IPO. He has also been working on creating a cable-television station and developing a financial enterprise.

"I'm having a blast," he said.

In a parliamentary system, a candidate for Prime Minister, after losing an election, often returns to a prominent seat in parliament. It doesn't work that way in the United States. Here, you make your own way: you give speeches, write memoirs, accumulate a fortune, find a righteous cause. Sometimes a reporter might come calling, but not often. In any case, Donna Brazile, Gore's campaign manager in 2000, said, "When it was over, the Democratic Party kicked him to the curb," preferring to forget not only the Florida catastrophe but also Gore's own misplays: his mutating personality in the three debates with Bush; his reliance on political consultants; his inability to exploit Bill Clinton's enduring popularity and his failure to win Clinton's Arkansas, much less Tennessee; his decision not to press immediately for a statewide recount in Florida. Now, everywhere he goes, Gore is faced with crowds who despair of the Bush Administration and see in him all that might have been, all the what-ifs. *The heartbreak of a lifetime.* Sometimes people approach him and address him as "Mr. President." Some try to cheer him up and tell him, "We know you really won." Some tilt their heads, affecting a look of grave sympathy, as if he had just lost a family member. He has to face not only his own regrets; he is forever the mirror of others'. A lesser man would have done far worse than grow a beard and put on a few pounds.

More than Franklin Roosevelt, or even John F. Kennedy, Gore was raised to be President. His father, Albert Gore, Sr., a senator who was known to look as noble as a Roman statesman, expected it of him. When Gore's mother was pregnant with Al, Gore Senior told the editors of the Nashville *Tennessean* that if his wife gave birth to a boy he didn't want to see the story tucked deep in the paper. After Al was born, the headline read, WELL, MR. GORE, HERE HE IS, ON PAGE 1. Six years later, the Senator planted a story in the *Knoxville News Sentinel* about how young Al had coaxed his father into buying him a more expensive bow-and-arrow set than they had planned to get. "There may be another Gore on the way toward the political pinnacle," the story said. "He's just six years old now. But with his experiences to date, who knows what may happen." By the time Gore made it to Harvard (the only school he applied to), he was informing his class of his ultimate ambition. His first run, in 1988, after he had spent just a few years in the Senate, was less an act of youthful presumption than a hurried attempt to win the White House in his father's lifetime.

Gore is fifty-six years old. After the 2000 race was finally resolved, some of the people around him consoled him by telling him to "remember Richard Nixon," how Nixon lost the Presidential race in 1960, lost the California governorship in 1962—informing the press that it would no longer have him to "kick around anymore"—and then came back to win the White House in 1968. Somehow, when that advice is mentioned to Gore today, it is neither consoling nor enticing. If John Kerry wins in November, that would likely spell the end of Gore's career in national politics; if Kerry loses, there would still be strong figures in a prospective field for 2008, not least John Edwards and Hillary Clinton.

"Basically, the answer is, I do not expect to ever be a candidate again," Gore said. "I really don't. The second part of the answer is, I haven't ruled it out completely. And the third qualifier is, I don't add the second part as a way of signaling coyness. It's merely to complete an honest answer to the question and it in no way changes the principal part of the answer. Which is, I really do not expect that I will be a candidate. If I did expect to be a candidate again, I would probably not feel the same freedom to let it rip in these speeches the way I am. And I enjoy that. It feels"—and there was that word again—"it feels liberating to me." Running again for the Senate or accepting a Cabinet position, he said, was also out of the question.

Gore, along with no small part of the country, is convinced that had things turned out differently in Florida in 2000, had the conservatives on the Supreme Court not outnumbered the liberals by a single vote, the United States would not be in the condition it's in: the front page would not be describing chaos in Iraq, record budget deficits, the roll-back of numerous environmental initiatives, a diminishment of civil liberties, a curtailment of stem-cell research, an erosion of American prestige abroad. Gore does not admit to any bitterness, but it is plain in nearly every speech he gives; and while the feeling may be partly personal—who could blame him?—it runs to a deeper, more public-minded sentiment than the disappointment of his own, or his father's, ambitions.

"Here you have a guy who worked all his life to achieve the one thing he wanted—to be President of the United States—and it was there, in his grasp," Tony Coelho, Gore's campaign chairman in 2000, said. "He felt Clinton hurt him, but nevertheless he worked his butt off and brought it off. He won the most votes, by half a million, but then the Supreme Court steps in and it's gone. It is hard for any of us to understand what that means or how it feels. The truth is that Gore is really a policy guy, not a political guy, and for him to feel that he was on the cusp of the ultimate policy job, that he could affect policy and the world like no one else, and then nothing—well, imagine that!"

In a little while, a new friend of Gore's, an eccentric musician and visual artist named Robert Ellis Orrall, was going to swing by to take him and Tipper to the Belcourt.

"You'll like Bob," Gore said, smiling. "But I'm warning you: he does his own thing. He's a crazy kinda guy."

Gore delivered that last sentence in what I came to think of as his Mr. Goofy voice. When he wants to undercut something he is saying, to indicate that he knows he is speaking in a cliché or taking on a stentorian or pompous tone, he uses the Mr. Goofy voice, stretching his face into a kind of clownish expression and affecting a tone more suited to a television dinosaur. Then, there is the Herr Professor voice, Gore as lecturer. Gore didn't really want to talk politics at first, but when the subject of the press came up he seized on it and gave, at my best estimation, a twenty-minute discourse on the degradation of "the public sphere," a phrase coined by the German philosopher Jürgen Habermas in the nineteen-sixties. (One tries, and fails, to imagine the current President alluding to the author of *Moral Consciousness and Communicative Action.*) "He's a ve-rrry interesting guy," Gore said. "Why am I just finding out about him?"

It's easy to see that Gore, lacking public office, likes to teach. In his uninterrupted answer, he mentioned the brain-imaging center at New York University; *The Alphabet Versus the Goddess,* by Leonard Shlain; *Broca's Brain,* by Carl Sagan; an Op-Ed piece in the *Times* about the decline of reading in America, by Andrew Solomon; the lack of research on the relation between the brain and television—"There is just *nothing* on the dendrite level about watching television"; Gutenberg and the rise of print; the sovereign rule of reason in the Enlightenment; individualism—"a term first used by de Tocqueville to describe America in the eighteen-thirties"; Thomas Paine; Benjamin Franklin. "O.K., now fast-forward through the telegraph, the phonograph." O.K., but we *didn't* fast-forward: first, there was Samuel Morse, who failed to hear the news of his wife's dying while he was painting a portrait—"You know, he has a painting in the White House, if I remember correctly"— and therefore went out and invented a faster means of communication. "Now fast-forward again to Marconi . . . now that's an interesting story"; the sinking of the *Titanic;* David Sarnoff; the agricultural origin of the term "broadcast"; moving right along to "the nineteen visual centers of the brain"; an article on "flow" in *Scientific American;* the "orienting reflex" in vertebrates; the poignancy and "ultimate failure" of political demonstrations as a means of engaging the aforementioned public sphere—"I mean, what do you really have? A crowd of people holding posters with five words on them at most hoping for a TV camera to come along for a few seconds of airtime?"—and, finally, Gore's own 1969 Harvard thesis, on the effect of television on the Presidency and the rise, at about that time, of image over print as a means of transmitting news. This was all a way to talk about the cable-television station that he is developing.

"What kind of station will it be?" I asked.

"Well, I really can't talk about it," he said. "Not yet."

What Gore does care to talk about, and what he has talked about openly and in language shocking in its contrast with his old stilted caution, are the failures of the man who prevailed in 2000.

"You're free to speak clearly," I offered.

"I'm unplugged," he said.

A few minutes later, Robert Ellis Orrall arrived. A charming man in his late forties with close-cropped hair and an earring, Orrall has a vibrant sense of performance, insofar as he is always performing. He began telling jokes the moment he arrived, and Gore seemed to relax completely in his presence.

Tipper Gore, wearing a cotton sweater and hot-pink pants, came out on the patio to greet Orrall.

"How *are* you, Bob?"

"Just fine, Tipper, but a little nervous. They asked me to introduce Al at this thing, so I've got this little speech . . ."

A slight breeze of anxiety riffled Gore's features. Orrall gave every indication of being an unpredictable stage presence. It was one thing to clown around on the patio, quite another when you're introducing the former Vice-President in front of a few hundred supporters.

"I hope you, um, wrote it down, Bob," Gore said.

"I got it right here," Orrall said, patting his pocket.

The four of us walked out to the driveway and climbed into Orrall's car, an incommodious Volkswagen Golf. The former Vice-President opened the front door, fastidiously folded in half, and inserted himself through the narrow space available, as if through a mail slot. Once inside, he shifted his legs, zigging them up and to the right, forming with them what seemed to be an especially complicated letter in the Cyrillic alphabet. Then he very slowly closed the door on himself. There were no major injuries. Tipper climbed in back.

Orrall steered out of the driveway and headed toward the theater. There were no sirens, no trail cars besides the normal run of traffic.

Gore smiled and said, "Bob, you could pretend like you're Secret Service, but you'd have to be wearing an earpiece instead of an earring."

"I'll do my best," Orrall said.

"Please do!" Mr. Goofy said.

Orrall is a performer of parts, and one of them is as "Bob Something," the chief songwriter and singer for a farcical band called Monkey Bowl. Monkey Bowl might be described as a cross between the Fugs and Ali G.

As we drove, Orrall produced a Monkey Bowl CD titled *Plastic Three-Fifty,* which listed such songs as "Stupid Man Things," "Hip Hop the Bunny," and "Books Suck." The second cut on the disk was called, simply, "Al Gore."

Not long after they met, through a mutual friend, Orrall played an early version of the song for Gore. Gore liked it so much that he added a touch of his own.

"Let's play it," Orrall said, and he slipped it into his CD player. After an infectious string of guitar chords and backbeat, Orrall started singing:

> *Al Gore lives on my street,*
> *Three-twenty-something, Lynwood Boulevard.*
> *And, he doesn't know me*
> *but I voted for him. Yeah, I punched the card!*
> *I don't know how he lives with knowing,*
> *That even though he won the popular vote*
> *He still lives on my street, right down the street*
> *From me.*

Soon, everyone in the car started laughing, maybe Gore most of all, and Tipper was whacking her palm against her knee in time with the drums:

> *One time, I had a bike*
> *And I was a kid, and someone stole it from me*
> *And still I'm mad about that,*
> *Carrying anger, I just can't let it be.*
> *I need to be more forgiving, I know it,*
> *'Cause even with the popular vote,*
> *Al Gore lives on my street, right down the street,*
> *From me.*

After another verse comically contrasting Orrall's childhood defeat and self-pity to Gore's historical disappointment and recovery, the chorus takes its climactic turn:

> *Life isn't fair, don't tell me, I know it*
> *'Cause even with the popular vote,*
> *Al Gore lives on my street, right down the street from me [repeats]*
> *President Gore lives on my street, right down the street from me.*

Finally, the song seemed to be ending, but then came the voice of Gore himself: "Hey, man, I like your song, but you need to get over all that stuff. Hey, this is a great neighborhood!"

Everyone applauded, and Orrall kept driving.

After a while, we started talking about Michael Moore's movie *Fahrenheit 9/11*, and the opening scenes, which show perhaps the most painful scene in Gore's political life—the day he had to preside over a joint session of Congress in his role as President of the Senate as it certified the votes of the Electoral College, a process that was repeatedly interrupted by various African-American members of the House who tried, and failed, to gain the floor and object to the proceedings. It was Gore, of course, who had to follow the rules of order and send them to their seats, all the while knowing that his defense of decorum and law would be seen as a kind of self-flagellation, a defense of a man he disdained, or would come to disdain.

"It's unbelievable, that scene," Orrall said.

There was a long pause, and then Gore said, "We haven't had a chance to see it yet. We were on vacation when it came out." Gore made it sound as if he had missed an opportunity to see *Harold & Kumar Go to White Castle*, but Tipper said, "I'm not sure I could watch it."

Gore remarked that he had been on Al Franken's radio show not long ago. "I called in from Nashville," he said. The guest was Michael Moore.

Franken went into his New Age therapist Stuart Smalley routine, and, with both Gore and Moore on the line, said, "Now, Michael, is there something you'd like to say to the Vice-President?"

In 2000, Moore and others on the left gave support to the third-party candidacy of Ralph Nader, who was campaigning on the notion that there was no difference between Gore and Bush. Without Nader in the race, Gore would likely have won the Presidency, even excluding Florida.

"We're really sorry, Al," Moore said.

Gore laughed as he recalled the story: "I gave it a big pause and said, 'For what, Michael?' And then he gave a whole complicated explanation about how he was voting in New York State, which wasn't in play, and how Nader had promised not to campaign in any swing states, and blah-blah-blah. So I said, 'That sounds *aw-fully* complicated, Michael.' " (Afterward, I listened to the exchange on the Internet. Franken remarked that it was really "not a full-on apology" and Moore made sure to tell Gore, "You're more liberal than you were four years ago.") Later, Gore told me, "I did see *Bowling for Columbine.* I really appreciate what he's trying to do, but I wouldn't have thought before seeing the movie that anyone could have aroused any sympathy in me for Charlton Heston. And yet he did. . . . I'm sure there is some of that in *Fahrenheit 9/11.*"

Orrall pulled the VW into the parking lot of the Belcourt Theatre. Someone pointed him in the direction of a space that had been saved with an orange traffic cone.

"Hey!" Gore said. "We've got an orange cone!"

As the Gores went through a side door, they met Bob Titley, one of the co-founders of the Music Row Democrats. Nashville is a center of the music industry, and the area around Sixteenth Avenue, where all the main recording and publishing companies have their offices, is called Music Row. For the most part, the country-music business is Republican. But there have always been exceptions, as when one of the Dixie Chicks said, last year, that she was ashamed of having Bush as President. When the Dixie Chicks were roundly denounced, a number of executives and songwriters in Nashville decided to start the new group.

"Is there any reason you haven't invited me to one of your Kerry-oke nights?" Gore asked Titley.

"We were saving you for a really big night," he said.

Orrall took the stage, plugged a performance he was making that evening at a local club, the Bluebird Café, and efficiently introduced the day's speaker. "He won the popular vote . . . and he lives down the street from me!" Gore, who was now wearing a jacket and tie, came out to a standing ovation, and he was smiling broadly and waving and doing that mouthing-gratitude-delightedly-pointing-out-friends-in-the-crowd thing that politicians do. He had torn into the Bush Administration quite often lately, and he knew well the particulars of his indictment.

When the crowd finally quieted down, he thanked a few people and said, "Hello. I'm Al Gore, and I used to be the next President of the United States."

Everyone laughed. He kept his practiced deadpan. "I don't find that particularly funny," he said.

Everyone laughed again. "Put yourself in my position. I flew on *Air Force Two* for eight years. Now I have to take off my shoes to get on an airplane.

"Not long ago, I was on Interstate 40 going from here to Carthage. We were driving ourselves. I looked in the rearview mirror. There was no motorcade. You heard of phantom-limb pain?" At around dinnertime, at the Lebanon exit, he went on, the Gores found a Shoney's—"a low-cost family restaurant"—and the waitress made a fuss over Tipper and then went to the next booth and said, "He's come down a long way, hasn't he?" Not long afterward, Gore said, he flew to Nigeria on a Gulfstream V to give a speech on energy. In that speech, he told the story about what had happened at dinner back in Tennessee, carefully explaining what a Shoney's was. On the way home from Africa, the plane stopped to refuel in the Azores. While Gore was waiting on the tarmac, a man came running with an urgent message, "Mr. Vice-President! You have to call Washington!" and handed him some wire copy.

"I wondered what could be wrong in Washington," Gore said. "Then I realized—a whole *bunch* of things."

It turned out that a reporter in Lagos had mixed things up and written a story saying that Gore had "opened a low-cost family restaurant called Shoney's."

Well, Gore said, "later, I got a letter from Bill Clinton saying, 'Congratulations on the new restaurant.' See, we like to celebrate each other's successes."

Gore has masked his outrage about the 2000 election with a distinct blend of uncomplaining poise and media-age irony which keeps him separate in our minds from the three men in American history who have shared his peculiar fate: Andrew Jackson, Grover Cleveland, and Samuel Tilden.

When Jackson lost the election in 1824 to John Quincy Adams despite winning the popular vote, he never ceased charging fraud and raging against the "cheating and corruption and bribery" of the system, to say nothing of the treachery of Henry Clay, who traded his own electors to Adams for the office of Secretary of State. Four years later, Jackson ran again and won.

Cleveland, running for reelection in 1888, lost the electoral vote to Benjamin Harrison but quickly assured his supporters that he would be redeemed. Take care of the furnishings in the White House, his wife, Frances, told staffers—we'll be back. Cleveland gained his second term, and his revenge, four years later.

Tilden was different. A New York Democrat, Samuel Tilden was a reform-minded governor who made a high-minded challenge to Rutherford B. Hayes in 1876. Tilden seemed the clear winner of the popular vote, but when disputed returns came in from four states, particularly Florida, Congress appointed a special electoral commission, which was controlled, in the main, by the Republican Party. The commission voted on partisan lines to give Hayes the electoral votes in question, and Tilden lost. He was viewed as intelligent but awkward and remote; he was criticized for being too weak, too hesitant to challenge the commission with the necessary ferocity. Instead of pressing the case politically, he decamped to Europe, and eventually retreated to Graystone, his estate in Yonkers. Faced with the decision of whether to run in 1880, Tilden wrote a letter declining: "I desire nothing so much as an honorable discharge." He rarely left Graystone, and died in 1886. On Tilden's tombstone was engraved "I Still Trust the People."

Al Gore handled his defeat and, ultimately, his decision to stay out of the 2004 Presidential race in ways that echoed Tilden's. After the Supreme Court decision, and after Gore decided not to pursue a "scorched earth" strategy of undermining Bush's legitimacy in the press and in the courts, he gave a concession speech on December 13, 2000, that will be remembered as demonstrating nearly perfect equanimity and pitch, a speech that exalted the rule of law and seemed to go a long way toward cooling the public war and his own inner rage. To write that speech, Gore drew on the bitter defeat in 1970 of Al Gore, Sr., at the hands of a race-baiting opponent. "As for the battle that ends tonight," he said, "I do believe, as my father once said, that no matter how hard the loss, defeat might serve as well as victory to shape the soul and let the glory out."

Gore's tone was elegiac, but, like Tilden, he still faced a decision, and it was solely within the Gore family that the decision would be made. Even during the campaign, Gore was surrounded mainly by paid professionals, not loyalists. And, afterward, his circle, such as it was, fractured and went its own way. Unlike Clinton, who could draw on a huge pool of friends for advice, Gore lacked the gift, or the patience, for showing gratitude, for keeping in close touch. Donna Brazile complained that she had never got so much as a thank-you note for her service in 2000, and many who had worked for Gore or who had given serious money to the campaign reported similar experiences. "He treated people poorly," said Robert Bauer, one of Gore's aides during the Florida battle. "He was cold, aloof, condescending, ungrateful. There were legendary stories about how he treated people with a lack of gratitude. There is a strange character in Gore. . . . He is an isolated man." Other aides were less harsh, saying that Gore was brusque and demanding but not unkind. Yet, once freed of the apparatus and the requirements of a political campaign, Gore really did savor his time alone, thinking, reading, writing speeches, surfing the Internet. "One thing about Gore personally is that he is an introvert," another former aide said. "Politics was a horrible career choice for him. He should have been a college professor or a scientist or an engineer. He would have been happier. He finds dealing with other people draining. And so he has trouble keeping up his relations with people. The classical difference between an introvert and an extrovert is that if you send an introvert into a reception or an event with a hundred other people he will emerge with less energy than he had going in. An extrovert will come out of that event energized, with more energy than he had going in. Gore needs a rest after an event; Clinton would leave invigorated, because dealing with people came naturally to him."

Gore ran for President in the shadow of Clinton: in the shadow of Clinton's talents and his mistakes—most of all, the affair with Monica Lewinsky, the supreme gift to the Republican opposition. After it became clear that Clinton had lied to his wife, to Gore, to everyone, that he had, in fact, carried on the affair, the Clinton-Gore relationship, which had been more formal than advertised, collapsed nearly into silence. Gore's choice for his running mate, Joe Lieberman, was heavily influenced by Lieberman's moral denunciations of Clinton.

"I could not persuade Gore to use Clinton," Tony Coelho, the campaign chairman, said. "Gore felt strongly that there were people who wouldn't support him if he did. To a great extent, Clinton was dismissive of his own errors. So, to him, infidelity was not that big of an issue. To Al

Gore, it meant something. Al is a loyal and committed husband to Tipper. They are like teenagers in love, so the act was not to be dismissed. For him, it was real. He felt that Clinton had never publicly owned up to it. They would meet—Clinton and Gore—because we would schedule things. It was strained, even hostile at times. Al is a guy who would rather deal head-on than pretend, and he tried that with Clinton. Clinton would just as soon laugh it off and move on."

Not long after September 11, 2001, Gore visited Clinton in Chappaqua, New York. Their fallen relationship now seemed repaired. Nearly everyone in the Gore camp still believes that Clinton dearly wanted to see his Vice-President succeed him, but some suspect that he was not entirely displeased that the defeat left more room on the political stage for Hillary in 2008. The relationship between Gore and Hillary had long been complicated, sometimes cool.

In the summer of 2001, Gore had ended his silence and launched a public critique of the Bush Administration with a speech in Florida. However, after the terror attacks, he declared Bush "my Commander-in-Chief," a gesture meant to promote unity and not offend the national mood. But by September 2002, as the Bush Administration started its march toward a war in Iraq, Gore ended his discretion with a withering speech at the Commonwealth Club, in San Francisco, aimed at the Administration's foreign policy. Gore, who was one of the few Democrats to vote in favor of the 1991 resolution in Congress endorsing the first Gulf War, now said that an American-led invasion of Iraq would undermine the attempt to dismantle Al Qaeda and damage the multilateral ties necessary to combat terrorism:

> If we quickly succeed in a war against the weakened and depleted fourth-rate military of Iraq, and then quickly abandon that nation, as President Bush has quickly abandoned almost all of Afghanistan after defeating a fifth-rate military power there, then the resulting chaos in the aftermath of a military victory in Iraq could easily pose a far greater danger to the United States than we presently face from Saddam.

Gore's challenge to the Bush White House to present real evidence of a link between Saddam Hussein and 9/11 was, in both tone and substance, more critical than any speech yet delivered by the candidates in the Democratic field. Suddenly, the prospect of a Gore candidacy hit the media in a wave.

"I wasn't surprised by Bush's economic policies, but I was surprised by the foreign policy, and I think he was, too," Gore told me. "The real distinction of this Presidency is that, at its core, he is a very weak man. He projects himself as incredibly strong, but behind closed doors he is incapable of saying no to his biggest financial supporters and his coalition in the Oval Office. He's been shockingly malleable to Cheney and Rumsfeld and Wolfowitz and the whole New American Century bunch. He was rolled in the immediate aftermath of 9/11. He was too weak to resist it.

"I'm not of the school that questions his intelligence," Gore went on. "There are different kinds of intelligence, and it's arrogant for a person with one kind of intelligence to question someone with another kind. He certainly is a master at some things, and he has a following. He seeks strength in simplicity. But, in today's world, that's often a problem. I don't think that he's weak intellectually. I think that he is incurious. It's astonishing to me that he'd spend an hour with his incoming Secretary of the Treasury and not ask him a single question. But I think his weakness is a moral weakness. I think he is a bully, and, like all bullies, he's a coward when confronted with a force that he's fearful of. His reaction to the extravagant and unbelievably selfish wish list of the wealthy interest groups that put him in the White House is obsequious. The degree of obsequiousness that is involved in saying 'Yes, yes, yes, yes, yes' to whatever these people want, no matter the damage and harm done to the nation as a whole—that can come only from genuine moral cowardice. I don't see any other explanation for it, because it's not a question of principle. The only common denominator is each of the groups has a lot of money that they're willing to put in service to his political fortunes and their ferocious and unyielding pursuit of public policies that benefit them at the expense of the nation."

The rumors were that Gore would choose whether or not he would challenge Bush before the end of 2002. History will record that he declared his non-candidacy not on December 15, on *60 Minutes,* but, rather, a day earlier, when he appeared as the guest host of *Saturday Night Live.* In the opening monologue, Gore said, "The good news about not being President is that I have my weekends free. The bad news is that my weekdays are also free. But I just want to say at the outset, tonight is not about rehashing things from the past. I mean, we all know there are things I should have done differently in the 2000 campaign. Maybe at times I was too wooden and stiff and I sighed too much and people said I was too patronizing. Patronizing, of course, means talking to people like they're stupid."

In a sketch that parodied his selection process for a Vice-Presidential candidate, Gore was soaking in a hot tub with "Joe Lieberman." Al Franken, playing a self-help therapist in another sketch, told Gore that, when he was in his bearded phase, "I think it's pretty clear that you were in a humongous shame spiral." And, later, with Martin Sheen showing him around the soundstage of *The West Wing,* Gore settled dreamily into the President's chair on the Oval Office set.

"Say, John," Gore asked John Spencer, who plays the chief of staff. "Could you do me a small favor?"

"Of course."

"I'm going to stand here at the window with my back to you and I'd like you to step up to the desk and say, 'Mr. President, the Joint Chiefs want an answer.'"

These were not the stunts of a man preparing to run for national office.

The next night, dressed in a proper suit and wearing a properly sober expression, Gore made it official. He told Lesley Stahl, "I've come to closure on this." A rematch with Bush, Gore felt, would be counterproductive; it would focus too much on 2000. Others around Gore accepted that but also said that Bush seemed popular, even unbeatable at the time. In the *Times* the next morning, Katharine Seelye, a reporter who had tormented Gore during the campaign with what he thought was her endless sniping at his gaffes, real and imagined, declared Al Gore "liberated."

At the Belcourt Theatre, after the opening volley of self-deflations, Gore moved on from praise of the "Clinton-Gore Administration" to a scathing critique of the Bush Administration. He rehearsed all the themes that had obsessed him for many months: the headlong rush to war, the manipulation of intelligence, the rollback of civil liberties, the "shame" and "betrayal" of Abu Ghraib, the exploitation of the war to manipulate the election campaign. ("He's . . . *using* the war! *Using* the division! *Fostering* the fear!") The one new spice of the day was a denunciation of Bush's nominee to head the CIA, Porter Goss, who had attacked John Kerry on the floor of the House of Representatives. Goss, Gore declared, was an inadmissibly partisan choice.

Gore's main policy speeches, which have been organized by Move On.org and the American Constitution Society for Law and Policy, are stripped of the sort of pedantry that sometimes wanders into his conversation. For the most part, they are cogent presentations of the anti-Bush critique familiar to readers of the more liberal editorial pages and columnists. What gives them their added force is the speaker himself, the authority of his having won the popular vote, and his Senate and White House credentials on foreign policy, the environment, and nuclear proliferation.

When I saw Gore deliver one of these speeches in Washington, and when I watched the others on tape, he was far less formal and awkward than he had been during the 2000 campaign. The shadow of Clinton's preternatural performance skills hangs over Gore (just as it does now over Kerry), and here and there, in an effort to show passion, Gore turns his volume dial a little into the feverish zone. He begins to shout, to sweat, to meander past the borderline of passion into the wilderness of hysteria. But only rarely. Those overheated moments, of course, were the ones featured most prominently not only on Fox but on CNN, where Soledad O'Brien informed viewers with all due objectivity that Gore had indulged himself in a public "rant."

Gore's Republican and conservative critics were both ferocious and mocking. The news outlets owned by Rupert Murdoch were especially quick to show Gore at his sweatiest, and quoted his most incendiary language. Writing in the *New York Post*, John Podhoretz declared, "It is now clear that Al Gore is insane. . . . A man who was very, very nearly President of the United States has been reduced to sounding like one of those people in Times Square with a megaphone screaming about God's justice." David Frum, a former speechwriter for Bush, wrote of Gore's "emotional deterioration" and suggested that he "ought to seek out for his own good a cool and quiet darkened room." And Charles Krauthammer, a columnist for *The Washington Post* who was once a practicing psychiatrist, went on Fox News Channel's *Special Report* and delivered a diagnosis: "It looks as if Al Gore has gone off his lithium again."

Among Gore's allies, the reaction was mainly positive, but not purely so. One said that Gore was "playing both ends of the game," combining the "MoveOn.org shtick" and a new life in big banking. "The speeches make me sick," the friend said, pointing especially to the use of "gulag" to describe American-run prisons. "I can't imagine a scenario of return. He's linked himself to the extreme left wing of the Party with these speeches. He'd say it's not true, but it is." That tends to be the view of some who put faith in Gore's New Democrat half, the Gore who was tough on deficit spending and ready to use the big stick in Bosnia and Kosovo. But most of his allies, the more liberal and the more forgiving ones, endorsed the tone of the attack as precisely what his speeches four years ago lacked: clarity, conviction, even fearlessness. Eli Attie, a speechwriter for Gore who now writes scripts for *The West Wing*, said, "These are fierce times, and Gore's responding to them with fierce, passionate language. What's he got to lose, really?" Lisa Brown, who was counsel to Gore in the White House, said that, while Gore has moved left, "I don't think he's crossed the line into conspiracy thinking."

When Gore finished his speech at the Belcourt, he won another standing ovation. Offstage, he posed for pictures. His collar was saturated, his face was reddened. It had not been particularly hot onstage.

On the ride back to Belle Meade, Gore started theorizing about the November election. "Twenty-eight elected Presidents have run for a second term and almost none of those elections were close," he said. "Ten were defeated, and there were eighteen victories. Of the ten defeats, they include one who won the popular vote. The exceptions are Ford and Truman, but neither one of them was elected in the first place. And Truman's election has the memory of closeness because of that incorrect newspaper headline, but it was actually about three or four points, if memory serves. This all implies that the election is a referendum on the incumbent. In information-theory terms, the voters have so much more information on the incumbent because they have had four years to watch him, and the opponent is a subsidiary question: Will the challenger be reasonably O.K.?"

Gore, of course, believes that Kerry is more than reasonably O.K. The two men went to the Senate together in 1984 and shared some of the same qualities: intellectual seriousness, aloofness, a background of privilege and high expectations. They were hardly friends.

When I asked Gore about their relationship, he said, "In the first year, it started off as . . . um . . . competitive. We worked on some of the same issues in the same way, and that can be a formula for a difficult relationship. But he took the initiative to reach out to me and to identify the fact that he felt the relationship was not what it could be and should be and asked to sit down and talk about it and jointly create a basis for a much better working relationship. I appreciated that and was impressed by that. In the aftermath of that, we almost always worked together extremely well."

Five years ago, Kerry was wondering aloud whether he, and not Gore, should be the Party's nominee to succeed Clinton.

"He did make noise about it, to me," Gore said. "He was straightforward with me about it. He told me why, exactly what his thinking was. He thought he'd be a good candidate, it might be his last shot, he might well do it, and blah-blah-blah. I told him why I thought it would be a mistake to do it and obviously I had a self-interest in saying it."

Did Kerry feel that Gore was damaged-goods-by-association after the impeachment? I asked.

"He didn't couch it in terms of criticism of me or my prospects but, rather, in his belief that he could do a better job or be a better candidate." Gore smiled. Then he un-smiled and spoke . . . very . . . carefully. "I wasn't angry. If he had thought those things and pursued those options and didn't talk to me about it, well, that might have made me angry." When it came time for Gore to choose a Vice-Presidential nominee, his short list included Kerry and John Edwards.

Back at the house, Gore took off his jacket and tie and sat down at the dining room table. Dwayne served a lunch of lamb chops fanned out over a bed of seasoned greens. Another servant set down large pitchers of water and iced tea.

As Gore tucked into his chops, he said he was quite convinced that Kerry would win in November.

"Bush's failures have been spectacular," he said. "The evidence of deceit, miscalculation have combined to produce in the minds of a lot of people a growing conviction that it's really not good for America."

Then why were the polls showing the race as being so tight?

"I always try to tell people that it's going to be very close and it's extremely important that everybody do their part, but my own prediction is that in the end it's probably not going to be that close. I think it's in the process of tipping right now. Also, the Republican right wing has launched a kind of civil cold war in a very ruthless fashion."

Gore kept an open laptop at hand as we ate. (He and Tipper have matching Apple G4s. "What did you expect?" she said. "I live with the man who *invented* the Internet.") He bookmarks the Internet to some of the more expected outlets—the *Times, The Washington Post,* Google News—but also to left-leaning sites like mediawhoresonline.com and truthout.com. From his reading, online and elsewhere, he has grown more convinced that, in the wake of the Goldwater collapse, in 1964, and the anti–Vietnam War movement, American conservatives were determined to "play a long game" and organize themselves, ideologically, financially, and intellectually, to win national elections and carry out a conservative revolution. Gore is interested in a memorandum written at the request of a committee chairman of the U.S. Chamber of

Commerce by a Virginia attorney named Lewis F. Powell, Jr., and dated August 23, 1971, just two months before Nixon nominated Powell to the Supreme Court. The Powell memorandum portrays the American economic system as "under broad attack" by well-funded leftists, who dominate the media, academia, and even some corners of the political world. The memo describes a battle for the survival of free enterprise, and calls for less "hesitation" and "a more aggressive attitude" on all fronts. The memo was marked "confidential" and was distributed to chambers of commerce and leading executives around the nation.

As a Supreme Court Justice, Powell turned out to be a moderate, but the conservative movement did help its favored candidates, not least Ronald Reagan. I asked Gore if he thought that Hillary Clinton, in the midst of the Lewinsky period, had been right to raise the specter of a "vast right-wing conspiracy."

"It's hard to separate the phrase from all the dicta that have grown up around it," he said. "It stands for something it wasn't originally intended to mean. The word 'vast' is accurate; the phrase 'right-wing' is accurate; it's the word 'conspiracy' that people want to modify, because it implies to many who hear it something that I don't think Hillary intended when she used it. I'm sure my phrase 'civil cold war' is vulnerable to even worse misinterpretations."

Gore was quick to distinguish the Bush Administration from any predecessor. Things were "much worse" now, in his view, than in the nineteen-eighties. "The experience of the Reagan Administration was in many ways disappointing to the right wing," he said. "It was satisfying to have a champion who won the hearts of so many Americans and was so eloquent as a presenter of many of their ideas, but it was deeply disappointing to them that he bowed to reason far more than they would have wanted. The largest tax increase in history was not the Clinton-Gore increase in '93 but what Reagan did in '82. That was really disturbing to them. His arms-control initiatives, which I was a big part of, were very troubling to people like Richard Perle, who is very prominent in the genesis of the Iraq policy. There was a determination, in the aftermath of the Reagan experience, to prepare themselves for the next opportunity they had. So that they would be comprehensive and uncompromising across the board. Then, when Gingrich and his crew succeeded, in '94, they laid the foundation for the identification of all the discrete levers of power and particular programs, policies, offices, agencies that needed, in their view, to be transformed. . . . Bush, as a candidate, basically shook hands with this collection of groups that were bound together to respect each other's respective self-interest. What they had in common was that they were all powerful and had a set of objectives that were counter to the public interest."

Gore refreshed himself with a long sip of tea. The chops and the greens had been dispatched and a fruity granita, served in tall crystal cups, had been placed before us. He polished off the ice and checked his laptop. Then he began talking about the disappearance of the Soviet Union and the old "bipolar" world.

"One consequence is that there is an emergent triumphalism among market fundamentalists that has assumed an attitude of infallibility and arrogance that has led its adherents to be dismissive and contemptuous of values that are not monetized if they don't fit into their ideology."

What's missing? I asked.

"Families, the environment, communities, the beauty of life, the arts. Abraham Maslow, best known for his hierarchy of needs, had a dictum that if the only tool you use is a hammer, then every problem begins to look like a nail. Translating that into this discussion: if the only tool you use for measuring value is a price tag or monetization, then those values that are not easily monetized begin to look like they have no value. And so there's an easy contempt, which they summon on a moment's notice for tree-huggers or people concerned about global warming."

And yet the Bush ideology is tinged with religious belief, I said. Not everything comes with a price tag attached.

Gore's mouth tightened. A Southern Baptist, he, too, had declared himself born again, but he clearly had disdain for Bush's public kind of faith.

"It's a particular kind of religiosity," he said. "It's the American version of the same fundamentalist impulse that we see in Saudi Arabia, in Kashmir, in religions around the world: Hindu, Jewish, Christian, Muslim. They all have certain features in common. In a world of disconcerting change, when large and complex forces threaten familiar and comfortable guideposts, the natural impulse is to grab hold of the tree trunk that seems to have the deepest roots and hold on for dear life and never question the possibility that it's not going to be the source of your salvation. And the deepest roots are in philosophical and religious traditions that go way back. You don't hear very much from them about the Sermon on the Mount, you don't hear very much about the teachings of Jesus on giving to the poor, or the Beatitudes. It's the vengeance, the brimstone."

Tipper had gone out to lunch with Bob Orrall's wife, Christine, and now they were back.

Recently, Tipper had bought three designer flyswatters and wanted to show them off.

"Flyswatters?"

"You can catch them with your hand, Al, but check these out."

Tipper produced three extraordinarily artful flyswatters and laid them out on the dining-room table.

"Hey, Christine," Gore said, "how do I call up Bob's paintings on the Internet? I want to show . . ."

Christine, a woman far less theatrical than her husband, told him.

Gore typed in the correct URL and the right thing happened. He had not looked so delighted all day.

"Bob does these paintings about all these childhood traumas of his and then he writes about it on the canvas."

"We were in marriage counseling," Christine said, "and then he started doing these things about childhood memories instead."

"That must have been cheaper than therapy," Gore said.

"Well, we're still married!"

Gore swung his laptop around and started calling the paintings up on the screen and reading the captions. One of them showed a group of people gathered around a child at an amusement park. The writing on it said, "Don't throw up at Disneyland. Everyone acts like you broke the law or something, and your parents try to pretend you're someone else's kid. Then they mark off the area like it's a crime scene and these guys who clean it up are wearing radiation suits. I'm not kidding. Then it's 'Well I think we've had enough for one day,' and back to sharing a bed with your brothers at the Howard Johnson Motor Lodge."

Gore was laughing very loudly. "That was traumatic, wasn't it?" he said. Then he started clicking again on the laptop. "Where's the one where he was so fat he was hiding pencils in the rolls of his belly?"

Then Gore said, "Now this has become a profit center for your family, hasn't it?"

"Lucinda Williams bought five of them," Christine said. "You know, she really—"

Gore interrupted. There was real excitement in his voice, half sincere, half Mr. Goofy.

"Look, honey, I committed news!"

Gore had Googled his speech at the Belcourt, and there was a story on the wires about it. The first paragraphs were about his criticism of Porter Goss.

Before Christine left, she and Tipper and Al made plans for the weekend. They might have dinner, go hear some music at the Bluebird or somewhere.

Gore kept looking at the computer screen.

"As a general rule, where news is concerned, if you are the President you have a traveling press corps, and if you are the Party's nominee you do, too," he said. "But with those two exceptions, outside of the Scott Peterson trial, nothing—a speech, a proposal, something in the democratic discourse—nothing will be national news unless it occurs within a ten-minute cab ride of downtown Manhattan or downtown Washington, D.C. Los Angeles, Chicago, St. Louis—they don't exist. This thing here about the speech? It'll just be a little AP storylet. That's about it."

Gore's one moment to transcend the storylets of the wire service this year was his appearance at the Democratic National Convention, in Boston, in late July. Gore had not intended to stay long. The Party, now led by people who were putting their hopes in John Kerry's prospects, was, by all appearances, willing to give Gore only a tertiary role at the convention. Rather than remind Democrats of what could have been, rather than arouse any sense of anger or regret, they seemed intent on hiding him. Donna Brazile was right: he had been cast to the curb. The convention began on a Monday, and that evening was designated "formers" night, with Gore, Jimmy Carter, and Bill Clinton all speaking. But, with the broadcast networks shaving their schedules to minimal coverage, they were giving airtime only to Clinton. The winner of the 2000 popular vote would be the stuff of MSNBC, CNN, and ABC's digital operation. "We're only in town for Al's speech and then we're all getting out of here," said Carter Eskew, who was Gore's strategist in the last campaign. "We've been here, done that, if you know what I mean. This is someone else's party."

"This is a pretty emotional time," said Gore's aide Josh Cherwin, an ex-fund-raiser for the Democrats in his mid-twenties. "This should have been a moment of glory, Gore's renomination. Instead, it's pretty damn painful."

I met Gore early on Monday at the Four Seasons Hotel. On the way over, I'd read a story in the *Times* on Gore's Boston appearance, by Katharine Seelye. Gore was made, once more, to look slightly ridiculous.

Gore had promised to do a video greeting for all the state delegations that were having "kickoff" breakfasts in hotel ballrooms around town.

He and Cherwin arrived at the room for the bargain-basement broad-cast looking bleary-eyed. The convention speech was especially impor-tant for him to get right, even if it was not terribly important to anyone else. This could be his last time at the podium.

Now all Gore had to do was take a seat, look into a camera, and say a few nice words to the delegates—about as routine a political task as can be imagined. And yet the makeup woman worked on him as if she were preparing him for the opening close-up in *The Good, the Bad and the Ugly*. After around twenty minutes of having his pores detailed, Gore smiled gamely and said, "This may be the most professional makeup job for a webcam ever."

"It's actually not a webcam, sir," someone said. "It's videoconferencing."

"Ah. And that's not just a mute button," Gore said, fumbling with a switch in front of him. "It's an *activation device.*"

Everyone else was quiet in that it's-too-early-no-coffee sort of way. Gore, however, seemed desperate to be cheerful.

The director asked Gore to test the sound level on his microphone.

Gore nodded and began to speak in the husky whisper of Ronald Reagan: "Ladies and gentlemen, in one minute we will begin . . ."

None of the young technicians seemed to get the reference. The makeup woman did and she smiled.

Then something strange happened—strange if you have never been in the presence of Al Gore. At the instant he was asked to perform, to speak into the camera, his whole body straightened. He smiled a little . . . too much. The smile seemed a form of pain, almost. His voice started into that up-and-down Southern rhythm he used to do, which was meant to be charming and soothing but so often seemed patronizing and irritating. (One kept hearing the echoes of an old *Saturday Night Live* debate parody: ". . . and then ahm gonna put it in a . . . lockbox.")

Finally, he said, "My heart is full and extremely grateful for the opportunity to serve that you gave me." It was over. Gore got up from his seat and, all around town, delegates were free to eat breakfast.

Gore and Cherwin thanked everyone and went back to Gore's suite. The place looked like the workroom for a hurried college thesis, assum-ing that the student had a thousand dollars a night to spend for a room with a view of the Public Garden. The garbage cans were overflowing with shredded paper. One wall was covered with sheets of paper con-taining hastily written outline points for the speech.

"I've been up pretty much all night," Gore said. "It's a bad habit I've always had, but I just can't seem to shake it."

The convention speech, he knew, could not resemble the anti-Bush speeches that he had been delivering around the country. The language had to be tamer; he had to deliver a concise, politic address, making sure to thank Bill Clinton, pay extensive tribute to John Kerry, and, above all, give no ammunition to the Republican response teams. To make excessive reference to the 2000 election was simply not permissible.

"They look at these speeches pretty closely," he said. "They don't want any Bush-bashing in there." He smiled at the ludicrous idea of it. "No Bush-bashing at the Democratic Convention! It reminds me of the time Steve Martin was giving a speech in honor of Paul Simon at the Kennedy Center Honors a couple of years ago, and he said, 'It would be easy to stand here and talk about Paul Simon's intelligence and skill, but this is neither the time *nor* the place.'"

Gore spent another hour at the Four Seasons greeting old friends— the hotel was the omphalos of the convention, its center for major politicians, Party bureaucrats, and money people. Gore went down in the elevator with his daughter Kristin, who worked in Los Angeles as a writer for the animated series *Futurama* and had lately finished a comic novel about political Washington. Like her father, Kristin Gore healed her wounds, at least in part, under a comic bandage. Before publication, one interviewer had asked Kristin why she hadn't written the novel sooner after the election, and she said that she wanted to avoid a book that sounded like "Sylvia Plath Does D.C."

Gore, who was wearing a dark suit, and Kristin, who was wearing a T-shirt and running shorts, climbed into the backseat of a Cadillac, the staff got into a minivan, and the mini-motorcade headed for the Fleet Center. After clearing security, the Gores went through a series of back hallways and tunnels heading toward the locker rooms that were serving as greenrooms. As we were walking, Kristin took a sharp breath and said, "This is going to be a strange week." Gore had to stop every minute or so to greet people. Some seemed delighted to see him, others did that tilted-head sympathy thing.

"It's old-home week here!" Gore said as someone kissed him on the cheek.

Jim King, who has been a stage manager for Democratic conventions for years, accompanied Gore to the stairway that led to the stage.

"Hey, Jim! Where's the rest of you?" Gore said.

We walked up the stairs and onto the stage. The convention activities would not start for four or five hours. The seats were nearly empty. The vast ceiling of the Fleet Center was crammed with red, white, and blue balloons, all held back with netting. They were John Kerry's balloons. While Gore was looking at the ceiling, King was telling him to watch out for the cables and various other hazards that could cause embarrassment and a broken ankle.

"Is this the OSHA part of the briefing?" Gore said.

That night, at a few minutes to eight, more than two hours before the network broadcasts, Governor Bill Richardson, of New Mexico, introduced the former Vice-President: "a visionary . . . a fighter . . . one of this country's greatest leaders and patriots, and on Election Day 2000 the man who the people chose to be the President of the United States."

Gore came out waving and smiling, and said, "My friends, fellow Democrats, fellow Americans: I'm going to be candid with you. I had hoped to be back here this week under different circumstances, running for reelection. But you know the old saying"—here it came—"You win some, you lose some. And then there's that little-known third category."

Big laugh in the hall.

"I didn't come here tonight to talk about the past. After all, I don't want you to think I lie awake at night counting and recounting sheep. I prefer to focus on the future, because I know from my own experience that America is a land of opportunity, where every little boy and girl has a chance to grow up and win the popular vote. In all seriousness . . ."

Gore received an ovation of just over a minute before his speech and about thirty seconds after it. The initial self-deprecation, then the direct, yet restrained, indictment of the sitting President, then the gestures of support for Kerry and gratitude for Clinton, were all well marshaled, well written, and inoffensive to the barons of the convention. The politician known in 2000 for his dramatic exasperation, his awkward self-presentation, had been modest, intelligent, and poised.

No matter. By night's end, all anyone talked about was Bill Clinton's dazzling performance. The networks had ignored Gore, and most papers gave him only storylets. By the time John Kerry arrived in Boston to accept the nomination, Gore was gone, watching it all in his living room with friends in Nashville.

Al Gore will not bleed for public consumption. He will not rehearse his old resentments—against the Clintons, against the press, against Katherine Harris and Jeb Bush, against the Supreme Court, against Ralph Nader, against Bob Woodward ("Don't get me started"). We spoke for hours, and at the first mention of the 2000 election Gore stopped every-thing. He wasn't going there—not with any specificity, anyway. He said, "Let me pause for a moment. When I called you and invited you to come to the speech and the convention, I told you that the reason I made an exception to not doing interviews now is because I've had so many experiences where the initial premise of the story becomes the leading edge of a wedge to open up a much broader discourse." Gore now spoke with many pauses, which is the measure he takes when he wants to get something just right for print. "I don't mean to convey any distrust . . . but just to convey my sense of caution—there's an element of self-soothing here—I don't really want to get into a full dialogue on the 2000 campaign, because at another time and in another venue I may want to treat that fully. I use a different standard in deciding what to say and not to say about the 2000 campaign, because I think more time needs to pass both for me and for most of the people who would read what I have to say about that. I think it's still a very . . . Forty-nine per-cent of the people are still not ready to hear what I have to say about it without assuming it's not distorted by partisan motives on my part. . . . At the right time, I'll have a lot to say about it. I myself need more perspec-tive on it." The language was formal, the voice as pained as it was cau-tious. "There is so much inside of me related to the election of 2000 that, even though I know pretty much what I want to say, it takes more time. It's taken more time for me to feel that it is in a form that it can make the maximum contribution that I can make to extruding deeper meanings out of that election. Now, that may be a banality on stilts . . ."

Among the columnists and political professionals, Gore squandered no small amount of his remaining political capital last year when he endorsed Howard Dean for the Democratic nomination. At the time, pre-Scream, Dean seemed the likely nominee, and Gore appeared to add an establishment credential. But soon, post-Scream, post–free fall, even Dean himself admitted that his candidacy had begun to plummet at the precise moment of the endorsement, making it seem the ultimate kiss of death.

Many of Gore's former aides told me that they thought he endorsed Dean because the Vermont governor was running the sort of campaign—grass-roots, Internet-generated, hellbent—that he wishes he had run in 2000. That "psychoanalytic" interpretation, Gore said, was nonsense. The real reason was that, above all, Dean was the one candidate who, like Gore himself, was speaking out in unalloyed opposition to the war in Iraq.

"I think Bush put forward a counterfeit large vision," Gore said. "The war in Iraq was postured as a big idea. Well, it was a big dumb idea. And, again, I don't think he's dumb, but I think that idea is dumb."

Gore remains engaged, serious, credentialed. It is still easy to imagine him as a good, if unloved, President. And yet one trait persists—and it is a trait that he shares with George W. Bush. He is extremely reluctant to admit a mistake, even a small one. Midway through our talks in Nashville, I asked him what was the biggest mistake he had ever made in politics. He paused, made false starts, paused again, and recalled that in the campaign four years ago he had a prepared response for just such a question. But he couldn't remember what it was.

"Maybe it was my sugar-subsidies vote?" he ventured.

I asked him about his failure to alert his former running mate, Joe Lieberman, that he was endorsing Dean.

"I, uh, consider Joe a friend," Gore began. "I feel badly that his feelings were hurt. And, uh, I think that some people in his campaign convinced him that this might be a positive by trying to use it. I actually tried many times to call him before the public announcement, and could not."

Did he think that the Lieberman campaign had tried deliberately to gain political advantage from the incident?

"I, uh, don't know that for certain, so I won't say it. The only important thing is that I failed to personally tell him before the announcement."

Just before dinner, Gore checked his Treo.

"Hey," he said as we were walking near the pool. "I just got an e-mail about Jim McGreevey. He's gonna resign as governor in New Jersey. Can you guess why? Let's play multiple choice."

I guessed "C"—the right answer—and Gore did a Mack Sennett double take.

"Whoa! How'd you know that?"

Dwayne laid out an early dinner for three outside: blackened salmon, greens, good white wine. We had to leave soon. Norah Jones and her band were giving a concert that night at the Grand Ole Opry House, about half an hour away. Before eating, we had talked about the two Bush Administration figures who had also been in the Clinton-Gore circle: Colin Powell and George Tenet.

Gore said that he still considered Powell a friend, "but it's transparent to everybody that he was marginalized. Because the right wing distrusted his values and instincts, he was made a figurehead, largely. . . .

We've seen them"—Powell and his wife—"socially and I like him and respect him a lot, but I think he has been (a) badly treated by this Administration and (b) allowed himself to be used in ways that have been harmful to him—more important, harmful to the country. He should have resigned, in my opinion. Absolutely. I winced quite a few times when I watched him during his presentation to the United Nations. That was a very painful experience to watch. . . . I am not accusing him of knowingly cooking the books. I think it's far more complex and nuanced than that.

"I think that one thing that both Powell and Tenet share is a feeling of personal debt to President Bush and the Bush family. In both cases, the personal debt came to play a larger role in determining their decisions on when they should draw the line and say, 'Enough. I can't go along with this.' "

We ate quickly and headed for the Cadillac. Gore drove; Tipper, with directions on her lap, showed the way. Gore told a very funny story about a secret meeting with the former Russian Prime Minister Viktor Chernomyrdin ("the sober one") which he declared "off the record for national-security reasons."

Tipper's directions were flawless and Gore followed them—a rarity in the history of the marital institution. When we arrived at Opryland, a parking spot had been saved for the Gores.

"There's no more motorcade," Tipper said as we got out of the car. "It's just me."

We'd arrived five or ten minutes before the opening act came out, and Gore preferred to wait in the shadows rather than take his seat and have to be himself, say hello, perform.

When the lights went down, we scurried to our seats.

The Gores enjoyed the concert—they both know a lot about the rock and roll of their generation and the current country-music scene—but in between acts a few people came over wanting time, wanting to connect.

"Norah Jones *and* Al Gore . . . in one night!" someone said.

Another man came over and he and Gore started talking, in great detail, about some schoolchildren in Whitwell, Tennessee, who had made a Holocaust memorial out of millions of paper clips.

After the concert, the Gores were in a good mood and offered to drive me around Nashville before dropping me at my hotel. Gore was even thinking about stopping by the Bluebird if there was time to catch Bob Orrall's show. We passed by the music offices on Sixteenth Avenue, the clubs downtown, the waterfront, the Ryman Auditorium, the Ernest Tubb record store.

Tipper squirted some amber goo on her hands and rubbed them together and squirted some on her husband's hands when we were waiting at a red light.

"Hand cleanser," she said in a professional tone, turning toward the backseat. "Want some? We've been shaking a lot of hands."

We were talking about whether Gore was going to write a book, and I asked him if he had read the then No. 1 best-seller on the nonfiction lists. Gore laughed and said, "I haven't read Clinton's book. I hear he talks a lot about losing the Presidency of his grade school!"

We passed the Southern Baptist Convention building. Earlier in the day, Gore had made a point of telling me that he and Clinton used to pray together in the White House. I asked him which church in Nashville he and Tipper attended now.

There was a pause in the front seat.

"We're ecumenical now," Gore said, finally.

Tipper said with a laugh, "I think I follow Baba Ram Dass."

"The influx of fundamentalist preachers have pretty much chased us out with their right-wing politics," Gore added.

This was obviously a detail in a broadly painful subject. Tennessee, which was never particularly liberal, had rejected Al Gore in 2000, a loss that led to the loss of his dream.

"It makes you wonder how you ever got elected to Congress in the first place," I said.

Gore didn't deny it. "Sometimes I wonder that myself," he said.

(2004)

Mrs. Graham

In my boyhood as a reporter, I nearly killed the matriarch of the liberal-media conspiracy. This was in 1988, and I had recently been assigned to *The Washington Post*'s bureau in Moscow. In an otherwise blissful spring of journalistic overload, a time when the merest cough in the Kremlin merited front-page attention, it came about that the *Post* and its sister publication, *Newsweek*, were being awarded a plum: an interview with the General Secretary of the Communist Party. Katharine Graham, the General Secretary of the Washington Post Company, and a plane-load of senior editors would soon arrive in town to conduct it.

This was not entirely to the good. Great risk was involved, or so one heard. Mrs. Graham—one always referred to her as Mrs. Graham, even in private and at great distances—did not travel in the style of the British Raj, but she was not arriving on a Eurailpass, either. Attention would have to be paid. The cost of failure was incalculable. The legends of correspondents and their varying abilities to cope with a royal visit were countless. There was the Latin-American correspondent for the *Post* who wandered the continent for weeks in advance, arranging hotel suites, hairdressers, and interviews with heads of state from Caracas to Tierra del Fuego. He was quite a success. But there was also a certain Africa-based correspondent who carved his own career coffin by arranging for a balloon safari over the Masai Mara at dawn; just as the sun was glinting off the savanna and the balloon was rising above a herd of grazing giraffes, Mrs. Graham is said to have turned to the correspondent and announced, with a profane burr, "You know, I didn't travel all the way here to be a fucking *tourist.*" It is said that the correspondent ended up as a recipe checker in the food section. Perhaps it was true. We in Moscow had neither the time nor the luxury that would allow us to confirm these legends. One did not want to spend the remainder of one's career taste-testing lima beans.

As is true of any royal visit, there were many logistical problems to be worked out. As the junior man in the bureau, I was given the task of finding the hairdresser. I would not insist that Moscow was short on luxury in those days except to note that I did not so much find a hairdresser as create one. At one of the embassies, I found a young woman who was said to own a blow-dryer and a brush. I rang her up and explained the situation. Gravely, as if we were negotiating the Treaty of Ghent, I gave her an annotated copy of *Vogue*, a mug shot of Mrs. Graham, and a hundred dollars.

"You're on," she said.

This was my most important contribution to the interview with the General Secretary of the Communist Party. On the appointed day, I put on my good blue suit, fired up the office Volvo, and proudly drove the hairdresser to Mrs. Graham's suite at the National Hotel. Apparently, the interview went well. It was featured, with a photograph, in the next day's edition of *Pravda*. Mrs. Graham looked quite handsome, I thought. A nice full head of hair, and well combed. I felt close to history.

A few days later, I was assigned to show her and her close friend Meg Greenfield, the *Post's* editorial-page editor, around the city that was then known as Leningrad. Following the lead of my successful colleague the Latin-American correspondent, I tried to schedule every minute of the two days allotted me. The first night's entertainment was an easy choice: the Kirov Ballet at the Mariinsky Theater. For the second, I went with the upbeat, down-market option: the circus. Mrs. Graham seemed not to mind the nasty benches or the almost very funny clowns. She was in a good mood. The interview had been heady stuff. The General Secretary had "revealed" his plans for a joint United States–Soviet space mission to Mars, and we led the paper with that world beat. At one point, Mrs. Graham asked for ice cream. I got it for her. But then, at intermission, she seemed to tire. As enormous cages and nets were being assembled in the circus ring, she declared, "I think it's time to go."

I panicked. My limousine driver had been given strict instructions—and a sizable bribe—to wait outside in case of emergency. This being Russia, however, I could not bet with any confidence against the possibility that he was at this very moment converting his cash into a refreshing liquidity at some local *boîte*. "Sure, we can go," I ventured, "but the second act has some really great animals." I began to describe Misha the Bear, who wore skates on his hind paws and played ice hockey.

Mrs. Graham blinked and said, "I think it's time to go."

As I began to lead the way down the steps, a bus-size babushka—the usher—fixed me with a hard look and said, *"Nel'zya."* Impossible. You can't go.

It is not usually advisable, or possible, to argue with a Soviet bus, but my priorities were clear. I had visions of that fellow in the balloon, high above the plain, floating into journalistic obscurity, so I did what one cannot ordinarily do with a babushka. I insisted. Then I lied. I told her that this woman, this very *important* woman, was gravely ill and in need of immediate medical attention. The babushka melted.

"But hurry," she said. All around was the loud mewing of big cats and small children.

With me in the lead, the three of us walked down a ramp and past what appeared to be a coffin-size box with open slats. I passed the box without incident. So did Meg Greenfield. Then Mrs. Graham started past it. Suddenly, an enormous claw lunged out of the box and toward the innocent calf of the chairman of the Washington Post Company.

To this day, I cannot say what the beast was—a leopard, a cougar, a jaguar—but I can still see its talons not an inch from the hose and flesh of my proprietor. She, too, saw it, felt its heat, and began running for the exit. The car, at least, was waiting and its driver was sober. But what of it? I would be recalled to the home office. I would be lucky to cover high-school softball in Prince William County.

But then Mrs. Graham was laughing. She was flushed, delighted. "My God!" she said, covering her pearls with the tips of her fingers. "That was some circus! I almost rather died!"

Needless to say, for years I regaled all who would listen with my Katharine Graham story. The story, of course, revealed nothing of Mrs. Graham. During that Leningrad trip, the only moment that hinted at something mysterious and human came when we were in a map room at the Hermitage Museum. Mrs. Graham spotted a map of the Aegean and Black Seas and began to talk about a cruise she had taken in the summer of 1963, not long after her husband died. The subject of the cruise seemed to cause her, so many years later, intense pain—pain beyond the loss of her husband. "I never should have gone," she said. And then nothing more. It was a fleeting, mystifying moment, but a very real one. There was, of course, no way to press the point.

For nearly all *Post* reporters and editors, even those few who ventured to call her Kay, she was the woman who signed our checks, a Queen Mother with a lockjaw voice that sounded, to us, like money. But those who worked in the *Post*'s newsroom knew one infinitely reassuring fact about Mrs. Graham: that at the most important moments of her professional life she did the right thing. She went ahead with the publication of the Pentagon Papers, and she backed her reporters and editors during Watergate, when the Post Company's survival was under threat and the paper was all alone in pursuing the story. In doing so, she and her editor, Ben Bradlee, dragged the *Post* out of the sea of the ordinary and made it great, made it a rival of *The New York Times*. But even this was hard to understand. How could a woman reared in such exquisite privilege— one whose circle of friends, among them Robert McNamara and Henry Kissinger, Lyndon Johnson and Nancy Reagan, rarely widened beyond the most powerful élites of Washington and New York—take such risks?

Her story was not easy to figure out. When a young woman named Deborah Davis published a biography in 1979 called *Katharine the Great*, Mrs. Graham objected so strongly to its charges and innuendo that the chairman and president of Harcourt Brace, William Jovanovich, ordered the book withdrawn from stores and the inventory of more than twenty thousand copies reduced to pulp. "I cannot tell you how pained I am by the circumstances which have caused you, quite unnecessarily, distress and concern," Jovanovich wrote in a cowering letter to Mrs. Graham. "If we should ever meet again, I would like to tell you some of my thoughts on what I have come to recognize as a kind of 'editorial blackmail,' in which persons say that if you reject a work . . . you are repressing free expression and limiting the truth."

Few suggested that *Katharine the Great* was a first-rate book, or even a solid one—it was flatly written and salted with highly suspect, even paranoid, material—but one had to wonder if Mr. Jovanovich would have done the same for anyone else. There are plenty of lousy biographies in this world, and they languish on musty shelves, ignored—but whole. Jovanovich caved, then pulped. Mrs. Graham, for her part, wrote back to him, "I was full of admiration anyway for what you did and the way you did it." To round out this unlovely episode, Davis finally sued her publisher for libel and breach of contract in 1982 and received a hundred-thousand-dollar settlement. The book has been republished twice by small presses.

Until recently, Katharine Graham, considering her influence, has been almost invisible. She hardly exists in Woodward and Bernstein's books, and she is portrayed in cardboard terms almost everywhere else. An exception is David Halberstam's 1979 book, *The Powers That Be,* which provides a vivid group portrait of the men and women behind the *Post,* CBS, *Time,* and the *Los Angeles Times.*

All that changed with the publication of Katharine Graham's own *Personal History.* This is a surprising piece of work on every level. As far as I know, Katharine Graham had not written much since her early days on the *Post,* when she wrote a magazine column and was the anonymous author of such editorials as "On Being a Horse," "Mixed Drinks," and "Spotted Fever." And yet I don't know of a more complex autobiography by an American business figure, certainly not one that allows such moments of weakness, embarrassment, and pain. There is plenty of material in *Personal History* to satisfy the most obvious expectations— all the familiar episodes of the *Post's* history are replayed, and famous faces bob into sight as if in a capital version of *Grand Hotel*—but more interesting is the degree to which this memoir is a description of the muggy intimacy of the world of Washington and the way one powerful woman learned to live her life there.

For all its glamour and great personages, *Personal History* is a litany of humiliations, incidents in which the memoirist faults herself for lack of judgment, of independence, or of strength. For example, what I could not have known at the Hermitage is that after the suicide of her husband, on August 3, 1963, and the funeral, Mrs. Graham sent her eldest son, Donald, back to his internship at the *Times,* sent her two younger sons, Bill and Steve, back to summer camp, and promptly flew off to Europe to meet her eldest child—her daughter, Lally—and a group of very O.K. friends for the Aegean cruise.

"That decision may have been right for me," she writes, "but it was so wrong for Bill and Steve and even for Don—so wrong that I wonder how I could have made it. . . . This is, for me, the most painful thing to look back on. It's hard to remake decisions and even harder to rethink non-decisions. Sometimes you don't really decide, you just move forward, and that is what I did—moved forward blindly and mindlessly into a new and unknown life. . . . In effect [Bill and Steve] lost both parents at once. Up to that time I had been a fairly present mother, attending school functions, driving teams to sports events, trying to be back in the afternoons when the kids got back from school. All that was mostly over now, though I tried to be with them as much as possible." This is not the sort of moment one could hope to find in the self-examination of Andrew Carnegie or Colonel McCormick, much less of Bill Gates or Rupert Murdoch.

Graham's insecurity as a woman, as a publisher, and as a parent has clear and painful origins. So does her imperious carriage. Her beginnings were at once privileged and starved. Even considering the style of rich American families in the early part of the century, her parents, Eugene and Agnes Meyer, seem to have exceeded the norm for emotional reticence. Eugene Meyer was a Jew who might have preferred not to be. "Money, my father's being Jewish, and sex" were taboo subjects at home. Katharine, born in New York in 1917, was baptized when she was ten to satisfy the Lutheran side of the family; to satisfy the demands of class, the Meyers had their own pew at St. John's Episcopal Church, on Lafayette Square—"the President's church." (Katharine did not seem to realize she was part Jewish until she was at Vassar.) Meyer began his financial career by investing six hundred dollars his father had given him for not smoking until he was twenty-one. By 1906, Meyer had made several million dollars by investing in securities; by 1915, he was worth between forty and sixty million. He was intent, however, on making his mark in public life as well as on the stock exchange. He came to Washington in 1917 as a dollar-a-year man for the Wilson Administration; and, while he was holding a variety of positions on the War Industries Board, the Farm Loan Board, and the Federal Reserve Board, the Meyers became friendly with Bernard Baruch, Oliver Wendell Holmes, Charles Evans Hughes. It was not long before he began looking around town to buy a newspaper.

Katharine's mother, Agnes Meyer, was descended from Lutheran ministers. She was a woman of inchoate ambition—an ambition that took the shape mainly of ambitious friendships and painfully comic intellectual pretensions. She pursued hard the company of the well known. When she traveled to Paris, she took up with Brancusi and Rodin and Stein and Satie; she took fencing lessons with Mme. Curie. Later, she developed an infatuation with the work of Thomas Mann and seems to have made endless demands on the author's time and patience. Mann was once asked whether Agnes was German. He replied, "Oh, yes, very. She is a Valkyrian type with something else—a mixture of Valkyrie and Juno."

Agnes's ambitions were fueled by resentment of her station as a wife and mother. (The Meyers had five children, of whom Katharine was the fourth.) "She had not thought about what marriage entailed in the way of relationships to spouse and children," Graham writes. "I'm not sure she was ever really able to. Insofar as she was capable of love, I think she loved my father and us, but she was highly complex, and at times deeply unhappy." In her own memoir, Agnes wrote of rebelling against the responsibilities of marriage; she behaved, she said, "as if the whole world were in a conspiracy to flatten out my personality and cast me into a universal mold called 'woman.' "

Katharine saw her parents only sparingly. Agnes was perennially engaged in writing books-in-progress. When she spoke to her daughter, it was often in the barbed rhythm of insult. Eugene served Agnes breakfast in bed every morning; he ate at the bedside table. Sometimes Katharine glimpsed her parents as they were dressing to go out, or as Agnes was being massaged and manicured in preparation for the evening's entertainment. Even when Katharine was the publisher of the *Post,* David Halberstam writes in *The Powers That Be,* she felt as if she were in her mother's shadow. She once took the time to introduce her friend the architect I. M. Pei to Agnes.

Pei was talking, and Katharine said, "I didn't know that."

"What's surprising about that?" Agnes said. "You've never known anything."

"I can't say I think Mother genuinely loved us," she writes. "Toward the end of her life, I was a success in her eyes, and perhaps that is what she loved. Yet, with all her complexity, I felt closer throughout my early childhood to my mother than to the very distant and rather difficult figure of my father." It was a loyal nanny, Powelly, who "supplied the hugs, the comforting, the feeling of human contact, even the love that my mother did not."

Katharine, by her own account and in the accounts of others, was a tall and awkward girl with a "manly stride," but she was also intelligent, and she absorbed the lessons of her social class well. She attended the Madeira School, in McLean, Virginia, one of the few girls' schools intent on training young women for a career. The founder, Lucy Madeira Wing, believed that God was a woman and tried to mold the girls into "Shavian Fabians," an army wielding its noblesse oblige.

At Vassar and at the University of Chicago, Katherine took an interest in left-wing politics, which were very much in the air, but always her sense and her sense of breeding prevented her from taking what seemed like extreme steps. She rebuffed Norman O. Brown's invitation to join the Communist Party. In England, she lunched with Harold Laski, but then went off to Salzburg to meet her mother, who "treated us to the Hotel Bristol and tickets to the music festival there." While a friend went on to visit the socialist experiment in Moscow, Katharine, on the stern advice of her father, did not. She supported Roosevelt, but her political values were essentially conservative and well within the boundaries of the American upper classes.

Despite Katharine's fear of living out her life alone and unaccomplished, she soon met one of the brightest young men in her Washington circle—Philip Graham, a protégé and clerk of Supreme Court Justice Felix Frankfurter. Graham was from a Florida family whose financial prospects, while far from dire, were a matter of occasional drama. Graham's father had had trouble coming up with the funds to send him to Harvard Law, but managed to do so. Phil stunned Katharine by proposing marriage to her almost instantly, and he followed up the proposal with an insistence that they set out for Florida and a life without family money. His anxiety as a son-in-law was in place before the wedding vows.

From the start, Katharine was dazzled by her husband's intelligence and wit, his ability to light up a room: "He began to liberate me from my family and from the myths they had propagated." But she was resentful as well. For all his seeming irreverence and liberality, Phil Graham was no less domineering than so many other husbands of his day:

> Always, it was he who decided and I who responded. From the earliest days of our relationship, for instance, I thought that we had friends because of him and were invited because of him. It wasn't until years later that I looked at the downside of all this and realized that, perversely, I had seemed to enjoy the role of doormat wife. For whatever reason, I liked to be dominated and to be the implementer. But although I was thoroughly fascinated and charmed by Phil, I was also slightly resentful, when I thought about it, at feeling such complete dependence on another person. . . . I didn't think much about it at the time, but this was the beginning of a pattern that I can see now was quite unhealthy. I was expected to perform all the pulling and hauling; Phil gave directions and put the fun in my life and the children's. Gradually, I became the drudge and,

what's more, accepted my role as a kind of second-class citizen. I think this definition of roles deepened as time went on and I became increasingly unsure of myself.

Despite Phil Graham's constant self-flagellation about being the son-in-law of a rich and powerful clan, he did not shy from the advantages for long. Eugene Meyer had bought *The Washington Post* at auction for eight hundred and twenty-five thousand dollars in 1933, and in 1946 he made Phil its publisher. The Grahams ran their rather expensive household out of Katharine's trust fund; meanwhile, Meyer gave Phil nearly three times as many shares of *Post* stock as he gave his daughter. "Phil received the larger share of the stock because, as Dad explained to me, no man should be in the position of working for his wife. Curiously, I not only concurred but was in complete accord with this idea."

To get a sense of how momentous were Katharine Graham's two decisions in the nineteen-seventies—on the Pentagon Papers and Watergate—it is crucial to understand just how poorly she had been prepared for such decisions by her family, her legendary husband, and the atmosphere in which she had always lived. These days, the *Post* is usually thought of as the second-best paper in the country, after the *Times*—or, if not the second-best, then at least tied for that honor with *The Wall Street Journal* and, stretching some, the *Los Angeles Times*. Under Phil Graham, the *Post* had a well-respected editorial page and was otherwise a mediocrity; it was not even the best paper in the city. Phil's greatest successes were in business: buying and absorbing the *Times-Herald* in 1954, purchasing *Newsweek* (for a song) in 1961, and making inroads against the dominant paper in town, the *Evening Star* (which folded in 1981).

It is hard to remember now just how far in front the *Times* was after the Second World War. Even before Adolph Ochs bought the paper, in 1896, the *Times* had earned its record for rigor when it went after Boss Tweed. Under Ochs, the *Times* institutionalized the notion of nonpartisan, objective reporting. As a way to solidify this code, Ochs developed the idea of a "paper of record."

Under Philip Graham, the *Post* had no prayer of even pretending to match the standards of the country's best paper. He was simply not interested in the *Times* ideal so much as he was in making the *Post* a player in Washington and, perhaps more, in being a player himself. The *Post* was his instrument, his means of being listened to. In the summer of 1949, there were race riots in Washington over the integration of a city swimming pool. The paper sent out a young reporter named Ben Bradlee to cover what was happening, but Bradlee could barely find his story in the paper: it was buried deep inside, and nearly all mention of race and violence had been excised. Bradlee was incensed, and said so in terms both loud and profane. Graham heard him. "That's enough, Buster," he said, and he dragged Bradlee into a meeting with two officials from the Department of the Interior and with Clark Clifford, from the Truman White House. Graham instructed Bradlee to recount what he had seen and heard, and after he had done so the publisher and the three officials worked out a deal: as long as all the city pools were shut down for the time being and would be integrated the following year, the paper would print nothing more of what had happened.

Which is precisely the wrong way to conduct business as the publisher of a newspaper. But that is the way Phil Graham wanted it. And he wanted many things. He wanted Estes Kefauver to head an anticrime commission and told him so, repeatedly, until Kefauver did it. In later years, he wanted to mold the career of his friend Senator Lyndon Johnson. While publisher of the *Post*, he grew so close to LBJ that he wrote speeches for him and advised him on civil rights and key appointments; he even had power of attorney for Johnson and went out and found him a house to buy. At dinner at Joseph Alsop's one night early in 1961, Graham continually offered political advice to the new President, John Kennedy. "Phil," Kennedy said, "when you get elected dogcatcher I will listen to you on politics." But in fact Kennedy had listened to him. Without Graham working as a go-between at the 1960 Democratic Convention, Kennedy might never have picked Johnson as his running mate. When Johnson had announced he was running for President that year, Phil Graham helped write the speech; he even "ended up on his hands and knees, crawling around at the last minute to retrieve one of Lyndon's contact lenses, which had popped out." This is a posture unbecoming to a publisher of newspapers. James Reston, who was then a friend of the Grahams and was the most eminent figure at the *Times*, repeatedly declined offers to go to the *Post*. Phil Graham, he said, was "too hot for me, too involved in politics, felt too deeply about people, even his own people on the paper."

Nor did Phil Graham always have the mettle to stand by his best people. During the McCarthy era, the *Post* acquitted itself well, especially in the reports of Murrey Marder, but when everyone from the *Chicago Tribune* to a two-bit conservative publication entitled *Plain Talk* attacked the *Post* as Washington's *Pravda*, Graham showed dangerous signs of capitulation. At one point, he wanted to fire the highly respected editorial writer Alan Barth, who had dared to defend the right of Earl Browder, the former Secretary General of the Communist Party in America, not to name names before a Senate subcommittee. Graham's mentor, Felix Frankfurter, talked him out of firing Barth, but Graham did print an apologetic note in the paper undermining the original editorial. Graham supported Eisenhower in 1952 and, in the service of that support, censored the work of his greatest star, the cartoonist Herblock, in the last two weeks of the campaign.

In the late nineteen-fifties, Phil Graham's health and behavior also presented increasingly difficult problems—problems that might have been solved with medication, if he had not refused it. He was a manic-depressive. For years, Katharine witnessed her husband's violent mood swings—his periods of heavy drinking, his bizarre behavior, his prolonged depressions. And yet his periods of lucidity and humor, of lively intelligence, were frequent enough to confuse her and delay any sense of reckoning. With time, Katharine was becoming more and more troubled, less and less secure. The two most powerful presences in her life—her mother and her husband—were both clearly suffering from psychological problems, yet Katharine still felt inferior to them. "My mother seemed to undermine so much of what I did, subtly belittling my choices and my activities in light of her greater, more important ones," she writes. "As for Phil, at the same time that he was building me up, he was tearing me down. As he emerged more on the journalistic and political scenes, I increasingly saw my role as the tail to his kite—and the more I felt overshadowed, the more it became a reality." Phil Graham began referring to his wife, who by 1952 had given birth to four children, as Porky; to heighten the joke, he gave her as a present a French butcher-shop head of a pig. "Another habit of his that emerged during those years was that, when we were with friends and I was talking, he would look at me in such a way that I felt I was going on too long and boring people. Gradually, I ceased talking much at all when we were out together." She "felt like Trilby to his Svengali"; she felt as if he had "created" her, that she was totally dependent.

"Even now I can't sort out my feelings about this; it's hard to separate what was a function of Phil's terrible affliction, which manifested itself only later, and what was more basic. The truth is that I adored him and saw only the positive side of what he was doing for me. I simply didn't connect my lack of self-confidence with his behavior to me."

The end of this increasingly painful marriage was prolonged and extremely public. In 1962, Phil Graham met Robin Webb, a young Australian woman who had been working in *Newsweek*'s Paris bureau, and he began appearing with her at *Newsweek* bureaus all over the world. Katharine soon learned of their affair, when she picked up the phone and "heard Phil and Robin talking to each other in words that made the situation plain."

Not long after Phil left her, Katharine sent him a desperate telegram:

> Mascots are for loving helping and listening. You are stuck with me as a mascot repeat mascot. The moment of happiness you gave me is more help than most people are given in a lifetime, Thank you for it. I'm here if you need me and I love you.

Phil wrote a letter in return that Katharine rightly describes as "pretty strange":

> Dearest Kay—
> One morning when you were despairing I tried to help you by words. I told you how lonely it had been when I had visited my Far Country and how I could not get near enough to help you in your Far Country. And by the words you came near enough for help and I touched you and we went for a walk and were again in life.
>
> I have now gone. Gone not to my Far Country but to my Destiny. It happens to be a beautiful Destiny and I shall be there while it is beautiful and while it is not.
>
> I did not go to help you. I did not go because I did not want to help you. I went because it was my Destiny. And by now "helping" you I believe and I pray I shall *help* you.

Soon Phil began telling his friends that he was going to divorce his wife and marry Robin Webb. He also began making public scenes— once launching into an obscene tirade during a speech, and, on another occasion, punching out a detective at an airport. At one point, President Kennedy dispatched a Presidential plane to get him from Phoenix to Washington.

What made the situation even more complicated was the status of the *Post*. Not only did Phil own the majority of the stock but he also believed that his efforts as publisher entitled him to ownership. To win the paper, Phil employed the most feared lawyer in Washington, Edward Bennett Williams. Katharine knew that her husband and her old way of life were lost to her, but, fearful though she was of confrontation and of Williams, she was determined to fight for the paper.

She did not have to. In the summer of 1963, Phil seemed to be getting better—he was undergoing treatment at a psychiatric center in Maryland—and there was even hope of resuming a normal life at home. On an August afternoon, Phil and Katharine went together to their farm, Glen Welby:

> We had lunch on two trays on the back porch at Glen Welby, chatting and listening to some classical records. After lunch, we went upstairs to our bedroom for a nap. After a short while, Phil got up, saying he wanted to lie down in a separate bedroom he sometimes used. Only a few minutes later, there was the earsplitting noise of a gun going off indoors. I bolted out of the room and ran around in a frenzy looking for him. When I opened the door to a downstairs bathroom, I found him.

Phil Graham was forty-eight when he died. His widow was left to confront all the myths and all the insulations that her marriage, her class, and her sex had imposed on her. In middle age and in a state of grief, she suddenly found herself in charge of a newspaper that had yet to show any signs of greatness, and of a group of men who regarded her with, at best, considerable suspicion. In meeting after meeting, in Washington and New York, she was the only woman in the room, and not a self-confident one at that. She had not yet developed the steely mask that would later trouble the sleep of her adjutants. Before making speeches, she shook with terror; in the face of unsettling news, she had the unfortunate habit of breaking down in tears. The pressures were enormous and her preparation for them slight. She had to learn to be a publisher and, what was more, to be a far better publisher than her husband had been. ("One area that, surprisingly, started to shift under my feet was the *Post's* editorial quality. I hadn't realized that the *Post* wasn't perfectly okay.")

Surrounded by her male editors and executives, Graham could recognize in herself the same reflexes of deference she had learned as a daughter and as a wife. When she suggested to the *Newsweek* editors that it might be a good idea to hire Aline Saarinen, of the *Times*, to edit the back of the book, they brushed the suggestion off, saying that the closings were too late, that "the physical demands" of the job would be too much. Graham found herself agreeing: Saarinen would not get an offer.

I adopted the assumption of many of my generation that women were intellectually inferior to men, that we were not capable of governing, leading, managing anything but our homes and our children. Once married, we were confined to running houses, providing a smooth atmosphere, dealing with children, supporting our husbands. Pretty soon this kind of thinking—indeed, this kind of life—took its toll: most of us *became* somehow inferior. We grew less able to keep up with what was happening in the world. In a group we remained largely silent, unable to participate in conversations and discussions. Unfortunately, this incapacity often produced in women—as it did in me—a diffuse way of talking, an inability to be concise, a tendency to ramble, to start at the end and work backwards, to overexplain, to go on for too long, to apologize.

Women traditionally also have suffered—and many still do—from an exaggerated desire to please, a syndrome so instilled in women of my generation that it inhibited my behavior for many years, and in ways still does. Although at the time I didn't realize what was happening, I was unable to make a decision that might displease those around me. For years, whatever directive I may have issued ended with the phrase "if it's all right with you." If I thought I'd done anything to make someone unhappy, I'd agonize. The end result of all this was that many of us, by middle age, arrived at the state we were trying most to avoid: we bored our husbands, who had done their fair share in helping reduce us to this condition, and they wandered off to younger, greener pastures.

Circumstances seemed to conspire in challenging Graham. Some companies thought the *Post* such a potentially profitable property, and Graham such an unlikely figure to run it, that they came to her with offers to buy it. To the surprise of some, she easily warded off the blandishments of Samuel I. Newhouse (once with a somewhat duplicitous Theodore Sorensen as her agent) and the Times-Mirror Company. From the start, she was intent on keeping the paper within the family and eventually passing it on to her children.

But that did not mean she was strong in all things. Phil Graham's world had been the world of the powerful, and his widow did not want to offend its leading members. At one meeting with LBJ in 1964, in his bedroom, she sat in an armchair while the President lay down on the bed. "I then talked in terms I had inherited from Phil and in a way I would never have done later—and that embarrasses me now," she writes. "I told him I had the feeling that he thought my point of view was different from Phil's, but that in general Phil and I had agreed. I said that, much as I admired and loved President Kennedy, Phil personally had got along with him much better than I had. I also said that I admired the legislation he himself had got passed and was for him and wanted to make sure he knew it."

On the first great story of her era as publisher—the war in Vietnam—the *Post*'s performance was nearly an embarrassment. While the *Times* and the two wire services, AP and UPI, were infuriating the White House with reporting that showed the contrast between the official statements of the generals and the dire situation in the field, the *Post* could not keep pace.

In 1967, Katharine wrote a letter to Johnson (not quoted in the book) expressing enormous empathy: "These times are so difficult that my heart bleeds for you. . . . The only thanks you ever seem to receive is a deafening chorus of carping criticism. Unlike Phil, I find it hard to express emotion. I can't write in the eloquent words he used. But I want you to know I am among the many people in this country who believe in you and are behind you with trust and devotion."

Her obeisance was institutional and political, not merely personal. In the beginning, even Richard Nixon got the same treatment. On the eve of the first Moratorium against the war, the *Post* published a nasty editorial (also not quoted in *Personal History*) that tried to set the paper apart from the antiwar movement. "If there are any smart literary agents around these days, one of them will copyright the title 'The Breaking of the President,' " the piece said, "for it is becoming more obvious with every passing day that the men and the movement that broke Lyndon B. Johnson's authority in 1968 are out to break Richard M. Nixon in 1969. . . . There is still a vital distinction . . . between the constitutionally protected expression of dissent . . . and mass movements aimed at breaking the President." Eventually, the debate over the war led to a shift in the editorial page—the conservative Russell Wiggins was replaced by the more liberal Philip Geyelin—but the *Post* never completely distinguished itself on Vietnam.

Katharine Graham's establishment position on the war did not go unnoticed. In 1966, Truman Capote, her neighbor at the UN Plaza, where she kept a New York apartment, threw his famous Black-and-White costume ball for her. ("I had a French dress—a Balmain design, copied at Bergdorf Goodman," she writes. "It was plain white crêpe with slate-colored beads around the neck and the sleeves. The mask was made to match, also at Bergdorf's, by Halston, who was then still making hats.") Graham considered the ball a kind of coming out for a "middle-aged debutante." But in Pete Hamill's column in the *New York Post* she was suddenly Marie Antoinette. Hamill interspersed a faux-sprightly account of the party ("And Truman was just marvelous!") with accounts of the war in Vietnam: "The helicopter landed in a scrubby open field six miles north of Bong Son."

In 1965, Graham helped herself and the paper immeasurably by hiring Ben Bradlee, *Newsweek*'s charismatic bureau chief in Washington and a friend of the Kennedys. Bradlee had been Phil's friend, not hers, but he pushed for the job of managing editor, pushed with his customary blend of charm and vulgarity ("I'd give my left one" for the job, he told her at lunch one day), and she melted. Over the years, she would fire an endless line of *Newsweek* editors and *Post* executives, but in Bradlee she had found someone who from the start satisfied her in every respect: élan, strength, social class, and talent. And, under Bradlee's urging, she began spending the money necessary to create, among other things, a first-rate foreign staff. With Graham's support, Bradlee was soon firing the lazy and the mediocre, the racist and the dull, and he then set about raiding top-flight papers around the country for their best talent. The talent level in the newsroom began to shift, and so did the culture of the place. By 1968, reporting and editorials on Vietnam by Ward Just and a few others helped change the atmosphere of reverence on the pages of the *Post*, and that change had its effect on the thinking of the publisher—so strong an effect that when the *Times*, thanks to Neil Shee-han and his source, Daniel Ellsberg, began printing the Pentagon Papers, on June 13, 1971, Bradlee felt wounded, and, with Graham's encouragement, pushed his staff to find its own copy of the documents. By June 17, thanks to his national editor, Ben Bagdikian, he had his own set of papers.

Graham had every reason to refuse or defer publication of the Penta-gon Papers. The *Times* was immediately in trouble with the White House and the courts. The Post Company had gone public just two days before getting the papers, and publication could easily have affected its stock prices for the worse. Moreover, Graham was acutely sensitive about the image of the *Post* as a liberal newspaper and, as a result, had chosen a law firm with close connections to the Republican Party; not surprisingly, her lawyers urged her to delay publishing or not to publish at all.

To a reporter, and especially a reporter now, this does not seem an especially vexing decision. If you have the goods, you publish. But in the spring of 1971 the Supreme Court had not yet declared its strong support of press freedoms to the degree that it would in the Pentagon Papers case; moreover, the *Post* itself did not yet have the financial standing or the self-possession to go forward simply and with confidence. Graham was gambling every sort of inheritance that was important to her: the paper, her fortune, and, perhaps most important, the judgment of the ghosts who crowded around her. If there was one journalist she admired more than any other, it was her friend James Reston, and it was Reston who, despite his many virtues, had famously said, "I will not have *The New York Times* muckraking the President of the United States." But in the end she made her decision.

"All right," she told Bradlee on the telephone, in the midst of a reception at her house, with the *Post*'s lawyer counseling caution in her free ear. "Let's go, let's publish." And by doing that she opened the way to Watergate and to the *Post*'s position as a rival of the *Times*.

Week after week, the leading figures of the Nixon Administration lambasted Graham and the *Post* for the Watergate stories. Charles Colson, for one, tried to dismiss the conspiracy as fiction—a charge that, if true, would probably have ruined the paper forever. "The charge of subverting a whole political process, that is a fantasy, a work of fiction rivaling only *Gone with the Wind* in circulation and *Portnoy's Complaint* for indecency," Colson said. "Mr. Bradlee now sees himself as the self-appointed leader of . . . the tiny fringe of arrogant élitists who infect the healthy mainstream of American journalism with their own peculiar view of the world." The fact is, though, that two days after making that statement Colson talked to Howard Hunt about the need to supply more financial help to the defendants in the Watergate trial.

John Ehrlichman, Ronald Ziegler, H. R. Haldeman, and Nixon himself all charged the *Post* with disloyalty. Nixon told his men to "treat the *Post* absolutely coldly" and spoon-feed "scoops" to its local rival, the *Star*. He also vowed to "do a number" on the *Post*, and to go after the Graham family's broadcasting licenses. The reporters and editors might have got a nervous thrill from the Administration's hysteria, but Mrs. Graham did not. In the midst of the crisis, she wrote to Ehrlichman, saying, "What appears in the *Post* is not a reflection of my personal feelings. And by the same token, I would add that my continuing and genuine pride in the paper's performance over the past few months—the period that seems to be at issue—does not proceed from some sense that it has gratified my personal whim. It proceeds from my belief that the editors and reporters have fulfilled the highest standards of professional duty and responsibility."

At about the same time, she was on a cross-country flight and ran into Senator Bob Dole, who was then working as chairman and chief hatchet man for the Republican National Committee. In speeches, Dole had accused her paper of waging an ideological vendetta against the President.

"By the way, Senator, I didn't say I hated Nixon," she told Dole.

"Oh, you know," he said, "during a campaign they put these things in your hands and you just read them." (Dole admitted the same to a *Times* reporter after the 1996 campaign. He never really meant it when he spent weeks vilifying the *Times* for bias, he said.)

Graham had undeniably, historically, made the right decision, and in the years to come she supported the investigative efforts of the *Post;* but she never stopped showing signs of her ambivalence about her social and political role. As she grew older and more self-confident, she could be imperious, even frightening to her editors and executives, but her desire to please, or at least to get along with, those in power never entirely faded. In the early days of Watergate, she tried, in rather submissive terms, to build a personal bridge to the one man who exceeded even Nixon in his public hatred of the *Post*—Spiro Agnew. Her gesture "in retrospect seems to me undignified, considering the awful slamming we were taking from him," she writes. "I think my behavior was a combination of a rational idea—that it was better to be talking to people who hated us or disapproved of us than not—and that good old-fashioned encumbrance of mine, the desire to please."

Not long after Watergate, she worried about "over-involvement" and a newspaper's need to guard against "the romantic tendency to picture itself in the role of a heroic and beleaguered champion, defending virtues against overwhelming odds." Watergate, she writes, "had been an aberration, and I felt we couldn't look everywhere for conspiracies and cover-ups."

Mrs. Graham's personal relations with the powerful and the once powerful became, if anything, even more visible after Watergate. Robert McNamara, Henry Kissinger, Lawrence Eagleburger, George Shultz, Paul Nitze, Douglas Dillon, McGeorge Bundy, Jack Valenti, Joe Califano: her list of establishment friends is long and decidedly nonpartisan. If she has been cool to any Presidents since Watergate, they have been the two Democrats, Jimmy Carter and Bill Clinton, not least because they came to town with the greatest suspicion of old-line Georgetown—Katharine Graham's Washington.

Ronald Reagan made sure to accept invitations to Mrs. Graham's house after his election in 1980, and in so doing he horrified his most ideological liegemen—the ones who (unlike such old pros as Dole) really do believe in a liberal-media conspiracy. At a meeting of the Religious Roundtable, Howard Phillips, the head of the Conservative Caucus, warned darkly, "You cannot always have Kay Graham going to your cocktail parties and smiling at you. If by June the Washington establishment is happy with Ronald Reagan, then you should be unhappy with Ronald Reagan." In the coming years, Mrs. Graham formed an especially close friendship with Nancy Reagan. During the 1988 visit to Moscow, I remember, Mrs. Graham said that perhaps she ought to telephone Nancy and tell her about the lengths that the Kremlin was going to in preparing for an imminent summit. The editors around her grumbled almost inaudibly, but just enough, it seemed to me, to dissuade her from making such a call.

"I see nothing wrong with the fact that people in power often deal with others on more than one level," she writes. "Sometimes you become friends with people with whom you work because of some common interest or just because you have to work together. But there are also relationships that start out that way yet cross over to become real friendships that last forever. Some of my deepest friendships began with an administration person whom I got to know because of my association with the paper."

To read *Personal History* is to understand how ridiculous is the right-wing image of Graham as the matriarch of a liberal-media conspiracy. Her allegiance to democratic capitalism is no less firm than that of William F. Buckley, Jr., and her inherent faith that the establishment élites will do the right thing is nearly absolute. She really does seem to believe that Watergate was an aberration.

There is no doubt that the majority of reporters at papers like the *Post* are themselves more liberal than the general population: a recent poll showed that eighty-nine percent of Washington-based correspondents voted for Clinton in 1992. But that statistic has to be balanced by the conservatism of nearly all publishers. The *Post* pursued Watergate as a news story, not as an ideological crusade. It similarly (if with less success) pursued Iran-Contra and Bill Clinton's ethical failures. By contrast, *The Wall Street Journal*'s editorial page ignored Watergate and Iran-Contra as ideologically inconvenient and pursued Whitewater with the foam visible on its lips. If one compares the approach of the liberal media (the *Post*, the *Times*, etc.) with that of the increasingly powerful conservative media (the *Journal* editorial page, the *Weekly Standard*, *The American Spectator*, etc.), it is preposterous to say that the rules of the game are the same.

Katharine Graham is now seventy-nine, and the *Post* is in the hands of her son Donald, who is fifty-one. His temperament, his interests, and his style are quite different from his mother's. He does not travel the globe to interview foreign leaders. He does not live in Georgetown. His friends are, for the most part, not especially famous. His most passionate political interests are local. As a publisher, Don Graham may never face a pair of crises as critical as the Pentagon Papers and Watergate. But, if he does, the decisions should not be as hard for him as they were for Katharine Graham. He does not have to invent himself, nor does he have to invent a set of principles. There is an example to follow.

(1997)

•

In 1998, Katharine Graham won a Pulitzer Prize for *Personal History*. Although the Washington Post Company was now in the hands of her son, she remained an active voice and, along with Ben Bradlee, who had retired in 1991, an important symbolic presence for the paper. In July 2001, while Mrs. Graham was attending a media conference in Sun Valley, Idaho, she took a bad fall and, a few days later, died of her injuries. She was eighty-four.

The funeral at the Cathedral Church of Saint Peter and Saint Paul—known to everyone in D.C. as the Cathedral—took place on a broiling, humid morning. More than three thousand people attended, including Vice-President Dick Cheney, the Clintons, Alan Greenspan, Bill Gates, Warren Buffett, the staffs of the *Post* and *Newsweek*, a raft of foreign diplomats, the better part of both houses of Congress, and so on. The sheer volume of political, financial, and media power packed into the Cathedral suggested a scene from an old-fashioned Washington pot-boiler, a novel by Irving Wallace or Fletcher Knebel. The eulogists were the Graham children, Ben Bradlee, Arthur Schlesinger, Jr., Henry

Kissinger; the pallbearers included Barry Diller, Vernon Jordan, and Robert McNamara; and among the ushers were Lloyd Cutler, the de la Rentas, Barbara Walters, Mike Nichols, Diane Sawyer, and Bob Woodward. Even the presiding clergy, an Episcopal priest, was a "notable": Senator John Danforth of Missouri. With the Cathedral filled, and the service about to start, one heard from the back the frantic footfalls of two New York worthies insistently making their way to the front: the financier Ron Perelman and his wife, the actress Ellen Barkin. Yo-Yo Ma played a Bach allemande, and the National Symphony Orchestra, along with the Kennedy Center Opera House Orchestra Brass Ensemble, performed works of Respighi, Gabrieli, and Handel. Mrs. Graham's coffin was carried down the long aisle in a processional as decorous as any royal funeral.

In the years after, newspaper proprietors and editors have faced a range of new challenges. The Internet promises to increase the readership of the *Post,* but the problem of earning money from the Web, as the traditional paper's circulation declines, remains a riddle. Editors are now faced with far more criticism and transparency (which is to the good), but also a government prepared to shut out, attack, and even prosecute honest reporters (which is unambiguously dangerous). At Gannett, Knight Ridder, the Tribune Company, and the networks, the demand for unreasonable profits is undermining the quality of American journalism. During Watergate, Katharine Graham was prepared not only to publish and support her reporters but also to protect them by every means available to her. Her values, as well as her courage, seem increasingly endangered.

The Masochism Campaign:
Tony Blair

Not long before making a series of visits to No. 10 Downing Street, I was reading the novel that everyone in London seemed to be poring over in the cafés and on the benches in St. James's Park—Ian McEwan's *Saturday*, which is set on February 15, 2003, the day of the worldwide antiwar demonstrations. The central character is a middle-aged neurosurgeon named Henry Perowne. He is prosperous, fortunate in his wife and two children, happy, yet haunted by the onset of middle age; and although he is not especially political, he is pained and ambivalent about Tony Blair's support of the American-led invasion of Iraq. At one point, Perowne recalls meeting Blair. As a member of the Royal College of Surgeons, he'd been invited to the opening of the Tate Modern, where he and his wife, Rosalind, were among four thousand guests. Perowne wanders into a huge gallery and suddenly finds himself next to Blair, who is, as ever, eager to shake hands, to forge a connection.

"I really admire the work you're doing," Blair says. "In fact, we've got two of your paintings hanging in Downing Street. Cherie and I adore them." Clearly, Blair has taken Perowne to be one of the Tate's artists, and, after thinking it through, Perowne decides on honesty.

"You're making a mistake," he says.

"And, and on that word, there passed through the Prime Minister's features for the briefest instant a look of sudden alarm, of fleeting self-doubt," McEwan writes. "A hairline fracture had appeared in the assurance of power."

To follow British politics these past weeks, to watch Blair campaign for a third term—Election Day is May 5—is to witness a politician putting himself in the way of any audience, any camera, anyone who will have him. His aides call it "the masochism campaign." The punishment is daily and takes many forms. During a televised meet-the-voters session in Coventry, Blair's declaration that he had improved the National Health Service was answered by Mrs. Valerie Holsworth, who told him that she had so despaired of finding an available NHS dentist that she'd used her husband's pliers to yank her own rotten teeth—four of them. As proof, she readily displayed her gums. Blair winced in sympathy. At a Downing Street press conference, a tabloid reporter reacted to the Government's proud announcement of a hike in the minimum wage by asking Blair, "Would you be willing to wipe someone's bottom for this 'higher' minimum wage?" And, at a lunchtime session at No. 10 with British journalists, I heard a reporter say that Blair had appeared on the cover of *Attitude,* a magazine much like *Out,* which led him to ask the Prime Minister, "Are you a gay icon?" In every case, one saw the "hairline fracture in the assurance of power," the Halloween rictus, a practiced yet futile attempt to mask embarrassment or anger with a game expression that hopes to project sincerity, patience, and (the essential category of pollsters) likability.

The masochism campaign is a kind of political rope-a-dope, the idea being that through constant exposure to Blair's kindly endurance, his lucid, if canned, explanations, the electorate will eventually weary of its lingering anger and distrust—primarily over Blair's unwavering support of George W. Bush—and will come around to conceding that the Conservatives, under the forgettable Michael Howard, have little to offer but fear-mongering on issues like asylum-seeking immigrants from Asia and Eastern Europe, and that the left-leaning Liberal Democrats are still a marginal party in the House of Commons promoting, as one Blair aide airily put it, "the ideology of bicyclists."

In a sense, after eight years of crisis and grating propinquity, Blair has to revive the notion of his own charm. When he came to power, in 1997, as the standard-bearer of New Labour, he ended eighteen years of Tory rule and the distinct possibility that Labour would never head a government again. Blair did not possess quite the glamour of a Kennedy, but, compared with his managerial predecessor, John Major, he was positively vibrant, promising a progressive revival as thorough as Margaret Thatcher's conservative revolution. He was just forty-three, the youngest Prime Minister since the Napoleonic Wars. His majority in the House of Commons was the biggest since 1935. He became the first Labour Party premier ever to last two consecutive terms, winning votes not just among the urban élites and the urban poor, the Labour base, but among traditional Tory voters in the suburbs of Middle England. Now, despite a rudderless opposition, Blair will be relieved if he wins a third term with a less gaudy majority in the Commons than he has enjoyed. His campaign's only anxiety is a sullen apathy among Labour voters. The Tories point to the 1970 campaign, when Harold Wilson's Labour Government held a decisive lead only to be dumped from office by the Tory Edward Heath.

The masochism campaign is a daily operation. One morning, I stood in one of the second-floor drawing rooms of No. 10 as a group of television technicians set up their cameras, microphones, and lights for a taping with Little Ant and Little Dec, two ten-year-old adorables who specialize in faux-naif celebrity interviews for an ITV variety show called *Ant and Dec's Saturday Night Takeaway*. Little Ant and Little Dec sat jammed together into one of Downing Street's better armchairs waiting for the Prime Minister. They wore little black suits and their hair was pomaded. Their names are Dylan McKenna-Redshaw and James Pallister, and they are the Mini-Mes of the show's oleaginous grown-up stars, Ant and Dec.

"Boys! Sit up straight!"

This was the voice of Georgie Herford-Jones, the show's producer. Herford-Jones, who resembles the young Linda Evans, had complete command of her puppies. When she barked, they straightened in the chair, and when she raised a brow they commenced rehearsing the wiseacre questions that had been scripted for them. The idea was to be both cute and rude, a kids-say-the-darnedest-things routine. They'd interviewed the midfielder David Beckham, Posh Spice's husband. "You and your wife just had your third kid," one question went. "My dad says you must be at it like rabbits. What does he mean?" They asked Angelina

Jolie, "How big is your mouth?" Bruce Willis was so offended by the pre-pubescent grilling that he walked off the set, earning himself a couple of jabs in the tabloids.

Finally, Blair appeared, wearing no jacket but a genuine smile.

"How ya doin', boys?" he said, settling into a chair opposite Little Ant and Little Dec.

Blair's press aides, David Hill and Hilary Coffman, stood out of cam-era range and looked eager.

"Seven, eight million people watch this Saturday nights," Hill whis-pered to me. "For this country, that's huge." Hill had said, repeatedly, that Blair had to "reconnect" with the British public, especially voters who rarely watched the news or read the papers. If some of Blair's natu-ral liberal constituents were staying home to protest his fealty to Bush, he needed new, more forgiving voters. *Saturday Night Takeaway* was the perfect forum in which to show Blair as "accessible, clear, nice."

Little Ant and Little Dec were ready to begin.

The Prime Minister nodded distantly. Low clouds of preoccupation encased him. Not only were the latest polls too tight for absolute com-fort; the Pope was on his deathbed and, in a few hours, Blair had a Cabi-net meeting where he would face his saturnine Chancellor of the Exchequer, Gordon Brown. The closest of comrades fifteen years ago, Blair and Brown have run the country in tandem for eight years yet, at times, barely speak. Brown, who had hoped to lead the Party himself, has always bridled at his sidecar position in the arrangement, and his aides regularly leak word of his particular resentments to the conflict-hungry press. For the duration of the campaign, and for the sake of party comity, Blair and Brown would have to behave rather like an angrily divorced couple who must come together on their daughter's wedding day; the price of a spat now could be Blair's election and Brown's ambitions.

The tape rolled. The questions began:

"You run the whole country. Have you always been that bossy?"

"When your children are cheeky, do you ever say, 'How dare you speak to the Prime Minister like that!'?"

"My dad says you've got to be mad to do your job. Are you mad?"

The biggest political story that week had been a campaign by the young television cook Jamie Oliver, "The Naked Chef," to improve school lunches, which are notoriously foul. Little Ant moved in.

"What were your school meals like?"

Before going up to St. John's College, Oxford, Blair attended Fettes, a posh boarding school in Scotland. In Britain, boarding-school food, with its rissoles fried in grease and its wan Brussels sprouts, is no better than the rest, but, still, Blair is rarely eager to remind anyone of Fettes and thus kept his answer vague.

"Have you actually tasted a Turkey Twizzler?" Little Ant persisted. Turkey Twizzlers, a fatty processed food, had never been on Blair's menu. Another dodge.

With each question, Blair parried in a pleasantly harrumph-ish sort of way, but it became increasingly clear that he had been only casually briefed. In any case, it was impossible to imagine an earlier Prime Minister—Gladstone, Asquith, Churchill, Eden, Macmillan, Thatcher—coping with the inquisitions of Little Ant and Little Dec. Informality was part of Blair's "American" style—"Call me Tony," he told everyone, and everyone did—but now the cost of informality was plain.

Then things got worse. After Blair mentioned that as a student he'd been in a rock-and-roll band called the Ugly Rumors, Little Dec said, "When my aunt makes a smell, she says, 'Oh, my, I think I started an ugly rumor.' Is that where the name comes from?"

Well, no, Blair said, it comes from a Grateful Dead album that—

"If you make an ugly smell, do people pretend not to notice because you is the Prime Minister?"

And then it came: the strained rictus, the hairline fracture . . .

Off-camera, Linda Evans beamed at her little darlings. She occasionally asked them to repeat a flubbed question and kept gesturing for them to sit up in their chair. Blair looked over at her, as if for a sign that this agony was about to end.

"Why does the Labour Party have flowers as its logo? Isn't that a bit . . . girlie?"

The grilling was over at last, but now there was an exchange of presents. One of the boys picked up a shopping bag and handed over several gifts: a bouquet of cheap flowers, some crummy memorabilia from the show, a pair of panties and a pink boa for Blair's wife, Cherie.

"That's for Cherie? What can I say?"

"Say thank you," Little Dec said.

Blair looked over toward the cluster of aides. "I don't believe this!" he said, mock indignant. "I'm not used to interviews like this. I'll try to see who got me into this."

"Yesterday they did Ozzy Osbourne," the father of one of the boys told me.

"How much of this will they use?" Blair asked as he wearily rose from his chair.

"About half."

"I can think of some things to cut out," he said.

Linda Evans informed the Prime Minister that he had to film another scene. Blair had already devoted forty-odd minutes to the Little Ones and he rolled his eyes. And yet he obeyed. Linda Evans told him that the boys would sit on a couch next to a telephone and that he, Blair, would suddenly enter. "You come into the room and you say, 'Good morning, boys. Have you been looked after?' "

Blair nodded moodily, as if he had just received a stern rebuke from the Chancellor of the Exchequer.

We all moved to the next room for the shot. Suddenly, Cherie Blair arrived. Someone had put Little Ant and Little Dec on her schedule, too.

"Hi, guys!" Cherie said brightly.

"This is Little Ant and Little Dec," the Prime Minister said, in just about the same voice one might say, "These are the McCrary twins and they have come to kidnap the children and shoot the dog."

"You're not really called Little Ant and Little Dec, are you?" she said. "You're much cuter than the big ones."

"I was just asking them if they spent more time reading or playing on the PlayStation," Blair said.

"I still read loads," Cherie said. "You must read. It's really important. I love cuddling up in bed with a good book."

"Thank you, dear," the Prime Minister said. "That's what twenty-five years of married life gets you, boys."

Cherie was told that the pink boa was for her. She fingered it and tried to think of something clever to say. All she could manage was "Well! It's been lovely! But I have to go do something about the Olympics!" London is in the hunt to win the Summer Games in 2012. Then she beat it down a flight of stairs.

"Are you jealous of the Queen?" Little Ant asked Blair.

"No. She's the Queen and I'm not."

"Really?"

This was beginning to sound like outtakes from *Krapp's Last Tape.*

"Well, she's Queen for a long time. Prime Ministers aren't," Blair said, as he waited for a cue to leave the room and reenter. "What do you want to do when you grow up?"

"Direct," Little Dec said.

At last, Linda Evans said, "Could I get you coming through the door?"

"This one?" Blair asked, pointing. She nodded. He left. He came back in, smiling. Beckett had now bowed to Feydeau.

"Hi, boys! Have you been looked after?"

Little Dec said, "A nice man called George Bush just called. He's bringing pizzas . . ."

"Whoa!" Linda Evans said, waving her arms. She didn't like the shot. "Um, could we do that once more?"

Blair squinted murderously.

"Right," he said, recovering. "So, I say . . ."

And then he went out the door once again.

A few seconds later, he came back in. The tape was rolling.

"Hi, boys. Have you been looked after?"

"A nice man called George Bush just called. He's bringing pizzas."

Then Tony Blair sighed and said, "Is he bringing one for me?"

After all that, the Prime Minister required what White House schedulers call "a little bit of alone time." I was brought to a waiting room downstairs. Blair lives and works in what must surely be the least commodious headquarters of any leader of a major industrialized state. Downing Street is a small cul-de-sac off Whitehall, and No. 10 is a large, somewhat worn seventeenth-century town house. (The Blairs and their four children, who range in age from four to twenty-one, live in an apartment above No. 11. The Browns are next door. There is a jungle gym in the backyard.) The Prime Minister does not even have an officially designated office. Margaret Thatcher used a room on the second floor. John Major read documents at the enormous table in the Cabinet Room. Blair occupies a room just outside the Cabinet Room known as the den, which is just large enough for a couch, a desk, and two armchairs.

By the time Blair greeted me in the den, he seemed well over the depredations of Little Ant and Little Dec.

"It was a piece of fun, that's all," he said gamely, and yet, he went on, "it's always a battle, isn't it, between the modern world in which we live, in which people expect their leaders to be a lot more accessible . . . and the dignity of the office. And you've got to be careful that you don't compromise the one in the attempt to enter into the other."

There is a tendency for political criticism to be sharper among the chattering classes of London than in, say, the Midland suburbs and towns, where concern for foreign policy is dwarfed by issues like binge drinking and discipline in the schools. Nonetheless, it was remarkable how many people had turned on Blair. Even early in his first term, there were those who considered him unbearably pious, prone to empty idealism and windy intellectual pronouncements—a spinner, a glad-hander.

As far back as 1997, the joke was that if you called the Downing Street switchboard after hours the answering machine would say, "Please leave a message after the high moral tone." He was Bambi, and Phony Tony. He wasn't especially smart, it was said, nothing like the Labour giants of an earlier generation: Denis Healey, Harold Wilson, Tony Crosland, Richard Crossman. At Oxford, he'd earned a second-class degree, and, well, doesn't *everyone* at Oxford get a second-class degree just for breathing? Blair's mentor, the late Roy Jenkins, a colossal figure in Parliament and the biographer of Churchill and Gladstone, echoed an old remark about FDR when he told a writer for *The Spectator* that Blair had "a second-class mind" and "a first-class temperament." Unfortunately for Blair, most people seemed to remember only the former. He'd been an actor in school—he'd played Mark Antony, and Captain Stanhope in *Journey's End*—and now he was capable of changing his rhetoric, even his accent, as the occasion warranted. Wasn't he just a British version of Bill Clinton with a more settled domestic arrangement? "Blair's like a very sweet pudding," one senior Tory MP told me. "The first mouthful is nice, but then it becomes nauseating—the easy emoting, the quivering chin . . ."

It was relentless. Perhaps only in England—the one country where, it is said, the people feel Schadenfreude toward themselves—could a Prime Minister with such promise, and, over time, real accomplishments, be whacked around so mercilessly.

After the war in Iraq, it was something else, more serious. Blair and his team were roundly blamed for "sexing up" an intelligence dossier that had been compiled on Iraq and for presenting conjecture on weapons of mass destruction as incontrovertible fact. Worse, Blair was seen as the "poodle" of Bush and the Pentagon neoconservatives, ignoring domestic opinion and the ambiguity of the intelligence estimates simply to rush into the arms of the American President. So now he was Tony Bliar. And Tony Blur. And the Right Honourable Member for Texas North. Last year, a small group of members of the House of Commons undertook what was, in effect, an impeachment initiative against Blair, with a motion called "Conduct of the Prime Minister in relation to the war against Iraq." If successful, it would be the first impeachment since the proceedings brought against Lord Melville, the First Lord of the Admiralty, in 1806, for embezzlement. Some of Blair's own diplomats thought that he had fudged the case on Iraq. One of his former First Secretaries at the United Nations, Carne Ross, told the BBC, "I personally don't trust him, no. . . . I'm afraid the government did not tell the whole truth about the alleged threat that Iraq posed. That's why I think it's a tawdry story." The rhetoric of his opponents could be unhinged. In the *Guardian,* once the newspaper of Blair's electoral base, Harold Pinter was quoted as saying, "Blair sees himself as a representative of moral rectitude. He is a mass murderer."

One afternoon, I met with Peter Kilfoyle, a Labour traditionalist in the Commons—"Not Old Labour," he insisted. "Vintage Labour"—at the Pugin Room, one of the many tearooms inside Westminster. Kilfoyle represents a lower-income constituency in Liverpool. He had been such an early enthusiast among the Party's Old Guard that he'd earned a spot as a minister. He resigned in 2000.

Kilfoyle represents what one journalist called the "flat-cap and pass-the-fish-and-chips" wing of the Party, and, in the end, sounding much like some of Clinton's critics in the Democratic Party, he found Blair to be a trimmer, insensitive to the poor, and inauthentic. "I once took him to a football match," Kilfoyle said. "He showed up in a dark suit and a polo sweater. I said, 'Tony, what the hell? You look like an Apache dancer!' He called Peter Mandelson"—one of Blair's closest advisers at the time—"to ask what he thought. He needed reassurance on how to play the part.

"He's lost his way completely," Kilfoyle continued. "He's trying to re-create the Labour Party, and he's trying to recast it in his own image. The Labour Party was an ideological party and now it's a cult of personality." The Pugin Room was crowded, loud, and smoky. Kilfoyle lit up his fifth Silk Cut of the hour and said, "Look, we all mobilized behind Tony Blair after eighteen years of opposition. Those around him treat him like Chauncey Gardiner in *Being There.* . . . The best government was post-war Clement Attlee, who really changed this country: with welfare benefits, the health service, massive renewal programs. This Government has just flitted around the edges."

When I asked Kilfoyle if he would support Blair this time around, he smiled and said only, "No comment."

"I'm a critical friend," he said. "If your friend is pissed and says, 'Give me the keys, I'll drive,' you can't say O.K."

It really is remarkable how unwilling Blair's antagonists—whether Tory or Labour—are to give him credit for what's gone right in the past eight years: the lowest rate of inflation since the nineteen-fifties; a sharp decline in unemployment; sustained economic growth for every year in office; a historic breakthrough in the Northern Ireland dispute, leading to the 1998 Good Friday agreement and a near-cessation of violence on all sides; the establishment of a parliament in Scotland, an assembly in

Wales, and a mayoralty in London; an improvement in—or, at least, an end to the deterioration of—public services; an increase in the number of doctors, nurses, and dentists (sorry, Mrs. Holsworth!) and a reduction in the waiting period for surgery. Perhaps the most significant of Blair's achievements was to lead the rescue of the Labour Party, which, in the Thatcher-Major years, had seemed destined for marginality as the English working class declined in number.

Blair risked everything in his decision to support Bush, and, when his case for war turned out to be unfounded, he lost the confidence and trust of much of the population. He will almost certainly win May 5, but will he win convincingly enough to rule? Or will he suddenly be afloat, a lame duck paddling in the wake of Gordon Brown? Chris Patten, the last British governor of Hong Kong and an avatar of the British political establishment, said, "Never, after eight years, can it be glad, confident morning again. The young leader would look shop-soiled even without Iraq. But Iraq showed the gap between the image and the reality. . . . The real question to be asked about Blair is whether he sacrificed the objective with which he entered office—of making Britain comfortable in Europe—and sacrificed it to President Bush."

The debate over Blair and Iraq centers on two vexed and related subjects: the nature of the Prime Minister's core convictions and the efficacy of the "special relationship" between the United States and Britain.

Two and a half years ago, as Blair made plain that he would be America's strongest political and military ally, Roy Jenkins rose in the House of Lords, and, like Mark Antony in his funeral oration, began with tribute:

> I have a high regard for the Prime Minister. I have been repelled by attempts to portray him as a vacuous man with an artificial smile and no convictions. I am reminded of similar attempts by a frustrated Right to suggest that Gladstone was mad, Asquith was corrupt, and Attlee was negligible. My view is that the Prime Minister, far from lacking conviction, has almost too much, particularly when dealing with the world beyond Britain. He is a little Manichean for my perhaps now jaded taste, seeing matters in stark terms of good and evil, black and white, contending with each other, and with a consequent belief that if evil is cast down good will inevitably follow. I am more inclined to see the world and the regimes in it in varying shades of gray.

Although it was left unsaid in which particular shades of gray Roy Jenkins saw the Iraqi Baathists, he was undoubtedly right to see a moralist in his protégé. When Blair was at Oxford, in the early seventies, he impressed no one as a budding politico; he was not an activist, nor did he join the Oxford Union or any political groups—not even the student Labour Party. (In fact, his father was a Tory who revered Margaret Thatcher.) He read law, but he also had time for history and political theory, particularly the works of Christian socialists like R. H. Tawney, and, through an older friend at Oxford, an Australian-born vicar named Peter Thomson, he came to read the work of John Macmurray, a Scottish philosopher whose left-of-center Christian thought—a disdain for raw individualism, a yearning for solidarity without collectivization— anticipates the work of some of the American communitarians, as John Rentoul, one of Blair's biographers, writes. Like Blair himself a quarter century later, Macmurray was a philosophical triangulator, rejecting the prescriptive designs of socialism yet accepting its softer Sermon on the Mount generalities. "If you really want to understand what I'm all about," Blair once said, "you have to take a look at a guy called John Macmurray. It's all there."

When Blair was at Oxford, religious observance in England was already in decline, and yet he became observant and was eventually confirmed in the Anglican Church. As a young barrister, he married a colleague, Cherie Booth, who had been reared in the Labour Party and the Catholic Church. Blair often took communion at Cherie's church, in Islington, in North London, until, in 1996, Cardinal Basil Hume wrote to him and asked that he, as an Anglican with sufficient access to Anglican churches, desist. Blair wrote back obliging the Cardinal, but, with a drop of acid in his pen, added, "I wonder what Jesus would have made of it."

As a Labour Party activist and then as an MP from the constituency of Sedgefield, Blair continued speaking about politics in moralistic terms. He was not at all rooted in the socialist, Labour vocabulary of Michael Foot and Tony Benn, following instead the Victorian path of such Liberal Party lights as Gladstone, Asquith, and Lloyd George. He did not, like Gladstone, wander the night streets of London looking to redeem the souls of prostitutes, but he did write with the starch of a parson invoking the awfulness of moral relativism. "Christianity is a very tough religion," he wrote. "It is judgmental. There is right and wrong. There is good and bad."

Blair attends church nearly every Sunday and is said to read the Bible daily (he has even said that he's read the Koran three times, including once when he was on vacation in Portugal), yet he learned over time to avoid mentioning religion in a political context. Statements like "Jesus was a modernizer"—which sounded to some as if the leader of New Labour had brought the Son of God into his fold—caused him enormous grief. In contrast to the United States, where it is nearly a requirement for high office to advertise belief, only seven percent of the British population attends church regularly, and displays of public piety are scorned as sanctimonious. In 2003, Blair drafted his speech to the nation on Iraq, closing with a solemn "God bless you." His aides, a fairly godless lot, replaced the offending phrase with a simple "Thank you." But the staff cannot undo the image. The satirical magazine *Private Eye* still calls Blair "the Vicar of St. Albion," and the television interviewers Jeremy Paxman and David Frost have both tried to get a rise out of him by asking if he prayed with George Bush—an idea sure to unnerve many Britons. In one of our interviews, I tried to ask Blair about his religious background, and, predictably, he would not answer.

"It leads to all sorts of highways and byways having nothing to do with politics," he said. "I learned my lesson when I actually gave an interview about religion and I was asked the question three times: 'Are you saying that if you are a Christian you have to vote Labour?' Each time, I said no, and the headline was something like 'If You're a Christian, You Have to Vote Labour, Says Blair.' The fact is, you never, ever, ever, in our politics, get into this argument and get out of it without people misconstruing it."

Blair saves his high principles for large occasions. Faced with humanitarian crises in the Balkans and in Sierra Leone, he began to invoke his nineteenth-century predecessors and to make a moral case for military action. On a trip to Bulgaria in 1999, he talked about Gladstone's campaign in the eighteen-seventies to bring attention to atrocities committed there by the Turks. "Today, we face the same questions that confronted Gladstone over one hundred and twenty years ago," he said. "Does one nation or people have the right to impose its will on another? Is there ever a justification for a policy based on the ethnic supremacy of one ethnic group? Can the outside world simply stand by when a rogue state brutally abuses the basic rights of those it governs? Gladstone's answer in 1876 was clear. And so is mine today."

In many ways, Thatcher had prepared the way for New Labour. Not only had she presided over the privatization of major utilities and the contraction of failing industries such as coal and steel; she also showed how a Prime Minister could answer Dean Acheson's postwar challenge when he said that Britain "has lost an empire and has not yet found a role." Like Harold Macmillan before her, Thatcher saw Britain's role as America's closest ally—British Athens playing wise man to the Roman-American superpower.

During the Second World War, the choice, rooted in national interest, had been clear. Churchill told de Gaulle, "Each time I have to choose between you and Roosevelt, I shall always choose Roosevelt." Afterward, Britain wavered between contradictory impulses, between its European allies and its Atlantic alliance. In 1956, during the Suez crisis, when Britain, France, and Israel colluded to seize the canal from Egypt, Anthony Eden acted without Washington's support—a miscalculation that provoked President Eisenhower to unprecedented anger. Britain was forced to withdraw from the canal, and the crisis left the country with a warning: that it should never again ignore America's interests or defy Washington. During the Vietnam War, however, Harold Wilson turned down Lyndon Johnson's request to send troops to Southeast Asia. Then, in the eighties and early nineties, the trend shifted once more. Thatcher's embrace of Ronald Reagan was absolute, a Tory-Republican version of the Athens-Rome model; and, after Saddam Hussein invaded Kuwait, Thatcher bolstered George H. W. Bush's confidence in the run-up to the Gulf War, telling him, "This is no time to go wobbly."

In the late nineties, when the Europeans and the Clinton Administration were slow to act in Kosovo, Blair repeatedly urged the West to move more forcefully. His remonstrations helped bring on the first major deployment of NATO troops since the pact was signed, a half century earlier. The action in Kosovo raised new questions about the conduct of foreign policy, particularly the use of force against sovereign states that had not attacked a neighbor. In 1879, when Gladstone was facing similar questions about humanitarian intervention, he made the Victorian moralist's case:

> Remember the rights of the savage, as we call him. Remember that the happiness of his humble home, remember that the sanctity of life in the hill villages of Afghanistan, among the winter snows, is as inviolable in the eye of Almighty God as can be your own.

If he was right about being "morally forced" toward intervention, Gladstone wrote in his diary, then he could consider his work in politics the "great and high election of God."

In 1999, Blair led an England that would brook no mention of the

Almighty in politics and had long ago lost the capacities of an imperial power; nevertheless, he was prepared to urge on the world—the new "interdependent world," as he said constantly—an end to Realpolitik and the revival of a morally based interventionism. Blair wrote a speech entitled "Doctrine of the International Community," which he delivered at the Economic Club of Chicago. The modern world, Blair said, could no longer avoid intervening in the sort of crises that it had seen in Bosnia and Rwanda. He laid out five criteria for action:

> First, are we sure of our case? War is an imperfect instrument for righting humanitarian distress; but armed force is sometimes the only means of dealing with dictators. Second, have we exhausted all diplomatic options? We should always give peace every chance as we have in the case of Kosovo. Third, on the basis of a practical assessment of the situation, are there military operations we can sensibly and prudently undertake? Fourth, are we prepared for the long term? In the past, we talked too much of exit strategies. But, having made a commitment, we cannot simply walk away once the fight is over; better to stay with moderate numbers of troops than return for repeat performances with large numbers. And, finally, do we have national interests involved? The mass expulsion of eth- nic Albanians from Kosovo demanded the notice of the rest of the world. But it does make a difference that this is taking place in such a combustible part of Europe.

During the 2000 U.S. election campaign, Blair's circle was fairly indis- creet in betraying its hope that Al Gore would defeat George Bush. The Clinton-Blair relationship had been one of like-minded brothers (with Clinton in the role of the wise, if erratic, older brother), and Blair's lieu- tenants, including his chief of staff, Jonathan Powell, had learned many of their campaign techniques and media gambits by observing James Carville, George Stephanopoulos, and Paul Begala in Clinton's first cam- paign, in 1992. Together, they promoted a fuzzy "third way"—liberal on social issues such as abortion, the environment, and race, centrist on economic issues such as welfare and deficit spending, and increasingly interventionist abroad.

Initially, there seemed little chance that a Bush foreign policy would, in any way, resemble the tenets laid out in Blair's Chicago speech. In 2000, Condoleezza Rice published an article in *Foreign Affairs*, "Pro- moting the National Interest," which was Kissingerian in its emphasis on national interests and its disdain for "humanitarian intervention" and nation-building. And yet the first piece of advice that Clinton gave Blair after Bush, in effect, was declared President by the Supreme Court was distinctly nonpartisan. "Be his friend," Clinton told Blair at Chequers, the Prime Minister's weekend retreat. "Be his best friend. Be the guy he turns to."

After Blair held his first serious meeting with Bush, at Camp David in February 2001, he told an aide that Bush was "strong, straightforward, with an underlying seriousness. You know where you are with him. I like him." As Bush said at their press conference, "He put the charm offensive on me." Asked whether they shared some interests, Bush cracked, "Well, we both use Colgate toothpaste."

One morning, Blair and his entourage set off to campaign in the town of Gravesend, east of London. The ostensible aim was to promote the development of industries and infrastructure along the banks of the Thames, but the real reason was to reach the swing votes of the county of Kent. Blair got into the backseat of his car—a bottle-green Jaguar Sovereign—and, along with his press aides, David Hill and Hilary Coffman, and some other assistants, I climbed into a van. After a breakneck, bendy ride to Canary Wharf, we boarded a kind of *bateau-mouche* and embarked on an hour-long journey on the river. All along the way, Blair gave a string of interviews, careful always to repeat key facts about the multibillion-dollar Thames Gateway development project. He repeated the same phrases—"biggest brownfield project in Western Europe," "concern for the environmental questions," etc.—with precision. He had mastered the briefing book.

David Hill stood off to the side and, with an ironic glint of admiration, watched his man at work in front of the cameras and tape recorders.

"You familiarize him, then you wind him up and let him go," he said.

The Blair team disembarked at Gravesend, did a public event on the pier with local pols and businesspeople about the development program, took a walkabout along "the historic High Street" (snap, snap, sound bite, sound bite), and then we hustled back to the waiting vans. In the rush, we almost lost track of Blair's Jaguar.

"Do you remember that episode of *The West Wing* when Josh and Toby miss the motorcade and they're left behind in Indiana?" Hilary Coffman said. "We can relate."

A couple of minutes later, we arrived at a train that would take us from

Gravesend back to Charing Cross Station, very close to Downing Street. There was no special train, not even a reserved car; the Blair crowd remarked on "how non–White House" it all was. Blair took a seat near a window and a few aides squished in next to him, including John Prescott, Blair's deputy PM. Prescott, who comes from a family of miners, railway-men, and union officials, attended Ruskin College, Oxford, on scholar-ship in his late twenties; as a young man, he worked as a steward on a cruise ship, and when he won a seat in the Commons Tory MPs like the toff Nicholas Soames used to shout at him, "A whiskey-and-soda for me, Giovanni! And a gin-and-tonic for my friend!" Prescott has a meaty, Old Labour face; he is tough and is a skillful Party enforcer. Once, when Blair angered him, he called him a "fucking Jesus Christ." One of Prescott's main tasks is to serve as arbiter of the dysfunctional partnership between Blair and Gordon Brown. As the train rolled along, I could hear Hill qui-etly briefing Blair on some upcoming events, at one point saying, "And the message is . . ." Blair took notes on a white legal pad. As the train picked up more passengers, he cheerfully told his security guards to let some in to fill the few empty seats in our part of the car. "As opposed to the right wing, we need all positive messages," Hill was saying. "Clear . . . refined message . . . forward . . ."

The commuters seemed underwhelmed to be in the presence of their Prime Minister. A man carrying the *Daily Telegraph* sat down, glanced once at Blair, opened his paper, and never stopped reading. A little girl asked her mother, "Mummy, is that Tony Blair?" Sensing an interest, Blair invited her to come over and take a picture with her cell-phone camera. The mother, an Italian immigrant, told Blair that Silvio Berlus-coni would never take such a train.

"I imagine not," Blair said.

For much of the hour-long trip into town, I was able to sit near Blair and ask him about Iraq. From almost the day he took office, Blair had been telling visitors to No. 10 that he was appalled by the intelligence reports he was reading on Saddam's intentions and his weapons programs. "I don't understand why the French and others don't understand this," he said in 1997 to Paddy Ashdown, then the leader of the Liberal Demo-crats. "We cannot let him get away with it."

The Al Qaeda attacks in New York and Washington marked the end of the Bush Administration's hope of running the inward-looking foreign policy envisioned in Rice's *Foreign Affairs* article. "We are all internationalists now," Blair had said in Chicago, and, as Clinton had advised, Blair quickly became Bush's most steadfast ally, signing on for the military efforts in Afghanistan and Iraq. No other country provided nearly as many troops for the U.S.-led incursions. I asked Blair if he thought the United States could have gone to war in Iraq without Britain, which had given the invasion at least the appearance of an international coalition.

"I don't know," Blair said. "I think the United States, in the end, would do whatever was necessary for its own security. But it was important that we did not leave this up to the United States alone. I also profoundly believe that September 11th was an attack on the free world, not on the United States. It was an attack on America because America is the leading power of the free world. If America hadn't been, and Britain was, it would have been an attack on Britain. Let's not be daft about this. This alliance with America has stood my country in good stead."

Part of Blair's problem is that despite his differences with the Administration over everything from the Kyoto environmental accord to foreign aid, to say nothing of Labour's far more liberal domestic policies, much of the British public now sees his brand of interventionism as indistinguishable from the neoconservatism of the White House "Vulcans." And yet Blair seemed not to mind.

"What I think is interesting is that people can come to the same position from different perspectives," he said. "The idea that our ultimate security lies in the spread of the values of democracy and freedom is an idea I feel very comfortable with as a progressive. Now, that doesn't mean you go and alter every regime in the world that doesn't correspond with those principles. But it does mean that where we have taken those steps to intervene, you do have faith in the people—whether it's in Iraq or in Afghanistan or, indeed, in Palestine and the Lebanon—to decide their own future."

Is there in fact much difference between the American neoconservatives and Blair's liberal interventionism?

"I don't spend too much time trying to analyze that," he said. "I just say what I think is right in a situation. And in the end we had to take a decision on Saddam. You could have left him there or you could have removed him, and I thought it was better to remove him. . . . What used to be just a moral cause is now also a cause in our own self-interest, which is why the conservatives and the progressives can unite around it."

Sometimes, I said, it seems as if Blair has more admirers in the United States than at home.

"It's kind of people to be good about me in the United States, but right now I need that here," Blair said. "Iraq has been a very divisive issue. There's no point in disputing that. The most important thing now is to concentrate on the future, though, because it must be the case that in a battle between the Iraqi people—and it's now clear that the Iraqi people want democracy with all the guarantees and rights and freedoms that we take for granted—and a gang of terrorists and insurgents, it's pretty obvious whose side we should be on, even for those people who opposed the original conflict. I think there is a sense now of change spreading across the Middle East. Let's leave aside what the reasons for that are, but what's happening in the Lebanon, the announcement made by the President of Egypt about democratic elections, what's already happened in a country like Afghanistan is amazing after decades and decades of brutal repression.

"Sometimes these issues have to be judged on a long time scale and you have to accept that. I hope and believe that when people look back they will see this as something that brought about change, as something good not only for Iraq and the region but also for our country here."

In the months preceding the war, Blair often denounced the history and the nature of the Baathist dictatorship, but he built his case for war on a legalistic argument that Saddam had repeatedly defied UN resolutions on the possession and development of weapons of mass destruction. After the invasion, when no such weapons were found, Blair was attacked by politicians and public figures across the political spectrum—including in his own Cabinet—for selling the war on the basis of dubious intelligence. Two independent inquiries, the Hutton and Butler reports, cleared Blair of the charge that he had deliberately lied to the British people, but his credibility suffered immeasurably. What happened?

"I don't know," Blair said as the train rolled past the fenced-in back-yards of suburban London. "The best that I can go on is what the Iraq Survey Group has found. Two things we do know: Saddam had WMD and we haven't found them."

If he had known that Iraq's weapons program was so diminished, would he have gone to war based on Saddam's "intentions" to build more WMD and on a human rights case?

"The legal case for war rested on breaches of UN resolutions, but in February 2003, I made a speech in Glasgow where I described the relevance of the nature of the regime," he said. "And the truth is, what the relevance of the nature of the regime did mean was that, one, obviously, any risk of WMD in the hands of a regime such as this was greater than WMD in the hands of a relatively benign regime. And, secondly, it meant that removing that regime was in itself not a bad thing to do. On the contrary, it's a good thing to do. Now, the legal case had to be based on the breaches of UN resolutions. That's the distinction, really. Again, contrary to the history of this, I think that, for all of us looking at this, the nature of the regime was a very important context in which that legal case was examined. In terms of the legal case, ah, it was about WMD."

Blair squirmed at this line of questioning. He could not, politically or otherwise, bring himself to say that the war was fought on a false premise. "So you are saying no, in other words?" I said.

"In the end, the issue was to do with breaches of UN resolutions with respect to WMD," Blair said. "A better way of putting this question is: 'But for September 11th, is this a discussion we would have been having?' And the answer to that is no. What September 11th did was change my thinking fundamentally. I then thought that all those worries I'd had about WMD and proliferation were thrown into sharp relief and I thought, No, the one thing we must make absolutely sure of is that this nexus of repressive states, the development of WMD, the development of this type of virulent and extreme form of terrorism—you've got to put a stop to it. What does that mean? It means take the security measures that are necessary. It means sending a signal right across the world that from now on in if you develop this in the face of UN resolutions you're going to face trouble. Now, that was the reason for taking on Iraq. It wasn't because I suddenly thought Iraq was going to invade Britain. I didn't. We never put the case on that basis. But the importance of enforcing the international will vis-à-vis WMD was brought home to me by September 11th and therefore the place to start was Iraq, because Iraq was in breach of UN resolutions going back a number of years."

Blair paused and then continued, "Now, I personally think that since then there has been an imperfect dialogue with Iran, but at least Europe and America are working together on it. Libya is giving up its WMD. The A. Q. Khan network, which was very dangerous indeed, has been effectively shut down. North Korea is an issue, but the world is focused on it. It's not been allowed to fester. The security reason, for me, for taking the action—and without the security reason you couldn't have taken it simply on human rights grounds—the security reason was very much linked to my perception that, post–September 11th, the whole game had changed. The balance of risk had changed. If, in the situation previously, the balance of doubt was toward inaction, after September 11th the balance of doubt, always, for me, fell with action."

. . .

According to Peter Stothard's book *Thirty Days,* one of several informative accounts of the debate over Iraq in Britain, less than a week before the Commons voted on the war Blair told one of his aides, Sally Morgan, "What amazes me is how many people are happy for Saddam to stay. They ask why don't we get rid of Mugabe, why not the Burmese lot. Yes, let's get rid of them all. I don't because I can't, but when you can you should."

That remark, and others like it, showed Blair's increasing disenchantment with the left. Even though, in Clintonian fashion, he had moved his party to the center, he never imagined in 1997 that so many readers of the *Guardian,* say, would abandon him. (Similarly, many readers of the *Guardian* would never have imagined that a Labour Prime Minister would tighten up on civil liberties or court Rupert Murdoch, the über-purveyor of right-leaning media, as assiduously as Blair has.)

When I asked Blair about his exasperated remark at Downing Street, he said, "The biggest scandal in progressive politics is that you do not have people with placards out in the street on North Korea. I mean, that is a disgusting regime. The people are kept in a form of slavery, twenty-three million of them, and no one protests! You get a hundred thousand people out in the street of just about any European capital to protest about America, which, for all its faults, is a free country!

"The left has two impulses, which come into conflict with each other, though both of those impulses are perfectly good," Blair went on. "One is peace, and the other is intervention to help people. Peace is great. But, if you're living with a tyrannical regime, you don't have much peace."

I asked Blair about all the mistakes and even disasters that followed the fall of Saddam: the American failure to anticipate mass looting, the insurgency, the unending casualties, the torture at Abu Ghraib prison.

"On that I take a slightly heretical view," he said. "I think that when anything like that happens it's ghastly and terrible and should be condemned immediately and dealt with. But I also think that people are cleverer in the Middle East, in Iraq and places like that, than we often give them credit for. And what they see is something terrible happening and the U.S. acting on it, the U.S. politicians under pressure, the U.S. soldiers responsible being prosecuted. I think people say these things happen, but the difference between a democracy and a dictatorship is that in a democracy when something terrible happens someone is held to account and in a dictatorship they're not.

"I had meeting after meeting about post-war planning, but all the post-war planning was really on the basis of humanitarian collapse," Blair continued. "I mean, that's what one thought was going to happen. That's what we were warned about." Only if the coalition successfully provided Iraq with the rudiments of a working, secure democracy, Blair said, would the insurgents fade. "Because how can they then turn toward the people in the Middle East and elsewhere, to Muslims the world over, and say, 'This is the terrible Satan exploiting and demeaning our people and preventing us from having our religion,' when people in Iraq are actually freer to worship in Iraq than they were and they've got a democracy!"

Blair's own frustrations were clear. The absence of WMD in Iraq had left him feeling unmoored, evasive. I thought of McEwan's Perowne and his attempt to get behind Blair's earnest mask in the days before the war:

> Perowne wonders if such moments, stabs of cold panicky doubt, are an increasing part of the Prime Minister's days, or nights. There might not be a second UN resolution. The next weapons inspectors' report could also be inconclusive. The Iraqis might use biological weapons against the invasion force. Or, as one former inspector keeps insisting, there might no longer be any weapons of mass destruction at all. There's talk of famine and three million refugees, and they're already preparing the reception camps in Syria and Iran. The UN is predicting hundreds of thousands of Iraqi deaths. There could be revenge attacks on London. And still the Americans remain vague about their post-war plans. Perhaps they have none. In all, Saddam could be overthrown at too high a cost. It's a future no one can read. Government ministers speak up loyally, various newspapers back the war, there's a fair degree of anxious support in the country along with the dissent, but no one really doubts that in Britain one man alone is driving the matter forward. Night sweats, hideous dreams, the wild, lurching fantasies of sleeplessness?

Now, with the main fighting likely over, it remains unclear how history will judge Blair. Conor Gearty, a human-rights advocate who works in the same law chambers as Cherie Blair, told me that he was against the war and Blair's conduct of it, and yet he will sometimes ask his students at the London School of Economics if they can imagine Blair and Bush one day being declared heroes, for having opened the way to a democratizing wave in the authoritarian states of the Middle East. "My students just laugh," Gearty said. "But I admit it's not inconceivable."

In all the best accounts of Blair's diplomacy—Stothard's *Thirty Days*, Peter Riddell's *Hug Them Close*, John Kampfner's *Blair's Wars*, the Hutton and Butler reports, and the BBC documentary *Iraq, Tony & the Truth*—the Prime Minister is convinced that Saddam is in violation of UN resolutions. He is not deliberately misleading Britain, but, at the same time, he appears too willing to accept unsubstantiated intelligence as absolute and to advertise that evidence as fact to the public. "At the heart of the problem was a culture clash: between the worlds of John le Carré's George Smiley and 'The West Wing,' between cautious words, caveats, and nuances of the Joint Intelligence Committee and the megaphone communications of 'spin doctors' and the twenty-four-hour news cycle," wrote Peter Riddell, a columnist for the London *Times*. "The more public intelligence assessments are, the more that any qualifications and uncertainties disappear. Tony Blair and the Government were certainly at fault in not highlighting the doubts."

Even some of Blair's closest advisers appeared to know that they were playing a reckless game in preparing a dubious dossier for the leadership and for public consumption. In an e-mail that was sent in September 2002—and that was revealed publicly a year later—Jonathan Powell, Blair's chief of staff, told the chairman of the Joint Intelligence Committee, John Scarlett, that while the "dossier is good and convincing for those who are prepared to be convinced . . . the document does nothing to demonstrate a threat, let alone an imminent threat, from Saddam."

Peter Oborne, the political editor of the conservative *Spectator*, told me he thought that Blair could be a "broken" man as a result of the loss of trust. "This all matters because of a hundred thousand Iraqis killed, Abu Ghraib, a shameful thing for which no one was sacked," Oborne, who has just published a book on lying in British politics, said. "The readiness to break international law, to lie to voters and the international community, to ignore proper process, the sheer arrogance. It is the most evil and destructive and barbaric act of my lifetime and it has shaken my faith. Those WMD did not exist and we were told that they did. . . . As a result, the entire political system has suffered a catastrophic collapse in trust in Blair himself."

Although some historians might well agree with Blair that the destruction of the Baathist regime—despite the casualties, the terrible postwar planning, Abu Ghraib—prevented further violence by Saddam and his sons and led to regional change, the antipathy to, even hatred of, George Bush among some Britons is so intense that Blair's most unforgivable sin seems to be his second-banana role in the Anglo-American alliance. This impression was only exacerbated when, in early 2003, Defense Secretary Donald Rumsfeld told the press that the coalition could live without British military help, or when White House aides such as Scooter Libby, Vice-President Dick Cheney's chief of staff, openly mocked Blair's calls for a (doomed) second resolution in the Security Council. "Oh, dear, we'd better not do that or we might upset the Prime Minister," Libby said, according to Philip Stephens's biography of Blair.

The British have not soured on the United States so much as they have come to long for a Prime Minister who will remove the taint of subservience from the relationship. Last year, English audiences went to see *Love Actually*, a lighter-than-air comedy starring Hugh Grant as an improbably handsome, love-starved Prime Minister. People broke out in applause during a scene in which Prime Minister Grant, during a joint press conference at No. 10 with a libidinous (Clintonian) cowboy (Bushian) American President, played by Billy Bob Thornton, says that the relationship is no longer special. "I fear that this has become a bad relationship," he says, "a relationship based on the President taking exactly what he wants and casually ignoring all those things that really matter to Britain." And yet those applauding audiences knew that the *Love Actually* moment was as improbable under Tony Blair, or any modern Prime Minister, as Don Corleone's ascension to the papacy. Around the Downing Street offices, aides are quite sure that Blair will win, but they do not pretend that the Bush-Blair quandary has been fully resolved. "The problem is Bush," one of his senior advisers told me. "The monumental obligation to Bush has brought out latent anti-Americanism. People are concerned about trust and Blair's judgment. The fact that he has done the wrong thing on Iraq means they have grave concerns about his judgment."

In order to win back the left, the official said, Blair has to show that he is pushing the Americans to act more forcefully on the Israeli-Palestinian dispute, on aid to Africa, on climate change. "It doesn't balance Iraq," the official said, "but if you are a voter who needs permission to vote for Blair, even grudgingly, you can say at least he is O.K. on the Palestinian question or public service." For conservative voters, Blair needs to show that he is active in what another official called "Rudy Giuliani politics": getting rid of public drunkenness, eradicating annoyances like graffiti, getting control of discipline in the schools. The leaders of the Conservative Party concede that they can win only through apathy and protest votes; their overall voice in this campaign, one Tory MP told me, is "more Dole in '96 than Bush in 2000, more bleak than hopeful." And that should be telling. Simon Jenkins, who writes a column in the London *Times* that regularly attacks Blair, told me that, as long as the economy stays at its current level, "people feel quite good. And they are prepared to give credit to the smiling chap at the top. There is no one else but Tony Blair."

President Bush has not yet paid much of a political price for the mistakes that accompanied the Iraq war. The Abu Ghraib torture scandal outraged world opinion, yet Rumsfeld had to endure little more than a day's questioning on Capitol Hill. Recent government investigations showed the entire intelligence bureaucracy to have been utterly mistaken on the question of Iraqi WMD. But there were no resignations of consequence—George Tenet stepped down as CIA chief, but then was awarded the Medal of Freedom. During the Presidential debates, Bush could not name a major mistake that he had made in his first term; the words "Abu Ghraib" were never uttered in the debates by either Bush or John Kerry.

Blair has endured far more criticism, but he, too, may pay a minimal price at the polls. Recently, I was watching him on a television chat show called *The Wright Stuff*, in which an unctuous host named Matthew Wright put the Prime Minister through yet another hour of the masochism campaign. (He called him Tony no fewer than twenty times.) At one point, Wright ran a tape for Blair of voters telling the camera what they wanted from him:

> WOMAN: I would like Tony Blair to get rid of bureaucracy in hospitals, so that nurses could actually get on with their job. . . .
> MAN: I want equal rights for fathers.
> YOUNG WOMAN: I want Tony Blair to improve schools by giving teachers more power.
> MAN: I want smoking banned in public.
> WOMAN: I want university fees abolished.
> WOMAN: I want honesty from the government.
> MAN: I want regional government for the Northwest.
> MAN: I want immigrants not to be treated like criminals.
> YOUNG WOMAN: I want Tony Blair to introduce congestion charges all over Britain, so it will encourage people to use public transport.

YOUNG WOMAN IN HEAD SCARF: I want Tony Blair to stop doing what the American government says, and more what the British public thinks.

WOMAN: I want Tony Blair to stop putting pressure on moms like me to go back to work.

"It's a long list," Blair said. But he could only be pleased. Only one person, the woman wearing a *hijab,* said a word about foreign policy; everything else was domestic bread and butter.

Blair is concentrating on winning his way back into the affections of the British public inch by inch. He will take any meeting, it seems. A reception for the British Society of Magazine Editors at Downing Street did not appear to feature the opinion magazines—the *New Statesman, The Spectator,* or *Prospect.* It cast a wider net: *CosmoGirl!, Waitrose Food Illustrated, Motorcycle News,* fashion magazines, travel magazines. I sat next to the editor of *Spirit & Destiny.* I asked her what was in her magazine and she said, "Alternate lifestyle, health, and just a hint of witchcraft." Blair opened the meeting by saying, "A special thanks to the lady from *Flower Arranger* magazine who brought some flowers for Cherie."

Some of the questions were serious—about human rights in China, European alliances, the campaign—but there were more on things like "the BikeSafe campaign" and, more than once, the Prime Minister's opinion of Turkey Twizzlers. Then someone asked Blair whom he would choose as Chancellor of the Exchequer "if Gordon Brown were to be hit by a bus."

Blair is unshakable, and yet he paused, as if to catch his breath. "Well, that would be a really good one to speculate on," he said. "Actually, I saw him this morning and he is in very good health."

When the group of editors had fairly exhausted their cache of questions, something in Blair clicked—"Be a good host! Show them around!"—and, with a tinge of been-there-before irony, he gave the briefest of No. 10 house tours.

"Right," he said. "Well, we're in the state dining room." He pointed to one side of the room. "There's the silver. It's best to leave that alone." Then, pointing to a huge painting over his shoulder, "There's a portrait of King George. When he was around, we still had America."

Blair went back downstairs to his den. When I asked him what, if any, criticisms he had of the Bush White House, he was, as ever, careful, even indulgent. He said that the Administration's policies on everything from the environment to aid for Africa were not so much right wing as they were victims of bad press.

"The key is to understand where the Administration is coming from," he said. "The Administration is not saying Africa is unimportant. They are hardheaded about the need for good governance, anti-corruption, conflict resolution, as well as debt relief. Contrary again to what people think, they do accept the importance of tackling climate change and moving beyond the carbon-based economy. But they are going to be very hardheaded about how you do that and how it affects economic growth and living standards.

"It's a question of persuasion and also understanding where America is coming from, rather than *reading* about where the Americans are coming from, because my experience is often completely different."

Blair's delicacy about the United States is such that he seemed to dismiss the importance of anti-Americanism in Britain, especially in the universities and among the political élites and the media.

"It's a fashion!" he said. "For people to run down the relationship, to say Britain gets nothing out of it, to say I'm a poodle of America and all that stuff. . . . If you listen to any of the people doing chat shows or any of the rest of it, there's an underlying culture of mocking the relationship, saying it doesn't matter, et cetera. That's just the way it is. But if you are taking the long view and say, 'What's really in the interests of the country,' you just have to stand up and properly explain to people why the relationship is important and that we do share certain values.

"There's a part of the media in Britain that is anti-European, there's part that's anti-American, and there's a part that is anti both alliances," he continued. "Which is a bizarre position to try to put yourself in with Britain in the early part of the twenty-first century, as opposed to Britain at the end of the nineteenth century. . . . Sometimes you have to bring people back to the fundamentals and say, O.K., so you don't like this or that aspect of a policy. Are we really saying you want to give up this relationship with Europe or America? Of course not. It would be daft. No country in its senses would do that in this day and age, when, unless you are the size of China, India, or the U.S., the very thing that gives you purchase on all sorts of international situations which have a direct bearing on the interests of your country are these alliances. These are the two pillars of British foreign policy, and we'd be crackers to give up either."

.   .   .

Last spring, Blair was thinking about whether to stand again. In 1994, he and Gordon Brown had a private dinner at a restaurant called Granita, in the North London neighborhood of Islington—an event that is the folkloric mystery of contemporary British politics. Both Blair and Brown have their designated leakers; the Brown leakers contend that Blair promised Brown that, after two terms as Prime Minister (or, alternatively, ten years as Party leader), Blair would step aside for Brown; and, in the meantime, Brown would have unprecedented authority in the broad realm of domestic policy. Blair told me, as he has told everyone else, that "you don't make deals" with such positions, and no such deal was made at Granita. What is clear is that Blair saw what had happened to Thatcher, who had once said that she would go "on and on"—a bit of presumption that was laid low when her own party threw her out and then replaced her with John Major. And so Blair decided to run for a third term but, unlike Thatcher, promised that he would not attempt a fourth.

"Nobody could go on for four terms," he said. "The country wouldn't want it."

In the past couple of weeks, Brown and Blair have again closed ranks, appearing together on the campaign trail and even in a gauzy ad put together by Anthony Minghella, the director of *The English Patient*. Brown's televised support has helped Blair widen his lead.

In moments of crisis, the press often reaches for a bit of physical description to match what it imagines must be Blair's exhaustion or despair. He is "ashen-faced." His "hair is thinning." He has lost weight. I didn't see any of that. He still looks preposterously youthful, despite episodes in the past year of cardiac arrhythmia. Yet Blair did one the favor of denying that he was always in absolute command even as the polls were breaking his way.

The job "is utterly relentless," he said. "You are dealing with a multiplicity of issues the whole time. And the decision-making process stops with you. That's an amazing thing—when every decision stops with you. How do you make sense of that? It's by recognizing that it's a privilege to do it, that you can do it only for a limited time, and that the only way to make the most of it is to keep your nerve, do what you think is right, recognize you won't please all of the people all of the time—in fact, pleasing some of the people some of the time is quite an achievement. And, whatever judgments are made at the time, history may take another view."

(2005)

•

Five days before the May 5th election, the London *Sunday Times* published a formerly secret memorandum, minutes of a meeting of Blair and several of his top security, foreign policy, and intelligence officials, held seven months before the war. The document showed clearly that the British leadership understood that President Bush, despite what he had pledged, was determined to invade Iraq no matter what Saddam Hussein did in regard to his weapons programs. "Military action was now seen as inevitable," said the document, which summarized a report to Blair from Richard Dearlove, then the head of MI6, British intelligence. Dearlove had just returned to London after meetings with Administration officials in Washington. "Bush wanted to remove Saddam through military action, justified by the conjunction of terrorism and WMD. But the intelligence and facts were being fixed around the policy." *Facts were being fixed around the policy.* The disclosure of the memorandum deepened the impression that Blair had not been entirely straight with the British public, that he had done too little to challenge Bush. Even those who defended the war, even those who saw the war as having a good result—the end of the Saddam regime—if fought on largely false premises, were dismayed by Blair's flexible relation to the truth and to George W. Bush.

In the end, the election results were about as weak for Labour as Blair's advisers could have imagined. A combination of low turnout, protest votes for the Liberal Democrats, and a stronger showing by the Conservatives in the last couple of weeks of campaigning failed to keep Blair out of office—he won his third term—but the Labour majority in Parliament was reduced by a hundred votes, an enormous drop that spelled the difference between easy mastery and near-deadlock.

On July 7, 2005, while Blair, Bush, and the rest of the leaders of the major industrialized countries were meeting at Gleneagles in Scotland, four London suicide bombers—three in the Tube and one on a bus—killed fifty-six people and injured hundreds. Two weeks later, four more bombers tried for a repeat performance. The speculation about whether Tony Blair would resign in favor of Gordon Brown faded, at least for the moment.

High Water

On September 10, 1965, President Lyndon Johnson had lunch in the Roosevelt Room—the Fish Room, as FDR called it—with several aides and half a dozen ambassadors of modest-sized countries. Then he returned to the Oval Office for a routine round of meetings and telephone calls—a fairly ordinary, crowded day amid the growing crisis of the war in Vietnam. At 2:36 P.M., according to copies of Johnson's daily diaries, the President took a call from Senator Russell Long, of Louisiana. The day before, Hurricane Betsy had made landfall on the Gulf Coast. Storm gusts were up to a hundred and sixty miles an hour, and in New Orleans levees had been breached, causing much of the city to flood overnight, especially the neighborhoods of Bywater, Pontchartrain Park, and the largely black and impoverished Ninth Ward. The Army Corps of Engineers later reported as many as eighty-one deaths, a quarter-million people evacuated, and water levels of up to nine feet. Hurricane Betsy was the worst disaster to strike New Orleans since the cholera epidemic of 1849 and the yellow-fever epidemic of 1905.

Russell Long, the son of Huey Long and an old friend of Johnson's in the Senate, had a simple goal. He wanted to convince the President of the urgency of the crisis and have him come immediately to Louisiana. Their conversation is rich with emotional and political manipulation. Long made it clear to Johnson that to delay, or to send a subordinate, could easily have consequences in the 1968 election:

SENATOR LONG: Mr. President, aside from the Great Lakes, the biggest lake in America is Lake Pontchartrain. It is now drained dry. That Hurricane Betsy picked the lake up and put it inside New Orleans and Jefferson Parish, the Third [Congressional] District. . . . If I do say it, our people are just like . . . It's like my home— The whole damn home's been destroyed, but that's all right. My wife and kids are still alive, so it's O.K. Mr. President, we have really had it down there, and we need your help.

PRESIDENT JOHNSON: All right. You got it.

LONG: Well, now, if I do say it . . . we've lost only one life so far. Why we haven't lost more I can't say. . . . For example, that damn big four-hundred-year-old tree fell on top of my house. My wife and kids were, thank God, in the right room. So we're still alive. I don't need no federal aid. But, Mr. President, my people—Oh, they're in tough shape. . . . If I do say it, you could elect Hale Boggs and every guy you'd want to elect in the path of this hurricane just by handling yourself right.

Now, if you want to go to Louisiana right now—You lost that state last year. You could pick it up just like looking at it right now by going down there as the President just to see what happened. . . . Just go, and say, "My God, this is horrible! . . . These federally constructed levees that Hale Boggs and Russell Long built is the only thing that saved five thousand lives." See now, if you want to do that you can do it right now. Just pick one state up like looking at it—you lost it last time. If you'd do that you'd sack them up. [Louisiana congressman] Ed Willis is sitting on this telephone and he knows like I do that all you've got to do is just make a generous gesture, he'd get reelected, a guy that's for you.

JOHNSON: Russell, I sure want to. I've got a hell of a two days that I've got scheduled. Let me look and see what I can back out of and get into and so on and so forth and let me give you a ring back. If I can't go, I'll put the best man I got there.

LONG: So now listen, we are not the least bit interested in your best man. . . . I'm just a Johnson man. Let's—

JOHNSON: I know that. I know that.

LONG: . . . Just make it a stopover. . . . You go to Louisiana right now,
   land at Moisant Airport. [Imagining a news story] "The President was very much upset about the horrible destruction and
   damage done to this city of New Orleans, lovely town. The town
   that everybody loves." If you go there right now, Mr. President,
   they couldn't beat you if Eisenhower ran.
JOHNSON: Um-hmm. Let me think about it and call you back.

Johnson hung up. He met with Bill Moyers, Larry O'Brien, J. Edgar
Hoover, and others. He accepted an award from the leaders of the World
Convention of Churches of Christ. Then, at 5:03 P.M., he boarded a
helicopter on the South Lawn, and it ferried him to Andrews Air Force
Base. From there the President—along with Russell Long and Representative Hale Boggs, the key congressional powers in Louisiana, and
officials from the Red Cross and the Army Corps of Engineers—flew to
New Orleans on *Air Force One*. "The President spent a good deal of the
time talking w/ Senator Long and Cong. Hale Boggs during the flight,"
the diary says. "Also worked in his bedroom w/ [his assistants] on mail
that had been taken on the flight. Afterwards, the President napped for
about 30 minutes before arrival in New Orleans."
   Even at the airport, Johnson began to get a sense of the damage
wrought by Betsy. "Parts of the roofing of the terminal were torn away
and several of the large windows were broken," the diary reads. "The
members of the Presidential party had seen from the air a preview of
the city—water over ³⁄₄ of the city up to the eaves of the homes, etc." At
the urging of the mayor of New Orleans—a diminutive conservative
Democrat named Victor Hugo Schiro, whom Johnson referred to as
"Little Mayor"—the President decided to tour the flooded areas. His
motorcade stopped on a bridge spanning the Industrial Canal, in the
eastern part of the city, and from there the Presidential party saw whole
neighborhoods engulfed by floods. They could see, according to the
diary, that "people were walking along the bridge where they had disembarked from the boats that had brought them to dry land. Many of them
were carrying the barest of their possessions and many of them had been
sitting on top of their houses waiting for rescue squads to retrieve the
families and carry them to dry land." Johnson talked with a seventy-four-
year-old black man named William Marshall and asked about what had
happened and how he was getting along. As the conversation ended,
Marshall said, "God bless you, Mr. President. God ever bless you."
   In the Ninth Ward, Johnson visited the George Washington Elemen-

tary School, on St. Claude Avenue, which was being used as a shelter. "Most of the people inside and outside of the building were Negro," the diary reads. "At first, they did not believe that it was actually the President." Johnson entered the crowded shelter in near-total darkness; there were only a couple of flashlights to lead the way.

"This is your President!" Johnson announced. "I'm here to help you!"

The diary describes the shelter as a "mass of human suffering," with people calling out for help "in terribly emotional wails from voices of all ages. . . . It was a most pitiful sight of human and material destruction." According to an article by the historian Edward F. Haas, published fifteen years ago in the *Gulf Coast Historical Review,* Johnson was deeply moved as people approached and asked him for food and water; one woman asked Johnson for a boat so that she could look for her two sons, who had been lost in the flood.

"Little Mayor, this is horrible," Johnson said to Schiro. "I've never seen anything like this in my life." Johnson assured Schiro that the resources of the federal government were at his disposal and that "all red tape [will] be cut."

The President flew back to Washington and the next day sent Schiro a sixteen-page telegram outlining plans for aid and the revival of New Orleans. "Please know," Johnson wrote, "that my thoughts and prayers are with you and the thousands of Louisiana citizens who have suffered so heavily."

Hurricane Katrina was more devastating than Betsy. The death toll is sure to be many times as high and the physical damage far more extensive and enduring. And yet to see the city of New Orleans a week after the flood, to see the ruin, was to be shocked much as Johnson was forty years ago. New Orleans is never abandoned easily. Driving along St. Charles Avenue, through toxic puddles that once belonged to the Mississippi River or Lake Pontchartrain, you saw a painted sign on a door reading, "Still here. Cooking a pot of dog gumbo." Another, next to a branch of the Whitney National Bank, read, "I am sleeping inside with a big dog, an ugly woman, two shotguns and a claw hammer." By the time Hurricane Rita had reflooded parts of the city, there was almost no one left in town.

The last holdouts, especially the poorest among them, wore a look of delirium. They seemed to sense that to leave now, with no savings, with no resources, meant to leave forever. On a desolate corner in the Ninth

Ward, I sat on a curb with an old woman who had been refusing rescue for more than a week. She wore a soiled housedress. She was very old and could not have weighed more than seventy-five pounds. "I'll be here to the end," she said. There was a bottle of warm beer in a paper bag at her feet. She didn't drink from it. She was just dazed by the sun and the heat and the emptiness of her street. She was firm in her belief that all her neighbors, now in shelters in Lafayette, Houston, Pensacola, God knows where, were the lost ones. "Plain fools," she said. The street smelled of low tide in a tidal swamp. She said, "They're jealous of me. I got forty-four dollars' worth of meat in that icebox inside, and they ain't gonna take it from me. Nobody gonna lock me out of my home."

Although there were no looters now and very few residents, the streets were still being patrolled in fantastic numbers by—and this is a random sampling—the New Orleans Police, New Orleans SWAT teams, the New York City Police Department, the Sacramento Fire Department, the Greenbelt, Maryland, police, private Blackwater security contractors, the Louisiana Department of Wildlife and Fisheries, the 82nd Airborne, National Guardsmen, San Diego lifeguards, Surf Zone Relief Operations, and, in yellow T-shirts, Scientology Disaster Response teams. The Scientologists pitched a tent outside Harrah's Casino with a sign reading "Something Can Be Done About It," and offered massage "assists" to the police.

Eddie Compass, the superintendent of the New Orleans Police Department, was holding court in front of Harrah's. I got to know Compass years ago, when he was an up-and-comer in the department, and Jack Maple, who helped set the New York department right in the early Giuliani Administration, came down as a paid consultant for the NOPD. Maple was a natural for New Orleans; he was his own Mardi Gras float. He was fat and funny and wore a homburg, spectator shoes, and sharp suits, and smoked a huge Mexican cigar. In many American cities, the combination of tech-era prosperity and the sort of innovative policing techniques that Maple had helped to develop were driving crime rates down. Yet Maple, like so many consultants before him, could do little about the poverty and corruption in New Orleans. He died a couple of years ago, and now Eddie Compass, who has barely aged, was saying that he missed him. "We could use the Fat Man now," he said. "Everything else we tried failed." Five hundred of his officers—roughly thirty percent—did not initially report in the crisis. "Either they went home to take care of their families, went missing, or, God forbid, worse." Compass himself was AWOL for the first three days of the crisis. Two of his officers, including his spokesman, committed suicide during the flooding. The jails, like everything else, were non-functional, and he was keeping nearly two hundred prisoners—looters, mainly—in a makeshift lockup in the local Amtrak station. Now the streets were so militarized—and so depopulated—that the city resembled a war zone with no enemy.

"Right now," he said, "New Orleans may be the single safest city in the United States."

Hurricane Katrina destroyed the structures, comforts, and protections of civilization, and the poorer you were, the more exposed you were to high water. Stripped of electricity, air-conditioning, medicine, safety, food, clean water, doctors, transport, firm ground—stripped of everything that seemed necessary to live in New Orleans—people were left with a gesture of political correctness. Within a day of the bowl of the city filling, TV commentators had instructed viewers that the people fleeing town were under no circumstances to be called refugees: "These are Americans!" Not Bosnians, not Kosovars, not Bangladeshis—Americans. And yet, of all the New Orleanians I met—in the city, or in the Cajundome, in Lafayette, in downtown Baton Rouge, in the churches and parks of New Iberia, at the Astrodome in Houston—none gave a damn for the terminology. They'd fled danger and now they were homeless, with few prospects or none at all.

At a house where I was spending the night, I sat out on the porch until early morning listening on a transistor radio to the most powerful signal on the airwaves: WWL, 870 AM. It was a strangely efficient way of scanning the misery that had hit the Gulf Coast. The host was Garland Robinette, a sonorous broadcaster with a long history in town as a television anchor. Robinette's show was a catchall for rumors, the debunking of rumors, interviews, speculation, and a kind of regional disaster therapy.

"This is Alexandra in Algiers Point. I'm still looking for my sister, Lee Ann. If you hear anything, please call. . . ."

"Elise, you're still looking for your family?"

"The people of the Allstate National Catastrophe Team are standing by at 1-800-54-STORM."

"Ray from Houma" called to say that at Louis Armstrong Airport two people posing as FEMA officers were telling people they had to pay fifteen dollars each to get on any buses leaving New Orleans. People traded information about gas, electricity, food supplies, and rental properties throughout the South. There were news bulletins: the floodwaters are contaminated with *E. coli*, rotting flesh, spilled petroleum. Washington is sending fifty-two billion dollars. Watch out for fake website charities: there are "so many the FBI can't keep up with them." Here's how to get generators and chainsaws from John Deere. Here's how to begin filing insurance claims. A few days after the storm, WWL joined in a consortium of rival stations to form United Broadcasters of New Orleans, and they were now reaching thirty-eight states and thirteen countries. The moment that brought WWL the most attention was Robinette's interview with Mayor Ray Nagin while people were still trapped in the Superdome and in the Convention Center, and Washington, particularly the White House, seemed to be on extended summer vacation. Unlike Lyndon Johnson, President Bush was slow to respond to the emergency—so slow, in fact, that his staff felt compelled to prepare a DVD of network newscasts to impress upon him the scale of the floods, the chaos, and the suffering. "God is looking down on all this," Nagin said, "and if they are not doing everything in their power to save people they are going to pay the price. Because every day that we delay, people are dying and they're dying by the hundreds, I'm willing to bet you. . . . Don't tell me forty thousand people are coming here. They're not here. It's too doggone late. Now get off your asses and do something, and let's fix the biggest goddam crisis in the history of this country."

One morning, I set out on Interstate 10 for St. Gabriel, a small town fifteen miles south of Baton Rouge, where federal officials had converted a warehouse into a morgue. As rescue workers found more bodies in attics and hospitals and nursing homes, they sent most of them to St. Gabriel. The death toll was a matter of speculation, and yet twenty-five thousand body bags were on their way to Louisiana. On the road, I listened to an interview on WWL with Kathleen Rhodes Astorga, of the Rhodes Funeral Home chain, in New Orleans and Baton Rouge.

"We do jazz funerals, celebration-of-life ceremonies, all kinds of funerals," she said. "We just want it to be with dignity and respect."

The host lowered his voice to a timbre indicating solemnity and said, "These people have drowned, spent days in the water. Do you, um, think people should just go with your judgment on whether there should be a closed casket and put a picture on it?"

Rhodes agreed. "Thinking closed casket is not a bad idea," she said.

I pulled up to the St. Gabriel morgue. A fence surrounded the place, and the policeman at the door politely rebuffed any questions. "All I can tell you is nothing," he said. "And all I can give you is this." He handed me a sheet of paper:

Disaster Mortuary Operational Response Team (DMORT) Process
- As deceased victims are located by local emergency workers and volunteers they are taken to the collection site. A collection site is

a place where FEMA DMORT staff collects preliminary informa-
tion to help identify the victim. Information collected includes:
Address or location of victim
Any documentation associated with victim
GPS coordinates
Personal effects

- From the collection site, they are taken to the Disaster Portable
Mortuary Unit (DPMU) with dignity in a very respectful manner utilizing a police escort.

Ordinarily, WWL's studios are on the fifth floor of Dominion Tower,
an office building near the Superdome. But the windows blew in during
the storm, and WWL broadcast for a few days from a former waste-
disposal plant, in Jefferson Parish. Finally, the station moved its operations to a studio in Baton Rouge. One afternoon, I came by to meet with
the news director, Dave Cohen, a man in his thirties who wore a dirty
white undershirt and shorts that would soon be better incinerated than
washed. Every few minutes, his cell phone would bugle him to attention.
His ring tone is "When the Saints Go Marching In." He'd reach for his
hip pocket in a panic. "Yes! This is Dave!" His house, in Metairie, just
west of New Orleans, was flooded, but nothing, he said, like the Ninth
Ward.

Because his station was the most immediate, moment-to-moment
source of information in the region, I asked Cohen how it had felt to be
inside the hurricane. "Friday before the storm, we were feeling good,"
he said. "The National Hurricane Center said that this would really hit
the Florida panhandle, not us. We were barely in the 'cone of error' in
New Orleans. So I kicked off for the day on Friday at one o'clock and
went to the gym. But at around four my pager started going haywire.
Max Mayfield, the director of the National Hurricane Center, had
changed his prediction. There was a hundred-and-fifty-mile shift to the
west." It was going to be a problem to get people in the city to adjust. "In
New Orleans, people go home at lunch on Fridays," Cohen said. "All
year round. And Friday night was a football night. The Ravens were in
town to play a preseason game against the Saints at the Superdome. It
was also a big high-school football night, the jamboree games, which kick
off the season. People were out drinking, having a good time. They were
consuming very little media. But by Saturday morning we were told
there was mandatory evacuation for Plaquemines Parish, to the southeast, and some coastal areas, though not yet New Orleans. On Saturday,

Ray Nagin was still saying that we have time to watch this. A lot of people were clueless. They had no idea there were evacuations.

"We've always talked about the worst-case scenarios in Louisiana," Cohen continued. "They talk about 'slosh models'—computer-generated models on what would happen. The geography is obvious. If you are walking along the riverfront in downtown New Orleans, you are looking up at the Mississippi River. You look up at Lake Pontchartrain, up at the canals. When the water flows in, you have a city that becomes a tidal lake, with sharks and manatees and all the rest.

"By ten on Saturday night, Nagin was really concerned. He got a call from Max Mayfield saying that he should evacuate the city. And on Sunday morning Nagin issued a mandatory evacuation order. Sunday night, there were gale-force winds. We were told that if you weren't out by now it was too late, that—and this was the quote—'preparations to protect life and property should be rushed to completion.' We were broadcasting all of Sunday night. The power went out in the city. The eye of the storm wasn't even near us, but our windows in the downtown studio started cracking. And on Monday morning, while Garland Robinette was on the air, the windows blew in.

"Landfall was at six A.M. on the coast," he went on. "We feared that it would get to New Orleans at exactly ninety longitude, thirty latitude, and it got to 89.6. At one A.M., it went due north, and it felt like Christmas had come early. It was staying at 89.6 at two, three, four A.M. with one-hundred-and-fifty-mile-per-hour winds, but still it did not look like the worst-case scenario. Roofs were flying off houses, cars moved around in the wind, there were rapids in the streets, but still . . . On Monday night, there were reports that water was coming over the Seventeenth Street canal, which separates Orleans Parish and Jefferson Parish, to the west. The water was coming over in the dark. The levee itself is in Lakeview, an upscale lakefront neighborhood near where I-10 and I-610 split. At six in the morning, we were told that the levee had been ripped apart and water was pouring in. I went on the radio and said that eyewitnesses had said 'The bowl is filling.' So I said, 'Get out if you are to the east of the Seventeenth Street canal. That's the whole city. It's as bad as the Mississippi River breaking through. Lake Pontchartrain is emptying into the city of New Orleans. The water is rising and it's not going to stop. Get out now.'

"We started getting amazing phone calls: a woman in her house with a two-year-old on one shoulder, a five-year-old at her side, no formula, no food, 'What do I do?' And what can I tell her? I'm just a guy on the radio!"

. . .

Like so many other newspeople in town, Dave Cohen had been preparing forty-years-later reports on Hurricane Betsy when Katrina hit. Although LBJ and the local officials of New Orleans and the State of Louisiana responded to their crisis with far greater coordination and speed than their successors in 2005, the memories of Betsy remain bitter, and not only because of the suffering and destruction it caused. As Edward Haas has made clear, Betsy was followed within days by widespread rumors that Mayor Schiro had ordered floodwater pumped out of his own well-to-do subdivision, Lake Vista, and into the Ninth Ward. At the time of the flood, Schiro was in a race for reelection with another Democrat, the City Council President, James E. Fitzmorris, Jr. There were also stories that he had ordered the levees breached. Thomas E. Allen, of Hunt Foods & Industries, an ally of the Mayor's, wrote to him to say that two of his African-American servants "brought this tale to my wife yesterday and said that all of the Negroes were talking about it and were angry with you about it." Haas quotes Schiro's secretary, Marguerite Guette, who told the Mayor, "An old 71-years of age colored man by the name of Williams, who says you have helped him all of his life and who lives at 2630 Republic Street, called to say that he is very concerned about a rumor that is going around that may ruin you with colored voters. The rumor is that you cut the Industrial Canal to drown the colored people so that they would not vote in the coming election." An aide to the Mayor later reported that people claiming to be relief workers and Schiro supporters delivered bags of "supplies" to flood victims in the Ninth Ward. People opened the bags only to find spoiled food and soiled, useless clothing.

Four years ago, a play staged in New Orleans called *An Evening with Betsy* explored the old conspiracy rumors. And although among historians Schiro earns high marks for his handling of the flood (if not for his obstinate views on race), the rumors persist. "That theory is why older people in the Ninth Ward still keep hatchets in their attics," Dave Cohen had told me. "They remember what it was like to be trapped, with the water rising and no way to get to the roof."

The pattern in Katrina's wake is similar. Everywhere I went in Louisiana and Texas to talk to evacuees, many of the poorest among them were not only furious—furious at the President and local officials, furious at being ignored for days—but inclined to believe, as many did after Betsy, that the flooding of the city was, or could have been, a deliberate act.

In the town of New Iberia, south of Lafayette, a few hundred New Orleanians, nearly all of them African-American, were staying at a gym on the grounds of West End Park. It was dusk when I arrived, and people were wandering around the athletic field, shooing away clouds of mosquitoes, drinking bottles of cold water provided by the Red Cross, and recounting for each other, yet again, their exodus stories. "Biblical proportions"—everyone used that phrase, and why not? I went inside and noticed a couple of signs: "This is Our Home. Please Respect Us." "Evacuees and Volunteers Only Beyond This Point: Curfew 730, Lights Out 10, TV off at 10:30." Two of the Red Cross volunteers who had organized the shelter and were keeping it running told me that they had been at Ground Zero in New York four years ago and that, in many ways, this was worse. "A whole city ruined," one said. "More than a million people leaving their homes." "Biblical proportions," the other said.

A friendly man in his late thirties named Walter Hays sat down to talk. Hays is African-American, a Navy veteran who had been working as a fitter at Northrop Grumman. People had painful and fantastical stories to tell—floating a family to safety in an inflatable kiddie pool, nights in the Superdome or on the street, helicopter escapes in the arms of a soldier—and Walter Hays wanted to tell his. He was in New Iberia with a group of twenty-eight close family and friends, including three infants and several small children. The adults had vowed to bring everyone out together. He talked of the beautiful weather the day after the storm, and then, the next day, he said, "the water started coming out of the ground," rolling down the streets, streaming through the floorboards. In three hours, the water was at chest level. Hays filled an ice chest with papers and the group started out, halting for two days and nights, along with two thousand other souls, on the sweltering Claiborne Avenue overpass, near the Superdome.

"We had with us three-month-old twins, a two-month-old, no water," he said. "People were pulling guns. What we saw on that overpass was beyond imagining: there were suicides, people jumping off the bridge, older people who couldn't take it, there were dead bodies floating underneath, the whole overpass reeked of feces and urine. Fights broke out all the time. People tried to jump on whatever military vehicles went by, but of course they wouldn't let anyone on. There were choppers over our heads. We could see the touch-and-gos of the helicopters—it went on all night long, and no one got any sleep. It was so hot and humid. And the one thing I'll never forget is that the sky was so clear and full of stars. So clear because there weren't any lights from the city. And all night long the kids were crying, the adults were crying, old people crying."

In the days that followed, they made their way to higher ground. A heroin addict they met had been looting, and he gave them water, food, Pampers. He even let them bathe in his house. "And he went on looting," Hays said. "I can't really argue. If you're dealt lemons, you make lemonade." Walter Hays and the others knew they had to get out of town, but there was still no transport. A police officer told them they should break into cars and see if they could steal one. Hays and his best friend, a grocery-store manager named Chester Pye, went to a nearby bus barn. "A guy there showed me how to hot-wire a school bus. We got our hands all slashed up from pulling wires, and it seemed like all the batteries were dead. Finally, Chester finds a good battery, and we went looking for keys." They found one that fit bus No. 9322 and picked up the rest of the extended family and headed out of town. Along the way, near the Fisher housing project, in Algiers, someone shot at the bus and demanded to be let on, but there was no room. They kept going west on Route 90, getting as far as Houma, Louisiana. On the road to New Iberia, a police officer pulled them over. "I was scared," Hays said. "After all, we'd boosted the bus. The cop, a white guy, looked inside and saw it wasn't hot-wired. There was a key. And what did he do? He gave us a police escort and called another police escort as we left Raceland and we got the escort all the way to New Iberia. And in New Iberia an officer said to me, and I will remember this forever, he said, 'I want you to understand something. You think this is the end of life as you know it for you. But this is a new beginning. You have a lot of people pulling for you.'"

Walter Hays had been telling his story for a couple of hours, with many other details of disasters averted and kindnesses provided. By now many of his friends had gathered around him, adding clarifications and saying that, all in all, they were blessed.

"All along the way, things were strategically placed in our way by the Lord," Hays said, in agreement. "The dopehead who helped us, the bus key, the people in Houma, wading through the water, the bodies, the tiny infants who made it out, sleeping on the bridge, like it was a terrible desert. It's biblical, isn't it? After everything we've been through, if you aren't changed morally, spiritually, then you are dead inside."

And then, just at the point where the story seemed over, with a flourish of amens and thank-the-Lords, Tyrell Pye, Chester's nephew, said, "Now, just remember." He paused and lowered his gaze at me. "Remember," he said, "this was a premeditated disaster. They flooded the city. It happened on a pretty, sunshiny day, two days of rising water. You tell me: where the rich people at?"

And Chester Pye said, "How come the Seventeenth Street levee broke? It's a totally poor area. And once the water started coming to St. Bernard Parish it was, Oops, maybe we should start doing something?" The others nodded. They agreed with this no less than they agreed on the saving grace of God.

Except Walter Hays. He was unsure. "I just don't know about any of that," he said.

When I asked Chester Pye if he and his family would return to New Orleans, he said, "There's no reason to go back now. Back to what? Back as a tourist? The new New Orleans is going to be like Six Flags Bourbon Street, you know what I mean?"

The link between conspiracy theories and oppression is as old as racial conflict. Some early American slaves were convinced that their new owners were cannibals bringing them to the New World to eat their flesh. In Washington in the nineteen-eighties, there was often talk in poorer black communities about the Plan. This was a belief that the "white power structure" had a secret scheme to inexorably move the black population out of the District. Similarly, in shelters in Louisiana and Texas you heard the suspicion that the "higher powers" of New Orleans wanted to employ a policy of citywide gentrification through natural disaster, that a mass exile of poor African-Americans was "the silver-lining scenario." For most, it hardly seemed to matter that some wealthier neighborhoods in New Orleans, particularly Lakeview, did not escape damage.

At the Houston Astrodome, for instance, people made statements and asked questions that mixed the logical with the conspiratorial.

"Where were the buses?"

"Why is it, do you think, that the French Quarter and the Garden District are high and dry and the Ninth is flooded and gonna get bulldozed?"

"In Betsy I know the mayor blew up the levee to save those big homes on the lakefront. A lot of people believe that, especially the people who were on their roofs!"

"I couldn't leave. I was terrified. I didn't have any money, no car, nothing. Where was I supposed to go? They shoulda had some buses. It's me and my five kids. I live in Desire, the Ninth Ward. I think it was a setup to get black folks out of New Orleans forever. Look around. Who's here? Nobody but the black and the poor. They ain't got but ten white families in the whole Astrodome."

"This came from a higher power, the alpha and the omega."

At the Reliant Center, in Houston, Patricia Valentine, a fifty-four-year-old woman from Treme, a black neighborhood near the French Quarter, told me that her area was "waist high" in water and the restaurants down the street "got nothing." She was sitting in a wheelchair and said that she had no intention of returning home. "They can have New Orleans," she said. "It's a toxic waste dump now. I was in Betsy forty years ago: September 1965. And the levee broke. What are we, stupid? Born yesterday? It's the same people drowning today as back then. They were trying to move us out anyway. They want a bigger tourist attraction, and we black folks ain't no tourist attraction."

The best-known writer to come from the Ninth Ward is Kalamu ya Salaam. A poet, playwright, and civil-rights activist, Salaam used to go by the name of Val Ferdinand. When I told Salaam what I was hearing in New Iberia and Houston, he laughed, but not dismissively. He said, "The real question is why not?" He recalled that in 1927, in the midst of the worst flooding of the Mississippi River in recorded history, the white city fathers of New Orleans—the men of the Louisiana Club, the Boston Club, and the Pickwick Club—won permission from the federal government to dynamite the Caernarvon levee, downriver from the city, to keep their interests dry. But destroying the levee also ensured that the surrounding poorer St. Bernard and Plaquemines Parishes would flood. Thousands of the trappers who lived there lost their homes and their livelihoods. The promise of compensation was never fulfilled. That, plus the persistent rumors of what may or may not have happened during Hurricane Betsy, Salaam said, has had a lingering effect. "So when I heard on TV that there was a breach at the Seventeenth Street levee, I figured they'd done it again," he said. "Or, let's just say, I didn't automatically assume that it was accidental."

Lolis Eric Elie, an African-American columnist for the New Orleans *Times-Picayune,* told me he didn't believe that the levees were blown deliberately—"and most black folks with some education or money don't, either"—but he could "easily" understand why so many were suspicious. "Blacks, in a state of essential slavery, built those very levees that were blown up in 1927. When the ships came to rescue people, whites made damn sure not to rescue blacks in Mississippi because of their fear that the blacks wouldn't return to work the farms. If black life is not valued—and isn't that what you were seeing for days in New Orleans?— then the specifics of the explanations are irrelevant. You begin to say to yourself, 'How do you aid tsunami victims instantly and only three or four days later get to New Orleans? What explanation other than race can there be?' I believe the real explanation is manifold, but I can understand how people start believing these things."

In Washington, whites dismissed the Plan as part of the "pathology" of poverty. Nevertheless, in D.C. and other cities, legends of conspiracy persisted as the counter-narrative to the conventional view of inexorable progress and the growing black middle class. Many in the population left behind could believe almost anything: that AIDS had been concocted in government laboratories as part of an anti-black conspiracy; that the government distributed crack in black neighborhoods as a genocidal practice; that the Klan has ownership interests in Church's Chicken, Kool cigarettes, and Tropical Fantasy soft drinks and uses them all to damage the health of African-Americans and even to sterilize them; that between 1979 and 1981 the FBI took part in a string of murders of black children in Atlanta. Scholars such as Patricia Turner, at the University of California, the author of *I Heard It Through the Grapevine,* have written extensively on the role of rumor and conspiracy theory in the African-American community, especially among the poor (and also on the phenomenon of wild rumors about blacks among whites), and they make a convincing case that these counter-narratives emerge from decades of institutional racism and from particular episodes in American history, such as the use of hundreds of poor African-Americans, between 1932 and 1972, as lab rats in U.S. government trials, known as the Tuskegee experiments, on the effects of syphilis.

John Barry, in *Rising Tide,* his book about the 1927 flood, quotes a *New York Times* account of a levee breach in Washington County, Mississippi, in 1912. An engineer who had run out of sandbags "ordered . . . several hundred negroes . . . to lie on top of the levee and as close together as possible. The black men obeyed, and although the spray frequently dashed over them, they prevented the overflow that might have developed into an ugly crevasse. For an hour and a half this lasted, until the additional sandbags arrived." The *Times* called the idea "brilliant."

New Orleans was sixty-seven percent African-American at the time of Katrina. It always had a substantial black population—it was one of the leading slave markets—and decades of migration starting at the time of Reconstruction made it even larger. The city was, in per-capita terms, the wealthiest in America before the Civil War and the wealthiest in the South until the nineteen-twenties. No more. Few of the improvements in urban America—the growth of the black middle class, the decline of the murder rate, greater attention to inner-city schools—have taken firm hold in New Orleans. There is hardly any industrial base, no major corporate headquarters, no homegrown businesses on the scale of FedEx in Memphis, Coca-Cola in Atlanta, the Hospital Corporation of America in Nashville. Colonel Terry Ebbert, the head of Homeland Security in the city, told me, "Drugs are the biggest business in town, bigger than tourism." Small wonder that at school-board meetings of Orleans Parish parents may think the worst—for example, that magnet schools are part of an overall plan of educational disenfranchisement. Small wonder that they might believe that the break in the levees was a plot.

"Perception is reality, and their reality is terrible," said Jim Amoss, the editor of the *Times-Picayune*. "We are talking about people who are very poor and have a precondition to accept this belief. Lots are cut off from mainstream news and information. They are isolated in shelters and they know a thing or two about victimization. It fits well into a system of belief."

In 1900, after a hurricane killed thousands in Galveston, Texas, the city died as a port and the rise of the port of Houston began. After the floods of 1927, John Barry writes, the city fathers of New Orleans began their long decline into insular stagnation, Huey Long rose to power as governor of Louisiana, and Herbert Hoover, who led the rescue program, was elected President.

Catastrophe and displacement are not subjects only for the history books. The fate of a city can change in a single turn of the weather. According to polls, huge numbers of people now living in shelters say they will not go back to New Orleans. Few have insurance policies or even bank accounts, credit cards, or savings sufficient to start over. Many of them are sick or unemployed. As Hurricane Rita bore down on Texas last week, there were still roughly a hundred and fifty thousand evacuees in Houston alone. A poll conducted jointly by *The Washington Post,* the Harvard School of Public Health, and the Henry J. Kaiser Family Foundation showed that fewer than half the evacuees in shelters will move back, and there was nothing in my days of conversations in Houston, New Iberia, Lafayette, and elsewhere that made that figure seem exaggerated. Certainly, much of the white establishment was not displeased at the prospect of a smaller city, a New Orleans stripped of its poor by a terrible storm and levees unable to withstand it.

Kalamu ya Salaam told me that he thought the suffering was far from over. Hurricane Rita has made recovery even more difficult. For the moment, people are focused on the grace of their own survival, and are grateful for the small and large acts of compassion that have come their way. And yet, he said, "you are going to see a lot of suicides this winter. A lot of poor people depend entirely on their extended family and their friends who share their condition to be a buffer against the pain of that condition. By winter, a lot of the generosity and aid that's been so palpable lately will begin to slow down and the reality of not going home again will hit people hard. They will be very alone.

"People forget how important all those Social Aid and Pleasure Clubs are for people. It's a community for a lot of folks who have nothing. Some people have never left New Orleans. Some have never seen snow. So you wake up and you find yourself beyond the reach of friends, beyond the reach of members of your family, and you are working in a fast-food restaurant in Utah somewhere and there is no conceivable way for you to get back to the city you love. How are you going to feel?"

(2005)

Part II

Into the Clear:
Philip Roth

The summer before last, Philip Roth left his house in rural Connecti-cut to make one of his periodic raids on Babylon. He visited a few friends, got his hair cut, and, just before heading home, dropped by the offices of *The New Yorker*. Over sandwiches, he talked first about the Yankees, who were enjoying a summer of blissful accomplishment, and then, less happily, about the Clintons, who were not. Over the next year or so, when we met in New York or at the house in Connecticut, Roth proved as funny and as intense as his friends had said he was. "Philip is an unbelievably fierce man," the biographer Judith Thurman said. "His senses are quick and raw—he's the opposite of phlegmatic." When Roth is in the mood, he is a deft mimic (he can do any voice from the febrile ramblings of the sports-radio team Mike and the Mad Dog to the plummy anti-Americanisms of Harold Pinter); he is funny in the way a great Catskills comedian might be were that comedian also possessed of an immense linguistic gift. But on that summer day, while the country seemed to rock between pious concern and giggling fits, Roth was not at all in the mood. His dark, expressive eyes were deadly serious. It was the summer of Monica, a season drenched in a "treacherous and subversive pleasure: the ecstasy of sanctimony," as Roth eventually put it. This was the season of "that depends on what your definition of 'is' is," of the Starr report and oral-sex jokes in the office, and the rage and the accusations and the ceaseless chatter that plumped the ratings. Many of Roth's most persistent themes were coming into play: betrayal, false piety, a flawed man's struggle with the repellent and the libidinous—and now, while he was wondering what Clinton might do, Roth straightened and said, only half in jest, "Maybe he should get on TV and talk frankly about adultery." Maybe he could talk about the complexity of a long and difficult marriage, about frailty, and maybe he'd dare to ask if he is really so alone in his weaknesses. But there was, of course, no political sense in that. Then Roth said, "Why don't you get a bunch of novelists to write about this?" Why cede a national discussion of morality, of men and women, to *Hardball* and *The Beltway Boys*? In the end, however, one of the few writers to say no to the idea was Philip Roth.

As it turned out, he couldn't spare the time, because he was writing a novel set in the summer of America's "purity binge, when terrorism—which had replaced communism as the prevailing threat to the country's security—was succeeded by cocksucking." He was writing *The Human Stain*, the book that now completes a trilogy on postwar American life. Before it came *American Pastoral*, which was set in the Vietnam era, and *I Married a Communist*, which took the McCarthy period as its backdrop. Roth is a storyteller who believes in getting quickly to the problem, to a character's predicament, and, in *The Human Stain*, in a voice unmistakable for its directness and outrage, he swiftly sketches the moral and political weather in which his characters will move:

> It was the summer in America when the nausea returned, when the joking didn't stop, when the speculation and the theorizing and the hyperbole didn't stop, when the moral obligation to explain to one's children about adult life was abrogated in favor of maintaining in them every illusion about adult life, when the smallness of people was simply crushing, when some kind of demon had been unleashed in the nation and, on both sides, people wondered "Why are we so crazy?", when men and women alike, upon awakening in the morning, discovered that during the night, in a state of sleep that transported them beyond envy or loathing, they had dreamed of the brazenness of Bill Clinton. I myself dreamed of a mammoth

banner draped dadaistically like a Christo wrapping from one end of the White House to the other and bearing the legend "a human being lives here." It was the summer when—for the billionth time—the jumble, the mayhem, the mess proved itself more subtle than this one's ideology and that one's morality. It was the summer when a president's penis was on everyone's mind, and life, in all its shameless impurity, once again confounded America.

Roth does not attempt a fictional treatment of historical players, as Don DeLillo has done with Lee Harvey Oswald in *Libra* and with J. Edgar Hoover in *Underworld*. Rather, in each book of the trilogy, history intrudes without rational explanation into the lives of ordinary people. Many years ago, in the comic experiment of *Our Gang*, Roth thrust a grotesquely drawn President into the foreground—his Nixon, Trick E. Dixon, seemed to rise from a swamp of American iniquity—but now, in his late career, he works more in the tradition of Stendhal or Tolstoy, who put their Fabrices and Pierres, not Napoleon, in the foreground. History here is not scenery; history permeates the story, the minds of the characters, and the moral fabric of the book. In *American Pastoral*, a Jewish-American Adonis, Seymour (Swede) Levov—a good son, an all-state athlete who inherits his father's glovemaking factory in the ruins of Newark—marries a former Miss New Jersey, and moves to the stone house of his dreams in sylvan Old Rimrock; he loses everything that matters in his life when his daughter Merry "brings the war home" to New Jersey by blowing up the local post office. In *I Married a Communist*, a silent-film star, Eve Frame, betrays her husband, a radio actor and idealistic communist named Ira Ringold, in a marital rage fueled by the climate of accusation during the McCarthy years. She publishes a memoir (ghostwritten by a gossip columnist) accusing him of spying for the Soviet Union. The book she writes is called *I Married a Communist*.

The Human Stain portrays a contemporary version of "the indigenous American berserk": the leftish and reactionary pieties, the pervasive and knowing gossip, the impoverishment of the language, the atmosphere of political and sexual inquisition. The main character, Coleman Silk, is a classics professor with "an autocratic ego," who teaches at the small New England college of Athena. Some of Silk's colleagues resent him because, when he was dean of the faculty, he forced deadwood professors into retirement and was thought to be harsh and insufficiently impressed by the more voguish modes of writing and teaching. These colleagues seize on an opportunity for vengeance when Silk, faced with the continued absence of two students, innocently asks the class while calling roll, "Do they exist or are they spooks?" As it turns out, the missing students are black. It hardly matters that Silk does not know that: for his one-word infraction, for "spooks," he is accused of racism, humiliated in front of his colleagues, and, finally, driven out of his job. The incident is so traumatic, so inexplicable, that when Silk's wife dies he blames the college. The novel's secret, revealed in chapter 2, is that Silk himself is black. Silk endured a childhood of bigotry and, like Alexander Portnoy before him, he yearned to free himself of the burdens and obligations of the "We," of the group; but, unlike Portnoy, he had the perversity and the will—and the skin tone—to succeed. He trips the historical and ethnic lock. Or he thinks he has. ("Was it the social obstruction that he wished to sidestep? Was he merely being another American and, in the great frontier tradition, accepting the democratic invitation to throw your origins overboard if to do so contributes to the pursuit of happiness?") Silk's "victory," his defection from his race and his own family, now helps to ruin him. As the world takes him for an aging Jewish racist, he is destroyed in a battle he cannot fight by a We he cannot escape.

In these late novels, Roth's narrator, Nathan Zuckerman, is no longer the singular and central presence he was in middle-period novels of the eighties like *The Ghost Writer, Zuckerman Unbound, The Anatomy Lesson,* and *The Counterlife.* Roth has aged Zuckerman considerably (and relieved him of his prostate and potency, for good measure); Zuckerman is more in the background, a recording—and imagining—angel. Once Roth's subject had been the vocation of a writer; now he has turned outward and toward a narrative of American history. He is using the novel as a vehicle for middle-class tragedy in which history happens to, rolls over, even destroys, ordinary men and women: a businessman, an actor, a teacher. Roth is no longer a Wunderkind; he is sixty-seven, and the books reflect it. His voice is still charged, an endlessly pliable instrument of comedy and impersonation, but that voice has also darkened, its comedy is deeper, the story it tells is more tragic and painful. You find yourself laughing loudest just at the moment when the abyss widens. The funniest scene in *The Human Stain* comes when a damaged Vietnam veteran tries to overcome his trauma and his hatred of Asians by forcing himself to go with his local support group to a Chinese restaurant ("They count as gooks!"). His mates talk him through the wonton-soup course as if he were in a Mekong Delta firefight: "Okay, Les, we got it under control. You can let go of the menu now. Les, let go of the menu. First with your right hand."

Silk, a reader steeped in Homer, Sophocles, and Aeschylus, careers toward a familiar Attic fate. After his banishment from Athena College and his wife's death, his one consolation is a consuming affair with Faunia Farley, a much younger woman who works as a janitor and farmhand. For this, too, Silk is condemned, pursued, and destroyed. His most avid accuser is a young professor of French literature named Delphine Roux, who "exposes" Silk's affair with Faunia, sending him an anonymous letter that reads, "Everyone knows you're sexually exploiting an abused, illiterate woman half your age."

The insidious phrase that resonates throughout the book is "everyone knows."

"Everyone knows" is the invocation of the cliché and the beginning of the banalization of experience, and it's the solemnity and the sense of authority that people have in voicing the cliché that's so insufferable. What we know is that, in an unclichéd way, nobody knows anything. You can't know anything. The things you know you don't know. Intention? Motive? Consequence? Meaning? All that we don't know is astonishing. Even more astonishing is what passes for knowing.

Philip Roth lives in a town that, strictly speaking, lacks a town. There is a post office, but not much else. He lives in northwest Connecticut, where there are towns like Sharon, Litchfield, and Kent, with restaurants, antique stores, craft stores, libraries, schools, weekend warriors in SUVs. "Up here, there's no beach, there's no town, there's no place for anybody to go, so all you have to do is stay at home," Roth said. We were driving in his Volvo along the banks of the Housatonic River. Suddenly, he went into *Deliverance* mode: "Well, o' course, we got the *rivah heah,* yessir we do!"

We drove through the hills. New York was a dreary mess of cold rain, but here the river was icy, clear as gin, and there was snow in the woods and in the trees. Roth, still playing the hick Virgil, piped up again, saying, "We got a bridge. Would you like to see a *real* bridge? Yessir!" He also made up an entire history of a flood near the bridge. "*Dang* near swamped the *en*-tire town, it did!"

Roth grew up in Newark (urban eastern Jersey is his Yoknapatawpha, his Combray), and he has spent long stretches in Chicago, Manhattan, Iowa City, Rome, and London. His house, a gray two-story clapboard, was built in 1790. It is not easy to find, which is, for the owner, part of the attraction. Not long ago, Roth bought twenty acres to add to the forty he already owned. Since his separation from the English actress Claire Bloom, seven years ago, he has lived alone. He has very few visitors. In *The Ghost Writer*, the older writer Lonoff says of Zuckerman that "an unruly personal life will probably better serve a writer like Nathan than walking in the woods and startling the deer. His work has turbulence—that should be nourished, and not in the woods." No longer. Enough unruliness. If turbulence remains one of Roth's dominant literary tones, "Order in living" is now his credo. "Philip lives like he's at Fort Dix," his friend Ross Miller, who teaches literature at the University of Connecticut, told me. "Everything precise and hospital corners." Roth wakes early and, seven days a week, walks fifty yards or so to a two-room studio. The front room is outfitted with a fireplace, a desk, and a computer set up on a kind of lectern where he can write standing up, the better to preserve a bad back. There are pictures here and there of his family: his father, Herman, who sold insurance for Metropolitan Life; his mother, Bess; his older brother, Sandy, who used to be in advertising and now paints. Most of Roth's books are in the big house, where they run, room after room, in alphabetical order by category.

When I came to visit, it was a late-winter morning, and the snow was piled high around the studio. Roth was wearing a blue Shetland sweater, green corduroy pants. Often there is tweed. He dresses like a graduate student of the late fifties. He led me to the back room. There was a team photograph of the 1947 Brooklyn Dodgers. There were free weights, a lifting bench, and an exercise mat. He had quintuple-bypass surgery eleven years ago and is determined to keep in shape. He stays out here all day and into the evening: no telephone, no fax. Nothing gets in. In the late afternoons, he takes long walks, often trying to figure out connections and solve problems in the novel that's possessing him.

"I live alone, there's no one else to be responsible for or to, or to spend time with," Roth said. "My schedule is absolutely my own. Usually, I write all day, but if I want to go back to the studio in the evening, after dinner, I don't have to sit in the living room because someone else has been alone all day. I don't have to sit there and be entertaining or amusing. I go back out and I work for two or three more hours. If I wake up at two in the morning—this happens rarely, but it sometimes happens—and something has dawned on me, I turn the light on and I write in the bedroom. I have these little yellow things all over the place. I read till all hours if I want to. If I get up at five and I can't sleep and I want to work, I go out and I go to. So I work, I'm on call. I'm like a doctor and it's an emergency room. And I'm the emergency."

.   .   .

Not long before I went up to see Roth in Connecticut, I was reading the text of a conversation he had had with the French philosopher Alain Finkielkraut, and, faced for the millionth time with the "Are you the guy in your novels?" question, Roth had pointed out a passage from Virginia Woolf's 1915 novel *The Voyage Out*. A would-be writer says, "All you read a novel for is to see what sort of person the writer is, and, if you know him, which of his friends he's put in. As for the novel itself, the whole conception, the way one's seen the thing, felt about it, made it stand in relation to other things, not one in a million cares for that."

Considering the extent to which Roth has used his own life and character in fiction (in that way he is similar to Céline, Genet, and Gombrowicz), and even considering the degree to which he has been vacuumed up occasionally as an object of gossip, there's no mystery why he might like that passage of Woolf's. One night, I went with Roth to Columbia University, where he met with a graduate seminar led by his friend the novelist David Plante. They were reading *Operation Shylock*, in which the main character, "Philip Roth," arrives in Israel in the year of the Demjanjuk trial only to be tortured by a double, an imp of the perverse, named Pipik, who goes around Jerusalem announcing that he, in fact, is Roth. Sooner or later, one of the Columbia students asked Roth if the story was "true."

No, it isn't, he said gently: "None of this seems like autobiography to me. It seems like fiction. Not to say that one doesn't draw on one's experiences, but what counts is the use you make of it." Life is the amorphous thing and, to the artist, it feels nothing like art, the made thing, the considered thing. Both in life and in *Operation Shylock,* Roth endured a mental breakdown after taking the tranquilizer Halcion, but whereas in life the breakdown was to no good purpose, except to be endured, in the novel the breakdown works to heighten the narrator's violent and confused encounter with Israel. Roth went through this explanation patiently, but when the subject finally turned to the made thing, to the novel, he brightened. "Every Jewish exigency, pain, and antagonism flows through 'Roth,' " he told the students. "In *Finnegans Wake,* there is the character Humphrey C. Earwicker, who sleeps with absolutely everything flowing through his mind, and Joyce uses the initials H.C.E. as 'Here Comes Everybody.' Well, in *Operation Shylock* you have 'Here Comes Everybody Jewish.' Leon Klinghoffer. Jonathan Pollard. Menachem Begin. Meir Kahane. All these names were passing through the collective Jewish brain at the time, and I wanted to get inside the Jewish mind."

Roth's career began, forty-three years ago, with much the same project: writing about Jews. And, as a result of his fearlessness and bravado, of his aversion to a pious literature of virtue and victimhood, his public reputation began with scandal, distortion, and a wound. It was a modest scandal at first, and then became the sort of full-scale storm that may well be looked back upon as a curious relic.

Years later, Saul Bellow remarked that critics often thought of him, Bernard Malamud, and Roth as a small company of Jewish haberdashers, "the Hart, Schaffner & Marx" of American letters. But influence doesn't work in the mimetic or genetic way most critics would have it. Roth, as an undergraduate at Bucknell and later as a graduate student at the University of Chicago, did indeed read both Malamud and Bellow. In Malamud he saw "harsh fables" about urban immigrants; but they were fables about Roth's Yiddish-speaking elders, not his contemporaries, and they were written in the minor key of immigration rather than in the broad C major of full-fledged American immersion. In Bellow, particularly in *The Adventures of Augie March*, Roth sensed something more congenial, more liberating, a narrator with an aggressive native voice, far more American than immigrant Jew. The novel opens with a declaration of citizenship, not nostalgia: "I am an American, Chicago born." For Roth, "the spine of American literature" in the twentieth century is Faulkner and Bellow, and although Roth has never written like Bellow—no reader would ever mistake those two voices for each other—it was *Augie March* that gave him permission to cut loose, to write not of a victimized European generation living in the shadowland of immigration but of a younger generation steeped in America, in its freedom and talk, its energies and superabundance.

For Roth, growing up in New Jersey in the forties was never about getting beaten up, about pogroms or tortured shopkeepers. "My experience," Roth said, "had been about our aggression, our going out into Newark, three or four of us, wandering the streets at night, shooting crap in back of the high school with flashlights, girls, going after your date to this gathering place called Syd's on Chancellor Avenue and telling your sex stories. It was that verbal robustness, people talking, being terrifically funny, playing ball, competing, the energy flowing out . . . Appetite. Maybe that's the word. It was the appetites that were aggressive."

Then, in March 1959, *The New Yorker* published "Defender of the Faith," a story about a Jewish recruit at an Army base in Missouri at the end of the Second World War, who tries to wangle special treatment out of his Jewish sergeant. The germ of the scandal lay, first, in the fact that the recruit was a devious kid playing on the guilty fellow-feeling of his officer and, second, in the fact that the story wasn't being published in a Jewish magazine or in a quarterly. Roth had certainly published stories about Jews before, including "You Can't Tell a Man by the Song He Sings," in *Commentary,* and "The Conversion of the Jews," in *The Paris Review,* but those were relatively small journals for highbrow readers who were used to far more radical ideas and jokes. *The New Yorker* was something different. The magazine published many Jewish writers, including J. D. Salinger, S. J. Perelman, and Irwin Shaw; Isaac Bashevis Singer's stories, translated from the Yiddish, eventually became a mainstay; but the aura of the place in 1959 was more Bronxville than Upper West Side.

Roth did not anticipate anything other than the simple pleasures of early publication. He was living in a two-room basement apartment in the East Village, and, on the day the magazine was to appear, he kept going up to his neighborhood kiosk asking, "You got it yet?" When it finally came in, he bought four copies.

"I'd open it and close it, and look at it from here and look at it from there, and read it, read it and then the words would just blast out of my mind and it all made no sense. It was terribly thrilling." A few days later, his editor at the magazine, Rachel MacKenzie, called, saying they were getting a lot of letters, many of them angry. Then came a call from the Anti-Defamation League, and then word that rabbis around the city and beyond were decrying the story in their sermons. His sin was simple: he'd had the audacity to write about a Jewish kid as being flawed, as being aggressive and conniving, as being interested in money—and he had done it in a national magazine. He had violated the tribal code on Jewish self-exposure: Not in front of the goyim! The letters poured in, both to the magazine and to Roth:

Mr. Roth:
With your one story, "Defender of the Faith," you have done as much harm as all the organized anti-Semitic organizations have done to make people believe that all Jews are cheats, liars, connivers. Your one story makes people—the general public—forget all the Jews who have lived, all the Jewish boys who served well in the armed services, all the Jews who live honest hard lives the world over.

One letter came to the Anti-Defamation League from a prominent rabbi, reading, "What is being done to silence this man? Medieval Jews would have known what to do with him."

Roth was not so much frightened by the hostility as he was engaged. He was not a young twenty-six; he was ambitious, he'd traveled, he'd taught at the University of Chicago, he'd been in the Army. There was something exciting (at first) about getting a reaction to his stories, a reaction out in the world, beyond his circle of friends and editors.

"I was not in flight from it and I wanted to find out who these people were," Roth told me. "Suddenly, I was the center of controversy with these rabbis, all of whom were my seniors by thirty years, and who had constituencies, who had congregations."

For a while, the scandal seemed mild, manageable. *Goodbye, Columbus,* a collection that included "Defender of the Faith," won the National Book Award in 1960, and Roth was invited to speak to campus Hillel groups and synagogue congregations. Usually, the questions were polite, easily absorbed. But then, in 1962, Roth, while teaching in Iowa, was invited to be on a panel at Yeshiva University, the academic bastion of Orthodox Judaism, in Washington Heights. "I felt that I was obliged to do this, I wanted to do it, and it seemed to me tied up with writing," Roth said. "I had written something that provoked this response and I had to be responsible to it. I don't know how at twenty-eight, twenty-nine, thirty I could have responded any differently. Now I might respond to it by just letting the fiction speak for itself."

The panel was called "The Crisis of Conscience in Minority Writers of Fiction," and it also included Pietro di Donato, the author of a proletarian novel called *Christ in Concrete,* and Ralph Ellison, whose 1952 novel, *Invisible Man,* was starting to come under attack from radical black nationalists. That night at Yeshiva was a slaughter. The students practically ignored the outsiders, Ellison and Di Donato, and focused on their own, on Roth. They battered him, asking him over and over, in one form or another, "Mr. Roth, would you write the same stories if you lived in Nazi Germany?" (This is much the same question that the imperious Newark judge Leopold Wapter asks Nathan Zuckerman, almost two decades later, in *The Ghost Writer:* "Can you honestly say that there is anything in your short story that would not warm the heart of a Julius Streicher or a Joseph Goebbels?") Over and over, Roth answered, "But we live in the *opposite* of Nazi Germany!" And he got nowhere.

"Finally, in about the eleventh round," Roth recalled, "when Ralph had a feeling I couldn't come out for the twelfth, he came out and said, 'What's going on here?' Ellison said that he had gotten mail from black readers furious with him for having depicted incest in a black family—a sharecropper who sleeps with his daughter. A typical letter asked how he could write such a scene while the civil-rights movement was just starting. Ellison told the audience his only answer was to insist on a novelist's independence: 'I am not a cog in the machinery of civil-rights legislation.' "

The Yeshiva students listened politely to Ellison—and then went right back to pummeling Roth. After the program ended and Roth was trying to leave the stage, the students who had been most antagonistic gathered around him, surrounded him, shouting. One even shook his fist, crying out, "You were brought up on anti-Semitic literature!"

"Yes?" Roth said. "And what is that?"

"English literature," came the answer. "English literature is anti-Semitic literature!"

Later that night, at a postmortem at the Stage Delicatessen, Roth looked up from his pastrami sandwich and told his friends, "I'll never write about Jews again."

In fact, Roth's next two books, *Letting Go* and *When She Was Good,* were his least antic, his least Jewish. But that restraint did not satisfy him, either. The incident at Yeshiva, the urge to speak with a voice that came more from Newark than from the graduate-school seminar rooms, the desire to write in a prose as energized as the sixties, led him toward *Portnoy's Complaint.* This time, there was no innocence, no accident involved. He set out thinking, You want outrage? I'll give you outrage!

The gestation period of *Portnoy's Complaint* was long, complicated, and chaotic. Its first incarnation was a two-hundred-page riff called "The Jewboy," based on a Newark childhood. Then came the draft of a play called "The Nice Jewish Boy"—"in its way a less comforting, more aggressive *Abie's Irish Rose,*" Roth called it—that was read as a work-shop exercise at the American Place Theatre in 1964, with Dustin Hoff-man in the main role. Then, after finishing *When She Was Good,* in 1966, Roth wrote a long monologue "beside which the fetid indiscre-tions of *Portnoy's Complaint* would appear to be the work of Louisa May Alcott." The piece featured a slide-show lecture about the intimate organs of the famous and a lengthy disquisition on the subject of adoles-cent masturbation. There came yet another manuscript, this one titled "Portrait of the Artist," which focused, in part, on a Jewish family, the Portnoys. Finally, there was a short story, "A Jewish Patient Begins His Analysis": the breakthrough of the story was setting it in the office of a psychoanalyst—the setting, eventually, for *Portnoy's Complaint.* This gave the rage and obscenity, the performance-piece comedy, a literary frame, a context for unfiltered confession.

"I needed permission, and permission came with casting the book as a psychoanalytic confession," Roth told me. "The theater of the analyst's office says the rule here is that there are no rules, the rule here is no inhibitions, the rule here is no restraint, the rule here is no decorum." The novel that resulted had little to do with Vietnam, civil rights, or any other political question of the sixties, but in its openness, in its unhinged comedy and freedom, it was a book of its time. Alexander Portnoy tells all to his shrink, all of it: the joy of his Jewish neighborhood in Newark—

> *White bread, rye bread,*
> *Pumpernickel, challah,*
> *All those for Weequahic,*
> *Stand up and hollah!*

—the passionate grip of his overweening goddess-mother, Sophie, "who could accomplish anything. . . . She could make jello, for instance, with sliced peaches *hanging* in it, just *suspended* there, in defiance of the law of gravity"; the bathroom agonies of his life-weary father, who chews vainly on Ex-Lax and dried fruit "by the pound bag" and falls asleep on the toilet, a man who, "in his retirement now, has really only one subject into which he can sink his teeth, the New Jersey Turnpike." Portnoy confesses his adventures in masturbation: ejaculating into a cored apple, into a baseball glove, into a Mounds-bar wrapper, into an empty milk bottle, into "Lenore Lapidus's big fat red-hot brassiere!" and (in perhaps the most famous solo performance since Lindbergh crossed the Atlantic) into a piece of refrigerated liver, the Portnoy family dinner. Portnoy yearns to be good, to lash himself to the mast of respectability, and at the same time rages against all the ropes that would bind him there—family, religion, taboos:

> Look, am I exaggerating to think it's practically miraculous that I'm ambulatory? The hysteria and the superstition! The watchits and the be-carefuls! You mustn't do this, you can't do that— hold it! don't! you're breaking an important law! *What* law! *Whose* law! They might as well have had plates in their lips and rings through their noses and painted themselves blue for all the human sense they made! Oh, and the *milchiks* and *flaishiks* besides, all those *meshuggeneh* rules and regulations on top of their own private craziness! It's a family joke that when I was a tiny child I turned from the window out of which I was watching a snow-

storm, and hopefully asked, "Momma, do we believe in winter?" Do you get what I'm saying? I was raised by Hottentots and Zulus! I couldn't even contemplate drinking a glass of milk with my salami sandwich without giving serious offense to God Almighty. Imagine then what my conscience gave me for all that jerking off!

Portnoy's Complaint was a best-seller (more than four hundred thousand copies sold when it came out, in 1969) and became as much a part of the popular culture that year as Woodstock and the Mets. Roth had crossed over; he had already gained a serious reputation, but now he also showed that he could shift easily from low burlesque to high drama. And yet there were repercussions that would haunt him for decades. Not only did *Portnoy's* success vault Roth into the bizarre and disorienting realm of American celebrity (the gossip columnist Leonard Lyons wrote that he was dating Barbra Streisand; they'd never met); it also conflated the character Portnoy and his author to such a degree that anyone—anyone!—felt free to identify Roth as an erotomaniac who prowled Broadway looking for shiksas. Jacqueline Susann went on the *Tonight Show* to promote *The Love Machine* that year and told Johnny Carson that she might like to meet Philip Roth, her rival for the No. 1 spot on the *New York Times* best-seller list, "but I wouldn't want to shake his hand." Jacqueline Susann! The intimacy of Roth's voice seemed to invite this sort of thing. It still does. To this day, on Broadway, people will stop him to make a joke about masturbation or delicatessens.

Even Roth's parents, who collected all the reviews and clippings as trophies, had to endure the sneers of people around them who assumed they were the models for the Portnoys and that Philip was somehow anti-Semitic. "Our folks were wonderful about it," Roth's brother, Sandy, told me. "Their friends were not great readers, they just repeated crap that other people said."

The book was, in the main, badly read. Of course, *Portnoy* was hilarious and profane, but many of Roth's critics and readers seemed to miss the pain in the comedy, the violence done, say, when a father betrays his son and pays the boy's Gentile girlfriend a hundred dollars to get lost, and then ends up in a horrible fight in the basement with his son. What people missed, too, was Portnoy's paradox, his desire to defect—to be free of the suffocating We, the family, the congregation, the ethos of victimhood and virtue, all of it—and, at the same time, the equally powerful desire to listen to his mother, to cut off his affair with his lover, Monkey, to be a good boy, to pay proper respect to history, to be a good son, a good Jew:

Oh, to be a center fielder, a center fielder—and nothing more!

But I am something more, or so they tell me. A Jew . . . Can't you see, my dear parents, from whose loins I somehow leaped, that such thinking is a trifle barbaric? That all you are expressing is your *fear*? The very first distinction I learned from you, I'm sure, was not night and day, or hot and cold, but *goyische* and Jewish! But now it turns out, my dear parents, relatives, and assembled friends, who have gathered here to celebrate the occasion of my bar mitzvah, it turns out, you schmucks! you narrow-minded schmucks!— oh, how I hate you for your Jewish narrow-minded minds! . . . Jew Jew Jew Jew Jew Jew! It is coming out of my ears already, the saga of the suffering Jews! Do me a favor, my people, and stick your suffering heritage up your suffering ass—*I happen also to be a human being!*

Perhaps it's hard now to imagine how transgressive this all was thirty years ago, hard to picture the outrage, so much more intense than what had been aroused by "Defender of the Faith." To this day, ethnic fiction too often asks to be loved purely for its affiliations, its purity and virtue; this was a voice in *struggle* with its affiliations, in rebellion against purity. It did not ask to be loved, and it often wasn't. Certainly not by the ethnic leadership. Once more, rabbis took to the pulpit. The reaction among many Jewish intellectuals was as hysterical as it had been in the Hadassahs of suburbia. One of the most censorious essays came from Gershom Scholem, the distinguished Jewish scholar and the author of definitive studies of Jewish mysticism. Scholem wrote about *Portnoy* in the Israeli daily *Ha'aretz,* branding it a "revolting book," worse than "The Protocols of the Learned Elders of Zion" because it provided anti-Semites with "authentic evidence" of Jewish perfidy:

> This is the book for which all anti-Semites have been praying. I daresay that with the next turn of history, not long to be delayed, this book will make all of us defendants at court. We will pay the price, not the author. . . . I wonder what price k'lal yisrael [the world Jewish community]—and there is such an entity in the eyes of the Gentiles—is going to pay for this book. Woe to us on that day of reckoning!

Saul Bellow, who first met Roth at the University of Chicago in the fifties, told me, "Gershom Scholem was a Jew who left Germany and settled in Jerusalem and was likely to draw a parallel between the United States and the Germany he left behind, and he saw symptoms of this terrible problem in Philip's work and in me as well. He was mistaken. These things didn't mean what he thought they did. I think Scholem had in mind Nazi Germany and not the United States."

Less understandable, and far more wounding to Roth, was an assault by Irving Howe, in *Commentary* in 1972. Howe was not an émigré. As an eminence in both literary journalism and left-wing politics, he knew the American context as well as anyone, and yet, after showing early support, he now declared Roth "an exceedingly joyless writer" whose "unfocused hostility" is the "ground-note" of his sensibility. He attacked not merely *Portnoy* but its author as well, warning of a "deficiency" in Roth's character, an emptiness beneath the "comedian's shuffle and patter."

"The cruelest thing anyone can do with *Portnoy's Complaint* is to read it twice," Howe wrote. "An assemblage of gags strung onto the outcry of an analytic patient, the book thrives best on casual responses; it demands little more from the reader than a nightclub performer demands." In an insult sure to resound with the *Commentary* audience, he compared Roth not to Aristophanes or Swift but to Harry Golden: "Between 'Portnoy's Complaint' and 'For Two Cents Plain' there is finally no great difference of sensibility." In the very magazine that had helped launch Roth's career, Howe, the respected elder, was undermining Roth's seriousness, his authenticity. (This was the same Howe who excoriated Ralph Ellison and James Baldwin, in a 1963 essay in *Dissent,* for not being, in essence, sufficiently black.)

Howe's review in *Commentary* represented a terrible rebuke for Roth, and it gnawed at him for years. In *The Anatomy Lesson* (1983), Roth transforms himself into Zuckerman and Howe into the insufferable Milton Appel, and, with barely concealed rage, writes that Appel "had unleashed an attack upon Zuckerman's career that made MacDuff's assault upon Macbeth look almost lackadaisical." To this day, Roth keeps on his wall a drawing made for him by his friend the artist Philip Guston, depicting a stabbed and bleeding critic, a pipe dangling from his lips.

And yet Scholem, Howe, and the damning rabbis were not alone. *Portnoy* was a difficult book even for the most sympathetic reader. At the time, a strong supporter like Bellow could not fully embrace the comic extravagance of Roth's novel.

"I didn't get much of a kick out of *Portnoy's Complaint* back then," Bellow said. "Maybe there was a shred or two of respectability still clinging to me then. I wasn't *down* on it. I was amused, but it wasn't pure joy.

"I'm not sure Philip always realizes that he is being outrageous," Bellow went on. "He feels a writer should provoke—and he should, if that is the way he is inclined—but he can't expect to evade the results of this provocation. Philip is a radical. He feels he should treat the bizarre as if it were perfectly normal."

Roth told me he was never naïve about the provocative nature of some of his books, but the attacks, along with the freakish feel of celebrity, helped drive him out of the city and to an increasingly solitary way of living.

"I felt visible and exposed," he said. "Somebody who had just read *Portnoy's Complaint* would come up to me and say, 'I don't eat liver anymore.' It was funny the first seven thousand times I heard it." For a while, Roth lived in Woodstock, New York, near Philip Guston, and then he bought the house in Connecticut, and he has lived there, for the most part, ever since.

Working in Connecticut, and often for part of each year in London in the late seventies and eighties, Roth became a consistently prolific and evolving writer. The book-chat cliché that dismissed him as a gifted comedian who had then dived headlong into his own pool of Narcissus was always a vulgarity, on the same low level as dismissing Updike as a preternaturally skillful writer of surfaces or, for that matter, Dickens as a writer of potboilers. Many novelists are read dismissively, but it's been doubly so for Roth.

There are welcome surprises sometimes. Last year, Roth received an invitation to an all-Roth literary conference in Aix-en-Provence. He had not been to Europe for a decade, and he was reluctant to interrupt his work for even a few days. His friends had to convince him that basking in the Mediterranean sun and meeting with a group of serious readers of his books hardly amounted to a sentence to Elba. Once Roth was in Aix, he was delighted: his books were for sale and, evidently, read; the mayor gave him the key to the city; he was celebrated everywhere he went; on the main roads and side streets of Aix, red banners bearing his portrait and the words "The Roth Explosion" flapped in the breeze—a detail that, as Roth told his French hosts, "has made me understand a little about what it must have been like to be Chairman Mao."

Sitting each day in the audience of a large auditorium, Roth heard panels of American and French critics discuss his later novels; from the stage, he led two master classes. The classes were more like literary press

conferences and the questioners were, in the main, local graduate students, young men and women educated to a crisp in the great French
fryer of Continental literary education, with its bubbling Derridian rhetoric and dubious wordplay. Roth, who learned to read at Bucknell and
the University of Chicago a half century ago, was dumbstruck as he was
pressed on the significance of his characters' names: Seymour (Swede)
Levov, it means "love"? Lev? Lion? And, Seymour. It means See-more?
See-more, yes? And what about Merry? Is she the Mary? Christ's Mary?
There were questions about numerology, about the "tripartite nature" of
American Pastoral: its three generations, its three parts, its three family
members. Then the subject turned to the Talmud and Hebrew philology
(Roth's Jewish learning is modest, and he speaks Catskills Yiddish and no
Hebrew). On all these matters, Roth suggested to the French students
that perhaps they were reading with a "subtlety that is misplaced." He
hoped instead that they would begin to think of *American Pastoral* as a
book less about the mysteries of its names than as one about the costs of
a revolutionary period in American life, about "the uncontrollability of
real things," the inability to explain random events and catastrophes in a
good man's life.

Later, when I asked Roth about such readings, he laughed, and said,
"It's like baseball. Suppose you and I went up to the ballpark together,
and there's a guy next to us with his kid. And he was saying, 'Now, what I
want you to do is watch the scoreboard. Stop watching the field. Just
watch what happens when the numbers change on the scoreboard. Isn't
that great? Now, do you see what just happened up there? Did you see
what happened? Why did that happen?' And you say, 'That guy is crazy.'
But the kid imbibes it and he goes home and he's asked, 'How was the
game?' And he says, 'Great! The scoreboard changed thirty-two times
and Daddy said last game it changed only fourteen times and the home
team last time changed more times than the other team. It was really
great! We had hot dogs and we stood up at one point to stretch and we
went home.'

"Is that politicizing the baseball game? Is that theorizing the baseball
game? No, it's having not the foggiest idea in the world what baseball is."

Not long ago, Norman Manea, a Romanian émigré writer and one of
Roth's closest friends, invited Roth to speak to a class at Bard College
about his 1995 novel *Sabbath's Theater,* an incendiary portrait of Mickey
Sabbath, a broke and despairing Falstaff who refuses every social propri-
ety or sexual regulation. Manea feared that his students would attack
Roth for the usual reasons: that his portrayal of women was insufficiently

"sympathetic," that his ideas about sex were retrograde, that the hero Mickey Sabbath was neither heroic nor congenial, that the book failed the compassion test. "Of course, the day before, I tried to prepare them, to show them that there were some women who are this way, others another, and that Drenka, the main female character, is equal to Sabbath in her erotic proclivities," Manea said. "These are women, after all, not cats. They are different. I had to explain that to demand that everyone female be nice is just like when I was in Romania and they said that all the characters who were workers had to be nice workers." As a way of showing that the rude and the obscene are not new to Western litera-ture, Roth read from Rabelais. That seemed to work. At a subsequent session, on *I Married a Communist*, things did not go so well. Near the end of that class, Roth read to the students from an account of the trial of Andrei Sinyavsky and Yuli Daniel, two of the leading literary dissidents in the Brezhnev period. In the transcript, the judge demands to know from Daniel why he writes such unpleasant things about "the Soviet peo-ple." Daniel replies that these are not "the Soviet people" but, rather, characters in his book. "Even in the writers' union," Daniel says, "they don't ask that we write only about nice people."

But Roth's tactic only seemed to make matters worse.

"Philip could not make them see the novel from a more literary point of view and not politicize everything," Manea said.

Although it has been many years since some of the grandees in the Jew-ish establishment attacked Roth, it is still a commonplace to hear that his novels never paint a rounded portrait of a female character, that they are somehow "hostile" to women. At one point in *Sabbath's Theater*, Roth lampoons such reductive thinking when he quotes from a young woman's notes in a college lecture course. Of Yeats's poem "Meru," she writes, "Class criticized poem for its lack of a woman's perspective. Note unconscious gender privileging—*his* terror, *his* glory, *his* (phallic) monuments."

Roth's friend the Irish novelist Edna O'Brien told me, "As regards women, Philip has been mistakenly accused of not liking or understand-ing them. That's tosh! Take Faunia, his most recent heroine: she is gen-erous, funny, astute, and, like many a woman, castigated for her sexual robustness. She stands in extreme and salutary contrast to Monica Lewinsky, whose come-hither carried the hidden resolve of betrayal."

Roth does not like to talk much about these things, for fear of arousing more argument and hostility. His opinion about the state of reading, in the academy and in the culture generally, seems now to be what makes him most unhappy.

"Every year, seventy readers die and only two are replaced. That's a very easy way to visualize it," Roth said. By "readers," he said, he means people who read serious books seriously and consistently. The evidence "is everywhere that the literary era has come to an end," he said. "The evidence is the culture, the evidence is the society, the evidence is the screen, the progression from the movie screen to the television screen to the computer. There's only so much time, so much room, and there are only so many habits of mind that can determine how people use the free time they have. Literature takes a habit of mind that has disappeared. It requires silence, some form of isolation, and sustained concentration in the presence of an enigmatic thing. It is difficult to come to grips with a mature, intelligent, adult novel. It is difficult to know what to make of literature. That's why I say stupid things are said about it, because unless people are well trained they don't know quite what to make of it."

We were sitting at Roth's kitchen table, and I could see that he was eager to change the subject. We'd talked about this before, and it made him anxious; he sensed that saying these things would make him seem crotchety and sour, hostile to his audience. But I said, "Go further."

Roth straightened in his chair. "Go further? You wanna know? All right. Well, I think that the whole effort of certainly the first half of the twentieth century, the whole intellectual and artistic effort, was to see *behind* things, and that is no longer of interest. To explore consciousness was the great mission of the first half of the century—whether we're talking about Freud or Joyce, whether we're talking about the Surrealists or Kafka or Marx, or Frazer or Proust or whoever. The whole effort was to expand our sense of what consciousness is and what lies behind it. It's no longer of interest. I think that what we're seeing is the narrowing of consciousness. I read the other day in a newspaper that I occasionally see that Freud was a kind of charlatan or something worse. This great, tragic poet, our Sophocles! The writer is just not of interest to the public as somebody who may have an inroad into consciousness. The writer is only interesting in terms of how much money did he get and what's the scandal. That's all they're interested in. Why? Because the other stuff is useless, they don't want it. There has always been a debate over what literature is and what it's for, because it is a mysterious thing, and the mysterious side of existence, certainly for secular people, is not an urgent problem.

"I'm not a good enough student of whatever you have to be a student of to figure this out, but one gets the sense—and not just on the basis of the death of reading—that the American branch of the species is being retooled. I see the death of reading as just an aspect of this. I have to see it that way, otherwise it's just cultural whining, and cultural whining is boring. It's an aspect of some great shift that's occurred—been going on for a while—in that which interests the most intelligent members of American society."

In this period of Roth's maturity, his book sales have been modest, ranging between thirty and forty-five thousand in hardcover. The *Portnoy* days are long past. But this, he said, is hardly the point: "It doesn't make any difference really if a hundred thousand read the book or ten thousand or five thousand, frankly. Five thousand people is a lot of people. And, as a friend of mine said about five thousand readers, 'If they came through your living room one at a time they'd leave you in tears.'

"So when I talk of the death of reading, I'm not saying, 'Poor me, or poor the other guy, we don't have the readership.' I just mean that this great human endeavor has come to an end, when we're talking about the serious novel, and that is worth marking. I'm sixty-seven years old and writing now in 2000. I started publishing in 1959 in *The New Yorker.* Believe me, I know. If it were otherwise I'd be delighted. But I'm not despairing, I tell you. How can you be despairing about this and spend ten hours a day writing? I'd do it anyway."

In 1993, just as he was reaching a point of real mastery, Philip Roth met with a crisis. As an artist, he had deepened his subject, moving to a more varied cast of characters and a sense of place—and, above all, toward deeper feeling, a more tragic voice. There were a couple of lesser books along the way—*The Facts* and *Deception*—but there were three books as fine as any he'd ever written: *The Counterlife;* a memoir of his father's dying, *Patrimony;* and *Operation Shylock. The Counterlife* employs postmodern devices—the playing and replaying of scenes—and at the same time is drenched in emotion, not least the narrator's outrage over English anti-Semitism. In many ways, *Operation Shylock* is *Portnoy* brought to the next level of comedy and psychological tumult. But, while Roth was now writing well, his life was coming apart. Crippling back pain, the disintegration of his marriage to Claire Bloom, and a deep depression left him undone. And yet, eventually, with the help of his friends, Roth was somehow able to turn back to his work with greater concentration than ever before. With that sense of having survived a crisis, there came a liberating feeling of aesthetic release, and he began to write *Sabbath's Theater.*

"Philip was falling apart," Judith Thurman said. "He was antic and unbelievably depressed and overwhelmed. He felt trapped and run to ground by a life he didn't want to be living. He was also deeply exasperated by the condescension from reviewers and their clichés: Roth the enemy of the Jews, the bugbear of feminism, the hysteric, the narcissist—all of that, though he cared about that less. So the response was 'I'm going to do what I'm doing for me and the twenty-five people I care about. I'm going to retire to the country and write my books.' So out of chaos came this hunkering down."

Ross Miller: "What happened to him was essentially acknowledging that even the strongest human being can be brought to his knees by an almost farcical combination of a bad marriage, a bad back, death. All the things he satirizes in *The Anatomy Lesson* happened to him: the sudden loss of vitality, the collapse—and then the recovery, which gave him a sense of freedom."

Norman Manea: "Philip now has the internal structure of a soldier. He is close to his mates, his friends and family in the trenches; there is solidarity there and he will not betray that. This is crucial for him. *Sabbath's Theater* was written after this great crisis, and he just locked himself up and ate from a can and wrote. . . . I have changed a lot since I came here from Romania, but Philip has changed more. He went from being a social guy with the world in his fist to being a very reclusive man, very reluctant to reenter the chaos of the world. He created a strong, artificial order that became his natural order.

"He paid a heavy price, but he was lucky that, having paid it, he was compensated by literature."

Once, when we were talking about his career, I asked Roth when he had felt the happiest. Sometimes, when he is talking about books, he pauses for just a moment, the better to gather a well-formed argument. But now he answered immediately, definitely: When was he happiest? "When I was writing *Sabbath's Theater,*" he said.

"But why?" The moment just after all that pain.

"Because I felt free. I feel like I am *in charge* now."

There was a time, in the eighties, when writing was hard for Roth, when hundreds of pages would end up in the trash before a novel would begin in earnest: "I'd sit there and think, I can't stand this, I can't stand myself, I can't stand being in this room, I can't stand the frustration of this room. That's what it was: the drip, drip, drip of the frustration. It was like an acid drip." But now there is tremendous fluency. Not to over-rate the importance of personal crisis in the creation of an imaginative literature—thousands endure tragedy without any art coming of it—but Roth was able to convert personal crisis, a period when he thought he might never write again, and to pull himself out of that and onto a plane of mastery. "Like Charlie Parker, Philip can play what he hears now," Ross Miller said. "Writing is easy for him now, where it was once hard." Of course, Roth's fluency in writing his recent books could not have hap-pened without the many years of labor, any more than Parker could play his improvisations without thousands of hours practicing chord changes. The craft and the imagination would not be there, would not be on call, without this singular sense of devotion and the time and the quiet and the health it seems to require.

"I don't think Philip has ever been this happy, certainly not since I've known him," Judith Thurman said. "He now lives the life he's always wanted to live without the beholdenness to others except to the people he cares about. He's like a graduate student/monk. There are not a lot of moving parts to his life now. Complicated domestic arrangements, the needs and conflicts of family life, are all Rube Goldberg machines, and he now does without that. When you are younger, you're propelled by a lot of unslaked desires. Now there is this one thing: the work."

Over the years, Roth has let himself be diverted at times from the work. He taught at the University of Pennsylvania and Hunter College. He conducted a series of interviews with Aharon Appelfeld, Ivan Klíma, Milan Kundera, Isaac Bashevis Singer, Edna O'Brien, and Primo Levi—a collection that will one day be published as "Shop Talk." For Penguin, he edited the influential "Writers from the Other Europe" series, a paperback publishing project that brought Kundera, Tadeusz Borowski, Bruno Schulz, Ludvík Vaculík, Tadeusz Konwicki, and Danilo Kiš to the attention of American readers. There were lectures and readings, there were PEN reports to write and trips to Prague and Jerusalem, there were op-ed pieces to write for the *Times,* there were petitions to sign, readings to give, there were love affairs, friendships, elderly parents. Now there is work, and that is nearly all. For a long time, Roth kept two small signs near his desk. One read, "Stay Put," the other, "No Optional Striving." Optional striving appears to be a category that includes every-thing save writing, exercise, sleep, and solitude.

"It's a wonderful experience," Roth said. "That act of passionate and minute memory is what binds your days together—days, weeks, months—and living with that is my greatest pleasure. I think for any novelist it has to be the greatest pleasure, that's why you're doing it—to make the daily connections. I do it by living a very austere life. I don't experience it as being austere in any negative sense, but you have to be a bit like a soldier with a barracks life, or whatever you want to call it. That is to say, I rule everything else out of my life. I didn't always, but I do now."

When we first started these interviews, in late winter, Roth told me he was "between books" and was thinking about what might follow *The Human Stain*. A couple of months later, he was kidding around about long-ago Newark and said, "I was born before panty hose and frozen foods." And then he added, "That's a line from my next novel." It turned out that he had written over a hundred pages. At that moment, he recalled the fleeting period in an athlete's life when the vectors of his physical abilities and his mastery of the game—his experience, intelligence, and imagination—meet at the highest possible point. Although *Sabbath's Theater, American Pastoral, I Married a Communist,* and *The Human Stain* are all novels set on the abyss, all of them shot through with the comedy of failure and decay, the sense of exhilaration in their author is unmistakable.

"I have to tell you that I don't believe in death, I don't experience the time as limited. I know it is, but I don't feel it," Roth said. "I could live three hours or I could live thirty years, I don't know. Time doesn't prey upon my mind. It should, but it doesn't. I don't know yet what this will all add up to, and it no longer matters, because there's no stopping. And this stuff is not going to matter anyway, as we know. So there's no sense even contemplating it, you know? All you want to do is the obvious. Just get it right, and the rest is the human comedy: the evaluations, the lists, the crappy articles, the insults, the praise.

"I want only to respond to my work. I don't want to respond to all that stuff. It's not important. It was, and it is for others at a certain time, but it can't be important anymore.

"If I'm healthy and strong and writing every day, who cares? Whatever problem is raised for me by what I'm writing, I think, Don't worry about it, all it takes is time. That's all it takes. I don't worry anymore that I don't have what it takes to solve the problem. There are no interruptions, and I've got all the time in the world. Time is on my side."

(2000)

•

Roth's pace has not slackened. *The Human Stain* was the final install-
ment of what he called the American trilogy. In 2001, he published
a novella, *The Dying Animal*, which completed the "David Kepesh
trilogy"—the earlier books were *The Breast* (1972) and *The Professor of
Desire* (1977)—and, in 2004, he published *The Plot Against America*,
which seemed to confound his gloomy statements about the limits of
his readership when it quickly became his biggest-selling book since
Portnoy's Complaint. In 2005, the Library of America began to publish
the first volumes of Roth's complete works, beginning with *Goodbye,
Columbus.* Later, he finished a short novel called *Everyman.*

One day we were taking a walk near his apartment on the West Side.
"The only part of this walk that gives me pause," he said, "is this," and he
pointed to an obelisk just outside the doors of the Hayden Planetarium.
As we got closer it came clear that the names engraved on the stone were
those of the American winners of the Nobel Prize. Roth smiled. Saul
Bellow had died just a few weeks before, a loss that had affected Roth
deeply. He pointed to Bellow's name and said, "Well, they certainly got
that one right."

No Longer, Not Yet:
Don DeLillo

In the spring of 1988, the editors of the *New York Post* sent a pair of photographers to New Hampshire with instructions to find J. D. Salinger and take his picture. If the phrase "take his picture" had any sense of violence or, at least, violation left in it at all, if it still retained the undertone of certain peoples who are convinced that a photographer threatens them with the theft of their souls, then it applied here. There is no mystery why the *Post* pursued its prey. For whatever reasons (and one presumes they are not happy reasons), Salinger stopped publishing long ago—his last story, "Hapworth 16, 1924," appeared in *The New Yorker* in 1965—and he has lived a reclusive life ever since. His withdrawal became for journalists a story demanding resolution, intervention, and exposure. Inevitably, the *Post* got its man. The journalists took Salinger's picture. The paper ran a photograph on the front page of a gaunt sixty-nine-year-old man recoiling, as if anticipating catastrophe. In that instant, the look in Salinger's eyes was one of such terror that it is a wonder he survived it. CATCHER CAUGHT, the headline screamed in triumph.

On the day Salinger's picture appeared in the *Post,* another novelist of stature, Don DeLillo, began thinking about the inescapable and mystical power of the image in the media age, and, closer to home, about his own halfhearted attempts to keep his distance from the mass-media machinery. From the start, he had been shy of exposure outside the exposure of the work itself. When he published his first novel, *Americana,* in 1971, he had asked that the author's note on the jacket read, simply, "Don DeLillo lives and works in New York City."

After living in the Bronx and Manhattan for many years, DeLillo and his wife, Barbara Bennett, eventually settled a half hour's train ride north of the city, in Westchester County. They both work at home: DeLillo as a novelist in his upstairs study, Bennett as a landscape designer. (She used to be an executive at Citibank.) DeLillo does not teach, he rarely gives readings, and he keeps interviews to a minimum. When friends would ask his credo, DeLillo would say he lived by the words of Stephen Dedalus: "Silence, exile, cunning—and so on."

But what DeLillo learned from the picture in the *Post,* and what he has very likely learned through his friendship with Thomas Pynchon, is that the price of complete withdrawal is also great. Not long after seeing the picture of Salinger, DeLillo began writing *Mao II,* a book with a novelist named Bill Gray at its center. At one point, Gray says, "When a writer doesn't show his face, he becomes a local symptom of God's famous reluctance to appear. . . . People may be intrigued by this figure but they also resent him and mock him and want to dirty him up and watch his face distort in shock and fear when the concealed photographer leaps out of the trees."

There was a time when people who aspired to be a part of something called "the American reading public" felt vaguely obliged to buy, and even read, the fiction of the moment. One felt guilty about missing *A Perfect Day for Bananafish, The Adventures of Augie March,* or *The Group.* There is now more anxiety, probably, about missing *Pulp Fiction* a month after its release than about never reading the latest Saul Bellow novel. Occasionally, a serious novel carries with it a sense of popular urgent appeal and elbows its way past the bilge and onto the best-seller list. The most recent example is Pynchon's *Mason & Dixon*—a phenomenon that may have as much to do with the author's long silence and the exquisite packaging of the book as with the novel itself.

It will be interesting to see what happens with DeLillo's new novel, *Underworld*. DeLillo is sixty, and this, his eleventh book, is his longest, most ambitious, and most complicated novel. The length is in excess of eight hundred pages; the ambition is to portray the American psyche during its Cold War ascendance, beginning with Bobby Thomson's home run to win the 1951 National League pennant at the Polo Grounds for the New York Giants and ending with an underground explosion on the plains of Kazakhstan after the collapse of the Soviet empire. At the center of the novel is a man named Nick Shay, who, as a teenager, shot and killed a waiter in the Bronx; the novel follows Shay, and America, from Thomson's homer, that singular moment of citywide postwar joy, to a jaundiced maturity. Shay grows up to be an executive specializing in the management of waste. Just as DeLillo's 1988 novel, *Libra,* was a kind of fictional biography of Lee Harvey Oswald, *Underworld* also contains imagined public characters, a wealth of them, including J. Edgar Hoover, Frank Sinatra, Jackie Gleason, and Lenny Bruce, as well as Cold War artifacts like a "long-lost" film by Sergei Eisenstein called *Unterwelt,* the subway graffiti and murals of inner-city guerrilla painters, a documentary on the Rolling Stones, satellite photographs, and the play-by-play monologue of the Giants broadcaster Russ Hodges.

In the labeling process that passes for popular criticism, DeLillo has been called "the chief shaman of the paranoid school of American fiction"—and not without reason. Even DeLillo allows that the thread running through his books is about "living in dangerous times," about plots and conspiracies, about troubled men in small rooms. But, for all the cramped spaces and sweaty foreboding in the novels, *Underworld* included, what's usually missing from the critical work about DeLillo is the humor, the way the language undercuts, even redeems, the darkness of the landscapes. *Underworld* is the black comedy of the Cold War; it is full of sentences that capture, with the choice of the odd word, a moment in American history. Here is Shay in a contemporary restaurant:

> The waitress brought a chilled fork for my lifestyle salad. Big Sims was eating a cheeseburger with three kinds of cheddar, each described in detail on the menu. There was a crack in the wall from the tremor of the day before and when Sims laughed I saw his mouth cat's-cradled with filaments of gleaming cheese.

Although DeLillo has never had a best-seller, Scribner paid nearly a million dollars for *Underworld,* and Scott Rudin, the producer of *Clue-*

less and *The First Wives' Club,* has bought the movie rights. With a mixture of amusement and resignation, DeLillo has agreed to do his public
part, but he has tried to keep things within reason. When he and I first
talked on the phone to arrange a meeting at his house, DeLillo said, "I'd
ask that you not tell anyone where I live, specifically speaking. You can
say Westchester." We met, then, on a summer morning at the agreed-
upon hour at the agreed-upon unmentionable train station.

   To meet DeLillo, at first, is to meet someone who seems to have
sanded away all trace of authorial ego or personal affect: his voice is a
flat, wry monotone with just a trace of Bronx; he wears enormous and
very thick glasses; his clothes tend toward mail-order jeans, denim work
shirts, chinos. His life is equally Dionysian: four hours of writing in the
morning, a few miles around a local high-school track at midday ("trees,
birds, drizzle"), and then more writing, on into the early evening. Sometimes he will go see a movie. Sometimes he will rent one. DeLillo once
said, "A writer takes earnest measures to secure his solitude and then
finds endless ways to squander it." He has learned not to squander it
much, if at all. When DeLillo started writing, in the mid-sixties, he
worked sporadically, and it was only over time that he developed his athlete's focus and rigor, the sense of responsibility, that has allowed him to
publish so steadily since *Americana.*

   "I didn't become serious about fiction for a long time," he said as we
settled into his spare living room. The room is decorated with a few
antiques, a few books, some CDs, and fresh flowers. "I didn't have the
ambition, the sense of discipline. I had no idea what was demanded of a
writer who wanted to be serious about his work, and it took me a long,
long time to develop this. It didn't occur to me then that much more
was demanded out of me, and much more was at stake in day-to-day
work. You know, you become a better writer by getting older, by living
longer."

   DeLillo did not map out the architecture of *Underworld* and then
begin. The process was much more intuitive, mysterious, flounder-
ing. There was never an outline. The writing began with a twenty-five-
thousand-word burst—a set piece, which became the novel's prologue.
It opens with a black kid named Cotter Martin sneaking into the Polo
Grounds and then, like a movie camera that widens its focus, takes in the
crowd. The opening, which first appeared as a novella called "Pafko at
the Wall" in *Harper's,* is one of the most extraordinary performances in
contemporary American fiction. DeLillo is able to get the wise-guy
interplay among the Hollywood biggies in Leo Durocher's private box

(Gleason vomiting on Sinatra's lisle socks), the fears and pleasure of Cotter in his fugitive seat, the animal movements of the crowd, the action on the field, the city's ecstatic reactions beyond, even J. Edgar Hoover surreptitiously studying a small reproduction of a Brueghel painting ("the meatblood colors and massed bodies"). Hoover, sitting in his box, knows that while the game is being played the Soviet Union is secretly testing a nuclear weapon in Kazakhstan, and he thinks, What secret history are they writing? DeLillo's focus, his camera, seems to career around the ballpark, from scene to scene, face to face, mind to mind, taking it all in, as if at once.

After the home run has been hit, he ends the set piece by focusing on Russ Hodges, the broadcaster:

> This is the thing that will pulse in his brain come old age and double vision and dizzy spells—the surge sensation, the leap of people already standing, that bolt of noise and joy when the ball went in. This is the people's history and it has flesh and breath that quicken to the force of this old safe game of ours, and fans at the Polo Grounds today will be able to tell their grandchildren—they'll be the gassy old men leaning into the next century and trying to convince anyone willing to listen, pressing in with medicine breath, that they were here when it happened.
>
> The raincoat drunk is running the bases. They see him round first, his hands paddling the air to keep him from drifting into right field. He approaches second in a burst of coattails and limbs and untied shoelaces and swinging belt. They see he is going to slide and they stop and watch him leave his feet.
>
> All the fragments of the afternoon collect around his airborne form. Shouts, bat-cracks, full bladders and stray yawns, the sand-grain manyness of things that can't be counted.
>
> It is all falling indelibly into the past.

While the Giants were playing the Dodgers for the '51 pennant, DeLillo was in a dentist's office on Crotona Avenue in the Bronx. He was, naturally, a Yankees fan, so he was mainly waiting it out to see who the next National League victim would be. Thomson's homer was not for him what it was for Giants fans. But forty years later, as he read an anniversary account of the game in the newspaper, he began to think about the event, how it seemed unrepeatable, the communal joy of it married, as it was on the front page of the *Times* in 1951, to the nuclear explosion in Kazakhstan. "Somebody seemed to be wanting to tell me something here," DeLillo said to me.

For a long time, DeLillo has been interested in the passage in John Cheever's journals where he wrote, after attending a ballgame at Shea Stadium, "The task of an American writer is not to describe the misgivings of a woman taken in adultery as she looks out of a window at the rain but to describe 400 people under the lights reaching for a foul ball . . . [or] the faint thunder as 10,000 people, at the bottom of the eighth, head for the exits. The sense of moral judgments embodied in a migratory vastness."

"I had no idea this would be a novel," DeLillo said. "All I wanted to do was write a fictional account of this ballgame, and, for the first time ever, I was writing something whose precise nature I could not gauge. I didn't know whether I was writing a short story, a short novel, or a novel. But I did know that the dimensions of the Polo Grounds were my boundaries. I had no idea that I would go beyond this until after I finished.

"The prologue is written with a sort of super-omniscience. There are sentences that may begin in one part of the ballpark and end in another. I wanted to open up the sentence. They become sort of travel-happy; they travel from one person's mind to another. I did it largely because it was pleasurable. It was baseball itself that provided a kind of freedom that perhaps I hadn't quite experienced before. It was the game."

After the prologue, *Underworld* cuts to 1992 and begins to work backward through the years of the Cold War, so that the day of the game, October 3, 1951, and the day Nick Shay shoots the waiter, October 4, 1951, are separated by forty years of narrative. The mechanical device that travels through the narrative as it weaves back and forth in time is the baseball—the baseball that Bobby Thomson hit into the seats at the Polo Grounds, the ball that Cotter Martin grabs and takes home, the ball that collectors, Nick Shay included, covet as a talisman of history. Many of DeLillo's old themes are in *Underworld:* the increasing power of the image and the media in the modern world; the uncertainty of American life after the Kennedy assassination; a sense of national danger; men and women who live outside the mainstream of ordinary life and language. There is even the whiff, here and there, of that most singular DeLillo trademark: paranoia. But, more often, *Underworld* is a darkly funny satire of postwar language, manners, and obsessions.

DeLillo takes a Nabokovian delight in the American language. Just as the names of American schoolchildren are catalogued in *Lolita* as if they were Homeric ships, DeLillo lists the words of the fifties—"breezeway," "crisper," "sectional," "broadloom," "stacking chairs," "scatter cushions," "storage walls"—and recounts the small tragedy of a housewife at that techno-crazed moment in history: "She'd recently bought a new satellite-shaped vacuum cleaner that she loved to push across the room because it hummed softly and seemed futuristic and hopeful but she was forced to regard it ruefully now, after Sputnik, a clunky object filled with self-remorse."

DeLillo's most curious feat of literary discipline until now was his determination to look away from his native ground, the Fordham section of the Bronx. It is hard to imagine a writer keeping such vivid local color out of his work for so long. On a stifling, fly-blown morning this summer, DeLillo led me down Arthur Avenue, the heart of the Italian Bronx, past grocery stores and pasta joints, and said, "There was a Mob hit here when I was a kid—a mobster killed while he was buying fruit. I think it must have been a model for that scene in *The Godfather* when Mario Puzo has Don Corleone getting shot while he's buying fruit in the street. He was a mobster from City Island who came here to shop. There were actually three events like that when I was growing up. One was the uncle of a kid I knew. And the other was in a liquor store." On feast days on Arthur Avenue, the women dressed in brown robes and pinned dollar bills to the plaster flanks of Jesus. On summer nights, the area was dense with games—stickball, softball, stoopball, bocce—and radios were playing and the fire hydrant sprayed and on the roof the women yelled down at the kids for killing the water pressure. Dion and the Belmonts lived up the street. John Garfield went to P.S. 45 when he was still Julius Garfinkle. Paddy Chayevsky's *Marty* was filmed in the neighborhood, and when it came out "we felt as if our existence had been justified," DeLillo said.

"I'll show you the old house," he said, and he headed to the corner of 182nd Street and Adams Place. The house is a narrow, three-story building with patchy asbestos shingles. DeLillo grew up here with his parents, both immigrants from Italy, his sister, his aunt and uncle, and their three kids. An old man was sitting on the front steps. He had a broad belly that stretched and belled out the T-shirt he was wearing. It read, "You Idiot, Your Fly Is Open." Shy and friendly, DeLillo said hello and said he'd lived here many years ago.

"You wanna again?" the old man said, with a thick southern-Italian accent. "I sell you a hunnert twenny-five thousand."

DeLillo smiled and said, "See this brick gate? My father built that!"

"A hunnert twenny-five thousand," the man replied.

We were by now sweating, parboiled, but there was nothing much open. Finally, DeLillo found a pastry and coffee shop that featured working air-conditioning. After we sat down, I asked him why he'd waited until he had filled a substantial shelf with novels before turning to the Bronx in his fiction. In *Underworld,* Nick Shay grows up in an apartment building near DeLillo's old house.

"I needed to wait thirty years before writing about it to do it justice," DeLillo said. "I needed this distance. Also, I needed to write about it in a much larger context. I couldn't write a novel about a background and a place without putting it into a deeper setting. I plunged into the Bronx in my early stories, but the stories weren't very good. I wouldn't even care to look at them now. They were a kind of literary proletarian story. They were about working-class men under duress. I remember one was about a man who'd been evicted from his house, and he was outside sitting on the sidewalk surrounded by his possessions."

DeLillo went to Cardinal Hayes High School ("where I slept") and to Fordham University ("where I majored in something called communication arts"). His father worked as a payroll clerk at Metropolitan Life, in Manhattan. "You know that Graham Greene book called *England Made Me?* New York made me," DeLillo said. "There's a sensibility, a sense of humor, an approach, a sort of dark approach to things that's part New York, and maybe part growing up Catholic, and that, as far as I'm concerned, is what shapes my work far more than anything I read. I did have some wonderful reading experiences, particularly *Ulysses.* I read it first when I was quite young, and then again when I was about twenty-five. And this was important. I was very taken by the beauty of the language— particularly the first three or four chapters. I can remember reading this book in a part of my room that was usually sunny. It was a very strong experience. But I didn't read as a kid, and certainly no one read to us. This was not part of our tradition. People spoke, and yelled, but there wasn't much reading. I didn't take to nineteenth-century English material at all. It was a great struggle, a great burden, I couldn't concentrate on it. Once, I had to write a paper on a Dickens novel, and Dickens, of course, is easy. I just read the Classic Comics version and managed to get through. It's a struggle to emerge from a place like the Bronx and settle in a place like Manhattan. It represents an enormous journey that involves manners, language, what you wear, almost everything."

Today, Fordham is an easy train ride south for DeLillo, and when he was thinking about the Bronx sections that dominate the last few hundred pages of *Underworld* he would visit the neighborhood: the alleys of the apartment house where Nick Shay grew up, the projects a mile to the south, the cathedral-like Paradise movie theater on the Grand Concourse, which has since been gutted and left to rot. DeLillo, like any New Yorker, talks about neighborhood in narrow terms. When we passed Bathgate Avenue, he pointed out the street sign and said, "I keep out of there. That's Doctorow's turf." There are still plenty of Italians along the spine of Arthur Avenue, but there are also blacks, Hispanics, Albanians, Bosnians. Walking these streets helped him summon the faces and the mortar of the place, but it also helped him remember the psyche of the times—the way people knew what they knew, the way they so rarely lived in the larger world, except when they took the Third Avenue El downtown into Manhattan and glimpsed other lives through open apartment windows. And since *Underworld* is about the greater world, about the Cold War, his trips helped him remember how he and his neighbors had lived in threatening times.

"In those days, the way you absorbed the news was different," he said over the hiss and gurgle of the espresso machine. "You would have to go to the movies to really see something. There would be a cartoon and a short on the explosion of the hydrogen bomb. It was part of the entertainment, somehow—an extension of the movie."

In 1959, after college, DeLillo moved to a tiny apartment in Murray Hill, the sort of place where the refrigerator is in the bathroom. At first, he had a full-time job as a copywriter at Ogilvy, Benson & Mather. His friends were other copywriters, funny, sophisticated guys "who were like a combination of Jerry Lewis, Lenny Bruce, and Noël Coward." They went together to the galleries and the Village Vanguard, to the movies that were coming out of Italy and France. In the meantime, DeLillo started work on *Americana*.

It was a tentative start, but after a few years, once DeLillo got a handle on his novel and convinced himself that he was a real writer, he quit Ogilvy, Benson & Mather. To make a little money, he took freelance jobs writing copy for furniture catalogues, dialogue for a cartoon, a script for a television commercial. In 1971, *Americana* was published and was pronounced promising, and in 1975 he married Barbara Bennett. They have no children.

"It's a very lucky life for me," DeLillo said. "I've not been distracted by many of the things that other novelists are distracted by. I earn enough money to make a living at it, for one thing. I learned to live very,

very cheaply. And family complications have not been a source of difficulty for me, as they are for almost everyone else."

DeLillo's early novels—*Americana, End Zone, Great Jones Street, Rat-
ner's Star, Players,* and *Running Dog*—and then the triumphant run of
The Names, White Noise, Libra, Mao II, and *Underworld,* radiate a sensibility tempered in the sixties and seventies. But, unlike some of his
contemporaries and friends, DeLillo has kept mainly to the political
sidelines. "I took part in a number of war protests, but only as a sort of
marcher in the rear ranks," he said. "I was very interested in rock music.
At the same time, I have to say that I didn't buy a single record. I listened
to it on the radio. I let the culture wash over me. I used marijuana, not
frequently but more or less regularly. I found the sixties extremely interesting, and, at the same time that all this was happening—enormous
social disruption—I also felt that there was a curious ennui, a boredom,
which actually may be part of my first novel. I think it's something I
sensed around me, which would seem to be completely at odds with
what you were seeing and hearing in the streets. I suppose what I felt for
much of this period was a sense of unbelonging, of not being part of any
kind of official system. Not as a form of protest but as a kind of separate-
ness. It was an alienation, but not a political alienation, predominantly. It
was more spiritual."

When DeLillo was a young man in the city, he often went to look at
the Abstract Expressionists at the Museum of Modern Art. This summer, we met one afternoon at the museum and walked through exhibits
featuring the great Soviet poster artists of the twenties, the Stenberg
brothers, a series of photographs by Cindy Sherman, and a history of
the still life that began with a Cézanne and ended with a flat white slab
covered with milk, the sight of which caused DeLillo's to say, "Nice
milk."

Later, over lunch at the museum restaurant, I asked him about the
way those museum visits might have influenced his work; how, for that
matter, all the excitements of his youth—Joyce, Italian and French
movies of the sixties, bebop, and rock music—figured in his novels.

"That's very difficult for me to answer," he said. "But the influence is
almost metaphysical. I don't think I could make any kind of direct connection. I think fiction comes from everything you've ever done, and
said, and dreamed, and imagined. It comes from everything you've read
and haven't read. It comes from all the things that are in the air. At some

point, you begin to write sentences and paragraphs that don't sound like other writers'. And for me the crux of the whole matter is language, and the language a writer eventually develops. If you're talking about Hemingway, the Hemingway sentence is what makes Hemingway. It's not the bullfights or the safaris or the wars, it's a clear, direct, and vigorous sentence. It's the simple connective—the word 'and' that strings together the segments of a long Hemingway sentence. The word 'and' is more important to Hemingway's work than Africa or Paris. I think my work comes out of the culture of the world around me. I think that's where my language comes from. That's where my themes come from. I don't think it comes from other people. One's personality and vision are shaped by other writers, by movies, by paintings, by music. But the work itself, you know—sentence by sentence, page by page—it's much too intimate, much too private, to come from anywhere but deep within the writer himself. It comes out of all the time a writer wastes. We stand around, look out the window, walk down the hall, come back to the page, and, in those intervals, something subterranean is forming, a literal dream that comes out of daydreaming. It's too deep to be attributed to clear sources."

I asked DeLillo if he recognized himself when he read academic criticism or journalistic reviews of his work.

"Not really," he said. "What's almost never discussed is what you and I have just been talking about: the language in which a book is framed. And there's a good reason. It's hard to talk about. It's hard to write about. And so one receives a broad analysis of, perhaps, the social issues in one's work but rarely anything about the way the writer gets there."

The most vivid political critique of DeLillo has come from the right, a barrage that began, in 1985, with Bruce Bawer writing in *The New Criterion* and was then backed up, double-barreled, in *The Washington Post* by George Will and the paper's book critic, Jonathan Yardley.

In his essay "Don DeLillo's America," Bawer began with the dubious assertion that while one can always find DeLillo's books in stores it is very hard to find some titles by Fitzgerald, Hemingway, or Faulkner. Even more mystifying than the Barnes & Noble angle was Bawer's idea that DeLillo's novels are not believable novels but, rather, "tracts, designed to batter us, again and again, with a single idea: that life in America today is boring, benumbing, dehumanized." He went on, "It's better, DeLillo seems to say in one novel after another, to be a marauding, murderous maniac—and therefore a *human*—than to sit still for America as it is, with its air-conditioners, assembly lines, television sets, supermarkets, synthetic fabrics, and credit cards. At least when you're living a life of primitive violence, you're closer to the mystery at the heart of it all." A novel such as *White Noise,* Bawer wrote, is studded with cheap left-wing "Philosophy McNuggets."

Will, for his part, interrupted his ruminations on the 1988 Presidential race to take offense at *Libra,* a novel speculating on the character and responsibility of Lee Harvey Oswald, as "sandbox existentialism" and "an act of literary vandalism and bad citizenship." He treats DeLillo as if he were a certifiable crackpot, wielding an un-American weapon—a gift for prose. That DeLillo would dare call into question the veracity of the Warren Commission, or that he would speculate about the psychology of a murderer and the culture itself, "traduces an ethic of literature." And that DeLillo would describe the writer as an outsider in that culture is merely a "burst of sophomoric self-dramatization," because, after all, "Henry James, Jane Austen, George Eliot and others were hardly outsiders." Will went on, "DeLillo's notion of the writer outside the mainstream of daily life is so radical" that it "stops just a short step from declaring the writer as kin to Oswald, who, as a defector, was the ultimate outsider."

"I don't take it seriously, but being called a 'bad citizen' is a compliment to a novelist, at least to my mind," DeLillo said. "That's exactly what we ought to do. We ought to be bad citizens. We ought to, in the sense that we're writing against what power represents, and often what government represents, and what the corporation dictates, and what consumer consciousness has come to mean. In that sense, if we're bad citizens, we're doing our job. Will also said I blamed America for Lee Harvey Oswald. But I don't blame America for Lee Harvey Oswald, I blame America for George Will. I don't think there is any sense in *Libra* in which America is the motive force that sends Oswald up to that sixth-floor window. In fact, Oswald is interesting because he was, at least by his own lights, a strongly political man, who not only defected to the Soviet Union but tried to assassinate the right-wing figure General Walker about seven months before the assassination of President Kennedy. In that seven months his life unraveled. I think he lost a grip on his political consciousness, and on almost everything else around him. And I think he became the forerunner of all those soft white young men of the late sixties and early seventies, who went around committing crimes of convenience, shooting at whatever political figure or celebrity happened to drift into range." DeLillo said he didn't pretend to know the answer to the assassination riddle, though he thought there was probably a second gunman. When DeLillo visited the sixth floor of the Texas School Book Depository museum, he wrote in the guestbook, "Still waiting for the man on the grassy knoll."

DeLillo has no idea how *Underworld* will be absorbed into the culture, if at all. He seems not to worry about it. In fact, he doesn't think that the increasingly marginal status of the serious novelist is necessarily awful. By being marginal, he may end up being more significant, more respected, sharper in his observations. Not long ago, DeLillo wrote a letter to his friend the novelist Jonathan Franzen. DeLillo's letter sounds very much like reassurance to a successor:

> The novel is whatever novelists are doing at a given time. If we're not doing the big social novel fifteen years from now, it'll probably mean our sensibilities have changed in ways that make such work less compelling to us—we won't stop because the market dried up. The writer leads, he doesn't follow. The dynamic lives in the writer's mind, not in the size of the audience. And if the social novel lives, but only barely, surviving in the cracks and ruts of the culture, maybe it will be taken more seriously, as an endangered spectacle. A reduced context but a more intense one. . . . Writing is a form of personal freedom. It frees us from the mass identity we see in the making all around us. In the end, writers will write not to be outlaw heroes of some underculture but mainly to save themselves, to survive as individuals.
>
> P.S. If serious reading dwindles to near nothingness, it will probably mean that the thing we're talking about when we use the word "identity" has reached an end.

In *Libra,* in *Mao II,* and now in *Underworld,* DeLillo has increasingly brought the world of power and celebrity into his work—the world of contemporary history. It's likely that he will continue in that direction.

"I think the press of public events has got stronger in the last several decades," he told me. "It's the power of the media, the power of television. But also, I think, there's something in people that, perhaps, has shifted. People seem to need news, any kind—bad news, sensationalistic news, overwhelming news. It seems to be that news is a narrative of our time. It has almost replaced the novel, replaced discourse between people. It replaced a slower, more carefully assembled way of communicating, a more personal way of communicating. In the fifties, news was a kind of sinuous part of life. It flowed in and out in a sort of ordinary, unremarkable way. And now news has impact, largely because of television news. After the earthquake in San Francisco, they showed one house burning, over and over, so that your TV set became a kind of instrument of apocalypse. This happens repeatedly in those endless videotapes of a bank robbery, or a shooting, or a beating. They repeat, and it's as though they're speeding up time in some way. I think it's induced an apocalyptic sense in people that has nothing to do with the end of the millennium. And it makes us—it makes us consumers of a certain type. We consume these acts of violence. It's like buying products that in fact are images and they are produced in a mass-market kind of fashion. But it's also real, it's real life. It's as though this were our last experience of nature: seeing a guy with a gun totally separate from choreographed movie violence. It's all that we've got left of nature, in a strange way. But it's all happening on our TV set."

The day we were talking, television was filled with images of the fashion designer Gianni Versace shot dead on the street in Miami Beach. DeLillo was interested not so much in the murder itself as in the instantaneous packaging of the murder, its sudden appearance on every screen and thus in millions of conversations. "People talk about the killing, but they don't talk about what it does to them, to the way they think, and feel, and fear," he said. "They don't talk about what it creates in a larger sense. The truth is, we don't quite know how to talk about this, I don't believe. Maybe that's why some of us write fiction."

Underworld ends with the fall of the Soviet Union and its conflict with the West. As DeLillo thinks about the era we're living in, and writing about it, he has also been thinking about a passage in Hermann Broch's novel *The Death of Virgil*. "He uses the term 'no longer and not yet,' " DeLillo said. "I think he's referring to the fact that his poet, Virgil, is in a state of delirium, no longer quite alive, and not yet dead. But I think he may also be referring to the interim between paganism and Christianity. And I think of this 'no longer and not yet' in terms of no longer the Cold War and not yet whatever will follow." But six months after finishing *Underworld,* he added, the germ of something really new has not yet shown itself.

On the way to the station to drop me off for the train back from Westchester County to the city, DeLillo said, "What happens in between is I drift, I feel a little aimless. I feel a little stupid, because my mind is at odds. It's not trained on a daily basis to concentrate on something, so I feel a little dumb. Time passes in a completely different way. I can't account for a day, a given day. At the end of a day, I don't know what I did."

(1997)

Exit the Castle:
Václav Havel

On his last weekday in Prague Castle as the President of the Czech Republic, Václav Havel taped a brief farewell address to the nation and then took a telephone call from George Bush. Havel, who came to office thirteen years ago wearing borrowed trousers that flapped high around his ankles, now wore an exquisitely tailored navy blue three-piece suit, a white shirt, and a tie that had undoubtedly done its duty at summit meetings and memorial services. A clutch of efficient aides scurried around his office door. A steward with a napkin folded over his arm delivered a glass of white wine. Sunlight streamed through tall windows, and chandeliers lent a glow to the flowers and the Oriental carpets.

The American President might have been surprised to learn that Havel's castle makes the White House seem inelegant, but Bush probably remembered the place well. Just a few months earlier, he had been to the Castle for a NATO summit—the first ever in a former Warsaw Pact capital. Bush, his Defense Secretary, Donald Rumsfeld, and dozens of generals and other politicians were treated not merely to the usual working meetings but also to theatrical performances organized by Havel himself. The NATO visitors watched an ersatz eighteenth-century dance (complete with powdered wigs and simulated copulation) that might have been considered obscene had it not been so funny. They listened to booming renditions of the "Ode to Joy," a souped-up "Marseillaise," and John Lennon's "Power to the People."

"I didn't understand anything," Rumsfeld remarked as he headed toward dinner. "I'm from Chicago."

When I got a chance recently to ask Havel about his NATO productions, he smiled and said, "I didn't want it to look like just another meeting of politicians and generals, so I shaped those arrangements, to a great extent. The ballet was set in Central Europe and featured Mozart's music, and it also included elements of the American grotesque, to underline the Euro-Atlantic character of the gathering. It may have been on the verge of what Mr. Rumsfeld and certain others could tolerate."

Awkward and shy, Havel is a curiously natural director. Forty-odd years ago, he started out as a stagehand and a playwright. He was an acolyte of Beckett and Ionesco—the theater of the absurd. The sense of the absurd extends to his own life. There is surely no modern biography that is more improbable yet dramatically coherent. Havel's is the rare life, Milan Kundera has written, that resembles a work of art and gives "the impression of a perfect compositional unity." Consider: a bourgeois boy becomes a bohemian playwright; he then becomes a dissident, who, for the crime of writing subversive essays and helping to organize a subversive movement called Charter 77, is encouraged by the regime to master the art of welding in a reeking Czech prison; finally, in late November 1989, everything implodes and he is leading demonstrations in Wenceslas Square, and hundreds of thousands of people are shouting *"Havel na hrad!"* ("Havel to the Castle!"); within days, he is the head of state, working in the same hilltop redoubt that served as a seat of power for dynasts of the Bohemian kingdom and the Hapsburg monarchy, for the emissaries of Berlin and the satraps of the Kremlin.

During the uprising, which quickly became known as the Velvet Revolution, and for a while afterward, there were graffiti around town proclaiming, *"Havel je král"*—"Havel Is King." The King tried to demystify his Castle. He ordered the costume designer for the movie *Amadeus* to create red-white-and-blue uniforms for the palace guards. (Communist-era guards wore khaki.) He himself at first refused the suits that his friend Prince Karel Schwarzenberg brought him. "I can't wear any of these!" Havel said. "I'd look like a gigolo." In jeans and sweater, he rode a scooter through the Castle halls. He threw a "festival of democracy" in the courtyards, with jugglers and mimes performing while he wandered around drinking Pilsner and greeting his guests. Later on, when he discovered that the chandeliers in the gilded Spanish Hall were outmoded, a couple of typical visitors, Mick Jagger and Keith Richards, paid for new fixtures. For weeks, he drove his staff crazy as he monkeyed around with the remote control, dimming the lights, then brightening them again.

"When I first came here, there were many things that I found absurd," Havel told me in his office. A sly, can-you-believe-it smile creased his face. "For example, it seemed to us on the first day that there were three rooms, close to where we're sitting now, which you couldn't enter. When we finally got inside, we discovered a kind of communications facility for contacts within the Warsaw Pact. So we took advantage of that and sent a New Year's greeting to Mikhail Gorbachev. Later, I heard from confidential sources that the KGB chief, Vladimir Kryuchkov, didn't really appreciate the fact that we'd found those facilities."

Within a few months of Havel's ascension, the euphoria of the Velvet Revolution began to fade. The poetry of those winter weeks, the theatrical press conferences and the street rallies, yielded to the prose of governing a ruined state. No more scooters, no more sneaking out of the Castle for a drink at a local pub. Havel allowed that he felt "strangely paralyzed, empty inside," fearful that dissent and governing were hardly the same. "At the very deepest core of this feeling there was, ultimately, a sensation of the absurd: what Sisyphus might have felt if one fine day his boulder stopped, rested on the hilltop, and failed to roll back down," he told an audience in Salzburg. "It was the sensation of a Sisyphus mentally unprepared for the possibility that his efforts might succeed, a Sisyphus whose life had lost its old purpose and hadn't yet developed a new one."

Havel had been preceded by dictators and, therefore, had to learn to be a President nearly on his own. He borrowed from many examples, especially from the humanism of Tomáš Garrigue Masaryk, the President of the First Czech Republic after the First World War, and from his friend Richard von Weizsäcker, the President of Germany. (The powers of the Czech presidency are based largely on the postwar West German model; the President is secondary to the Prime Minister in domestic affairs but has great authority in making appointments and in foreign policy.) At times, Havel felt thoroughly insufficient, a fraud. A familiar Prague voice, the voice of Kafka, told him what anyone who has grown up in a police state knows instinctually—that it could all end as easily as it started.

"I am the kind of person who would not be in the least surprised if, in the very middle of my Presidency, I were to be summoned and led off to stand trial before some shadowy tribunal, or taken straight to a quarry to break rocks," he told a startled audience at Hebrew University, in Jerusalem, less than six months after taking office. "Nor would I be surprised if I were to suddenly hear the reveille and wake up in my prison cell, and then, with great bemusement, proceed to tell my fellow-prisoners everything that had happened to me in the past six months. The lower I am, the more proper my place seems; and the higher I am, the stronger my suspicion is that there has been some mistake."

In Havel's thirteen years as President—first of Czechoslovakia and then, after the Slovaks and the Czechs divided into two states, in 1993, of the Czech Republic—many of his advisers repeatedly begged him to delete, or at least soften, these public moments of self-doubt. What effect would they have on an exhausted people waiting for the radical transformation of their country? (Imagine Chirac or Blair, Bush or Schröder beginning a national address with an ode to his midnight dread!) Havel, however, would not be edited. The Presidential speech was the only literary genre left to him now, his most direct means of expressing not only his personal feelings but also the spirit of the distinctively human politics he wanted to encourage after so many decades of inhuman ideology. "Some aides tried to stop him, but these speeches had a therapeutic value for him," Havel's closest aide, Vladimír Hanzel, told me. And yet, at times, Havel seemed not a President so much as Kafka reading from his diaries, providing an inventory of what haunted him:

> Then there is a powerful feeling of general alienation . . . an experience of unbearable oppressiveness, a need constantly to explain myself to someone, to defend myself, a longing for an unattainable order of things, a longing that increases as the terrain I walk through becomes more muddled and confusing. . . . Everything I encounter displays to me its absurd aspect first. I feel as though I am constantly lagging behind powerful, self-confident men whom I can never overtake, let alone emulate. I find myself essentially hateful, deserving only mockery.

Political gossip, to say nothing of political journalism, abhors stasis, and Havel's last days in office were on the calendar of Prague's columnists and parliamentarians for so long that it became an article of faith that he was "just like Mikhail Gorbachev"—a figure of historical magnitude who had overstayed his welcome, popular abroad but not at home. Of Gorbachev that was certainly true. On Christmas night, 1991, when he resigned his office and handed over the nuclear codes to his hostile inheritor, Boris Yeltsin, his poll ratings were in the single digits. Havel's case is quite different. His popularity rating when he took office was more than eighty percent; he leaves with around fifty-five percent. Even for heroes, such endurance is rare. In 2000, Lech Walesa, the Solidarity leader, ran again for the Polish Presidency. He received one percent of the vote.

Havel surely has detractors: the "lost generation" of pensioners and workers who could not cope with the dizzying cultural changes and the rising cost of living; leftists who still resent the collapse of Communist ideology; right-wingers who find his economic thinking fuzzy and his speeches naïve and too philosophical. Some intellectuals, like the social theorist Ernest Gellner, thought that Havel's rhetoric of love triumphing over evil had been admirable, perhaps, but "absurd, indefensible" as an explanation for the fall of Communism; that softness, Gellner wrote, had allowed members of the old regime to escape unpunished and to reap enormous profits in the new economy. There were also subtler, more personal forms of resentment. One morning, I had coffee with a theater director in his late seventies, who had known Havel since he was a young man. It was clear that the director disliked Havel, not for reasons of official policy but, rather, because of Havel's "moralisms," his insistence, after the Soviet invasion in August 1968, that Czechs try to resist the regime by "living in truth." Even now, Havel's purity stung the director; it was a lingering and deeply personal rebuke. The old man had not signed Charter 77; to do so was an almost suicidal crossing. Only hundreds of people dared go that far, he said, while "the rest just wanted to live."

Although the Czechs have suffered none of the violence that has plagued other countries in the region, especially Yugoslavia and Romania, the transition has not been purely pacific. Far from it. Despite Havel's objections, Czechoslovakia split. The "lustration" campaign to bar from certain jobs informers and other guilty people from the old era was a confused and traumatic process. "Why so much velvet?" some asked. Why appoint a Presidential team of inexperienced exiles and dissidents and tarnished Party hacks? Havel was sui generis to the end: he did not form a lasting party or movement; he had admirers, he had aides, but he has no real inheritor. In fact, as he left office, parliament could not settle on a successor.

Havel's most serious and persistent enemy through the years has been his political doppelgänger, the former Prime Minister Václav Klaus. For a decade, their relationship became the running story of Prague politics. Klaus is a technocrat and a Thatcherite—and, it must be said, a steely and arrogant man. He has always resented the "intellectuals in the Castle," and accused Havel of being a "half-socialist," in "love with state power." In 2001, he said of Havel, "I don't believe what he says, what he stands for, what he does. I don't understand his civil society. For me it is an empty phrase. . . . He is the most elitist person I have ever seen in my life. I am a normal person. He is not."

And yet, with those notable exceptions, almost everyone is quick to point out the dimensions of Havel's moral and political achievements, his importance in the reshaping of Europe. For a country that had lost so many of its best minds to deportation, Holocaust, exile, emigration, and suppression, Havel embodied a sense of the future and of Czech idealism. As a dissident and then as President, he was the most incisive Czech voice on reviving civil liberties and human rights, on restoring a sense of public responsibility at a moment of post-Communist apathy and greed. Havel was a playwright and essayist who wrote as if censorship did not exist; when he became a politician, he behaved as if his country, small as it is, were indispensable to the reordering of Europe. With his moral authority and moral glamour, he exerted an outsized influence. Bill Clinton, Tony Blair, and other leaders of the major powers were deeply influenced by him. The rapid expansion and redefinition of NATO is, in no small measure, Havel's doing.

One afternoon, I went to a farewell reception for Havel at the Castle. Hundreds of Castle aides, past and present, gathered in the Spanish Hall, under the Rolling Stones' chandeliers, and milled around, drinking beer, eating sandwiches, and lining up to say goodbye to their old boss. Havel posed for snapshots, accepted advice and best wishes—sometimes with pleasure, sometimes with the grimace usually reserved for a periodontist. Havel possesses a charisma peculiar to the shy. He is rather small, with tiny hands that play nervously at his lapels. He tends to speak to the floor or to your shoulder. Everyone leaned in to listen. Everyone laughed at his jokes.

Nearby, I ran into Michael Zantovský, one of his closest associates over the years. Zantovský had been a dissident and was the author of a book about Woody Allen; after the revolution, he'd been ambassador to the United States.

"I think this is the fifth or sixth farewell party, and there's more to come," Zantovský said merrily. "There was the so-called underground farewell, and, of course, at that one everyone got drunk." Then the diplomat waxed grand. "This is the end of an era," he said. "It means the end of transition, it means the end of changes and setbacks and new beginnings, you name it. What's going to happen now is that we will become a country like any other in Europe. Maybe I'm cynical, but these moments in history, for a person or a country, come and go. It's like Andy Warhol's fifteen minutes of fame, and ours was Havel's Presidency—especially the first years. Sometime in the future, it may come again, but at this point we are no more glamorous than Belgium or the Netherlands. As Brecht said, 'Unhappy the land that is in need of heroes.' I hope we don't need another." He drank to that.

Václav Klaus may despise Václav Havel, but he has a point: Havel is not a normal man. "I am just beginning to understand how everything has, in fact, been a diabolical trap set for me by destiny," Havel said on a recent trip to New York, his last as President. "I really was catapulted overnight into a world of fairy tales."

Havel was born in 1936, before the sellout of Czechoslovakia at Munich and the Nazi occupation, before the Communist putsch. He was born to good fortune. His father was a wealthy businessman, and his parents had a broad circle of highly educated friends. The family employed a cook, a governess, a maid, a gardener, and a chauffeur. The Havels wanted their sons, Václav and Ivan, to graduate from Oxford or Harvard. As boys, they went to boarding school. When the Communists took power, in 1948, the Havel family properties were confiscated, and, in an act of reverse social engineering, the regime barred bourgeois children like Václav from the better schools. Had it not been for the putsch, Havel once said, he would likely have "gone on to study philosophy at the university, attended . . . lectures on comparative literature, and, after graduation, I would have ridden around in an imported sports car without having done the least thing to deserve it."

With a spotty formal education, Havel gravitated to the theater, particularly the Theater on the Balustrade, which was a center of bohemian artists. His younger brother, Ivan, a cognitive scientist, said, "Coming from a bourgeois family, my brother was exposed to literature and many interesting people, but he felt bad, slightly guilty about it. In his literary circles, he was the rare bourgeois and he was embarrassed by it." This was Prague in the sixties, a more relaxed time, and Havel quickly adapted to a life of late-night discussions in smoky kitchens and the Café Slavia, beer and Becherovka, love affairs, samizdat, and rock and roll. His musical tastes ran to the Velvet Underground and, especially, to the Plastic People of the Universe. In his twenties and early thirties, he wrote a series of plays—*The Garden Party, The Memorandum,* and *The Increased Difficulty of Concentration*—that were all understood by their audiences as implicit critiques of the regime: its stifling "automatism" (a favorite term of Havel's), its inhuman language. Those plays, which were produced abroad as specimens of the cultural thaw, became emblems of the Prague Spring permitted by the Party reformer Alexander Dubček.

In the mid-sixties, Havel, to the despair of his mother, married a poor yet regal young woman named Olga Splíchalová. Until her death from cancer, in 1996, Olga was a levelheaded balance to Havel's idealism and to his trusting nature; she was a practical intelligence and, through years of harassment and imprisonment, an indefatigable support. "Olga and I are very different," Havel once said. "Olga's a working-class girl, very much her own person, sober, unsentimental, and she can even be somewhat mouthy and obnoxious; in other words, as we say, you can't get her drunk on a bun. . . . In Olga, I found exactly what I needed: someone who could respond to my own mental instability, to offer sober criticism of my wilder ideas, provide private support for my public adventures."

After the Soviet Union invaded Prague, ousted Dubček, and instituted a period of hard-line "normalization" that lasted for more than twenty years, the Communist Party banned Havel's works. For his part, Havel moved to a country house that he and Olga called Hrádeček (the Little Castle), and he veered increasingly toward a position of full-time dissent. Thrilling as *The Garden Party* was for young audiences in Prague, this next phase was even more important—and, perhaps, even more appropriate to Havel's real talents. "Havel has been a politician since the sixties," the novelist Ivan Klíma told me. "His plays were exciting in their time and place, they had great meaning, but they tend to lose their context now, especially abroad."

Far more ambitious, and more lasting, were Havel's dissident essays, particularly an open letter to the Communist leader Gustav Husák and *The Power of the Powerless,* which served as the most extensive theoretical underpinning for Charter 77 and Czech resistance. Havel's prose reached its audience in a variety of subterranean ways: in typewritten, carbon-copied manuscripts; in books that were published abroad and then smuggled back into the country; or as broadcasts on Radio Free Europe. (As President, Havel repaid RFE by making it possible for the studios and offices to move, in 1995, from Munich to Wenceslas Square.)

If Solzhenitsyn was the great witness of Communist oppression within the imperium, Havel was its most acute moral clinician. "Havel synthesized ideas that were in the air here and, as it turned out, all over the totalitarian world," Ivan Havel said. In those two essays, he describes the "entropy" of life under Communist oppression, the myriad everyday means by which every man and woman is "subjected to a prolonged and thorough process of violation, enfeeblement and anesthesia." When I visited Havel at the Castle, his aides were packing his effects, including a painting of a Communist-era sign reading, in Slovak, "Workers of the World Unite!" In *The Power of the Powerless,* Havel asks his reader to imagine the manager of a grocery who puts that sign in his store window, "among the onions and carrots":

> What is he trying to communicate to the world? Is he genuinely enthusiastic about the idea of unity among the workers of the world? . . . He does it because these things must be done if one is to get along in life. It is one of the thousands of details that guarantee him a relatively tranquil life.

The power of totalitarian ideology, he wrote, is that it acts as "a veil behind which human beings can hide their own fallen existence, their trivialization, and their adaptation to the status quo. . . . It is rather like a collection of traffic signals and directional signs, giving the process shape and structure. This metaphysical order guarantees the inner coherence of the totalitarian power structure. It is the glue holding it together, its binding principle, the instrument of its discipline."

Havel describes dissent not as an alternative political ideology but, rather, as an individual's insistence on his own humanity, on thinking and doing things, even the smallest things, honestly. In the mid-seventies, Havel had to make his living by working in a brewery, and, in *The Power of the Powerless,* he recalls a dispute at the plant. A worker there spoke out to his bosses about ways to improve production. He was not an intellectual or a political rebel, just someone with an idea on how to produce beer more efficiently. But he had dared defy his bosses, and that could not be tolerated. All too often, Havel wrote, living normally "begins as an attempt to do your work well, and ends with being branded an enemy of society."

And so it did with Havel. As an analyst, he wrote that the system could not tolerate even the slightest challenge, because its existence depended for its survival on unanimity. As a result, Havel knew that the knock on the door could come at any time. In a samizdat interview, he said, "I've put together something I call my 'emergency packet,' containing cigarettes, a toothbrush, toothpaste, soap, some books, a T-shirt, paper, a laxative, and a few other small things." He took this bundle along with him every time he left his house.

With good reason. Between 1977 and 1989, Havel was imprisoned several times and in many different cells. His longest term lasted from 1979 to 1983, and his singular relief from the drudgery of those years was writing a weekly letter home. *Letters to Olga,* filled with everything from complaints about his hemorrhoids and Olga's inconstancy as a correspondent to ruminations on Being and political responsibility, is his most personal book, perhaps his best. Havel wrote the letters under terrific pressure, including that of a pro-Nazi warden who made sure the letters included no mysterious erasures or codes. Working in the laundry, he said, "I hid my rough drafts in a mountain of dirty sheets stained by millions of unborn children, and I would revise them during the noon break, while trying to avoid being seen by informers."

The only visitors allowed were Olga and Ivan. They were permitted to come four times a year for half-hour visits. When I asked Ivan about those visits, he laughed ruefully. "I saw him more often when he was in jail than I do now," he said.

One night during Havel's frenetic last week as President, there was a gala held in his honor at the National Theater, a black-tie-and-evening-gown affair with lots of television cameras outside and government ministers and pop stars in the audience. I went along to the gala with Jiří Pehe, a former exile who had returned to Prague after the revolution and become one of Havel's closest advisers. He told me that the gala had been organized by Havel's second wife, an actress named Dagmar Veškrnová, whom everyone knows, simply, as Dása. Unlike Olga, who had impeccable dissident credentials, Dása was a movie and television actress who, during "normalization," appeared occasionally in productions of Shakespeare and Strindberg but more often in mediocre comedies; she once played a topless vampire. The gala, Pehe said, was controversial because the musical lineup would run more to Andrew Lloyd Webber than to Havel's favorites, Lou Reed and Frank Zappa. He was not exaggerating. Sometimes I thought I was watching a taping of a Bob Hope Christmas special. Dása had even invited Karel Gott, an oleaginous crooner who was the epitome of "cooperative" under the Communists. Some of Havel's old Charter 77 friends, including the singers Jaroslav Hutka and Vlasta Trešnak, boycotted the event. Prague is the smallish capital of a smallish republic; often enough, its politics are the politics of a village. Some Czechs, it seemed, could never forgive figures like Gott; others could never forgive Havel for marrying Dása.

"Olga was much more than a partner," Pehe told me. "Havel was a bohemian and did wild things, and there were many other women, but he always went back: she was a tough, moral lady. She treated him like a boy, in a sense, and he liked that, he needed that corrective. When she was gone, a part of his universe collapsed. He remarried too quickly, in the humble opinion of the public."

In Havel's opinion, Dása saved his life. A chain smoker and a veteran of Czech jails, Havel had suffered from pneumonias, a perforated bowel, and various other illnesses. "He's nearly killed himself in the job," Havel's friend the writer Timothy Garton Ash said. "He's been close to death several times." The closest call came in late 1996. Havel's doctor found a spot on his lungs and treated him for pneumonia. Havel continued suffering fevers and double vision. Finally, doctors determined that he had cancer and removed half his right lung. (Just before going into the operating room, Havel was shown on television smoking with his Minister of Health.) Dása fired the doctor who had misdiagnosed Havel. (She also summoned a faith healer, but never mind.) The crisis was not over. One day at the hospital, according to Havel's biographer John Keane, Dása went to visit him in intensive care. He was on a ventilator and seemed to be choking. Dása called for help, rescuing him. A few weeks later, Havel and Dása married.

With the image of Olga still strong in the public mind, Havel felt compelled to explain himself to the nation. "Before she died, Olga said I should remarry," Havel said. "At the time, I ruled it out categorically, and I was resolved to end my days alone. She was convinced that I can't live alone and that I shouldn't. She was right, and life itself confirmed that when I was lucky enough to get to know Dása."

At the gala, Havel sat in the Presidential box with Dása and gazed down at the stage with utter delight. He was egalitarian in his applause. He clapped for Karel Gott and he clapped for Ivan Král, a former exile who sang a ballad by the Plastic People of the Universe and then Patti Smith's "Dancing Barefoot." But Havel's greatest visible pleasure came when an actor walked to the lip of the stage and read the text of a denunciation of the leaders of Charter 77, published in the Communist Party newspaper *Rudé Právo* twenty-five years ago under the headline THE SHIPWRECKED AND THE SELF-APPOINTED. At the time of that article, the Party leader Gustav Husák had confidently announced that the Charter 77 movement would collapse and Havel and "the hired puppets of these campaigns will end up in the dustbin of history." It all seemed like a punch line now.

Another day at the Castle, this time in the company of Oldrich Cerny, a compact fellow with perfect English. For many years, Cerny made his living dubbing Hollywood movies in Czech. When he was a teenager, he saw *The Garden Party* and asked to meet the playwright. Cerny eventually became friends with Havel and ran errands for the coalition of forces called Civic Forum, which was at the center of the revolution. After Havel took office, James Baker, who was then George H. W. Bush's Secretary of State, delivered to the Czechs a CIA briefing book outlining everything the Americans knew about the security forces under the Communists. Havel, whose English is limited, asked Cerny to translate the documents; later, he asked him to become his national-security adviser. Every time Cerny mentioned that title to me, he smiled and made the universal sign for ironical quotation marks. "I wasn't exactly Condoleezza Rice," he said.

After the revolution, he continued, "we were babes in the woods, and so I went to the West for help." Officials from MI6 and the CIA helped the Czechs rebuild the security system, ridding it, above all, of its function as a private police and army force for the government. Even now, years after leaving the Castle, Cerny, like so many others, can't forget the arrival. He said, "When we first went into the Castle, it was so strange—sparsely furnished in the Communist style of a taste for the distasteful, with huge fake leather chairs that made you freeze in the winter and stuck to the back of your trousers in summer."

We took a walk to the old summer residence, a two-story villa, on the Castle grounds.

"This was Husák's house," Cerny said as we strolled past a guard and approached the front door. "I still have the key."

We went upstairs. Cerny started rapping his knuckles against the walls and the ceilings, which were unusually low. "When we first got here, I noticed that my cell-phone reception was very bad," he said. "It turns out that Husák was paranoid. He had all the ceilings reinforced with concrete. Turns out he thought someone was going to fire cruise missiles at him."

Cerny took me to the basement. And there was Husák's favorite indulgence: a swimming pool with a wave machine. "He was quite a swimmer," he said.

Early in his Presidency, Havel lived for a few months in Husák's house. Naturally, this was a torture. "I find myself in the world of privileges, exceptions, perks, in the world of VIPs who gradually lose track of how much a streetcar ticket or butter costs, how to make a cup of coffee, how to drive a car, and how to place a telephone call," he said. Eventually, he got used to it all, though he never refilled Husák's swimming pool. There was too much work to do, thousands of documents to consider, a broken state to rebuild.

"From what I know, Havel cannot wait to step down," Cerny told me. "He is exhausted, and he is not a healthy man. He also takes things very hard. When it became clear that the President couldn't save everyone's life, it became a ritual for young Czech journalists—almost as a rite of initiation—to write terrible things about Havel, and he never got used to that. There was even a psychosomatic aspect to this: he would get depressed and his body began to ache."

The day after leaving office, Havel was scheduled to take a five-week vacation abroad. He is always coughing, and warm weather has been good for his lungs. At times, he has said that he might work on an "absurdist play" or a book-length conversation with Timothy Garton Ash and Adam Michnik. His aide Vladimír Hanzel told me that Havel had not kept a diary in office and so there would not likely be a memoir, or not in the traditional sense. One morning, I read in *The Prague Post* that Havel in fact would write a memoir, but that it would be "somewhere between Henry Kissinger and Charles Bukowski."

In a sense, he's been writing that memoir all his life. I remembered reading a short piece of his, from 1987, in which he recalled walking near the National Theater and, by chance, seeing Gorbachev, who was in town for a summit with the Czech Party leaders. He caught sight of the Soviet leader amid the crowds and the bodyguards:

> All of a sudden I find myself feeling sorry for him. I try to imagine the life he must lead, all day long in the company of his hard-faced guardians, no doubt with a full agenda, endless meetings, negotiating sessions, and speeches: having to talk to a great many people; remember who is who; say witty things but at the same time make

sure they are the *correct* things to say, things that the sensation-seeking outside world can't get hold of and use against him.

In my meeting with Havel at the Castle, I recalled that passage for him, and he laughed. I asked him if, in some way, he had become what he had pitied.

Havel shrugged and began speaking, all the while staring at the carpet. "I remember," he said. "Of course, I met Gorbachev about two months after I was elected President. We went to Moscow, for my first visit to the Kremlin, and we met for eight or nine hours. At first, Gorbachev looked at me as if I were some kind of exotic creature—the first living dissident he ever saw, who was coming to him as the head of a state that had been part of his realm. But, gradually, we developed a kind of friendship, which had even begun to develop at the end of that first long visit to the Kremlin." Havel lifted his head and smiled. "I used to be a smoker then, and, after two hours of our conversation, I asked Gorbachev whether I could have a cigarette. He said, 'Yes, please, go ahead and smoke.' He didn't call to his staff, but, all the same, somebody suddenly appeared with an ashtray. There must have been microphones there, I suppose."

A year after Havel came to power, there was a crisis in Iraq, and now, as he was leaving office, he was involved in another. Earlier in the month, he had spent hours with his aides at his country villa, discussing the problem, and that day, in *The Wall Street Journal,* there was a letter signed by Havel, along with seven other European leaders, which essentially agreed with the Bush Administration's position. I asked him why.

"I think it's not by chance that the idea of confronting evil may have found more support in those countries that have had a recent experience with totalitarian systems compared with other European countries that haven't had the same sort of recent experience," he said. "The Czech experience with Munich, with appeasement, with yielding to evil, with demanding more and more evidence that Hitler was truly evil—that may be one reason that we look at things differently than some others. But that doesn't mean automatically that a green light is to be given to preventive strikes. I always believed that every case has to be judged individually. The Euro-American world cannot simply declare preemptive war on all the regimes that it doesn't like."

Havel coughed and took a sip of wine. I asked him why he thought a policy of containment could not work in Iraq more or less indefinitely.

He put his glass down and said, "Civilization has changed. Today, any crazy, practically any crazy person can blow up half of New York. That was hardly possible fifteen or twenty years ago. That's not the only reason. On the whole, the world has changed. There once was a bipolar world, a balance of two great powers, who made agreements on weapons reductions, so that they were capable of destroying the world seven times instead of ten. Now we live in a multipolar world. . . . Of course, the question is: When is the best time for action? Should it have happened a long time ago? That is a political issue, a diplomatic issue, a sociological issue. But, generally, it's a matter of the functioning of the world's immune system, whether the world can deal with such a case of extreme evil before it is too late."

On Sunday night, February 2, Czech radio and television broadcast Havel's farewell address. He took pains to thank his wife and his supporters. To all those who felt disappointed "or have simply found me hateful, I sincerely apologize and trust that you will forgive me." Havel flashed his country the peace sign and his work was done.

(2003)

The Exile:
Solzhenitsyn in Vermont

On the morning of January 7, 1974, the leadership of the Communist Party of the Soviet Union convened to draw up battle plans against a grave threat to Communist ideology and power: a writer and his manuscript. Leonid Ilyich Brezhnev, the General Secretary of the Party, sat at the head of the conference table and opened the meeting. "Comrades," he began, "according to our sources abroad and the foreign press, Aleksandr Solzhenitsyn has published a new work in France and in the United States—*The Gulag Archipelago*."

By then, Brezhnev's health was beginning to fail. He worked only four or five hours a day, his burden soothed by frequent naps, massages, saunas, and snacks, and by round-the-clock attention from his doctors. His speech was slow, slurred. "I am told by Comrade Suslov that the Secretariat has taken a decision to develop in our press a debunking operation against this work by Solzhenitsyn and its appearance in bourgeois propaganda," Brezhnev went on. "No one has had a chance to read the book, but its essential contents are already known. It is a filthy anti-

Soviet slander. We have to determine what to do about Solzhenitsyn. By law, we have every basis for putting him in jail. He has tried to undermine all we hold sacred: Lenin, the Soviet system, Soviet power— everything dear to us. . . . This hooligan Solzhenitsyn is out of control."

Yuri Andropov, the chief of the KGB at the time and a future successor to the Party throne, did not wait long before offering his recommendation. He was by far the most intelligent of the Politburo members, and it is plain from reading the minutes of the Politburo session (a stack of classified documents stamped "Top Secret" in the Party archives) that Andropov's was the decisive voice. Better than anyone else, he understood the threat Solzhenitsyn's work posed to the regime. Back in 1962, when Nikita Khrushchev approved the publication of Solzhenitsyn's *One Day in the Life of Ivan Denisovich,* as a way of discrediting the Stalin era, a great cultural thaw had already begun—one that so unnerved the Communist leaders that they eventually called it off, banned Solzhenitsyn from print, and, in 1964, "retired" Khrushchev "for reasons of health." But Solzhenitsyn's literary mission, the process of giving voice to the sixty million victims of Soviet terror, went on secretly, and even collectively. Much of *Gulag* was based on the hundreds of letters and memoirs that former prisoners had mailed to Solzhenitsyn after *One Day* was published. Andropov had an intuitive sense that this new work could do as much, in its way, to undermine Soviet power as all the nuclear arsenals in the West.

"I think Solzhenitsyn should be deported from the country without his consent," Andropov said, according to the Politburo minutes. "Trotsky was deported in his time without getting his agreement. . . . Everyone is watching us to see what we will do with Solzhenitsyn—if we will mete out punishment to him or if we will just leave him alone. . . . I maintain that we must take legal action and bring the full force of Soviet law against him."

Andropov then fueled the already evident anger of the other members with terse descriptions of Solzhenitsyn's "impudence"—his meetings with foreign correspondents, his brazen flouting of Party control over literature and over publication abroad. (The manuscripts of *Gulag* and other works had been microfilmed by Solzhenitsyn and his wife in Moscow and smuggled by friends and other contacts of theirs to publishers in the West.)

Nikolai Podgorny, the chairman of the Presidium, was furious, and indignantly defended Andropov's proposal to suppress Solzhenitsyn against any prospect of a righteous response abroad. "In China, there are public executions," he said. "In Chile, the Fascist regime shoots and tortures people! In Ireland, the English use repression on the working people! We must deal with an enemy who gets away with slinging mud at everybody."

"We can send Solzhenitsyn away to serve his sentence in Verkho-yansk," beyond the Arctic Circle, said Alexei Kosygin, the Soviet Premier, a "liberal" in the eyes of many foreign analysts. "Not a single foreign correspondent will go visit him there, because it's so cold."

No matter what was done, Brezhnev said, the Solzhenitsyn affair would pass. The regime was unshakable. "In our time"—in 1968—"we did not worry about acting against the counterrevolution in Czechoslovakia," he said. "We did not worry about throwing out Alliluyeva"—Stalin's rebellious daughter, Svetlana. "We survived it all. And I think we'll live through this."

As the General Secretary droned on, the object of the Politburo's fury was at work, writing in a small extra room of a friend's dacha in the village of Peredelkino, about a half hour's drive west of Moscow. As he had been doing since his prison days, he wrote in a tiny scrawl, in small notebooks, the better to conceal his notes and manuscripts in the event of a search; after a day's work, he would go into the garden of the dacha and burn his early drafts. Solzhenitsyn had always been an avid listener to foreign radio stations on shortwave, and when he heard the news that *Gulag* had been published abroad he allowed himself just a moment's satisfaction. Then he went back to his writing table. Remarkably, he was able to shut out the world—the world of the Politburo, of denunciations, of censorship—and work fourteen to sixteen hours a day. While his wife and their three young sons stayed at their apartment, in downtown Moscow, Solzhenitsyn was spending six days a week in Peredelkino, as a guest of the family's close friend Lidiya Chukovskaya, who was the author of *The Deserted House,* a remarkable short novel about Stalin's purges. In Peredelkino, the light was better, and there were no children, no phone calls, to distract him.

"Aleksandr Isayevich slept and worked in an extra room and kept a pitchfork near his bed, as if that would protect him against an attack," Chukovskaya told me many years later, at her apartment in Moscow. She recalled how solicitous he was of her, how reluctant he was to disturb her work. Sometimes Chukovskaya would wander into the kitchen and find a note taped to the refrigerator door: "If you are free at nine, let's listen to the radio together." Sometimes Solzhenitsyn would go outside for a walk, but never through the village. Instead, he would pace back and forth across the dacha's small garden. When Chukovskaya asked him if he ever grew bored wearing the same tracks in the turf, he said, "No. I got used to it in jail."

"Wherever Solzhenitsyn happened to dwell and wherever fate cast him, he never for a moment ceased to be the absolute master of his own life," Chukovskaya once wrote. His working schedule was broken down not by the hour but by the minute. "A long chat (except about work, or the creative process) would have been relaxation, idleness—and Solzhenitsyn and idleness are two quite incompatible things. It was as if, at a certain moment (I do not know why or when), he had sentenced himself to imprisonment in some strict regime camp, and was now rigidly enforcing that regime. He was convict and guard rolled into one, and his own surveillance of himself was perhaps more relentless than that of the KGB."

Not only was *Gulag* now out in the West; it was also being read in Russian over Radio Liberty—a phenomenon that ensured even greater outrage in the Kremlin. Yet, despite the sensation, Solzhenitsyn did not sense quite how precarious his situation, and his family's, had become. He was not completely naïve: on New Year's Day of 1974, he had drawn up a list of possible reprisals that the regime might take against him— a list that included imprisonment, internal exile, and even murder, but he thought a press campaign and petty harassment the most likely punishment. He had no idea that the Party was now choosing among the most Draconian options.

On February 7—just a month after that first Kremlin meeting—he wrote in his diary, "Forecast for February: Apart from attempts to discredit me, they aren't likely to do anything, and there will probably be a breathing space."

That same day, Andropov sent a top-priority memo to Brezhnev saying that the West German chancellor, Willy Brandt, was willing to accept Solzhenitsyn as an exile. "We have to act quickly, before Brandt changes his mind or Solzhenitsyn gets wind of the plan," Andropov said. "There will be costs, but unfortunately we have no alternative. The unlawful acts Solzhenitsyn has already committed have inflicted on us costs more profound than those which will come up abroad in the case of expulsion or arrest." Andropov began mapping out a minute-by-minute plan to arrest Solzhenitsyn and hustle him out of the country before he or his family had a chance to react.

Late in the afternoon of February 13, Solzhenitsyn, who had returned to the family apartment, was arrested there, and locked in a cell of the Lefortovo Prison. Later that evening, he was charged with treason, and the next day KGB guards shuttled him to Sheremetyevo Airport and put him on an Aeroflot jet bound for Frankfurt. The plane had been delayed on the ground for three hours in Moscow, the passengers were told, because of "the fog."

For many years now, a sign has been hanging outside the Cavendish General Store, in southern Vermont:

NO DIRECTIONS TO
THE SOLZHENITSYN HOME

Ever since the Solzhenitsyn family moved from Zurich to Vermont, in the summer of 1976, the residents of Cavendish—all one thousand three hundred and twenty-three of them—have been vigilant in protecting the privacy of their Nobel Prize winner. When James Jeffords, the state's Republican senator, who was then in the House of Representatives, came to visit some years ago, he had to explain at length his station in Washington before anyone would help him find the Solzhenitsyn house.

"They say the family is moving back to Russia come May," the counterman at the general store told me this winter. "I'm thinking of taking down the sign and seeing what it'll get at Sotheby's."

Cavendish was in a deep freeze when I arrived in town. The bed-and-breakfast places in the area were filling up, mostly with skiers heading for the slopes in Ludlow, two towns to the west. A few snowmobiles ripped through the hills. That evening, I ate dinner at a local restaurant, with a pro football game blaring on screens in every corner. As I watched John Madden work the telestrator, it seemed inconceivable that just a couple of miles away Solzhenitsyn was in his workroom, writing. Certainly it was not strange that a writer lived in Cavendish: after all, what place would better fulfill the perennial literary fantasy of escape and quiet?—but this was Solzhenitsyn, a survivor of the camps, who knows nothing of John Madden, who speaks little English and rarely leaves his property. Just up the road, in the hills, was the man who wrote this sentence (in *Gulag*) about the inability of the comfortable to imagine the capacities of evil:

If the intellectuals in the plays of Chekhov who spent all their time guessing what would happen in twenty, thirty, or forty years had been told that in forty years interrogation by torture would be practiced in Russia; that prisoners would have their skulls squeezed within iron rings, that a human being would be lowered into an acid bath; that they would be trussed up naked to be bitten by ants and bedbugs; that a ramrod heated over a primus stove would be thrust up their anal canal (the "secret brand"); that a man's genitals would be slowly crushed beneath the toe of a jackboot; and that, in the luckiest possible circumstances, prisoners would be tortured by being kept from sleeping for a week, by thirst, and by being beaten to a bloody pulp, not one of Chekhov's plays would have gotten to its end because all the heroes would have gone off to insane asylums.

Solzhenitsyn's exile in America remains, to the last, an astonishment. Living in what must be the most serene state in the union is a Russian whose destiny is singular and, at the same time, nearly identical to Russia's. Solzhenitsyn, born in 1918, just months after the Revolution, was a captain on the East Prussian front during the Second World War, and survived; he was arrested in 1945 for making jokes in letters to a friend about Stalin ("the man with the mustache") and was sentenced to a total of eight years in the Gulag (spending one year in a prisoners' research center) and to "perpetual" internal exile in Kazakhstan, and survived; while he was still in Kazakhstan, he also survived a case of stomach cancer that doctors assured him was terminal; and, despite the best efforts of the Politburo, he not only survived his battle with Soviet power but won it. Now, after twenty years in exile, at the age of seventy-five, he is returning home. Solzhenitsyn will die in Russia, not a pariah but a free man. Is it too much of an embarrassment in the age of irony to think that his homecoming is somehow biblical?

The next morning, I turned off the main street in Cavendish and headed up a steep road, past power lines, past a graveyard, past trailers and rotting tractors and handsome vacation houses, to the fence surrounding Solzhenitsyn's property, his mythic barrier against the world. In Russia, and even in the West, the legend was that the fence was huge, forbidding, perhaps electrified, as if it guarded a prison camp. When he first moved to Cavendish, *The Washington Post* headline was SOLZHENI-TSYN'S BARBED-WIRE FREEDOM. The fence turned out to be nothing much, a pitiable chain-link job. After moving in, Solzhenitsyn came to a town meeting in 1976 and apologized to his neighbors for getting in the way of snowmobilers and hunters: "I am sorry for that and ask you to forgive me, but I had to protect myself from certain types of disturbances." He said he did not expect to be bothering them long: "The Russian people dream of the day when they can be liberated from the Soviet system, and when that day comes I will thank you very much for being good friends and neighbors and will go home."

The driveway winds past a brook, now frozen and banked with snow. Down a slope, there is a small waterfall, a pond, a tennis court. Solzhenitsyn had always dreamed of having a court, but it seems that he finds fifteen minutes of play quite enough. His wife used to make fun of him for wanting to play such a "bourgeois game," and his sons long ago nailed a proletarian basketball hoop over the garage door.

"Thank goodness you found us," Natalia Dmitriyevna Solzhenitsyn said, in Russian. "I thought you got lost."

"I did, a little."

"Well, it happens all the time."

"The birches here look Russian," I said.

"But they aren't, really," she said. "The birches here are fat, even a little gnarled. In Russia, they are tall and thin and straight."

Natalia Dmitriyevna is a handsome woman in her mid-fifties. She began her professional life as a mathematician, but when she married Solzhenitsyn, in 1973 (both had been married once before), she became absolutely vital to his work, and to his existence. She is his assistant, his editor, his mediator with the outside world, his lion at the gate— a woman of fierce energy. In the days between his exile and her own, she managed to smuggle his entire archive, a vast trove of papers compiled over decades, from Moscow to Zurich. She has raised four children and runs the household with only the help of her mother, Ekaterina Svetlova.

Thanks to the vigilance of Cavendish and Natalia Dmitriyevna, Solzhenitsyn works undisturbed, adhering to the same schedule every day of the year. He wakes at around six, has a cup of coffee, and begins work. There is a lunch break in the afternoon, and he continues working until late in the evening, sometimes through the night. He works, eats, and sleeps, and that is about all. For him to accept a telephone call is an event. He rarely leaves his fifty acres; home is all he needs. After the family bought the house—an old two-story farmhouse—in 1976, they built a three-story "working house" next door. In bad weather, Solzhenitsyn does not even have to go outside to get there. The houses are connected by a long concrete tunnel that joins the two basements. The main house is comfortable, yet unspectacular; it looks like a modest ski lodge, airy and filled with light, but the furniture is absolutely ordinary, functional, and the floors are carpeted in plain, almost industrial, colors. Solzhenitsyn's books have been published in more than thirty languages, so the family is quite prosperous, even though all the royalties from *Gulag*, by far his top-selling book, are channeled into a fund used to aid political prisoners and their families. The Russian Social Fund, which Natalia administers, "is far richer than we are," she said.

There is something at once frenetic and peaceful about the Solzhenitsyn household. Everyone has a job to do, and everyone does it with efficiency and evident pleasure. Upstairs, Natalia has her own office, where she runs what is, in essence, a literary factory. For Solzhenitsyn's latest works, she sets the type on an IBM composing machine, and then she sends the typeset pages to Paris, where their friend Nikita Struve runs the Russian-language YMCA-Press. Struve has only to photograph the set pages, print them, and bind them. Natalia has set all twenty volumes of Solzhenitsyn's *sobranie sochineny*—his collected works. Only now that Solzhenitsyn has completed his series of immense historical novels, *The Red Wheel,* is either author or amanuensis able to concentrate on the move back to Moscow.

The children—Yermolai, Ignat, and Stephan, and their older half brother, Dmitri Turin—have also been very much a part of the Solzhenitsyn enterprise. During the family's first years in Cavendish, they began the day with a prayer for Russia to be saved from its oppressors. They went to local schools, and when they came home in the afternoon their father gave them further lessons in mathematics and the sciences (Solzhenitsyn had been a schoolteacher in Russia) and their mother tutored them in Russian language and literature. Until the boys began leaving home for boarding schools and college, they, too, helped with literary chores, setting type, compiling volumes of Russian memoirs, translating speeches. Now they are spread across the world. Dmitri lives in New York, where he restores and sells vintage motorcycles. Yermolai, after two years at Eton, went to Harvard, and while he was there he studied Chinese and had a part-time job as a bouncer at the Bow & Arrow, a Cambridge bar; he is now living in Taiwan and wants to begin working soon in China. Ignat is studying piano and conducting at the Curtis Institute of Music, in Philadelphia, and has performed around the world, to spectacular reviews, including a series of triumphant concerts with his father's old friend Mstislav Rostropovich last September in Russia and the Baltic states. Stephan is a junior at Harvard and is majoring in urban planning.

Ignat and Stephan were home for winter vacation, and I asked them if their father ever stopped working.

Ignat smiled slyly and replied, "No, he's never said, 'Today I'm just gonna chill out, take a jog, and blow off this *Red Wheel* thing.' Not one day."

"Chilling out is not exactly his thing," Stephan added.

"So, fine. Why can't the West get over this?" Ignat said, growing more serious. "Why is his working all the time such an annoyance? Why is it so bad that he lives in Vermont and not the middle of Manhattan?"

"They assume he must be weird," Stephan said.

Natalia led me to the working house, where Solzhenitsyn was waiting. While he was writing *The Red Wheel,* he often stayed in the working house for many days straight, replicating the way he would hole up for weeks and months at various dachas in and around Moscow before his exile. The first floor has its own Russian Orthodox chapel, with skylights and icons, and there is also a library of books and documents that Solzhenitsyn gathered for use in *The Red Wheel.* Sometimes he works on the third floor, where there is a vast skylight, but in winter the room is frigid. We met in his main work area, on the second floor.

Even physically, Solzhenitsyn is a figure out of time. He has an astonishing nineteenth-century face: a Tolstoyan beard; blue, almost Asiatic, eyes; thinning, swept-back hair. In recent years, though his face has grown more lined and he has gained weight, he still does not look seventy-five but, rather, looks lived-in—at ease in an old brown cardigan and a woolen shirt. We sat across from each other at a small table, where he had prepared himself for our talks with a set of handwritten notes and a few volumes of his collected works, sprouting bookmarks. I asked him if he had read the documents describing how the leadership decided on his exile.

Solzhenitsyn nodded. "It is strange, but we did not foresee this last step," he said, in a voice that seemed too high-pitched for his grave face and his presence. "My wife and I had become so impertinent. We felt that nothing would happen to us, and we would manage once more to stay on our feet. The pressure had reached such a high level, but, even so, various friends came to our place and said, 'You know, it's extraordinary, there is such tension all around, and yet here there is peace and quiet and the children are falling asleep.' So, yes, in this instance my intuition failed me."

Where Solzhenitsyn's intuition proved keenest was in his prediction when he arrived in the West that his books would surely be published in the Soviet Union and, what was more, that he would himself return to a liberated Russia. In the depths of the Cold War, he told Malcolm Muggeridge, on the BBC, "In a strange way, I not only hope, I am inwardly convinced that I shall go back. I live with that conviction. I mean my physical return, not just my books. And that contradicts all rationality." It was a firm and intimate belief that even contradicted Solzhenitsyn's dire analysis of Soviet ruthlessness and Western accommodation. During the two years the Solzhenitsyns lived in Zurich, friends in Europe remember thinking that the exile was indulging in delusions when he spoke of inevitable return. "When I met with him in Zurich just after he was exiled, in one of the very first conversations we had, he said, 'I see the day when I will return to Russia,' " Nikita Struve had told me in Paris. "It seemed crazy at the time to me, but it was a real conviction, a poet's knowledge. He *sees*. The man *sees*."

"It's true. In my heart, I sensed that I would return," Solzhenitsyn was saying now. "All of us in prison in the forties were certain that Communism would fall. The only question was when. Perhaps I even exaggerated the danger of Communism, perhaps even consciously, to inspire the West to stand more firmly. But remember—countries were falling to Communism one after another."

Ignat, who sat down at his father's side, smiled at this last remark, as if he were remembering something fondly. In fact, he was. Later, he told me how when the boys were newly arrived in Vermont their father sat with them on a boulder on their property and told them that the rock was really a flying horse and that when the time was right it would fly them all back to Russia.

"I always trusted Aleksandr Isayevich's feeling, his intuition, that we would return," Natalia Solzhenitsyn said. "He has this uncanny ability to see certain things that I do not and most people do not. It is not mystical. There is just a certain level of profundity that sets him apart. But I have to admit there were times when my own faith weakened. In the early eighties, when there was a new wave of arrests, when Andropov came to power, things looked very grim. Those were dark times, and it was very hard to believe that we'd be going home. I was losing faith."

That faith returned only gradually in the mid-nineteen-eighties, as the Soviet Union began showing some signs of reform under Mikhail Gorbachev. But even then maintaining it was not easy. As glasnost flourished, in 1988, Solzhenitsyn's works were excluded from the process. At the time, I asked Yegor Ligachev, the most powerful conservative in the Politburo, why the leadership had so far refused to publish Solzhenitsyn, and he grew angry—every bit as fierce as Andropov had been fourteen years earlier.

"We have sacred things, just as you do," Ligachev said.

But it was not just a question of the conservatives. Even the self-described liberals in the leadership could not face the prospect of permitting the publication of Solzhenitsyn's books in the Soviet Union. In the autumn of 1988, Sergei Zalygin, the editor of the journal *Novy Mir*, thought he had the tacit approval of the leadership to publish Solzhenitsyn, and he printed an announcement on the back cover saying that the process would begin in future issues. In the middle of the night, *Novy Mir*'s printers got a "stop work" order from the Central Committee, and the covers, at great expense, were torn off more than a million copies of the magazine. The Politburo's ideology chief, Vadim Medvedev, told a press conference soon after that that Solzhenitsyn's works were impermissible, since "they undermine the foundations on which our present life rests." It was only in late 1989, when the regime had clearly lost its hold on society, that Gorbachev let Zalygin go forward. Solzhenitsyn insisted that *Novy Mir* begin with *Gulag*.

Solzhenitsyn did not return to Russia at the first opportunity, mainly because he did not see how rushing home, and jeopardizing the chance to finish *The Red Wheel*, would help anyone. Instead, like the rest of the world, he followed the fall of the Soviet Union in the press and on television.

"In August of 1991, my wife and I were incredibly excited to watch Dzerzhinsky's statue taken down outside the KGB building," he said. "That, of course, was a great moment for us. But I was asked at the time, 'Why didn't you send a telegram of congratulations?' You know, I felt deep inside that this was not yet a victory. I knew how deeply Communism had penetrated into the fabric of life. Afterward, for two years, we tap-danced about, and what were we doing? What was Yeltsin doing? We forgot everything else and fought one another. The same is true now. All is in decay. It's too early to celebrate. Why was I silent about Gorbachev for several years? Thank God, something did begin! But everything that began was done wrongly. So what do you do? Celebrate or weep? What can you say? I could not have gone over there and had a glass of champagne with Yeltsin in front of the parliament, the White House. The heart is not yet joyful."

Solzhenitsyn finished the fourth volume of *The Red Wheel* in late 1991—the series runs to more than five thousand pages—and I asked him (against the evidence) whether exile had depleted his language and imagination.

"The thing is, I came to the West when I was fifty-five years old," he said. "I had had an amazingly rich and varied experience of life. As a writer, I did not need any addition to this experience but, rather, the time to process it. Purely for my work, the eighteen years in Vermont have been the happiest of my life. Simply put, over eighteen years I have not had one creative drought. Seven days a week, three hundred and sixty-five days a year, without holidays or vacations, I worked, and that's all there is to it. Such conditions, from this point of view, in terms of books and writing and just day-to-day life, I had never had before and will never have again. This was the richest period of my creative work.

"The loss was the pain inside me, the separation from the homeland, from its spaces and people, from interaction. Raising children as Russians in the West was extremely difficult, and it is only thanks to Natalia Dmitriyevna that we have been able to do this, because one usually becomes engulfed in the country in which one lives. So this was our loss. Now, when we are about to go back to Russia, we hope to recover from this loss, but not in the sense that the pain will go away. In fact, the pain will only increase, because of the horrifying circumstances in Russia. One might have thought that after the fall of Communism Russia would encounter serious problems. But it was hard to imagine that with leader after leader, and year after year, everything would worsen continuously. We are faced with incredible hardship for years to come. I am sure that I will not have the chance to work so calmly again. I know that I will be torn apart by people's tragedies and the events of the time."

But what of his language? Many exiles say that this is the most telling loss.

"I have always been surrounded here by Russian manuscripts, and I write in Russian," he said. "I studied English and German as a schoolboy, but I have not been able to study them further since coming to the West. I do read in English and German, but I was not able to develop my conversational skills. If I need to read letters in those languages, or articles, I do it. I am constantly immersed in the Russian language." Gesturing toward the woods and the fields of snow outside the window, he said, "And we really have a piece of Russia here. Once, my wife and I traveled across this country from the Pacific to the Atlantic; then I went by myself to conduct research—to the Midwest, mostly. But I simply could not allow myself the time to take a trip around America just to get to know the country. I had only two choices: to write *The Red Wheel* or not. To write it, I had to give it my full attention. Maybe, if I were not returning now to Russia, I might change my way of life on account of finishing *The Red Wheel*. But now it is time to go back to Russia. There simply was not the time. One cannot encompass everything. Our history has been so hidden. I had to dig so deep, I had to uncover what was buried and sealed. This took up all my years."

In terms of the effect he has had on history, Solzhenitsyn is the dominant writer of the twentieth century. Who else compares? Orwell? Koestler? And yet when his name comes up now it is more often than not as a freak, a monarchist, an anti-Semite, a crank, a has-been, and not as a hero. One afternoon in Cavendish, I was in the kitchen with Natalia and Stephan, and I asked whether Solzhenitsyn planned to make any public appearances, any speeches, before leaving Vermont for Moscow this spring.

"Who would ask him to speak in America?" Natalia said. "Who in America wants to hear him?"

"Face it, Mom," Stephan said. "It hasn't worked out here."

Solzhenitsyn chose to live in the United States mainly because of its *prostranstvo,* its size and space. In Paris, Nikita Struve told me, "Aleksandr Isayevich went to America so he could live far from the world—the world not in the religious sense but in the most ordinary sense. You could never do that in Switzerland or France. When everything is close together like that, anyone can just drop by and knock on the door, ring the buzzer. In Vermont, it's not so easy. He lives, and has always lived, like an *otshelnik,* a hermit. Like a monk. No one has ever done this to quite the same extent. People said Gogol was crazy when he didn't go out. But, look, great writers are almost always considered crazy. Great writers are a different sort of people."

I told Struve what he already knew—that Solzhenitsyn's reception in the United States had been troubled from the very start.

"Americans do not generally live with fences around their homes, and Americans want you to live the way they do," Struve said. "There are always a lot of people who resent it when there is someone in their midst who is higher than they are. The man in question must be crazy, because he doesn't come out and live among them. Solzhenitsyn lived in America as if it were always foreign. And this Americans didn't like. He lived in Vermont, but it was his special Vermont. He didn't have to 'get to know' the West. He never went about making himself into a great 'Western thinker.' That just was not his job in life. Solzhenitsyn was at war against Soviet power—the pen against power. This was his literary work, and he carried it out absolutely."

Soon after his arrival in this country, Solzhenitsyn accepted invitations to speak to the AFL-CIO in New York and Washington, at the Hoover Institution, in California, and, most notoriously, at the 1978 Harvard graduation ceremonies. In those speeches he excoriated the West not only for weakness in its negotiations with the Soviet Union but also for a general cultural and civil collapse. To him, the rot of Western life was evident in billboards and tabloids, in the lyrics of rock music and the exploits of Daniel Ellsberg. He delivered those perorations in an elevated, angry, almost Grand Inquisitor–like tone, a tone rarely heard in the West. Here he was, in a typical pitch, at Hoover:

> Freedom! To fill people's mailboxes, eyes, ears, and brains with commercial rubbish against their will, television programs that are impossible to watch with a sense of coherence. Freedom! To force information on people, taking no account of their right *not* to accept it or their right to peace of mind. Freedom! To spit in the eyes and souls of passersby with advertisements. Freedom! For publishers and film producers to poison the younger generations with corrupting filth. Freedom! For adolescents of fourteen to eighteen to immerse themselves in idleness and pleasure instead of intensive study and spiritual growth. . . . Freedom! To divulge the defense secrets of one's country for personal political gain.

Somehow, it was all too fierce and sarcastic, too impolitic. This was not Sakharov; this was not a lovable man. Solzhenitsyn gave Americans little reason to relax or to admire themselves. Two of his supporters, the scholars John Ericson, of Calvin College, and John Dunlop, of the Hoover Institution, have compiled book-length collections of writing largely about the reaction to Solzhenitsyn in the West. Even in the years before Solzhenitsyn arrived in this country, the attacks came from high and low, and they were endless. In 1974, before becoming the main book critic at *The Washington Post,* Jonathan Yardley wrote for the Knight-Ridder chain that Solzhenitsyn was a "not-very-thinly-disguised Czarist." Writing the next year in the *Guardian,* Simon Winchester referred to Solzhenitsyn as the "shaggy author" and the "hairy polemicist," and declared that he had become "the darling of the redneck population." There was this headline in the London *Daily Mirror* in 1976: SOLZHENITWIT. Writing in the London *Sunday Times,* Alan Brien reviewed the essay "Letter to the Soviet Leaders" with total disdain: "Is Aleksandr Solzhenitsyn a crank? His open, unopened letter to the Soviet Government certainly bears a superficial resemblance to those lengthy screeds which flop on the desk of every journalist from time to time, even down to the passages underscored and printed in capitals, full of contradictory assertions, obsessive fears, Falstaffian escalations of statistics." And on it went, year after year. As recently as 1993, *The Boston Globe*'s former Moscow correspondent, Alex Beam, published an opinion piece in the paper under the headline SHUT UP, SOLZHENITSYN.

Some Russian émigrés also came to resent Solzhenitsyn, partly because he showed them no great sympathy and had urged them to stay in the Soviet Union. His exile, he argued, was unique, because it had been forced—as if dozens of dissidents had not been given a choice between departure and brutal punishment. The comic novelist Vladimir Voinovich, who lives in Germany, portrayed in his novel *Moscow 2042* a Solzhenitsyn-like figure as a combination of imam and holy fool. "At a certain point, Solzhenitsyn's quality of being uncompromising in his struggle against the system became something else," Voinovich told me. "I began to notice an atmosphere of authoritarian impulses even in his work, and certainly in his demeanor. I defended him, but after a while I got the impression that after he had written anything or said anything you either had to fall in line and agree or you were an enemy. He could be so unjust, unceremoniously casting people out of his circle for some slight, usually imagined."

Vasily Aksyonov, an émigré who is the author of *The Burn* and many other novels, and who is more sympathetic to Solzhenitsyn, said that the prickly relations with the outside world were natural. "Solzhenitsyn's greatest problem is his isolation," Aksyonov said. "Look at J. D. Salinger. People assume that because Salinger has holed himself up in the country and made an obsession of that isolation he must be crazy. The same with Solzhenitsyn. He is like some sort of owl up there in the woods. And so, even though people can be unfair, he, too, is to blame for the negative myth. The couple of times I have seen him on television, he has turned out to be a perfectly normal, truthful person. He is not a living monument."

One of the absolute low points of Solzhenitsyn's reception in the West occurred at the highest levels. For a while, in 1975, President Gerald Ford considered inviting Solzhenitsyn to the White House, but he and his advisers soon thought better of it. The Secretary of State, Henry Kissinger, sent a memo through his executive assistant, George Spring-steen, to Ford's national-security adviser, Brent Scowcroft, saying, "Solzhenitsyn is a notable writer, but his political views are an embarrassment even to his fellow-dissidents. Not only would a meeting with the President offend the Soviets but it would raise some controversy about Solzhenitsyn's views of the United States and its allies. . . . We recommend that the President not receive Solzhenitsyn." When I called Ford in Colorado recently to ask about the incident, he spoke blandly about the need to avoid offending the Kremlin during sensitive arms negotiations. "It's the old never-ending conflict between foreign-policy concerns and domestic political concerns," he said. "As a matter of principle, we made the right decision." But it seems that he was rather less measured about it at the time. According to his former press secretary, Ron Nessen, Ford called Solzhenitsyn "a goddamn horse's ass" and said that the author wanted to come to the White House merely to get more lecture dates and publicize his books.

No one enjoyed Solzhenitsyn's dismal clashes in the West more than his former tormentors. In a memorandum to the Council of Ministers dated January 4, 1976, the KGB chief, Andropov, wrote gleefully about Solzhenitsyn and "the fall in interest in him abroad and in the USSR." Andropov admitted in the memo that the KGB had helped promote, through its agents and contacts, "material useful to us" condemning Solzhenitsyn and his "class-based hatred of the Soviet power." Andropov was pleased to report that the compromising material, much of it insisting that Solzhenitsyn was an anti-Semite yearning for a return of the tsars, "has brought about a reevaluation of his personality and has successfully brought up, and strengthened, doubts about the reliability of his distorted 'work.' "

What the KGB did not point out was that Solzhenitsyn's reception was actually varied. In Europe, and especially in France, the publication of *Gulag* and the exile itself in 1974 immediately changed the intellectual landscape. Suddenly, a generation that had grown up under the spell of Jean-Paul Sartre's brand of leftism and a powerful Stalinist Communist Party now turned to the avatar of anti-Communism. Largely thanks to Solzhenitsyn, the *nouveaux philosophes*—former Marxist thinkers like André Glucksmann and Bernard-Henri Lévy—took a strong anti-Communist stance and assumed an intellectual authority in France. American thinkers did not change as markedly as those in France had, because fewer of them had lived under any illusions about the nature of the Soviet regime. Orwell, after all, had been published and absorbed, and anti-Stalinist redoubts on the left—including *Common Sense*, Dwight Macdonald's *Politics*, and, most important, *Partisan Review*—had done a great deal to obliterate lingering fantasies about the Soviet Union even among former Communist sympathizers. Still, the American intelligentsia, especially on the left, was not entirely convinced of the accuracy of all that Solzhenitsyn had reported—or, at least, they had not focused on it sufficiently, concentrating more on the war in Vietnam or on their own dalliances with Castro's Cuba. Susan Sontag, who shocked an audience of left-wing intellectuals and activists at New York's Town Hall in 1982 simply by equating Communism with Fascism and suggesting that the *Reader's Digest* may have been more accurate than *The Nation* in its assessment of Communism, admits that she had been taken aback by Solzhenitsyn and *The Gulag Archipelago.*

"It was January of 1976, and I was having a long conversation with Joseph Brodsky," Sontag told me recently. "We were both laughing, and agreeing about how we thought Solzhenitsyn's views on the United States, his criticism of the press, and all the rest were so deeply wrong. And then Joseph said, 'But, you know, Susan, everything Solzhenitsyn says about the Soviet Union is true. Really. All those numbers—sixty million victims—it's all true.' Until then, I must have felt that it was an exaggeration or one-sided, somehow. I don't really know what kind of inner reservations I had. But at that moment something gave way."

Brodsky, for his part, told me, "I was not surprised, really, that Susan had been so shocked. Maybe I found it revolting and idiotic. But I have a theory of why these things don't seep through, and that is a theory about self-preservation, mental self-preservation. Western man, by and large, is the most natural man, a mental bourgeois, and he cherishes his mental comfort. It is almost impossible for him to admit disturbing evidence. Plus, when you add in the phenomenon of geography, which was very real until recently, and add into it the particularity of Soviet reality, even just the difficult names—when you add all that in, you have a considerable barrier, a mental fence that was constructed especially by the Western left. It was mostly among the intellectuals, the educated classes. Sometimes education results only in obfuscation."

The habit of willful obfuscation regarding the Soviet Union has a long and painful history among some of the most revered intellectuals of the century. The desire to wish away the catastrophe of the Soviet Union makes for a depressing psychological portrait. George Bernard Shaw, for one, declared, "We cannot afford to give ourselves moral airs when our most enterprising neighbor"—the Soviet Union—"humanely and judiciously liquidates a handful of exploiters and speculators to make the world safe for honest man." Elsewhere Shaw said, "Mussolini, Kemal, Pilsudski, Hitler, and the rest can all depend on me to judge them by their ability to deliver the goods and not by Swinburne's comfortable notions of freedom. Stalin has delivered the goods to an extent that seemed impossible."

While the likes of Shaw's stupidities became less common with time, many intellectuals on the left remained hesitant to denounce the Soviet Union. The reasons were various, but perhaps the most important was the liberal aversion to joining ranks with anti-Communism as a movement. Joseph McCarthy was repellent, and so was the senator who greeted Solzhenitsyn most noisily: Jesse Helms. Often the leading anti-Communists were so harebrained in their rhetoric or so repugnant in their positions on other issues—race and the war in Vietnam being but two—that there was no way the left could find a common language with them. What remains a wonder is how resistant the "anti-anti-Communists" were to the figure of Solzhenitsyn. Oddly, Solzhenitsyn's children, as bridges between their father and the American world they grew up in, understand as well as any scholar the barrier that developed between the writer and his newfound land.

"My father spent his entire life fighting the Communist system, and, understandably, there was no relativity involved: they were evil and that was that," Yermolai told me before he left for Taiwan. "It was a question of a battle to the death that was black and white and requiring courage. Having gone through the Western system—through the Vermont schools and Harvard and all the rest—I guess I've been inculcated with the more relative way of things, leaving a door open for merits on both sides of issues. But you should know that it wasn't like my father was some kind of anti-Western ogre at home. It's true we didn't watch television that much when we were young. Nothing like the national average. But I remember watching the '86 World Series with my mother—the Mets and the Red Sox—and we listened to rock and roll, all the usual things."

Visiting the Solzhenitsyns makes them immediately less alien. It somehow humanizes the father to see Ignat's room, with its hand-drawn emblems of the New York sports teams on the wall, or to hear Stephan mimic the Linda Richman *Saturday Night Live* shtick, to his mother's indulgent incomprehension. Even when it comes to the attacks on Solzhenitsyn, the sons are ironic, American.

"I suppose in the age of political correctness we should all feel emotionally victimized," Ignat said.

At lunch in the kitchen, Solzhenitsyn himself reminded me of a dyspeptic uncle. He sat at the head of the table and took delight in announcing the day's news from Russia, and giving his grumpy commentary. ("Isn't it about time Yeltsin cracked down on crooks?") When he was done, he quietly forked his way through a plate of hamburgers, beet salad, and potatoes, excused himself, and returned to the working house.

Back in the study, I asked Solzhenitsyn about his relations with the West. He knew that things had gone wrong, but had no intention of making any apologies. "Instead of secluding myself here and writing *The Red Wheel*, I suppose I could have spent time making myself likable to the West," he said. "The only problem is that I would have had to drop my way of life and my work. And, yes, it is true, when I fought the dragon of Communist power I fought it at the highest pitch of expression. The people in the West were not accustomed to this tone of voice. In the West, one must have a balanced, calm, soft voice; one ought to make sure to doubt oneself, to suggest that one may, of course, be completely wrong. But I didn't have the time to busy myself with this. This was not my main goal."

I remarked that I had recently heard a lecture in New York given by Solzhenitsyn's biographer Michael Scammell, and that at the end all the questions from the audience had boiled down to "Why doesn't Solzhenitsyn like us?"

The notion that he is "anti-Western" is wrong, and "arose out of the inordinate sensitivity and superficiality of Western correspondents," he said. "My speeches to the AFL-CIO in 1975—and I would not take back a single word of them—were built in the following way: one speech against the Communist state and the second against Communism as an ideology. Both of them were absolutely correct. I said there, 'Do not help us. Fine. But, at least, don't help dig our graves.' Immediately, the next day, the press was in an uproar, saying that Solzhenitsyn wants to destroy détente and go to war with the Soviet Union. Never in my life did I ever call for liberation by the West. Nor did I ask for the West to fight for our sake, or even help. I said only, 'Just do not help our executioners.' They asked about détente. I said, 'Yes, I am for détente, but only so that all cards are on the table. Otherwise, what really happens under détente is that you are being deceived.' For example, in the speech to the unions, I noted, 'Please understand, you are being deceived. There are still POWs in Vietnam. They will not be released, because they were tortured.' The whole Washington press corps had a great laugh at my expense. What a stupid thing he has dreamed up! Everything has been counted up and is in order! And now we see today that they say not everyone was returned, but back then they laughed.

You see, the whole atrocity of Communism could never be accommo-
dated by the Western journalistic mind. I spoke on the basis of my experiences in the Gulag.

"Most Americans understood what I was saying, even if the press did
not. The press did not understand, because it did not want to and
because I had criticized them. But how can I not criticize the press?
How can the press aspire to true power? No one elected it. How can it
aspire to an equal level with the three branches of government? The
people in the press can be either scoundrels or good—it's all a matter of
chance. The press does very often play a positive role. In Russia today,
the press is unraveling what our criminal oligarchy is up to. Even though
most of the Russian press depends on the government for financial support, there are still excellent articles. How can one not value the press?
But there must not be abuses, and in relation to me there have been
staggering abuses."

It is a curious thing: Václav Havel is almost universally admired, even
loved, in the West; Solzhenitsyn is not. And yet Havel's essays and
letters show an admiration of and an affinity with some of Solzhenitsyn's
greatest obsessions: the need for a spiritual dimension in politics, the
need for the East to see Western capitalism and democracy with a
clear eye, without romanticism. I suggested to Solzhenitsyn that part of
his problem might be one of his glaring differences with Havel: while
Havel revels in Western pop culture, and writes affectionately about
the Rolling Stones and Frank Zappa, Solzhenitsyn calls pop culture
"manure."

"Well, these things, after all, are the pits of Western culture," he said.
"This is not to the credit of the development of Western culture. This is
the image I use: that it is manure that flowed under the Iron Curtain,
and it influences the unformed, the youth. They have no idea what
thinkers or writers there may have been in the West. They just hear rock
and roll and wear some sort of T-shirts with something on them. This is
dangerous for the younger, unprotected part of the population. Maybe
they'll develop badly. They need to be protected. Our youth is in terrible
straits."

The charges that have hurt Solzhenitsyn most in the West are those of
anti-Semitism and authoritarianism. There exists a lingering suspicion
that Solzhenitsyn's critique of secularism in the West and his Russian
patriotism are somehow a combustible combination—one that spells
trouble for Jews and other non-Russian minorities. The charges are
preposterous—nowhere does Solzhenitsyn support a theocracy—and

yet they persist. (In the Soviet Union, the Kremlin's original "accusation" was that he was a Jew—"Solzhenitsker"—and a bourgeois counter-
revolutionary.) The most comprehensive set of charges was published in
the American Jewish magazine *Midstream* in 1977. There a Russian
émigré named Mark Perakh blamed Solzhenitsyn for, at best, a thought-
less attitude toward Jews. He noted that in the second volume of *Gulag*
the majority of the camp commandants shown in a full-page gallery of
photographs were Jewish, and that in *Lenin in Zurich* the evil "genius"
supporting Lenin was Parvus, a German Jew. (Solzhenitsyn, for his
part, says that the pictures in *Gulag* were the only ones available at the
time, and that the historical characters in *Lenin in Zurich*, Parvus
included, are portrayed accurately and according to reliable records and
witnesses.)

"In the magazine *Midstream*, I was charged with anti-Semitism
because nowhere in *One Day in the Life of Ivan Denisovich* did the
word 'Yid' appear," Solzhenitsyn said. "The word doesn't appear, and
therefore I am an anti-Semite! The author is sure that in the camps
there was no more urgent question than the Jewish question. He
thinks they all sat around and condemned Jews all day and said 'Yid.'
Well, in this book no one uses the term, so I must be hiding the facts—
and why would I do that unless I was an anti-Semite? Meanwhile, in
reality, there were informers being knifed, there were uprisings against
the authorities, there were murders with machine guns spraying all
around. There were no more than five or six Jews in the whole camp.
The same thing with the accusation of tsarism—that I want to return
to the past. There is not a single passage of mine that has been shown
me in which I say that I want to return to the past, that I want priests in
power, a theocracy.

"Anti-Semitism is a prejudiced and unjust attitude toward the Jewish
people as a whole. My own work has no such attitude. The press has
said, 'Please make such a statement.' But there exists in this country the
presumption of innocence. Why should I suddenly come forward with a
statement that I am not an anti-Semite? It would be as if I were to make
the statement that I am not a thief, that I have not stolen anything. If I
am accused of actually stealing from someone, then I would come forward and deny it. So, if somebody were to show where, specifically, I
exhibit an unjust or prejudiced attitude toward the Jewish people, if
they would show me one such quotation in my work, I would gladly
defend myself. But nobody has ever pointed out such a passage, and yet
I am still asked to make the statement that I am not an anti-Semite."

. . .

Solzhenitsyn will make no farewell tour of the country he has lived in for eighteen years, but he did make the rounds of Western Europe last fall. He visited Nikita Struve in Paris, met with Pope John Paul II in Rome, and said his farewells to old friends in Switzerland and Germany. The trip to Europe was mostly personal, but there were two public speeches—one in Liechtenstein, one in France—that conveyed a good sense of Solzhenitsyn's current thinking and of a distinct shift, if not in his views, then in his emphases and his tone.

At the International Institute for Philosophy, in the village of Schaan, Solzhenitsyn rehearsed many of his old themes for the people of Liechtenstein: the failure of the West to recognize the scale of evil in the Soviet Union, the lack of an ethical dimension in politics since the rise of secularism. But, even if he sounded to me and others there much like a preacher, there was less fire and brimstone than there had been at Harvard sixteen years ago. Gone was the old astringent tone, gone were the scathing images and sarcastic phrases. He called for a saner, more limited role for modern technology, a search for a spirituality that would allow men and women to move beyond self-absorption and fear of death. A pleasant, almost New Age modesty had leavened his rhetoric. Small is beautiful. Man is lost without belief.

A few weeks later, in the town of Lucs-sur-Boulogne, Solzhenitsyn spoke to a crowd of thirty thousand gathered to commemorate the massacre of ninety thousand Frenchmen by the revolutionary Jacobin government between 1793 and 1795. It was a remarkable event, probably the most important public appearance that Solzhenitsyn has made since Harvard. On the dais, he attacked violent revolution, all attempts to remake a society at one bloody moment. The uprising of the Vendée and its brutal suppression were, he said, parallel to the Bolsheviks' suppression of peasant uprisings in Tambov and in western Siberia in the early nineteen-twenties:

> That revolution brings out instincts of primordial barbarism, the sinister forces of envy, greed, and hatred—this even its contemporaries could see all too well. They paid a terrible enough price for the mass psychosis of the day, when merely moderate behavior, or even the perception of such, already appeared to be a crime. But the twentieth century has done especially much to tarnish the romantic luster of revolution which still prevailed in the eighteenth

century. As half-centuries and centuries have passed, people have learned from their own misfortunes that revolutions demolish the organic structures of society, disrupt the natural flow of life, destroy the best elements of the population and give free rein to the worst; that a revolution never brings prosperity to a nation, but benefits only a few shameless opportunists, while to the country as a whole it heralds countless deaths, widespread impoverishment, and, in the gravest cases, a long-lasting degeneration of the people. . . .

I would not wish a "great revolution" upon any nation. Only the arrival of Thermidor prevented the eighteenth-century revolution from destroying France. But the revolution in Russia was not restrained by any Thermidor as it drove our people on the straight path to a bitter end, to the abyss, to the depths of ruin.

Later, when I met with Solzhenitsyn, I asked him why he had been so sweeping in his judgment. Was the American Revolution, too, a catastrophe?

"No," he said. "By 'revolution' I mean a violent overthrow of power within a particular country which claims human lives. Such revolutions have occurred in France, in Russia. The word 'revolution' is being applied to any change today. That is not what I mean by 'revolution.' The American Revolution, to me, was not a revolution. This was a national liberation—like Italy liberating itself from Austria, like the unification of Germany in the nineteenth century. I condemn revolution because it undermines the strength of the nation instead of allowing evolutionary development."

Solzhenitsyn soon heard ringing agreement with this from the Kremlin. On January 10, 1994, the government's new Commission for the Rehabilitation of Victims of Political Repression issued a report condemning Lenin and the Bolsheviks for the suppression of the Kronstadt Rebellion of 1921. The sailors of Kronstadt, who had initially supported the Bolsheviks and a socialist system, staged demonstrations calling for fair elections, a representative parliament, and other reforms repugnant to the new regime. The Bolsheviks declared war on the "counter-revolutionary conspiracy" and crushed the uprising with mass executions, deportations, and jailings. Aleksandr Yakovlev, the chairman of the commission, declared that Kronstadt proved that Bolshevik terror was Lenin's singular contribution to Russia. Stalin "was just the Great Continuer of Lenin's Task," he said. "It all began under Lenin."

In Vermont, Solzhenitsyn has kept his own counsel for years, preferring to work on his literary projects and keep his opinions on Russian politics to himself. In his only major American interview since the rise of Gorbachev, which appeared in *Time* in 1989, he held fast to one ground rule: there could be no questions about politics in the Soviet Union, the better to avoid his showing any signs of undue euphoria or discouragement. In 1990, Solzhenitsyn published his long essay *Rebuilding Russia*, which called for an end to the Soviet empire and the evolutionary development of democracy. But even in *Rebuilding Russia* he remained reticent about the dominant Russian personalities of the past seven or eight years. Why, I asked him, did he think the Soviet Union finally collapsed? What role did he think Gorbachev played?

"I can say I was the first person to predict that the Soviet Union would collapse, and to declare that this was necessary," he replied. "Not only did Gorbachev not want to hear about this; President Bush and other Western leaders also said the Soviet Union must remain intact. To me, it had been clear for many years. To all of us in prison, it was clear that Communism could not stand on its own. Ironically, Communism, which is based on the theory that the economy is the basis of all human activity, collapsed for economic reasons. Its economy was completely absurd. It could survive only with an iron grip. When Gorbachev first tried to ease that iron grip, the process of collapse accelerated. Gorbachev did not have in mind the negation of socialism. Even when he came back from captivity after the attempted coup in August of 1991, he said once again that our 'choice' was socialism. By no means did he intend to part company with socialism. He wanted only to rearrange things slightly and give the *nomenklatura* economic influence. There were clearly dirty economic transactions going on. Under Gorbachev, the debt more than quadrupled. The country never saw that money.

"Gorbachev imagined he would give glasnost to the Moscow intelligentsia, and, with its help, and with the help of the press, he would tame the extreme conservatives in the Party. But glasnost immediately spread to the whole country and to the nationalities question. The nationalities question sprang up everywhere, and the most extreme chauvinistic points of view developed. He could not cope with that. He could not imagine where all this would lead. In general, Gorbachev and his circle were locked into a Marxist ideology, and they were shortsighted. For example, about Eastern Europe. He could not foresee what would happen there. He wanted to replace their Ligachevs with their own Gorbachevs and leave it at that. But as soon as he touched something all these 'velvet revolutions' happened right away."

Solzhenitsyn gave almost no credit to Gorbachev, maintaining that expedience or necessity or cynicism motivated all he did. But what of Gorbachev's decision to withdraw from the arms race and end the Cold War?

"This was not cynicism," Solzhenitsyn said. "He really understood that the country was in such a difficult economic situation that sustaining the tension of the old rivalry with the West was no longer possible. The Cold War was essentially won by Ronald Reagan when he embarked on the Star Wars program and the Soviet Union understood that it could not take this next step. Ending the Cold War had nothing to do with Gorbachev's generosity; he was compelled to end it. He had no choice but to disarm."

In contrast to his denunciations of Gorbachev, Solzhenitsyn has generally backed Yeltsin, and even issued a statement of support last October when Yeltsin ordered the storming of the rebellious parliament.

"I both support Yeltsin and criticize him," Solzhenitsyn said. "I support him because—well, Gorbachev was not sincere in all his pronouncements, while Yeltsin was. Yeltsin truly decided to cut off ties with the Party. You might have seen on TV in 1990 how he walked out of the Party Congress with everyone sitting down looking at him as if they were wolves. And in August of 1991, when he read his pronouncement from the top of a tank, he acted courageously again. One cannot even compare him with Gorbachev. Yeltsin truly wanted what was best.

"But immediately after August of 1991 Yeltsin committed a series of mistakes, and very serious ones. That September, he could have easily dissolved the Supreme Soviet, dispersed the local soviets, and closed down the Communist Party, and nobody would have dared to object. There was such a surge of enthusiasm then! Everyone wanted this done, but he did not do anything. And so two years later—in October of 1993—he was forced to carry on this horrifying carnage in Moscow. In 1991, he could have done it with clean hands.

"Second, there is his indifference to the twenty-five million Russians now living abroad. He made no statement about this. God forbid we should have some sort of war over this as in Yugoslavia, but Yeltsin should have said, 'We take note that there are twelve million Russians in Ukraine, seven million in Kazakhstan, and in all negotiations we will always remind you of this and will seek a political solution to this question.' But he did not do this. He simply said, 'I accept all the borders,' and let it go at that. It was Lenin who established these false borders— borders that did not correspond to the ethnic borders. They were set up in ways to undermine the central Russian nation—as conscious punishment. The Donetsk and Lugansk regions supported the Cossacks in their fight with the Bolsheviks, and so Lenin cut those regions off from the Don as punishment. Southern Siberia rose up massively against the Bolsheviks, so he gave the region to Kazakhstan.

"As far as Ukraine is concerned, I was perfectly well aware of the mood of Ukrainian nationalists twenty years before Moscow ever heard about it. I spent time with such people in the camps. I know their intransigence. They were raised in Galicia, and they wanted absolutely to be separate. I greatly respect the Ukrainian people; I have great sympathy for them. I myself am part Ukrainian. If you want to be separate, by all means, go ahead, please. But within the borders of the true Ukraine. The historical Ukraine, the place where Ukrainians really live.

"So it has turned out that twenty-five million Russians all of a sudden live outside Russia. This is the biggest diaspora in the world. The leaderships of Ukraine and Kazakhstan are both extremely shortsighted. They have taken upon themselves a task that culturally cannot be worked out. For example, in Kazakhstan they will have to turn those Russians into Kazakhs. So what do they begin to do? They begin to rename villages. They make it a criminal act to speak out against the exclusivity of the Kazakh language. In Ukraine, they are eliminating Russian schools."

In the past two years, I said, the Russian Army has meddled consistently in the "near abroad," the former republics of the Soviet Union, in a clear attempt to reestablish at least some of the power that Moscow lost with the collapse of the union. Does Russia really have the right to send troops into Tajikistan, Armenia, Azerbaijan, and Georgia the way it has done?

"Interference in Georgia, in Armenia, and Azerbaijan? God forbid!" Solzhenitsyn said. "This sphere of influence, this military presence, is a remnant of imperial thinking. It must not be there. Of course, there is also a technical explanation. Why has Russia conducted itself this way? After the breakup of the Soviet Union, Russia found itself with no protected borders. You could do anything you liked, bring in anything across the borders: drugs, radioactive materials, arms, and so on. And so, in panic that the borders could not be quickly fortified, Russia decided to protect the old borders. But we must restructure, adjust. We must stop insisting on the right to take action in the breakaway republics.

"By the way, there is a huge Islamic nucleus on the rise. There was a conference of Islamic nations in Alma-Ata in 1991, and there they proclaimed the creation of a greater Turkish region, from Anatolia to Altai.

This is what they have in mind. I would not necessarily say that this is better for the world than a Russian presence in Central Asia. But let events take their course. Let the world deal with this problem. Maybe it is a threat, but it is not our business to interfere."

Finally, I asked about what are probably the two most pressing problems in Russia today: the collapse of the economy, and the advent, after the December elections, of a powerful opposition force dominated by hard-line nationalists, neo-Fascists, and Communists.

"Yeltsin's economic mistakes are enormous," Solzhenitsyn said. "Yeltsin felt the need to adopt any reform as soon as possible. We had Yegor Gaidar, a theorist who sat in his office under the influence of the International Monetary Fund, which itself exhibited total ignorance of the situation in Russia. Gaidar adopted a free-market policy, thinking that once prices were freed you would solve everything, because competition would begin and then the prices would stabilize and fall. He predicted first that they would stabilize in a month, then in two, then in four. So this is how this reform, which made no sense economically, began. It showed no compassion toward the people. The government never even asked what the people will do. Its own people live well, after all. Gaidar said after a year of the reforms, 'Yes, we had thought there might be a popular uprising, but it did not occur.' Yeltsin went even further, saying, 'I congratulate the people for not rebelling.' It's as if I were to meet you on the street, rob you, strip you, and congratulate you for not offering resistance.

"This is why the people, desperate and not knowing how to express themselves, expressed themselves the way they did in the December elections. They said, in effect, 'Anyone but you!' Those who voted wished primarily to voice their protest against this reform, against this conduct of our government. Their only recourse was to vote for those who showed their sharp disagreement with the reform. And that was who? The Communists, the agrarians, the women's party, and Vladimir Zhirinovsky. No one even knows who is in these parties. It is only because Zhirinovsky spoke so sharply against the current policy that he received so many votes. It was not a choice *for* Fascism, and it is not a choice *for* Communism. I receive letters saying, 'We feel thrown out into the cold. No one needs us. We cannot in any way influence what is happening.' This is not democracy. We have an oligarchical merger of Communist *nomenklatura* and the shadow economy. Our people have no influence.

"You know, I've never seen Zhirinovsky on television. They say that he has great eloquence and had tremendous impact on his listeners. I don't know if this is true. But, judging by his actions, he is a clown. I can't take him seriously."

Hitler was also a clown at first, I said.

"In terms of being a clown, Zhirinovsky outpaces even Hitler," Solzhenitsyn said. "I've never encountered this level of unending lunacy. It is a joke at every step of the way. Now, more important, people speak about the danger of Fascism in Russia. For me, the word 'Fascism' is used instead of 'National Socialism.' National Socialism is based on racism—without racism National Socialism is inconceivable. That is its basis and its theory. Racism, as a state policy, is possible only in a very homogeneous country, such as Germany, not in a multinational country like Russia. The danger is not Fascism, as many say it is, but is, rather, that it is possible to come to power merely on slogans refuting current policy."

During our conversation, Natalia Dmitriyevna joined us. I remarked that when I was in Moscow a couple of months earlier I had been disturbed to hear about how the city police had carried out wholesale arrests against Armenians, Azerbaijanis, and Chechens under the pretext that they alone were responsible for the soaring crime rate. I was even more disturbed to read polls in *Izvestiya* showing that the overwhelming majority of Muscovites were all for the arrests.

Somehow, the Solzhenitsyns did not see the issue as a matter of civil liberties. "You know, this question is first of all a criminal question," Solzhenitsyn said. "The Caucasians created a real Mafia, and in the Moscow and St. Petersburg regions they have monopolized the arms and restaurant trades."

"I saw this with my own eyes," said Natalia, who had been back to Russia twice since the ban on the family was lifted. "It is monstrous. There is nothing national about it. It's a criminal situation in Moscow when every father fears for his daughter walking at night. Those people are all armed to the teeth. They occupy every market. I saw myself how the old Russian women from the Moscow suburbs who try to sell some radishes or green onions have to work outside the subway stations, because they have been driven from the markets. Every market stall has to be bought for a huge sum, and, of course, none of the women could afford that. Those people have completely taken over life in Moscow, and I'll be the first to applaud if they are driven out—not because they are Chechen but because they are bandits. They have behaved like an occupying army that conquered the country."

. . .

In *The First Circle,* Solzhenitsyn made the famous remark that in a tyranny a real writer is like a second government. Whether it was Pushkin, Tolstoy, or Herzen under the tsars, or Akhmatova, Pasternak, or Mandelstam under the Bolsheviks, the role of the writer in Russia has been singular. But if all goes well in Russia, that kind of authority will, happily, vanish.

"When I said that a writer is like a second government, I meant it in the context of a fully totalitarian regime," Solzhenitsyn told me. "And, indeed, one can see today, in the newly published documents of the Politburo, that the members were concerned with my personal fate as seriously as if I were a whole state. In this sense, there was no exaggeration. But in a free society this formula no longer applies. Moreover, literature, like so much else in Russia, is now in a state of terrible degradation. At the moment, literature means very little. And yet I still hope that my books may help serve moral goals. I still hope to be useful in some way. I cannot write simply to be able to say, 'Look how cleverly I have fashioned this.' I refuse to see literature as amusement, as a game. I think that you ought not to approach literature without a moral responsibility for every word you write."

Solzhenitsyn's approach to literature, as a reader and as a writer, is as antimodernist as some of his political positions are. In our talks, he was disdainful of some of the contemporary writers in Russia, who tend to look for inspiration to, say, the sexual narratives of the Marquis de Sade or the formal hijinks of Italo Calvino rather than to Russian realism. He cannot abide experimentalism for its own sake, or pure pleasure as a literary end. To Solzhenitsyn, even Vladimir Nabokov was ultimately a disappointment.

"I don't take anything away from his artistic force," he said. "I nominated Nabokov for the Nobel Prize, but he did not receive it. At the same time, I am grieved that Nabokov, who came from a family that participated so avidly in the affairs of Russia, and who could have written so much and compiled even more material on the Russian Revolution a long time before me—well, I am grieved that he washed his hands of it and busied himself only with literary successes. I am pained by this. I do not understand it. I do not understand how this is possible.

"As it happens, I do not like *Lolita* at all. It seems to me in bad taste. But he has some fine novels—*Invitation to a Beheading* and many others. I rate him very highly. But I don't like *Lolita,* because in my opinion it is an unworthy play on sexuality."

Over the years, a loose critical orthodoxy has evolved about Solzhenitsyn's collected works. *One Day in the Life of Ivan Denisovich* is the
undisputed masterpiece. *The First Circle* and, to a lesser extent, *Cancer
Ward* are important works not only of political comment but also of
realism; it's as if, in the land of socialist realism, Solzhenitsyn took a
debased form and gave it life. *Gulag*, too, is generally considered a
masterwork, but of what is less clear. Memoir? Political analysis? Documentary prose? No matter. The three volumes of *Gulag*, like *One Day*,
will endure.

Solzhenitsyn sees his own work differently from nearly everyone else
in the world. In 1937, when he was still a convinced Communist, he
dreamed of writing an epic history leading up to the October Revolution
of 1917, and he even began making notes and writing early sequences.
The Red Wheel has been the obsession of Solzhenitsyn's writing life. As
his politics changed—especially in prison, where his labored defenses
of Marxism, he has said, "shattered like glass"—so changed *The Red
Wheel*. Eventually, he came to believe that the October Revolution, celebrated in Bolshevik mythology as a popular revolt, was actually a coup
d'état carried out in circumstances of complete chaos. More important, he felt, were the historical events beginning with the First World
War and climaxing in the February Revolution—the overthrow in early
1917 of the tsar and his short-lived replacement with the Provisional
Government.

"When I began to study the February Revolution, I understood, first
of all, that it is the central event of modern Russian history," Solzhenitsyn said. "I came to understand its weaknesses, its flaws, and how it
was already doomed to result in October. Doomed. I understood this
because by April of 1917 Lenin was already laughing at it. Everything
lay at his feet. So, gradually, my emphasis shifted in time to February.
Then I realized that to explain the February Revolution I had to explain
how tsarism and society had developed by that time. And so I went back
all the way to the end of the nineteenth century, even though I was
rebuked in the West for admiring the tsar and for calling for a return to
the past. The émigrés, meanwhile, chided me for writing an insulting
book about the last tsar, Nicholas II. But the truth is that I describe him
as he was. I do not praise him or rebuke him. I simply portray him as he
was."

The Red Wheel is formally quite different from anything Solzhenitsyn
has written before. Alternating with the historical narrative are long
biographical set pieces, actual newspaper clippings, and other experi-

ments, which borrow from sources as varied as John Dos Passos and Tolstoy. But most striking to Russian readers, perhaps, is Solzhenitsyn's language—his use of Russian words that have fallen into disuse. For many
years, Solzhenitsyn has made it his business to compile such words, even
assembling a dictionary with thirty thousand entries. Although Solzhenitsyn has been using such language ever since *One Day in the Life of
Ivan Denisovich*, it is this unusual lexicon, more than the formal experiments, or even the sheer immensity, that seems to trouble the Russian
writers who have read all or part of *The Red Wheel*.

   "The language is not at all appropriate," Vasily Aksyonov told me. "It's
very strange to be reading a conversation between Imperial Guards and
find them talking like two peasants. In *The Red Wheel* Solzhenitsyn is at
his best only when he is writing about something that he knows
absolutely, that he is close to. The sections on Lenin are great. But there
is so much that is uneven. His descriptions, for example, of Russian village life are false, and his writing about old Petersburg society is also not
a success. It's too far from him."

   Joseph Brodsky was even more critical. "What Solzhenitsyn has done
overall is tremendous, but I am not a complete champion," he said. "I
can't approve of his stylistic endeavors. He is a writer with natural gifts
and talent. But I think he suffers from this desire, widespread in the
twentieth century, that a Russian writer should have his own distinctive
style. Solzhenitsyn had reason to doubt that he was in possession of such
a commodity, despite the grace of *One Day in the Life of Ivan Denisovich*. In a sense, he went shopping for a style, and he wound up with two
things. First, he wanted to tap the dictionary. He forged or coined words
that have Slavonic roots but are not really Russian. There is Russian
grammar and, to a certain extent, vocabulary there, but it's Slavic, not
Russian. More important, in *The Red Wheel* he decided to enliven
things because of the extraordinary threat of monotony. And so he is
relying on the sort of filmlike technique in Dos Passos, with headlines
and documentary material spliced in. Sometimes it seems there is more
scissors and paste than actual scribbling, if you know what I mean. It
looks grotesque to my eye. It reflects a groping for a style. It's as if he
saw Proust with his style of elaboration, Beckett's dead-end style, Andrei
Platonov's cul-de-sac syntax, and he knew he needed something to call
his own."

   When I summarized such criticism for Solzhenitsyn, he seemed more
interested than dismissive. "My language is this," he said. "There is a
river flowing along, and you can take water from the surface or you can

reach in deeper and take from a lower stream. I take from the lower streams of the river of our language. In Russia, because of the general decline of Russian culture, there is a general decline in the language. If you now say to a Russian words like 'briefing,' 'establishment,' 'consensus,' everyone will understand. But as for Russian words, they will ask, 'What is this?' They are losing the Russian language. It is because our people are now losing the richness of their language and snapping up Anglicisms that my language seems somehow strange. Of course, it would be a lot easier to write more simply, but I don't need to do that. I am trying to rescue the old richness of the language. There is a layer just below the day-to-day language which is dying off for lack of common use. That's the layer I am trying to rescue. On this point, Brodsky is not correct. I don't try to reach for incomprehensible words or Old Slavonic, and I don't make up any words. I take from what exists. When I compiled and published this dictionary, I gave there examples of use by twenty or twenty-five Russian authors. This is the responsibility of the writer. Without this, the writer is pale and flat, and then he has nothing."

   The Red Wheel, which Solzhenitsyn finished in 1991, consists of *August 1914*, *November 1916*, *March 1917*, and *April 1917*. Because public interest in Solzhenitsyn was still high when Farrar, Straus & Giroux published an early version of *August 1914*, in 1972, it sold well. "We were right behind *Jonathan Livingston Seagull* on the *Times* best-seller list," Roger Straus, the publisher, told me. "We sold hundreds of thousands of books." But, Straus said, when he publishes *November 1916*, in 1995 or 1996, he expects to print somewhere between twenty-five thousand and fifty thousand copies. "The truth is that I'd consider myself lucky to sell that many," he said. "The interest is just not there anymore." Solzhenitsyn's French publisher, Claude Durand, of Fayard, said much the same thing: "The young just do not know who Aleksandr Solzhenitsyn is." In Russia itself, the publishing industry, like the rest of the economy, is in a state of free fall, and *The Red Wheel* languishes, unpublished. Solzhenitsyn is resigned to the likelihood that the books he considers the centerpiece of his work will not be read properly and completely until the next century. In the meantime, many of the Russians and non-Russians who have read parts of the books have expressed disappointment, even boredom. "The everyday response is based on a kind of tiredness," said Alexis Klimoff, a professor at Vassar, who has translated several of Solzhenitsyn's works. "One of the problems of reading *The Red Wheel* is: who has the time? You practically need a grant to read it all. It's thousands and thousands of pages, which, if you wish to make a serious judgment, need to be read together. It's physically exhausting, and people are unlikely to have the opportunity to do that. Reading it becomes a matter of 'Oh, hell, life is too short.' Which is true enough. But it is irresponsible in some fundamental sense."

The critics who have read *The Red Wheel* measure it against *War and Peace*. The two works differ in many ways, not least in that Solzhenitsyn wants his work to stand as reliable history, a definitive account of Russia's chaotic march toward the rise of Bolshevism.

"The fact is that Tolstoy's work on *War and Peace* was not very similar to mine on *The Red Wheel*," Solzhenitsyn said. "I won't compare the two works themselves but, rather, their respective aims. Leo Tolstoy wrote in the eighteen-sixties about the events of 1812—approximately fifty years after the fact. But in that time Russian society itself had hardly changed. There was an aristocratic Russia that still existed; everyday life was much the same. Therefore, his task was easier in the sense that he was describing the same world at an earlier stage. He could have easily transported the people of his world into his novel, because it was much the same circle. I started in 1937 but really began writing seriously in 1969, and from 1969 to 1917 is about the same time difference, but I wrote, I can say, about an entirely different world, a new planet. Pre-revolutionary Russia and then the Russia in which I have lived were cut off from each other. They were different worlds. I had to transport myself into a country that no longer existed. So I did not have the chance to transport today's people into the books."

Not long ago, I drove to the village of Troitse-Lykovo, on the western outskirts of Moscow. The main road out is the Rublyov Highway, a kind of golden pathway for the Kremlin élite, past and present, who have their dachas west of the city. On Friday afternoons, black Chaika limousines roar along the highway, often seizing the empty middle lane—known as the Kremlin lane—the better to start the weekend a few minutes early. Aleksandr and Natalia Solzhenitsyn are building a house in "dachaland"—on a ten-acre site that, as it happens, is where the fabled military strategist Marshal Mikhail Tukhachevsky once lived. The Solzhenitsyns razed the old wooden house and are now building a V-shaped brick house. There will be a working wing, with room for archives, a library, and research assistants, and there will be a living wing, with six bedrooms and various living areas. A high wooden fence painted green surrounds the property. If the house is not ready for the

Solzhenitsyns' arrival, in May—and, considering the pace of construction work in Russia these days, this is a near certainty—they can live in a five-room apartment they own in downtown Moscow.

While I was living in Moscow, from the beginning of 1988 to the end of 1991, most intellectuals had begun to realize that it was inevitable that Solzhenitsyn would be published and would return home. The cultural figures on the right wing—the editors of journals such as *Nash Sovremennik (Our Contemporary)*—were hopeful, figuring that Solzhenitsyn would present a hard-line nationalist alternative to Andrei Sakharov and the more Western-oriented radicals. Many of the liberals were terrified. Vitaly Korotich, who was the editor of the reformist magazine *Ogonyok* ("Small Flame"), told me then that it was entirely possible that Solzhenitsyn would return to Moscow as "an Ayatollah Khomeini." The publication of *Rebuilding Russia*, in 1990, brought an enormous letdown for the right and a relief for the reformers: the essay was anti-empire and pro-democracy. Russian and non-Russian reformers said that the piece showed traces of Solzhenitsyn's distance, his difficulty in grasping events he could only see on television or read about in the press, but, all in all, there was relief.

These days, opinions in Russia about Solzhenitsyn are emotional and mixed. A political poll taken in St. Petersburg last November showed that forty-eight percent of the respondents would like to see Solzhenitsyn as President of Russia, despite his stated refusal ever to hold office. Only seventeen percent picked Boris Yeltsin. But in more rarefied circles—among intellectuals, especially—a more ironical attitude toward Solzhenitsyn has formed. I found the attitude ranging from indifference to mockery:

"Solzhenitsyn is late. Developments have accelerated way ahead of him. He must realize he is coming back to a world that is utterly foreign to him."

"He should have come back when the Communists were driven out. Where was he? He has nothing to say anymore. This *Red Wheel* of his is the work of a graphomaniac. I tried to read it and fell asleep every time."

"Maybe if he'd come after Sakharov died, in December of 1989. The reaction to Sakharov's death, the outpouring, was an indication of how much one honest man meant in those days. But the time for a single heroic figure has passed. Solzhenitsyn's authority is based only in the past."

"I suppose he'll come back and play the role of Tolstoy, the great writer who gives us all advice, the prophet who accepts visitors and wears a great beard. The beard is very important in this role."

Solzhenitsyn is well aware of the range of attitudes that awaits him. Not only has his wife been back—three times now—but his sons have also been to Russia. Moreover, hundreds of Russians have sent letters to Cavendish telling Solzhenitsyn what they have heard said and what they themselves feel about his return home.

"Many await my arrival with hostility," Solzhenitsyn told me. "There are those who weep for Communism and consider me its main destroyer, the main person at fault. Some fanatics are literally saying they want my neck. Second, the mafiosi understand that if I was not going to make peace with the KGB, I certainly would not with them. Third, there are those who believe in myths: for example, that I will return and become the head of Pamyat"—the nationalist hate group—"or the head of the right wing. They cannot understand that I want nothing to do with power or any political position. Finally, there are the powers that be. I do not avoid making critical comments. In Europe, or with you here today, I do not avoid criticizing today's authorities or the current reforms and how they are being conducted. I speak out sharply and will continue doing that. I will not be surprised if I am denied access to television after a while. In other words, life will not be easy in any respect. But I am going because I have fulfilled my literary duty and now I must try to fulfill my duty to society to whatever extent I can. How it will turn out I don't know."

In our time together, Solzhenitsyn repeated several times that he had no interest in politics, that he would never run for political office or accept an appointment of any kind. I asked him if he would play the sort of role that Sakharov did in the late nineteen-eighties—that of a moral compass for a country that is adrift.

"My role can be only moral," he said. "What other role can I have? But the situation is changing very quickly. Many years have passed since Sakharov's death. In fact, there is no guarantee that Sakharov would have remained as influential and as much admired as he was. The situation is changing so quickly that it is difficult to say how much my moral efforts will resonate and be successful. The fact that my books have not been read—this also interferes a lot. You can't get them. People say, 'Who is Solzhenitsyn? Oh, yes, he's the guy they kicked out, he did something long ago.' But there are no books. This makes it very difficult."

One of the most remarkable aspects of Solzhenitsyn's journey is that he can finish it. In May, the moment his plane lands at Sheremetyevo Airport, where the KGB escorted him to the waiting jet twenty years ago, his life will be complete. As a writer, too, he has finished all he has wanted to, restoring the memory of the Soviet holocaust, giving voice to the lost. Now his literary old age does seem Tolstoyan: Tolstoy, in his last years, his great novels done, worked on much shorter fiction, honing valedictory stories like "Hadji Murad" and "Alyosha the Pot" to perfection with ten, fifteen, twenty drafts.

"There is no sense in beginning a big project at my age," Solzhenitsyn said. "But I am very much interested in the short form, and I am beginning to work in it again. It's not just a question of age. I began with short stories, but the task ahead was always first my novels, then *Gulag*, and then *The Red Wheel*, and I had to fulfill those tasks. Finally, I have the chance. Now I will replenish my impressions of life in Russia, of today's Russia, and I will definitely write short stories. For the moment, while I am still in Vermont, I am working on stories using materials from the twenties and thirties, because I cannot write about today's Russia without personal impressions of it. I remember well these things from my youth. And then, now that I have finished *The Red Wheel*—this huge beast now felled—there are many loose ends left over, and it is unclear what to do with them. I have a mountain of leftover material that has to be sorted out."

The Solzhenitsyn house in Cavendish was strewn with packing crates. There were brand-new suitcases heaped in the guest room. The Solzhenitsyns are not selling the Cavendish house, preferring to keep it, at least for now, as a base for their children. Although Yermolai will probably spend the next couple of years working in China, Stephan is still at Harvard, and Ignat is still at the Curtis Institute. They all say they intend to move to Russia, to be of use to Russia, but probably not anytime soon. The center of the household, though, has almost put America behind him.

"It's as if we no longer lived here," Solzhenitsyn said. "In spirit, we have already gone. I await different trials and different tasks. I am ready for this, and I thank God I have the strength for it now. Naturally, I have been following intensively what has been going on in Russia, and I am well informed. But meeting with specific people and learning about their specific fates—that still awaits me. The specific situations in particular cities, in farms and factories—that awaits me. I will need, first of all, a period of reacquaintance, to get a sense of the lower depths of life in Russia. I have to take careful note of it, the way an artist would—of today's situation and the people's mood."

Was he returning with any optimism at all?

"If it took Russia seventy-five years to fall so far, then it is obvious that it will take it more than seventy-five years to rise back up," he said. "A hundred or a hundred and fifty, we can guess. It is very difficult to find a country in modern history that was systematically destroyed for as long as seventy-five years. And it is important to remember that the destroyers destroyed selectively: not just anyone but those who were the most intelligent, those who might protest, those who could think on their own—the life force of the people."

"But, of course, it will be a happy day, returning," Natalia said. "Even now, it is as if a terrible weight had been lifted from us. Just the knowledge that we will finish our lives in Russia is a great relief. When I was back, I got pleasure just from being surrounded by the Russian language. I remember being in the Metro and hearing that banal voice: 'Careful! The doors are closing. . . . The next stop is . . .' But it was in Russian! Just to pass stores that say '*Moloko*' and '*Khleb*' instead of 'Milk' and 'Bread.' The pleasure in that!"

It was time for me to go. Natalia had fed us all one last time. Ignat played a Schubert sonata. Natalia loaded me up with files, clippings, and a Christmas cake to take home to my family. We all agreed to meet again, in Moscow. As a final question, I mentioned to Solzhenitsyn that I remembered his speech in Liechtenstein, when he said that modern man, by putting himself at the center of the world, fears death because death thus becomes the end of all things—and I asked him if he feared dying now that he was seventy-five.

"Absolutely not," he said, his face lighting up with pleasure. "It will just be a peaceful transition. As a Christian, I believe that there is a life after death, and so I understand that this is not the end of life. The soul has a continuation, the soul lives on. Death is only a stage, some would even say a liberation. In any case, I have no fear of death."

"And where will you be buried?"

"I've made a preliminary choice," Solzhenitsyn said. "Maybe I'll change it later, but I have one in mind. It's in central Russia, and I invite you to come there after I have gone."

(1994)

Part III

Deep in the Woods:
Solzhenitsyn in Moscow

Not long ago, during the White Nights, I took a walk from the gates of the Kremlin, past the underground shopping mall on Manezh Square, and up Tverskaya Street, the ground zero of Russian neo-capitalism. There was a time when it was no simple matter to get, say, a bowl of borscht on this street. Now it's entirely possible to order (as one strolls at random) a *macchiato* at Coffee Bean, a calzone at Sbarro, a Cadillac sedan, a ten-thousand-dollar ball gown, VCRs, DVDs, and, should you still desire it, a bowl of borscht. Every year brings a new accretion of commercialism to Tverskaya—more stores, more restaurants, more hotels. Depending on the state of things, there are even some Muscovites who can buy as well as look.

Suddenly, there was a thunderclap and a flash summer storm. Rain fell in cool sheets. I ducked into the Young Guard bookstore. It was crowded but not unpleasantly so; it was clean and air-conditioned, a helpful sales staff roamed the floor, and the shelves were filled with the collected works of authors who, little more than a decade ago, were

banned by Soviet censors. As I was riffling through a memoir by an actor
I'd met—a film star who once gave a public performance of Joseph
Brodsky's poems when that was something dangerous and delicious—
the store manager came on the loudspeaker, and, in the beguiling voice
of unembarrassed salesmanship, more Kmart than commissar, she said,
"Respected shoppers! Please note that today we are featuring a new title,
which can be found near the cashier's desk. It's a volume by the Nobel
Prize–winning author of *The Gulag Archipelago*, Aleksandr Isayevich
Solzhenitsyn. The book is called *Two Hundred Years Together*, a history
of Russian-Jewish relations."

No one stopped, no one seemed in the least surprised. In fact, in
the next half hour, hardly anyone dropped by to check out this curious
new book. In contemporary Russia, history has been ruthless in its
speed, and the public's memory is fickle. Solzhenitsyn is eighty-two. For
younger people, especially, his name marks just another event in a half-
remembered Soviet past: the Revolution, the camps, Stalingrad, Yuri
Gagarin . . . Solzhenitsyn. When Solzhenitsyn returned to Russia in May
1994, after twenty years of forced exile, he was welcomed by a mixture of
celebration, derision, and indifference. Some younger writers seemed
determined to carve out a place for themselves by declaring the old man
a reactionary egomaniac, a bore, passé. These harsh greetings, along
with a generally negative critical reception to his cycle of historical novels, *The Red Wheel*, left Solzhenitsyn resentful at times, though he was
loath to admit it.

Browsing the shelves, I picked up a volume of Solzhenitsyn's short
stories published last year. The second half of the book is taken up with
the tales he's written since coming home: "Ego," "On the Extremes,"
"Apricot Jam." The first half is made up of those early, classic stories
that reordered the politics and the literature of the Soviet Union in
the early sixties: notably, "An Incident at Krechetovka Station" and
One Day in the Life of Ivan Denisovich. As one reads "Matryona's
House," there comes a chill, a foreshadowing of the author's exiles and
returns:

> During the summer of the year 1956, I came back at random from
> the hot, dusty desertlands—simply to Russia. No one was waiting
> for me or had invited me anywhere, because I had been detained
> from returning for a little stretch of ten years. I simply wanted to
> get back into the heart of the country—out of the heat, into wood-
> lands with rustling leaves. I wanted to cut myself loose and get lost

in the innermost heart of Russia—if there were any such thing—
and live there.

Solzhenitsyn, like the narrator of his story and like millions of others,
made his way back west after "a little stretch" in the camps—the myriad
islands of the gulag archipelago—and in internal exile. He returned and
for twenty years wrote, mainly in secret, the story of Soviet tyranny.
When *The Gulag Archipelago* was published abroad, in 1974, the Soviet
leadership arrested Solzhenitsyn, put him onto a plane, and sent him to
the West. In exile, he not only dreamed of his return, he was confident of
it—just as he was confident of the regime's collapse.

On May 26, 1994, Solzhenitsyn and his wife, Natalia, flew from their
home in Vermont to Magadan, on the Sea of Okhotsk, which had been
one of the principal centers of the gulag system. For the next two
months, he and his family traveled by train toward Moscow, stopping in
Vladivostok, Khabarovsk, Irkutsk, Krasnoyarsk, Novosibirsk—seventeen
stops in all. It was a return not without a sense of occasion and ego: the
BBC made a documentary and paid for special railway cars. Solzhenitsyn
hardly "lost" himself in innermost Russia this time. Crowds came to hear
him speak at every stop, he signed books, he appeared on local television; it was the grandest author tour in history. But there was also a great
poignancy in the journey. Solzhenitsyn had done as much as any man to
bring an end to seven decades of oppression in Russia, and it was
unlikely that he would ever travel that extensively in his own country
again. This was at once a return, a welcome, and a farewell.

When the convoy finally arrived in Moscow, Boris Yeltsin, who had
become the first President of a post-Communist Russia, tried to win over
Solzhenitsyn, just as he had tried to win over Andrei Sakharov, in the late
eighties. Vyacheslav Kostikov, Yeltsin's former press secretary, wrote in a
memoir,

> His aides sought to put him in an overbearing frame of mind. He
> was told: "Who is this Solzhenitsyn? After all, he is not a classic, not
> a Leo Tolstoy. And what's more, everyone is tired of him. Well, he
> suffered under totalitarianism, and, yes, he is an expert on history,
> but there are thousands more like him! While you, Boris Niko-
> layevich, are one of a kind." Yeltsin, however, chose a different
> tone. The conversation proceeded easily and very frankly, without
> any attempts to paper over the political differences. They talked for
> four hours and even had a little vodka.

The meeting may have been friendly, but Solzhenitsyn's critique of Yeltsin, on television and in two short books of political writing—*The Russian Question at the End of the Twentieth Century* (1994) and *Russia in Collapse* (1998)—only intensified. Solzhenitsyn blamed Yeltsin for breaking up the old union without regard for the interests of the twenty-five million Russians who now found themselves abroad in the former Soviet republics; for economic reforms that "impoverished" the nation; for behaving "like slaves" to the West and selling out Russia's interests to the International Monetary Fund and NATO; for promoting corruption; for failing to establish any real democratic institutions on the grassroots level. Solzhenitsyn declared that in Russian history there had been three *smuty,* or "times of troubles": the political upheaval in the seventeenth century that established the Romanov dynasty; the revolutionary year of 1917; and now, the post-Communist crisis. Solzhenitsyn was no longer saying the unsayable—most of his opinions were common fare and none were forbidden—but his tone was no less fierce than it had been in *Gulag.* By declaring the present, but not, say, the nineteen-thirties, a time of troubles, he relegated Yeltsin to a ring of Inferno even lower than Stalin's.

In 1998, on Solzhenitsyn's eightieth birthday, Yeltsin still seemed eager to please the writer and awarded him the highest of all state honors, the Order of St. Andrew. Solzhenitsyn turned it down. "In today's conditions, when people are starving and striking just to get their wages, I cannot accept this award," he said. "Maybe in many years' time, when Russia overcomes its insurmountable problems, my sons may be able to accept this award." When Yeltsin left office, on the eve of 2000, Solzhenitsyn was furious that the new President, Vladimir Putin, had granted his predecessor immunity from prosecution. Solzhenitsyn declared that Yeltsin "along with another one or two hundred people must be brought to book."

By now, Solzhenitsyn had managed to alienate almost everyone. The Communists despised him, of course, and the hard-line Russian nationalists, who had once hoped he would be their standard-bearer, found him too liberal. The liberals, who looked west for their models, could not take seriously Solzhenitsyn's view of the West as a trove of useless materialism and a wasteland of spiritual emptiness. Nor could they abide conservative positions such as his support for the reinstatement of the death penalty.

When Solzhenitsyn first arrived in Moscow, he was cited as a possible successor to Yeltsin. This was always a fantasy, but it did indicate his enormous prestige. And yet with time, and with Solzhenitsyn's weekly exposure on television, the majority of the public soured on him or grew indifferent. His television appearances were canceled. He fell in the political ratings and then disappeared from them. He began to appear less and less in public. But still he continued to write. I was able to obtain, through his sons Ignat, a concert pianist and conductor in Philadelphia, and Stephan, an urban planning and environmental consultant in Boston, an advance copy of the first volume of *Two Hundred Years Together* and made plans to pay him a visit on the outer edge of the capital.

As it happened, I arrived in Moscow just after George W. Bush had met with Putin in Slovenia. Bush had come into office vowing that he would not be seduced by a Russian leader the way he thought Bill Clinton had been by Yeltsin. And so it was a matter of hilarity among the former Russian dissidents I saw that Bush, after one short day in Putin's presence, declared that he had "looked the man in the eye" and found him to be "very straightforward and trustworthy." "I was able to get a sense of his soul," Bush said. It appeared to mean little to Bush that Putin had rebuffed him on missile defense, or that Russia was still waging war on the Chechens, in the south, and on the media in Moscow, or that Putin was making increasingly friendly overtures to Iran. In the absence of knowledge and preparation, Bush relied on metaphysical self-confidence. What he found in the soul of a career KGB officer was "a remarkable leader." It reminded a Russian friend of mine of the moment in *Annie Hall* when Alvy Singer describes how he was thrown out of college for cheating on his metaphysics final; he had looked into the soul of the boy sitting next to him.

The vast majority of Russians were apparently every bit as enamored of Vladimir Putin. Putin's approval ratings, after a year and a half in office, were around seventy percent. People admired him because he appeared not to suffer from the sins of Yeltsin. Where Yeltsin was bombastic and unpredictable, Putin is steady, purposefully dull. Where Yeltsin was a tsar, Putin is chief bureaucrat. He has tamed his own language—he once vowed to kill the Chechens even "in their outhouses"—and now he wants to "put an end to the resistance by illegal armed formations." At least in imagery, he has delivered on a promise of stability. It seems for the moment not to matter that this stability has less to do with Putin's sobriety than with the high price of oil. The country's economic comeback after its August 1998 crash resembles the stability of the Brezhnev era: Russia still does not produce much that the world wants except natural resources.

Putin's opposition is easy to define—an aging cadre of followers of the Communist Party and some liberals, like Grigory Yavlinsky, of the Yabloko Party—but, for the moment, they pose no great threat to him. What's more, there is little nostalgia for the old battles. So many of the warriors of the late eighties and the nineties have scattered, died, or been discredited. And some of the contemporary figures who put themselves forward as avatars of democracy were hardly heroic. Until Putin brought low the NTV network—the only independent, privately owned national television outlet in the country—and replaced its leadership, its most prominent broadcaster was Yevgeny Kiselyov, who hosted a Sunday-night newsmagazine show called *Itogi.* Kiselyov's reputation was based on a showy fearlessness; and yet he seemed to have no ear at all for the ordinary Russian or for the poor. One night, he went on the air and coyly revealed, by way of humanizing himself, that he had a terrible weakness for clarets of exceptional vintages. To prove it, he took viewers on a tour of his considerable wine cellar. This was not exactly Andrei Sakharov with his net shopping bag and shabby suit.

One afternoon, I dropped by the House of Journalists, on the Boulevard Ring Road, where a group of human-rights activists was holding a conference. During a break, I met for coffee with Aleksandr Podrabinek, an old friend who, since 1987, had been publishing an independent newspaper called *Ekspress-Khronika,* which reported news that the bigger papers and the networks ignored. Podrabinek is a small, almost impish man in his late forties. From 1978 to 1983, he was forced to live in eastern Siberia in both labor camps and internal exile, for the sin of having written a book, *Punitive Medicine,* about the Soviet regime's use of psychiatric hospitals to deal with political dissent. He had no illusions about Yeltsin, and remains a fierce opponent of the war in Chechnya, but for all Yeltsin's mistakes, he said, the country was leaving a relatively "golden" era and moving somewhere darker. "The idea of democracy has failed to capture the popular imagination to any great degree," he said. "Yeltsin was a man of broader views and vision than Putin. Now we have someone who has the intellect of an Army sergeant. He gives people simple orders and he obeys simple orders. He has no great vision except the creation of a vertical construct of power."

Putin spent most of his adult life as a KGB officer, but his résumé gives off a different, more varied, resonance in Russia than it does

abroad, Podrabinek said. Even Sakharov once said that, despite the
KGB's role in the terror of the Communist regime, it was also a bastion
of competency, of people who understood what was really going on
behind the official façade. "It doesn't really matter to most people that
Putin was a KGB officer," Podrabinek said. "The idea of reputation is not
a major one here. People elect bandits as governors knowing they are
bandits—in the Far East, for example. Or they elect a KGB officer or a
hard-line Communist. They vote for those people whose names are most
in front of them. Russia's mentality is too easy to shape, as has been
shown over and over."

As the human-rights movement in Russia has shifted to the margins,
its newspapers and conferences are often funded either by Western
foundations or not at all. *Ekspress-Khronika,* with a peak circulation of
sixty-five thousand, used to run on the largesse of the National Endowment for Democracy; now the sense of urgency is gone, and so is much
of the movement's financial support. Podrabinek has not been able to
publish the paper for a year. When I asked him about this, he just
laughed. "Soon it will be like the old days—just a few dissidents and
some kindly Westerners bringing in money secretly in their belts and
shoes. But, remember, it is possible to slide backward a long way, especially if the West does not bother to pay much attention. . . . What we
really need, I think, is a new generation of politicians who are willing to
say that Russia, just like everyone else, needs a normal democratic system. Until that, maybe we will wander in the desert for forty years."

A few hours later, I met with one of Podrabinek's colleagues at the
conference, Ludmilla Alexeyeva, who is the chairman of the Moscow-
Helsinki human-rights group. Alexeyeva is in her seventies. She lives
just off the Old Arbat, the pedestrian mall, which has long featured ven-
dors selling T-shirts of high post-Soviet irony; a favorite, advertising
"McLenin's," juxtaposes Vladimir Ilyich in profile and the Golden Arches.
Alexeyeva immigrated to the United States in 1977 and then came back
to live in Moscow in 1992.

"The biggest problem we have is the problem of law, the judicial system," she said. "The constitution was rewritten in 1993, so there are new
laws, but no one knows these laws, no one follows them. The judges are
corrupt, ignorant, or they are old enough so that all their legal 'thinking'
and habits were formed in Soviet times. Nearly all of these judges take
the Soviet view that the goal of the court is, above all, to protect the
interest of the state. There is little or no thought to the individual."

When I suggested that the fall of the Communist state, the popularity of Putin, and a general decline in politics as a Russian obsession had led to the marginalization of the human-rights movement, Alexeyeva disagreed, and gave an indulgent smile.

"Not marginalized," she said. "Changed."

In the old days, the movement was composed of extremely small groups of urban intellectuals gathering secret petitions, furtively meeting with Western visitors, and risking jail at every turn. Nowadays, it has taken the shape of a loosely knit national legal aid society. In the cities and the provinces, young lawyers with a firm grasp of modern juridical practice and ethics have set up shop in offices and courts.

"There are thousands of such people," Alexeyeva said. "That's not marginalization. That's a real step forward."

One cloudy afternoon, I drove out of Moscow to the village of Peredelkino. During the Soviet period, the government encouraged the Writers' Union to allocate dachas in Peredelkino to writers, especially to writers who were ideologically reliable, but also to true artists like Pasternak and Rostropovich. (At one point in the sixties, Solzhenitsyn lived with friends here.) Some of the Peredelkino dachas have been bought up by young businessmen—there's a lot of high-end construction going on behind the old green gates—but there are still a great many writers around. I'd come out to see Lev Timofeyev, an economist who had been sent to a prison camp in the Urals under Gorbachev, in 1985, for having written and distributed a book on the illegal, or shadow, economy. Along with dozens of other political prisoners, Timofeyev was freed in 1987 and became an active figure in the pro-democracy movement. In the nineties, he regained his bearings as a scholar, publishing a series of books on the illegal economy and narco-business. He also writes shorter pieces for *Izvestia* and *The Moscow News* and teaches at the Russian State University for the Humanities. He looked younger than he did ten years ago.

"Well," he said sheepishly as we greeted each other at the gate to his dacha. "I divorced and married a young wife. It happens."

We went inside to a screened porch and a table laden with peaches, grapes, wild strawberries, and a bowl of cherries.

"The last time we saw each other, you know when it was?" Timofeyev said. "It was inside the White House on the last night of the putsch." That was August 21, 1991, the night the KGB-led coup collapsed and, with it, the Communist regime. By Christmas night, Gorbachev had transferred power to Yeltsin and the Soviet Union was dissolved.

Timofeyev was in agreement with his colleagues in the human-rights movement on Chechnya and the assault on the press, but he was far more sanguine than many of the others I met. Timofeyev's view of the economy is far different from the standard analysis: that Russia is suffering from the rise of a small number of ruthless oligarchs who came to control major industries through their political connections.

"Not one person in Russia lives outside the reality of a shadow Russia," he said. "As soon as you leave your house or apartment in the morning, you find yourself in a world of bribes, contraband, unregistered activity, 'black cash,' and the rest." Outside, it began to thunder—one clap was so loud I jumped from my chair—then came rain. A cool mist drifted through the screen. "This is not something to do with the oligarchs," Timofeyev went on, "nothing to do with the big businessmen you read about in the papers, but everyone—peasants, teachers, workers in a factory, everyone. And, in this sense, nothing really changed between the Soviet period and now. It changed only in quantity, which became infinitely greater. The shadow economy is a normal market of buying and selling. After all, there used to be prices for everything before: positions in the Communist Party were the assets then, and they were worth something and you paid for them. Now the fruits of the market are different, but there are no laws or structures to give meaning to a true market economy. The examples are everywhere. My neighbor here just went to get a driver's license, but it soon became clear that the only way to get this was to pay two hundred dollars to the guy who gives the exam. He gives fifteen or twenty of these exams a day. He can't keep all the money—he has to distribute it around a little—but it's a living. . . . This system works, but it is not productive like an open economy. It only maintains daily life, it's a kind of holding pattern.

"I am an economist, so what interests me most about Putin is that. In Russia, it will be impossible to have democratic change that is serious without a developed market economy. And, in that regard, I think Putin and his team have done more in a year than Yeltsin and his team did in ten years. Yeltsin, of course, laid the groundwork, and he probably needed that time. But Putin has done well. Most important, there is finally a flat income tax of thirteen percent. Before, hardly anyone paid taxes at all. This is a major advance. There is now a law on land for non-agricultural use, legislation on trial by jury. And there is an overall tendency to avoid any reactionary economic thinking. Considering what some people were expecting, I can't ask for much more."

In 1989, I had gone with Timofeyev to a theatrical production of *One*

Day in the Life of Ivan Denisovich. When I mentioned that I was going
to visit Solzhenitsyn the next day, Timofeyev reacted like the other former prisoners and dissidents I had met in the past. He thought that
Solzhenitsyn's achievements, especially *One Day* and *Gulag,* were so
great and his independence and integrity were so beyond judgment that
to criticize him, even to engage his ideas critically, was wrong.

"I have a great many disagreements with Aleksandr Isayevich, but I
have no wish to argue with him," Timofeyev said. "There is probably no
life in the entire twentieth century that has so many pluses next to it. No
one in this century, at least no one in Russia, except Sakharov, is on his
level. So he can say what he wants, it's his right." Timofeyev paused, and
then he went on, saying, "But, at the same time, his influence has diminished. When, many years ago, he wrote his essay 'Zhit' ne po lzhi!' "—
"Live Not by Lies!"—"our reaction was the same as your reaction to that
thunderclap a little while ago. The effect was that startling. But when I
heard him on television I have to admit that it was clear to me that he is a
fact of literary life still, but not really a crucial actor in political or social
life."

Had Solzhenitsyn lost his moral authority since coming home? I asked.

"In the modern world, moral authorities are proof of a society's inability to live a decent life," Timofeyev said. "To have to rely so much on
someone like Solzhenitsyn or Sakharov is a sure sign that something is
wrong. Nowadays, I can express myself not by quietly identifying myself
with a figure like that but by writing, reading, voting, doing business,
whatever it is. This is a good thing. Society needs a Solzhenitsyn in a time
of emergency, far less so now."

The next afternoon, Natalia Solzhenitsyn picked me up at my hotel in a
gray Volvo. She is a highly intelligent and energetic woman in her early
sixties, and she has helped her husband in every way possible: while
Solzhenitsyn wrote, often staying in his study for days at a time, she ran
the household, raised their three sons (a son from her previous marriage,
Dmitri, died in 1994), carried out research, typed and retyped manuscripts, edited a series of volumes on Russian history, administered a
fund for camp veterans using the proceeds from *The Gulag Archipelago,*
organized the family archives, and planned their move home. In Vermont, Natalia was Solzhenitsyn's liaison with the world; she retains that
function here, dealing with publishers, reporters, readers, harassers. I
doubt if Aleksandr Isayevich has picked up a ringing telephone in

decades. Natalia grew up in Moscow, and knows every street and alley, but her husband is not a real Muscovite; he is from a provincial city, Rostov, and in his work celebrates, even romanticizes at times, the verities of village life. Their house is in Troitse-Lykovo, a verdant pocket along the Moscow River, a place that only now, with urban sprawl, can be called part of the capital.

"At first," she was saying in the car, "when we returned home, Aleksandr Isayevich would come downtown for various things a couple of times a month. Then it became once a month."

"And now?" I asked.

"And now almost never. Aleksandr Isayevich doesn't really live in Moscow. He lives in the woods."

The traffic in Moscow has grown horrendous in recent years. It took us three-quarters of an hour to drive the ten miles west to Troitse-Lykovo. Finally, Natalia turned off the main road and onto a narrow, pitted lane. We passed some small cottages and then pulled up to a tall gate painted forest green.

"We don't have automatic openers in Russia yet," Natalia said as she cheerfully hopped out of the car. She unlocked the gate and pushed it open. The effect was incredible: we were suddenly looking into a pristine wood. She got back in the car and slowly rumbled past a small house where her eldest son, Yermolai, and his wife were living and then pulled up to the main house, which is shaped like a wide-open "V." The place, which they'd had built for them, was modern, airy, elegant—not something you see very often in Moscow, even now. If Natalia had told me that she had airlifted the house in from Aspen or Telluride, I might have believed her. Members of the old Politburo, including the notorious secret police chief Lavrenti Beria, used to live in the area. Natalia mentioned that Putin's Prime Minister was living a few doors down the road but was soon to move.

As we were walking toward the house, we saw Natalia's mother waving from a window. She is the same age as Solzhenitsyn, but her health, Natalia said, is better than her husband's. In recent years, Solzhenitsyn has had two heart attacks and suffers from intense back pain. Since coming home, he has continued working—short stories, prose poems, essays on other writers, political writing, as well as *Two Hundred Years Together*—but his energy, his urgency, is nothing like it had been. When he was writing *The Gulag Archipelago*, he would make two writing days out of one: he would get up at one A.M. and work until nine; take a break and then work again until six, eat dinner, go to bed at seven P.M., sleep till one, and then start again—all while expecting a knock on the door. He slept with a pitchfork near his bed.

Natalia led us to a library, and Solzhenitsyn met us there. He looked much as he had when I first met him, in 1994—the same nineteenth-century beard and furrowed brow, the same safari jacket. But now he walked quite slowly and used a cane; he was more subdued in conversation, more likely to fall back on familiar nostrums. When I asked if he ever thought his work would be finished, he said, "This all depends on my health. If I'm still alive but bedridden, then I'll have to stop working, of course. But as long as I can move, even with the help of a cane, I'll go on working."

Every Soviet and Russian leader since Khrushchev has had a Solzhenitsyn strategy. For decades, it was repression; now it is seduction. Putin and his wife, Lyudmila, came calling last year, flowers in hand. Not long after that visit, I met Putin in New York and asked him about his time with Solzhenitsyn. "Oh, he had quite a lot of interesting ideas," he said blandly.

Now Solzhenitsyn was saying, "The meetings with Yeltsin and Putin were relatively brief and just once each, so it would be a mistake to make too much of my personal impressions. I watched Yeltsin, though, for ten years from afar, so I can judge him as a historical figure. I feel that Yeltsin permitted an enormous devastation of Russia. One might have imagined that things could not have got worse than the point to which Communism had brought us. It seemed that any effort at all would bring something better. On the contrary. Yeltsin managed to bring Russia even lower. He supported thieves. Our national riches and resources were privatized nearly for free, and even the new mobsters are not asked to pay any rent. The state has become a pauper.

"As for freedom of speech, that's the great achievement of Gorbachev and his policy of glasnost. Yeltsin just did not interfere in this process. As for the attack on the Communist Party, this also began before Yeltsin. From the end of the eighties, many Party functionaries fled their Party positions to join commercial concerns. They fled like cockroaches. So when Yeltsin came to power, the Communist Party no longer existed as a monolith. Yeltsin in his clash with the Supreme Soviet allowed state power to weaken, and then"—in October 1993—"he rushed to another extreme, firing with tanks on the White House. The rest of the world did not call out loudly enough or reprimand him enough. He was considered a great champion of democracy even while he did this. And then Yeltsin established an autocratic regime. Democracy has not been established in Russia. Democracy has had no time to establish itself."

As for the current President, Solzhenitsyn said, "The first thing to ask is, Who put Putin into power? Yeltsin did it, with the help of [the notorious oligarch Boris] Berezovsky. To analyze this phenomenon of a KGB man in power, you have to analyze how he came into power. If he had come into power as the result of a KGB coup, it would have been one thing, but we had something else. I met Putin only once, and since then I've had no contacts. I got the impression of a businesslike person. . . . During our meeting, I made several suggestions, but he has followed none of them."

Nearly thirty years ago, it became clear that Solzhenitsyn had a distinctly different opinion of the West than many other dissident thinkers. In speeches at Harvard and in front of the AFL-CIO, Solzhenitsyn railed against the weakness and the naïveté of the West, attacked those who criticized the war in Vietnam, warned of godlessness and junk culture. Nothing that has happened since—not even the collapse of the Communist regime—has changed his mind about this.

"When the Iron Curtain was still standing, the cheapest fashions still made their way here: tawdry fashions, rock and roll, drugs, *popsa*— everything cheap, the cheapest possible things. When the Iron Curtain came down, the situation became even more complicated. It wasn't only the manure that came through. There were many Western influences that came in, different qualities, different types of things, and I wouldn't say all of them were negative. But my fellow-countrymen welcomed all of it with an open soul, everything! We thought a period of universal happiness would begin. Gorbachev and then Yeltsin withdrew our troops from Europe without any conditions. I'm now reading a memoir about how Gorbachev told the West, 'Are you sure you won't expand NATO to the east?' And they answered, 'Oh no, no, no.' It never occurred to Gorbachev to get a written document guaranteeing this. He just believed in their word and that was it. That was how we greeted the West. That's how things started, in that spirit. Then we became extraordinarily disillusioned when we began to understand the arrogance, the real policies, of the Western powers." In the seventies, Solzhenitsyn charged the West with weakness before the Soviet Union; now the West is too aggressive with Russia.

Solzhenitsyn's book on Russian Jewry is a peculiar one. For many years, he has had to face accusations of anti-Semitism. The reasons are complicated. His view of the world, shaped by an intense devotion to Russian patriotism, Russian suffering, and Russian Orthodoxy, is alien to many former dissidents, who have not hesitated to call him a hard-line nationalist, a tsarist, a Slavophile. What's more, an intellectual like the mathematician Igor Shafarevich, who had once been allied with Solzhenitsyn, is, inarguably, anti-Semitic. In the seventies, some third-rate critics seemed to encounter his books with an accountant's pencil, tallying "positive" and "negative" portraits of Jews, and sometimes found him wanting. Solzhenitsyn, in fact, is not anti-Semitic; his books are not anti-Semitic, and he is not, in his personal relations, anti-Jewish; Natalia's mother is Jewish, and not a few of his friends are, too. It is true, however, that, as a Russian patriot, Solzhenitsyn has written of "the incomparable sufferings of our people," and, as such, clearly does not believe in the uniqueness of Jewish suffering in the past two centuries or in the idea of the Jews as a symbol of persecution. Much of the new book is taken up with putting Jewish suffering into a wider context of Russian suffering; there is an insistent effort made to point out that the vast majority of the population, especially the serfs and then the peasantry, were deprived of their rights just like the Jews. Solzhenitsyn does not exactly deny the persecution of Jews—the pogroms, the restrictions on university admissions, the general prejudice—but there is also a tendency to highlight any exaggeration of tsarist oppression or to measure Jewish suffering against the sorry state of nearly all Russians. In his text, Solzhenitsyn often seems irritated that there is a "taboo" against discussing "the Jewish question," that one must either endorse certain notions of Jewish history and suffering or risk being branded a bigot. And yet, even as he describes and condemns the large number of Jews who took part in the revolutionary movement against the tsar, he is quick to disavow "conspiracies" and blames Russians and Russian failures—from the "arrogance of the nobility" to the "abandonment" of the peasantry—for the Revolutions of 1905 and 1917. "The highest circles of St. Petersburg nonetheless succumbed to the seductively simple explanation that Russia was in no way organically diseased, and that the whole Revolution was nothing but a vicious Jewish plot, part and parcel of the worldwide Judeo-Masonic conspiracy. There was one explanation for it all: the Jews!" he writes in *Two Hundred Years Together,* and goes on to say that, in fact, "it was our own Russian weaknesses that determined our sorry history's downward vector."

This is a serious subject with a gigantic literature, but it is puzzling that, at this point in his life, Solzhenitsyn decided to take on a two-volume history. Beyond his classics—*One Day in the Life of Ivan Denisovich* and the three volumes of *Gulag*—there are books in

Solzhenitsyn's oeuvre that are arguably dull or dated or minor but never tangential. *The Red Wheel* is marred by long, wooden passages and artificial-sounding dialogue, yet there is no doubt about its intent and ambition; Solzhenitsyn set out to write a cycle that would encompass nearly everything that led to the Russian Revolution. *Two Hundred Years Together* seems anomalous, not at all essential. He considers it a scholarly work and is quite proud that there are hundreds of footnotes. In fact, he ignores most contemporary scholarship. Could it possibly be that, at his age, he wanted to write this to rebuff the old attacks?

"For fifty-four years, I was working on *The Red Wheel*, from 1936 to 1990," Solzhenitsyn said. "And during that time I came across many facts and points of view about Russian history beginning in the nineteenth century until now. There were various themes I came across which were subsidiary to *The Red Wheel*. One of them, not the only one, was the theme of the common life of Russians and Jews. This theme would emerge now and then and become a topic of discussion in earlier years, so from decade to decade this theme has accompanied my work on *The Red Wheel*. I felt it should be treated in its way, but if I had included it in *The Red Wheel* it would have created a wrong accent. It would have looked like an attempt to explain the Revolution because of the interference of the Jews." He dismissed the idea that he was responding to "criticism."

"Criticism is a balanced judgment, and this wasn't that. In this case, there were just groundless, fantastical attacks, and I could only answer with surprise. Why was *Ivan Denisovich* accused of being anti-Semitic? Well, it's because one of the characters, Tsezar Markovich, worked in an office instead of laying bricks. The prototype of Tsezar Markovich, Lev Grossman, was a lifelong friend of mine. There was a lot of this rubbish."

Officially sanctioned anti-Semitism in Russia, for all its historical resonance—especially for the children and grandchildren of Russian-Jewish immigrants—has virtually disappeared. In his book and in conversation, Solzhenitsyn readily acknowledged the presence and persistence of anti-Semitism among many Russians, but he also was quick to add that he had felt the sting of anti-Russian prejudice. "There is a lot of it. Radio programs on Radio Liberty, where you would hear the most contemptible and denigrating programs—these were often Russian Jews, and Russians were spoken of as *Untermenschen*."

After a while, Solzhenitsyn seemed tired, and I turned the subject to perhaps the most painful one. I asked him if he thought that the new order of things in Russia had diminished his moral authority, and whether that might even be a good thing, as Lev Timofeyev had suggested.

Solzhenitsyn looked down at the table and thought this over awhile. Then he said, "I know from the many personal letters I still get that for many people I am a source of trust and moral authority. But I cannot really say if I am a moral authority or not. I do feel that for humanity— not society but for humanity—moral authority is a necessity. The course of world history and world culture shows us that there are, and should be, moral authorities. They constitute a kind of spiritual hierarchy which is absolutely necessary for every individual. In the twentieth century, the universal tendency, not only in the West but everywhere, was to destroy any hierarchies so that everyone could act just as he or she wants without regarding any moral authority. This has already been reflected in, and has influenced, the whole of world culture, and the level of world culture has been lowered as a result."

Solzhenitsyn let me know that my visit was drawing to a close.

"I'm not working with the old speed," he said. "My workday is different, because once or twice a day I stop to take a rest. I never used to do that. And in the evening I feel tired and go to bed fairly early. In the morning, I feel strong, but this strength doesn't last as long as it used to. It's hard to walk, even to stand. I have to use that cane over there. I have some problems with my spine, so even sitting is a problem now." One of the prose poems he has written since his return to Moscow is called "Growing Old":

> How much easier it is then, how much more receptive we are to death, when advancing years guide us softly to our end. Aging thus is in no sense a punishment from on high, but brings its own blessings and a warmth of colors all its own. . . . There is even warmth to be drawn from the waning of your own strength compared with the past—just to think how sturdy I once used to be! You can no longer get through a whole day's work at a stretch, but how good it is to slip into the brief oblivion of sleep, and what a gift to wake once more to the clarity of your second or third morning of the day. And your spirit can find delight in limiting your intake of food, in abandoning the pursuit of novel flavors. You are still of this life, yet you are rising above the material plane. . . . Growing old serenely is not a downhill path but an ascent.

When he was a younger man, always under assault from the authorities, Solzhenitsyn used to take breaks and pace, like an infantryman, back and forth, in the woods. He viewed his writing life as a war waged against tyranny, and he viewed himself, he always said, as a soldier. And so I asked him now if he still saw himself that way, as a soldier in writer's clothing. Solzhenitsyn smiled, something he does not do very often or easily with visitors.

"No," he said. "It doesn't feel like that any longer." Then we said our goodbyes, and he slowly got out of his chair, took up his cane, and went to another room to lie down.

(2001)

The Last Tsar

In the late-decadent period of the Soviet regime, when the Communist Party was ruled by a succession of half-dead men in half-lit hospitals, a youngish customs inspector named Oleg Vasiliyevich Filatov woke on a summer morning as the heir of shoemakers and schoolteachers but finished the day convinced that he was the heir to the imperial dynasty of the Romanovs. Time has only hardened Filatov's conviction that one day the Russian people will recognize the truth and crown him Tsar of All the Russias.

This was in the summer of 1983. Filatov was working at Pulkovo Airport, the main Leningrad airport. For a salary of a hundred and thirty rubles a month, he searched commercial shipments for narcotics and illegal currency; he went through the suitcases of foreign tourists with an eye out for pornography (on the way in) and icons (on the way out).

Filatov lived in a modest apartment on the edge of town. He was thirty years old. He had recently married, and to introduce his bride to his parents and siblings he flew south with her to Astrakhan, a city on the

Caspian Sea famous for its sturgeon and caviar. Filatov's parents, after living for many years in the cold of the north of Russia, had retired to a village near Astrakhan where they lived in a small house surrounded by a garden and fruit trees—cherry trees, peach trees, apricot trees. Members of the family were coming to the reunion from all directions.

Oleg especially looked forward to seeing his father, Vasily, who had reared his children on a rich diet of classical music, Russian theater, and exquisite manners. Oleg also cherished a certain mystery in his father. He revered the old man, and yet he felt that there was, within him, a secret, a history, that he could not quite reach. Vasily Filatov had told his children that he was born in Shadrinsk, a small city in the Urals, where his father repaired shoes. Vasily's health had always been miserable. The Soviet Army had declared him the equivalent of 4-F. He suffered from heart problems, hardening of the arteries, severe back pain, and much more.

Once, while the family was living in Orenburg, Vasily took Oleg fishing; Oleg was ten. "When he took his shirt off I saw scars on his back, and I poked at them and asked him what they were from," Filatov told me one morning over tea. "The scars were two, three, four centimeters long. He moved with great difficulty. His right foot was bigger than his left and he had two ribs missing, and there was a deep scar on his left arm. When I asked him how he got that way, he said, 'There was a revolution, and people killed and hurt each other. There was a war over property. There were bad people. And these are the scars.' If he nicked himself working in the garden, his legs would swell and ache. He'd have to stay in bed for a week. He prayed all the time. He played chess with himself as a way to deal with the pain. He was always on special diets. My mother brought him meat, and he ate it raw. Sometimes he drank bull's blood. He ate all kinds of herbs and nettles. Until 1975, he would never see a doctor. I realized early on that my father was not like other people."

Vasily was in his seventies, and, considering the state of his health, his children—Oleg and two daughters—were delighted to see that he was in a fine mood. One afternoon, in the midst of the reunion, the Filatov family gathered in the garden. It was sunny and there was a warm breeze blowing through the fruit trees. Everyone sat drinking tea in the Russian style, with sugar and jam.

As a way to get a conversation going with his new daughter-in-law, Anjelica, Vasily asked her about her family. She was from St. Petersburg, she said, and before the Revolution members of her family made embroidery for the royal family.

Vasily then began to tell her something about his own family, saying that his family name, Filatov, was Greek—derived from Filaret, the name of a patriarch of the Orthodox Church in the seventeenth century. Vasily rarely spoke in the first person, but, for some reason, he did so now. He talked about being an orphan of the Civil War, about how his mother had been executed "because she loved Chopin's waltzes," and how his father had died of consumption, shortly after the First World War. The family members inched their chairs closer, for they had never heard Vasily speak so frankly and in such detail about the past. Then he said that he had been left homeless as a boy, wandering the dismal orphanages of middle Russia.

"Gorky already wrote about the life I led," Vasily said. "And that's how it went, more or less."

Some months later, at another family meeting, Vasily went on to tell his story from a different angle. He began to describe the Ipatiev House, the private house in the Urals city of Ekaterinburg where the Bolshevik secret police kept the imperial family under guard in 1918. Sometime after midnight on July 17, 1918, the police woke the Romanovs and their few remaining retainers and shot them all dead. Lenin had decided that he had best not provide the Whites—the opposition in the ongoing Civil War—with a symbol.

As it happened, Vasily said, "not everyone" had been killed that night at the Ipatiev House—in fact, Alexis, the son of the Tsar, had survived and had been piled onto a truck with the corpses. Clearly, the executioners thought they had killed everyone, but the boy regained consciousness. It was raining. The truck stopped near a pond, and the guards began to unload their cargo. Before they could get to Alexis, the boy—thirteen years old, and a hemophiliac, who had been so sick in recent months that his father had to carry him from room to room—crept away from the truck and hid. Out of sight, he found a railroad track, and on his knees he crawled more than three miles to a railway station. But there he came across four guards. They seized him, threw him into a shallow pit, stabbed him with bayonets, and left him for dead. Later, two other guards, the brothers Andrei and Alexei Strekotin, found Alexis, and they were kind to him. The Strekotin brothers had known Alexis at the Ipatiev House, and they helped the boy escape. He was then taken to Shadrinsk, two hundred kilometers from Ekaterinburg. There a man named Mikhail Gladkikh took him to his sister's family.

. . .

Oleg Filatov understood well what his father was telling him: Alexis was his father.

"This family had had a son who had died of influenza," Oleg said to me. "And so they gave my father the name of the dead son, Vasily Filatov. For two months, Alexis lived as a peasant boy, and his terrible wounds slowly healed. Surely he was the only boy around who spoke fluent French, German, and English, as well as Russian, and was beautifully schooled in music, literature, and theater. Eventually, Gladkikh began moving Alexis around the country, the better to keep him away from the advancing Red Army, which was slowly overwhelming the Whites. He took him to the city of Surgut, where he was treated for his hemorrhaging and malnutrition. They cured him, using raw walrus meat for the bleeding, and they fed him deer meat, frozen fish cut in thin slices, and tinctures of pine trees."

By early 1921, Alexis—now Vasily—was on his own, moving around Russia from orphanage to orphanage with extraordinary speed and stealth. Between 1921 and 1930, he lived in Yalta, Baku, Magnitogorsk, Nizhny Novgorod, Kostroma, Yaroslavl, Tula, Kaluga, Moscow, Batumi, and Tbilisi. He was in such constant motion that he left behind almost no records of his childhood. These were still the early years of Soviet power, and the levels of police control and restricted movement which would become characteristic of Stalinism were not well established. The Soviet Union was still a disorganized and permeable construct. Not until 1930, when Vasily seems to have shown up in the oil region of Tyumen and begun studying to be a teacher, did his life become an established fact, registered officially in the Soviet bureaucracy. Vasily lived in the Tyumen region until 1967, when he and his wife moved to Orenburg; they retired to Astrakhan in 1970. "Does it make any sense to tell you how stunned we all were?" Oleg said. The family's urge to tell their father's story was overwhelmed only by the more powerful impulse toward self-protection.

"There was no repeating it, no blabbing," Oleg said. "People could die as a result. We had to protect ourselves and protect his rescuers if they were still alive. We didn't know if we'd be sent to prison or to psychiatric hospitals. . . . After he told us that one time, he never repeated it. He told me, 'Only madmen talk about this twice.' He was my father, how could I not believe it? And how could I check it out in a book or look into it? This was the Soviet system—a repressive, closed system."

Mikhail Gorbachev came to power in March of 1985, and not long afterward, under the liberal policy of glasnost, it became possible to write or talk more freely about the history of Russia and the Soviet Union. Publications such as *Moscow News, Ogonyok,* and *Literaturnaya Gazeta* began to print details about pre-Revolutionary Russia, including the captivity and execution of the Romanovs. But the Tsarevich would not live to see his story recognized.

On October 24, 1988, Vasily Filatov died of heart failure. "Only his eyes signaled his pain and my heart was torn to pieces," his wife, Lidia, wrote later. "I couldn't help him. He was dead before the ambulance came." Vasily Filatov was buried outside Astrakhan.

"My family got together, and we agreed that we would slowly begin telling his—our—story," Oleg Filatov, who is now in his mid-forties, said. "Today I can talk about it. But even now I can't say everything."

On July 17, Russia will hold the first royal burial ceremony since the death of Alexander III, in 1894. After eighty years of mystery and scandal, scientists have determined that a cache of bones found outside Ekaterinburg in 1979, and excavated twelve years later, are in fact the remains of Nicholas II and his family. There are two bodies missing, those of Alexis and one of the daughters—most likely Maria. The investigators believe that the execution team probably burned those two corpses down to ash, but, feeling that their time was limited, they merely buried the rest.

The ceremony will be as strange and as improvised as any other ritual in the new Russia. Some members of the extended Romanov family who have been living in France, Spain, and other foreign countries are expected to fly to Ekaterinburg (named Sverdlovsk by the Soviets) for a "farewell" ceremony. In mid-July, the bones, accompanied by the Romanov relatives and officials from the Russian government, will be flown to St. Petersburg. The relics will be transported from Pulkovo Airport in a kind of funeral cortège to the Peter and Paul Fortress, which Peter the Great founded in 1703, along with the city. The Fortress, a brick pile on the banks of the Neva, was used as a military outpost and as a prison by the tsars. Lenin's brother, Aleksandr Ulyanov, was imprisoned there after he took part in a plot to kill Alexander III. Elsewhere in the Fortress is a cathedral where generations of Romanovs are buried.

One afternoon, I went with Oleg Filatov to the cathedral to visit the dead he calls his forebears. Filatov's hair and beard are blond, nearly white-blond, the color of summer-bleached wheat, and his beard and mustache are trimmed in a way that evokes none other than Nicholas II.

His eyes are pale blue, backlit, like a Siberian wolfhound's, and he suffers from a condition that makes his eyes quiver in their sockets. He
wore a light polyester suit and carried a briefcase. When we first met and
I asked even the most politely doubting questions, he turned steely
and unpleasant ("So don't believe me! What difference is it to me!"),
but after just an hour or so he proved good-humored, to say nothing of
lucid.

"Doubt is the first step toward reason, even in me," he said after
he'd become more accustomed to my questions. "Of course, I have
doubts. How could I not have doubts? My wife, that first time she saw
my father, didn't say anything. My mother-in-law reacted by calling him
a saint. What can I say? If we learned that my father told the truth, we'd
be the happiest people on earth."

Since the fall of Communism, in 1991, Leningrad has been renamed
St. Petersburg, as it was known when the tsars were still in power. As is
appropriate to the mercenary times, Filatov now works in a bank, though
he is by no stretch a member of the privileged tribe of "new Russians."
He still lives in a small apartment. And yet when Filatov takes buses
and trains to the city center, when he passes by the old Winter Palace,
or when he visits the tombs, he does so with a preternatural sense of
ownership.

As we entered the Fortress, we saw sunbathers standing flat against
the brick. Very few bothered with what one normally calls a bathing suit.
The women wore fantastic foundation garments—industrial foundation
garments—and the men, no matter how fat, wore tiny nylon underpants.
Everyone's skin was the color of soap. It had been a long, gray winter,
and now the weather was glorious. The mosquitoes were out. People sat
on the grass eating homemade sandwiches and drinking bottles of German and Danish beer.

"Peter and Paul, this is a sacred place, a place to go and meditate, to
ponder yourself," Filatov said as we entered the gates.

We passed the commandant's house, the prison, and several smaller
buildings before coming to the whitewashed cathedral.

"This is the building where all the tsars' families are buried," Filatov
said. "The family church is Kazan Cathedral, on Nevsky Prospekt—that
was a museum of atheism for years—but this is the burial place."

We put a few rubles in a collection jar and stepped inside a cool,
vaulted transept, with a stone floor; all around, in no discernible pattern,
were the white marble and jasper tombs of the Romanovs: Catherine the
Great, Peter III, Anna Ionovna, Peter the Great. We stood for a while in

silence near the tomb of Nicholas's father, Alexander III. A group of German tourists milled around us; they were led by a stout woman holding aloft a long stick with a red ribbon tied around it.

"It must be strange to come to this place and believe that this is your family cemetery," I said.

"It's no longer strange," Filatov said. "This is what my life is."

Filatov led me down a hall and into the area of the cathedral where the burial ceremony is scheduled to take place. The chapel was blocked off by a makeshift white gate. Filatov peeked through a crack in the gate.

"If they made a mistake in identifying the remains, I don't know what will happen," he said. "I'm afraid they are mistaken and these aren't even the true remains. And where are the other two bodies? What are they actually putting into these graves?"

We walked back near the tombs. Oleg was quiet for a long time, and then he started talking about money. He said there were "huge" accounts abroad: twenty-seven billion dollars in the United States, he guessed, six billion in a bank in Tokyo—all money that belongs, by rights, to the Romanov family.

"Nicholas was allocating funds for the First World War to buy arms, and the deal was that if the arms did not come the money would be returned," he said. "The money was just kept there accumulating high interest."

"Do you think about the money becoming yours?" I said.

"If the courts certify that I'm the person and they have to pay the money—well, I don't think about this much. This has to be proved on a state level."

We left the cathedral and passed a man carrying a monarchist placard. He walked right past Filatov.

"I've met with some monarchists in town, but I'm afraid a lot of them are just clowns," Filatov said.

That was the striking thing about Filatov: for a man who felt in his heart that the crown of the tsars was due him, he did not appear to be one of those whacked-out souls who are convinced that they are the President of Freedonia or the King of Lilliput. Rather, his carriage was more like that of someone who thought that his father and he had both been passed over for the general manager's slot at the Red October concrete plant, but that one day justice would prevail.

"For now, my name is Oleg Filatov," he said. "Why should I go around calling myself Romanov? If and when the people decide I am a Romanov, then I'll be Romanov."

On the way out, we saw a crowd of about a hundred people watching a group of mimes perform the sort of absurdist drama that one might have seen many summers ago in Greenwich Village. Three young men in prison outfits pranced around with marionette cockroaches while a woman dressed in a witch's outfit tried to hit the bugs with a gigantic loaf of rye bread. As it turned out, this was part of a festival in honor of Daniil Kharms, a comic writer of the early Soviet period whose specialties were children's poetry and anarchic miniatures called *sluchai,* or incidents. Filatov stood a while with the crowd and watched the crone smack the roaches with her loaf.

"Let's go home," the Tsar said. "I think I've had enough."

The revolution that Gorbachev ignited in the late eighties was, to a great degree, a recovery of the past, a reevaluation of Russian and Soviet history, which began with an assessment of the Stalin era and worked its way back toward 1917. When I was living in Moscow during that period, I'd pick up every magazine and search it for historical reassessments— history was the news—and one of the most astonishing moments came when a playwright and historian named Edvard Radzinsky published the written testimony of Yakov Yurovsky, the secret-police officer in Ekaterinburg who was charged with killing the imperial family. The Yurovsky "note," as it is called, had been buried in the Soviet archives for seven decades until Radzinsky, who was doing research for a book on Nicholas II, published it in the May 19, 1989, issue of *Ogonyok.*

The little that had been written about the execution of the Tsar in Soviet textbooks made the event seem ordinary, benign, an inevitable outcome of all popular revolutions. The fact is, though, that the way in which the Bolsheviks went about the execution said a great deal about them and the violent regime they were establishing. Richard Pipes, in his history of the Revolution, notes that before the Russian Revolution two other European monarchs were killed in revolutionary upheavals: Charles I, of Great Britain, in 1649; and Louis XVI, of France, in 1793. Charles was tried by a specially constituted High Court of Justice, which allowed the King a defense. The execution took place in full view of the public. Louis XVI was tried before the Convention, which sentenced him to death by majority vote only after a prolonged debate. The King had his own counsel, and his execution, too, was carried out in front of the public—a daytime beheading in central Paris.

Without romanticizing these earlier events, it is fair to say that the

Bolsheviks took an entirely different course—one far more secretive and brutal. Nicholas, of course, resigned his office in the face of the February revolution and was exiled with his family to Tobolsk by Aleksandr Kerensky's provisional government. After Lenin ousted Kerensky, the Bolsheviks took custody of the imperial family and kept them under a kind of listless house arrest. Alexis's diary from January 1918 reveals a schedule of aimless amusement and nervous waiting:

1/6/18

Got up at 7. Had tea with Papa, Tatiana, and Anastasia. We played cards. Maria is dressed and walking around the rooms. At 6 o'clock we played hide and seek and shouted and made a terrible noise.

1/7/18

The whole day was just like yesterday.

1/9/18

The whole day was just like yesterday.

Then, in March 1918, the Bolsheviks moved the Romanovs to Ekaterinburg, and the family was set up in the house of Nikolai Ipatiev, a retired Army engineer. The house, a white two-story structure, was quickly converted into a prison, with an improvised palisade and a round-the-clock seventy-five-man guard. At first, according to Pipes, Nicholas and his family were still permitted to drift through their days: they rose at nine, took tea at ten, lunch at one, dinner between four and five, tea at seven and supper at nine, and went to sleep at eleven; there was lots of reading and praying; when the weather was fair, Nicholas would carry the sickly Tsarevich, Alexis, to the garden, where they would play a game of bezique or the Russian version of backgammon, called trictrac. Occasionally, a local priest was allowed to visit the family to lead them in prayer.

Back in the capital, Lenin, Trotsky, and the rest of the Bolshevik leaders tried to figure out what to do with the Romanovs. Trotsky proposed a trial, but Lenin never acted on the suggestion. Fearing a wave of White troops in Ekaterinburg, Lenin felt the need to act sooner rather than later. By July, Yurovsky had taken charge of the Romanovs. His orders were clear. Yurovsky scouted possible burial places in the area around Ekaterinburg and found some abandoned mine shafts in the nearby village of Koptyaki. He assembled an execution team and a sufficient cache of arms.

On July 17, shortly after midnight, Yurovsky woke the Romanov family's doctor, Yevgeny Botkin, and told him to wake the others, have them dress, and go to the basement. Yurovsky told Botkin that there was unrest in the streets of Ekaterinburg and this was a safety measure. At around two, the family, as well the doctor, the cook, a maid, a valet, and the girls' King Charles spaniel, Jemmy, came down the stairs. The Tsar led the way, carrying his son; Nicholas and Alexis wore field shirts and forage caps. Then came Alexandra and her four daughters. They all wore dresses. Two chairs were brought into the basement—one for Alexandra and one for Alexis. A detachment of executioners armed with revolvers was waiting in a small room next door.

"When the party entered," Yurovsky wrote, "I told the Romanovs that in view of the fact that their relatives continued their offensive against Soviet Russia, the Executive Committee of the Urals Soviet had decided to shoot them. Nicholas turned his back to the detachment and faced his family. Then, as if collecting himself, he turned around, asking, 'What? What?' [I] rapidly repeated what I had said and ordered the detachment to prepare. Its members had been previously instructed whom to shoot and to aim directly at the heart to avoid much blood and to end more quickly. Nicholas said no more. He turned again toward his family. The others shouted some incoherent exclamations. All this lasted a few seconds. Then commenced the shooting, which went on for two or three minutes. [I] killed Nicholas on the spot."

According to witnesses' accounts, bullets ricocheted everywhere—some deflected by corsets worn by the daughters which had jewels sewn inside them. Finally, the soldiers stopped shooting and inspected the bodies. They noticed that some were still breathing, and those that showed a trace of life were shot in the head, point-blank, or stabbed. Yurovsky recalled that he himself shot Alexis in the head twice.

The corpses were loaded onto a truck. Almost a day passed before the burial party at last put the bodies in a ditch by the side of the road. One of the guards later boasted that he could "die in peace because he had squeezed the Empress's ———."

"The bodies were put in the hole," Yurovsky wrote, "and the faces and all the bodies generally doused with sulfuric acid, both so they couldn't be recognized and to prevent any stink from them rotting. . . . We scattered it with branches and lime, put boards on top, and drove over it several times—no traces of the hole remained. The secret was kept." The Romanov dynasty, which had begun with the election of Mikhail Romanov as Tsar on February 21, 1613, had come to an end.

"The decision was not only expedient but necessary," Trotsky wrote in his diary years later. "The severity of this punishment showed everyone that we would continue to fight on mercilessly, stopping at nothing."

Six weeks after the executions, the Bolsheviks began their campaign of fierce and random cruelty against enemies real and imagined. The campaign would come to be called the Red Terror.

The Bolsheviks hid the truth about the executions, not because they had a sudden attack of moist moralism but, rather, because they wanted to sidetrack their opponents, to keep any enemies still harboring thoughts of monarchist restoration in a state of confusion. It would be better to keep them guessing about the status of the Romanov family.

The Bolsheviks did announce almost immediately that Nicholas had been killed. Lenin ordered reports to be published in *Pravda* and *Izvestia,* and by July 22, 1918, the news was appearing in European and American papers that the Tsar had been shot because "a counterrevolutionary conspiracy" to free him had been uncovered.

Those same reports, however, said that the other members of the family had been sent to a "place of security." The Bolsheviks sustained this myth for nine years. The disinformation effort was so thorough that even the most expert foreign intelligence officers and diplomats could not unmask it. Sir Charles Eliot, the British high commissioner for Siberia, went to Ekaterinburg and filed a report to Foreign Secretary Arthur Balfour, in London, saying that on July 17 "a train with the blinds down" had left Ekaterinburg and "it is believed" that the surviving members of the family were on it.

All in all, it was a brilliant deception, one that even the Romanov relatives in European exile believed. In 1920, the White investigator Nikolai Sokolov came to Western Europe with a box containing small bits of bone, blood-soaked soil, and two small bottles of congealed fat—which he said were the remains of the Tsar. They have never been scientifically tested; they are kept at the Russian Orthodox Church of St. Job in Brussels, "in Memory of the Martyred Tsar Nicholas II and His Family." In 1924, when Sokolov published a report, entitled "Judicial Enquiry into the Assassination of the Russian Imperial Family," declaring that everyone had been killed and all the bodies completely destroyed by acid and fire, the Romanovs still refused to accept the news.

Nearly from the instant of the execution of the Romanovs to the present day, there have been reports of one or another member of the family who escaped the slaughter. The history of fraud is long and populous and never seems to stop growing. Not long ago, a friend in Moscow sent me a copy of an article in the historical journal *Istochnik* ("Source"), about a young Siberian peasant named Aleksei Shitov, who, in the early twenties, had become convinced by a group of people that he was, in fact, Alexis. Shitov was not a hemophiliac, nor had he the slightest notion that he was from the imperial family, but somehow he came to believe in his royal origins. Eventually, the local secret police arrested Shitov and his "followers"; some were executed and others were sentenced to long prison terms.

Although there have been many would-be Romanovs in Russia, there have been even more abroad. In the twenties, the émigré press and White Russian circles in Western Europe percolated with rumors that Nicholas or Alexis or one or another of the daughters was hiding out somewhere. In 1920, there was a sighting of the Tsar in London, his hair now white. Then there were rumors of Nicholas hiding out in the Vatican, of the entire family on a ship in the White Sea, sailing eternally to and fro, never coming to land. And there was the self-proclaimed Anastasia, who was seen in Siberia trying to get to China. She was arrested and sent to various prisons and camps in Russia. In 1934, she wrote letters from a prison hospital in Kazan to the Romanovs' English relative King George V, appealing to him, in French and German, to come to her aid. When she died, in 1971, the head of the hospital wrote that "except for her claim that she was Anastasia she was completely sane." Robert Massie's excellent book *The Romanovs: The Final Chapter* is filled with such colorful tales, including the epic story of the most successful of all the Anastasia impostors, Anna Andersen, a wily Polish-born loon whose career as a claimant began with a suicide attempt in Germany shortly after the execution of the Romanovs and continued with a magical transformation into Anastasia in a mental hospital. Andersen managed to sponge off half the royalty in Europe. And then there was the clubbable gent in Arizona whose success with the lonely women of Scottsdale was not at all diminished by his insistence that he was Alexis Romanov. Mr. Romanov never seemed to suffer a moment's problem with his hemophilia; he even played polo without overmuch fear of the mallet. He also marketed a line of vodka.

In Moscow, I met with Edvard Radzinsky, whose books on the Tsar and on Stalin, along with countless appearances on television, have turned him into one of the biggest celebrities of the post-Soviet period. He lives in the Aeroport section of Moscow, a neighborhood that had largely been the province of the Writers' Union. Radzinsky is a friendly fellow who has been made absolutely radiant by his fame and fortune. (His book *The Last Tsar: The Life and Death of Nicholas II* was a best-seller in the United States for Doubleday; Jacqueline Kennedy Onassis was his editor.) When he greeted me at the door, he was accompanied by a beautifully groomed Borzoi roughly the size of a pony. His study is furnished with heavy Russian antiques, expensive prints, and a computer. After he showed me the memorabilia of his success—the foreign editions of his books, newspaper clippings attesting to the top ratings of his television documentaries—he settled down in an armchair to tell me about his own experience of living Romanovs.

"After I published the Yurovsky note in *Ogonyok*, in 1989, I got constant phone calls," Radzinsky said. "This was a time when people in the Metro were poring over *Ogonyok*, the period of first truths, and I got non-stop calls and letters by the thousand. One day a woman called. She sounded nervous. I invited her to my house. She came and told me that the Yurovsky note was a mistake, that all the Romanov daughters had survived the executions. She offered to show me their graves. I was shocked. My book on Nicholas II was ready. I had eyewitness reports of the execution from seven different people who took part in the shooting. They were testimonies that had been taken in different places and at different times. But she said, 'I'll show you the graves.'

"So we went on a long trip to the Orenburg region. Once we were there, we had to continue on by horse to a tiny village. I'd stopped all my work to do this. She was about forty, forty-five. She said she hadn't seen the graves herself, but her relatives had. She told an incredible story: after the executions, three girls soon appeared in this village, and then a fourth. Anastasia, she said, had come last and separately. She took me to the cemetery in this village, and there were graves marked for Tatiana, Maria, Olga, and Anastasia Romanova, with their real historical birth-dates and then dates of death, all in the early nineteen-sixties. The people in the village told me that the girls had come and had hidden in basements there and were protected. No one betrayed them, even though they lived through Stalin's time! This was a real achievement, like keeping Anne Frank alive. Then, after Stalin died"—in 1953—"they lived outside the basements, aboveground. A priest who was priest for three or four villages also helped them. His church was used partly for worship and partly to store potatoes. The girls lived in secret and wore dark clothes for many years, because they were mourning the deaths of Alexis, the Tsar, and their mother, Alexandra. The girls never explained to anyone how they survived, and they told the priest only that they were the Tsar's daughters.

"I believed it! I decided that it was a great secret. But when I returned to Moscow that changed. Now I got a call from Sukhumi from someone saying he was Alexis's son and that Alexis was still alive. Strange: he had a Georgian accent. He invited me to Sukhumi. But then I got a letter from Kalinin from a woman who wanted to give me some documents. She told me she was the great-granddaughter of Nicholas II and her mother was dying in Kalinin and wanted to see me. So I went. I saw this ancient woman who said she was Olga: she was old and wrinkly and had dead eyes, but when she talked about her life in Tsarskoye Selo her eyes shone. She said she had no memory of the executions, that she had lost consciousness. But she was saved by one of the executioners. She showed me the wounds in her side. But, unfortunately, I'd already seen Olga in her grave!

"Then I got letters about a story of Alexis ending up in the Gulag. I believed—well, not belief, exactly. The others had no documents. I got a letter from a hospital in Petrozovodsk. He'd been in the Gulag and had been moved to a hospital. They found traces of hemophilia and an unde-scended testicle, which is rare, and he knew a lot about Tsarskoye Selo. The key thing with Alexis is that the body has still not been found. There is no trace. So the story of Alexis raises suspicion. So I really began to hesitate about this man. Now, though, I don't believe it."

What once caused Radzinsky a great deal of anxiety and doubt now amuses him. Even today, he routinely gets letters from around the world: an Alexis in Australia who drives a bus, a grave of Alexis in Miami, another grave somewhere in Canada.

"Gorbachev told me that when he was in power he even got letters from Cuba about would-be royalty," Radzinsky said. "Before, it wasn't a matter of money. It was a form of madness. Here in Russia, we had no way of knowing about Anna Andersen or the Greta Garbo movie about Anastasia. People wanted a miracle, a fairy tale. So these rumors are out of control, as they were at the time of the 'false Dmitri' who pretended to the throne in the seventeenth century. We are a country of impostors. It's deep in the Russian soul.

"Now Russia is a country of scandals. This had been a very boring society before, and now we are full of sensationalism. People want their share of attention. All the letters begin, 'My name is Romanov, and I have begun to think that I am a descendant of the Tsar.' "

When I went to see an investigator at the Russian Procurator's Office in Moscow, he mentioned that "an odd guy" named Nikolai Dalsky had called, claiming that he was Nicholas III. He went by the name Nikolai Dalsky-Romanov.

Dalsky, as I'll call him until history proves otherwise, asked me to meet him at his rather grand-sounding Institute for New Thinking. The institute, it transpired, was a walkup in a garbage-strewn courtyard. When I arrived, I asked for Comrade Romanov, and a plump cleaning woman rolled her eyes and pointed down a hallway.

Dalsky did not disappoint. He wore a dark military uniform with epaulets. His tie clasp was in the shape of an imperial double eagle. He wore tinted aviator glasses and had a fiercely trimmed mustache and a nice head of hair. His office was decorated as a Tsar-in-waiting's should be: an official portrait of Dalsky and his wife, Natalia, in full royal gear against the background of a leopard-skin rug; a Tibetan scroll; a Russian flag; a small portrait of Nicholas II; candles; plastic flowers; and a picture of a pulchritudinous pop star called Anastasia. Dalsky was flanked by some strange-looking men, including a self-proclaimed duke with a ponytail, who deferred to him as if he were nothing less than the person he claimed to be.

"We are tolerant of all information about us even if it's twisted," Dalsky informed me. "We never sue."

Immensely relieved, I was ready to begin our talk, but what actually began was his opening aria, which went on for quite a while. "No one was shot in the Ipatiev House. The execution was staged, and we don't really know who was executed there," Dalsky said. "The Emperor and the Empress and their children were put in mental institutions. Or that can't be ruled out. They were kept there, died there, and their remains were put in a collective grave. This is not ruled out. . . . My father, Alexis, died in 1965 of a massive hemorrhage that began near his heart. Before that, he had episodes of hemorrhaging but not like those when he was young. Tibetan medicine helped him get over his hemophilia, not Rasputin, as everyone thinks."

Dalsky showed me a snapshot of his "coronation," which he said took place on December 19, 1996, in a cathedral in Noginsk. His wife was crowned Tsarina.

"We talked with God," he said, "and followed the church bells with two metropolitans and a bishop. There were representatives of the people there, too, and a procession with a cross. I am the spiritual presence of Russia."

When I asked him if he was getting ready to live in the Kremlin, he said, "Live in the Kremlin? Well, I would not want to outrun events. But

I won't make a secret of the stakes and my qualifications. I'm well educated. I can name every city in America. I can tell you the regions they have there, the foreign policy. And this is a rare thing." He also claimed to speak English and all the major European languages.

"Do you speak Italian?"

"*Parlare.*"

"English?"

"I yes understand."

"*Parlez-vous français?*"

"*Si.*"

As I was getting ready to go, I asked Dalsky if he knew that other son of Alexis Romanov's—Oleg Filatov, of St. Petersburg.

"We've studied Filatov's materials, and we've concluded that he is masterminded by the special services," Dalsky said. "He has nothing to do with the Tsar's family."

"You know," I said, "I have to tell you that you really don't look much like your grandfather Nicholas II."

"No, it's true," Dalsky said. "I don't look like Nicholas. But I'm the spitting image of Alexandra."

Neither Dalsky nor Filatov will attend the burial of the Romanov bones on July 17th. Nor will Alexy II, the Patriarch of the Russian Orthodox Church. And, since the Patriarch and the Church hierarchy are not taking part, Boris Yeltsin, who craves the Church's political support, will also keep his distance. The reason for their nonattendance tells a great deal about the new Russian state and its profound crisis of identity.

To begin, there is no reasonable doubt that the remains being shipped from Ekaterinburg to St. Petersburg are those of the imperial family. That much has been established by two genetic testing sessions, in England and the United States. The investigation has been led by a government-appointed commission that includes members of the government and the Russian legislature, scientists, an archaeologist, a criminal investigator, the head of the state archives, and Metropolitan Juvenaly, a subordinate of the Patriarch.

The Church has decided neither to endorse nor to denounce entirely the commission's findings. "It's like playing a game of heads and tails and calling 'Edge,' " said Vladimir Solovyov, the investigator from the Russian state prosecutor's office who has been on the commission from the start. "They won't deny that the genetic tests tell us beyond a shadow of a doubt that the bones are the Romanovs, but they do keep saying, 'Well, look at science in the nineteenth or eighteenth centuries. It was all overturned.' "

Pavel Ivanov, the chief geneticist on the panel, said, "The church people told me, 'We've waited seventy-odd years, and if you're not one hundred percent sure, then we can wait another seventy years.' If you say it's ninety-nine-point-nine-hundred-and-ninety-nine percent certain, it's not enough for them. And as for two missing bodies, we can't say anything about them. Maybe they were killed and burned. It takes a long time to burn a corpse down to nothing, and the burial team did not have unlimited time. They didn't have enough gasoline, and the gas burns off quickly. So they refused to burn them all. There was no time."

The Russian Orthodox Church is an especially conservative church, filled with clerics dubious of science and of modernity in general, but its position is even more complicated than that. The Church, which was undermined and infiltrated by KGB informers under Soviet rule, does not want to contradict too starkly the Orthodox Church Abroad, which has already canonized Nicholas and maintains that the July ceremony is a travesty. The Patriarch in Moscow has announced that he will send no representatives to the ceremony at Peter and Paul, and it is likely that only some local clerics will appear.

The Church's tactics have led to some bewildering behavior in the government. Yeltsin is no monarchist, of course, but for years he has tried to expropriate for himself and for the fledgling state the grandeur of the Tsarist past. He enjoys being called Tsar Boris by his aides in private, and would have loved to come to St. Petersburg for a grand burial ceremony. Such a ceremony would seem to Yeltsin almost like a coronation of himself, a passing of the torch after an eight-decade-long Communist interregnum. Yeltsin would also like to relieve a burden of guilt: in 1977, when he was the Sverdlovsk Party leader, he was put in charge of destroying the Ipatiev House. But without the Patriarch Yeltsin simply cannot go. He cannot afford to be out of synch with the one institution in the country that symbolizes Russianness at a deep level for tens of millions of people. And so the burial ceremony will be far less grand than originally planned, and many groups that were going to attend, such as the Russian Noble Assembly, will probably stay home.

In the meantime, some of the more extremist opponents of the ceremony are accusing scientists like Ivanov, the geneticist, of participating in a Judeo-Masonic-Bolshevik plot against Mother Russia that began with the overthrow of the Tsar in 1917. Among the chief doubters are

Vladimir Osipov, a writer for a right-wing nationalist journal called *Moskva*, and a former dissident who was arrested and imprisoned for his Christian activism in the sixties and seventies. I met Osipov after we both attended a press conference given by various members of the commission in Moscow. Sitting off in a corner of the conference hall, Osipov said that the burial ceremony was the last step in "an ongoing plot" to destroy once and for all Russia's "innate path of development"—namely, monarchy.

"Ivanov is probably not a Chekist, just an ambitious professional," Osipov said, "but it all looks like a plot. Nicholas was a symbol of the state, and his abdication was pointless, crazy. They killed the Tsar of a great state, a great power. There are witnesses that the head of Nicholas II was taken to the Kremlin as proof of his execution! We know that Trotsky was shown this head as proof. The subject is almost mystical in character."

Then what, I asked, is behind the plot?

Osipov adopted the nodding of a sage. "One cannot rule out the idea that Yeltsin wants to get his hands on the Romanov money," he said.

In fact, money is an issue: the new tomb will be made not of marble but, rather, of wood covered with "marble pattern" paper. The writer Gely Ryabov, who was instrumental in uncovering the bones in the first place, said that perhaps the Yeltsin Administration should sell off one of its Mercedes limousines and buy a real marble tomb, to provide the Romanovs a decent burial.

What a confused and confusing place Russia is! This depressing spectacle—the seriocomic parade of pretenders, the implacable doubt about government motive and scientific result—goes back to hundreds of years of obscurantism and the lethal reign of history-obliterating Communism.

"Of course they're the real bones," Radzinsky told me. "But this is a typical Russian story. It's impossible to do anything serious correctly in Russia. Everything is about politics and delay. We are unable to make normal, legal decisions. This burial should unite the country, and instead ends up dividing it. People are suspicious of anything done by the government, even a DNA test. Pavel Ivanov says these are the real bones of the Tsar, and yet intelligent people on the street still come up to me and, conspiratorially, they pull me over and whisper, 'Edvard, are these really the bones of the Tsar?' "

Vladimir Solovyov, the chief investigator, said ruefully that all the confusion is heightened because the execution of the Romanovs was the "point between the old Russia and the new Russia, an event that defines everyone: the Church, the Church's relations with the people, the Bolsheviks. All this goes back to the question Who are we? It may not be important to the average man on the street, but it is essential to intellectuals, patriots of a certain kind, royalists. But now we are ending in confusion, with no resolution. On July seventeenth, in St. Petersburg, we'll have something new: the Tomb of the Unknown Tsar."

But what about Oleg Filatov? I couldn't help thinking that his best claim to the throne of the Romanovs was his beard (which really had a fine shape to it, very much like that of Nicholas II) and his fantastic, if mistaken, loyalty to his father. "My father understood life in terms of the Russian prince's obligation to procreate and defend the family and the state," Filatov said. "He felt he had survived, procreated, and protected us."

With the help of a couple of local scientists, Filatov has collaborated on a book about his family's claim, which will soon be published in St. Petersburg. The book, which I read quickly one night at my hotel in St. Petersburg, is fairly dull and absolutely unconvincing. It has lots of pseudoscientific stuff about handwriting, appearance, genealogy, and the rest, but the most obvious element is completely missing: a DNA test. Wasn't it preposterous to think that anyone, much less a hemophiliac, could survive the Ipatiev House shootings? Did Filatov really believe that, in an era without clotting agents, his father could make do with bull's blood and nettles? Sure, Alexis's remains have not been found, but hadn't Yurovsky testified to putting two bullets in his head? And why hadn't Filatov had a genetic exam? (The only Romanov pretender who did was Anna Andersen; after she died, scientists tested a tissue sampling, and it proved her to be a fraud.)

When I asked Filatov these questions, he sighed. He'd heard them before, of course. He said he'd appealed to everyone from the Russian government to the international court in The Hague and been turned down for help. He is counting on a court decision and outside donations to help facilitate the tests he needs.

"Otherwise I'll be told how crazy I am," he said.

Filatov tried at times to soft-pedal his claim, saying that he was not really insisting on his inheritance so much as fulfilling a promise to his father. "It was his cross to bear, and I cannot free myself of it," he said. "The subject scares people off. Maybe there will be a time when we'll get private donations. The university, perhaps, or maybe your article will cause people to donate. I'm immune to insult now. The moment I give up is the moment I die."

He went on to say, "My father had told me, 'When you're forty, you'll learn everything.' " In 1993, I was forty, and that's when I thought about all this seriously. On April 3, 1994, I had a vision of the Holy Virgin, and she told me, 'Have you forgotten what your father told you?' "

I asked him if he'd had other visions. Filatov looked as if he wanted very much to answer, but he didn't.

"I don't want to do myself any harm," he said. "Some will invariably say, 'Oh, he's another one, he's crazy.' "

The greatest price Filatov has paid for his loyalty to the dreams of his dead father is his estrangement from Maksim, his son from an earlier marriage.

"Maksim was born in 1981 and is being brought up in another family," Filatov said. "It's been a long time since I've seen him. They won't let me see him, because the family is against it. They don't want the boy to be traumatized. They're against it because I remain loyal to my parents. But I could not abandon them. The time will come, though, and he will know."

(1998)

The Translation Wars

In the early seventies, two young playwrights, Christopher Durang and Albert Innaurato, collaborated on a satire about nineteenth-century Russian literature called *The Idiots Karamazov*. In their liberal interpretation of Dostoyevsky, Father Zosima is a gay foot fetishist. Which causes the angelic monk Alyosha to wonder, "How can there be a God if there are feet?" The main character is based not on any figure in Dostoyevsky but, rather, on his first and most enduring English-language translator, a woman of Victorian energies and Edwardian prose, Mrs. Constance Garnett.

In the first production of *The Idiots Karamazov*, at the Yale Repertory Theatre, Garnett was played by a student at the drama school named Meryl Streep, who portrayed the aged "translatrix" as a muddled loon. The mangling of the translator's craft is a main plot point. The Russian for "hysterical homosexual," Mrs. Garnett insists, is "Tchaikovsky." When she recalls for the audience the arduous process of translating *Karamazov*, she confuses the four brothers with the *Three Sisters*, a stumble that leads inevitably to the musical number "O We Gotta Get to Moscow!" Mrs. Garnett closes the proceedings by reciting a conjugation of the verb "to Karamazov."

Poor Mrs. Garnett! Translators suffer a thankless and uneasy after-life. (Or they never get that far: until the King James commission, English translators of the Bible were sometimes burned at the stake or strangled—or, as in the case of William Tyndale, both.) Translators are, for eternity, sent up, put down, nitpicked, and, finally, overturned. The objects of their attentions dread their ministrations. Cervantes complained that reading a translation was "like looking at the Flanders tapestries from behind: you can see the basic shapes but they are so filled with threads that you cannot fathom their original lustre." And yet they persevere: here comes Edith Grossman, four centuries later, quixotically encountering the Don and his Sancho on behalf of a new generation of English readers.

Without translators, we are left adrift on our various linguistic ice floes, only faintly hearing rumors of masterpieces elsewhere at sea. So most English-speaking readers glimpse Homer through the filter of Fitzgerald or Fagles, Dante through Sinclair or Singleton or the Hollanders, Proust through Moncrieff or Davis, García Márquez through Gregory Rabassa—and nearly every Russian through Constance Garnett.

As a literary achievement, Garnett's may have been of the second order, but it was vast. With her pale, watery eyes, her gray hair in a chignon, she was the genteel face of tireless industry. She translated seventy volumes of Russian prose for commercial publication, including all of Dostoyevsky's novels; hundreds of Chekhov's stories and two volumes of his plays; all of Turgenev's principal works and nearly all of Tolstoy's; and selected texts by Herzen, Goncharov, and Ostrovsky. A friend of Garnett's, D. H. Lawrence, was in awe of her matter-of-fact endurance, recalling her "sitting out in the garden turning out reams of her marvelous translations from the Russian. She would finish a page, and throw it off on a pile on the floor without looking up, and start a new page. That pile would be this high—really, almost up to her knees, and all magical."

Without Garnett, the nineteenth-century "Rooshians," as Ezra Pound called them, would not have exerted such a rapid influence on the American literature of the early twentieth. In *A Moveable Feast*, Hemingway recounts scouring Sylvia Beach's shelves for the Russians and finding in them a depth and accomplishment he had never known. Before that, he writes, he was told that Katherine Mansfield was "a good short-story writer, even a great short-story writer," but now, after reading Chekhov, she seemed to him like "near-beer." To read the Russians, he said, "was like having a great treasure given to you":

> In Dostoevsky there were things believable and not to be believed, but some so true they changed you as you read them; frailty and madness, wickedness and saintliness, and the insanity of gambling were there to know as you knew the landscape and the roads in Turgenev, and the movement of troops, the terrain and the officers and the men and the fighting in Tolstoy. Tolstoy made the writing of Stephen Crane on the Civil War seem like the brilliant imagining of a sick boy who had never seen war but had only read the battles and chronicles and seen the Brady photographs that I had read and seen at my grandparents' house.

Among the most astringent and authoritative critics of Garnett were Russian exiles, especially Vladimir Nabokov and Joseph Brodsky. Nabokov, the son of a liberal noble who was assassinated at a political conference, left Russia in 1919. He lived in Europe until 1940, when he came to the United States. In *Lectures on Russian Literature,* there is a facsimile of the opening pages of his teaching copy of the Garnett *Anna Karenina.* On the blank left-hand page, Nabokov has written a quotation from Conrad, who told Garnett's husband, Edward, "Remember me affectionately to your wife, whose translation of Karenina is splendid. Of the thing itself I think but little, so that her merit shines with greater lustre." Angrily, Nabokov scrawls, "I shall never forgive Conrad this crack"—he ranks Tolstoy at the top of all Russian prose writers and *Anna* as his masterpiece—and pronounces Garnett's translation "a complete disaster." Brodsky agreed; he once said, "The reason English-speaking readers can barely tell the difference between Tolstoy and Dostoevsky is that they aren't reading the prose of either one. They're reading Constance Garnett."

Garnett's flaws were not the figment of a native speaker's snobbery. She worked with such speed, with such an eye toward the finish line, that when she came across a word or a phrase that she couldn't make sense of she would skip it and move on. Life is short, *The Idiot* long. Garnett is often wooden in her renderings, sometimes unequal to certain verbal motifs and particularly long and complicated sentences. The typescripts of Nabokov's lectures, which he delivered while teaching undergraduates at Wellesley and Cornell, are full of anti-Garnett vitriol; his margins are a congeries of penciled exclamations and crabby demurrals on where she had "messed up." For example, where a passage in the Garnett of *Anna* reads, "Holding his head bent down before him," Nabokov triumphantly notes, "Mark that Mrs. Garnett has decapitated the man." When Nabokov was working on a study of Gogol, he complained, "I have lost a week already translating passages I need in *The Inspector General* as I can do nothing with Constance Garnett's dry shit."

A less imperious but no less discerning critic, Kornei Chukovsky (who was also a famous writer of children's books), esteemed Garnett for her work on Turgenev and Chekhov but not for her Dostoyevsky. The famous style of "convulsions" and "nervous trembling," he wrote, becomes under Garnett's pen "a safe blandscript: not a volcano, but a smooth lawn mowed in the English manner—which is to say a complete distortion of the original."

Garnett (1862–1946) was one of eight children. Her father was paralyzed, and when Constance was just fourteen her mother died of a heart attack from the exertion of hoisting her husband from chair to bed. Constance won a scholarship to read classics at Newnham College, Cambridge, and after graduation she married a publisher, Edward Garnett, the scion of a family of English literary aristocrats.

When the Garnetts were setting up housekeeping, Edward began to invite various Russian exiles as weekend guests. Constance was entranced by their stories of revolutionary fervor and literary ferment. In 1891, when she was confined with a difficult pregnancy, she began to learn Russian. Soon, she tried her hand at translating minor pieces, beginning with Goncharov's *A Common Story* and Tolstoy's *The Kingdom of God Is Within You* and then moving on to her favorite of the Russians, Turgenev. In 1894, she left behind her infant son and her husband and made a three-month trip to Russia, where she drove long distances through snowstorms by sleigh, visited experimental schools, and dined with Tolstoy at his estate.

When Garnett returned to England, she began an ascetic lifelong routine of housekeeping, childrearing, and translating. Mornings, she made porridge for her son David, and then, according to her biographer Carolyn Heilbrun, "she would go round the garden, while the dew was still on the plants, to kill the slugs; this was a moment of self-indulgence." Garnett was a sickly woman, suffering from migraines, sciatica, and terrible eyesight, and yet her ailments did not deter her from working as a translator. She turned down an offer from Tolstoy's close friends Louise and

Aylmer Maude to collaborate on a translation of *War and Peace* and did it on her own. (So, too, did the Maudes, her only rival in Tolstoy.) Garnett went nearly blind working on *War and Peace*. She hired a secretary, who read the Russian text to her aloud; Garnett would dictate back in English, sometimes grabbing away the original text and holding it a few inches from her ailing eyes.

Hemingway recalls telling a friend, a young poet named Evan Shipman, that he could never get through *War and Peace*—not "until I got the Constance Garnett translation." Shipman replied, "They say it can be improved on. I'm sure it can, although I don't know Russian."

Richard Pevear was living in Manhattan in the mid-nineteen-eighties when he began reading *The Brothers Karamazov*. He and his wife, a Russian émigrée named Larissa Volokhonsky, had an apartment on the fourth floor of a brownstone on West 107th Street. To earn money, Pevear built custom furniture and cabinets for the emerging executive class in the neighborhood. He had always earned just enough to get by: in New Hampshire, he cut roses in a commercial greenhouse; he worked in a boatyard repairing yachts. He'd published verse in *The Hudson Review* and other quarterlies, and he'd worked on translations from the languages he knew: French, Italian, Spanish. He'd translated poems by Yves Bonnefoy and Apollinaire, and a philosophical work called *The Gods*, by Alain, a teacher of Jean-Paul Sartre and Simone Weil.

Larissa was born in Leningrad; her brother Henri is a poet who was a rival of Brodsky. While Larissa was still living in Russia, she learned English, sat in on a translation seminar, and, using a smuggled copy of *The New Yorker*, translated a story by John Updike. After she emigrated, in 1973, she translated *Introduction to Patristic Theology*, by John Meyendorff, a Russian Orthodox priest and thinker.

One day, when Richard was reading *Karamazov* (in a translation by one of Garnett's epigones, David Magarshak), Larissa, who had read the book many times in the original, began peeking over her husband's shoulder to read along with him. She was outraged. It's not there! she thought. He doesn't have it! He's an entirely different writer!

As an experiment, a lark, Pevear and Volokhonsky decided to collaborate on their own *Karamazov*. After looking at the various translations—Magarshak, Andrew MacAndrew, and, of course, Constance Garnett—they worked on three sample chapters. Their division of labor was—and remains—nearly absolute: First, Larissa wrote out a

kind of hyperaccurate trot of the original, complete with intersti-
tial notes about Dostoyevsky's diction, syntax, and references. Then,
Richard, who has never mastered conversational Russian, wrote a
smoother, more Englished text, constantly consulting Larissa about the
original and the possibilities that it did and did not allow. They went back
and forth like this several times, including a final session in which
Richard read his English version aloud while Larissa followed along in
the Russian. Their hope was to be true to Dostoyevsky, right down to his
famous penchant for repetition, seeming sloppiness, and melodrama.

When they had a text they liked, they sent a copy to an editor at Random House. It came back with a brief letter that said, in Richard's reading, "No, thanks. Garnett lives forever. Why do we need a new one?"
Then they tried Oxford University Press. The editors there sent the text
along to an Oxford don, who objected to Alyosha Karamazov being
called an "angel"; in the margin he wrote instead "good chap"; another
marginal note said, simply, "balls." Oxford University Press turned them
down. They did not despair. Pevear and Volokhonsky had in the meantime armed themselves with enthusiastic letters of endorsement from
some of the country's best Slavic scholars—including Victor Terras, at
Brown; Robert Louis Jackson, at Yale; Robert Belknap, from Columbia;
and Joseph Frank, Dostoyevsky's supreme biographer, from Stanford—
and sent the manuscript out to Holt, Harcourt Brace, Farrar, Straus &
Giroux, and a couple of others. There was only one bite: Jack Shoemaker, from North Point Press, a small house in San Francisco (now
defunct), called, offering an advance of a thousand dollars—roughly a
dollar per page. They estimated that the translation would take five to six
years—more than twice as long as it took Dostoyevsky to write the novel.
Although translators of long-dead authors do not have to share royalties,
the arithmetic was unpleasant. Pevear called back and shyly asked if,
perhaps, North Point could come up with a bit more money. Shoemaker
offered six thousand. "P/V," as they would come to be known in the academic journals, went to work on *The Brothers Karamazov*. In time, they
would become the best-selling and perhaps the most authoritative translators of Russian prose since Constance Garnett.

A few months ago, I visited Pevear and Volokhonsky in Paris. They
moved to France in 1988, convinced that France would be cheaper than
the Upper West Side. They live in a small ground-floor apartment on a
side street called Villa Poirier. They are both in their early sixties and

have two grown children. Pevear is a mild, friendly man with a gray goatee and the sort of untraceable accent that comes off a little high-end. Volokhonsky is earthier, more reserved than her husband, though hardly retiring. Sometimes Pevear would barge uninvited into his wife's sentences, but she did not easily relent. The rooms are spare and light, and reminded me of apartments I had visited in many Russian cities, apartments of a particular intellectual variety, with the entranceway lined with bookshelves and volumes in Russian, English, French, and other languages. Russian intellectuals always seem to display pictures not only of the family but also of their cultural icons; Larissa kept photographs above her desk of John Meyendorff and another venerable Orthodox thinker, Alexander Schmemann.

Pevear and Volokhonsky made it clear that their work is a collaboration—her Russian, his English—but they work in adjoining offices, alone. "We don't want to work over short passages together," Pevear said. "Larissa does an entire draft first. The first draft for *The Brothers Karamazov* took two years, and thankfully we had an NEH grant"—for thirty-six thousand dollars—"which we stretched out."

"We thought it would last forever!" Larissa said. "We'd never had anything like that kind of money. We moved to France illegally on a tourist visa, and it was finally a policeman who told us that we needed to 'regularize our situation,' as he put it."

Unlike Garnett, who started small and then worked her way up to the big, baggy monsters of Dostoyevsky and Tolstoy, Pevear and Volokhonsky began with the bulkiest and most complex masterpiece imaginable. *The Brothers Karamazov* is, to use Mikhail Bakhtin's famous term, the most polyphonic of Dostoyevsky's novels, the one with the most voices, tones, and textures braided into the text. Tolstoy and Chekhov are far clearer, more serene; perhaps, among the main nineteenth-century texts, only Gogol's *Dead Souls*, with its singular vocabulary and jokes, is as difficult for a translator.

"We thought, if we can do this together, we should start with the book that meant the most to us and had suffered the most from previous translators," Pevear said. "Dostoyevsky's marvelous humor had been lost. *The Divine Comedy* is divine, a religious work, but it's also funny; there are comic moments. The same with Dostoyevsky, and the comedy comes when you least expect it. Ilyusha is dying. His shoes are outside the room. His father is banging his head against the door. A prestigious German doctor comes from Moscow to treat the boy. The doctor comes out of the room after seeing him and the father asks him if there is any hope. He says, 'Be pre-pared for an-ny-thing.' Then, 'lowering his eyes, he himself prepared to step across the threshold to the carriage.' Dickens would never have joked at such a moment. He would have jerked all the tears he could have from us."

"Yes, that's true," Larissa said. "Translators too often look for the so-called Russian sensibility, and, lo and behold, they find it: the darkness, the obsessiveness, the mystic genius. All of that is there, of course. But there is also a lightness, a joyful Christian lightness, too. There are deaths, suicide, the death of a child, Ivan goes mad, Mitya goes to prison—and yet the book ends with joy."

Dostoyevsky's detractors have faulted him for erratic, even sloppy, prose and what Nabokov, the most famous of the un-fans, calls his "gothic rodomontade." "Dostoyevsky did write in a hurry," Pevear said. "He had terrible deadlines to meet. He wrote *Crime and Punishment* and *The Gambler* simultaneously. He knew that if he didn't finish *The Gambler* on time he would lose the rights to all his future books for the next nine years. That's when he hired his future wife as a stenographer and dictated it to her. Tolstoy was better paid, and he didn't even need the money. And yet Dostoyevsky's roughness, despite the rush and the pressure, was all deliberate. No matter what the deadline, if he didn't like what he had, he would throw it all out and start again. So this so-called clumsiness is seen in his drafts, the way he works on it. It's deliberate. His narrator is not him; it's always a bad provincial writer who has an unpolished quality but is deeply expressive. In the beginning of *The Brothers Karamazov*, in the note to the reader, there is the passage about 'being at a loss to resolve these questions, I am resolved to leave them without any resolution.' He stumbles. It's all over the place."

"And this is how people speak," Volokhonsky said. "We mix metaphors, we stumble, we make mistakes."

"Other translators smooth it out," Pevear said. "We don't."

In his preface, Pevear points out that the narrative voice in the novel is full of hedged assertions, mixed diction, wandering syntax, weirdly incorrect compound modifiers ("Ivan Fyodorovich was convinced beyond doubt of his complete and extremely ill condition"), "fused" clichés (as when he refers to a monk from Obdorsk as "the distant visitor"—combining "visitor from far away" and "distant land"). In order to re-create some sense of the tone of the original, Pevear and Volokhonsky have to rely on their own literary instincts, but they have also devised a set of guidelines. For instance, they will not use an English word that the Oxford English Dictionary says came into use after the publication of the novel they are translating. In the Sidney Monas *Crime and Punishment*, the translator uses "pal" instead of something like "old boy." "We won't do that," Pevear said, making the face of a child who has inadvertently eaten a Brussels sprout.

Also, Volokhonsky said, "Dostoyevsky doesn't use slang, really, though sometimes there is a vulgarism. For example, he uses *profiltrovat'sya*—'to filter through,' say, into a society—or *stushevat'sya*, which Dostoyevsky seems to have invented, meaning 'to efface yourself out.'" There are no real obscenities. In *The Demons*, a Holy Fool—a religious idiot savant—curses, but Dostoyevsky uses dashes instead of the word itself. Pevear and Volokhonsky are hardly prudes, but their reading tastes have limits. Even when they desperately needed the money, they refused an offer to translate Victor Erofeyev's fantastically dirty novel, *Russian Beauty*. Nor did they find much to admire in a recent scandalous text from Russia, Vladimir Sorokin's *Blue Lard*. "It was the only book I ever asked to have removed from my house," Volokhonsky said. "I said, 'Take it back, rid me of its presence. We are not amused.'"

To compare the Garnett and the Pevear-Volokhonsky translations of *The Brothers Karamazov* is to alight on hundreds of subtle differences in tone, word choice, word order, and rhythm.

"These changes seem small, but they are essential. They accumulate," Pevear said. "It's like a musical composition and a musician, an interpretation. If your fingers are too heavy or too light, the piece can be distorted."

"It can also be compared to restoring a painting," Volokhonsky said. "You can't overdo it, but you have to be true to the thing."

Volokhonsky's sense of fidelity has obvious roots: she is confounded by any translation that has little sense of the original's qualities as they play on a Russian ear and sensibility. Pevear's fidelity to Dostoyevsky's "sloppiness" comes from a rather grand ambition. "I began as a writer, as a poet, not as a translator, so I started out with that set of problems," he said. "It seemed to me that English prose had become textureless, flavorless, flat, naïve, a kind of dull first person. 'I woke up. I saw the window. I felt very bad. The sun was rising over the hills.' Now, Dostoyevsky writes often in the first person, but there's a richness of texture and idea and voice. So one subliminal idea I started out with as a translator was to help energize English itself.

"Hemingway read Garnett's Dostoyevsky and he said it influenced him," he continued. "But Hemingway was just as influenced by Constance

Garnett as he was by Fyodor Dostoyevsky. Garnett breaks things into simple sentences, she Hemingwayizes Dostoyevsky, if you see what I mean."

The Pevear-Volokhonsky translation of *The Brothers Karamazov* won almost uniformly positive reviews and the PEN prize for translation. "In the *Wichita Eagle*, we got an amazing full-page review with the headline KARAMAZOV STILL LEADS CREATIVE WAY," Pevear said as we broke for lunch one day. "The only problem is that they used a photograph of Tolstoy."

Traditionally, translating was part of a Russian writer's work. Before the nineteenth century, the sum total of great Russian literature—after taking into account a twelfth-century epic, *The Song of Igor's Campaign*, a few comic playwrights, and some stars of the Westernizing eighteenth century, such as Derzhavin, Radishchev, and Karamzin—was relatively negligible. The upper, reading classes automatically thought of literature as a European import. Some read the works in translation, others in the original. In *Eugene Onegin*, Pushkin provides us with Tatiana Larina's reading list—"From early on she loved romances, / they were her only food"—and it is all foreign: Richardson, Rousseau, Lovelace, Sophie Cottin, Madame de Staël. And in Chapter 2 of Pushkin's story "The Queen of Spades" an old countess calls on a young officer, her grandson:

> "Paul," cried the Countess from behind the screen, "send me some new novel, only pray not the kind they write nowadays."
>
> "What do you mean, grand'maman?"
>
> "That is, a novel in which the hero strangles neither his father nor his mother, and in which there are no drowned bodies. I have a great horror of them."
>
> "There are no such novels nowadays. Would you like a Russian one?"
>
> "Are there any Russian novels?"

During the Soviet period, citizens were deprived of censored works but could read countless translations: Boris Pasternak's *Hamlet*, Vasily Zhukovsky's *Odyssey*, Nikolai Gnedich's *Iliad*. Pushkin paid epigrammatic tribute to Gnedich:

> *Poet Gnedich, renderer of Homer the*
> * Blind,*
> *Was himself one-eyed,*
> *Likewise, his translation*
> *Is only half like the original.*

As part of the Revolution's project to educate the masses, Maxim Gorky initiated a publishing house in 1918 with the plan of producing at least fifteen hundred volumes of "the most outstanding works of world fiction"; the project came to a halt in 1927, having turned out a hundred and twenty books. As socialist realism was imposed on Soviet writers, one form of permissible resistance, of finding an inner freedom, was to read translations of foreign writers. No private library was complete without Hemingway, Faulkner, London, Fitzgerald, Steinbeck, Salinger—all officially permitted as "progressive writers" exposing the "ulcers of the capitalist world." There were also stodgy classics that had long ago gone out of fashion in the English-speaking world (especially Sir Walter Scott), as well as some minor writers like A. J. Cronin and James Aldridge. It was common, as in the case of Aldridge, for writers to be translated because they were Communists or, at least, sympathizers. Among the essential pillars of culture in the Soviet era was the journal *Innostrannaya Literatura—Foreign Literature—*which published stories and novels in translation.

One of the forbidden lights of Russian literature during the Soviet era was Vladimir Nabokov. None of his books, not the early Russian-language novels written in France and Germany or the later works, written in English when he lived in the United States and Switzerland, were approved by the authorities. He was considered dangerously "anti-Soviet" and banned outright. Even his translation of *Eugene Onegin*—with its three accompanying volumes of commentary (notes so Nabokovian, so joyful, intricate, and erudite, that they seem like the apparatus to one of his novels, like the "commentary" of *Pale Fire*)—even this was impossible to find in the pre-Gorbachev Soviet Union except in illegal, smuggled editions.

Pevear and Volokhonsky told me that they considered Nabokov's *Onegin* one of the great triumphs of translation, even though it is nothing like their own work. Nabokov, who regarded *The Gift* and *Lolita* as his best novels, thought that his *Onegin* was perhaps the most important project of his life and, at the same time, like all translation, innately futile. In 1955, just as he was setting out on the project, he published a poem in *The New Yorker* on the impossibility, the insult, of translation:

> *What is translation? On a platter*
> *A poet's pale and glaring head,*
> *A parrot's screech, a monkey's chatter,*
> *And profanation of the dead.*

The parasites you were so hard on
Are pardoned if I have your pardon,
O Pushkin, for my stratagem.
I travelled down your secret stem,
And reached the root, and fed upon it;
Then, in a language newly learned,
I grew another stalk and turned
Your stanza, patterned on a sonnet,
Into my honest roadside prose—
All thorn, but cousin to your rose.

The poem, which is written in Pushkin's signature stanza form—fourteen lines, a hundred and eighteen syllables in iambic tetrameter, with a regular scheme of feminine and masculine rhymes—is both tribute and apology, to Russian and to Pushkin.

Nabokov worked on *Onegin* for nearly a decade. His intention, as he makes clear in the introduction, is not to provide a traditional "poetic" rendering, a pleasurable English *Onegin*, like Avrahm Yarmolinsky's, James Falen's, or Charles Johnston's noble attempts. Such efforts, he felt, had necessarily ended in failure.

Not long before publishing his own *Onegin*, Nabokov took to the pages of *The New York Review of Books* and, like the lepidopterist he was, picked the wings off a translation by Walter Arndt—which, to his rage, went on to win the Bollingen Prize. Nabokov could not bear Arndt's "Germanisms," his freewheeling sacrifice of semantic accuracy for rhythmic "beauty." Of all the sins of a translator, he would later write, "The third, and worst, degree of turpitude is reached when a masterpiece is planished and patted into such a shape, vilely beautified in such a fashion as to conform to the notions and prejudices of a given public. This is a crime, to be punished by the stocks as plagiarists were in the shoebuckle days."

For his part, Nabokov intended to provide the reader with a literal-minded "crib, a pony," as he once told an interviewer. "And to the fidelity of transposal I have sacrificed everything: elegance, euphony, clarity, good taste, modern usage, and even grammar." He had no hope for *Onegin* as an English poem. His purpose was singular and clear. Just as Dante wrote *The Divine Comedy* to move a reader toward Scripture (or so he said), Nabokov wrote his translation to inspire his reader to know the poem in Russian:

It is hoped that my readers will be moved to learn Pushkin's language and go through EO again without this crib. In art as in science there is no delight without the detail, and it is on details that I have tried to fix the reader's attention. Let me repeat that unless these are thoroughly understood and remembered, all "general ideas" (so easily acquired, so profitably resold) must necessarily remain but worn passports allowing their bearers shortcuts from one area of ignorance to another.

Despite the stubbornly eccentric and unlovely texture of Nabokov's *Onegin,* the work was generally well reviewed, especially by those who understood and accepted his intention and did not go looking for an English poem. The most notable exception was Edmund Wilson, who decided in July 1965 to wage battle against the translation in the pages of *The New York Review.*

Since 1940, just after Nabokov's arrival in the United States, Wilson and Nabokov enjoyed a warm friendship, a constant Dear Volodya–Dear Bunny correspondence full of mutual instruction, jocular competition, and traded enthusiasms. They were perfectly matched: both were self-confident, supremely intelligent, and well trained in the art of polemics. Wilson had been extraordinarily kind to Nabokov, making introductions for him that led to teaching jobs, a Guggenheim fellowship, contracts with book publishers, and publication in *The New Yorker* and *The New Republic.* And yet there was an uncommon, almost frightening honesty in the relationship. Wilson did not hesitate to tell Nabokov that he did not like *Bend Sinister, Lolita, Ada,* and other major works. (He never bothered to read *The Gift.*) Nabokov, despite his debts to Wilson, treated him, especially on Russian matters, with a breezy condescension: "Dear Bunny, I am going to steal an hour from Gogol and thrash out this matter of Russian versification, because you are as wrong as can be." Wilson was bemused by many of Nabokov's literary judgments, his disdain for Mann's "asinine" *Death in Venice,* Pasternak's "vilely written" *Dr. Zhivago,* Faulkner's "corncobby chronicles"—anything that smacked of journalese, local color, big ideas, or political propaganda. And yet, for a quarter century, despite any friction or jealousies, the friendship seemed to thrive on its directness. "I like you very much," Nabokov told Wilson in 1945, to which Wilson replied, "Our conversations have been among the few consolations of my literary life through these last years—when my old friends have been dying, petering out or getting more and more neurotic." In the end, however, the relationship could not survive Wilson's attack on Nabokov's *Onegin*. The assault was too fierce, too presumptuous, and Nabokov's amour propre was never quite restored.

Despite his imperfect, book-learned Russian, Wilson betrayed no doubt that he was capable of taking on Nabokov. In the course of his career, he learned several languages in order to "work up" his projects: Russian and German to write on Marx and Lenin in *To the Finland Station*, Hebrew for *The Dead Sea Scrolls*, Hungarian to read Endre Ady and other poets. He was especially earnest about his Russian, consulting grammars, Dahl's dictionary (a more antiquarian sort of Russian *OED*), and, quite often, his émigré friend.

When it came to Russian literature, the correspondence between Nabokov and Wilson was rather like that between an amused, patient teacher and an eager, overreaching student. Wilson's publication of "The Strange Case of Pushkin and Nabokov," in *The New York Review of Books*, was an assault from the back of the class:

> This production, though in certain ways valuable, is something of a disappointment; and the reviewer, though a personal friend of Mr. Nabokov—for whom he feels a warm affection sometimes chilled by exasperation—and an admirer of much of his work, does not propose to mask his disappointment. Since Mr. Nabokov is in the habit of introducing any job of this kind which he undertakes by an announcement that he is unique and incomparable and that everybody else who has attempted it is an oaf and an ignoramus, incompetent as a linguist and scholar, usually with the implication that he is also a low-class person and a ridiculous personality, Nabokov ought not to complain if the reviewer, though trying not to imitate his bad literary manners, does not hesitate to underline his weaknesses.

Wilson not only disapproved of Nabokov's "bald and awkward language"; he also discerned in his friend a desire to "torture both the reader and himself" by "flattening out" Pushkin. In *The Wound and the Bow*, Wilson found the key to imaginative art in the injuries and humiliations suffered by a writer in his youth—in Nabokov's case, the humiliation of being stripped of his homeland, of being forced to wander the world far from his home and his language. Nabokov's revenge, he feels, is "sado-masochistic," and it expresses itself in an infuriating perversion of Pushkin:

Aside from this desire to suffer and make suffer—so important an element in his fiction—the only characteristic Nabokov trait that one recognizes in this uneven and sometimes banal translation is the addiction to rare and unfamiliar words, which, in view of his declared intention to stick so close to the text that his version may be used as a trot, are entirely inappropriate here. . . . He gives us, for example, *rememorating, producement, curvate, habitude, rummers, familistic, gloam, dit, shippon* and *scrab.*

In all, Wilson accused Nabokov of "actual errors in English," an "unnecessarily clumsy style," "vulgar" phrases, immodesty, inaccurate transliteration, a "lack of common sense," a "tedious and interminable appendix," a poor grasp of Russian prosody, an "overdone" commentary that suffers from "information which is generally quite useless," and— "to try to get all my negatives out of the way"—"serious failures" of interpretation. The particulars take up the bulk of Wilson's attack, though he closes with some lapidary tribute to Nabokov's mini-essays on Pushkin's period, cohort, and influences.

After reading Wilson's piece at home in Montreux, Nabokov cabled the co-editor of the *Review*, Barbara Epstein, in New York: "Please reserve space in next issue for my thunder." If Wilson saw his essay as simply an elaboration of an ongoing game, his target did not. Nabokov, whose sense of humor was so supreme on the page, was not at all amused, and his counterattacks, published in *Encounter* and *The New York Review*, filleted Wilson personally as well as in the philological particulars:

As Mr. Wilson so justly proclaims in the beginning of "The Strange Case of Pushkin and Nabokov," we are indeed old friends. I fully share "the warm affection sometimes chilled by exasperation" that he says he feels for me. In the 1940s, during my first decade in America, he was most kind to me in various matters, not necessarily pertaining to his profession. I have always been grateful to him for the tact he showed in refraining from reviewing any of my novels. We have had many exhilarating talks, have exchanged many frank letters. A patient confidant of his long and hopeless infatuation with the Russian language, I have always done my best to explain to him his mistakes of pronunciation, grammar, and interpretation. As late as 1957, at one of our last meetings, we both realized with amused dismay that despite my frequent comments on Russian prosody, he still could not scan Russian verse. Upon being challenged to read *Eugene Onegin* aloud, he started to do this with great gusto, garbling every second word and turning Pushkin's iambic line into a kind of spastic anapest with a lot of jaw-twisting haws and rather endearing little barks that utterly jumbled the rhythm and soon had us both in stitches.

Like an admiral commanding a flotilla that his underfunded opponent cannot hope to match, Nabokov lords his superior command of Russian language and prosody over his opponent. After a while, his methodical counterattack seems unfair:

In translating *slushat' shum morskoy* (Eight:IV:11) I chose the archaic and poetic transitive turn "to listen the sound of the sea" because the relevant passage has in Pushkin a stylized archaic tone. Mr. Wilson may not care for this turn—I do not much care for it either—but it is silly of him to assume that I lapsed into a naïve Russianism not being really aware that, as he tells me, "in English you have to listen to something." First, it is Mr. Wilson who is not aware that there exists an analogous construction in Russian, *prislushivat'sya k zvuku*, "to listen close to the sound"—which, of course, makes nonsense of the exclusive Russianism imagined by him, and secondly, had he happened to leaf through a certain canto of *Don Juan*, written in the year Pushkin was beginning his poem, or a certain "Ode to Memory," written when Pushkin's poem was being finished, my learned friend would have concluded that Byron ("Listening debates not very wise or witty") and Tennyson ("Listening the lordly music") must have had quite as much Russian blood as Pushkin and I.

Wilson never relented in his argument that Nabokov's translation was nearly unreadable as a poem (and here he was right), but, with time, he seemed to regret the affair. On rereading his original article, Wilson admitted that he had sounded "more damaging" than he had intended. But it was too late. The correspondence with Nabokov, once so robust and warm, now dwindled and ceased. Wilson felt the loss acutely. There were a few last desultory letters in the years left to them, but Nabokov could never fully forgive the *Onegin* affair and other slights, including a wounding passage about his wife, Véra, in Wilson's memoir *Upstate*. A quarter century of intense friendship ended. In a letter to the *Times*

Book Review in November 1971, Nabokov wrote, "I am aware that my former friend is in poor health but in the struggle between the dictates of compassion and those of personal honor the latter wins." Wilson died in June 1972.

Pevear and Volokhonsky may be the premier Russian-to-English translators of the era. They are certainly the most versatile and industrious and the only such team in which one member, Richard Pevear, does not really speak the language. Pevear told me that he has not even spent much time in Russia—just one three-week trip to St. Petersburg to meet his wife's old friends and family.

"I've never been curious to see Russia," he said during one of our conversations in Paris. "I'm not curious to see the city of Moscow. Should I be?"

Larissa looked faintly embarrassed by her husband's incuriosity. "I don't know what to say."

By listening to Larissa talk with her émigré friends in Paris, by reviewing thousands of small matters of translation, Pevear has certainly picked up a great deal of Russian, but not its outlandishly rich vocabulary, the complicated grammar, with its maddening verb conjugations, shades of tense, reflexivities, cases, endings, gerundial gymnastics.

Parenthetically, it's impossible for me not to sympathize with him. Russian was the bane of my academic life. I've never given a subject more time and concentration only to feel broken before the task. In college, to the dismay of the two émigrée dominatrixes who were my teachers, I spent hundreds of hours poring over a brown-and-blue text called Stillman and Harkins (and, later, a more advanced green one by Charles E. Townsend), hundreds more hours in language laboratories mispronouncing verbs, and all to very little avail—so little that I dropped out of school for a year and, upon return, shifted to the sunny promise and mathematical logic of French. Later, I resumed my Russian studies with a young tutor from Novosibirsk, who, upon hearing me attempt a participial phrase with a reflexive, heavily prefixed verb of motion in the anchor position—a maneuver that I considered the triple salchow of my conversational repertoire—winced, as if stabbed, rolled her eyes into the back of her skull, and, upon recovery, seemed eager to return to the communal apartment she had once shared in central Siberia. She produced a blue text called *Russky Yazyk dlya Vsyekh*—"Russian for Everybody"— a beginning grammar published in Moscow, and said, "So, we start from page one, yes?"

As a teacher, Nabokov reveled in the difficulties of the language almost to the point of serene confidence that no student would ever quite surpass what he called the *Kak-vy-pozhivaetye-ya-pozhivayu-khorosho* (How-are-you-I-am-fine) level of Russian. Nabokov was especially focused on pronunciation. "Please take out your mirrors, girls," the future author of *Lolita* instructed his students at Wellesley, "and see what happens inside your mouths." Many of his students went into his courses hoping to read Tolstoy in the original (as I did) and left satisfied if they could mutter a simple "These boys are standing on those bridges."

Larissa Volokhonsky is a less imperious professor to her husband than Nabokov ever was to the women of Wellesley. Her drafts and proofs provide literal renderings of the original and plenty of signposts, but the final authority is his. "In English I make mistakes," she said, "but there is enough to explain to Richard what is going on in the Russian text and to collaborate."

Since the great success of *The Brothers Karamazov*, Pevear and Volokhonsky have translated (for a variety of publishers) all of the major Dostoyevsky novels and many of his stories; Mikhail Bulgakov's *The Master and Margarita*; a selection of Chekhov's short stories and one of his short novels; and, most famously, Tolstoy's *Anna Karenina*.

Strangely, Pevear spoke readily, and with confidence, about Tolstoy's language. He said that the hardest part of starting a long project like *Anna Karenina* was "getting the voice," capturing the narrative tone that will run throughout the book. "Tolstoy's style is the least interesting thing about him, though it is very peculiar," he said. "It seems like most, translators included, are insensible to the crudeness of Tolstoy's style, but Tolstoy liked to be crude, he was crude provocatively. *Anna Karenina* is interesting very often for how the prose is deliberately not smooth or fine. Nabokov apologizes for Tolstoy's bad writing. But Tolstoy himself said the point is to get the thing said and then, if he wasn't sure he had said it, he would say it again and again."

Pevear and Volokhonsky agree with the majority of their critics that they are best at Dostoyevsky and, perhaps, Tolstoy. Gogol is notoriously difficult for everyone, Chekhov deceptively simple.

"Chekhov has his own difficulties," Larissa said. "His tone seems to be very simple and ordinary, almost banal, and yet it is very hard to catch. It almost falls into trivia, near-cliché."

Richard interrupted, saying, "Yeah, there is a weary rhythm. 'And they saw . . . And then they could see . . . And if it was clear they could move on . . .' One thing after another, without any evident passion, a monotony. Look at 'The Steppe' "—one of Chekhov's best-known longer stories. "The rhythms and paragraphs are on the same level all the time. The task is to maintain that level without falling into banality. Remember, this is the author of 'A Boring Story.' He takes banal people and puts them into banal situations, but he has hope for them. As a doctor, he knew that life is horrible, and if we all knew that, we would hang ourselves. And yet there is a hidden source of light in his work; the source is unknown and unclear. He talks of the horror of life in 'In the Ravine.' And yet there is radiance somewhere in the corner. Dostoyevsky was a Christian and so there is a transcendent clear light. With Chekhov, the light is milder, but it is there."

Pevear and Volokhonsky finished *Anna Karenina* in September 1998—or so they thought. Despite their growing reputation in the United States, they failed to impress the editors at Penguin in London. "They told us the book was unreadable," Pevear said. "They told us it had to be more 'reader-friendly.' But Tolstoy himself is not reader-friendly! They said it was not at a stage to be copy-edited."

Pevear thought that he had solved the problem by taking out some of Tolstoy's more repetitive or overemphatic passages. "Then we got a persnickety copy editor who kept telling us that things might read obscene in a way we hadn't intended," he said. "For example, Kitty says, 'I love balls.' This editor was good enough to tell us that this might read funny. But Kitty liked going to balls! What were we supposed to do? And one sentence read, 'Did you come recently?' Oh, it was all pretty painful. And then they started blue-penciling in alternate translations from Rosemary Edmonds, dozens and dozens of times. I was out of my mind with rage. There were more than a hundred cases of that. It took me two weeks, working twelve-hour days, to restore everything."

Finally, in 2000, the book was published in the U.K. Penguin sold a few hundred copies in England. At Viking Penguin in New York, Caroline White, a senior editor, ordered a print run of thirty-two thousand, with the hope that some strong reviews would mean that the new edition would displace Garnett, the Maudes, and other translations on the academic market.

Then, one day in the spring of 2004, White called Pevear in Paris. She had big news. Oprah Winfrey was selecting *Anna Karenina* for her book club. Neither Pevear nor Volokhonsky quite understood the commercial implications. In fact, they had no idea who Oprah Winfrey was. "I thought she was a country singer," Richard said.

White informed them that Viking Penguin would print an additional eight hundred thousand copies of their translation in a single month.

Soon the buses, subways, and coffee shops of America were filled with people reading Tolstoy. I asked Richard and Larissa what "the Oprah moment" meant for them.

"It means I have an accountant," Richard said.

Notes from Underground now sells eight thousand copies a year, *Crime and Punishment* twelve thousand, *The Brothers Karamazov* fourteen thousand, *Anna Karenina* twenty thousand. Flush, though not rich, Pevear and Volokhonsky split their time between the apartment in Paris and a farmhouse in Burgundy. They have been thinking about future projects, including the stories of Nikolai Leskov, famous for "Lady Macbeth of the Mtsensk District." But they cannot look too far ahead, because the publisher Everyman has engaged them to translate the novel that E. M. Forster insisted was the greatest of all, and that is certainly the longest volume in the nineteenth-century lineup: *War and Peace*. Volokhonsky is about two-thirds of the way through with her first draft, and Pevear about six hundred pages into his.

"There is a real challenge in *War and Peace*, a vast amount of historical detail," he said. "The novel has five hundred historical figures and fictional figures, so we have to write commentaries for the historical ones, which are the vast majority. In the battle scenes, we have to come up with the words for particular kinds of guns and cannons, for military tactics. There is a huge hunting scene, so we have to find very particular words for the wolves, the foxes, the kinds of dogs, the horses, the color of the horses, their gaits, the shape of their paws and hooves and the way they wagged their tails. Tolstoy knew all this as second nature. Or the terms of fashion and high society. In the opening scene, the aunt, *ma tante*, is dressed in 'high ribbons.' Elena Kuryagina is dressed in *listya i mokh*—'leaves and moss.' What do we do with that? We'll have to call our friend Sasha Vasiliev, a stage designer, who has a collection of old stage costumes."

Their deadline is at the end of 2006. Although they prefer Dostoyevsky to Tolstoy, they are finding *War and Peace* to be immensely satisfying. "Even when people go to war, with tragedy and grief, there is still a safe and harmonic world," Larissa said. "Natasha has babies while living in a world that might not be there tomorrow."

Pevear, especially, has read some of the theory about translation: Walter Benjamin, José Ortega y Gasset, Roman Jakobson, and, of course, Nabokov. He said that he takes the most inspiration from a turn-of-the-century French poet and translator named Valéry Larbaud. At the end of our last conversation in Paris, Pevear went to his shelves and pulled down a volume in French, and read a prayer by Larbaud addressed to St. Jerome, who translated the Bible into Latin. Following the line with his finger, Pevear squinted and, slowly, translated: "Excellent Doctor, Light of the Holy Church, Blessed Jerome. I am about to undertake a task full of difficulties, and from this moment on I beg of you to help me with your prayers so I can translate this work into French with the same spirit with which it was composed."

Pevear snapped the book shut and picked up the Maude translation of *War and Peace,* which he'd been reviewing for his own work.

"I know how he feels," he said. "It's the same thing that sits on our heads when we start up."

Early this fall, Penguin announced the publication of a new translation of *War and Peace*—it was by Anthony Briggs, a British academic. Briggs, who won generally positive reviews, sounded like an attractively modest sort. One of the British papers, *The Daily Telegraph,* quoted him as saying, "Professional translators are generally mediocre people like me, not great poetic geniuses." The *Times Literary Supplement* published a short, curious article pointing out that Briggs had, unlike some of his predecessors, rendered all Tolstoy's French into English and even spelled out some of General Kutuzov's obscenities. (Tolstoy had obscured the profanity with ellipses.) What Rosemary Edmonds, the last translator of the novel, had as "It serves them right, the b— b—s!" Briggs has as "They asked for it, the fucking bastards!"

In the meantime, Pevear and Volokhonsky were working on their translation at their farmhouse in Burgundy. I wrote to them about the Briggs approach and hoped for a response, even a prickly one. It came a couple of weeks later:

> We're well and had a busy but fruitful summer. I'm about to lose the battle of Austerlitz (W&P vol 1 pt 3). . . . About your questions: I don't know how "new" it is to translate the French passages in *War and Peace.* Edmonds keeps only the *"Eh bien, mon prince"* of the opening speech, but puts the rest in English, whereas Tolstoy has the first ten lines in French, along with many other extended dialogues in the opening chapters. There are also French words and phrases all through the novel. The Maude and Garnett versions translate all of it into English, as they do, for instance, Napoleon's letter to Murat, and the German of Weyrother's dispo-

sition before Austerlitz. If, as you say, Anthony Briggs also trans-
lates it all, then as far as I know ours will be the only version that
DOESN'T. We do as Tolstoy does, and, like the Russian editions of
the novel, put the translations in the footnotes.

Tolstoy used French for a reason, or for several reasons: to give
the tone of the period; to play on the ironies of a French-speaking
Russian aristocracy suddenly finding itself thrown into war with
France; to suggest a certain frivolity and uprootedness in characters like Prince Vassily and the witty Bilibin. . . . Interestingly, when
Napoleon banters with his troops, he does so in French, but when
he talks seriously, Tolstoy lends him Russian.

About Kutuzov's purple patch, again we'll do as Tolstoy did. He
would never have written out "fucking bastards," and in any case
Briggs has not been very inventive. None of us can figure out what
epithet Tolstoy had in mind for Kutuzov, but it seems to have
involved the mistreatment of mothers.

With best wishes from us both . . .

(2005)

Post-Imperial Blues:
Vladimir Putin

On a murky day twenty years ago, I sat in a Soviet railcar (Helsinki–Leningrad; rain-drizzled windows) reading a collection of stories by Vladimir Nabokov. There was then, as there no longer is, an illicit thrill in crossing over, West to East: the neat Finnish streets and houses thinning, then vanishing, near the border; just minutes later, the signs of Soviet dilapidation. A puttering Zhiguli towing another Zhiguli by a rope along a muddy road; waterlogged posters ("Communism = Soviet Power plus Electrification of the Whole Country!") nailed to the sides of a shack; a scaly drunk in a padded jacket, oblivious of the rain, stomping his boots in a puddle. The train stopped with a creak at the border town of Vyborg. The ventilation coughed and went still. A trio of clean-jawed men in uniform—they could not have been more than twenty years old—climbed on board and made their way down the aisles, checking passports and visas, making cursory searches of our bags. As agents of state security, the guards tried to affect a haughty expression, but they managed to radiate only nervousness, the sense that, just as they were watching us, someone of greater consequence was watching them.

By the time the guards reached my row, they had already gathered a small stack of Bibles tied together with twine and a cache of German skin magazines. They looked through my duffel bag and saw nothing of interest. Then one of them extended his index finger and tipped back the book of stories in my hand in order to examine its foxed cover. The cover illustration was of a generically pretty girl with shimmery light hair, though curiously un-Russian, more like a model for the House of Breck. The guard paused and narrowed his eyes. The book was not *Lolita,* but it was Nabokov, illegal all the same. Authors are banned not by title; they are banned whole. He *knew.* And yet he looked me over and moved on, leaving me to my counterrevolutionary pleasure.

A few minutes later, the train eased once more into the trip eastward, the pleasingly numb hours of birches and rain, the villages going by. Soon it was dark and the windows were fogged. I turned to "The Visit to the Museum," in which a Russian émigré finds himself wandering through a provincial museum in France. In a dreamlike state, he comes to realize that he has passed through a magical portal into his native land, into Russia, and yet he has the dawning sense that this is not quite his Russia. Everything is vivid: the coolness of the air, and "the stone beneath my feet was real sidewalk, powdered with wonderfully fragrant, newly fallen snow." But as he approaches a shoe repair shop and sees the word "shoe," he realizes that something is wrong; there is no *tvyordy znak,* no "hard sign," at the end of the word. The hard sign was largely eliminated by the Bolsheviks. They'd set out to remake the world, including its orthography:

> I knew irrevocably where I was. Alas, it was not the Russia I remembered, but the factual Russia of today, forbidden to me, hopelessly slavish, and hopelessly my own native land. . . . Oh how many times in my sleep I had experienced a similar sensation! Now, though, it was reality.

Nabokov left Russia in 1919 on a ship called the *Hope* and became a permanent exile: Berlin, Paris, Cambridge, Ithaca, Montreux. His revulsion for what had become of Russia was such that in "The Visit to the Museum" he could never bring himself to call the place "the Soviet Union."

The train slowed. The suburbs of Leningrad, then the ghostly apartment blocks of the outer city, sluiced by. With a jolt, we arrived. The
Finland Station. The doors opened with a rubbery kiss. The air that
rushed in was damp and cold and smelled of cheap tobacco. On the platform, I bought a roll stuffed with a few pebbles of bluish meat. I needed
help getting around, and so, for a few kopecks, I bought a copy of
Pravda and a map and set off on my way.

"The Visit to the Museum" is a story steeped in the exile's nostalgia.
When I return to Moscow now, I find myself thinking that this state
of temporal, even historical, disorientation also resembles a quality
within Russia, within Russians. Twelve years after the collapse of Communism and the Soviet Union itself, Russians live in a state of historical disjunction and simultaneity. The kopecks I spent at the
Finland Station are no longer in circulation; *Pravda*'s readership has
dropped from nine million to a hundred thousand; in some cities,
many of the street names on the map have been changed to new or pre-
revolutionary names; in others, the streets are still named for Lenin,
Labor, the Red Banner. Russians exist in an economy that is neither
socialist nor capitalist; they live in distinctly Soviet apartments, in Soviet
conditions, and yet in television commercials they are comfortable,
clean, rich, in a Scandinavian sort of way. In the larger cities, even in
smaller, unexpected places, every material delight or spiritual degradation known to the modern world is available for cash or credit; and yet
there are still thousands of towns and villages where men and women
wear high boots and walk on muddy roads that are just as they were in
the time of the tsars.

Not long ago, I took a room in Moscow on the city's main commercial
drag, Tverskaya Street. In the nineteenth century, Tverskaya was among
the most fashionable streets in Russia: Tolstoy lost a fortune playing
cards at the English Club; the food stores supplied the tsars. In the
Communist era, the English Club became the Central Museum of the
Revolution, and Food Store No. 1 still had its chandeliers but hardly any
food. Now the delicacies, the caviar and the crab—at Tokyo prices—are
back. Few can afford them; many come just to gaze, the way they once
did at Lenin's cap and his Rolls-Royce at the museum devoted to his
memory.

When consumerism (legal and not) began to appear in the early
nineties, it seemed to matter only to a few wealthy Russians and foreign-

ers. This was the era of "the New Russians": vulgar, brash, and, often enough, criminal. It was the era of American gangster movies, bullet-proof windows, strip joints, porn palaces, casinos with naked women swimming in enormous fish tanks.

The grotesqueries and the poverty of the first years of post-Soviet life are still reality. The naked women still swim in their tanks. Gangsters abound. But now, in the post-revolutionary era, there is something else in evidence in Moscow and in many other cities: a certain stifling calm, an indifference to politics, a slowly growing middle and professional class, a more normal commercialism, a sense that while a new Russia—independent, prosperous, and linked to the West—has not yet been achieved, not by a long shot, it is no longer inconceivable. And the embodiment of modern times in Russia is its President, Vladimir Vladimirovich Putin.

Putin is not a man of imagination or spark. He is stern, intelligent, competent, blandly agreeable—an authoritarian bureaucrat thrust forward in history. His is the bearing of the vigilant listener, of the intelligence agent. After he joined the KGB, he used to tell his close friends, "I am a specialist in human relations." His language is usually flavorless in a particularly Soviet fashion. His gaze is flat, even dead, and gives nothing away. That is why most Russians thought it riotously funny when President Bush declared in 2001 that he had "looked the man in the eye" and got a "sense of his soul." They had never had the privilege.

Rather than mark himself completely a man of the future, a democrat, a European—or, to the contrary, a Soviet, a man of traditional autocratic values—Putin has achieved the distinction of seeming everything to nearly everyone. His embrace of the ideals of the democracy movement in Russia—a free press, constitutionalism, civil liberties—is slight. He never fought for an end to Communism; he merely inherited a set of post-Communist realities. Putin is, first and foremost, a *gosudarstvennik*—a statist—who values the growth and stability of Russia before all else. If that means prosecuting a media baron or a business leader who displays even a trace of political ambition, so be it. If that means filling the state bureaucracy with thousands of former intelligence officers, then it must be so. And yet, paradoxically, no less than Mikhail Gorbachev or Boris Yeltsin, Putin has decided that Russia does not have an ideologically or mystically determined "special path" of development; rather, Russia's destiny is allied to Europe and to the United States—its future might even include membership in the European Union and NATO.

Yeltsin staked his historical reputation on destroying the Communist system and the empire known as the Soviet Union. Putin has cast himself as a man of evolution. He makes gestures toward the old order, partly to soothe the bruised feelings of the Russian people. He praises the honesty of the dissident hero Andrei Sakharov, but he also has kind words for Stalin's dubious military acumen. Although Putin is realistic about Russia's diminished standing in the world, and even admits (up to a point) to a history of horrific cruelty and loss, he constantly assures his countrymen that theirs is a nation of historical greatness and that greatness, in some new form, will surely return. At the celebrations this spring for the three-hundredth anniversary of his native St. Petersburg, he lauded the city's *imperskii blyesk*—its "imperial splendor." The pro-Kremlin party in parliament, United Russia, uses figures such as Pushkin and Stolypin, the early-twentieth-century economic reformer, to advertise its virtues.

Putin, who was appointed acting President when Yeltsin suddenly resigned, on December 31, 1999, won election in 2000, with fifty-two percent of the vote. He will surely win reelection in 2004. His popularity rating runs to more than seventy percent. Some new Russian textbooks describe his childhood in the hagiographic terms once reserved for general secretaries of the Communist Party.

For now, Russia is lucky, floating along on a tide of profits from the oil-and-gas industry. The ruble is strong, world energy prices are high, inflation is declining, and economic growth, for the fifth year in a row, is robust. Nevertheless, Putin's opponents, be they Moscow liberals or provincial Communists, complain that oil provides only a fleeting security; they talk of *zastoi*—stagnation—a term evocative of the Brezhnev era. A website called vladimir.vladimirovich.ru features dozens of absurdist *anekdoty* about Putin's cold-bloodedness, his neo-Soviet habits; political jokes have not been in such fashion since the days of the last Kremlin dinosaurs, in the early eighties. "The atmosphere is not as oppressive as it was under Brezhnev, but it's sickening, and it says a lot, that such a website would appear and gain such popularity," said Masha Lipman, a political analyst at the Carnegie Moscow Center. Putin's supporters just shrug. They welcome the lethargy.

"Putin arrived as the man to stop the revolution," Gleb Pavlovsky, a bumptious intellectual with a dissident past who cultivated an image as the shadowy operative in Putin's last campaign, told me. "This is why the theme of his election campaign was Thermidor. His message to voters was that this will be the end of revolution.

"Putin is an unrealized Louis Philippe," Pavlovsky went on. "He prefers family life and would like to keep his workday to eight hours and forget about it afterward. He's like the rest of the country in that way. After twenty years of revolution and surprises, people are tired. They're exhausted by the notion of thinking about an entirely new world, a new state, a new form of economy and thinking—new everything! And so they forgive Putin his weaknesses, because they know he feels the same things that they do."

When Yeltsin handed power to Putin, Putin, in turn, handed Yeltsin a package of comforts (the dacha, security, cars, drivers, etc.) and, more important, a grant of legal immunity. By the time he left office, Yeltsin was despised by so many people, and by so many politicians, that there was always the chance that he could become the object of prosecution. His rash and disastrous decision to unleash a war in Chechnya, the new economy of corrupted winners and resentful losers, and the collapse of basic industries and social services all made it impossible for most Russians to give Yeltsin credit for making the break with Soviet Communism. Indeed, the majority resented what the West most celebrated: the demise of the Soviet Union.

Yeltsin and "the Family"—a team composed of his daughter Tatyana Dyachenko, various business tycoons, and several close aides such as Valentin Yumashev (who married Dyachenko) and the chief of staff, Aleksandr Voloshin—gave Putin the Russian Presidency mainly because he seemed competent and loyal. Putin ascended, in part, because after a decade of revolution hardly any political reputations had survived. As Boris Nemtsov, one of the many Kremlin ministers once thought to have a chance to succeed Yeltsin, told me, "Revolutions eat their young, to say nothing of their young politicians." In less than four years, Putin was summoned to work as a Kremlin aide, then was made chief of intelligence, then Prime Minister, then President. "Yeltsin's people created Putin out of a pot of clay," Leonid Parfyonov, one of Russia's leading television journalists, said. "We don't have a real party system, so the Kremlin gave birth and breath to this man."

Yeltsin has complained publicly only once about his successor. That was when Putin supported an effort to reinstate the Soviet national anthem, composed, with Stalin's approval, in 1943. Putin called on the deeply conservative writer Sergei Mikhalkov, who co-wrote the

Soviet-era lyrics ("Party of Lenin, the strength of the people / To Communism's triumph, leads us on!"), to write some new verses to suit the modern era:

> *From the southern seas to the polar region*
> *Spread our forests and fields.*
> *You are unique in the world, inimitable.*
> *Native land protected by God!*

Yeltsin took the revival as an affront. He had replaced the Soviet red flag with the tsarist-era tricolor, and the hammer and sickle with the two-headed eagle, a symbol originating in the fifteenth century. Throughout the Yeltsin era, when a national anthem was called for, orchestras played Mikhail Glinka's 1833 hymn, "A Patriotic Song"—a tune without lyrics. Putin's anthem was an offense to the leaders of the democracy movement.

"This is the music that accompanied the murder of tens of millions of people!" Aleksandr Yakovlev, a close adviser to both Gorbachev and Yeltsin, told me. "The entire literary and musical and artistic intelligentsia spoke out against it—Rostropovich, Solzhenitsyn, all of them! But Putin felt he had to make some sort of compromise with the Communist Party," which is still the leading opposition party in the country. "He also decided to revive the state prize called the Order of Lenin. And yet Lenin was a criminal who should be tried for crimes against humanity!"

Putin's reasoning for having what Russians call a "postmodern" collection of symbols—some tsarist, some Soviet, some sui generis—is part of his everything-to-everyone strategy. Most Russians do not regret the loss of Communist ideology or their dominion over Eastern Europe, but they do mourn the past greatness of the "inner empire," the non-Russian republics that are now on their own. The Soviet Union, like the tsarist empire before it, commanded respect and fear in the world, and the anthem was consonant with that sense of position. Putin always wins applause when he tells a crowd, "Anyone who does not regret the collapse of the Soviet Union has no heart, but anyone who wants it restored has no brain." Putin's anthem is a hymn to past greatness and a promise of return—a popular and unifying sentiment. And so Putin felt he could summarily dismiss Yeltsin's objections. "We respect the first President, we listen to his opinions, and take them into account making decisions," he said. "But we act on our own."

· · ·

In Moscow and St. Petersburg, I rarely met anyone who did not say of Putin that he is "a good guy," "a normal fellow," "trying his best." He is even more unassailable in the provinces. To be sure, there were plenty of urban journalists and intellectuals who told me that they find Putin weak, indecisive, or, more often, a closet authoritarian guilty of war crimes in Chechnya and determined to stifle dissent and an independent judiciary. For some, he resembles Alexander III, the conservative tsar who followed Alexander II, who liberated the serfs. "This is a time of an inert public," Aleksei Venediktov, the chief editor of the independent radio station Echo of Moscow, said. "Putin has no understanding of democracy in the Western sense. For him, order precedes everything else in the social contract."

But that is an élite, minority view. Putin is equally popular among poor retirees, who often vote Communist, and young professionals, who barely remember the world before Gorbachev's perestroika. Yeltsin, too, came to office with high approval ratings, but he quickly exhausted those reserves by instituting painful (and often botched) economic reforms and committing, as with Chechnya, horrendous mistakes. Putin is intent on husbanding his rating, not merely because it will ensure reelection but also because such a rating represents the very idea of his Presidency: post-revolutionary calm.

In private, Yeltsin objects to a great deal more than the Stalinist anthem. "Now Boris Nikolayevich complains about Putin all the time," one politician close to Yeltsin told me. "It's not just the symbols. It's everything they stand for. He thinks Putin is too cautious. I think if he didn't depend on Putin for his well-being he would be a lot more open about it. As it is, he sits at home and bitches to the people he thinks he can still trust. And Putin knows this. Putin's relationship is easier now with Gorbachev than it is with Yeltsin. Sometimes it's easier to get along with your grandfather than it is with your father."

Yeltsin, since leaving the Kremlin and transferring custody of the nuclear-weapons codes to Putin ("Take care of Russia!" he told his successor as he walked out the door), has lived almost obscurely, in a village about an hour from the capital, at the same gated dacha compound that he used while he was in power. In the last several years of his Presidency, Yeltsin was a feeble sight. He was often drunk, sometimes in public, and almost always sick. Weeks would go by with Yeltsin bedridden, incommunicado. "Boris Nikolayevich is reviewing documents," the

Kremlin press service would tell reporters. "You should see him now," one of his closest advisers, Anatoly Chubais, told me not long ago. "Boris Nikolayevich has not looked so healthy in years. He barely drinks. He swims."

In Yeltsin's totalist scheme of the world, you were with him or against him. Putin, by contrast, has repeatedly said, through statement and gesture, that he bears no grudges, makes no judgments, about the past. At his inauguration, in 2000, Putin invited his former boss at the KGB, Vladimir Kryuchkov, who engineered the failed 1991 coup against Gorbachev and has never apologized for it. "We have nothing to regret," Kryuchkov said at a roundtable meeting of former KGB chiefs. "We only tried to save the Union. It's those who unleashed the present chaos who should think about repentance."

"Kryuchkov was a true believer in Communism, who sided with the coup plotters," Putin has said, "but he was also a very decent man. To this day, I have the greatest respect for him." Another of the plotters, the former Soviet Prime Minister Valentin Pavlov, went out of his way to celebrate the new regime. "Today, they are trying to do what we attempted to do in the Soviet Union in 1991," he said. On the tenth anniversary of the defeat of the coup, two years ago, Putin made sure to draw no attention to an event that he knew the world recalled with joy and his countrymen with profound ambivalence: there were no Kremlin parades, no official speeches. The President went trout fishing in Karelia.

At a dinner at "21" hosted by Tom Brokaw a few years ago, I sat with Putin, his translator, and some other media guests. Putin spoke only when addressed. (And, unlike Yeltsin, he hardly touched his wine.) He parried our questions with reluctant, cursory answers and even an occasional charmless roll of his eyes. In the interviews he has granted to Western outlets, generally before a foreign visit, he seems to go out of his way to be as boring as possible. When he spoke to students and invited guests at Columbia University a couple of weeks ago and at a meeting with American reporters at his dacha outside Moscow recently, he droned on in a style familiar to the reader of *The Collected Speeches of Yuri Andropov*. As I sat with him at the "21" dinner, I felt that I had been with such men dozens of times in Moscow—ascetic former officers of the KGB who were, thanks to their preparation and years abroad, comfortable in any setting yet who often betrayed a steely disdain for all the ignorance and opulence around them. ("I am not sure you understand what you are talking about," he told Katie Couric at one point.)

With time, it's become clear that Putin's blandness and reserve are only in part a matter of innate character and professional posture; they are also a tactical choice, a determination that Russia endured long enough Gorbachev's soliloquies and Yeltsin's unpredictable and autocratic nature. This year, one of the most popular television programs in the country was a serialization of Dostoyevsky's *The Idiot.* In the novel, the narrator says of Russia that "people are constantly complaining that we have no practical men," that the civil service is filled with incompetents who let the crops rot in the fields and the trains smash into one another. Although Putin is late to every appointment, he has carefully cultivated an image as Russia's first practical man, a distinctly un-Russian efficiency expert. Putin, the saying goes, "is our German."

Putin's grandfather was a cook for Stalin at one of his country estates near Moscow. During the Second World War, Putin's mother nearly starved to death during the nine-hundred-day Nazi blockade of Leningrad (at one point, she fainted from hunger and was thrown onto a stack of corpses); his father was wounded at the front and survived only because one of his comrades dragged him across the frozen Neva River to safety; one child, a son, died of diphtheria.

Putin was born after the war, in 1952. He grew up in Leningrad, and, like so many in that city, he and his family lived in a *kommunalka,* a communal apartment, where there was no bath, no hot water, and plenty of rats. "My friends and I used to chase them around with sticks," Putin once said. He was a mediocre student and spent most of his time playing in the city courtyards. If he had a real ambition, he got it from reading thrillers. "Even before I graduated from school, I wanted to work in intelligence. It was a dream of mine, although it seemed about as likely as a flight to Mars," he told the interviewers for a book-length conversation called *First Person,* published in 2000. "Books and spy movies like *The Sword and the Shield* took hold of my imagination. What amazed me most of all was how one man's effort could achieve what whole armies could not. One spy could decide the fate of thousands of people. At least, that's the way I understood it.

"In order to find out how to become a spy, sometime back around the beginning of the ninth grade I had gone to the office of the KGB Directorate," Putin continued. "A guy came out and listened to me. 'I want to get a job with you,' I said. 'That's terrific, but there are several issues,' he said. 'First, we don't take people who come to us on their own initiative. Second, you can come to us only after the Army or after some type of civilian higher education.' I was intrigued. 'What kind of higher education?' I asked. 'Any!' he said. He probably just wanted to get rid of me. 'But what kind is preferred?' I asked. 'Law school.' And that was that. . . . When I accepted the proposition from the Directorate's personnel department, I didn't think about the [Stalin-era] purges. My notion of the KGB came from romantic spy stories. I was a pure and utterly successful product of Soviet patriotic education." Putin studied law at Leningrad State University, and in his fourth year was recruited to join the KGB.

Eventually, Putin was assigned to work in East Germany. A tremendous amount of journalistic energy has been spent trying to discern what Putin actually achieved in East Germany, and the answer is, clearly, not a lot. Dresden, where he was stationed, was a third-rate assignment, as opposed to, say, Berlin. Putin collected information on visiting foreigners, he spent time trying to cultivate agents and sources, but he never had the chance to emulate the heroes of *The Sword and the Shield.* His work was, in the main, dull. There were many idle days and nights in Dresden for Putin, his wife, Lyudmila, whom he married in 1983, and their two young daughters. "We used to go to a little town called Radeburg where there was one of the best breweries in East Germany," he said in *First Person.* "I would order a three-liter keg. You pour the beer into the keg, you add a spigot, and you can drink straight from the barrel. So I had 3.8 liters of beer every week. And my job was only two steps from my house, so I didn't work off the extra calories." Putin gained twenty-five pounds in Dresden.

The most eventful time in Putin's career as a spy came in his last weeks in Dresden, when signs of the collapse of Communism—and the Berlin Wall—became plain. Rather than face a potential insurrection and exposure as agents of the Soviet oppressor, Putin and his colleagues at the KGB and the East German secret police, the Stasi, began to burn their files. "We destroyed everything—all our communications, our lists of contacts and our agents' networks," he said. "We burned so much stuff that the furnace burst. We burned papers night and day. All the most valuable items were hauled away to Moscow." Crowds began to demonstrate around the Stasi buildings and the KGB outpost. "Those crowds were a serious threat. We had documents in our building. And nobody lifted a finger to protect us. . . . These people were in an aggressive mood. I called our group of forces and explained the situation. And I was told, 'We cannot do anything without orders from Moscow. And Moscow is silent.' . . . But that business of 'Moscow is silent'—I got the feeling then that the country no longer existed. That it had disappeared."

Putin experienced Moscow's silence not as an ideological loss but, rather, as a betrayal of loyal professionals. He was a salaried satrap of the empire, and, as if in an instant, there was no empire, no rivalry with the United States, no stature, no money. Putin was ill-prepared for this. He and his family had not experienced at first hand the changes that Gorbachev had initiated in Moscow, the revelations about the Soviet past, the protests against the Party and the KGB. One former KGB associate told me that if Putin had had any sort of future after Dresden he would have been assigned to the KGB's central headquarters, in Moscow. Instead, he was charged with watching foreign students at Leningrad State University—a lowly calling. The KGB was already beginning to cut back on personnel as it became clear that the Cold War was over, and it was equally clear that Putin's intelligence career was coming to an end.

Before it did, however, he encountered Anatoly Sobchak, a law professor at the university and a leading democrat, who would soon become mayor. A man of liberal ideals but a hopelessly inept administrator, Sobchak eventually hired Putin to help him run the city. Putin proved adept at learning the new rules of the market, though many of the deals he made collapsed. Boris Fyodorov, who served as Finance Minister under Yeltsin, told me that in those days he met "a dozen times" with Putin. "He was always extremely careful. He didn't look you in the eye. He mostly listened. He was still living in a communal apartment"—with his wife and daughters—"and he talked only about business and politics."

When the coup plotters sent tanks into Moscow on the morning of August 19, 1991, Yeltsin led the resistance there; in Leningrad, the leader of the resistance was Sobchak. Putin, despite his KGB background and his high regard for Kryuchkov, returned from vacation to help his boss. Sobchak, with Putin working the phones in the Mariinsky Palace, rallied the city against the coup; the demonstration on the square behind the Hermitage rivaled the biggest rallies in the capital.

The post-coup euphoria was pervasive in Leningrad; Sobchak, like Yeltsin, was enormously popular. But as the years passed, and as Yeltsin's Kremlin came to resemble a Byzantine court, with warring factions of business barons and security chiefs, idealists like Sobchak became less welcome. Sobchak came up for reelection in 1996, and the most conservative faction in the Kremlin, led by Yeltsin's personal bodyguard, Aleksandr Korzhakov, propped up an opponent named Vladimir Yakovlev, who won by less than two percent.

"When Sobchak lost the election, Putin submitted his resignation," Sobchak's widow, Lyudmila Narusova, told me. "He said, 'Better to be hanged for loyalty than live rich from betrayal.' " Sobchak lived for a while with his family at his dacha outside St. Petersburg and then accepted a job in Moscow, in the Kremlin's property office. Even out of power, Sobchak remained a focus of attack: the St. Petersburg press became filled with accusations of corruption. In 1997, Sobchak, who was in his fifties, suffered a heart attack, and Putin, calling on his old connections in the KGB, organized a private plane to smuggle Sobchak to Paris for medical treatment. When Sobchak died of another heart attack, three years later, Putin wept at the funeral. "He did not die of natural causes," he told Narusova.

Putin's demonstrations of fealty to Sobchak were a crucial part of what led Yeltsin and the Family to accelerate his career and, finally, to appoint him tsar. "They figured that he was a man of loyalty," Anatoly Chubais said, "and that his loyalty was transferable."

Not long after he became President, Putin said he would tame the small group of self-described "oligarchs" who had used their political connections to take ownership, or control, of the oil industry; banking; mineral, chemical, and metal plants; construction and real-estate concerns; and, the most political of the economic sectors, the media. In 1996, the oligarchs had joined forces to help Yeltsin win reelection over the Communist Party candidate; they acted out of pure self-interest. "Don't forget the seriousness of that threat," said Yegor Gaidar, the most liberal of Yeltsin's many prime ministers. "A return of the Communists to power in Russia really would have been a terrible danger for the world. Expectations are always high after a revolution and people are invariably disappointed, and so the Communists come to power again." The benefits accrued to the oligarchs after Yeltsin's reelection—the properties, the contracts—were incalculable.

As President, Putin soon met with the principal oligarchs and delivered a message: So long as you stay out of politics, you will be allowed to keep your properties, no matter how they were obtained. The Kremlin was already moving against the two who showed the greatest impudence: Boris Berezovsky, an industrialist and media magnate, whose political pretensions were too blatant for Putin to tolerate, and Vladimir Gusinsky, who had made his fortune in banking and Moscow real estate and his name by starting NTV, the first privately owned network in the country. Both were forced out of the country. Berezovsky lives mainly in London, where he has tried, with little success, to launch an opposition movement against Putin.

Gusinsky lives in Israel and in Greenwich, Connecticut; he lost control of NTV to a state gas monopoly, and now the network, while still less obsequious than the rest, is far less rambunctious than it had been.

The most prominent oligarch remaining was a moonfaced oil executive named Mikhail Khodorkovsky. A former officer in the Young Communist League, Khodorkovsky is now forty and, according to *Fortune,* wealthier than any other man or woman in Europe. During the Gorbachev era, he was among the privileged young people who were granted the chance to test the new semi-capitalist market. In the late eighties, Khodorkovsky used Communist Party sponsorship and connections to begin a successful bank called Menatep; and by becoming an adviser to the Russian government he had unparalleled access to crucial information. Eventually, Khodorkovsky got into the most lucrative of all Russian businesses, the oil business, and through his connections, and through a ruthless series of maneuvers, he came to run the newly merged oil conglomerate Yukos-Sibneft. His company is so wealthy, and the rest of the economy so weak, that Khodorkovsky, by his estimate, contributes seven percent of Russia's total tax revenue. He is worth around a billion dollars personally and told me that another eight billion is "under my control."

I met Khodorkovsky at his headquarters in Moscow, a glass office building that looked as if it had been airlifted from Houston. The Moscow of the twenty-first century is filled with such buildings. The old-style Soviet offices still functioning have the customary worn red runner carpets and smell like an overflowing ashtray; these offices have the smell of a new car, and they are invariably equipped with dozens of armed security men and six-foot-tall beauty queens dressed in Versace and Armani suits and bearing leather binders. Khodorkovsky grew up in a middle-class family, but his years of experience in

the Young Communist League business offices and in the new Russian economy show. Many of the figures in big business felt that in
the conference rooms of Europe and the United States a decade ago
they were regarded as rubes—"They treated us like educated monkeys," the banker Pyotr Aven complained—but Khodorkovsky betrays
no resentment. He seems at ease, self-contained, as if he had been born
to riches.

Although Khodorkovsky has never been as brazen in his political
ambitions as Gusinsky and Berezovsky, he discovered that he was not
immune from Kremlin pressure. Occasionally, Putin meets with the
leading business figures in Moscow, and at one such session, earlier this
year, the President attacked him sharply. When I asked Khodorkovsky
about it, he flushed and smiled. He told me that he had been called on
to talk about corruption involving a financial transaction between two oil
companies. "Evidently, this was not the first time the issue had been
raised with him, and it struck a raw nerve," Khodorkovsky said.

Putin, various sources told me, grew angry with Khodorkovsky and, in
paraphrase, told him to watch who was calling the kettle black where
corruption was concerned. Everyone, the President said, knew how the
men in the room had become so rich so fast.

Khodorkovsky does not feign innocence. "I don't set myself up as a
shining example," he told me. "Nor have I ever said that I've been a
model citizen. On the other hand, it's possible to develop and change,
especially in rapidly changing times. You can't just accord the right to
change to successive generations. My life is a good example of this. It
shows that in a single lifetime there can be two or more watersheds.
Until I was in my mid-twenties, I was raised as a model Soviet citizen. I
thought there was no other way to live. There were people, with more
humanistic educations, who thought there was something not quite
right with our lives. But not me. I thought it was all going quite well. It's
funny to hear myself saying this now, but it's true. Then, from twenty-
five till my mid-thirties, I was convinced that everything had been wrong
and that absolutely everything was permissible. You could get away with
not breaking any laws because there weren't really any laws. People,
even in the West, tried to say I broke the law, but they were never able
to prove it. Not everything was ethical. This is not something for me to
be proud of. Those were tough times; the way we dealt with minority
shareholders was not ethical. Then, from thirty-five onward, I've had a
third life. You can't be involved in business and engage in politics successfully. Many have tried. They are abroad now."

In his "third life," Khodorkovsky has championed "transparency" in corporate accounting and in the economy generally. He established a charitable foundation that has contributed huge sums to universities, the arts, and other causes. When he travels in the United States, he meets with top figures in Congress and the federal bureaucracy and mixes easily with other oil barons. These moves are as purposeful as Putin's seeming blandness. To encourage foreign investment, to borrow from foreign banks at normal rates, Russian businessmen like Khodorkovsky cannot have outlaw reputations. They must advance yet another generation or two, from John D. Rockefeller to David Rockefeller, from robber baron to scion of established industry.

"In the West, things evolved more slowly," he said. "It took more than one hundred years to develop contemporary society. We've started from scratch. But we have a model to look at. It's easier to do your homework when you have the answers."

A few weeks after we met, Khodorkovsky and his company came under attack from the Kremlin. Police arrested his partner and chief financial adviser, Platon Lebedev—himself a billionaire—on charges of theft, and prosecutors announced that they were investigating instances of tax evasion, fraud, and even murder. For weeks, there were interrogations, searches, threats. Analysts in Moscow said the affair was the result of an ongoing feud in the Kremlin between those who support the new capitalists and those who support the traditional bureaucracy. Khodorkovsky's involvement in politics, his support for potential opposition factions, was something neither Putin nor the security forces would tolerate. Putin, for his part, denied as "utter nonsense" that he is behind the pressure; it is just the law at work.

Putin may periodically lash out at the oligarchs, but, in general, the arrangements of power and influence have altered less than one might think. Putin, unlike his volatile predecessor, rarely fires anyone. Yeltsin's chief of staff, Aleksandr Voloshin, a bald and bearded man in his forties, has remained in place under Putin and, if anything, is more powerful than before. Two of the most influential aides, Igor Sechin and Viktor Ivanov, come from Putin's old haunt, the KGB's headquarters in St. Petersburg. And then there are smaller factions centered on the oil companies, the state gas monopoly, and other concerns.

There is constant talk in Moscow political circles about Putin's lack of commitment to democratic principles, especially civil liberties. When I asked Anatoly Chubais, who now runs the state's vast electric-power system, whether Putin was a democrat, he laughed and said, "Is Silvio Berlusconi a democrat?" (As it happens, Putin is personally close to the Italian leader; his family has vacationed with the Berlusconis in Sardinia.) "The question should not be if he is a democrat or not," Chubais went on. "There is a spectrum of democrats that ranges from, say, Berlusconi to Tony Blair. Putin is somewhere within the spectrum, but he is closer to Berlusconi than he is to Blair. What he is not is Fidel Castro."

Perhaps the comparison to Berlusconi is apt. Putin's control of the airwaves is, in its way, as complete as Berlusconi's. Putin has systematically neutered serious opposition in the media. In an international press-freedom index, Russia ranks a hundred and twenty-first out of a hundred and thirty-nine nations, according to the respected monitoring group Reporters Without Borders. Yelena Tregubova, a columnist at *Kommersant*, a leading daily newspaper in Moscow, told me that Presidential aides routinely call editors and threaten to "freeze out" their papers if they don't install "friendlier" correspondents at the Kremlin. Tregubova says that her own editor transferred her out of the Kremlin after feeling the pressure. "Putin reacts to criticism like a KGB person," she said. "Everything that is not praise is some kind of threat to him." At his recent meeting with American reporters, Putin admitted, "I don't like provocative questions."

Twelve years after the fall of Communism, there is no Soviet-style censorship at work, no Central Committee ideology department reviewing every news broadcast. Instead, in 1999, the Kremlin, which has full control of state television, installed a genial, like-minded fellow—Konstantin Ernst, a former scientist—to run Channel One, the main station. Putin and his advisers know they can rely on Ernst to keep matters under control. There are, of course, politicians and commentators who criticize the government. But within limits.

"Freedom of speech is a relative notion," Ernst told me one afternoon in his office, a sleek lair of steel and leather where several televisions were playing soundlessly. "It does not exist anywhere in its ideal form. It's like an ideal gas that does not exist in nature, only in theory. In reality, freedom of speech depends on the government, on the editors and producers. Everyone has a different sense of what it means."

Ernst admitted that he spoke from time to time with Kremlin officials, especially with Voloshin, and when I asked what would happen if they disagreed about editorial policy he flapped his hand and smiled, as if to dismiss so absurd a notion. "That's impossible," Ernst said. "It's easy for me to work here, because the Kremlin's foreign and domestic policy is always clear and understandable to me. A minimum of mistakes have been made. There is no mental distance between the majority view and government policy."

Putin's opposition is weak, sporadic, disorganized, and ill-defined. Although the Communists remain the biggest opposition party in Russia, they are an aging party, one that likely missed its chance to capture the Kremlin in 1996. The leading liberal opposition parties these days are small and timid: the Union of Right Forces, which is "liberal" in the Friedmanite-Thatcherite sense; and Yabloko, which is "liberal" in the European social-democratic sense. These factions are represented in the Duma by some intelligent voices, but they are pathologically incapable of forming a coalition and tend to draw nearly all their votes in Moscow, St. Petersburg, and a few other large cities. When they show any sign of influence, Putin easily coopts them or slaps them down.

I've known Grigori Yavlinsky since he was a young economist in the Gorbachev circle. Since 1993, he has led the Yabloko faction in the Duma. Now he is fifty-one, and he seems even more caustic, more frustrated than when I first met him. When I asked him about the opposition to Putin, he scowled and grew defensive. "Do you have a real opposition in Great Britain or Japan, much less in the United States?" he said. "So, if you are looking for one here, it's rather difficult. To have an opposition you need serious preconditions—an independent media, or at least media that are not all in one hand. You need independent financial resources, a civil society, a special environment. The Duma is filled with people who are on the take, as if they were staff members for the government administration or one interest or another. We have no independent elections. This is almost a corporate, semi-criminal system, and there are no alternatives that can be presented to the people. The system entirely serves one person."

Yavlinsky blamed Yeltsin for the "rotten" state of affairs. "We tried to bring the Yeltsin era to a close as soon as possible. His time was over in 1993," he said. "Everything that came after was counterproductive: Chechnya, the default in 1998, criminal privatization. But Yeltsin tricked us in a special way. He brought a successor onto the scene. And his system was cemented in place. This system can create one successor after another. So be prepared for a very long and winding road. In this situation, you can either be a dissident or help to create a civil independent party. You need a strategy and you need to keep on the vector of human rights, liberal policy, human dignity, private property. The challenge is to be independent while accepting money from the likes of Khodorkovsky"—Yabloko is almost completely funded by Khodorkovsky—"or keeping an open dialogue with Putin, and understanding the regional bureaucracy, which is as loyal as animals to the President. Either people wake up and act or you wait indefinitely for the appearance of a 'good tsar.' My task in this system is to create an independent Russian democratic party. Eventually, we have to overcome, we have to create a post-Yeltsin era. Maybe in twenty years we'll get there."

In the days when Moscow was still the capital of an empire, the city was militarized. It wasn't just a matter of the occasional parades on Red Square, with all the ICBMs and tanks rumbling across the cobblestones, and the Politburo members waving absently atop Lenin's tomb. Driving to work, you were forever following a troop truck with a sign reading *"Lyudi"*—"People"—tacked to a wooden back panel. Inside, a few dozen recruits in khaki uniforms sat on benches smoking and kidding around: there were recruits from every corner of the empire.

The Russian Army, the inheritor of the structures, arms, and tactics of the Soviet armed forces, is now a shambles: a psychological wreck, a material ruin. Conscription is still universal, but only notionally so. It's easy to bribe your way out of the draft for a couple of thousand dollars. It is only the least skilled, the least educated, who enlist. Many of the draftees are illiterate and in such poor physical condition that they are useless as anything more than cannon fodder in Chechnya or as targets of abuse for their predatory superiors. *Dyedovshchina,* the sadistic, often fatal, hazing of recruits, is ubiquitous: soldiers are routinely humiliated and tortured by their commanders, beaten with sticks, chains, chairs, anything at hand. Every year, thousands are wounded and hundreds are killed or commit suicide; thousands more go AWOL as a result of the abuse. The Russian Army is preposterously top-heavy—there are five times as many generals as in the American armed services—and, for many of those officers and commanders, life has been so leached of a sense of mission and pride that they destroy themselves with drink; their salaries are so low that they ease into a life of corruption, petty or grand. In a rare case of prosecution, Colonel General Georgy Oleinik, a former financial official in the Defense Ministry, was convicted last year of "misappropriating" funds; it seems he misappropriated four hundred and fifty million dollars.

Dmitri Trenin, a former career officer in the Soviet Army, is now a scholar at the Carnegie Moscow Center. He remains well connected at the Defense Ministry. When we met one afternoon for coffee, he described the ministry as a "ghost town," with innumerable generals sitting at their clean desks doing little more than trying to maintain some semblance of the status quo and their own positions. These generals and officers, Trenin said, suffer from "a huge inferiority complex." Having spent their careers as the heads of a colossal military machine preparing for the possibility of an Armageddon clash in Europe, they have refused to change strategy or tactics. Even as Putin talks about the possibility of Russia one day joining NATO, the Russian commanders still spend their energies devising ways to defeat it. Putin has so far been unwilling to reform the Army, to make it professional, smaller, more modern.

The Army has lost, in effect, its last three wars: after a decade of fighting, the Soviet armed forces retreated from Afghanistan; in 1994–96, Yeltsin foolishly tried to bomb Chechnya into submission, but failed; the revival of that war in the late nineties has, until now, resulted only in—as Russians say—the "Palestinization" of Chechnya, a conflict that now includes suicide bombers. The Russian troops in Chechnya are incapable of keeping any kind of peace in the region and routinely rape, harass, loot apartments, demand protection money from local merchants, execute prisoners, and even sell arms to the rebels. Key Chechen militant groups have accepted help from Islamic radicals, including Al Qaeda.

"As a nuclear power, Russia is still potent. It still makes Russia the No. 2 country in strategic nuclear power," Trenin said. "But, apart from that, this military is so bad that it is a miracle that people are willing to go to Chechnya and risk their lives for the meager pay that they get. The commander of the *Kursk* submarine"—which sank in 2000 owing to a mysterious explosion in the Barents Sea, killing a hundred and eighteen sailors—"got a salary of two hundred dollars a month. It is hard for me in Moscow to find a kid who will work here as an assistant for less than five hundred dollars a month. And this was a nuclear submarine with the power to annihilate a major country."

The politicians who support fundamental reform of the Army insist that Russia requires around five hundred thousand troops, not the more than one million in uniform today, and a total rethinking of its structures and strategy. Alexei Arbatov, the deputy chairman of the Duma's defense committee, told me, "We are still oriented toward a war against the West. This stems from Russian military strategy since the days of Peter the Great. To change this is like telling the astronomers to stop relying on Newton and Kepler."

Obsession with American power is universal. The Russians are obsessed with American power in their own way. Theirs is the reaction of the humbled rival learning to deal with an unaccustomed sense of weakness. This may be the most important emotion in all of Russian politics, and it shapes Putin's foreign policy almost completely.

Two of Russia's leading political pollsters, Aleksandr Oslon and Lev Gudkov, both told me that anti-Americanism in Russia is far different from what it is in, say, France. The feeling comes and goes. During the American military actions in Kosovo and Iraq, and during the last Winter Olympics, when Russian skaters were accused of winning a gold medal through bogus judging, antipathy toward the United States ran high. But then it faded. "Generally, Russians have a positive attitude toward the United States, but there is this complex of defeat and humiliation and even neurotic sensitivity that flares up," Gudkov said. "Fifty-five percent think the West and the United States are trying to colonize Russia, but the U.S. is still seen as a utopia because it is the most vivid example of a normal country."

Putin's attitude toward the United States has proved flexible. When he began his term of office, the foreign-policy élites in Moscow—the Foreign Ministry lifers, the generals and admirals—anticipated that Putin would "stand up" to the United States more than Yeltsin ever did. With the exception of fairly marginal liberal politicians, most believed that Yeltsin was capable of great bluster with Washington but in the end would cave in to every American demand and desire, be it in arms control, diplomacy, or trade. At first, Putin did seem a steelier, more readily offended negotiating partner than Yeltsin. Then came September 11.

"Right after 9/11, Putin gathered many politicians to talk about the role of Russia in the situation," Grigori Yavlinsky, the head of Yabloko, said. "The absolute majority of politicians said that Russia should be either neutral or even on the side of the Taliban. Only a few spoke up and said that we should support the United States."

Putin went with the minority, with the liberals. He was, as it happened, the first leader of a major foreign country to call George Bush and pledge his support. That support included giving the American military critical intelligence reports on the Taliban forces in Afghanistan. These moves allowed Putin to make the argument to the West that, at this stage, the war in Chechnya was not a brutal assault but, rather, another front in the war against terrorism, and Washington, which had always at least lightly protested Russia's actions in Chechnya, now no longer does so with any conviction.

Putin's decision on how to react to September 11 was easy compared with the question of Iraq. He was wary of an American invasion, and he came under heavy pressure from German Chancellor Gerhard Schröder and French President Jacques Chirac to join their opposition to Washington in the United Nations. He was also under heavy pressure at home. "People in the KGB and the military-industrial complex wanted to block Putin's 'American connection,' " Sergei Karaganov, a former foreign-policy adviser to Yeltsin, said. According to several well-informed diplomatic and intelligence sources, Putin was told by his generals and intelligence chiefs that the United States would have an impossible job finding physical evidence of any weapons of mass destruction and that an invasion would take months, if not years, to accomplish.

Putin does not seem to entirely trust his own Foreign Ministry to conduct day-to-day relations with the United States. During the Iraq crisis, he sent Voloshin, his chief of staff, to meet with officials at the White House. On other occasions, he has dispatched Dmitri Rogozin, the chairman of the Duma's foreign-affairs committee. Rogozin is an emotional nationalist, and is known around Moscow as a skeptic where the United States is concerned. "We see something of ourselves in America, for better or worse, and America is going through its golden age and we are at our nadir," he told me. "But we are having a roller-coaster ride, we are out of phase with each other. This is why our attitude to you is almost condescending."

When I asked Rogozin about the war in Iraq, he smiled and said, "Everyone in Europe thinks it's a calamity. But we shrugged and realized there was nothing we could do about it. . . . Before the end of the eighties, there were still some forces deterring you. There was the Soviet Union and the balance of pressures. Now, with this having disappeared, it's like in sumo wrestling. The United States simply fell forward for lack of an opponent, and you became responsible for everything. During the Cold War, both sides created their own cyborgs. We created the Palestinian cyborg. You created the Bin Laden cyborg, in Afghanistan. And suddenly these cyborgs were no longer under their masters. Now the United States has to fill the entire space, they are responsible for everything—and, therefore, they are to blame for everything."

Putin's view is clearly that Russia can no longer hope to be a rival or a counterweight to American power. It can only seek to influence that power in the interest, above all, of stability at home and abroad, for it is only under conditions of relative calm—stable oil prices, relative quiet along the southern borders, and integration with the West— that Russia can steadily develop. In the end, Putin played Iraq well, putting up a reasoned opposition to the war, but without damaging his relations with the United States. If anyone won that diplomatic battle, he did.

"Look, many in the Russian leadership resent the United States, but they have decided that it is better to adapt to American power and do the best they can, because the Middle East, Pakistan, and Iran—it can all go up in flames, in revolutions and wars," Karaganov said. "So we have to have someone to do the dirty job of keeping it all together. And that's the United States. And although you do stupid things, the United States is the only steamboat we can hitch ourselves to and go in the direction of modernity."

One afternoon, I went to the Kremlin to see Andrei Illarionov, one of Putin's top economic advisers. Illarionov is young, speaks fluent English, and is married to an American. I mentioned that on my way across Red Square and through Spassky Gate I'd noticed that workers were preparing for a parade. A gold tsarist-era two-headed eagle had been mounted on one end of the square and a vast Russian tricolor had been draped over Lenin's tomb. Putin's anthem would undoubtedly complete this postmodern picture.

"Yes, tomorrow is Independence Day," Illarionov said. "Not many people remember, but it's the day Russia was declared independent."

"And what of all these symbols?" I asked.

He shrugged. "These symbols reflect the complexity of Russian history, a fact of life," he said. "We've inherited the legacy of the Russian empire, seventy-three years of Soviet Communism, and, now, twelve years of independent Russia. Mr. Yeltsin tried to remove Lenin's body from Red Square, but the resistance from the Communist Party didn't allow it. Yeltsin reluctantly decided to postpone the action."

Illarionov had worked in the Yeltsin government, and I asked him to distinguish between the two Presidents.

"Mr. Yeltsin's was an era of revolution, and he was a revolutionary who set out to destroy the ancien régime," he said.

In the Putin era, I suggested, the world has all but stopped paying attention to Russia. Television stations and newspapers were closing their Moscow bureaus, or, at least, cutting back.

"Maybe the fact that we're not on the front pages all around the world is a good thing," he replied. "We've always dreamed of such a time. It's a sign of normality." Sometimes, he said, people forget the historical burden that Russia carries, and they focus instead on the decisions, and the personalities, that come and go. "There were seventy-five years of civil war with millions killed since 1917: war between red and white, then collectivization, then a real civil war again, industrialization, the purges in 1937, the Second World War—a war against Fascism, but also a kind of civil war in which one million people changed sides. Where else would you find this? Then the purges of the POWs, the war on cosmopolitans, a civil war against nationalities like the Chechens, the Volga Germans, the Crimean Tatars: twenty nationalities deported or wiped out. Another civil war. At the same time, tens of millions of people were raised on Communist ideology and ideals. You cannot change that overnight. It's like being raised in some kind of orthodox faith, an orthodox form of Islam, say. There is a serious response when you try to change their world. You need a time of calming down. So the state of people now, for the majority, is geared around a sense of survival. That's what's really wanted. That's who Putin is. That's how we live now, with history and histories all around us and everything all mixed up."

(2003)

•

Putin's "soft authoritarianism" has hardened with time. After a bogus trial, Mikhail Khodorkovsky was sent to prison in distant Chita. Opposition parties and movements have dwindled under constant pressure from the Kremlin. Putin has even threatened to eliminate organizations as benign as foreign think tanks, like the Moscow Carnegie Center. He has greeted signs of political independence in the region, particularly the "Orange Revolution" in Ukraine, with ill-concealed hostility and anxiety. In 2005, Freedom House, which tracks civil liberties and political rights in countries around the world, downgraded Russia's status from "partly free" to "unfree." It was the first time Russia had been ranked "unfree" since 1991. The next mystery of Russian politics is how Putin will manage his own succession when his second term is finished in 2008.

Part IV

The Afterlife:
Natan Sharansky

In the Land of Israel, nothing is more telling than the hat on your head. The followers of the late Lubavitcher Rebbe Menachem Schneerson tend to the felt fedoras once favored by sidemen in the old Ellington orchestra, while the Moroccan Sephardim wear the multi-colored embroidered caps that were de rigueur for bebop pianists at the Five Spot. A small knitted *kipa,* or skullcap, signifies the Modern Ortho-dox Zionist; a slightly greater circumference indicates a settler; a black velvet model is the mark of the ultra-Orthodox and (sometimes, but not always) the anti-Zionist. It is true: to be a discerning Israeli is to be no less an expert in hats than the millinery specialists at Bergdorf's. The really well versed can simply glance at the brim width, the crown height, and the fur type of a passing *shtreimel*—a kind of Hasidic sombrero worn on the Sabbath and on holidays—and identify the particular sect of the Hasid in question, his attitude toward Israel as a state, his income, his fealty to certain texts and chants, and the location of his ancestral vil-lage in Ukraine or Poland, Russia or Lithuania.

When the Soviet dissident and Jewish activist Natan Sharansky was released from the Gulag and allowed to emigrate to Israel, in 1986, not a few people in the cheering throng at Ben-Gurion Airport were curious to see what he would wear (or not wear) on his pale bald pate. During nine years as a prisoner of the Communist regime, Sharansky had become the emblem of Soviet Jewry, the most desperate realm of the Diaspora. Throughout his imprisonment, his weary and impish face projected the singular image of the persecuted Jew—an image on placards everywhere, at demonstrations outside the United Nations and the White House, outside the Elysée Palace and in Pushkin Square. An entire generation of Jews—in Europe, in Israel, and, most of all, in the United States—had measured its commitment to the postwar slogan "Never again!" by its commitment to the liberation of the Soviet Jews in general, and Natan Sharansky in particular.

In Mikhail Gorbachev's first months as General Secretary of the Communist Party, he parroted the familiar line on Sharansky, claiming that he, like Andrei Sakharov and other prisoners and internal exiles, was guilty of "anti-Soviet" behavior, of treason. That soon changed. One of Gorbachev's earliest and most important moves to make his peace with the West and seduce the intellectual classes at home was to release Sharansky and, not long after, to end the emigration restrictions on Soviet Jewry. Sharansky fast became the symbol of a historic exodus, Biblical in its scale. Since 1989, more than seven hundred thousand Jews have arrived in Israel from the former Soviet Union. Considering Israel's size, receiving them has been a feat of demographic agility even more impressive than, say, the United States absorbing the entire population of Canada and then making room for every Australian as well. It is hard to know exactly how many Jews are left in the former Soviet Union, but Sharansky says Israel should be prepared to absorb "hundreds of thousands more."

At first, Sharansky could not have been more ignorant of the identity politics of Israel. That is, he knew almost nothing of its hats. As a young dissident in Moscow, and then during his time in the Gulag system, he dreamed of finally getting an exit visa and making aliyah—immigrating— to an Israel of "brothers and sisters, a country unified in the essentials." Sharansky was one of many refuseniks who formed within themselves an image of a Promised Land by raking together whatever scraps of information they could find. On the Voice of America he heard half-jammed radio accounts of the Six-Day War. He read Leon Uris's novel *Exodus.* He absorbed the fevered, well-meaning descriptions of paradise from visitors from the West. He learned Hebrew in underground classrooms from smuggled textbooks. The refuseniks formed, quite naturally, a romanticized—or, at least, simplified—notion of Israel, an antidote to their day-to-day reality. Even Sharansky's marriage was an episode in romantic Zionism: he married Avital Stieglitz one day and she emigrated the next. At the airport, they made a pledge: "Next year in Jerusalem."

A lot of time has passed since Sharansky's arrival in Israel, but it is still startling to meet with him at his apartment, in the Old Katamon district of Jerusalem. When I was living in Moscow, I got permission to visit Perm-35, in the Urals, which was Sharansky's last prison camp. He had already been free for several years, but I went to his old barracks, his old punishment cell, and met his commandant, Lieutenant Colonel Nikolai Osin, a thick sausage of a man who scowled vermilion when I mentioned Sharansky's name. "There were never any political prisoners here!" Osin told me, and roared with laughter. And so to see Sharansky now, at liberty in Israel, surrounded by his wife and two daughters, by a riot of pink and purple flowers on his porch and the shattering desert sun and everywhere the pale Jerusalem stone, is a miracle. Somehow he has managed to sustain his life's drama. Sharansky is now a minister in the government of Benjamin Netanyahu, a man he once counted as a dear friend. In the past several months, however, he has found himself in the position of having to decide whether to withdraw his support and bring down the government or to stay in power and risk tarnishing what has been a peerless moral reputation in Israel.

"In prison, when people would ask about Israel there were never any questions about whom you felt closer to, the left or the right, the religious or the nonreligious," Sharansky said. "I never really knew much about this, and when I came I was suddenly besieged with these questions and issues and all the debates, and I had to think about these things. It was completely bewildering."

At first, Sharansky could be forgiven his bewilderment. On February 11, 1986, he began the day as a prisoner of the Soviet Union. KGB guards then flew him to East Berlin, and there he was told to walk across the Glienicke Bridge and into the West. Sharansky had grown so skinny on prison rations that, on worldwide television, his state-issued trousers nearly fell to his ankles as he walked to freedom. By nightfall, he was at the Western Wall in the Old City of Jerusalem, carried along on the shoulders of hundreds of jubilant Israelis. At the Wall, he prayed from a tiny Book of Psalms—a gift from Avital. He had been able to keep that book throughout his imprisonment in Lefortovo, Chistipol, and Perm-35. It was his talisman, his communion with the language and his people and his wife. Once Natan was thrown in prison, Avital had spent nearly every day campaigning for his release, and the moment they saw each other again, on the day of his release, Natan said, in Hebrew, *"Slichi le she'icharti k'tsat"* ("Sorry I'm a little late"). After the initial celebration in Jerusalem, Natan and Avital went to the Galilee for a brief vacation. One morning, Sharansky woke to the fragrance of a blossoming almond tree and the music of Palestine songbirds. He roused his wife and dragged their bed out to the balcony. "Look," he told her, "it's paradise." Nine months after their reunion, their first daughter, Rachel, was born.

But Israel does not permit its saints long honeymoons. Sharansky would have to decide about his public identity—his hat—and much else. Compounding the problem was the fact that, in his absence, Avital had grown close to the religious nationalist group Mercaz Ha'rav. Her circle was, in all ways, conservative. Politically, she was close to the settlers in Gaza and the West Bank. Avital was now a devout Orthodox woman and covered her head with a scarf. What sort of Israeli would her husband be? The speculation began.

"People were betting on whether I would put on the *kipa* or Avital would take off her scarf, because for Israelis it is impossible to stay in one room together if they haven't got their headgear together," Sharansky said. "This really irritated me. I didn't want to belong to any group. I wanted to belong to all of them together. But when I got out of prison and came to Israel I found very quickly that, while I had joined the greater Israeli people, everyone was in his own cell."

Sharansky carries his iconic status with a sheepish modesty. His vanity lies in his self-regard as a lifelong chess player, as one who can figure his way out of any strategic cul-de-sac. After a great deal of thought, he was convinced he had solved the riddle of the hat. "In 1974, there was a famous underground art exhibition in Moscow that was knocked down with bulldozers by the KGB," he said. "Some foreign tourists had brought me a souvenir—a hat that Israeli soldiers wore. I put it on and almost that very day I found myself at that exhibition fighting against the KGB. I felt like a real soldier. I had very sentimental feelings about that hat, but then I got arrested and lost it. So when I got to Israel I put on this hat, thinking, First of all, it's Army; second, it has a sentimental meaning for me; and, finally, let other people break their heads over this. Let them decide what kind of religious or not religious person I am."

The Army hat seemed to solve the identity problem. It represented an allegiance to the singular national institution—the national protector—and, at the same time, it was a particularly schlumpy Army cap, and so it projected a sense of unimportance, as if to say, O.K., I have covered my head, I cannot be accused of complete religious indifference, but I also have a secular, national allegiance, and without being too crazy about it, either. In any case, Sharansky did not tip his hand—or his hat—to any one ideology, religious sect, or community, and he was enormously popular across the political spectrum: an almost impossible feat in fractious modern Israel.

Sharansky's informality worked well for him. When he went to dine with the King of Belgium, he forgot all he had been told about the protocol of the occasion and addressed the King as "Mr. King." Mr. King was charmed. After wearing a tie to visit Ronald Reagan and Margaret Thatcher, he dispensed with the constricting garment forever. At the White House, Bill Clinton asked him why he didn't bother with a tie. "We have a special law in Israel," Sharansky said. "For everyone who was in prison more than nine years, they don't have to wear a tie."

For his first ten years in Israel, Sharansky kept his distance from elective politics and focused mainly on his de-facto leadership of the Russian emigration. This was no small burden. Hundreds of émigrés were arriving every day at Ben-Gurion Airport. To help the new immigrants, Sharansky founded the Zionist Forum, whose mission was to supplement the budget for immigrant absorption and build apartments and create jobs and institutions for the new arrivals. The Forum has raised millions of dollars, much of it from foreign donors.

But a little more than a year ago Sharansky entered the world of elective politics. He had thought about the decision for a long time. Even in a tiny landscape rich with survivors of war and persecution, Sharansky stood out. Was he risking his reputation, his moral authority? But in order to get closer, to exert more influence, he would have to run for parliament. While Sharansky was thinking it all over, his longtime friend Ari Weiss told him, "If you go into politics, you are going to have to forget what I have to say to you now, but listen: You have to realize that in politics your stature is inevitably going to be reduced."

Weiss knew what he was talking about. Before emigrating to Israel, he had worked on Capitol Hill as a key aide to the late Speaker of the House Tip O'Neill.

Sharansky made up his mind. "I have no doubt that's true," he told his friend, "but stature is of no importance if you don't use it." For the 1996 elections, he helped create a new political party, Israel B'aliyah, which is, first and foremost, the party of the new Russian immigration. The émigrés had first voted for Likud, then for Yitzhak Rabin and Labor, and now in their dissatisfaction they were ready to turn to their own. The Party's leaders are Russian. Its lingua franca is Russian. Its primary interests are the interests of Russian immigration. In almost none of its television and radio advertisements did the Party even bother to broadcast in Hebrew.

From the start, Sharansky's politics have been conservative. Like so many Russians raised on Soviet socialism, he holds views of economic policy that tend to the Thatcherite. Largely because he looks through the prism of a Soviet dissident who felt that the West was foolish ever to forge treaties with totalitarian states during the Cold War, he is convinced that Israel must beware of all dealings with the autocrats of the Middle East, including Yasir Arafat. An incident like last week's suicide bombings in west Jerusalem only hardens Sharansky's conviction that the Oslo peace process under the Rabin-Peres Labor governments went too far, too fast, and provided too few guarantees.

Sharansky knew that he could not count on the support of the Israeli left, and yet he was not a run-of-the-mill right-winger. First, he has behind him an enormous ethnic constituency. The politics of the new Russians are, above all, about the new Russians. Although the new Russians are reflexively distrustful of a settlement with the Palestinians, their first priority is economic. The Israeli government cannot spend or build fast enough to satisfy the demands of such a huge influx. They need funds for housing. They want jobs that match their remarkably high level of expertise as scientists, mathematicians, academics, doctors, and musicians. The hotels of Israel are still filled with Russian doctors changing the sheets. Sharansky was connected to that community and could rely on its support. He also had support among the sorts of nationalist and settler who saw him as a Zionist hero. He could even count on a few votes among liberals who admired him not so much for the content of his politics as for his character, his honesty, and his wit.

In 1996, for the first time, the electoral system allowed people to vote separately for a party in the Knesset and for a Prime Minister. As a result, the Russians and the Israeli conservatives could vote, say, for the Likud candidate for Prime Minister, Netanyahu, and for the Israel B'aliyah slate—Sharansky's slate—for the Knesset. I also spoke to some Israelis in Jerusalem, Tel Aviv, and Haifa who had voted for the Labor candidate, Shimon Peres, and Israel B'aliyah.

As a politician, Sharansky owes his charisma to his biography and his character. He is a mediocre stump speaker and a less than imposing physical presence. He is quite short, or, as Groucho Marx once said, "well over four feet": about five-three. His Hebrew is, to be charitable, limited in vocabulary, and it is marred by a heavy Russian accent. His English is better than his Hebrew. He is, however, funny and self-deprecating. He has little of the pride-in-suffering seen occasionally in famous dissidents.

When the balloting was over, Sharansky's new party had won seven seats in the parliament and, after the usual bargaining over a coalition government, got two seats in Netanyahu's Cabinet: Minister of Trade and Industry (Sharansky), and Minister of Absorption (Yuli Edelstein, another former political prisoner and a West Bank settler). It was an incredible victory, and totally unexpected, but in no time at all Sharansky had learned the cost of moving from dissidence to neutrality to partisan politics.

"Israeli politics is brutal because the logic of coalition politics is that you have to concede your principles to form a government," Yaron Ezrahi, a prominent political theorist, told me. "Israeli politics demands that. All party leaders cede principles. Sharansky was immediately subject to that cruel logic. He had to play by rules inconsistent with what had made him unique in the first place. In this respect, he was overwhelmed. Here is a guy who took on the Kremlin and won but now has to face the prospect of not being able to survive the warm embrace of Bibi Netanyahu."

Orwell wrote in his 1949 essay on Mahatma Gandhi, "Saints should always be judged guilty until they are proved innocent." Orwell admired Gandhi but was forced to ask himself, "To what extent did he compromise his own principles by entering into politics, which of their nature are inseparable from coercion and fraud?" Nearly every saint who has entered the realm of politics fails—or, at the very least, fails to keep his sainthood under repair. Nelson Mandela is the exception, not the rule.

Sharansky has been an enormous disappointment to many Israelis, especially on the left. For one thing, he has not shown himself to be overly concerned with the human rights of the Palestinians. Sharansky, who helped start Helsinki Watch, the leading human-rights group in the former Soviet Union, has been extremely reluctant to speak out even in cases of alleged torture and abuse of Palestinian prisoners. Civil-rights groups, many Laborites, and smaller liberal parties expected a different man, a crusader of another kind. "Sharansky writes in his book about helping other persecuted peoples as part of his own freedom, but in Israel he hasn't lived according to that," said Eitan Felner, the executive director of B'Tselem, a human-rights organization in Jerusalem. "It's like the first Zionists a hundred years ago, who came here as if there were no other people here. It's easy to talk about human rights when it's your own people."

In 1996, there was still great hope for Sharansky as a new politician. Most of the leading media outlets in Israel—two of the three major newspapers, state television, and state-run radio—are inarguably liberal, but Sharansky's triumph did not rankle them the way Netanyahu's did. Perhaps no liberal institution was more sanguine about Sharansky's rise to political power than *The Jerusalem Report,* the country's leading English-language magazine. A few years after arriving in Israel, Sharansky helped start up the magazine with his friends Hirsh Goodman, a native South African who had been the longtime defense correspondent for *The Jerusalem Post,* and Ze'ev Chafets, an irreverent author and columnist.

At *The Jerusalem Report,* Sharansky was a regular columnist and a moral force. As a reporter, he tagged along with the Army during its secret airlift of Ethiopian Jews out of Addis Ababa and wrote a moving dispatch; he wrote intelligent commentary on the collapse of the Soviet Union and on the problems of the arriving immigrants. Once, in the midst of the Gulf War, he invited the eminent religious scholar Rabbi Adin Steinsaltz to lecture the magazine's reporters and editors on the interpretation of libel laws in the Talmud. While everyone wore gas masks and listened, Steinsaltz spoke about the importance of avoiding *lashon harah*—malicious gossip.

"Natan's message was simple," Goodman told me one morning at the offices of *The Jerusalem Report.* " 'These are your roots. This is how the Talmud relates to slander, and the punishment is tremendous.' It was very illustrative, and it was very illustrative of Natan."

Goodman could not have been closer to Sharansky. Sharansky signed on Goodman's mortgage and was a witness at his wedding. Sharansky was so delighted with what he called "my first day job" that he inscribed a copy of his memoir, *Fear No Evil,* "To Hirsh, Who freed me from being a prisoner of Zion." Goodman did not vote for Sharansky—he was convinced that the Russians would end up a "Trojan horse for Bibi"—but he was not displeased that his friend had won.

"*The Jerusalem Report* was great," Goodman said, "but it wasn't his calling. He was destined for national leadership of some kind. Just as

Avital's destiny was to fight for his freedom, he saw his destiny as bring-ing a million Jews in from the former Soviet Union. Natan is a chess player, and that is crucial. He survived in jail by playing chess with the authorities. So in politics he saw that the only way to achieve his agenda is to play chess again, and Bibi is a piece on the board."

Several months after the election, Sharansky's old friends at *The Jerusalem Report* got a sense that he was fast becoming a rather conven-tional conservative minister and perhaps the most visible supporter of the West Bank settlers. Netty Gross, a friend and neighbor of Sharan-sky's, wrote a profile of him for *The Jerusalem Report*. Although the arti-cle was mild by the standards of Israeli journalism, Sharansky thought the piece was damaging, and certainly, compared with the worshipful press coverage he had accumulated in his years as a dissident-icon, it was. "Natan has a hard time with criticism," Gross said. "I think he really has to get off this hero business, this you-can't-criticize-me business. It's time for his handlers to tell him that he is part of a government—a gov-ernment that has to ask its kids to go die for it. I get the impression that criticism is seen as betrayal, and it's not."

Early this year, Sharansky found himself in the center of one of the worst political scandals in the history of the state—the Bar-On affair. Netanyahu, after his election victory, needed to appoint an Attorney General, a job that, under Labor, traditionally went to some liberal jurist from the courts or academe. Netanyahu, who was intent on bucking the Labor establishment, selected a relatively obscure Likud activist and attorney named Roni Bar-On. Bar-On had no great reputation in the law—he was better known as the chairman of Betar Jerusalem, one of the most popular soccer teams in the country—and quit almost immedi-ately. Two weeks later, a journalist for Israeli television reported that, in fact, the Bar-On appointment had been a favor to Aryeh Deri, who was the leader of Shas, the main party of the ultra-Orthodox Sephardim—Jews whose roots are in Morocco and other Muslim countries—and whose continued support was essential to the survival of the Netanyahu government. Deri is on trial for fraud and corruption, but, with his friend Bar-On as Attorney General, the report suggested that he was hoping to win favorable consideration.

The result was nationwide hysteria. The story, in effect, suggested that the Prime Minister had knowingly appointed as his chief law officer a man who might extend his good offices to Aryeh Deri in his time of trouble. The implication was that Netanyahu had cut a deal with the Devil.

Sharansky did not hesitate to respond. "If there is even ten percent of truth in Israel TV's story," he declared, "this government has no place in continuing to govern."

On April 21, the Attorney General appointed after Bar-On's resignation, Elyakim Rubenstein, and the state's attorney, Edna Arbel, issued a seventy-five-page report declaring that while there was insufficient evidence to indict Netanyahu, there had been "a real threat to the rule of law."

Netanyahu went on television and said that the Attorney General's report had completely exonerated him. He attacked the news media for trying "to undermine the legitimacy of the government." The Prime Minister had always been critical of the Israeli media, but this attack took on a particularly dark, Nixonian ring. There was not the slightest hint of regret in his words or in his voice.

After making his television statement, Netanyahu went home. At about two in the morning, he met with Sharansky. The two men had been friends for a decade. When the Labor establishment gave Sharansky minimal help in staging demonstrations abroad in the eighties, Netanyahu, as the United Nations representative, was quick to do what he could. Over the years, he and Sharansky had had many private meetings and Sabbath dinners. Usually, Netanyahu would go to the Sharanskys', because he is willing to drive on Saturdays. But in recent months they had grown apart. Netanyahu had been angry when Sharansky did not endorse him in the election campaign (Sharansky preferred to remain neutral, to preserve his party's independence from Likud) and had become even angrier when Sharansky pressed for a more significant Cabinet post than Trade and Industry. Sharansky, for his part, refused to be treated like the obedient protégé. He felt that the government was ignoring promises to his constituency, the Russians. What was more, he had begun to dislike Netanyahu's style as Prime Minister: he found him arrogant, condescending, uninterested in the contrary advice of his elected ministers. And now Netanyahu had been humiliated by Sharansky's "ten percent" remark. Indeed, even a generous reading of the report on the Bar-On affair made it clear that well over ten percent of the original television broadcast was true.

Netanyahu knew that Sharansky had it in his power to topple the government. Netanyahu controlled sixty-eight of the hundred and twenty seats in the Knesset. Of the sixty-eight, Sharansky controlled the seven legislators from his party and held sway over four more from an allied party, the Third Way, led by the Internal Security Minister, Avigdor Kahalani. The power to force new elections for both Prime Minister and the Knesset was, and is, in Sharansky's hands.

The two men negotiated for about an hour. In the end, Sharansky decided to back down. He could not bring himself to negate the 1996 election on the basis of a report that called for no indictments. He could not bear to open the way for Labor. Netanyahu promised that he would consult more with his ministers, that he would pay more attention to Russian issues, that he would set up an internal-appointments committee within the Cabinet that would include Sharansky. (Sharansky soon discovered, to his dismay, that the committee was a sham: Netanyahu simply ignored it.)

Goodman could not believe that his friend had stayed put. He had always known that Sharansky was a conservative, but now he saw him sticking with a government that surely did not pass the "ten percent" test. He was also incensed that Sharansky had voted for a new law that would give Orthodox rabbis de-jure control over religious conversions inside Israel—a law that was widely interpreted both in Israel and abroad as delegitimating Conservative and Reform Judaism. In his rage, Goodman went to his desk and wrote a column titled "Mr. Ten Percent" for the May 15 issue of *The Jerusalem Report*. "Rumor has it that Natan Sharansky is growing a beard these days," the column began. "Apparently, he can't bear to look at himself in the mirror anymore." Goodman charged that Sharansky had supported a conversion law that effectively disenfranchised half of world Jewry, and had done it only because "his personal political survival depended on his caving in to ultra-Orthodox ultimatums." The reason Sharansky did not move against a corrupt Prime Minister, Goodman wrote, was that the Russian Party was split and was not likely to win seven seats again in new elections. "It is therefore crucial for him that the current government survive and no matter what he may think of Netanyahu personally or his professional performance, he will continue to support him politically," Goodman wrote. "And because Natan Sharansky is essentially a person of principle, who understands better than anyone else that he has become just another cheap politician devoid of any principle other than that of political survival, rumors of his beard may very well be correct."

Goodman did not want to take Sharansky by surprise, so he slipped an advance copy of the column and a personal note into Sharansky's mailbox. The column ended their friendship.

When I went to see Goodman at his office at *The Jerusalem Report*, a few weeks after the column ran, he seemed to wear none of the journalist's customary self-satisfaction after thrusting the lance. "The whole thing pains me," he said. "Recently, I gave a lecture to a Jewish group in

Los Angeles, and there were six or seven hundred people there. At the mention of Sharansky's name, they booed! It was like a knife through my heart."

This spring and summer have been a thoroughly depressing time in Israel. Netanyahu's government is constantly at war with its opponents and with itself. The peace process, which Netanyahu promised to continue (if with greater caution), has deteriorated. The bombings in the west-Jerusalem market will undoubtedly make serious negotiations almost impossible for weeks, or months, to come. The suspicions and divisions that followed Yitzhak Rabin's assassination linger. When I was driving from Jerusalem to Tel Aviv to meet Sharansky, a newscast reported that fanatic Israeli nationalists had gone to the prison that houses Yigal Amir, Rabin's assassin, to celebrate Amir's twenty-seventh birthday, and had brought bottles of champagne.

Sharansky, for his part, was still smarting from the attacks on his integrity and political wisdom by Goodman and many others. Netanyahu, who was at least grateful that Sharansky's ten-percent remark had not led to something more disastrous for him, told me, "Natan's not cowed by the fact that he's taking a beating from the circles that adulated him before."

"I wouldn't say what Hirsh wrote was painful. It was just wrong," Sharansky said. "He was saying, 'You are a guy who once had principles and now you have no principles at all. You are a politician who only wants to survive in power and you know that your voters won't vote for you again.' It's bad enough that he doesn't understand my votes, but he doesn't understand me at all. To say of me that I'm a guy who wants only to be in power and that's all—well, he might as well say, 'You are a guy who wants to be seven feet tall and only play basketball.' It's not about me. By the way, I understand it. Hirsh can't stand the Prime Minister. To think that his friend had the ability to bring Bibi down and didn't do it made him angry."

"Will you ever respond to him?" I asked.

"It's not something to respond to," Sharansky said. "Someone tells you that you're a person without principles. What should I do? Say, 'Yes, I do have principles'? I show my principles by my life, and not by arguing about it. There's nothing to talk about. It's as if six years together were nothing. You can spend all that time together and not understand a thing about each other. There's no reason to reconcile. Why reconcile if that's the situation?"

Sharansky's metaphor for nearly everything in life is chess. Perhaps his greatest triumph, next to staring down the KGB, was defeating Garry Kasparov last year during a simultaneous match in Jerusalem. ("Natan is a reasonably good club player, and in a simultaneous game that can be dangerous," Kasparov told me. "But he should be pretty decent. He's the product of Soviet chess schools.") In his prison cell, Sharansky played game after game against himself—"and I always won." He approached KGB interrogations as if they were elaborate chess games, complete with wary openings, intricate developments, trade-offs, deceptions, endgames. One afternoon, I went with him to the opening of a chess center outside Tel Aviv sponsored by Kasparov and the Belgian philanthropists Sol and Sissy Mark. As the cameras surrounded Sharansky, the directors asked him to sit down and play a quick game. With anyone.

"Sit down!" Sharansky commanded me.

"Me?"

"You."

Each time Sharansky moved, he slammed his piece down on the board and whacked the clock. A thin stream of sweat started on the back of my neck. I lasted fourteen moves and considered it a triumph. The scene was broadcast that night on national television.

"For me, chess was always a great game, which helps to give life a frame, but it was never life itself," he told me later. "But, if there is something that is truly irritating about politics, it's that too often for the players the game is not just the means but the essence. It becomes difficult to concentrate, and you have to make constant efforts to remind yourself what you are here for. Frankly speaking, I'm not enjoying politics at all. But, you know, as long as you feel that you have some aims you want to achieve and you are moving in this direction, then you know what you're doing it for. Look, I didn't want to be a prisoner of conscience, either. But, once I did it and understood why I was doing it, I had to go forward."

To critics who felt that Sharansky was trying to have his integrity and his power, too—threatening to exert his moral and political power and then withdrawing for the sake of saving his seat in the Knesset and in the Cabinet—he said, "That's all nonsense. For me, it was not a matter of the left coming to power or the present government staying in. For me, it's whether I have the moral right to cancel the results of the last elections. Was there enough reason to do it? . . . If I were a real politician, I probably shouldn't have made the ten-percent statement. But I don't feel that it was wrong or even bad, or that I lost. . . . There was no criminal proof. . . . As one who knows very well the difference between suspicion and proof, I felt it was not."

In his ministry office, Sharansky hung a portrait of his "higher authority"—Andrei Sakharov, his mentor in the Soviet human-rights movement. The portrait is there as a reminder of Sakharov's example: his honesty, the purity of his intentions and of his language. "His expression was like a saint's—straight, pure, clear moral thought," Sharansky said. "This connection of simplicity and directness with his greatness, it was from the heavens. It was a very strange feeling, which I have practically had with no one else. So it's important to always remind myself that the distance from the heavens to the earth is very close and it all depends on you how close it will be. That is what that picture on my wall reminds me of all the time."

Old Katamon, where the Sharanskys live, was an Arab neighborhood until the rise of the Jewish state, in 1948, and the first Israeli-Arab war. The architecture is in the Arab style or, as with the Sharanskys' building, newer imitations of the Arab style. Unusually for Jerusalem, the area is mixed—religious and secular; there are cars on the street on Shabbat— but it is, in the main, well-to-do. Real-estate values have climbed so rapidly during the recent boom economy that one of the Sharanskys' neighbors figures their apartment is worth around three-quarters of a million dollars.

Sharansky lives well by Israeli standards. Shortly after he left the Soviet Union, he signed a book contract with Random House for a million dollars. The book, *Fear No Evil*, is an account of the subtle war between the political prisoner and his jailers. It did not, however, sell as well as the publisher had hoped, mainly because when it came out, in May 1988, Ronald Reagan was making nice with Mikhail Gorbachev in Red Square. The frisson of the Cold War was fast becoming a memory. "Random lost a lot of money," Peter Osnos, Sharansky's editor, recalls. "But, as Natan said to me, 'I know this was a dreadful disappointment to you, but it made it possible for me not to bend.' It enabled him to have a life."

Sharansky can walk into an elevator and people will begin to cry, to tell him how they read his book, how he changed their lives. He certainly could have become wealthy speaking at Hadassah luncheons and synagogue dinners from Oahu to Brooklyn Heights, but he did not. There are other Russians entering the realm of power politics (Yuli Edelstein; Avigdor Lieberman, Netanyahu's closest aide; Eduard Kuznetsov, a former dissident, who is the editor of the newspaper *Vesti;* and Larissa

Gershtein, an influential member of the Jerusalem city council), but, in the words of one Israeli journalist, "In the new Russian power élite, Natan and Avital are the tsar and tsarina."

While I was in Jerusalem, Israeli television broadcast a two-hour episode of *Hayim Sheka'elah*, a kind of *This Is Your Life*, devoted to the Sharanskys. Friends, colleagues, and admirers from all over the country and abroad gathered in a studio for six hours of taping. Both Sharanskys later told me that, while they were grateful for all the praise, finally the marathon rehash was tedious. "It's the past, and we have had another life for ten or eleven years," Avital told me one afternoon on the terrace of their apartment. "For years and years, I spent all my time talking about Natan and his case and our past in Russia. It's already boring to go on and on. You want to live." The only time that the past seems worth thinking about anymore is when they hold their "second seder," every February, commemorating Sharansky's arrival in Israel—an occasion for their two daughters to probe into their parents' story.

By all accounts, the Sharanskys have an extraordinarily close marriage, but the differences between them are also fairly clear. Natan attends synagogue only sporadically; in rare cases, out of the presence of Avital, he has been known to eat without maximal regard for the laws of kashruth. The Army cap was a means of satisfying not only the nation of Israel but also his wife. His gratitude to her is boundless. Avital, a shy woman by nature, had waged the most public of campaigns. A friend of mine recalls going to a bar mitzvah in Montreal and watching as Avital seized the occasion to make an impassioned plea for the Soviet Jews. In fact, Avital hoped not only for her husband's release but, secondarily, for her own release from a public life.

"Just before Natan got out of the Soviet Union, Avital told me that all she wanted to do in the world was darn Natan's socks and change diapers for their babies," David Bar-Illan, a friend of the family and Netanyahu's press spokesman, said. "When they finally came to Israel, they went north to Safed in the Galilee for a few days of vacation. I remember my wife came out of the bathroom at the hotel with tears in her eyes because she had looked out and seen Natan's socks and Avital's stockings drying side by side in the window. She had never forgotten what Avital had said."

Where Natan is rational, Avital is mystical, their closest friends say. Where he is merely wary of compromise with the Palestinians, she is adamantly against it. While Sharansky is capable of spending a long night at blues clubs in New York with his friend Ze'ev Chafets, Avital long ago exhausted her curiosity. When the Sharanskys were invited to Buckingham Palace to visit the royal family, Avital consulted a rabbi, and they concluded that there really was no sufficient reason to go.

There was Zionist feeling on Natan's side of the family, but Avital's parents were true believers, products of the Communist regime. She and her late brother, Mikhail Stieglitz, were their opposites, anti-Soviet rebels from a young age. "I left my parents so early. I ran away and never came back," Avital said. "We were so different. At the end of my mother's life, we brought her here, and she stayed for three months, until she died, but she was so sick I don't really know if she even recognized us. I know my own children will rebel, but we are in Israel, and there will not be such a terrible gap."

The greatest influence on Avital's life in Israel has been the followers of the late Rabbi Avraham Yitzhak Kook, the first Ashkenazi chief rabbi of Palestine. A messianic Zionist, he believed that God had given Jews what would later be known as "greater" Israel—a territory that includes the occupied West Bank. The Kookists were among the first Israelis to propound a religious-political interpretation of the Bible, and their influence began to grow under the leadership of Kook's son, Zvi Yehuda, following the Six Day War, in 1967.

During her campaign for her husband, Avital possessed a valiant glamour. A feature story in _The Washington Post_ called her the Audrey Hepburn of the Soviet Jewry movement. In Israel, she has withdrawn completely from public life. She has adopted the earnest, plain look of Mercaz Ha'rav women: long skirts, a scarf, a heaviness of bearing. She is kind and pleasant, but she also has about her a messianic air. When I asked her what she thought about the state of American Jewry, she said, "American Jews were tremendously helpful in saving Soviet Jews, and I think that cause was an enormous bridge between Soviet Jews and American Jews—it's as if they were cemented together by fate. But I hope after the Soviet Jews are saved that American Jews will save themselves and come to Israel. There is no life there. This is just who I am, but I just feel that way, in the sense of all the assimilation. They are not living fully. I have had the experience of not being in Israel, and I know that by their not being here they lose something of themselves. It's not real life. It's just spending time. It might be luxurious, it might even be interesting, but real life is when you have your own place and you are with your own people and you have your own way of life and are not worried that your children will become something else." Then she stopped herself and said, "Please, I don't want to offend anyone through this. It's just one Israeli housewife's opinion."

In replying to the same question, Natan was at pains to be more diplomatic. When we met a few days after I talked with Avital at the apartment, he said that, while he saw the "richness" in various American Jewish communities and would never presume to issue a call for mass aliyah, "I do feel that if you really want to be an active part of Jewish history, if you want to build the future of the Jewish people, then your place is in Israel. This is the place where you always feel that you are in the middle of things. . . . Here the life is much more meaningful. But to say that life in America is empty—I wouldn't say that."

The historical importance of Netanyahu's victory over Shimon Peres and the Labor government may well depend less on the policies and treaties Netanyahu enacts and more on the demographic and psychological shift in Israeli politics that he embodies. When I talked with him, he did not seem especially eager to expand on his relationship with Sharansky (they were still feuding). On one point, however, he did keep hammering away: he feels he has paid a price for attacking the Ashkenazi élite, the Jews with roots in European countries. "I had a visit not long ago from the dissident Vladimir Bukovsky, who told me the intellectual climate here is not Bolshevik but Menshevik," the Prime Minister said. "Have you read Paul Johnson's book *Intellectuals*? It's an interesting expression of the distance people feel from the regnant intellectuals. That's what happened here."

In the coastal cities like Tel Aviv, Haifa, and Hertseliya, and even in some neighborhoods of Jerusalem, there are still plenty of (hatless) Israelis who work in high-tech jobs, learn English and European languages, vote Labor, slowly reconcile themselves to a Palestinian state, and, in general, hope that Israel will gradually lose its eternal sense of imperilment and exceptionalism and become, at long last, a wealthy state, secure, pluralistic, and, perhaps, more ordinary. But while Western visitors and reporters are invariably drawn to that accessible sector of Israeli society, and while those voices still dominate journalism, literature, and the arts, the country is clearly becoming more religious, more Middle Eastern, and less European. Birth rates, for example, are far higher in the religious and Sephardic communities than among the secular Ashkenazim who have dominated the scene since the founding of the state. Ze'ev Chafets is exaggerating only slightly when he says that Israel has become, in a sense, a divided state: the secular, coastal state, with Tel Aviv as its capital, and the religious state of "Judea," with Jerusalem as its capital. The choice now, he says, is whether one wants to be a modern Israeli or a three-thousand-year-old Jew. In the 1996 elections, the "Judeans" won by a whisker.

"For people like me and my friends, it's almost the end of the world," Danny Rubenstein, a well-known liberal journalist on Arab-Israeli affairs, told me one afternoon at the greatest of all establishment meeting places, the veranda of the King David Hotel. "This new wave is totally against our values," he went on. "We were brought up to work, and the new people, especially the ultra-Orthodox, do not make work a value at all. They think that all my kids know or care about is MTV. They are like the Moral Majority. Their ideal for their children is that they become yeshiva students. They say to us, 'Give us lots of money, and we'll study in yeshivas and return the country to its basic values.' And we say, 'We'll give you billions, but not to study Kabbalah.'

"The ultra-Orthodox treat us like goyim, with such contempt. They don't serve in the Army, they don't care that we die. They don't even respect us. On Memorial Day, a siren goes off and everyone is supposed to stop and come out into the streets and be silent. They deliberately keep on walking. Maybe Israel is changing to some kind of ayatollah regime, some kind of coalition in which the leaders are ultra-Orthodox. My kids will never live in Jerusalem. Jerusalem to them is like Borough Park or Crown Heights."

The resentments on the other side are, of course, equally vehement. The ultra-Orthodox feel they have been stereotyped, mocked, as if all of them were as fanatical as the assassins of Rabin and of the Arabs at the Cave of the Patriarchs. The Sephardim have long felt left out of the Israeli élite: their income rates and their representation in the professions, business, the media, and big-time politics are much lower on the average than those of the Ashkenazim. Like Menachem Begin before him, Netanyahu campaigned as the champion of the non-élites: the Sephardim, the ultra-Orthodox, the settlers on the West Bank. But while the Ashkenazic secular community may still be at the center of Israel's high-tech economic explosion, its members are suffering the same sense of self-doubt and decline as the American WASP. "It turns out that we, the old Ashkenazi—the secular community, especially—are the dinosaurs," Avishai Margalit, a professor of philosophy at Hebrew University, said. "We lack identity and vitality. The vitality is in the other communities. But it's not the end of life. It's the end of a species—the species of Zionist propaganda and Jewish Agency posters. This is a country of immigrants, so you have to be ready for what comes."

Among the Ashkenazim, the sense of loss can be fierce, as with Rubenstein, or resigned, as with Margalit, but it is distinct. For that reason, the prospect of the arrival of a mass Ashkenazic diaspora—the Russian Jews—was thrilling, especially to the old élite. The Russians represented not only the European Jews who had survived the war but also a revival, of sorts. And yet, when Sharansky was released from prison and arrived in Israel, he was shocked and offended to discover that the country's leadership was skeptical about the prospect of a Soviet exodus.

"We had many conversations, with Shimon Peres and Yitzhak Shamir and with all leaders," Sharansky said. "Our estimation was then that four hundred thousand could come as a first big wave of immigration. It was difficult for people to believe. Of course, they figured that a person who has just come from prison still lives in a dream world. Peres felt that the Soviet Union always had such great potential, but because of a rigid Communist system couldn't use all its socialist potential. But now Gorbachev was making this a free country and a great country. 'And look,' he told me, 'now, with Gorbachev, Jews will be able to live as free Jews. Why would they leave? Of course, we have to attract them—or, at least, be friends.' But he was 'realistic.' Shamir was more skeptical. He felt that the Russians would not really be free, but if they were finally free they would all go to America. Why should they be interested in Israel?"

A couple of times a month, Sharansky gets in the backseat of a government-issued white Volvo and covers as much ground in one day as he can. He invited me along on one of his journeys, and we visited a newly expanded city north of Tel Aviv called Yokneam; a series of Druze villages; and, in Haifa, the Technion, Israel's equivalent of MIT or Caltech. Like a good politician, he sat through one interminable meeting after another, showed fantastic interest during every tour of a factory or housing project, made dozens of phone calls from the car, and ate more baklava than was probably good for him. Sharansky's knowledge of the intricacies of trade and industry began at about zero; he relies heavily on his staff. His more exact role is to delegate the detail work of the Ministry to the experts and concentrate most of his efforts on his greater goal: to accelerate the passage of three-quarters of a million Russians into the mainstream of Israeli life. It is, as it happens, an immensely difficult job.

At first, and even now, tremendous resentment has been directed

toward the Russians. It is a truism that all Israelis are agreed in their ado-
ration of aliyah and their equally ardent suspicion of the *olim*: that is,
they love immigration; it's the immigrants they aren't too crazy about.
Russians are thought to be, alternately, snobbish and low-rent. There is
resentment directed against the influx of so many musicians, scientists,
and professors, and resentment, too, against bleached-blond women
who are all, no doubt, prostitutes, and Mercedes-driving men, who are
all, no doubt, mafiosi. Groups like the Moroccans, who have been less
successful than many other groups, see the Russians getting enormous
breaks on apartments and wonder why they didn't get the same treatment upon their arrival, in the fifties.

The Ashkenazi élite, on the other hand, find the Russians presumptuous, unwilling to follow the normal pattern of immigration, in which the
first generation suffers its privations humbly and quietly and clears the
way for the second. It does not go unnoticed, either, that as many as
thirty percent of the new Russian immigrants were not born Jewish. "We
also don't understand their attachment to literature and culture. The
notion that any book other than the Bible could have such a hold on
them is weird," Eetta Prince-Gibson, an American émigré and journalist, said. "Plus, they're not begging to be a part of us, and that's insulting.
Also, there's that heaviness about them. They whine. There's that Russian style of speaking that makes us crazy, like a child whining. Israelis are
used to the idea that for the first generation immigration is tough. So
Israelis are tough about whining. It gets under our skin that Russians
think that the society we've created is not so great."

Most Israelis will admit that the Russians are learning Hebrew
quickly and have been willing to take jobs well below their qualifications.
What irritates them, however, is a certain sense of immediate entitle-
ment and, at the same time, a disconnection from Israel as a Zionist
enterprise, as a cause. "The idea that the Russian aliyah is consciously
related to the Zionist movement is, alas, a myth," Mikhail Grobman, the
best-known Russian artist in Israel, told me. "An essential thing to
remember about this immigration is that these Russians came here with
no real choice. Most of them would just as soon have gone to the States
or to Western Europe, but those places are essentially sealed off from
them. Culturally, Soviet man brings with him an expectation of the state
as a milk cow, and this causes problems. This doesn't disappear the
moment you arrive at Ben-Gurion Airport."

On the road tour, Sharansky met with a group of Russian scientists at
the Technion. Led by the eminent scientist Valentin Fainberg, they all

complained bitterly that they were getting tiny salaries, the worst laboratory equipment, and no access to scientific conferences. "Our situation is the situation of slaves!" one of the scientists cried out.

Sharansky has heard such complaints a thousand times. And, while he sympathizes with the Russians, he also knows that it is natural for the existing scientific establishment to want to guard its positions rather than open them up to competition. He was more encouraged when we visited the town of Yokneam, which had once been centered on an outdated metallurgical plant and is now a high-tech boomtown in the making. Hundreds of new apartments have been built to house Russian immigrants who will work in software firms and medical-technology companies. The local officials fawned on Sharansky, and that pleased him mightily.

"A year ago, in the best of circumstances, the head of the local population would have been invited for a five-minute meeting, if at all, to give his report, and then he'd be asked to leave, so that the more serious guys could discuss everything," he said. "It was my idea that in order to make integration immediate we have to sit at the table where decisions are made, and the only way to do this is to have political power."

In many ways, the Russian immigration resembles the German influx of the thirties. The populations have much the same profile: well educated, largely professional, and a threat to the Old Guard. "Every new immigration is like a heart transplant," Shimon Peres, the former Prime Minister, told me. "The heart has an extremely difficult time getting used to life in a new existing body. I remember when the German Jews came to Israel. The way we received them was shameful. I remember at school we behaved shamefully to the new German students. We told them they had to brush the teeth of the cows! It was awful."

The Germans had nowhere near the numbers of today's Russians, but they, too, started a political party—Aliyah Hadasha (New Immigrant Party), which was a kind of Central European liberal party. The Germans played a key role in helping to modernize the *yishuv*, the nascent Jewish state before 1948. As that population melted into Israeli society, the Party disappeared. Eventually, the Germans joined the Israeli élite.

"Our idea is much the same," Yuli Edelstein, Sharansky's conservative colleague in the Knesset and in the Cabinet, said. "The idea is to maneuver hundreds of thousands of us into the Israeli mainstream as quickly as possible. Who knows? We might even improve the country in the process."

There are those in Israel, especially on the right, who have grown disenchanted enough with the Netanyahu government to begin thinking about another standard-bearer. Possibly a Russian.

"Look, I never wanted to be a prisoner of Zion," Sharansky said. "I never wanted to be a member of the Knesset. And I don't want to be Prime Minister. I wanted only to be an international chess champion. Life just didn't work out that way. At each step, fate dictated what I had to do and what was demanded of me. So, if I won't have to, I won't be Prime Minister."

In 1992, the Israelis invited Gorbachev to the country. There was a dinner in his honor at the President's home. The Sharanskys were there and, like everyone else at the dinner, they stepped up to the receiving line to meet the former Soviet leader.

When it was Natan's turn, he said, "I'm glad to greet you, Mr. Gorbachev, on the same side of the barricades."

Gorbachev began to say something about Sharansky's "good works" in Russia and added, "You know, the first time I heard about you was 1985, during a summit meeting with Reagan in Geneva."

"Oh, yes," Raisa Gorbachev said. "Sharansky. The first time I heard about you was in 1985, when your wife was demonstrating for you."

"And here she is," Natan said, introducing his wife.

Avital had actually been arrested in Geneva, after she tried to pass a letter to Raisa Gorbachev that said, "Think about me when your husband comes home, or when you are playing with your children. Think about how I cannot be with my husband, how I have no children, because of how unjustly my husband has been imprisoned." The Gorbachevs, obviously, were playing dumb. Gorbachev had been on the Politburo that ruled while Sharansky was in prison.

When they returned to their table, Natan was (typically) amused and Avital was (typically) steamed. "It's all lies!" she muttered. "Once, when he was in London with a delegation, he was asked about Sharansky, and said, 'He's a spy!' It's all lies!"

Sharansky will never do anything in Israel to match the drama of his arrival. There is even the fear that his work as an ordinary Minister of Trade and Industry diminishes him. Recently, the newspaper *Ma'ariv* gave him low grades as a Cabinet minister. "There is a sense of loss, a loss of that original purity," Yaron Ezrahi, the political theorist, said. "But I suspect that Sharansky the mediocre minister cannot destroy Sharansky the icon. The minister is too weak, the icon too strong." Sharansky, for his part, shows no sign of wanting to be a curator of his own outsized image.

Even now, however, Sharansky is capable of the inspired, dramatic gesture. Last winter, he returned to Moscow for the first time since the KGB drove him to the airport, in 1986. Upon landing at Sheremetyevo, Sharansky had a moment of supreme satisfaction. "When I was in prison, I often dreamed of landing in Israel in an El Al plane—always an El Al plane—and being met there by my wife, Avital, and her brother Misha," he said. "But I never dreamed of landing in Moscow in an El Al plane."

Avital felt no sense of triumph. She hadn't even wanted to make the trip. "I don't have anyone there," she said. "Friends come here. Also, I don't feel any identification with this place—no nostalgia at all. But Natan pressed. When we landed, it was upsetting. All the snow and the ice—it brought back feelings of being young and being cold, it awakened unpleasant memories. There was something about it, kind of like when people go to Auschwitz and somehow swear they can hear the sounds of the past, the screams. When we were at the Moscow synagogue, in the eyes of my spirit I saw all the people we used to know, talking and laughing. It was a really spiritual experience."

The Sharanskys met with politicians and Jewish groups. They drank the ritual coffee around the ritual kitchen table with old dissident friends. They visited Sakharov's grave. They visited the grave of Natan's father, on the outskirts of the city. (The tombstone reads, "His soul will sleep in peace. His seed will inherit the Land of Israel.")

The pivotal moment of the trip, however, came when the Sharanskys visited Lefortovo, where Natan was first imprisoned and interrogated. Sharansky joked that ten years of labor camp had been the best preparation for ten years of Israel, and that his party's campaign slogan was "We Go to Prison First, Then the Knesset." But it was a serious trip, even an essential one. The prison had obviously been cleaned up for the occasion, and when Sharansky asked to see his old punishment cell, in the solitary-confinement area, the officials eyed each other sheepishly and said that they no longer had punishment cells—that things had changed. Hadn't he heard? The punishment cells were now used for "storage." Sharansky did not believe them and, in diplomatic language, said so. The officials were shamed, and relented.

"The cells in Lefortovo were tiny and cold, some of the worst," Sharansky said. "When they brought us to the cell, I asked them to leave my wife and me alone. I tried to describe what it was like. I told her how you take a cup of hot water and put it on spots all over your body to warm up in the cold. There is a tiny stool in the middle of the cell, and you can only sit for a few minutes at a time. For me, it was such a symbolic moment. I'd spent so many days sitting in the punishment cell just thinking about my wife in Israel, and then to think that almost exactly twenty years after my arrest you come here, where they threatened me, where they talked about putting me to death, where they read me testimony of foreign correspondents who supposedly betrayed me. . . . That was the most difficult thing. And to think that since that time one million people have left this big punishment cell—the Soviet Union—where the KGB had been looking in. And the regime doesn't even exist anymore! I realized it then, how much we had all survived, and how in the end this cell was the scene of my greatest victory."

(1997)

•

Sharansky had a long career as a Cabinet member, but in recent years his influence may have been greater in Washington than in Tel Aviv. In 2004, he published *The Case for Democracy: The Power of Freedom to Overcome Tyranny and Terror;* it became the one (and perhaps only) book that George W. Bush read and recommended publicly while in office. In his second inaugural address Bush said, "The survival of liberty in our land increasingly depends on the success of liberty in other lands," a line straight from Sharansky's book and one meant to justify the neoconservative project, everything from the decision to cease negotiating with Yasir Arafat to the invasion of Iraq. Over the years, Sharansky's influence on Elliott Abrams, Richard Perle, Paul Wolfowitz, Douglas Feith, and Dick Cheney—all former associates of Ronald Reagan and/or Henry Jackson, who became part of George W. Bush's orbit—has been acute. As Sharansky told *Newsweek,* "Many of them are my friends from those years. And in the last fifteen years, we kept talking to one another." In 2005, Sharansky resigned from the Cabinet to protest Ariel Sharon's plan to close settlements and withdraw from the Gaza Strip.

The Outsider:
Benjamin Netanyahu

If Paris is the City of Light, Jerusalem is the City of Opinion. Here it rains opinions. The desert blooms on the moisture of harangue. The rarest phrase in the fifty-year-long history of Israel is "No comment," and certainly no one has ever uttered the following sentence: "I have no comment on Bibi."

Left or right, everyone refers to the Prime Minister, Benjamin Netanyahu, by his childhood nickname, though familiarity in his case has not bred affection. The strangest thing about Netanyahu is that although he commands support—his stalling tactics on the peace process have won him a center-right majority—he commands little respect. One afternoon, I went to see David Bar-Illan, a former concert pianist who is among Netanyahu's closest aides and very few friends. On matters of policy, Bar-Illan is a spinmeister extraordinaire, the fellow who happily goes before the camera crews to defend the latest action of the Prime Minister. And yet when we were talking about Bibi's attempts to win over the ultra-Orthodox vote despite his own secular habits, even his admission of adultery, Bar-Illan rolled his eyes and spoke on the record in a way no Washington equivalent ever would.

"Finessing his being secular was nothing compared to other things, like adultery," Bar-Illan said. "One thing is to have an affair with a shiksa—but a married woman! With a shiksa, even the rebbes do it. But a married woman! Now Bibi'll go to synagogue on Rosh Hashanah, Yom Kippur, maybe he's gone to the Western Wall, or he'll say the phrase 'with God's help.' But he's not fooling anyone."

The rhetoric of Israeli democracy has always been noisier than the American brand, but talk about Netanyahu is unhinged. One of the first things I did on arriving in Jerusalem this time was to call Yitzhak Shamir, the previous Likud Prime Minister. Shamir picked up his phone on the first ring, as if he'd been waiting for the call all week. "Bibi?" Shamir said in his exhausted Old World accent. "He is not a very trustworthy man."

There was a long pause at the other end of the line, as if Shamir felt he had said quite enough to cover the subject. "He's too egotistical. I personally have no contact with him," Shamir went on. "He's a man who is not very popular. He's a talented, successful man. He made it at a young age. He had many advantages. But people don't like him. I wouldn't say he is admired. I don't believe he believes in anything. He has a huge ego. People don't like such people. I don't like him."

And so on. After Shamir had unburdened himself, I called Shimon Peres. Running on a platform of moving quickly on the Oslo peace accords with the Palestinians, Peres lost the 1996 election to Netanyahu, who captured the support not merely of the hard right but also of many Israelis who thought Yitzhak Rabin and Peres had gone too far, too fast. Peres also picked up on the first ring. He was leaving for China in five minutes, he said, but he managed to take ten to tear a hole in his successor. "We've lost so much, and for nothing," Peres said wearily. "Netanyahu's only consideration is his own coalition. He's always worried about losing power—that is always his first priority. In the meantime, we've lost the trust we built up, we've lost the Arab world, we've lost the respect we won throughout the rest of the world. All this makes it appear that we are a bizarre nation. To achieve peace and not follow through is bizarre."

Netanyahu, who is forty-eight, is the first Israeli Prime Minister to have been born after the founding of the state. As a result, perhaps, many Israelis sense in him a distinct lack of gravitas. He often strikes people as a younger man trying to make an impression and only suffering for it. When I went to interview Netanyahu, in his office, he began the session by lighting up a big cigar, a Davidoff. You knew it was a Davidoff because he left on the ring. Nor did he offer one to his guest. Bad manners? Low supplies? He then proceeded to fill the room with so much smoke that his young press aide, a friendly fellow from Dubuque named Michael Stoltz, reacted as if he'd been trapped in a garage with the car running. Stoltz could have died a slow death, I thought, and Netanyahu would not have stopped his pompous puffing.

The riddle of Netanyahu is that so many Israelis find him personally insufferable, and yet if there were an election tomorrow he would almost certainly defeat the Labor standard-bearer, his old military commander and role model, Ehud Barak. The Orthodox know all about Bibi's secular indiscretions—the pandering, the philandering. The far-right nationalists cannot yet decide whether he wants to kill the Oslo peace process (as they would like) or not. Both the Russian émigrés and the Sephardim know that he is not one of them. Nevertheless, these outsider constituencies believe that Bibi is better for their interests than the Ashkenazic élites of the Labor Party.

The left, of course, cannot bear Netanyahu. In their view, Bibi has "killed the peace," eradicated the historical chance symbolized by the 1993 and 1995 Oslo accords with the Palestinians. Bibi's enemies see him as an incompetent, unimaginative, and cynical politician with a singular gift for staying in office. "Netanyahu knows very well what he wants," Uri Savir, who had been Rabin's chief negotiator in Oslo, told me, "and the main thing is to steer Israel in the direction of a mutual-deterrence policy, because he does not really believe in real peace. He does not believe in a new quality of relations. He also sees everything through the eyes of a political animal and he wants to be reelected. Everything he does is to play to his right-wing constituency. To appeal to them, he uses the buzzwords that appeal to their ghetto mentality."

There are still many on the left who blame Netanyahu for helping to whip up an atmosphere of hatred that led to the Rabin assassination. Nevertheless, Bar-Illan insists that one day soon all Israelis will end up marveling at Netanyahu's guile and ideological agility. "Bibi wants to out-Begin Begin," Bar-Illan told me, meaning that he will do something even more shocking than Menachem Begin did when he signed the Camp David accords, in 1978, promising to give the Sinai back to Egypt and bringing about peace between Israel and its most powerful neighbor.

Israel is celebrating its fiftieth year as a state. Zionism has outlasted the two great threats of the twentieth century—Fascism and Communism—and yet the celebration is halfhearted. No small part of this is the sense that the occupation of the West Bank and Gaza has been in place, causing suffering and national erosion, since 1967; what's more, the country's leadership is thoroughly uninspired. Almost universally, left and right, Netanyahu is seen as a slippery pol—and a not particularly adept one, at that. During the 1996 campaign, Bibi promised the Orthodox that he, the most secular of men, would be the avatar of the Jewish state. He went to see the spiritual leader of the Sephardim, Rabbi Yitzhak Kaduri, and whispered in the rabbi's ear, "Leftists have forgotten what it is to be Jewish. They think they will put security in the hands of the Arabs—that Arabs will look out for us." Israeli Radio's microphone picked up these remarks.

During his two years in office, Netanyahu has become known for a series of flubs and fast ones. After winning the Likud nomination largely through a new, open electoral process, he supported the repeal of that process. He courted scandal by nominating an Attorney General whose main qualification was a tight connection to Shas, the Sephardic party. He defied his own intelligence chief and ordered the assassination of a Hamas leader, Khaled Meshal, in the Jordanian capital of Amman; when the plot to poison Meshal failed miserably (more Inspector Clouseau than 007) and became public, King Hussein was infuriated, and Israelis were bewildered. As Foreign Minister, David Levy said that he had a commitment from Netanyahu on social spending in Sephardic towns, and then resigned when Netanyahu reneged. Right-wingers remain furious about the redeployment of Israeli forces from the city of Hebron, in the West Bank.

Netanyahu's circle feels persecuted by the press. His defenders point out, for example, that he has not turned out to be militarily aggressive or ideologically unbending. Again and again, they mentioned "one of the few exceptions"—a long article by Ari Shavit published last December in the liberal daily *Ha'aretz,* headlined THE YEAR OF HATING BIBI. Shavit is a liberal intellectual who wrote that his own circle has been unduly vicious about Netanyahu. When I began reporting this story, Netanyahu's own father gruffly told me that I would invariably quote only his son's enemies, "the left-wingers." I invited him to give me a list of people I should call, and he did. Naturally, some on the list were ardent supporters, but others, while they said they supported Netanyahu's policies, admitted that they could barely stand the man.

One such was Yoash Tsiddon-Chatto, a reserve Air Force colonel and former Knesset member on the right, who went with Bibi to the Madrid peace talks in 1991. "Something about Bibi's personality creates an anti-rapprochement," Tsiddon-Chatto said. "I didn't ever think he would dodge and manipulate and weave and dodge the way he has as Prime Minister. I doubt if his father is so happy with the way his son has carried out his policies."

The father. Everywhere I went in Israel, when I asked about Netanyahu the same answer came back: "To understand Bibi, you have to understand the father." But while the Israeli press regularly describes Benzion Netanyahu as deeply conservative in his views and harsh in character, he is nearly a legend, a kind of secret. Benzion does not exactly hide from the world—he is a controversial scholar who has published a cascade of extraordinary books and papers on the Jews of fifteenth-century Spain—but he studiously avoids journalists. Like Bibi, Benzion Netanyahu and his wife, Cela, both regard the Israeli press, which is almost uniformly pro-Labor, with unconcealed contempt. "Bolshevik" is the term they use. They are not a great deal fonder of the American press. The *Times*'s coverage of Israel, Benzion told me, "often seems to me unbalanced and slanted toward the leftist side of Israel's public opinion." I was able to spend time with Benzion mainly because we share a book editor, a friend.

When the nation of Israel was founded, Benzion Netanyahu was on the fringe of its political life. Now he is its patriarch. His eldest son, Jonathan—Yoni—is a martyr of the Israeli Defense Forces, whose name is known to every Israeli schoolchild; the middle son, Benjamin, is the leader of the Likud Party and Prime Minister; and the youngest son, Iddo, is both a novelist and a radiologist.

Benzion, who is eighty-eight, is possessed of a clear mind, good health, and a forbidding personality. A cross word from him scatters the sparrows from the trees. After his son the Prime Minister makes a speech, Benzion sometimes calls to correct a grammatical mistake. "Bibi's Hebrew has gotten far better in recent years," he allows. Benzion is a secular man, and yet his judgments of Israel and history and much else are often so dark, so unforgiving, that he sometimes sounds like the harshest of Old Testament prophets. His views on everything from modern America to the ideological weaknesses and failings of various Israeli politicians, past and present, are often despairing.

Benzion's range of disapproval is breathtaking. Fifty years ago, at the time of Israel's birth, his politics were already on the edge, the outer feathers, of the right wing. As a young man, he was an aide to Ze'ev

Jabotinsky, the leader of the hard-line Revisionist movement. Among the early Zionists, the Revisionists were the underground fighters who argued that the Laborites, led by Ben-Gurion, were giving up too easily on territory that is now well beyond Israel. Benzion was part of a movement that saw Israel as laying claim to an area encompassing much of present-day Jordan. The pro-Jabotinsky hymn at the time went, "The Jordan has two banks: this one is ours, the other one, too." His vision, perhaps, is an anachronism and yet it is the vision that the current Prime Minister of Israel was raised on. Benzion looms above his son no less than Joseph Kennedy loomed above his clan, and his views are at the root of Bibi's sense of a menacing world.

When you meet Benzion, he does not seem so forbidding: he has little white tufts of hair and weary, narrow eyes, the eyes of a Chinese scholar. On the day Bibi was sworn in as Prime Minister, at the Knesset, in 1996, Benzion sat in the audience. Ari Shavit, of *Ha'aretz,* remembers seeing the old man and noticing that he betrayed no outward signs of pride or joy. "I was watching it on TV, and thought, My God, to be the son of this man, even if you become Prime Minister you can never satisfy him. This is really the key," Shavit said. "There is this person who pushes himself to the end, demanding the impossible, and even achieving it. It's like a constant internal tyranny. You can never stop. There is no celebration."

To say Benzion has no faith in a peace accord with the Palestinians or with any Arab nation is to state the obvious. Such treaties, to him, are the stuff of fools and naifs. "Jewish history is in large measure a history of holocausts," Benzion told me, "carried out by anti-Semitic leaders and factions that managed to take over whole countries or regions in times of anarchy, civil war, or rebellion. In the areas that fell under their control, all Jewish communities were wiped out. Hitler differed from them primarily in having become the sole, undisputed ruler of his country and in controlling a much larger area, which allowed him to murder many more Jews."

To a considerable degree, Bibi Netanyahu's internal struggle as Prime Minister is a struggle between an inherited ideology and the tug of political contingencies. His dilemma is always to what degree he can, or should, remain true to the ideals, the stubbornness, of his father. He may not always act on his father's imperatives, but he believes strongly in his father's rightness; the men share a keen sense of insular self-confidence, of being right when all others around them are innocent, bogus, mistaken. When I met with Bibi at his office, he fondly recalled to me how, in 1956, his father went to Ben-Gurion and told him that the Israelis, having just captured the Sinai, had to devise a strategy to keep it. Ben-Gurion had said that he would keep it for a thousand years. Why was Benzion worried about losing it?

"Because the U.S. will force you to," Benzion told him.

"Of course, he was right, unfortunately," Bibi said. "That was the first and last time an Israeli Prime Minister succumbed to an American dik-tat." It is not hard to imagine this anecdote playing in the Prime Minis-ter's head when American diplomats like Dennis Ross and Madeleine Albright sit with him in negotiations.

Both the Israeli left and the White House would argue that Bibi has slowed down the peace process so much that the Palestinians and such Arab states as Jordan and Egypt have lost hope. In recent weeks, Clinton Administration officials have urged Netanyahu to agree to withdraw from a full thirteen percent of the West Bank in exchange for Palestinian guarantees on terrorism. Netanyahu has balked at that figure, though he has indicated a willingness to pull back from nine percent of the dis-puted territory (perhaps even eleven percent). The point, he insisted late last week, at talks in Washington with Ross and Albright, was that any accord must preserve what he called a "territorial buffer" against Palestinian terrorism. Netanyahu, to be sure, continued to face intense pressure at home: Palestinians demonstrated against *al nakba*—"the catastrophe"—of the founding of Israel; riots broke out, and several Palestinians were killed by Israeli troops. And it is far from certain that Netanyahu's right-wing Cabinet, especially the influential Infrastructure Minister, Ariel Sharon, would agree to a settlement resembling the American plan.

Netanyahu's overall argument is that the left's dream of a new Middle East, of peaceful relations and open markets in a region of Arab dictator-ships, is fantasy. "The real Middle East is not this lovely palette of lovely colors," he said. "There are some very dark streaks there. More than streaks—large swaths of fundamentalism and dictatorial regimes. There is a battle on for the soul of this Islamic Arab civilization. I don't write them off. I think we can influence it, but first of all not in a major way and, in any case, in a way different from the way the left thinks. They think that if we make more concessions we'll defuse the time bomb, the mechanism that keeps this going. But this is much bigger than the battle with Zionism. It's a battle with modernity."

For the extreme right wing, however, Bibi has not always been firm enough with the Arabs. The Prime Minister's decision last year to cede authority over Hebron to the Palestinian Authority was, in their eyes, a betrayal of the 1996 campaign, and of Revisionist principles. Bibi's brother-in-law, a settler named Chagi Ben-Artzi, told me, "Bibi grew up in a family in which the principle of keeping the land, the entire land, in Jewish hands was a holy principle. . . . I've heard Bibi's father be very critical about the Hebron agreement. He said it is absolutely not justified. He didn't see any good reason to give Arafat more land before he carried out one single commitment included in the Oslo accords." Benzion denied that he had argued with his son about Hebron or Oslo in general; when Ben-Artzi made public his own opposition to his brother-in-law's policy, their relations soured.

Reflecting on his son and Oslo, Benzion later said, "What I can gather from the deeds and the statements of the Prime Minister is that he is struggling to obtain, within the limits of the Oslo agreement, and through the implementation of the commitments on the part of both sides, arrangements that are vital for the security of Israel and will minimize the outbreaks of large-scale terrorism and wars."

Bibi, for his part, dismisses all talk of paternal influence as "psycho-babble." His friends and colleagues who have known him for decades do not. Natan Sharansky, one of Netanyahu's current ministers and closest advisers, told me, "Look, there's no doubt that the father is crucial to Bibi, especially historically, in Jewish history and world history. In his day-to-day activities, it helps Bibi to somehow stay in focus. He gets caught up in the daily struggles, but he always has this view of history in mind."

What will Bibi do, then, in the coming months and years? Will he listen to the call of history and try to come to an agreement with the Palestinians? Or will he listen to the right-wing constituencies that will keep him in office? "I think Bibi is divided and sometimes paralyzed by the difference between his heart and his head," said David Makovsky, who covers diplomacy for *Ha'aretz*. "His visceral reactions are ideological, like his father's, but intellectually he's come to see that his visceral reactions are not always correct. The result is paralysis. Motion without movement in the peace process."

Benzion and Cela Netanyahu reared their sons in a spacious house, on Haportzim Street, in the Old Katamon district of West Jerusalem. They still live there. There was little wealth in Jerusalem in those days, and the

Netanyahus felt themselves quite nearly rich. Their car was American— a Henry J—and they had one of the few telephones in the neighborhood. Benzion edited the enormously popular *Encyclopedia Hebraica.* "And for that," he told me, "I got the highest salary in Jerusalem!" The house is now worth around a million dollars.

Benzion Netanyahu is known in scholarly circles around the world for his book *The Origins of the Inquisition in Fifteenth Century Spain.* In medieval studies, his thesis is considered revolutionary. The Jews were oppressed in Spain even after they had become converts to Christianity. Netanyahu challenged the traditional view that the Spaniards persecuted the *conversos* because many of them continued to practice their original faith in secret. Netanyahu's work contends that the long-held notion of the *conversos* as "secret Jews" is a romantic delusion. He argues that in fact only a very few of the New Christians practiced Judaism, and that the Inquisition was actually a historical moment in which the Christian monarchs developed a theory of racial hatred designed to uproot and demolish a perceived threat to their social and political order. Netanyahu writes that after two massive waves of conversion, in 1391 and in 1412, these New Christians began to assume powerful positions in politics and the Church. Since the Spaniards could no longer attack the *conversos* on the basis of religious faith, they devised tracts describing the *Jewish people* as an inherently polluted, contaminated race. For the first time, Netanyahu writes, a society devised a racial theory of Jewish inferiority, which laid the foundation for the Inquisition in Spain just as surely as the Nuremberg laws were the precursor to the Final Solution. After fourteen hundred pages, one is led to the darkest conclusion possible: that even if Jews go as far as to convert, and even if that conversion is thorough and official, it will not matter; the resentment of the Jews as a people will persist, even to the point of forced exile and mass murder.

I called on the Netanyahus on a fine spring morning. Cela Netanyahu let me in and then quickly went off to get her husband. Cela studied law at Gray's Inn, in London, but never practiced. Instead, she raised her three sons and, above all, was her husband's wife. She guarded him against distraction and traveled with him in the United States when there were no academic posts available in Israel. In all, Benzion and Cela lived in America for more than twenty years—first from 1940 to 1948, to work for the Zionist movement, and then from 1963 to 1977, to teach at various colleges and work on his books.

While I was waiting for Benzion, I walked over to the dining room.

When the boys were growing up, the dining room was their father's study, the nexus of the house. "When you went over there, you made sure not to disturb the old man," one family friend said. "That was the inner sanctum." Now a bust of Yoni dominates the room. Yoni was the only Israeli soldier killed during the commando raid on the airport in Entebbe, Uganda, in 1976.

Over the years, the Netanyahus have cultivated a sense of uniqueness about their family. "Their perception of themselves is as a major family in the history of Israel," one of Bibi's friends said. "The father is the great scholar and wise man. The eldest son, Yoni, is the martyred soldier. The middle son is the Prime Minister and savior of Israel. The youngest, Iddo, is the writer, who also practices medicine. Bibi's said that he thinks Iddo is 'Israel's new Hemingway.' No matter that Israel has truly great writers—A. B. Yehoshua, Amos Oz, Aharon Appelfeld, Meir Shalev. That's the way they think."

Finally, Benzion came in and sat down in an armchair. For a while he talked about his father, Nathan Mileikowsky, a rabbi who was born in Lithuania and helped run the famous Krinsky gymnasium, in Warsaw. As a leading Zionist orator, Nathan toured Europe and America making speeches in support of a Jewish state. When he brought his family to Palestine, in 1920, they came ashore in a small boat in Tel Aviv and changed their name to Netanyahu—"God-given."

Time and again in conversation, Benzion talked about the persistent specter of the left in Israel. He said much of the press in Israel is worse than *Pravda*, because in the old Soviet Union at least readers *understood* that their press was frequently lying. This, in modified language, is a familiar theme in Bibi's conversation.

Benzion studied medieval history at Hebrew University. Later, he was co-editor of a literary monthly, *Beitar,* and then of the Revisionists' daily newspaper *Ha-Yarden.* His contemporaries remember him as being extraordinarily intelligent and charming and, at the same time, arrogant and nearly seething with resentments and contempt. Even now, he radi-ates the same qualities, at once spinning a fascinating tale of old Jerusalem for his visitor and then talking with acid condescension (at best) about various constituencies and politicians in Israel. In his view, Arab fundamentalism and Asian nuclear power are the order of the future. He is a man of numerous and ferocious opinions, but is very wary of publicizing them—not least, perhaps, for fear of embarrassing his son.

It's hard to render the old man in print. For one thing, he is both fierce and irresistibly alive; for another, he insisted that our talks were "friendly chats," not a formal interview. But what comes through, so often, is a man who resents what he sees as the folly of others.

"There was always a strong myth of persecution in that family, always a grievance," I was told by Shalom Rosenfeld, a contemporary in the Revisionist movement who was later the editor of the leading newspaper *Ma'ariv*.

"There is a feeling of rejection by the academic establishment, which was dominated by the left and denied Benzion a decent job, and, as a result, the Netanyahus were forced to emigrate, which was very painful," Chagi Ben-Artzi, Bibi's brother-in-law, said. "Part of the background of the determination of Bibi to change Israel, to make it a more democratic society, to push the process of privatization, stems from that old resentment, because the left used the economic structure of the country to dominate Israel ideologically—anyone who was not politically correct was denied economic chances. That resentment is still there. It's not something for them that belongs to the past."

Ben-Artzi's facts are only partly correct. It's true that Benzion did not get a job at Hebrew University, but the university was tiny in those days, and there were hardly any positions available to anyone. For work, and for superior libraries, Benzion accepted jobs at Dropsie College, in Philadelphia, and at Cornell, in Ithaca, New York.

The family's sense of outsiderness has more to do with real politics than with academic politics. Some of Jabotinsky's followers, including Begin and Shamir, took to the underground, carrying out military missions against the British and the Arabs. Netanyahu was among the ideologues, the campaigners. In early 1940, he went to the United States to help Jabotinsky lobby American politicians on behalf of the Zionist idea. Jabotinsky died later that year, but Benzion stayed on for eight years, as director of the New Zionist Organization, meeting with such influential figures as General Dwight D. Eisenhower, Secretary of State Dean Acheson, and key members of Congress. "When we came with Jabotinsky, people laughed at us at first," Benzion said. "No Jew was dreaming of a Jewish state. 'Who will create it?' they said. 'The English will create it? The Arabs are against it!' Even Chaim Weizmann declared that it was impossible, that it was no more possible to create a Jewish state in Israel than it was in Manhattan."

When Benzion and his family returned to the new state in 1948, he took up the *Encyclopedia* and moved out of politics. Bibi's eventual rivals for the Likud leadership—the Jerusalem mayor Ehud Olmert, the former Finance Minister Dan Meridor, and Ze'ev (Benny) Begin—all come from right-wing political legacies. They are known as Likud "princes." Bibi was never grouped with the princes, because his father had made his life, finally, in academe. "I don't think my father would ever have been in politics," the Prime Minister told me. "He's not temperamentally suited."

But when I asked Bibi if he considered himself an outsider in Israel and in Israeli politics he did not deny it.

"You're damn right—outsider!" he said. "You don't have to psychobabble it!" Netanyahu could hardly have grown up with more privilege, and yet he is a Prime Minister elected by a coalition of outsider groups. His votes came from the Sephardim, the Orthodox, the settlers, the Russians—all groups who see themselves as excluded from the liberal Ashkenazic establishment. Like Ronald Reagan, Netanyahu successfully governs as an outsider: even as he wields power, he keeps complaining to his constituencies about the lopsidedly liberal press, the fearsome lefties in academe, all the while implying that *they* are the establishment, and that *they* hate you. It is a familiar, and familial, theme.

"I think the father is already within him—it's built in," one of Bibi's friends told me. "The father always talked about They. *They* don't understand a thing. *They* are naïve. *They* are fools. Always *they; them.*"

Israeli-Palestinian political debate is almost invariably, at root, a clash of historical narratives. No argument or incident is too ancient for consideration. The evidence for this rushes at you every day. One afternoon, while I was drinking a cup of coffee at a café in the Muslim quarter of the Old City and reading the papers, I came across a letter to the editor in *The Jerusalem Post* from David Wilder, a right-wing spokesman for the Jewish community in Hebron, who was responding to an article by a well-known figure in Palestinian politics, Daoud Kuttab:

> Sir,—Daoud Kuttab viciously attacked the Jewish community of Hebron in his article "At the boiling point" (March 1). Herewith is our reply to several of Kuttab's accusations: Kuttab refers to the "Ibrahimi mosque." This building is known to Jews as the Machpela Cave, the second holiest site to the Jewish people throughout the world. This site has served as a mosque only since 1267. The building was originally constructed as a site for Jewish worship, built by Herod, king of Judea, 2,000 years ago.

The key phrase here, of course, is "*only* since 1267."

To celebrate the fiftieth anniversary of the state, Israeli television has been showing a twenty-two-part documentary on Sunday nights called *Tekuma*, "Rebirth." I happened to catch one of the most controversial installments—an overview of the early history of the Israeli occupation of Gaza and the West Bank and the rise of Palestinian nationalism and violence. To American eyes, it seemed fairly ordinary: interviews-plus-film-clips fare—the sort of thing you might see on A&E or the Discovery Channel. There was Golda Meir, in both English and Hebrew, denying the existence of the Palestinian people; there was the squalor of the refugee camps in Gaza; and there, too, were the terrorist attacks in Tel Aviv and Jerusalem, the slaughter of Israeli athletes in Munich, a mother remembering how her two children were killed when a terrorist tossed a grenade into the backseat of her car.

The filmmaker, Ronit Weiss-Berkowitz, said in the Israeli press that even before her segment was shown on the air she began receiving death threats. "They call my home," she said, "and say, 'We will burn you,' 'You fucking Arabs,' 'You stinking leftist, we know where you live.' . . . I wanted to show, step by step, the creation of the ideology behind terrorism—which I reject, which I don't identify with, but whose roots I understand. I wanted to show why and how a Palestinian starts thinking of terror as a solution. We Israelis think we have a monopoly on blood, tears, and pain, but, of course, this is not true. We know our side in this story. I wanted to present the other side—loudly."

For the right wing, including the Prime Minister, the documentary series was an attempt by the leftist press to dominate the national narra- tive, to wallow in the guilt of "original sin"—the Jewish displacement and subjugation of Palestinian Arabs. Yoav Gelber, one of the show's aca- demic advisers, resigned and said that the segment belonged in a series marking "the fiftieth anniversary of the Palestinian Authority."

Bibi despises the men and women who run Israeli television—to him they are part of the leftist claque that has always dominated all cultural and media institutions in Israel—and when I asked him about *Tekuma* he waved in disgust. "It's a joke!" he said. "It's a joke! It's agitprop, it's agitprop, the small segment that I've seen. It's just not the facts. The presentation of the Palestinian side, what I've seen, is skewed beyond belief. It's the facts that I'm dealing with. The facts can have diverse interpretations, but there cannot be diverse facts. That, I think, is important."

In my talks with Benzion, he made it clear that he thought that the Jewish people might never recover from the murder of the European Jews; he also saw intermarriage and assimilation as posing great threats to the survival of the Jews. He insists that even present-day Israel, including the occupied territories, is but a fraction of what was originally promised; and to give up more land to the Arabs is extraordinarily dangerous, especially because a future Palestinian state could ally itself with such countries as Iraq and Iran—Israel's sworn enemies. "There is no doubt that many of the Arabs want to see the State of Israel destroyed," he said, "and they would end Jewish existence in the country if they had the chance to do it. Only the fear of retaliation keeps them back."

That is Benzion in conversation and it is Bibi in his 1993 book, *A Place Among the Nations*, which gives the most embattled reading possible to the history of Zionism and the Israeli state. When I talked to Benzion, he protested the idea of familial unanimity, but he did say, "There was no generation gap at all. We didn't agree on everything—this is not a family of robots—but our family has a coherence to it." However, he added later, "I am not involved in any measure or degree in shaping or influencing the policies or activities of the present government of Israel."

In *A Place Among the Nations*, Bibi's most sustained historical metaphor for the Israeli security predicament is Czechoslovakia before the Second World War; for him, the West Bank is the Sudetenland, the limited territorial pretext used by Hitler to overrun the entire country. When I asked Netanyahu about the comparison, he allowed that it was imperfect, but still one cannot read that book without sensing the author's parallel between the Germans and Arab aggression. The Czech metaphor is not one he indulges now as Prime Minister, but it has shaped his thinking since he was a young man.

If there was someone who really knew Bibi well, who shared with him the world of the family and a view of the world, it was his older brother, Yoni. In deciding what course to take with the Palestinians or with Syria, he has to cope with the legacy of his brother, a symbol of Israel's conflicts with the Arab world.

Along with their parents, Iddo, Yoni, and Bibi moved to Elkins Park, a Philadelphia suburb, in 1963, and went to a local high school. Each of the sons, in turn, went back to Israel for his Army service while their parents stayed in the United States. Yoni was the first to go, and he stayed in close touch with his brother through hundreds of letters, like this one, which was mailed after Bibi had been in a punch-up: "In my opinion, there's nothing wrong with a good fistfight; on the contrary, if you're young and you're not seriously hurt, it won't do you real harm. Remember what I told you? He who delivers the first blow, wins."

After the Six Day War, in which Yoni was wounded in the arm, he

wrote a letter to Bibi that evoked both the spirit of their father's tough-
ness and a determination not to remain in America: "The recruitment of
all these little terrorists only strengthens my consciousness as an Israeli.
If they come to fight, we—or at least I in the Diaspora—must certainly
do so all the more. My national consciousness is no doubt stronger than
that of the Arabs, I'm a much better fighter than they are, and so are all
Israeli soldiers."

In another letter to Bibi, Yoni wrote, "You're the only true friend I
ever had."

Because the country is so small, Israeli soldiers often go home for
weekends and vacations; each of the Netanyahu boys stayed with friends
of the family while their parents remained in the States. "Yoni lived like a
Gypsy, and this was strange in Israel," Yoni's friend, the scholar Avishai
Margalit, said to me. "To be a loner in Israel is unusual, and all three of
them were to an extent like this."

Bibi returned to Israel in 1967 and joined the élite reconnaissance
unit Sayeret Matkal. In the unit, he was regarded as intelligent and dili-
gent but not especially creative. He distinguished himself at a nighttime
raid on the Beirut Airport in 1968 and in the rescue of hostages aboard a
hijacked Sabena airliner in 1972. During the Sabena raid, Netanyahu
was one of the commandos who went on board dressed as mechanics; he
grabbed one of the hijackers, a woman, by the hair and slammed her into
a bulkhead, demanding to know where to find the hostages.

Bibi returned to the United States in 1972 to study architecture and
business administration at MIT. He raced home to his unit for the 1973
Yom Kippur War, but he made a life for himself in America, first as a student, then as a business executive in Boston. He gave right-wing lectures
on Israel, lectures that rang very much of Benzion. In 1973, he short-
ened his name to Ben Nitay. Netanyahu always denied to the Israeli
press that he had legally changed his name, and when *Ma'ariv* published
the legal documents recording the name change, filed in a court in
Middlesex County, Massachusetts, the Prime Minister's spokesman,
Shai Bazak, called the article "a malicious effort to contrive a sensational
story."

The years in the United States did nothing to push Bibi to the left. He
was very much for the war in Vietnam and deeply depressed by the con-
ciliatory turn Israel took under his father's old comrade Begin. When
Anwar Sadat came to Jerusalem, Avishai Margalit's sister-in-law threw a
party in Cambridge and invited Bibi.

"When he arrived," Margalit recalled, "he was totally grim-faced and said, 'What's the celebration? Now we'll relinquish the Sinai and they'll be on our border and there will be another war.' He was coming for a funeral, not a party."

No event shaped Netanyahu's future more than the death of Yoni, at Entebbe. On July 4, 1976—the American bicentennial—Yoni Netanyahu led a team of commandos to Uganda, where Israelis had been taken hostage by Palestinian and German terrorists. As the commandos stormed the airport building where the hostages were under guard, Yoni was gunned down, either from the control tower or from within the building itself. Bibi was in Boston at the time, and as soon as he heard the news he drove to Ithaca to tell his parents. His mother, Cela, seeing Bibi, ran to the door and, before he could say a word, said, "He's dead, isn't he?"

Many friends and acquaintances of the family told me that Yoni was the son who seemed destined for great things, perhaps first in the military, and later in politics. Had he lived, they say, Yoni might have been a chief of staff or a government minister.

Bibi was devastated. "If it wasn't for Yoni's death, I'm not sure Bibi would have gone into politics," Netanyahu's friend Uzi Beller told me. "He loved the States, especially the economy, the whole idea of a free market. He could easily have slipped into becoming an American businessman and made a lot of money." Bibi could not eat solid food for weeks after the funeral.

"The brother was the one person he really loved. This is crucial and underlies his loneliness," said Ari Shavit, of *Ha'aretz.* "I think that on the other hand they were both in the same position. They were both committed to the father. The father was from turn-of-the-century ideology and politics, though, and they realized they had to swim in a contemporary environment. So on the one hand they had to be loyal to this unique father figure, on the other hand they had to go out into the world and function. Losing Yoni was worse than losing someone you love. Bibi lost the one person who could understand him."

At the same time, Bibi saw Yoni not merely as a personal loss but as a national event, a figure in history. He was determined to make sure this was so. At the shiva, Bibi, his parents, and Iddo accepted the condolence calls of many Israelis. One of Yoni's friends arrived at the house and saw Bibi talking to Chaim Bar-Lev, a former chief of staff, then a Minister of Industry.

The friend recalled, "As soon as Bibi saw me come through the door, he left Bar-Lev, came to me, and, hardly saying hello, said, 'We've been at war for three hundred years with the Arabs and each generation needs a hero. Trompeldor fulfilled his role, and I'll make Yoni the hero of his generation.'" Josef Trompeldor was in the Tsar's Army and lost an arm in the war with the Japanese. After coming to Palestine, he was killed in a skirmish with Arabs in 1920 and became a hero, a legend of renewed Jewish heroism, especially for the right.

Because the Entebbe operation had been so spectacular, it was inevitable that Yoni's name would become a symbol. But, as Bibi had promised at the shiva, the family helped promote this. Bibi and Iddo edited a collection of Yoni's letters; more than sixty thousand copies have been sold in the Hebrew edition alone. Bibi also began a think tank called the Jonathan Institute, for the study of terrorism. To commemorate Yoni's heroism at Entebbe, Iddo wrote a book called *Yoni's Last Battle.* One former commando, however, a prominent military man named Muki Betser, who was at Entebbe, has been hostile to the Netanyahu family and was outraged over Iddo's book, which he thought inflated Yoni's role and downplayed the bravery of the rest. "I'm not sure Yoni would have liked what his little brother wrote," Betser told the Israeli press. In the early nineties, when it became clear that Bibi was emerging as a possible candidate for Prime Minister, the press began publishing stories about Yoni—all unproven—implying that he had made crucial mistakes during the Entebbe mission.

Iddo Netanyahu remains Yoni's main champion. Several months each year, he practices in the United States as a radiologist, a job that earns him enough money to live the rest of the year in Jerusalem with his family and write fiction. I met with Iddo at his house, in the Jerusalem hills. Like his father, Iddo was wary of being quoted, but he is clearly pained by the attacks on the Netanyahus.

Recently, Iddo published a novel in Hebrew entitled *Itamar K.* It can very easily be read as a thinly veiled political attack—and certainly the Israeli press has done so. The hero is Itamar Koller, a young filmmaker who discovers how hard it is in Israel to have right-wing views and still win respect as an artist and an intellectual. In refusing to embrace left-wing ideology, Itamar is rejected by the Israeli cultural élite. Itamar wants to make a movie, but funding goes instead to a left-wing homosexual, and Itamar is left behind with "untapped potential, with no way of knowing whether or not he could have realized it." The novel features set pieces on two filmmakers who cower before a former terrorist who is now a member of the Palestinian Authority. Itamar meets a writer who is infuriated by the "smiles on the faces of our ministers as they hand Bethlehem, the city where David was born, over to the Arabs." And so, once more, there is this loneliness, this singularity to the family—the Netanyahus versus the cultural hegemony of the left.

While Netanyahu's early family life is the stuff of Biblical complexity, his family life in adulthood, along with his relationships beyond the family, has been a feast for the tabloids. In the late seventies, Netanyahu married the first of his three wives, an Israeli woman named Micky, and they had a daughter, Noa. But in Boston Bibi met a woman named Fleur Cates, and when Micky learned of the affair she left him.

Netanyahu entered public life in 1982, when Moshe Arens made him his No. 2 at the embassy in Washington. Bibi made a name for himself on American television as the smooth Israeli who was everywhere, defending the Begin government's war in Lebanon. Later, Arens helped place Netanyahu as Israel's man at the United Nations, and there Bibi became an even more public figure with his support for Soviet Jewry and his attacks on Kurt Waldheim. Netanyahu went back to Israel in 1988 to win a seat in the Knesset and to be Arens's deputy at the Foreign Ministry. The marriage to Fleur, which was already troubled, fell apart once they were in Israel.

In 1989, Netanyahu was changing planes at Amsterdam's Schiphol Airport, and while he was on a moving walkway he spotted an El Al stewardess named Sara Ben-Artzi. "We were going in opposite directions," she once said, in an interview. "He looked at me until he had to turn his head backwards. Then, on the plane, he came to look for me."

Netanyahu married Sara in March 1991, when she was already several months pregnant. According to reports in the Israeli press, Netanyahu postponed the wedding at least once but was finally brought to heel by Yisrael Meir Lau, then the chief rabbi of Tel Aviv.

The Netanyahus now have two children. It would be folly to guess at the details of their marriage, but it is, by every outward sign, another troubled union. The first of several disasters came in January 1993, while Netanyahu was in a struggle for the leadership of the Likud Party. Sara received an anonymous phone call telling her that her husband had a "thing" for his image consultant, a married woman named Ruth Bar; what was more, the caller said, there existed a videotape of Bar and Netanyahu in "compromising romantic situations." Netanyahu's reaction was to go on television immediately and admit to his infidelity and, without naming names (everyone knew he meant his rival, David Levy), accuse members of his own party of "Mafia methods." This was "the worst political crime in Israeli history, perhaps in the history of democracy," he told viewers. He added that his only debt—"if I have a debt and I have a debt on this matter"—was to his wife and children.

As it happened, no videotape turned up, and now Netanyahu had to apologize to Levy. For his part, Levy called Netanyahu "Napoleon," "liar," "eel," and refused to speak to him or utter his name until 1996.

The Israeli press has reported that the Netanyahu marriage is sustained now by a series of guidelines laid out by Sara and family lawyers. Sources close to Netanyahu have said that Bibi felt he could not afford yet another divorce and still claim leadership of a conservative and religious political coalition. Netanyahu deflects the subject with various formulaic phrases of contrition and renewal, but his close aide David Bar-Illan was anything but evasive with me.

"The confession of adultery, the Sara business, this all hurt him more than I would have expected," Bar-Illan said. "For years in Israel no one cared about such things. Moshe Dayan screwed half the women in the Army and even got into trouble over it, but we said we didn't care. Everyone knew all about it and about other politicians and their affairs. But the atmosphere changed. It's the feminist thing, which is almost getting Victorian. When Bibi made his confession, it was not particularly subtle. It was hard to mistake what he meant, that he was accusing people in his own party. But it was a terrible mistake going on television and confessing to infidelity. The crime here is getting caught, and he wasn't caught."

Since he came to power, Netanyahu's marriage has remained a target for a hostile press. The tabloids have accused Sara of everything from plagiarizing work in graduate school to being a deranged "clean" freak. Her children's nanny, Tania Shaw, sued the family, accusing Sara of "enslavement" and mistreatment. A long report in the newspaper *Yediot Ahronot* featured such details as Sara's hurling shoes at her servants; in another account, Sara was described as bursting in on high-level government meetings and telling one of the Prime Minister's aides, a general, to get up, "you're sitting in my seat." The overall impression in the Israeli press is of a dim harridan who has her man by the neck. A member of the Knesset even declared that there should be legislation passed to restrain her.

Bar-Illan is supposedly a master of the press, but when I asked him about the marriage, on the record, with my pen and notebook out for all to see, he rolled his eyes and said, "Look, Sara is not the most stable woman in the world. . . . Now she only appears at the appropriate things, receptions for children, things for the retarded or the disadvantaged. And it works. It's O.K. Finally it's become boring to Israelis. Had she run half naked through the streets, it might have been something else, but it's under control."

Well, not exactly under control. Last year, Sara agreed to be interviewed on Israeli state television. She threw an incredible tantrum, accusing Knesset members of making passes at her, and said of Sonia Peres that just "because Sonia is not educated, and she washes dishes and plays cards—that doesn't mean I also have to do that." Sara then turned on her interviewer and finally walked out. She agreed to resume the interview only if the first part was destroyed; the tapes are now in a vault at the studios, but, Israel being Israel, the material leaked almost immediately.

In another interview, Sara insisted that her marriage was genuine and not at all politically motivated. "They cannot accept that we really love each other," she said. "Every time we hold hands it's supposed to be a show. You should see how often we hold hands when we're alone. It's unbelievable."

In a crude form, Netanyahu's personal situation recalls Bill Clinton's, but the comparison is weaker than it seems. Unlike Clinton, who has many layers of friends, both inside the White House and beyond, Netanyahu does not. He has forced out so many aides and ministers in his nearly two years in office that he is left mainly with yes-men. Two of Netanyahu's oldest friends, Uzi Beller, who is a doctor, and Gabi Picker, a dentist, rarely see him or talk to him anymore. "Nobody sees Bibi a lot," Beller told me. "Any leader has a small circle of intimates, and Bibi just doesn't." Bar-Illan said he considers himself one of Netanyahu's two or three closest confidants, but even he said, "Bibi is very hard to read emotionally. He's very closed. It's not possible to read what he feels, even with me. I never feel I know what's in his heart or mind. I don't know who does."

An Israeli journalist who has observed Netanyahu closely said, "It's a very difficult life he has. He is a prisoner in his office. The office is a very small room. With all that security, the moment he walks out, there are several guys at his side. Then he gets into a claustrophobic Cadillac. Wherever he goes, there are these really wild security arrangements. When he goes home, he goes to something worse. He actually has no place to relax, to unwind. All these problems—the press, his family, negotiations—all of it goes along with the idea that he has of the world as always hostile and him fighting everybody and everything all the time."

Netanyahu's few pleasures include good food (he has gained nearly fifty pounds since taking office), but while he likes luxury he does not like paying. He is notorious for rarely picking up a check. The left-wing newspaper *Kol Ha'ir* has reported that Netanyahu, in the past, tried to use his name to get discounts on goods and services. Even Netanyahu's most characteristic pleasure, his Davidoff cigars, seems to have exploded in his face. In April, the papers discovered that the government was spending some three thousand dollars a month on cigars that cost thirty dollars each. Netanyahu's spokesmen initially claimed that cigars had always been bought for foreign guests, as a kind of welcoming amenity, but then past Prime Ministers and their aides rushed in to deny it. Shamir, Netanyahu's ostensible colleague in the Likud, said the only niceties he ever offered foreign guests were a cup of tea "and maybe a cracker to go with it."

Netanyahu is certainly an outsider, too, in his relationship with Washington, for the White House is, in no small measure, a shrine to the memory of Bibi's shadow, Yitzhak Rabin. In Clinton's view, Rabin was the definition of gravitas, of historical risk-taking. There are pictures of Rabin both in the Oval Office and in the upstairs residence. Hillary Clinton prizes a crystal dove given her by Rabin. The President has kept his *kipa* from the funeral, and some sand from Rabin's grave is to be seen on a plate in his study. "It's almost a cult of Rabin here," one high-ranking White House official told me. "There's no one the President admired more or misses more."

When Bill Clinton came on the political scene, the great lions of the late–Cold War era were gone or were fading—Gorbachev, Thatcher, Mitterrand—and the statesman he came to look up to was Rabin. Their first meeting was at the Madison Hotel in Washington, during the 1992 Presidential campaign. In the realm of foreign affairs Clinton was a neophyte, and when Rabin uncorked a lecture about Middle East politics, which consumed fifty-five minutes of their allotted hour, Clinton was not insulted or bored; he was grateful. From then on, Clinton gravitated to Rabin as to a kind of father figure.

"It looked to me that Clinton saw Rabin as mentor," said Eitan Haber, one of Rabin's closest aides. "They spoke on the phone constantly, coordinating every step before anything became a problem, even the smallest step. Even their agreement not to kiss or hug Arafat onstage at the White House—to make it just a handshake—was coordinated."

Rabin's assassination, in 1995, was devastating for Clinton, and he responded by going to the funeral and spending hours with the Rabin family. (By contrast, when Netanyahu went to embrace Rabin's daughter, Dalia Pilosof, whom he had known as a student, she said, "Not now. Please, not now." Rabin's widow, Leah, made it plain that she preferred the condolences of Yasir Arafat.) With Shimon Peres now the Prime Minister, the relationship with the White House remained politically close but became personally more remote. Peres was more the ideologue—cool, Francophile, aloof.

In the 1996 Israeli election, however, Clinton made no secret of his preference for Peres over Netanyahu. The major factor, of course, was that Peres favored pushing the Oslo process ahead; Netanyahu's platform consisted of his alarm about Oslo and his resistance to American pressure.

American television viewers had come to know Netanyahu as "Americanized"—an MIT-educated Israeli politician with a perfect American accent and a feel for CNN and *Nightline*. But Netanyahu's America was antithetical to Clinton's: it was Ronald Reagan's America. Netanyahu's political friends were Richard Perle, Ronald Lauder, and Jeane Kirkpatrick. The journalists he favored were, of course, the ones who favored him: A. M. Rosenthal, William Safire, Charles Krauthammer. He yearned for the rise in Israel of the sort of neoconservative movement that had backed Reagan. He let Republicans on Capitol Hill know that he was one of them, a kind of Israeli Republican. And so while he spoke American, he was, and remains, deeply suspicious of the Clinton White House. *Of course* Clinton loved Rabin, he tells everyone. The Americans always love us when we are giving away everything and getting nothing in return.

When Netanyahu came to Washington for the first time as Prime Minister, he appeared determined to show everyone that there was a new man in office, one who would not be pushed around. Itamar Rabinovich, the Israeli Ambassador in Washington at the time, told me, "What I would have told Bibi to do on his first trip—not that he ever would have asked—is to have gone into the White House and said, 'Let's let bygones be bygones. I know you supported Peres in the election, but there are no grudges.' Instead, when they met, in July 1996, Clinton came out of the meeting saying that Netanyahu behaved and spoke in a tone that didn't seem to let on that he knew that Clinton was the President of a friendly superpower and that Netanyahu was the leader of a small nation who needs the superpower's support." In short, Clinton felt he had been insulted by the leader of a country smaller than Vermont that gets three billion in aid every year.

One Administration official described the personal chemistry between Clinton and Netanyahu as the same as that between the fractious White House pets, Buddy and Socks. When *Air Force One* and Netanyahu's plane were parked next to each other in Los Angeles last November, Clinton decided he didn't have time for even a brief meeting. Of the relationship, one Administration official later said, "We're treating him like the President of Bulgaria. Actually, I think he"—Clinton—"will go jogging with the President of Bulgaria, so that's not fair."

Netanyahu began a trip to the United States last January by accepting the hospitality of a group of Christian evangelicals—including Jerry Falwell, who'd been selling videos that accused the President of murder. Clinton was furious, but the next morning when he met with Netanyahu he jokingly suggested, "Now we're even." Both Netanyahu and David Bar-Illan told me that they had had no idea that Falwell was attacking Clinton so ruthlessly, and Bar-Illan tried to fall on his sword, saying that he had been encouraged by a Jewish contact in New York to meet with the evangelicals because of their support for Israel. Considering how closely Netanyahu and Bar-Illan follow the American scene, their protestations of innocence are hard to believe.

"The relations have never been more tense," a senior Israeli diplomat told me. "The ironic thing is that after Bibi came back from America having not accepted things, he became a hero to his people, like Saddam Hussein withstanding American pressure."

Norman Podhoretz, the former editor of *Commentary*, mainly supports Netanyahu's hard line with the Palestinians but admitted he was shocked at his performance. "He's done amazingly poorly, and I wouldn't have expected that of him," Podhoretz said. "He used to be able to seduce anyone. . . . But as a friend he's not a reliable person. It's like the Kennedys. If he makes a promise or appointment, he doesn't necessarily keep it. Then he'll depend on his charm, like Clinton. And the magic has gone out of that trick."

When I asked Netanyahu to characterize his relationship with Clinton, he took a long drag on his cigar and blew smoke through his smile. He is a bearish presence with a broad smile, and he never seemed more satisfied than now.

"It's *correct*," he said. "On a personal level there are interesting moments of affinity, because I think he has tremendous grasp of certain things that probably eluded his immediate circle. First of all, he's probably a much better politician than any of them. So he understands certain things from reading the lay of the land. He understands our political situation better than his people, especially those who led him to take the mistaken view of trying to influence the elections. . . . I have to tell you, personally, I like him. It's very hard not to like him. I wouldn't tell you we've developed warm and cozy relations. It's not true. It's possible. It just hasn't happened."

What Netanyahu has inherited from his father is a keen notion of Us versus Them, a sense that only fools can fail to see what he sees, that Jewish history is in perpetual danger of ending completely, and that Jewish history, considering the role of assimilation in the Diaspora, is in the hands of Israel and, in no small part, its Prime Minister.

"The Jewish people have had a history unlike any other people's because they lacked the elements of national survival," he said. "On the other hand, they didn't perish completely. They perished *mostly*. They were about ten percent of the Roman Empire at the time of the birth of Christ, so by any calculation they should be about a hundred and twenty million and not twelve million. The fact that we are ten percent of what we could be is based on many forces, but it is the inability to live in a coherent place with a coherent culture.

"It is not the idea of a diaspora. Other peoples have their diasporas. The Chinese have a diaspora, a far-flung diaspora, but they have a coherent center. We lost the coherent center and were dispersed. Normally what happens to a dispersed people is that they conquer new lands or they disappear. We didn't conquer new lands, but nor did we disappear, so we were always in the twilight of our existence. Between annihilation and assimilation, you could pretty much predict that the Jewish people would not survive the twenty-first or twenty-second centuries. What happened after the worst catastrophe in our history is that we somehow amassed the national will to re-forge a vital center for Jewish life here in Israel. I now think we have a Jewish future, here in Israel. It's true that, for the first time, the majority of Jews will be here in Israel sometime in the next decade. It'll happen, maybe even under my watch, I'm not sure. . . .

"You have to protect yourself. This is what the Jews didn't have. They didn't have the means to protect themselves against evil, the baser impulses of mankind. And they paid a price unlike any other people. We now have the means to protect ourselves."

(1998)

•

In 1999, Netanyahu lost the premiership to Ehud Barak. After Likud won it back two years later under Ariel Sharon, Netanyahu served in the Cabinet, first as Minister of Foreign Affairs and then as Finance Minister. Just days before the Israeli withdrawal from Gaza, Netanyahu resigned the Cabinet in protest. By staking out a position to the right of Sharon on concessions to the Palestinians, Netanyahu is clearly intent on regaining the office that he lost and pushing Israeli politics further to the right. In November 2005, when Sharon left Likud to form a new centrist party, the party fell into Netanyahu's hands and a clash became inevitable. And in January 2006, when Sharon suffered a catastrophic stroke, Netanyahu's fortunes seemed, once more, an open vista.

Rage and Reason:
Sari Nusseibeh and the PLO

Sari Nusseibeh, the Palestine Liberation Organization's chief representative in Jerusalem, is perhaps the most moderate adviser in the councils of Yasir Arafat. (He is also the only one to have worked on a kibbutz or to have written a graduate-school essay at Harvard on Wittgenstein and the role of jokes in philosophical discourse.) On many issues of moment within the Palestinian hierarchy—the morality of suicide bombings, the wisdom of Arafat's rejection of the Israeli offers at Camp David and at Taba, the refugees' demand for the "right of return" to historical Palestine—Nusseibeh disagrees, publicly and in all languages, with the hard men of the PLO and Hamas, and even with Arafat (to the extent that Arafat reveals himself). To him, "martyr operations" are blatantly "immoral," the flat rejection of the Israeli proposals a "major missed opportunity," and the right of return a painful delusion best forgotten. It is not obvious why Arafat, who craves the support and supposed authenticity of the maximalists of Hamas and Islamic Jihad, appointed a mild man in corduroy and tweed to run the East Jerusalem portfolio. As a scholar and as the scion of a distinguished family, Nusseibeh wields about as much street credibility in the refugee camps of Nablus as a duke among the sansculottes. He has no muscle to offer Arafat, no immediate value, except, perhaps, as an ornament of democracy. There is no argument to be made for Nusseibeh's power—unless one happens to believe in the power of restraint and rational thought.

Nusseibeh is fifty-three years old. He was born in the Sheikh Jarrah neighborhood of East Jerusalem. His forebears came to the city in the seventh century, with Caliph Omar. For centuries, the Nusseibehs have been involved in public affairs. Sari's grandfather was a top city official under the pre-1948 British Mandate, and Sari's father, Anwar, was, at various points in his career, a Palestinian warrior, the Jordanian Minister of Defense, the governor of Jerusalem, and Amman's Ambassador to the Court of St. James's. (His mother, Nuzha, was from a wealthy family in Ramle, a town between Jerusalem and Tel Aviv; they became refugees in 1948, losing their house and all their belongings, and resettling in Cairo and Jerusalem.) The signs of a Nusseibeh dynasty are abundant. For the past five hundred years, the family has been charged with holding the keys to the Church of the Holy Sepulchre in the Old City, which many Christians believe is the site of the Crucifixion. When it was time for Sari to send his eldest son, Jamal, to school, he sent him to Eton. As a boy, Jamal had participated in the first intifada—an uprising that was outlined in a Fatah paper called "The Jerusalem Document." The principal author of "The Jerusalem Document" was Sari Nusseibeh.

Nusseibeh came to politics obliquely, without a sense of calling. In 1968, just a year after Israel won the Six Day War and took possession of the West Bank, Gaza, and East Jerusalem—as well as gaining dominion over more than a million Palestinians—he was far away, reading philosophy at Christ Church, the most socially radiant of the Oxford colleges. (After university, Sari married Lucy Austin, the daughter of J. L. Austin, the Oxford don who wrote *How to Do Things with Words* and helped found the "ordinary language" school. They have four children.) Nearly every morning at eleven, Sari walked to the St. Aldates Church coffeehouse to meet with a young Israeli scholar from Queen's College named Avishai Margalit. "We talked politics in a sort of analytic way," Margalit, who now teaches philosophy in Jerusalem, told me. "There was no preaching to the other. It was melancholic talk, with me knowing that Israel was triumphalist and intoxicated after the war and him knowing that the Palestinians were in disarray. Sari was a sort of aristocratic kid, beautifully groomed and with great charm." Anwar Nusseibeh, who had been badly wounded in the war of 1948, sensed in his son a decidedly more pacific and private temperament. Margalit recalled, "His father said to me, 'I wanted to keep Sari outside of it because he would end up in trouble.' " As it happened, trouble could not be avoided.

After completing a Ph.D. in medieval Islamic philosophy at Harvard, in 1978, Nusseibeh began teaching at Bir Zeit University, in the West Bank, a center for both higher learning and elementary politics. At first, Nusseibeh kept out of public life, concentrating instead on problems of logic and moral philosophy; but eventually he was dragooned into academic politics—union issues and the like—and then into Palestinian politics generally. Nusseibeh was not mild in his opinions about the occupation. He demanded that the Palestinians in the occupied territories either be annexed as equal citizens of Israel (with the knowledge that in such an arrangement Arabs would eventually become a majority, ending the Jewish state) or, the more likely prospect, be made citizens of a new country, adjacent to Israel, called Palestine. And yet in the early eighties Nusseibeh outraged many of his fellow faculty members, and members of Arafat's Fatah organization, by attending a conference at Harvard to meet with Israeli politicians. As Palestinian politics grew more radical, Nusseibeh insisted on a rhetoric of moderation and on contact with the putative enemy. During the first intifada, he was quoted in the *International Herald Tribune* as saying, "I think it is a kind of exorcism to throw a stone at Satan," but he threw no stones himself and pressed for a "generally nonviolent" uprising. To call for the elimination of Israel, he argued publicly, was irrational; the Jews, he said, had a deep historical connection to Jerusalem just as the Arabs did. This was not, in all circles, a popular argument. One morning, on the Bir Zeit campus, several masked members of a Jordan-based branch of Fatah jumped Nusseibeh. He was badly beaten and one of his arms was broken.

Nusseibeh summoned up that day with a wry smile. "I remember it well," he said to me. "I'd just finished delivering a lecture at the university on liberalism and tolerance."

Not long ago, I met Nusseibeh at the Damascus Gate, one of the gates leading into the Old City of Jerusalem. Israeli troops and tanks were still in cities throughout the West Bank, and Colin Powell had been dispatched to the region, traveling everywhere and, it appeared, getting nowhere.

Nusseibeh sat on a stone step under a midday sun. He was in the company of a few dozen other Palestinians, and they were chanting slogans directed against Ariel Sharon and calling for his rapid demise. It was not an especially impressive demonstration, and Nusseibeh did not make for an impressive firebrand. He wore a slouchy baseball cap and a houndstooth jacket, and his expression, as he held up a hand-lettered anti-occupation placard and joined in the chanting, was sheepish. Over the years, he has repeatedly told friends that he would just as soon live a quiet academic life, one of teaching and contemplation and sabbaticals abroad—"Just like Avishai's life!"—and to see him now, hot and uncomfortable, was to take him at his word. He seemed both unhappy and out of place. And yet Nusseibeh is capable of absorbing every variety of political menace: anonymous telephone calls, hate mail, death threats. Even more unusual for someone in public life, he does not seem to mind being called irrelevant, as he often is. In January, when he declared that the Palestinians would be best served by the creation of a demilitarized state, Israel's Environment Minister, Tzahi Hanegbi, waved him off as an "esoteric character," and the right-wing Minister of Public Security, Uzi Landau, warned that Nusseibeh was trying to pull off some kind of "trick." Landau refers to Nusseibeh as "the pretty face of terrorism."

This was not the first time that Nusseibeh had been so accused. In 1991, during the Gulf War, he was jailed after Israeli military-intelligence officials said he had called the Iraqi Ambassador to Tunisia and described how better to target the Scud missiles that Baghdad was lobbing at Israel. After three months, Nusseibeh was released. He says that the charge that he helped Iraq in any way was "absurd," and that the Israelis had been tapping his telephone, collecting a file, and hoping to "nail" him since the 1987 intifada. In fact, such charges still come up. Recently, an article in *The Jerusalem Post* warned that Nusseibeh is a "con man," who plays the "good cop" in a media dumb show "orchestrated by Arafat." Nevertheless, leading politicians, including Israel's Foreign Minister, Shimon Peres, and its Defense Minister, Benjamin Ben-Eliezer, who are not in the habit of endorsing enemies of the state, have praised Nusseibeh as a courageous and trustworthy interlocutor.

Arafat clearly understands Nusseibeh's value. Until last year, Arafat's representative in Jerusalem had been another of the city's Palestinian dynasts, Faisal Husseini, and when Husseini died, of a heart attack, while traveling in Kuwait, Arafat turned to Nusseibeh. For months, Nusseibeh resisted, worrying that he would be a for-display-only appointment. More important, he thought that the second intifada, which followed Arafat's rejection of Israeli proposals for a final settlement and

Ariel Sharon's visit to the Temple Mount in September 2000, was not an effective uprising—"not really an intifada at all" but, rather, a series of terrible mistakes and improvisations that would lead to radicalization on the Palestinian side, a strengthening of the right wing on the Israeli side, and, above all, the bloody dissolution of trust on both sides. Nusseibeh finally took the job, but his forecast proved all too accurate.

After the demonstration, we drove to his office at Al-Quds, a university with six thousand students in East Jerusalem, where he is the President. Nusseibeh has bushy, graying hair and wears wire-rimmed glasses. In a frantic political realm, he moves laconically, thoughtfully. He slumped into a Naugahyde armchair and tried to cool off and smoke at the same time. An assistant came around with coffee. As Nusseibeh's attention alternated among the coffee, his cigarette, and a set of blue worry beads, he managed to describe the current disaster "through our prism," as if this were a kind of tutorial.

"The escalation has an internal objective dynamic," he began, blowing smoke to the ceiling. "Things moved from one stage to the next in a kind of inevitable way, leading to the point where people felt they had no way to react other than . . . this."

"This," of course, was a catchall category of violence, including so-called targeted assassinations, bus bombings, bat-mitzvah shootings, arrests, strip searches, bulldozers, stones, F-16s, Kalashnikovs, helicopter gunships, and, on March 27th, the Passover bombing at the Park Hotel in Netanya that left twenty-eight people dead, and Sharon's armored incursions into nearly every major city in the West Bank.

"A lot of this is Sharon's fault," Nusseibeh said. "He knew just how to elicit the kinds of reactions from us that would then be a justification for going one step further."

After fending off a few calls on his cell phone, Nusseibeh continued, "I look at it this way: before Camp David, when the Oslo accords were first signed, people assumed, and were told by their leaders, that this was a first step, and at the end of five years we were going to regain the territories occupied since 1967 and establish a state with East Jerusalem as its capital. So people went along with Arafat and this process. There were several positive steps taken. On the other hand, the Palestinians saw the Israelis doing things that were not consistent with withdrawal. They saw them continuing to confiscate territory and increase settlements. So they began to develop a kind of schizophrenia. If you were living in a place like Nablus or Jenin and were told by your leadership that things were going ahead and you heard about negotiators coming and going, you assumed it would happen. But, if you looked outside, you saw the opposite on your doorstep: territories being confiscated, settlements, lack of freedom of movement. And things were getting postponed—five years went to almost seven—so there was a sense of frustration among the population.

"When they went to Camp David and Arafat said afterward that we didn't get what we thought we should, people in the territories felt that their suspicions about Israel were vindicated. From the Palestinians' perspective, Barak did not come as far as they thought he should. So Arafat came out of Camp David feeling angry with Barak, and Barak, because he didn't get a proper or positive response and felt he went out on a limb, felt betrayed by Arafat and the entire PLO leadership. And Clinton, who wanted his Nobel Peace Prize, and wanted it to be done in ten days, also walked out feeling angry."

The biggest problem, as Nusseibeh sees it, is that neither side contained its anger, and so "the system of discussion was blown to smithereens." Each side indulged its worst suspicions about the other: an increasing number of Israelis felt that Arafat had been unmasked as a messianic terrorist who had never really wanted compromise except, perhaps, as a tactic; the Palestinians felt confirmed in their suspicion that Israel had no intention of giving up the settlements or their general dominance. According to Palestinians, Sharon's visit to the Temple Mount, the most disputed of all pieces of land, was the spark that set off the "cycle of armed violence." According to Israelis, the uprising had been planned months before.

As the violence accelerated, Arafat recognized that the leaders of Hamas and other Islamic radicals, with their calls for armed insurrection and the elimination of Israel from the map, were growing steadily more popular, while his own team, especially its members who were tied to the Oslo process, was seen as passé. And so Arafat began to encourage some of his younger lieutenants, including Marwan Barghouti and Jibril Rajoub, in the West Bank, and Muhammad Dahlan, in Gaza, to use the weaponry of the Palestinian police and security forces to create, in essence, a civilian army that could compete with Hamas and Islamic Jihad. Arafat's Fatah organization now sponsored the Al-Aqsa Martyrs Brigades, which was soon claiming responsibility for more suicide bombing attacks in Israel than even Hamas.

Nusseibeh, however, denies that the Palestinians were so calculating or so organized. "On the whole, the Palestinian reaction to the Israelis was basically haphazard, emotional, out of anger," he said. "Israeli action toward the Palestinians was very determined, planned, and cold-blooded. This is why I thought from the beginning that a strategy was being worked out to provoke the Palestinians and draw them into a battle of which they are not the masters—namely, of violent confrontation. The goal is the destruction of the Oslo process and the Palestinian Authority, to be followed by the implementation of a Sharonian regime of what peace should look like for the Palestinians. Which is basically to give the Palestinians something that they can call a state, maybe something like forty percent of the West Bank and Gaza, but under total security scrutiny by Israel." He added, "The good thing about Sharon is that he is a very systematic and straightforward thinker, and determined. He tells you what he wants to do and does it. Sharon has a vision."

In his narrative, Nusseibeh negotiated between history and apologia. He would not, for instance, argue that Arafat is innocent of incitement to violence. But he hints around the edges; Nusseibeh is brave but not a fool.

"Certainly Arafat is not a Gandhi," he said, with just a trace of a smile. "He is not someone who believes only in nonviolent action. He believes in the usefulness, the utility, of force."

Nusseibeh got another telephone call, this time from his wife, Lucy, telling him to come home. Their daughter had hurt her neck at a basketball game. Nothing too serious, but she was in the hospital.

"Sorry," he said. "We'll meet later." He left, with his bodyguards, and rode home in the backseat of his SUV.

A few minutes later, when I was back at my hotel in West Jerusalem, the sirens began.

Then the phone: an Israeli friend said he'd heard that there had been a suicide bombing at the Mahane Yehuda market in the midst of the pre-Sabbath shopping rush. Within five minutes, I was there, to witness the aftermath of an event that has taken place so many times: yet again, a young Palestinian wrapped with explosives had got as close as possible to as many Israelis as possible and pushed a button. It was a woman this time, twenty years old, Andaleeb Taqtaqah, from a small town near Bethlehem. A police spokesman said that the woman had tried to make it into the market, where scores of poorer shoppers were taking advantage of the last, closing discounts before dusk and the beginning of the Sabbath. Apparently, when she saw that the entrance was well guarded, she turned toward the bus stop nearby. Then she did what her masters in the Al-Aqsa Martyrs Brigades had trained her to do. Six dead, eighty wounded. A human head rolled down the street, we were told. Religious men trained to work at such sites put on sterile bodysuits and went around picking up body parts and scraps of flesh and putting them in garbage bags.

The wave of suicide bombings in Israel has steadily undermined the assumptions and the habits of everyday life. In Jerusalem, there are guards at the door of nearly every restaurant and café. People make all kinds of fine calculations. They try to sit at the back of public rooms or buses, the better to avoid the blast from a nervous bomber coming through the door. Parents of two children will send them to school on separate buses.

Many Palestinian leaders endorse suicide bombing as the answer to Israel's F-16s and Apache helicopters; the rest, the moderates, attempt to explain, if not justify, the phenomenon in terms of the frustrated hopes and the pressure of everyday life under Israeli occupation—never mind that the bombings began not at a time of deepest despair but, rather, in the mid-nineties, when Yitzhak Rabin and Shimon Peres, the initiators of the Oslo process, were in office. One prominent Palestinian spokesman, Ghassan Khatib, the director of the Jerusalem Media and Communications Center, told me that the occupation, with its check-points and its violence, "accumulates a feeling of bitterness and creates a spirit of revenge, a feeling of anger, and brings reaction in a way that people feel is the only way they can respond. In Ramallah, not long before these suicide activities, an Israeli tank shell killed a mother and five children. The Israelis said they were aiming at Palestinian police-men and mistakenly hit the civilians. You might believe them. I might believe them. But the perception of the public is what comes out of it."

In traditional Islamic theology, suicide is anathema. The Koran says that those who commit suicide are doomed to eternal damnation, for-ever repeating the act. There have been suicide attacks in the region, however, since the eleventh and twelfth centuries, when the Persian leader Hasan ibn al-Sabah led a group called the Assassins on raids of rival fortresses. The Islamic revolution in Iran ushered in the modern version. Now Iran supports Hezbollah in Lebanon and Islamic militants in the occupied territories and ships arms to Arafat. This has been a dis-tinctly violent period: recently, at the Grand Mosque in Mecca, Sheikh Abdul-Rahman al-Sudais gave a sermon, broadcast live, in which he prayed to Allah to "terminate" Jews, "the scum of humanity, the rats of the world, prophet killers, pigs, and monkeys." Suha al-Taweel Arafat, Yasir Arafat's wife, was quoted by *Al-Majalla*, a London-based weekly, as saying that if she had a son there would be "no greater honor" than to sacrifice him for the Palestinian cause: "Would you expect me and my children to be less patriotic and more eager to live than my countrymen and their father and leader who is seeking martyrdom?"

Leaders throughout the Palestinian movement have become emboldened by the lurid notion of liberation via a prolonged campaign of teenagers blowing up themselves and Israelis in restaurants and buses. What they see is that a suicide bombing, like no tactic before it, works; it is the ultimate terror act. Israelis go about their lives, but at the same time they are, in the profoundest sense, terrified.

That evening, when I went back to Al-Quds and met with Nusseibeh again, he told me he had learned of the bombing when the doctors at Hadassah Hospital, where his daughter was being treated for her neck injury, cleared out the emergency room in anticipation of the wounded who would surely come from the Mahane Yehuda market.

Nusseibeh was born a Muslim, but he is not a practicing one, he said. He does not believe, for example, in a real afterlife, for martyrs or anyone else. And yet when I asked him about suicide bombers he slowed down the rate of his conversation, as if he were being careful not to make a mistake. In front of whom—the authorities of religion or the PLO—it was hard to tell.

"Personally, I don't think that one should be afraid of death, nor should one be excessively in love with life," he said. "But that's another thing. A person, in my mind, who brings death to himself and who causes, in the meantime, death to innocent civilians, is not a martyr."

"What is he?"

"I think he has a problem, psychologically," Nusseibeh said.

"Is he a murderer?" I asked.

"I don't know that I would call him a murderer as such," he said. "A murderer is someone, perhaps, who seeks out a specific person and, in a premeditated way, goes off and kills him. In this case, if you just go and kill a group of people of whom you have no knowledge, it's more than a murderer. I don't know what . . ."

I asked Nusseibeh if Baruch Goldstein, a settler from Brooklyn who gunned down twenty-nine Arabs at the Tomb of the Patriarchs in Hebron in 1994, was a murderer.

Nusseibeh leaned back in his desk chair and propped his feet up on a window ledge. He took a long drag on his cigarette.

"Again, I wouldn't call him a murderer in that sense," he said. "I would call his act a terrorist act. I would call a suicide bomber's attack a terrorist attack. People killed in a terrorist attack are murdered. But I don't know if the person himself would be called a murderer. A killer? Hmm. I don't really know."

"This is a terrible semantic game, isn't it?" I said.

"It's not a game," he replied. "But, whatever it is, it's morally unjustified, by whatever name it goes by. . . . This is certainly abnormal, not normal, in a society that has this as a general state of mind."

Finally, I asked Nusseibeh if Arafat has ever expressed any reservations about the pervasive culture and celebration of martyrdom among the Palestinians.

"Uh, no," he said. "It's not just that he doesn't. In general, not many people do who are in a position of leadership. It's a social order, a social attitude, and people who partake of it are spread all over the community: the imams, the teachers, maybe mothers, and then, therefore, the kids. It's not Arafat. It's widespread, it's prevalent in society."

Jenin is a city of some thirty thousand in the northern region of the West Bank. It is known as a center for suicide bombers: a quarter of the bombers in this intifada so far have come from Jenin. Northern cities like Nablus, Tulkarm, and Jenin are generally poorer than central cities like Ramallah, and the politics there are more radical, the influence of Hamas and Islamic Jihad more pervasive. Iz al-Din al-Qassam, an Islamic preacher and a rebel against the Jews and the British in the thirties, was killed by British forces in a village near Jenin, and Hamas named its military wing after him. "For the Israelis he is a terrorist forefather and for the Palestinians he is the first martyr," Danny Rubinstein, a columnist for *Ha'aretz* who has been covering the Palestinians since 1968, told me. "He is a hero, like Jeanne d'Arc for the French."

Before the Passover bombing, the Israeli government had relied on targeted assassinations to go after the leaders of terrorist cells, using missiles, car bombs, exploding cell phones. Last year, Israeli security forces killed a leader of Islamic Jihad in the Jenin region at a booby-trapped public telephone. But now the operations in cities throughout the West Bank were less delicate and remote. On April 3, after encircling Jenin for several days and preparing reservists, Israeli Army officers ordered tanks, Cobra helicopters, and armored D-9 bulldozers into the city and its refugee camp.

Israeli Army officers said they expected that there would be some resistance, some shooting, as there had been elsewhere, especially in the refugee camp, but that it would soon subside at the sight of superior fire-power. Instead, the Palestinian fighters in Jenin, shooting rifles and set-ting off bomb traps from two- and three-story apartment buildings in the camp, held out for more than a week, and by the time the battle was over there were twenty-three Israeli soldiers dead. The number of Palestin-ian deaths remains in dispute; the Palestinians say there were hundreds, many of them civilians; the Israeli Army says the number was closer to fifty. The center of the refugee camp is, indisputably, a pulverized ruin.

When I first drove up to the outskirts of the city with some colleagues, the Israeli Army was not letting journalists in and had blocked the roads with checkpoints and tanks; far more important, it was turning away aid workers and ambulances. The Israelis claimed that there were still snipers and booby traps in the city, especially near the camp, and that they were concerned about safety, not public relations.

In an attempt to get around the roadblocks and reach the city center, we spent an hour crisscrossing some fields before a tank pulled up next to us and wagged its cannon threateningly. This was somewhat unnerv-ing. Then an Israeli reservist with wire-rimmed glasses and an ironic smile popped out of the hatch and ordered us to leave. We headed toward an outlying neighborhood of Jenin and knocked on the door of a tour guide in his thirties named Hassan al-Ahmad. Hassan told us what he knew of the assault on Jenin, describing it, as all the Palestinians we spoke with did, as a slaughter complete with executions and mass graves. Then someone asked him about the suicide bombings, twelve in March alone, which the Israelis said had led them to initiate what they called Operation Defensive Wall.

"Suicide bombers?" Hassan said.

His expression slackened, and he was quiet for a while. "Suicide bombers? You ask me? Honestly, I'll answer you. It's O.K. I don't think I ever thought it was O.K. before. But when I see this, and seventy-five percent of the Israeli people support Sharon, well, what can we do against these tanks? I have lived in Germany, in Europe, but I can't live in my own home with any security. They can drink coffee at night in the cafés of Tel Aviv but I can't in my home?"

Hassan's wife, who had just served us drinks, nodded in agreement.

Hassan said that there were still Palestinians who were prepared for a settlement, two states for two peoples, but "there are a lot of people who don't see it that way, who don't want compromise. They think that the Turks were here for four hundred years, and they left. The English were here in 1917, and they left in 1948. What is Great Britain now? It belongs to the States. And you hear from Hamas and Islamic Jihad that we will fight until the Israelis are gone, too. Arafat still has respect, and Israel has a serious chance with him. He has respect because he has fought for the Palestinian people for forty years. You know who comes after him? Rantisi. Zahar." Both are leaders of Hamas in the Gaza Strip.

A little later, we went back to the car to try again to reach the center of Jenin. This time, we succeeded. We parked in a narrow, shot-up alleyway and slowly walked toward the marketplace. The façades of the storefronts and the houses were cratered by tank and machine-gun fire. Every house that was still standing was pitted and charred. The Israelis had imposed a curfew, and the few people who dared come out onto the streets led us into houses that had been either destroyed or thoroughly trashed by soldiers searching for weapons. The streets were muddy, chewed up by tank treads. A couple of dusty dogs trotted along and then stopped when they felt the vibrations from a tank. On every wall along the way there were posters of Palestinian martyrs; the most common was of Abu Ali Mustafa, once the head of the Popular Front for the Liberation of Palestine, the second-largest faction of the PLO, after Fatah, and a supporter of terror attacks. Mustafa was decapitated by an Israeli missile last August while he was reading papers at his desk in Ramallah. In retaliation, less than two months later, PFLP gunmen assassinated an Israeli Cabinet minister, Rehavam Ze'evi, outside his room in a Jerusalem hotel.

Another tank rumbled down the street about a hundred yards away. A middle-aged man called us into an alley and over to a huge pile of concrete slabs.

"This was my home," the man, whose name was Assam Fashafsha, told us. "When they came in here, they called all the people out of their homes. In Arabic, on loudspeakers, they said, 'If you don't come out of your houses now, we'll knock them down with you inside.' This was at nine in the morning on the first day. And the tanks came in and destroyed it." Two of his relatives, a nephew and a sister-in-law, were killed, he said, when their house was bulldozed.

The fighting in Jenin was far worse than in any other city. Israeli officers said that after thirteen soldiers died in a booby-trapped building their attack intensified. The Palestinians we talked to, and those who spoke to the many other reporters who managed to get into Jenin, talked of Israelis bulldozing houses without waiting for them to be evacuated, of wounded fighters and civilians left to die in the streets, of strip searches, of people handcuffed for days, twenty and thirty to a room. In a Jenin hospital, a teacher in his forties named Ali Sereh described how Israeli soldiers used him as a human shield, having him walk down the street knocking on doors and telling people to come out of their houses. At the fifth such house, a confused Israeli sniper from another platoon shot Sereh in the leg and he was left in the street.

"I tried to ask for help, but the soldiers were unsympathetic," Sereh said. He said that someone from the neighborhood got to him, and he was passed from roof to roof, until, finally, he was delivered to the hospital.

The Israeli attack on Jenin has been heavily criticized by Amnesty International; there have even been suggestions that the Army committed war crimes. In Ramallah and Jerusalem, Palestinian spokesmen began to talk of another Srebrenica or Sabra and Shatila, charges that the Israelis dismissed as outrageous. The Israelis, in fact, said that it was the tactics of the Palestinian fighters that led to civilian deaths and the destruction of so many homes. If there was evidence of atrocities in Jenin, Guy Siri, the deputy director of the United Nations Relief and Works Agency for Palestine Refugees, did not find it. "Everybody was thinking mass graves in the way we think of Kosovo," he told *The Washington Post.* "I don't think we have seen that." A subsequent UN investigation came to the same conclusion and found no evidence of the sort of atrocities claimed by some Palestinian leaders.

Even in late April, as the Israelis were pulling out of Jenin and the other cities of the West Bank, government officials were thinking about going in again. In an interview at the Israeli Army headquarters in Tel Aviv, a senior general involved in planning told me, "If Powell fails, then there will be more violence and more escalation. Then maybe we'll have to take even more aggressive actions against the Palestinian leadership. Maybe if we are forced to carry out other operations, we will enter and conquer all of the Palestinian areas and crush their infrastructure and stay there. Not that it's pleasant, but we might be forced to do it."

In Jerusalem, people were watching and reading reports not only on Jenin but on the anti-Israeli demonstrations abroad and, of course, synagogue bombings and desecrations in Europe and Tunisia. Among Israelis, the fear was not merely of more suicide bombers—no one believed that Sharon's operation would stop the bombings completely. The fear was of international isolation and, worse, a poisonous impasse with the Palestinians and a regional war.

I was reading the galley proofs of *Six Days of War,* an excellent new history of the 1967 war by an Israeli diplomatic historian, Michael Oren, who had gained access to sources on all sides. We met at his office at the Shalem Center, a mainly conservative think tank in Jerusalem. Oren, who is in his mid-forties, was born in upstate New York and came to Israel when he was twenty-three. He fought in the Lebanon War in 1982, an experience that soured him for a while on Ariel Sharon; he and his fellow soldiers in the special forces were furious that Sharon had led them to Beirut, far beyond their initial mission.

At lunch, Oren said he thought that there was now, as there had been in 1967, a real chance of regional war against Israel, headed by Syria, Iran, and Iraq. "The dynamic of Palestinian leaders trying to drag the Arab states into a military conflict with Israel is recurring," he said. "You can close your eyes and it's 1967, but the idiom has changed from Arab nationalism to Islamic fundamentalism, to a great degree."

Oren's hopes for a solution are roughly in synch with Israeli public opinion. That is, he is "schizophrenic," the recurring word of the moment: he favors a Palestinian state with secure borders but, at the same time, supports Sharon's incursions as a necessary response to the "existential threat" that suicide bombers pose to Israeli society.

"Look, I am not sure that the Palestinian people know what they are about," Oren said at one point. "They have been offered a state so often: in 1937, they were offered a state, bigger than the Jewish state, by the Peel Commission, and they turned it down; they were offered partition in 1947 by the United Nations, and they turned it down; and then there was Camp David, and they turned that down. It raises the question, then, if a people cannot seize a historical opportunity, what kind of people are they? Instead, they are basing their identity on victimhood, and that feeds the suffering."

What Oren was saying was no longer common only among right-wing Israelis. For Oren, and for many Israelis left, right, and center, Arafat revealed himself as untrustworthy after he ended the negotiations with the Israelis in 2000 without offering a counterproposal, insisting, yet again, on the Jews' lack of a historical connection to the Western Wall and on the right of Palestinian refugees abroad to return to Israeli territory. Such a return, Oren said, "is a euphemism for not recognizing Israel's right to exist."

I mentioned Sari Nusseibeh and his statement, deeply unpopular among his own people, that the Palestinians will have to give up the right of return and recognize Israel's right to a secure existence if there is ever going to be a real peace.

Oren smiled indulgently, as so many Israelis and Palestinians do at the mention of Nusseibeh's name. "Sari is a wonderful guy," he said, "but how many divisions does he have?"

By car from the center of Jerusalem, it is fifteen minutes south to Bethlehem, ten minutes north to Ramallah, ten minutes east to Abu Dis. (Without counting the delays at military checkpoints, that is.) David Makovsky, the former executive editor of *The Jerusalem Post* and a diplomatic correspondent for *Ha'aretz*, told me, "What people have never understood is that the reason an Israeli-Palestinian settlement is so hard is that there is too much history and too little geography. When the Egyptians and the Israelis made peace, they suddenly had a hundred miles of desert between them. They signed a treaty and, for the most part, they never really saw each other again. The quality of relations after the treaty was a footnote, like a divorce. But with the Israelis and the Palestinians the quality of the relationship after they make a deal is at the core of everything, as with a marriage. And when the Israelis begin to think that what the Palestinians really intend is not land-for-peace but land-for-war, well, it doesn't bode well for the marriage."

And yet, in the current environment of resentment, someone like Sari Nusseibeh can work only at the margins. Recently, when Ehud Ya'ari, Israeli television's leading expert on Palestinian politics, was asked if Nusseibeh could succeed Arafat, he said, "The long answer is no."

"He is a prince with all the characteristics of a prince," Nahum Barnea, whose column in *Yediot Ahronot* is the most popular in Israel, said. "When it came to real struggle, he was not there. It's part of his grace. He will not come to a barricade, or get into a fight with police. He's a gentleman, but this is not a gentleman's war. This war is so far from any idea of gentlemen that it is unimaginable." What Nusseibeh represents is the persistence of the idea of compromise, a certain sympathy not only with his own people but with the Other. He, like certain Israelis, has the ability to think as critically about his brethren as about the Other. One of the tragic signs of what has happened since Arafat's decision to pursue an uprising is that a man like Nusseibeh is even less representative of his people than he used to be. To visit the neighborhoods of relatively pacific East Jerusalem, to say nothing of the enraged precincts of Gaza City and the West Bank, is to understand how thoroughly the "spirit of Oslo"—the spirit that allowed Nusseibeh to quit politics in 1993 and start thinking about a new and totally private academic life—has been destroyed.

One afternoon, I stopped in to see Nusseibeh again, and I mentioned to him that Abu Ala, a deputy of Arafat's who had done much of the negotiating for the Oslo agreement, had told Joshua Hammer, of *Newsweek*, that "there are a hundred thousand Palestinians willing to become kamikazes."

Nusseibeh was once again smoking and working his worry beads. He seemed genuinely cast down by the comment; this was Arafat's ally, Abu Ala, not the head of Hamas.

Then he sighed and said, "It is possible you will have this. People are so desperate, so crazy, so resentful, that it is natural to expect more of this. I'd expect more in the next months. It will be a very difficult, uphill struggle to return to the path of sanity. From our side, these acts of violence will be good reason for the Israelis not to give in. The break will not come—and this is the main point—unless somehow the Palestinians manage to develop a new pattern of thinking, a new state of mind among themselves, in the way they act with the Israelis."

He stopped for a moment, as if to consider his language carefully. Then he shrugged and when he spoke he used a curious metaphor.

"The Palestinians have to resurrect the spirit of Christ to absorb the sense of pain and insult they feel and control it, and not let it determine the way they act toward Israel," Nusseibeh said. "They have to realize that an act of violence does not serve their interest. This is a gigantic undertaking."

(2002)

The Spirit Level:
Amos Oz

A mos Oz is the best-known novelist in Israel. For eighteen years, he has lived in the desert outpost of Arad, a town of twenty-eight thousand, between Be'er Sheva and the Dead Sea. In the late afternoon, after a day at his desk, he often takes a seat at a café in the town shopping mall. He doesn't have to wait long before someone says hello or sits down to debate, perhaps even going so far as to denounce him for his public endorsement—first sounded in 1967, in the days after the Six Day War—of a two-state settlement with the Palestinians. Oz is a liberal, and the Russians who increasingly dominate the population of Arad are, for the most part, not. But he is always happy to talk, a "word-child," hyperarticulate. Fully formed paragraphs issue forth in conversation with a hypnotic, liquid ease. Sooner or later, his would-be debater is charmed and silenced.

Oz is in his mid-sixties, trim and, generously appraised, of medium height. He seems always to be squinting into a distant sun. When he first became famous, nearly forty years ago, reviewers and readers routinely commented on his rugged, emblematic looks: the light hair and light eyes, the deep tan, the spidery wrinkles near his eyes and the corners of his mouth. Dressed in rumpled chinos and a work shirt, Oz became part of the mid-century Zionist iconography: the novelist-kibbutznik, the Sabra of political conscience. His is still a handsome face but, depending on the angle or the expression, it now exists in a kind of temporal flux. A turn of the head this way and he is back in the vineyards and olive groves, a turn that way and he is a study-bound éminence grise. He wears bifocals on a string. Several years ago, he had his knees replaced. He walks as if on broken glass.

Oz is earnest, romantic, generous, sentimental, and pleasantly vain. He is well aware of his image, and is quick to make light of it. "European Zionist writing maintained that the moment the Jews set foot on Biblical soil they will be totally born again," he told me one morning in his basement study. "They will be a new race. Even physically they will change. They will become blond, suntanned. Both of my parents were dark. In a genetic-ideological miracle, they succeeded in having a blond son. Which gave them infinite pride and joy. They were raving at my blondness! They thought it was the sun, the air. It's Jerusalem! They used to call me *shaygets*. You know this Yiddish word and what's behind it? It's a little Ukrainian pig herder, who throws stones at Jews. I came from a long line of distinguished scholars and rabbis. Why would they be so happy to call their son a *shaygets*?"

Born in Jerusalem, Oz spent more than thirty years living on a kibbutz in central Israel, where he married and raised two daughters and a son. He moved to Arad in 1986. Until then, he had never owned anything more than some books and the clothes in his drawer. From the time he began earning serious royalties, with his 1968 novel *My Michael*—the story, told in a woman's voice, of a disintegrating marriage, set against the Suez War of 1956—he plowed all his earnings back into the general account of the kibbutz. "It wasn't until I was forty-six and moved to Arad that I had any private property, or even a checkbook," he said. "You will not find someone with a more exotic background this side of North Korea."

Oz is a man of nearly obsessive order: orderly sentences, orderly bookshelves. Every morning at around dawn and every evening at sunset, he leaves his modest house and makes his way to the desert. Arad is built on the flint, grit, and negligible scrub of the Negev. In the Book of Numbers, the Canaanite king of Arad battled Moses and his flock before the Israelites took the city. For three thousand years thereafter, the place made little impression. Set on a promontory with a view of Jordan, the Mountains of Edom, and the Dead Sea (a mercury gleam in the distance), modern Arad was founded in 1962 by the Israeli government, in the hope of shifting some of the growing population away from the cities of the coastal plain. The transformation came in an instant: the irrigation systems and the power grid, the housing—bungalows, concrete apartment blocks—the trees and the radar towers, the shopping mall. Arad was soon a frontier town as functional and as dull as the distant suburbs of Los Angeles.

One evening this summer, I went with Oz and his wife, Nily, on one of their desert rambles—first by car, then on foot. "The landscape here is no different than it was in the time of the prophets and Jesus," Oz said along the way. The hills are bare, but there are wolves, desert hares, jackals. There are Bedouin camps, oases. Oz takes his walks here to clear his mind of the latest news from Jerusalem and Gaza, to "keep perspective on eternity."

Nily, who has oil-black hair and a wit that is occasionally aimed at defusing the household star, smiles patiently as Amos makes observations that she has undoubtedly heard a hundred times. Amos and Nily met as teenagers on the kibbutz and have been married for forty-four years. Their children are grown and the distractions are few. On the drive, they showed me the oasis where their grandchildren go camping and ride camels when they visit from the suburbs of Tel Aviv and Haifa. We passed a few archaeological signs, Biblical sites. As if on cue, we passed a Bedouin camp, a goat, a camel, the desert tourist's equivalent of the Empire State Building.

"Amos," Nily said, tiring of the tour, "let's make sure we get back for a walk. The sun is getting low."

Oz stopped the car and, without fear of oncoming traffic, animal or automotive, swung back toward town.

Last year, Oz published a memoir called *Sipour Al Ahava Vehoshekh (A Tale of Love and Darkness),* one of the biggest-selling literary works in Israeli history. For many years, Oz has drawn on the facts and landscapes of his life for his novels. What made *A Tale of Love and Darkness* an event in Israel is the power with which it entwines the intimate story of an immigrant family—a lonely, depressed mother, a distant father, and their son—with the larger historical story: Europe's rejection, the frantic search for refuge among Arabs in Palestine, the idealism and the disappointments, the establishment of Israel and the war that followed. Amos is a precocious, secretive boy, a "ceaseless, tireless talker," confused by overheard news of death camps abroad and civil war at home; he is a boy who plots the history of a new country with toy soldiers and maps spread across the kitchen floor. The book is a digressive, ingenious work that circles around the rise of a state, the tragic destiny of a mother, a boy's creation of a new self. "I was, if you wish, the Tom Sawyer or Huckleberry Finn of history," Oz said. "To me it was like sailing alone on a raft on the Mississippi River, except it was a river made of books and words and stories and historical tales and secrets and separations."

In a novel like Philip Roth's *American Pastoral*, history seems to assault the characters, wreaking havoc on a desire for tranquillity; it arrives as a shock. That has never been possible in Oz's part of the world, where war and ethnic tension have been constants. "I know that for people in the West history is something that comes across the television screen," he said. "This whole book is saturated with history. It is not a piece of tragic chamber music played against a wide screen."

Oz's eldest child, his daughter Fania, teaches history at Haifa University. She told me that *A Tale of Love and Darkness* should be read, in part, as an argument about the history of Zionism. The book, she said, portrays Zionism and the creation of Israel as a historical necessity for a people faced with the threat of extinction. It acknowledges the original sin of Israel—the displacement and the suffering of the Palestinians—but, at the same time, defends Zionism against some on the European left and among the Israeli New Historians who challenge the state's claim to legitimacy even now, almost six decades after its founding. As Amos, Nily, and I were driving from the desert valleys to an area closer to town where we could take a walk at sunset, I mentioned his daughter's idea.

Oz quickly glanced back over his shoulder. "If there had been no Zionism, six and a half million would have been dead rather than six million, and who would have cared?" he said. "Israel was a life raft for a half-million Jews."

Some American, European, and Israeli intellectuals were now saying that the Zionist project was lost, and that the only future was binational, a state of both Arabs and Jews from the Mediterranean to the Jordan River—a state that would, given the realities of borders and birth rates, become majority Arab quite fast. Had Zionism, as it was conceived by his parents' generation, been a mistake?

"I don't think there was any real practical choice," Oz said. "When

anti-Semitism in Europe became unbearable, Jews might have preferred to go to the United States, but they had no chance in hell in the
thirties of being admitted to America." One of his grandfathers, in
Lithuania, applied for French, British, and various Scandinavian visas—
and he was rejected every time. "It was so desperate that he even applied
for German citizenship, eighteen months before Hitler came to power,"
Oz said. "Fortunately for me, he was turned down. The Jews had nowhere
to go, and this is difficult to convey today. People now ask, Was it good to
come here? Was it a mistake? Was Zionism a reasonable project? There
was no place else. There was a conference in Evian"—in 1938—"where
the problem of the Jewish refugees and the Nazi persecutions was discussed. It ended with practically just the Dominican Republic expressing its readiness to accept one or two thousand Jews, and a couple of
other countries. The Prime Minister of Australia said, In Australia we
have no problem of anti-Semitism, thank God. But we don't want to
encourage more Jews to come here. Otherwise, we might have anti-
Semitism." It was a time, as Chaim Weizmann, who became the first
President of Israel, described it, when "the world seemed to be divided
into two parts—those places where the Jews could not live and those
where they could not enter."

Oz parked the car at a curb that marked the end of Arad and the start of
the desert. We got out and looked into a long drop. Amos and Nily
walked hand in hand down a path that led to a huge, martial-seeming
piece of sculpture.

"I don't know what we did to deserve this lovely thing," Nily said as we
approached it. She rolled her eyes and smiled.

We did not hike far. Nily was wearing a long black cotton dress, and a
sharp breeze had come up suddenly.

Amos wanted to catch sight of the sun setting, and it was now at our
backs. We turned around and started toward the town. A few Ethiopian
men were sitting on the curb and sharing a large bottle of beer.

"Do you know what 'Addis Ababa' means?"

Oz knows a great deal. Nily is patient with this.

"What does 'Addis Ababa' mean?" she said sweetly.

The men glanced over and smiled, catching the drift.

Nily held up her hand and stopped us.

"Look down, look *here*," she said, pointing at a spot along the trail.
"Ants."

"A society of ants," Amos said. "Let's skip the metaphors. And watch."

They bent over and watched with the rapt fascination of a couple on safari.

The sun was pulsing orange and just inches from the horizon.

Nily smiled as Amos stood behind her and held her close. "I am glad to be alive," she said.

Amos waited awhile. It was darker, but it was not dark yet. He looked up. "I'm hungry," he said and headed to the car.

A few minutes later, we pulled up to a clump of low-slung commercial enterprises on the edge of town.

"Welcome to Mr. Shay's," Nily said. "The best Chinese restaurant in the Negev."

Mr. Shay, a Thai who had somehow come to Arad and married an Israeli, greeted us at our table. We were the only diners. I was concerned. But Mr. Shay turned out to be a fine cook and, though he is said to prepare a mean "kosher crab," I ordered the chicken.

We talked for a while about *A Tale of Love and Darkness.* Much of the book is clearly the result of memory and memory reconstructed from reading and conversations with older relatives. There are long excavations of Oz's origins, the lives of his grandparents and parents in Europe, a lost world of high culture, Jewish learning, ferocious anti-Semitism. Using the evidence, but also taking the liberties of a novelist, Oz tries to portray things as hidden to him as his father's love affairs and his mother's tortured inner life.

"I don't like to be described as an author of fiction," he said. "Fiction is a lie. James Joyce took the trouble, if I am not mistaken, to measure the precise distance from Bloom's basement entrance to the street above. In *Ulysses* it is exact, and yet it is called fiction. But when a journalist writes, 'A cloud of uncertainty hovers . . . '—this is called fact!"

A Tale of Love and Darkness ultimately amounts to the founding story of Israel as told through a child's eyes—a kind of Zionist *What Maisie Knew.* At a time when Zionism is under question, the book provides a dramatic, yet liberal justification for Israel's existence. Oz said that, while the conflict between the Israelis and the Palestinians is between "right and right"—between two legitimate claims demanding a decent and equitable divorce—what has been lost over time is the desperate conditions that preceded Israel's founding. Oz can only tell it as a story:

"The mother of the man who married my elder daughter is an unusual

Holocaust survivor. She was taken from Holland with her mother and sister to Ravensbrück, a concentration camp, where the mother died. The two girls were nineteen and eighteen. At Ravensbrück, the girls heard stories about Auschwitz from detainees who had been there but were not sent to their death because they came from mixed marriages. Then something happened that I think was unique in the history of the Holocaust. The Foreign Ministry in Berlin gave an order saying, Send those two girls to Theresienstadt. There they were introduced to Adolf Eichmann, and he and several S.S. commanders interrogated them. Eichmann asked what they knew about Auschwitz. He said, 'If you ever say a word about your life in Ravensbrück or what you know about Auschwitz, you, too, will go up in those chimneys.' At Theresienstadt, they were given work. Twice during the war, Eichmann saw those two girls.

"As it turned out, this woman grew up and was one of the witnesses at the Eichmann trial"—in Jerusalem in the early nineteen-sixties. "It was hard for her to testify. At the trial, Eichmann tried to say that he was just a cog in the wheel, that he hadn't even the capacity to decide on one life. I am telling you this story because, despite Eichmann's warning to the two sisters about being quiet, they did tell everyone they could in Theresienstadt. They talked about Auschwitz and the gas chambers, but not one person at Theresientadt believed them. They were called hysterical. So: how could people in Jerusalem or New York believe something that even the inmates of Theresienstadt refused to believe? Knowing is one thing. Believing another. Understanding another."

A few years ago, I tried to arrange a meeting with Oz in Jerusalem. He demurred, seeming to prefer almost any other place: Arad, or the apartment in Tel Aviv that he and Nily bought in order to spend weekends near their grandchildren. Now he said, "I don't often spend the night in Jerusalem. I'll go professionally or to see friends. It is hyperactive. Everyone is expecting something, either the messiah or disaster or both. Tel Aviv is becoming more and more Mediterranean, like the South of France, whereas Jerusalem is moving in the direction of—I don't know where, maybe like Qum, in Iran."

Oz was born Amos Klausner in Jerusalem in 1939. His parents, Yehuda Arieh and Fania, came from Eastern Europe, in the nineteen-thirties, speaking Yiddish, Russian, Ukrainian, and German. In Jerusalem, they spoke Hebrew with their son, Russian when there were secrets to keep. In those days, Palestine was predominantly Arab. Jerusalem was not. Except in the era of the Crusades, in the eleventh and twelfth centuries, there had been a continuous Jewish presence in the city. When Amos was born, the population was small—around a hundred thousand—and each neighborhood was distinct. The Klausners would walk from their basement apartment, on Amos Street, in Kerem Avraham, to see their more distinguished relatives in the neighborhood of Talpiot, and, Oz said, "it was in the same spirit that shtetl Jews would take the train to Warsaw to see the five-story buildings."

One morning, I met Oz at a hotel on the outskirts of the city, and we took a cab to Malchai Yisroel—Kings of Israel Street. Kerem Avraham, along with the neighboring enclaves of Geula and Mea Shearim, is almost completely Orthodox. Signs announced the opening of a new kosher butcher shop, the lecture schedules of prominent rabbis, a clothing store "for modest women." Oz pointed out an enormous walled-off compound that had first been an orphanage and then, after the British conquered Palestine, in 1917, was converted into the Schneller Barracks. The Schneller Barracks are a presence, the embodiment of the British Mandate, in many of Oz's stories and novels. When he was a boy, he and his friends used to take gum from the British soldiers and then turn around and shout "Nazi!" and throw stones.

"Imagine!" he said now. "This was one or two years after the British had been at war with the real thing." When Oz was seven, the Stern Gang, a Jewish terror organization, exploded a car bomb outside the barracks. "How I admired them for that!" he said in the same tone of self-mockery.

The day was brutally hot. Though the blocks are well planted with cypress and Jerusalem pine, today the trees seemed limp and singed.

In many neighborhoods of the city, Jews live in houses that were expropriated from Arab families during the war of 1948, what Jewish Israelis call the War of Independence and Palestinians call the *al nakba,* the catastrophe. With some relief, Oz said that Kerem Avraham was built on land bought by an English missionary, James Finn, who had the novel idea of a place where Jews could start a farm.

The overwhelming emotion in *A Tale of Love and Darkness* is of loss. Even Zionism itself felt, at that time, like a form of loss—the loss of a European culture that had rejected, and was now murdering, Jews. "Everyone in Jerusalem—Jewish Jerusalem—of those days missed something," Oz had said earlier. "Other places, other cultures, other languages, other people. It was, for most Jews, an exile, a refugee camp. But at the same time it was also a magnet for all sorts of lunatics, redeemers, world reformers, and self-fashioned messiahs. In this respect, it hasn't changed much; perhaps it is even more so. Everyone who had a way to salvage the Jewish people in three easy moves came to Jerusalem. It was full of prophets, bookbinders who prophesied, cashiers who prophesied, scholars who prophesied. And this was very exciting for a child, because for every fantasy that I could summon in my little mind I could find someone who would endorse my fantasy and say, 'Yes, yes, this little boy has a vision, he knows even better than Ben-Gurion.' "

We came to No. 18 Amos Street, a modest apartment block with a tiny hardware store in the center of what had been the apartment of one small family: the Klausners.

"It's more run-down than it used to be," Oz said as we climbed a few steps and looked at a small back garden. There had been fig trees, radishes, green onions, eggplants. Now little other than some scrubby grass seemed to grow.

"If you look at this spot here," Oz went on, "here is where my friends and I worked day after day, when we were all about seven, trying to build a rocket that we would aim and fire at Buckingham Palace. There was a problem with the fuel and the guidance system." When he was not plotting the overthrow of King George VI, Oz wrote what he calls "Biblical poems about the restoration of the Davidic kingdom through blood and fire." His father had studied literature and history in Vilna and Jerusalem and could read in sixteen languages, though he never found a teaching berth. He made his living as a librarian and, at night, wrote books and articles about comparative literature. On the Sabbath, Fania stayed inside alone, reading—Chekhov, Tolstoy, Kleist, Hamsun, Maupassant, Agnon, Flaubert—and the men would sit in the yard "discussing the problems of Bakunin and Nechayev and whether the German social democrats were too soft." Politics was the constant conversation, and nearly all the adults in the Klausner circle were right-wing Revisionists, suspicious of the Labor Zionists and their socialist dreams.

"The remarkable thing is that those people were not fascists," Oz said. "In their own view, they rejected any racist notion. They just happened to maintain that the Arab nation has a land mass three times as big as Europe, whereas the Jewish people have nothing, and that even if Greater Israel is given to the Jews and the Arabs are forced to migrate, that would mean for the Arabs a loss of zero point five percent of the Arab homeland. I am only trying to explain their view. . . . So yes, this Klausner environment was very right-wing, very militaristic, intoxicated by the fact that Jews can fight, and fight well. Thrilled by it in a childish way. Remember, this is two years after the Holocaust. In those years, the

Jews were never accused of being bullies or thugs; they were accused of being cowards who hide and will not fight back."

Oz looked in a window of his old apartment. The shades were drawn. When he lived there, every room, kitchen and bathroom included, was lined with books, and, among the books, there were small landscapes of Europe cut from magazines: lakes, forests, snow-capped mountains. "For years, throughout my childhood, my father and others would say to me, 'One day, Amos, not in our lifetime but in yours, this Jerusalem is going to evolve and become a real city,' " he said. "I didn't know what they were talking about. To me, Jerusalem was the only real city in the world. Europe was a myth.

"And yet deep down there was this longing and yearning. You walked in Rehavia, a kind of German-Jewish, fairly wealthy neighborhood of Jerusalem, you walked there on Saturday at siesta time, when the streets were absolutely empty, and you would hear from many windows the sound of pianos. They were all craving Europe, whether it was Chopin or Mozart or Brahms."

By the end of the Second World War, expectations about the founding of a Jewish state were intense: "We were in the corridor of the maternity ward, we were like the nervous parents waiting for what was happening beyond the door." One Hanukkah, as Oz's father lit the candles, he told his only child that, one day, "not in my lifetime but in yours," as many as a million Jews would live in the country: "It sounded like science fiction, a futuristic, wild speculation."

What came next, of course, is the diplomatic and military history of 1947–48: the United Nations declarations of two-state partition on November 29, 1947, and then the war that followed—Egypt, Syria, Transjordan, Lebanon, and Iraq on one side, the newly declared State of Israel on the other.

In his journalism and essays, in books like *The Land of Israel* and *Under This Blazing Light,* Oz harbors no illusions about the nature of that war—least of all about the displacement of more than seven hundred thousand Palestinian Arabs from their villages and cities and about their lives of misery in refugee camps throughout the region. At the same time, he argues, the Arabs were "under no obligation" to start a war after the U.N. partition plan. But in *A Tale of Love and Darkness* the narrator is not a disinterested historian; the point of view is that of a young boy seeing what he could see, listening to the broadcasts and speeches and rumors all around him. He describes collecting empty bottles to make Molotov cocktails, the suspension of school for an entire year, the rumor around the neighborhood that some families had fled the country and that one had stashed cyanide tablets "just in case."

"All of the Holocaust survivors had seen all this before, from the last weeks of August in 1939," Oz said about the first days of war. "The big change came on May 14, with the expiration of the British Mandate. That Friday morning, I saw with my eyes the British leaving the Schneller Barracks and then the Haganah"—the new Israeli Army—"rushing to take over. Then, on Friday afternoon, we were told that Israel is a nation now, it has a government, but one minute after midnight we were told that Israel is being invaded by five regular Arab armies, and that there was shelling and bombardment by artillery batteries. There was nowhere to send the kids, nowhere to go." For years, in Europe, Oz's father had seen graffiti in German and Russian and Ukrainian: "Jews Go Home to Palestine." Years later, as a citizen of Israel, he saw new signs: "Jews Out of Palestine."

At one point in the memoir, Oz writes that as a child he hoped to "grow up to be a book." When I asked him about it, he smiled and said, "There was fear when I was a little boy. People would say, Enjoy every day, because not every child grows up to be a person.This was probably their way of telling me about the Holocaust or the frame of Jewish history. Not every child grows up. I know the Israelis become tiresome when they say that the whole world is against us, but back in the forties this was pretty much the case. I wanted to become a book, not a man. The house was full of books written by dead men, and I thought a book may survive."

Fania's father had owned a mill in Rovno, in western Ukraine, and came with his family to Haifa, in 1934, to work as a carter on the docks. In the book, Oz describes his mother's knowledge, in the mid-forties, that, on the outskirts of Rovno, in the Sosenki Forest, "among boughs, birds, mushrooms, currants, and berries," the Nazis had slaughtered more than twenty thousand Jews, with submachine guns, in two days.

Even as a young boy, as he makes clear in *A Tale of Love and Darkness*, Oz was keenly aware that his mother was adrift and that relations between his parents had eroded. Fania became increasingly depressed, withdrawn. "Among the immediate reasons for my mother's decline was the weight of history, the personal insult, the traumas, and the fears for the future," Oz said. "My mother had premonitions all the time, probably because of the trauma of the Holocaust. She might have sensed that what happened to the Jews in her hometown would sooner or later happen here, that there would be a total massacre. This is not something she would share with a little boy, except perhaps obliquely, through some of the stories and fairy tales she told, the books she read, a hair-raising Schopenhauerian worldview."

By the end of 1951, Fania's black periods had become worse and more frequent. Amos and his father were, he writes, "like a pair of stretcher bearers carrying an injured person up a steep slope." In *A Tale of Love and Darkness,* the reader knows early on that Fania is doomed, and at the end of the book, as she wanders the streets in a downpour and, finally, takes her life with an overdose of sedatives, it is possible to get some sense of the son's loss and fury.

Only now, after reaching an age when he is old enough to be the father of his lost mother, Oz told me, can he look at those days with a certain detachment.

Fania Klausner killed herself in January 1952, Oz said, for countless reasons: "She died because, for her, Jerusalem was an exile. This climate and environment and reality was alien. And she died because her hopes, if she had any, that maybe a replica of her Europe could be built here, without the bad aspects of the Diaspora Jewish shtetl, were apparently refuted by the reality of the morning after." Fania was just thirty-eight years old.

"After my mother died, my father and I never talked about her," he said. "We never mentioned her name, not once. If we referred to her at all, it was as 'she' and 'her.' We had plenty of discussions, political discussions—he thought I was a Red—but never about her."

We came to Ben Yehuda Street, a pedestrian arcade lined with cafés, restaurants, bookshops, and trinket stores for tourists. The area around Ben Yehuda, one of the most crowded spots in Jerusalem, has been a popular site for suicide bombers.

Oz had not been back to his old neighborhood for a few years, and he was uncharacteristically quiet as we walked. Suddenly, he ducked into an alley, headed up a small set of steps, and then went looking for a favorite café.

"It's here somewhere," he said. "It's right . . . over . . . yes! . . . Here."

The sign read "Tmol Shilshom"—"The Day Before Yesterday"—the title of a novel by S. Y. Agnon. In Oz's youth, Agnon was the singular literary presence in Jerusalem, an immigrant from Galicia who wrote in Hebrew and, in 1966, won the Nobel Prize.

Oz mopped his brow and ordered a cold drink. Our walk through

Kerem Avraham had been a kind of exercise, a performance on request—the writer come home to the scene of the book, the scene of the crime. Oz seemed drained by it.

"We've just visited a place that no longer exists," he said. At least, not as it was in the life and books of Amos Oz. "When I visited Oxford, Mississippi, I had to run back to Faulkner's novels. The place was a fading reproduction of the real thing." Nearly half of Oz's books—among them *Where the Jackals Howl, My Michael, The Hill of Evil Counsel, The Same Sea,* and now *A Tale of Love and Darkness*—take place in one square mile of Kerem Avraham.

As a writer and as a teacher—he is a professor of literature at Ben-Gurion University, in Be'er Sheva—Oz says he is a committed "provincial." He is hardly ignorant of other literatures, but he is obsessed primarily with the storytellers, essayists, and poets who wrote in modern Hebrew and gave shape to cultural Zionism.

"Both of my parents knew Hebrew before they arrived in Palestine," he said. "They knew Yiddish, but Yiddish for them was shtetl talk, the talk of the previous generation, and so not to speak it was part of their rebellion against their own ancestors. For my mother, Yiddish was the language in which her parents quarreled. The Hebrew of my childhood was a language making its first steps in the open, like a creature bred and created in a laboratory or in a zoo and set free."

After seventeen centuries of near-dormancy, Hebrew was revived as a modern instrument by a small clutch of nationalists in Europe in the late nineteenth century. "There is a myth, according to which Hebrew was revived for ideological reasons by a genius of a madman, or a madman of a genius, called Eliezer Ben Yehuda, who reinvented Hebrew and invented thousands of words—and all of it is true," Oz said. "This is at the turn of the century here in Jerusalem. But, of course, not even a genius could persuade Norwegians to speak Korean one fine morning or Greeks to speak Portuguese. So what actually happened? In the last decade of the nineteenth century, with the growing influx of European Jews coming into Jerusalem, most of them not Zionists but ultra-Orthodox, who came for religious reasons, to get buried on the Mount of Olives—when they confronted the local indigenous Jewish population, the Sephardic population, there was no common language. The only way to ask directions to the Wailing Wall or to rent an apartment in the Old City was to resort to prayer-book Hebrew. If, a hundred years ago, you put on a desert island one thousand churchgoing Catholic French people and one thousand churchgoing Lithuanians, Latin would have been revived for the same reasons."

In addition, since the eighteenth century there had been writers who wrote in what most of the world considered a dead language: Chaim Nachman Bialik, Yosef Chaim Brenner, Micha Berdichevsky, and, later on, S. Y. Agnon. When Oz travels in Europe and the United States, giving readings and speeches, most audiences want to talk about current events, not literary influences, and, even for many Jewish audiences, Agnon and the rest of Oz's literary reference points are unfamiliar. It's as if Gabriel García Márquez's readers had never heard of Cervantes. "Agnon is an imagination on the level of Robert Musil and Hermann Broch," Oz said. "Why did he stick to Hebrew? Even if he had written in Yiddish there would have been a larger audience. Here is a writer who wrote realistic, mimetic novels in a language that no one really spoke. Part of it was probably ideology, neo-Zionism. Those writers were mesmerized by the beauty of Hebrew as a musical instrument, and there was also the nineteenth-century Romanticism—1848, the springtime of nations—and the interest in folklore, back to origins. This was going on all over Europe."

The renaissance of Hebrew is the most unqualified success of cultural Zionism. Ten thousand people spoke it at the turn of the century, three hundred thousand in the nineteen-forties, seven or eight million today. "This is more than the speakers of Danish worldwide," Oz said. "And more than the number of speakers of English in the days of William Shakespeare. So this is the big story of my life, more even than creating a state or drying the swamps or winning some victories on the battlefield."

Curiously, Oz has relatively little affinity for the Jewish-American novelists of his generation. He has read Bellow, Malamud, and Roth, and he is fully aware that some of his relatives had intended to make New York, and not Jerusalem, their promised land, and yet he seems not merely indifferent to those writers but even haughtily dismissive of their work and their subjects.

"Tongue in cheek, I can imagine myself having ended up as one of the Jewish-American writers of Russian background writing mostly about the neuroses of immigrants and their offspring," he said. "This probably would be my subject. I wouldn't be writing about the desert or the starry nights of the country. To some extent, as a reader I have some problems—and this is not a professional category and I wouldn't use it in my capacity as a professor of literature in the classroom—I have a certain problem with indoors literature. . . . So much of what I have to tell has to do with the open, the desert, the field, a kind of arid mountains around Jerusalem, the neighborhoods, the street, the garden, the kibbutz. I would feel claustrophobic."

.   .   .

Kibbutz Hulda, which grew over time to cover twenty-four hundred acres, lies just south of the road between Tel Aviv and Jerusalem. Jewish pioneers bought the land in 1904 from an Arab landlord, and in 1931 a group of young Zionists, who were followers of A. D. Gordon, a Tolstoyan visionary from Ukraine, established the kibbutz. Amos left home for Hulda when he was fourteen. He changed his name from Klausner to Oz, a Hebrew word for "strength," though when he arrived at Hulda he was hardly in possession of that. He was pale, weak, confused.

"The funny thing is, my new life was not far below the grain of my father's expectations, for the idea was always transmitted to me that you will have to be completely different," Oz said. "You will have to be simple, uncomplicated tractor drivers and soldiers."

I asked Oz why he didn't just run away to Tel Aviv, to the secular night life, to hedonism or books—anywhere but a place where the workday began at four in the morning.

"Tel Aviv was not radical enough—only the kibbutz was radical enough," he said. "The joke of it is that what I found at the kibbutz was the same Jewish shtetl, milking cows and talking about Kropotkin at the same time and disagreeing about Trotsky in a Talmudic way, picking apples and having a fierce disagreement about Rosa Luxemburg and Karl Liebknecht. It was a bit of a nightmare. Every morning you would wake up and you were in the same place! I was a disaster as a laborer. I became the joke of the kibbutz."

The other young people were already accustomed to the kibbutz life: the way children lived apart from their parents in a kind of barracks-dorm, the free and easy sexual life of the teenagers. "It was an old story: I was an Eastern European Jewish boy trying to assimilate into a society that had its accepted codes, even a particular set of accents and body language," Oz said. "It was a teenage *Lord of the Flies*, with better weather and a sensual permissiveness."

We pulled off the highway and headed down a road toward Hulda.

In the nineteen-fifties and sixties, Israel's communal farms were a khaki-colored banner of the Zionist project, its hardiness, its soft semi-socialism—though even then the kibbutzniks made up only four percent of the Israeli population. (Now it's less than two percent.) By the nineteen-eighties, young people were moving away from the kibbutz, rebelling against their earnest, idealist parents. The life was too hard, too plain. They grew tired of the lack of privacy, they wanted their share of the new proto-American consumerism in the cities.

Our first stop was a small graveyard shrouded by pines.

"Two-thirds of all my characters are here in this graveyard," Oz said.

As we walked, he pointed out one familiar grave after another: Pinchas Lavon, a Minister of Defense. The Zuckermans, Nily's parents. A pair of friends. An intellectual dandy known as the Count who argued philosophy and made his own wine. Then a row of twenty identical graves, all young men killed in battle on a single day in 1948. In the origins of those men, Oz said, was the story of the early state, and he read them as he walked along the row of flat stone markers: "Born in Poland. Born in Tripoli. Born in Russia. In Tel Aviv. Gaza. Czechoslovakia." After reading them all, he lingered awhile, and then he said, "Many here died in Israel without ever having lived in it, really. They came to Israel, and, within three weeks of independence, they died in battle."

We stopped at the grave of a young man who had been a student of his when he taught literature in the kibbutz school: "Died in the 1967 war." Then a four-year-old child, dead of drowning.

"I knew all these people, who hated whom, who loved whom, who was cheating with whom," Oz said. "It's an extended-family cemetery. We'll be buried here, too."

It was late morning, and most of the adults were working in the fields and the vineyards. The sun hammered down hard and the air was full of dust and everywhere was the smell of cow shit and hay. There are more than fifty buildings on the grounds. As the population has thinned, some of the buildings have been abandoned. We stopped by the low-slung concrete bungalow where Amos and Nily lived when they were first married. Kibbutz socialism was infinitely gentler than its East German cousin, but the architecture was just as brutal. The apartment was smaller than a freshman-dorm room. Oz smiled as he knocked on the door. In contrast with seeing the house on Amos Street, revisiting this place seemed to bring him pleasure. Oz wrote *My Michael* in the tiny bathroom. "I sat up smoking all night, sitting there with the toilet seat down, and a pad of paper and a book on my knees, writing," he said. "I wanted to become a simple, dumb tractor driver. But I began to write secretly. I couldn't resist it."

A rangy young man, shirtless, sipping a bottle of beer, let us in. He recognized the face.

"Amos Oz?" he said.

"The same," Oz said.

The young man smiled and showed us around—all four corners of the room. Oz inspected the corners carefully, joyfully, as if he were going to find his younger self under the mattress, behind the dust balls. Finally, he thanked his inheritor-tenant, stepped outside, and pointed to a large pecan tree.

"I planted it when my older daughter was born," he said.

We walked around the farm: to an abandoned arms depot; to the "children's republic," with a jungle gym, a school, and the long barracks where the children slept; and on to the dining hall, where Oz worked Saturdays as a waiter ("the fastest on the kibbutz"). The buildings have slouched, peeled, gone to seed. Across Israel it is widely speculated that, in a generation or so, there will be no more kibbutzim; the land will be turned into private farms or suburban developments.

"In a sense, the kibbutz left some of its genes in the entire Israeli civilization, even people who never lived on a kibbutz and rejected the kibbutz idea," Oz said. "You look at the West Bank settlers—not my favorite people, as you can imagine. You will see kibbutz genes in their conduct and even their outward appearance. If you see the directness of Israelis, the almost latent anarchism, the skepticism, the lack of an in-built class hierarchy between the taxi-driver and the passenger—all of those are very much the kibbutz legacy, and it's a good legacy. So, in a strange way, the kibbutz, like some bygone stars, still provides us with light long after it's been extinguished."

When Oz began publishing his first stories and asked for time off from his farming work to write, there was an intense debate among the elders: "Who is he, at twenty-four, to declare himself a writer? What if everyone calls himself an artist? Who will milk the cows and plow the land?"

Finally, after long discussion, Oz was given one day a week to write. (He taught for two days and spent three days in the fields.) With each book or so, he got an extra day to write. When *My Michael* became a best-seller, Oz continued the socialist practices of the kibbutz. "I became a branch of the farm, yet they still said I could have just three days a week to write," he recalled. "It was only in the eighties when I got four days for my writing, two days for teaching, and Saturday turns as a waiter in the dining hall."

Although their children never liked the kibbutz, Amos and Nily stayed on long past the peak years. But in the mid-eighties doctors told them that their third child, Daniel, was suffering from acute asthma and needed a change of climate. Arad has probably the cleanest, driest air in the country—"an asthmatic's mecca," Oz calls it—and the family moved there in 1986. "What kept me in the kibbutz was personal friendships, loyalty, also a certain sense that I didn't want to defect from a sinking boat," he said.

In *A Tale of Love and Darkness,* in his novels, and in conversation, there is little about his years on the kibbutz that Oz does not confront: the initial loneliness, the cramped atmosphere of labor and gossip and sex and dreams, the sense of living out a set of ideals and then seeing those ideals run down, fade. And yet there is almost no mention of his participation in the true Israeli universal: the Army.

In the late fifties, in the regular Army, he was part of a kibbutz-oriented unit called Nahal, and he was involved in skirmishes along the Syrian border. During the 1967 war, he served with a tank unit in Sinai; during the 1973 Yom Kippur War, when Israel nearly lost to the combined forces of Syria and Egypt, he was with a unit in the Golan Heights, on the Syrian border.

"It is difficult for me, either in an interview or in a book, to talk about the experience of fighting," he said. "I have never written about the battlefield, because I don't think I could convey the experience of fighting to people who have not been on the battlefield. Battle consists first and foremost of a horrible stench. The battlefield stinks to high heaven. It's hard to imagine the stench. This doesn't come across even in Tolstoy or Hemingway or Remarque. This stifling mixture of burning rubber and burning metal and burning human flesh and feces, everything burning. A description of the battlefield that does not contain the stench and the fear is not sufficient. It is where everyone around you has shit their pants." At one point, he talked about how he and his fellow soldiers thought for two or three days during the 1973 war that they would not live through the fighting and that Israel would be destroyed. "But I don't think I can describe that without resorting to clichés," he said. "I tried writing about it a couple of times a long time ago. I destroyed the drafts when I realized that language, at least mine, could not contain this experience. I could write about sex, I could write about the kibbutz, about envy, about sunsets, about howling jackals. Not this."

In the nineties, when Shimon Peres was thinking about retiring from the leadership of the Labor Party, he said that he could imagine three inheritors: Ehud Barak (who eventually became Prime Minister), Shlomo Ben-Ami (who became Barak's Foreign Minister), and Amos Oz.

"Ever since I was a little boy, I've been running this country in my head, and I do this today," Oz said. "I know what to do better than the

Prime Ministers." Then he smiled and became appropriately modest. "If I look at history, I know what to do, but this doesn't mean I can be Prime Minister. I know one or two things that Shimon doesn't, but I have a physical disability: I cannot pronounce the words 'No comment.' How can I be a politician?"

Oz is an ardent admirer of Václav Havel. He may even envy the way Havel, a political artist, was suddenly thrust into the role of statesman-visionary, becoming the first democratically elected President to govern in Prague since the rise of Communism. Oz emerged as a political actor just two months after the end of the 1967 war. He was twenty-eight, an obscure writer on a small kibbutz, but he had the nerve to send an article called "Land of the Forefathers" to the Labor newspaper, *Davar,* calling for the government to begin negotiations immediately with the Palestinians over the West Bank and Gaza. Like very few others at this moment of national exaltation, Oz gloomily forecast moral and political disaster should Israel retain the territories. "Even unavoidable occupation is a corrupting occupation," he wrote.

Support for a two-state solution—for an end to occupation and for a secure division of Israel and Palestine—is now a near-consensus position in Israel. Even Ariel Sharon, who is now acting to dismantle the Gaza settlements, concedes as much. But in 1967, as people around the world celebrated "tiny Israel's" triumph, as tourists from abroad began to flock to the liberated Western Wall, that position was considered off-the-board radical. At the kibbutz, Oz had clearly abandoned his right-wing Revisionist upbringing for a far more liberal politics, but even at Hulda he did not encounter unanimous agreement. Some demanded that he be fired from his teaching. His children were mocked in school. There were nasty letters in the right-wing press: "betrayal," "collaborator with the deadly enemies of Israel," "candidate for the local Judenrat." I asked him how he came to take such a bold public position at such an early moment.

"It was my imagination," he said. "I couldn't help thinking of my own childhood under the British in Jerusalem. As a child, I had nightmares—genetic, family nightmares—of uniformed aliens coming to our little street to kill us: the British, the Arabs, the Romans, tsarist soldiers, anyone from the long Jewish martyrology. My father bowed to the uniformed British, the same reaction he had in Lithuania. In 1967, suddenly I was the uniformed alien. I was in the West Bank in uniform with a submachine gun released for reserve service, and those Palestinian kids were willing to kiss my hand for chewing gum."

After the Yom Kippur War, advocates of the two-state solution were no longer considered members of the Flat Earth Society, and, in 1978, Oz, along with many other liberal activists and former Army officers and reservists, created the grassroots movement called Shalom Achshav—Peace Now. Most of his activism has taken the form of editorial writing. He has written countless columns, first for *Davar,* and then, when *Davar* folded, a decade ago, for the tabloid daily *Yediot Ahronot.* Although his positions are invariably left-wing, he seldom writes for the most élite left-wing paper, *Ha'aretz.* "In my political articles, I think of my audience as Edith Bunker," he said. "I can never convince Archie Bunker. He is beyond me."

Oz believes (as the pollsters do) that both the Israeli and the Palestinian publics support a two-state solution—a realistic, "clenched-teeth compromise"—but that neither Sharon nor the ailing Palestinian leader, Yasir Arafat, has the courage to carry the process to its conclusion. ("The patients are ready for the operation, but the surgeons are cowards," he says.) That is now fairly conventional wisdom, at least in moderate and liberal circles. What Oz adds to the political debate is an emotional, imaginative dimension. Dreamily (but aware of it), Oz tries to envisage a series of improbable gestures that would break the deadlock: "Suppose Sharon gave a Sadat-style speech to the Palestinian National Assembly expressing empathy, saying we'll do anything to heal the Palestinian wounds short of committing suicide, saying it will be hard but you will have an independent state with a share of Jerusalem. Suppose he said it on the anniversary of the massacre of Palestinians at Deir Yassin. Can you imagine the earthquake? And suppose Arafat went on Palestinian television and said that after a hundred years of bloody wars I finally realize that this is the Jewish national home, too. We need a two-state solution. Can you imagine? I realize this is not a likely scenario, but this is what was missing in the nineties. Imagine the reverberations in every Palestinian refugee camp and the entire Muslim world. But no one is ready to do it."

The four leading novelists in Israel—Oz, Aharon Appelfeld, A. B. Yehoshua, and David Grossman—are all on the political left, supporters of a Palestinian state, but they are distinguished by different emphases in their writing: Appelfeld by his memories of genocidal anti-Semitism in Europe; Grossman by his empathy with the Palestinians in journalistic accounts such as *The Yellow Wind;* Yehoshua by his connection to the non-European Jews, the Sephardim of North Africa and the Arab countries; and Oz by his liberal Zionism. Of the four, Oz is the best-known abroad, not only as a teller of tales but as a political artist. There is something about him—the lofty eloquence, the liberal opinions, the kibbutz-poster-boy good looks—that continues to draw crowds to his readings. Oz does not mind the attention, but he invariably finds himself out of step with his audiences. (When he is asked about Israel's new Security Wall, Oz has stunned more than a few on the left by saying, "The Wall, unfortunately, is a necessary thing. The only problem is that it's in the wrong place. It should run roughly along the 1967 borders.") In Europe especially, he is well to the left of the synagogue groups and to the right of more secular audiences. Over lunch one day, Oz described how in Europe he often gets the question "How long have you spent in Israeli prisons?"—the idea being that, somehow, the Israeli government does not permit contrary opinion. Among some younger writers and historians in Israel, too, Oz is rebuked because he continues to criticize both the Israeli and the Palestinian leaderships rather than seeing the situation as a version of the French disaster in Algeria.

"They're angry at me because I refuse the colonial analogy," Oz said. "Zionism may be a monster, but it is not a colonial monster. There was a strong element of self-righteousness and short-sightedness in the early Zionists, and they overlooked the presence of the Arab population and its significance. They had the self-righteousness of victims preoccupied with their own victimization to the degree that they could not even imagine that they could commit any kind of injustice to another. But then there is the problem of the left: in its struggle for the rights of the Palestinians, it overlooks the rights of the Jewish people."

I asked Oz why he had an especially hard time conveying his view in Europe.

"Many Americans and Europeans are sentimental about conflict resolution," he said. "They think the first thing to do is solve the hatreds, make friends out of enemies, and only then make peace. But, historically, deadly enemies, swearing inwardly to cheat and betray, sign peace treaties. This would be a divorce that results not in a honeymoon but in an emotional de-escalation that will take generations. Look at the Europeans. It took them a thousand years to make peace. Even as they wag their finger at us like a Victorian governess, they have a history of rivers of blood. I will risk a prophecy: it will not take the Middle East as long to make peace as it did Europe. And we'll shed less blood."

In the political imaginations of Israeli Jews and Palestinian Arabs, "Europe" continues to play an overwhelming role. "The Jews and the

Arabs had the same oppressors," Oz said. "The Europeans were guilty of anti-Semitism and the Holocaust, and the Europeans were guilty of colonialism in the Middle East and of the exploitation of the Arabs.

"In Brecht's poems, the oppressed join hands and march together. But the two children of the same oppressive parent can often be the worst of enemies. The Palestinians look at me, the Israeli, as an extension of white, sophisticated, colonizing Europe, which returned to the Middle East to do the same old thing: dominate, humiliate, like European crusaders. The other side, the Israelis, see the Palestinians not as fellow victims but as pogrom-makers, Cossacks, Nazis, oppressors in kaffiyehs and mustaches playing the same ancient game of cutting Jewish throats for the fun of it. You will hear this in many synagogues: they are pharaohs, the goyim, and we are lambs surrounded by seventy wolves. Neither party will ever give up this sense of victimhood and will forever dispute who was David and who was Goliath."

Oz is on the Israeli left, but he is not to be mistaken for a supporter of a bi-national state. In his novels, the Arab is the Other: the figure of fantasy, of authenticity, and, nearly always, seen from a distance. Oz grew up surrounded by but not among Palestinians, and he has not traveled much to Arab countries. An episode in *A Tale of Love and Darkness* that rings false is one in which young Amos and his family visit the home of a wealthy Arab family and Amos inadvertently causes a young Arab boy to suffer a severe accident.

Although in Israel most criticism of Oz comes from the right, he has been attacked from the left more and more in recent years as a younger generation enacts a kind of Oedipal battle against the founding generations. There is an Israeli version of "liberal parents, radical children" going on when scholars like Ilan Pappe, or the poet Yitzhak Laor, rebuke their elders for holding fast to the versions and iconographies of even liberal Zionism.

"They would ask, How can he be disengaged at such a time?" Oz said. "Why isn't he writing anti-Zionist pamphlets at this moment of colonial oppression? Then they criticize the subject matter—Jerusalem of the fifties, the kibbutz—as irrelevant, like a Wild West story for the younger generation."

Oz has no sympathy for Arafat—"He imagines himself as a combination of Che Guevara and Saladin"—but he does for the broader Palestinian claim. "The Arabs were deeply injured by the creation of Israel, by its relative prosperity, by what they regard as an endorsement of Israel by most of the West," he said. "The Palestinians were injured by the fact that they lost a significant part of their homeland. But this is not war of civilizations. Just the term—'the clash of civilizations'—is a hopelessly Hollywood thing, kind of like *Star Wars*. This is a conflict about hundreds of thousands of people who lost their homes, Palestinians and Jews from Europe and the Arab countries. There was one-hundred-percent ethnic cleansing of the Jews from the West Bank and Gaza in 1948. It is about one very small country inflicting a terrible, humiliating defeat on a people who have not had a military victory since the days of Saladin."

One afternoon, I met Oz in downtown West Jerusalem at a restaurant called Cavalier. It wasn't an ordinary lunch. The other guests were Israel Kantor, a lawyer and an old friend of Oz's, and Mo'en Khoury, a Palestinian Christian and a lawyer, who lives in Nazareth and has business in the occupied territories, Jerusalem, and elsewhere in the Middle East. A few months before, in March, Khoury's nephew George Khoury, a twenty-year-old student at Hebrew University, was jogging in the French Hill area of Jerusalem at around seven-thirty in the evening when he was shot in the head, the neck, and the stomach by a group of men passing by in a car. He was pronounced dead at the Hadassah University Medical Center. Initially, the news of the shooting was announced in the Palestinian press as a victory, and the Al-Aqsa Martyrs Brigades, which is linked to Arafat's Fatah organization, claimed responsibility for the killing. But when it became known that Khoury was Palestinian, and that his father, Elias, was a prominent lawyer who had contested land cases against Israeli settlements, Arafat's office called the Khoury home twice to apologize, and the Brigades declared George a *shaheed*—a martyr—and said the killing was a case of "mistaken identity." The Khoury family disdained the overture.

"This is a barbaric act that will not change my worldview, which includes deep faith in Palestinian rights," Elias Khoury said. He called on the Palestinian movement to stop encouraging terror and on religious leaders to denounce terror "in a loud and clear voice." He told Israeli radio, "Terrorism is blind. It does not discriminate between Jews and Arabs, or between the good and the bad."

Police caught three suspects who said they had been cruising the French Hill area looking for a Jew to shoot, and when they spotted a young jogger one assailant got out of the car and opened fire. One of the suspects had only recently been released from jail.

"I'm glad we could meet today," Mo'en Khoury was saying now. "Elias is going abroad today."

For a while, Khoury, Kantor, and Oz talked about George, and how he was planning to study law and go into the family business. Khoury recalled how his brother had led a fight against settlers in the nineteen-seventies in Sebastia and Elon Moreh. His father, Daoud, and twelve other people were killed in 1975 when a refrigerator packed with explosives detonated on Zion Square, close to where we were eating. Fatah claimed responsibility.

The violence of the past three years, Mo'en said, has been a catastrophe "all around." In Nazareth, a popular place especially among Christian tourists, "one hotel after another has closed," and one, which opened in 2000, has been converted into a prison. "The Pope's visit in March 2000 was supposed to be the beginning of a new era," he said. "It turned out to coincide with disaster"—the start of the second intifada.

They talked about the settlements for a while, agreeing that they had been ruinous for both the Palestinians and the Israelis. "The original sin of the Israeli Jews is that they thought too much about land and not enough about people," Kantor said.

The extended Khoury family, which is as close as it is prosperous, was interested in making public gestures that would demonstrate their feelings about the killing of George beyond their private grief. Kantor, who knew both Elias and Mo'en well, suggested that they read *A Tale of Love and Darkness* and consider the relatively rare and even expensive venture of underwriting a translation into Arabic. Oz has published twenty-five books, and they have appeared in dozens of languages; only two, *My Michael* and *Soumchi*, a novel for children, have been published in Arabic. Neither Oz nor Khoury thought that Arab readers would somehow be converted by *A Tale of Love and Darkness*.

"It's just a matter of knowing the other," Khoury said.

"It's a peek though the window," Oz said in agreement. "A chance to see the private lives of other people."

Finally, over coffee, Khoury agreed to underwrite the translation. The dedication of the Arabic edition would be an extended tribute to George, written by Amos Oz.

"Please see if that is acceptable to your family," Oz said.

"I certainly will," Khoury replied.

We left the restaurant. Khoury headed to his office in Nazareth, and Oz walked along the streets of Jerusalem, moving quickly, uneasy in the city of his birth, eager to get back to his home in the desert.

(2004)

After Arafat

After three decades of exile in Jordan, Lebanon, and Tunisia, Yasir
Arafat and the leadership of the Palestinian Liberation Organization returned to Palestine in 1994 and eventually made Ramallah the
PLO's administrative center. They refurbished a police compound,
which had been built under the British Mandate, and turned it into a
headquarters, their *muqata.* And there, Arafat was convinced, the Palestinians would negotiate the terms of an independent state and prepare
for the move to Jerusalem.

The *muqata* was never a very elegant compound, looking more like an
East German hospital complex than like the center of a fledgling country. Arafat was an incessant traveler, hooked on the glamour of the official visit, but when he was in Ramallah he worked and slept in a set of
small, modest rooms. Then, in late 2000, after final status negotiations
collapsed at Camp David, an era of promise ended and the second
intifada began; Israeli Prime Minister Ariel Sharon answered a series of
suicide bombings in 2002 with an overwhelming military operation

called Operation Defensive Shield. Suddenly, every major Palestinian city was under curfew, flooded with Israeli soldiers. In Ramallah, tanks converged on the *muqata* and ripped holes in the walls. At times, there was no electricity in the buildings, no communications. Cell-phone batteries were at a premium. And with the Israelis dropping hints that they might finally finish off Arafat, or at least deport him, the Palestinian leader became a prisoner in his own office. He received visitors in a dusty room that reeked of burst sewage pipes. Conversations were hard to hear over the sounds from the parking lot outside, the tanks swiveling their turrets, the tank treads gnashing the macadam. He protected terrorists even after he assured the United States that he was prosecuting them. At times, he seemed unhinged. "Pray for me to attain martyrdom!" Arafat said on Egyptian television. "Is there anything better than being martyred on this holy land?" When the Israelis relaxed their hold, last year, the Palestinians waited a long time before beginning any reconstruction on the *muqata.* They left some rooms a wreck, the better to dramatize their embattlement. They left the parking lot littered with debris—burned-out cars, oil cans filled with concrete—to make it harder for the tanks to return.

Less than three months ago, on November 11, 2004, Arafat died, of an undisclosed ailment, in a hospital outside Paris. He was seventy-five. His body was flown to the outskirts of Cairo for a military funeral the next morning and on to Ramallah for a Palestinian funeral.

Now Arafat, who envisaged for himself a founder's burial near the Al Aqsa Mosque, in Jerusalem, is entombed in the *muqata* parking lot. And Ramallah, like every other city in the West Bank and the Gaza Strip, remains surrounded by the surveillance technology and military hardware of the Israeli occupation forces. Nearly all Palestinians see Arafat as a patriarch, but few deny that his final years were a prolonged coda of political futility. The first intifada, in the late eighties, awoke Israelis to the moral disaster of occupation; the second, with its heroized suicides and targeted assassinations, has all but ended, and the most tangible result is more than four thousand dead, more Jewish settlements in the West Bank, more checkpoints, more suspicion, and a security wall. When Arafat died, the Palestinians were further away from statehood than they were when he first came to Ramallah, a decade ago.

Arafat was a revolutionary leader who treated the issue of succession without interest. Hussam Khader, a PLO leader in Nablus, once mocked Arafat's rejection of mortality by suggesting that perhaps he be elected "the god of Palestine." Some of his earliest brothers-in-arms, like Abu

Jihad and Abu Iyad, had been killed by the Israelis or by Arab rivals, like Abu Nidal; those who survived he often treated with contempt. According to one of his biographers, Saïd Aburish, Arafat used to call the PLO diplomats Saeb Erekat *gahel*, "ignorant," and Hanan Ashrawi *sharmootah*, "whore."

And yet there was little confusion among Palestinians over what was coming next. Even as Arafat lingered in Paris, only one man—a refugee and a senior figure in the PLO named Mahmoud Abbas—was taken seriously as a successor. Abbas, who goes by the name Abu Mazen, is a serene, uncharismatic man nearing seventy. He had been a member of Arafat's circle since the founding of Fatah, the dominant faction in the PLO, four decades ago. He served as Arafat's lead negotiator at the secret Oslo talks, in 1993, and at many other political initiatives. Abbas does not, as Arafat did, wear fatigues or a pistol on his hip. He has never played a military role in the movement. He wears a suit. The ashy bags under his eyes, the silvery hair and mustache, and his formal bearing give him the aspect of a certain kind of faded movie actor—Cesar Romero, say, in late middle age.

Last year, while both Sharon and the Bush Administration were ignoring Arafat, having declared him "the main obstacle" to negotiations and peace, Abbas served a four-month stint as Prime Minister of the Palestinian Authority. During that time, he repeatedly said that the "militarization" of the intifada against Israel—the shift from the rock to the suicide belt—had been a grave and self-defeating "mistake." He has also made it clear that he thought Arafat had undermined the cause in 1991 when he backed Saddam Hussein in the first Gulf War. These positions were received far more enthusiastically in Jerusalem and Washington than on the streets of Ramallah, Nablus, Gaza City, or Khan Yunis, and Arafat, who was not keen to share power, even when he had little, did nothing to help Abbas make progress in his negotiations with Israel. Arafat took to mocking his Prime Minister as a Palestinian Hamid Karzai, a reference to the Afghan President, who is generally considered among Arabs to be a stooge of the Bush White House. And soon, quite predictably, Abbas was gone, undercut by Arafat and replaced by a colorless bureaucrat known as the other of "the two Abus"—Abu Ala. Only death, it was clear, would loosen Arafat's grip on power.

The afternoon of Arafat's burial, the *muqata* parking lot was jammed with thousands of mourners, almost all of them men, many armed with pistols and AK-47s, which they fired into the air. Their show of chaotic grief was genuine—Arafat is regarded among his people as the man who created the Palestinian movement, unified its disparate factions, and then, through terror, diplomacy, theatrics, and his own peculiar persona, kept the cause before the world's wandering attention. But within a few days the emotion faded. The traditional forty-day mourning period seemed to last no longer than a week. Workmen erected a glass-walled mourning hall, but few visitors came. The talk in the press—Palestinian, Israeli, and beyond—was all of the future, of a vague sense of opportunity. The most prominent Palestinian pollster, Khalil Shikaki, reported that optimism had not run so high among ordinary Palestinians in five years. Even Arafat's most ardent admirers were pleased by the idea of a new start.

Abbas began his campaign for the Presidency of the Palestinian Authority on Christmas Day. His victory in the January 9 elections was deemed a near-certainty. There was only one other potential candidate with any mass following, Marwan Barghouti, a diminutive man of steely intelligence and ruthless measures. Barghouti, unlike Abbas, was fluent in the rhetoric of armed struggle but also had a deeper understanding of Israeli politics than most of his PLO elders. In the end, he decided that his candidacy was impractical. His decision was made in an Israeli prison, where he is serving five life sentences for his part in several terrorist operations. Abbas's only opponent of note was Mustafa Barghouti (distantly related to Marwan), a leftist and the head of a health-care relief agency, who advertised himself as a more pugnacious adversary of the Israelis; his most prevalent ad showed him in a confrontation with several Israeli soldiers.

Even before the campaign started, Abbas had moved out of his offices in northern Ramallah and occupied a suite in the *muqata.* Yet he was careful not to move into Arafat's old wing—those bare ruined halls and the artifacts within were being preserved as a kind of museum—and, despite all their disputes over the years, Abbas began every public appearance with a paean to the dead leader. Of all the factions, Fatah had the most money for advertising, campaign workers, television, travel. It could even feel safe in leaving the matter of turnout to a distinguished guest: the American actor Richard Gere filmed a commercial for Palestinian television, in which he said, "Hi, I'm Richard Gere and I'm speaking for the entire world. It's really important. Get out and vote."

Abbas knew that he was considered too stiff, too gray, too soft, too disapproving of "armed struggle." His election strategy was plain: he was Arafat Lite, people said, a man who would follow the Arafat line but without the autocratic style, without the fatigues or the cronyism or the calls for a "million martyrs" to march on Jerusalem. A ubiquitous Abbas campaign poster showed him and Arafat together, smiling, over the rubric "In Your Way, We Will Approach the Palestinian Dream."

One afternoon during the campaign, at a refurbished meeting hall in the *muqata*, I met with Nabil Aburdeneh, Arafat's closest aide, the sort one comes to think of as the whisperer, the briefcase man. He sat down in a pleasant, freshly painted room graced with new leatherette couches, a new rug, recessed lighting. Aburdeneh was full of enthusiasm for the election. Abbas, he said by way of endorsement, is "one of our historical leaders. He was behind Oslo, he was at Camp David, he was at Wye River"—during the Clinton Administration. "He was always involved with Arafat. Abu Mazen is taking all the posts of Arafat. He is the man of peace and the coming era." He continued, "We are going to test Sharon and the American Administration. All along, they said that Arafat was the obstacle. Well, now Arafat is not here. What now?"

In 1982, after the Israeli Army had invaded Lebanon in an effort to oust the PLO, Abbas flew to Moscow for a series of meetings. One of his sessions was with Meir Vilner, the Secretary-General of the Israeli Communist Party. Vilner told Abbas about an exchange he'd had with Sharon, who was then Defense Minister, in Jerusalem at the Knesset. "Vilner was leaving as Sharon was going in," Abbas writes in a 1995 memoir, *Through Secret Channels:*

> Their eyes met, but no words were exchanged. Sharon grabbed Vilner's shoulder and demanded, "Why do you not greet me? Why do you turn away from me?" Vilner replied, "I do not greet a bloodletter." "Are you talking about the Palestinians?" Sharon asked. "Yes," said Vilner, "I mean the blood of Palestinians, I mean the siege of Beirut. I mean your lust for killing. Don't you think they are human beings like us who also have rights?" As Vilner walked out of the door Sharon said, "One day you will realize that it is I who will establish the Palestinian state."

Twenty-two years later, Abbas was running for the chance to negotiate with a man whom he had always understood to be a butcher, an architect of the settlements in Gaza and the West Bank, but who now, with unprecedented popularity, had come to the point where he recognized the need for a Palestinian state. For decades, Sharon had rejected the notion that the Palestinians had any right to territory lost, mile by mile. Let Jordan, already a majority Palestinian state, take in its brethren, he would say. In the 2003 elections for Prime Minister, it was the Labor Party candidate, Amram Mitzna, who suggested that Israel restart the process by withdrawing, unilaterally, from Gaza. This is the position that Sharon has now assumed.

"I do not think that we have to rule over another people and run their lives," Sharon told an Israeli interviewer, Ari Shavit, in 2003. "I do not think that we have the strength for that." This was a calculation born less of moral reckoning than of demographic reality. With Jewish immigration plummeting and the Palestinian presence between the Jordan River and the Mediterranean growing, Sharon decided to begin a process of "disengagement," starting with a civil and military withdrawal from the Gaza Strip, in July 2005. Soldiers would be moved completely into Israel proper and more than seven thousand settlers would be uprooted—by force, if necessary.

During the campaigning last month, I met with many of Arafat's old confederates in the PLO and asked them if they shared the kind of optimism about a new start that was reflected in polls. They did not. The people, they insisted, were actually exhausted, demoralized. The intifada could not be counted a victory. Sharon was dictating the situation so thoroughly that most Palestinians were hoping for things far more modest than a final settlement: fewer checkpoints along the roads, military withdrawal from the cities. Sharon has said that he is willing to restart the international diplomatic process known as the Road Map, but he also reserves the right to slow things down, or even withdraw from the process. Hanan Ashrawi, the longtime PLO negotiator, told me, "Abu Mazen's prospects are very difficult. It seems that in Israeli political discourse the only acceptable Palestinian is a Zionist, one willing to give up on the right of return of refugees and one who refuses any dialogue with militant groups. They want a tailor-made Palestinian leader who will play the game by Israeli rules and then cannot possibly have the credibility to sell a deal to the Palestinian people."

Any sense that Sharon might be leaving Gaza as a first step toward a full and fair settlement was undercut last fall, when *Ha'aretz* published an astonishing interview with Dov Weissglas, a Tel Aviv lawyer who is one of Sharon's most intimate advisers. Weissglas acknowledged that the only reason Sharon had made a move was grudging Realpolitik; he had come to understand that "everything was stuck." The economy was weak, soldiers were refusing to serve in the occupied territories— "These were not weird kids with green ponytails and a ring in their nose who give off a strong odor of grass"—and unofficial plans for a two-state solution were gaining surprisingly high popular acceptance. However, Weissglas said, "The disengagement is actually formaldehyde. It supplies the amount of formaldehyde that's necessary so that there will not be a political process":

> It legitimizes our contention that there is no negotiating with the Palestinians. There is a decision here to do the minimum possible in order to maintain our political situation. . . . It thrusts [the Palestinians] into a situation in which they have to prove their seriousness. There are no more excuses. There are no more Israeli soldiers spoiling their day. And for the first time they have a slice of land with total continuity on which they can race from one end to the other in their Ferrari. And the whole world is watching them— them, not us.

The message was clear. Sharon was giving up Gaza—crowded, lawless Gaza, which even Yitzhak Rabin had once wished would "sink into the sea"—while planning to maintain far more of the West Bank than had been imagined in any of the previous talks with the Palestinians.

"Sharon seems to want to create a rump state in Gaza and that's all," Salim Tamari, a historian and sociologist at Bir Zeit University, in the West Bank, said, expressing a widespread view among Palestinian politicians and intellectuals. "Moshe Dayan thought that you could hold on to the territories and suspend sovereignty questions until the density of settlements had become a fait accompli. This is Sharon's logic, too. . . . I see Sharon's motives as Dov Weissglas expressed them.

"But this is shortsighted," Tamari continued. "It will only take a matter of months or a few years for the groups"—such as Hamas and Islamic Jihad—"to regain the ability to pull off military operations. In the thirty-seven years of occupation, Israel used every means of force— deportation, destruction of homes, imprisonment, assassination—to prevent resistance. It was never successful, and it's about time for the Israelis to realize that the use of force on their part cannot achieve security. Do they think they can keep the Palestinians in their cages forever?"

Yasir Arafat did not leave behind a democratic legacy. An autocrat to the end, he dominated politics, the press, the police, the flow of cash; he indulged sycophants, padded his own accounts, rewarded cronies, punished rebels, sometimes with beatings or jail. But, because the Palestinian movement has been a mixture of secularists and Islamists, capitalists and Communists, Arafat always had to maneuver, to include, to permit a modicum of debate, to a point unthinkable in nearly all the rest of the Arab world. "We had Baathists, Marxists, pro-Syrian people, pro-Jordanian, pro-Iraqi," Yasser Abed Rabbo, one of Arafat's principal negotiators, said. "What Arafat did, and it's to be praised, is that he brought this mosaic together into the PLO and it found a way of coexistence. Otherwise, we would have splintered into a thousand pieces. . . . This was the mother experience, the crucial experience, of the PLO. The experience of the rest of the Arab world would have given us something very different." The democratic example of Israel, Rabbo readily conceded, was also a profound influence.

By the New Year holiday, the campaign rolled along with an almost preternatural ease. As Abbas made stops in Gaza, the outskirts of Jerusalem, and the West Bank, he seemed suddenly to be adapting to the theatrical dimensions of elections, glad-handing, making spirited speeches. "We may be laying the foundations for the second working democracy in the Middle East," a Palestinian legislator, Ziad Abu-Amr, told me. "In Iraq, you Americans are imposing something. This democracy comes under the conditions of occupation and national struggle, but the Palestinian people are imposing their own regime. If the Palestinians can do this under duress, under occupation, then these other countries—Egypt, Syria, and the rest—cannot call their 'referendums' real elections."

A week before election day, I joined a few colleagues on a trip to the West Bank city of Nablus, where the fighting had been especially heavy during Operation Defensive Shield. Historically, Nablus was a mercantile center. For the Israelis, Nablus had distinguished itself as a center of terror: the old city (the Casbah), An-Najah University, and the nearby Balata refugee camp were all known as bastions of support for armed groups, and Beit Furik, a village outside the city, is widely known as a "cradle" of bombers the way some towns in the American South are known for their quarterbacks or spoon bread. In 2002, Sharon sent troops and about a hundred tanks and armored personnel carriers into Nablus to make arrests and, if necessary, kill fighters for the armed groups; the city is still under siege.

As we passed through an Israeli checkpoint and arrived at the outskirts of Nablus, we saw Arafat's local *muqata,* and it, too, was in ruins. The Palestinian police had left the rubble as a kind of monument; Arafat's bathtub was visible through a blasted wall. There were posters everywhere commemorating martyrs—children and teenagers who had exploded themselves, and Israelis, for the cause—and graffiti that said, "Jerusalem Is in Our Eyes."

At Balata, we met with Tayseer Nasrallah, the head of human rights for the refugee camp, where more than twenty thousand people live. The term "refugee camp" summons images of tent villages—and that certainly was Balata in the early nineteen-fifties—but the United Nations and other agencies long ago supplied money to help build rough-hewn apartment blocks and schools. To this day, Balata is contiguous with the city of Nablus but relies on few of its services. This insistent separation of cities and their camps is typical throughout the occupied territories. "Our concern in Balata is to keep the symbolism alive of the refugee camps," Nasrallah said. "The camp is the living witness to the Palestinian tragedy of 1948."

Nasrallah kept his office in a small cultural center that had been paid for by the government of Belgium. As a representative of the refugees, he had been on the stage with Abbas when he gave his first campaign speech; Nasrallah was determined to put the Arafat era behind him. "The personality of Arafat will never be repeated ever again. Inshallah, God willing," he said. "We suffered for having someone who was a symbolic, charismatic figure. We want someone who will understand our suffering, build institutions, and doesn't want to be considered a god. There is only one god in the sky."

But, once Nasrallah went beyond his general support for Abbas, the thorniest dilemmas of Palestinian politics—in particular, the problem of refugees—came into focus. More than seven hundred thousand Palestinians fled Israel in 1948. The Palestinians, including Abbas, insist that UN resolutions and international law give them the right of return—not merely to a new Palestinian state but, if they wish, to Jaffa, to Haifa, to Ramla, the cities of modern Israel. Yet, if there is one issue on which nearly all Israelis agree, it is that a full right of return will mean the end of a Jewish majority state, and cannot be permitted. Abbas himself is a refugee. He was born in 1935 in the town of Safad, in the Galilee; in 1948, his family left for Syria. In various speeches, he has reaffirmed the Palestinian position on refugees—that their right of return is absolute and complete—but his image as a conciliator persists. This does not entirely please most Palestinians. The impression is that, while he is serious about insisting on the borders that prevailed before the 1967 Six Day War, he is likely to compromise on refugees.

Nasrallah said, "We will accept a decision only after a referendum of all the refugees," including the ones in Jordan, Syria, and Lebanon. "Look," he said, "we are not seeking to throw the Jews into the sea. This land can absorb us all. If Jews can come from anywhere in the world, then Jaffa can accept us. Do you want us to go to China? . . . If they want a clean, purely Jewish state, they can go find it anywhere else in the world, but not here. This was not an empty land when they arrived."

A rainstorm pelted the roofs, but we could still hear the sound of drums outside—a parade of schoolchildren, Fatah scouts, pounding out the beat for the candidacy of Mahmoud Abbas. In Nablus, as in most Palestinian cities, many young people readily say that their greatest ambition is to die in the armed struggle against the Israelis, to hold a rifle or wear a suicide belt on the ubiquitous martyr posters. It was not hard to imagine that if Abbas and Sharon made no progress some of the scouts outside might one day be holding weapons instead of drumsticks.

Nasrallah's rationale for the terrorists in his ranks was a common one: "There is a motivation, they are terrorized. So the feeling is, Why not terrorize those who terrorize us? The message behind a suicide bomber is that. After Operation Defensive Shield, most young kids were willing to blow themselves up. In Balata, if you want to open an office for suicide bombers, it will do a better business than anything else. Israeli policies are creating new enemies every day."

In the short term, Abbas's most complicated internal political problem was persuading the fighters to put down their arms. In discussions I had with Israeli officials in Jerusalem and Tel Aviv—with Sharon, several of his close advisers, and his two Deputy Prime Ministers, Ehud Olmert and Shimon Peres; with intelligence chiefs; with the Foreign Minister, Silvan Shalom; and with Sharon's allies in the Knesset—not one of them seemed to think that Abbas had the means to unify the myriad Palestinian security forces and control terror for very long. They saw him as a man of positive intentions but little strength, and no real constituencies. "With your permission," one senior Israeli intelligence official said of Abbas, "I think he has olives, not balls."

The Palestinian Authority, which was established in 1994, as part of the Oslo accords, to run the territories until statehood, has been in free fall since the second intifada began, four years ago. Violence, corruption, factionalism, and Israeli pressure have eroded the P.A. When a former U.S. State Department official told Arafat last year that the P.A. was in danger of political ruin and financial bankruptcy, Arafat replied, "Let it collapse. It will be the fault of the Israelis and the Americans." More and more, the young leaders of the armed militant groups have been gaining stature as arbiters of the street, ignoring the P.A., and no potential Palestinian leader, not even Abbas, can easily control them. At the start of the campaign, fighters from Hamas and Islamic Jihad said that they would boycott the election. The leaders of the Al-Aqsa Martyrs Brigades—a secular group, affiliated with Fatah, and, in recent years, no less violent than Hamas—circled around Abbas and heard him out, to see if he was worthy of their trust. Abbas seemed to be gaining their support, but it was contingent. In Jenin, a city north of Nablus, the leader of the Brigades is Zakaria Zbeida. Released from jail in 1994 under the Oslo accords, Zbeida has been the city's kingpin; he reportedly once torched the P.A.'s offices when it failed to find employment for some of his fighters. Zbeida, who survived a bomb that blew up in his face while he was assembling it, is wanted for his part in a variety of terror missions, including an ambush of Israeli voters at a polling place, which led to the deaths of six Israelis and two Palestinian gunmen. When Abbas visited Jenin on a campaign stop, he won a great victory. He was hoisted onto the shoulders of Zakaria Zbeida.

To give us a sense of how the armed men in Nablus saw the campaign, Nasrallah invited to the office a Brigades fighter named Abu Muhammad. He was dressed in a black watch cap, fatigues, combat boots, and a kaffiyeh. He was around thirty, muscular, neckless, like a bouncer, and wore a dark beard so short that it seemed almost painted on his jawline.

"I'm wanted by the Israelis," he announced as he sat down. "I've been shot by them three times."

When?

"I'm not good with dates."

Abu Muhammad picked up a pack of cigarettes, stripped off the cellophane, and tried to shake one loose. Under the table, his foot was tapping furiously, keeping time, it seemed, with his own anxiety. He glanced at the doorframe, checking on his bodyguard. Like all fighters in town, he was under Israeli surveillance and he knew it. There were informers to look out for, post-midnight incursions into Balata and the Casbah. Abu Muhammad slept in a different place every night.

After a clumsy struggle, he finally freed one of the cigarettes. "We still have some activities attacking Israeli targets, but there are fewer of them," he said, lighting up. "We are waiting to see. The loss of Yasir Arafat has been great and we are waiting to see if the new situation fits or not. Why should we stop our operations when they still hunt us? . . . We have our reservations and conditions, but we'll vote for Abu Mazen. But we will not give up our rifles."

Someone asked if there was a Palestinian leader the armed men would have supported with real conviction. Abu Muhammad laughed.

"Of course, I prefer Marwan Barghouti," he said. "We call him the sheikh of our struggle."

When he was asked how long he was prepared to carry a gun, Muhammad said, "I'm a Fatah activist, but do you think I really want to do this? I was arrested in 1987, 1990, 1992. I had a ten-year sentence in 1992, but I was released in 1994 because of Oslo. Many of my closest friends are martyrs." His expression asked for sympathy, and the rhythm of his foot quickened. "I have three kids," he said. "Last week, I was called in to my daughter's school and, even though I was risking my life to go out in public like that, I went. The principal told me that my daughter was doing badly in school, that all she knows about is the names of the martyrs of the Al-Aqsa Martyrs Brigades. And it's not only her. They all wear pictures of the martyrs in pendants around their necks, like amulets."

In the Casbah that night, there was an election rally, a sullen, sodden affair. Aluminum sheets were set up over the warren of shops, but still the rain leaked through. The rally was set for six, and for an hour I sat with a very small crowd listening to PLO marching songs from the nineteen-sixties blare through a set of speakers. A few teenagers with AK-47s walked up and down the aisles, heedless of the fact that the barrels were pointed at people's faces, at my face. Finally, the governor of Nablus, Mahmoud Aloul, arrived. He had a seigneurial air and wore a cashmere overcoat. In Lebanon and Tunis, he had been an assistant to Arafat's deputy, Abu Jihad, and a member of the military wing of Fatah. He'd lost a son in the intifada, I was told—"shot while throwing stones."

Someone turned off the fight songs and Aloul stepped up to the microphone to deliver a speech commemorating the fortieth anniversary of Fatah. We have lost Arafat, he began. "He gave us courage. He gave us inspiration." The panegyric lasted around fifteen minutes. The governor never mentioned the name Mahmoud Abbas.

The next morning, at his office, Aloul seemed surprised when I asked about the missing man in his speech.

"It wasn't really the point," he said. "The point was Fatah, the party."

And then, like so many others, he said that Palestinian institutions, and not a single man, would now run the affairs of the Palestinian people. Mahmoud Abbas, he declared, was "an instrument of institutions."

"The Americans and the Israelis need to know that in order for Abu Mazen to succeed they have to give him something—free prisoners, lift the siege, help the economic situation," he said. "How can I tell a fighter, 'Don't fight,' when the Israelis are coming into the city to kill him?"

When Abbas came to Nablus a few days later, he delivered triumphant speeches in the refugee camp and at the university, and was followed around the city by a cheering procession. In the streets, many of the men closest to his side were armed commanders of the Al-Aqsa Martyrs Brigades. At least for now, his rhetorical gambit was working.

The Middle East is a region of messages explosively delivered. In Gaza City several years ago, when Islamic radicals wanted to inform the secular community that alcohol was impermissible, they burned down the Windmill Hotel, where drinking was allowed. Message noted. Now it is nearly impossible to get a beer anywhere in Gaza.

During the campaign, Abbas was on the receiving end of similarly indelicate communications. In Gaza City, just after Abbas began his campaign, members of the Brigades fired off guns in a mourners' tent while he was visiting, a gesture that terrified the candidate and his aides. The message seemed clear—Abbas was under threat of assassination—and it was received in an equally clear way: the leader of the faction that had done the shooting was quickly made a campaign manager. On days that Abbas spoke of the pitfalls of armed struggle, Hamas launched homemade rockets over the walls of Gaza; the people in the Israeli town of Sederot were also on the receiving end of these messages. Sharon's message was that Israel would not absorb attacks, no matter how minor: in retaliation for four mortars that nearly hit a school bus, an Israeli tank in Gaza fired on a group of teenagers in a strawberry field. Seven died, six from one extended family. The young men had fired the mortars, the Israelis said; the Palestinians maintained they were farmworkers. The mother of three of the boys went out into the field to collect the body parts of her children.

As Abbas and his entourage moved from city to city, he tried to balance his own messages. He kept criticizing the intifada, though he was careful not to besmirch the martyrs themselves. And just when he seemed to be crossing a line, seeming too soft, too much Sharon's man, he let loose a rhetorical rocket of his own. When he heard about the Israeli tank attack, he gave a furious speech in Khan Yunis and referred to Israel as *al adu el-sahyuni*, "the Zionist enemy," a term usually used by Hamas and its brethren organizations in Damascus and Tehran. Abbas is a man of calculation, and his remark was deliberately intemperate.

Later, when he returned to his office in Ramallah at the *muqata*, Abbas invited in the most famous political columnist in Israel, Nahum Barnea, of the tabloid *Yediot Ahronot*, and the paper's senior correspondent, Ronny Shaked. Barnea, who lost a son in a bus bombing, and Shaked greeted Abbas wryly, saying, *"Ahlan"*—"hello"—"we are the Zionist enemy!"

Abbas was apologetic. "When such a tragedy happens," he said, referring to the deadly mortar attack, "a person doesn't know what will come out of his mouth."

The campaign was full of indignities. In Rafah, the poorest, most lawless town in Gaza, Abbas was arriving at a campaign stop when someone in his entourage closed the car window on his right ring finger, chopping off the tip.

"I wrapped the finger in newspaper and went to speak," he told Barnea and Shaked. "Only when the rally was over did I go to the hospital." In the past, Abbas had said that Israel's military was capable of defeating "the Arab nation," all twenty-two states. And now he could not see why he was being criticized for being surrounded by men with AK-47s at nearly every campaign stop. "I do not understand why Israel is upset," he said. "Is it because they saw me being photographed with the Al-Aqsa Martyrs Brigades? I met with the Brigade people everywhere, and also with members of the other factions. We want to bring them all into the Palestinian framework. We will do this—on condition that Israel stops hunting them."

Mahmoud Abbas has spent much of his political life trying to balance the maximalism of party principle and the perils of negotiation. He has even been designated, at times, as a cleanup man for Arafat. In 1993, he was dispatched to Saudi Arabia to apologize for the PLO's support of Iraq in the Gulf War. Deeply knowledgeable about the debates among Zionist factions, he has been meeting with Israelis since the nineteen-seventies. He was a major presence at nearly every Palestinian negotiation with the Israelis since the thaw of the early nineties. The Arafat style was one of bluff, drama, flattery, purposeful contradiction, mystery, fog. Abbas is a logician, stern, arid. Yossi Beilin, the leader of the liberal Yahad Party, who spent hundreds of hours in meetings with Abbas, has written that he is "diffident . . . realistic . . . pragmatic but not moderate."

Some liberal politicians in Israel, including those who have known

Abbas for many years, told me that his orthodox statements on the refugee issue, for example, were merely a political necessity, and that, in the end, he was a leader prepared to take risks in order to achieve a two-state solution, Israel and Palestine as neighbors. "Abu Mazen resembles the successor to Fidel Castro," Beilin told me one evening in Tel Aviv. "Now, I haven't met Fidel's successor yet, but I know that he won't have the fatigues or the big cigar and he won't give seven-hour speeches.

"Abu Mazen is the natural successor to Arafat," he went on. "He was No. 2 in the PLO, so he is not an imposed leader. He's been there in Tunis and the territories. In an embryonic state, this is important. Plus, he's well liked in the Arab world. He has connections in the Gulf, Kuwait, Morocco, Saudi Arabia, Jordan, Russia."

Abbas is a devout Muslim, though he is adamantly secular in his politics. He has two sons, one who is a wealthy businessman. A third son died of a heart attack in 2002. Abbas has never carried a gun, never fought in a battle, aboveground or underground. One unsettling element in his past is his putative career as a part-time scholar. In the early nineteen-eighties, Abbas completed a doctoral dissertation at the Institute of Oriental Studies, in Moscow, about the alleged negotiations between some Zionist leaders and the Nazis for the relocation of German Jews to Palestine in exchange for their property. In 1984, Abbas published a version of his dissertation in Amman as a book entitled *The Other Side: The Secret Relationship Between the Nazis and the Zionist Movement.* (The Israeli documentary group Memri has on file a copy of both the dissertation, in Russian, and the book, in Arabic.) The dissertation is written in a near parodic Soviet style; the prologue endlessly, and irrelevantly, quotes the collected works of V. I. Lenin. In the book version, Abbas casts doubt on the scope of the Holocaust:

> During World War II, forty million people of various nations of the world were killed. The German people lost ten million; the Soviet people twenty million; and the rest were from Yugoslavia, Poland, and other peoples. But after the war it was publicized that six million Jews were among the victims, and that the war of annihilation had been aimed first of all against the Jews, and only then against the rest of the peoples of Europe. The truth of the matter is that no one can verify this number. Or completely deny it. In other words, the number of Jewish victims might be six million and might be much smaller—even less than one million. But a discussion regarding the number of Jews does not in any way diminish the atrocity of

the crime committed against them because the killing of a human being—any human being—is a crime that the civilized world cannot accept and humanity cannot comprehend. . . . It seems that the interest of the Zionist movement was to inflate the number of murdered in the war so as to ensure greater gains. This is what led it to confirm this figure, and to instill it in world public opinion, and by doing so, to arouse more pangs of conscience and sympathy for Zionism in general.

Abbas cites the research of Robert Faurisson, a French Holocaust denier, to the effect that Jews were not killed in gas chambers at Auschwitz. The dissertation is an ugly work and can hardly be dismissed as a youthful indiscretion: Abbas was in his late forties when it was published. His subsequent explanations ring hollow. When a reporter for the Israeli newspaper *Ma'ariv* asked Abbas about his book, he replied, "When I wrote *The Other Side,* in 1982, we were at war with Israel. Today, I would not have made such remarks." And, to *Ha'aretz,* he said that his work had been misunderstood, that the Holocaust was a "terrible, unforgivable crime against the Jewish nation."

Although Abbas and every other Palestinian continue to speak of an agreement that would provide a state contained by the 1967 borders, with East Jerusalem as the capital, and a compromise on refugees and the control of holy places, the Israeli political élite is operating in a different universe. Talk of an all-at-once settlement, like the one attempted by the Labor Prime Minister Ehud Barak at Camp David in 2000, is long past. Sharon has radically altered the terms of discussion and, at the same time, presented himself as the only figure able to move forward. In the same way that only de Gaulle could call on France to leave Algeria, or only Nixon could go to China, it is said, only Sharon can leave Gaza and dismantle settlements. Where the Labor Party failed, Sharon could, in his own, halting way, succeed.

The skeptical view (among some liberal Israelis and nearly all Palestinians) is that Sharon has not changed at all, and that to entertain such a notion is wishful thinking; rather, he is ceding Gaza only as a way to end a pointless and expensive occupation and, at the same time, to continue to perforate the map of the West Bank so thoroughly with Jewish settlements that it will be possible to give up no more than half the territory to any future Palestinian entity. "The real obstacle to peace has always been

Sharon and the collusion between Bush and Sharon," Hanan Ashrawi, the Palestinian negotiator, said. "This unilateral engagement serves Sharon, it gives him maximum demographic advantage and minimal geographic loss, it gives the impression of a political plan and negates the Palestinian side, undermining a Palestinian state. You are still an occupier, even if from a distance."

The opposite view (and there are many Israelis who hold it) is that it does not really matter what Sharon intends. He is neither young nor healthy, and if he successfully gives up Gaza, and the Palestinians are able to stifle suicide bombings and rocket attacks, and the Americans keep pushing the Road Map . . . well, more concessions will come. It is a future with none of the idealism of the Oslo days or the brinkmanship of Camp David, but it is a future. One of Sharon's Deputy Prime Ministers in the coalition government, the Labor leader Shimon Peres, told me that disengagement is a "very mediocre plan," but he was somehow more comfortable with Sharon's tactics than with Barak's attempt to leap over the abyss at Camp David. "Maybe Sharon hopes in his heart that he can get away with just Gaza. It doesn't matter," Peres said. "Facts are stronger than leaders. And the same will happen in the West Bank, even, for him, in the best conditions. There is a change. A few years ago, the idea that the Likud would talk about a Palestinian state—well, you'd have to be crazy. And here they are. They have given up the idea of Greater Israel. . . . Labor lost in actions, but we won in ideology. Sharon now speaks our language."

The Palestinians, like the Israelis, have lived with Ariel Sharon ever since the rise of the Israeli state, when the young commander was a protégé of David Ben-Gurion, the leader of the Mapai Party and the state's founding figure. Although Sharon heads the Likud Party, which inherited Ze'ev Jabotinsky's "Revisionist" yearning for Greater Israel—Menachem Begin came to power in 1977 under this banner—the Prime Minister is not a creature of steadfast ideology.

Part of the reason that Sharon can garner such widespread support for disengagement is the brutality of his biography. In the calculus of Israeli politics, no one can accuse him of being soft on the Palestinians. "Sharon is a man who knows only two states of mind," the Israeli political philosopher Avishai Margalit has written: "fighting and preparing for fighting." He is remembered both for his daring and for his ruthlessness. After serving in the 1947–48 War of Independence, Sharon became part of the legendary Unit 101 in the early nineteen-fifties, which carried out cross-border raids against fighters in Egypt and Jordan. Sharon led the attack on the Jordanian village of Kibbiya, in which more than forty houses were demolished, some with the families still inside. Sixty-nine people were killed, most of them women and children. As Minister of Defense under Begin, he was already the architect of the settlements program in the West Bank and Gaza and was the principal aggressor in the Lebanon war, ordering the Army to keep pushing north to Beirut. An independent Israeli panel, the Kahan Commission, determined that Sharon bore both "indirect responsibility" and "personal responsibility" for the slaughter by Christian Phalangists, while the Israeli military stood by, of hundreds of Palestinian men, women, and children in the Sabra and Shatila refugee camps.

As a politician, Sharon has never shown a shred of faith in even the most benign deal with the Arabs. In 1994, when the Knesset was nearly unanimous in approving a peace treaty with Jordan, Sharon abstained.

Ben-Gurion was both seduced and made anxious by Sharon, calling him "an original, visionary young man. . . . Were he to rid himself of his faults of not speaking the truth and to distance himself from gossip, he would be an exceptional military leader." Ben-Gurion's successors were even more astringent in their judgment. Golda Meir called Sharon a "danger to democracy" and, a decade later, Begin said that Sharon was capable of surrounding the Knesset with tanks. Even the settlers, who were his beneficiaries, were wary of him. When Israel and Egypt made peace, a quarter century ago, and Israel withdrew from Sinai, it was Sharon who took on the job of dismantling Yamit, the main settlement there.

Sharon, like any other head of state, is surrounded by aides and ministers, but his closest advisers hold no official post; perhaps the closest of all is his son Omri, a legislator in his late thirties, who seems to run his father's political operation from his cell phone. (Sharon's other son, Gilad, runs the family farm, said to be the largest private farm in Israel.) Bald, corpulent, cynical, and funny, Omri works his beat like a Chicago alderman, wheedling, pleading, trading, intimidating. At a small dinner in Tel Aviv one night—Omri had four platefuls of osso buco and loudly sucked the marrow from the bones—I listened to him describe how his father would sway a particularly recalcitrant rabbi in his nineties to support the governing coalition. "Everything can be done," Omri explained.

"Sharon doesn't trust anybody," Yossi Beilin told me. "He doesn't trust Likud, he doesn't trust Labor, he doesn't trust the Europeans or the British or even Bush, not the left or the extreme right. He depends on his sons, which is indicative of a paranoid person. Omri, a backbencher in the Knesset, is the director general of the country. It's unbelievable. Omri's importance is unhealthy. Israel remains a stable democracy, but it's unbelievable."

Even as early as 2001, Sharon introduced the vague notion that his country would eventually have to make "painful concessions." But, rather than get into specifics and risk the rejection of his own party, he used a deputy—in this case, the Deputy Prime Minister Ehud Olmert— to inflate a trial balloon, in December 2003, and let it float.

Olmert, a smart and cocky politician who was the mayor of Jerusalem before joining the Cabinet, told me how, in December 2003, on the thirtieth anniversary of Ben-Gurion's death, Sharon had been scheduled to speak near the burial place. The night before, however, Sharon called Olmert and said he was sick, asking if Olmert could fill in for him. Olmert comes from an old Revisionist family, which resented Ben-Gurion for agreeing to the United Nations partition of Palestine, in 1947, and for ordering Israeli soldiers in 1948 to fire on the cargo ship *Altalena,* which was carrying a huge arms cache and rebel fighters loyal to Menachem Begin. But if Olmert was still ambivalent about Ben-Gurion, he was loyal to Sharon.

He quickly agreed to give the speech. Sharon faxed Olmert a draft. The key passage quoted Ben-Gurion as saying that the Israelis "could have conquered" far more territory, but "Then what?" That state "would hold elections and we'd be in the minority. When we faced the choice of the complete land without a Jewish state, or a Jewish state without the complete land, we chose a Jewish state."

For Revisionist ideologues who believed in a Greater Israel, such pragmatism was still, a half century later, a heresy. And when Olmert read it at the ceremony the reaction was swift. "When I finished my speech, and I sat down," Olmert told me, "the speaker of the Knesset"— a Likud ideologue, Reuven Rivlin—"looked at me almost with tears and said, 'This is a disaster, this is the end. The end of Likud, the end of what we have been fighting for.' " (Rivlin, for his part, told me later in his office at the Knesset that he was indeed "heartbroken" to hear that his close friend, speaking in Sharon's name, had betrayed the principles of Jabotinsky, Begin, and Greater Israel.) A year later, when Sharon gave the memorial speech himself and echoed the same themes, Olmert concluded that Sharon had made his shift, in part, to deflect attention from a campaign finance scandal and because of pressure from the United States and the Europeans, who needed to see a show of progress somewhere in the Middle East.

Olmert said, "You ask me today, Do I believe that Judea and Samaria"—the Biblical names for the West Bank—"are the historical land of the Palestinians? Nonsense. There never was any Palestinian nation that lived there, there never was a clear, well-defined ethnic group that has created a national life other than the Jews. There were tribes, there were individuals, there were families, whatever. And most of the territories were rather empty. So, from a historic point of view, you can argue very strongly against the Palestinian claim. But what difference does it make? At the end of the day, there are five million Palestinians between the Jordan and the sea. This is the most fundamental fact."

Olmert, like everyone I spoke to in Sharon's circle, said that the boundaries that every mainstream Palestinian politician insists on for a final settlement—the 1967 borders—are "off the table." "But that doesn't mean that there will not be modifications," he said, lighting up a Cuban cigar. "For me, forever, these are parts of Israel. But maybe we will be forced to pull out from parts of Israel. Because we have to make a choice between Greater Israel and a Jewish democratic state. Why? Because I believe that in another ten years the entire setup will change. It will cease to be an Algerian-type conflict, and it will be a South African–type conflict. Algerian in the sense that this is entirely a confrontation between two nations. In a South African situation, [the Arabs] will say, O.K., we want Greater Israel, one person, one vote. The day that will be the main narrative, we've lost the game. It will become a Palestinian state with a majority of Palestinians with Palestinian government and a Palestinian leadership and Palestinian right of return, by a choice of the majority of the people in a democratic vote. What will we do then?"

I asked whether he thought Sharon's disengagement plan—no matter what the motive—would rescue his historical reputation abroad.

Olmert relit his cigar and slowly exhaled, his head nearly encased in smoke. "Who will remember Sabra and Shatila after the disengagement? Well, some Jewish historians!" He laughed and then puffed on his cigar. "Look," he said, "the world will finally focus on the main thing. This is the story of history, and you know it. Do you know how many flaws Churchill had before he became the historic figure of the twentieth century? Who remembers it now? This is a historic move by Sharon. I will have a footnote, but he will have the main chapter."

.   .   .

Sharon's offices are unimpressive—except for the security detail, which has multiplied since the Rabin assassination, a decade ago. The sense of threat has only increased. Two senior Israeli intelligence officials told me that they are worried for the lives of both Mahmoud Abbas and Ariel Sharon. "It's tense," one of them said. "We have reason to believe Hamas is trying to launch an assassination of Abu Mazen. And, within Israel, extremists"—especially among the settlers in the occupied territories—"understand that the removal of Sharon is the only thing that might stop disengagements."

Last fall, with the appearance in *Ha'aretz* of Dov Weissglas's indiscreet comments about using disengagement to put any further negotiations in "formaldehyde," Sharon and his circle were enraged, and since then his aides have been wary about speaking on the record. And yet they spoke, at least anonymously. One of Sharon's senior advisers took me into an office near the Prime Minister's and told me that everything now depended on Abbas's ability to stop terror. Sharon, he said, saw September 11, 2001, as the moment when the American Administration began to understand terror principally as ideological aggression that must be stopped at all costs.

"The European political vision was the other way around," the senior adviser said. "They saw terror as a by-product of political frustration. Not that the Europeans support terror. But in the European dialectic, unlike the American, terror is the natural outcome. From our intimate knowledge of the region for one hundred and ten years—which is when the major Jewish migration began—we have a different understanding of political terrorism. The rules are different in the Middle East.

"The problem now between us and the Palestinians," he went on, "is not the substance of the solution but the ability to implement it. Even if the Palestinians had gotten the 1947 territory, not that of 1967, even if all the refugees could come back, even if they got all of Jerusalem, not just a divided Jerusalem, what would happen the next day? There is not one person in the Palestinian Authority who is capable of turning to his people and saying, 'The game is now over,' the way Ben-Gurion did in 1948 on thirty percent of the land we have now. He was able to face down his opposition, including Menachem Begin, and say, 'Go to hell.' And the state was founded."

Sharon's adviser said it was understood that Abbas could not quash absolutely every terrorist, but the effort had to be impressive. "We at least want to see the Palestinians arrest them, kick the shit out of them, not welcome them like heroes," he said. After a while, the adviser and a press secretary took me across the hall to see the Prime Minister.

Sharon is seventy-six and alarmingly overweight. He seemed impatient, tired. Up the hill from his compound, near the Knesset, settlers from all over the occupied territories had set up a tent village and had been demonstrating, day after day, against disengagement. They waved orange banners and handed out bumper stickers and T-shirts that read, "The People Are with Gush Katif." A very few from the Gush Katif settlements, in Gaza, wore orange stars, as symbols of their victimhood and as an echo of the yellow Stars of David that Jews were made to wear under the Nazis. Most thought the symbol an outrage. Some settlers were talking about mass protests to block the disengagement this summer; already there had been clashes in the West Bank between soldiers and settlers when a tiny outpost—just two trailer homes—was disbanded. Privately, Sharon was said to be furious, but he was careful to show only sympathy.

"They are leaving their homes," he told me. "The disengagement plan is a heavy burden. It is painful for them and painful for me. But we have to do it."

Sharon was not ready to talk about concessions beyond Gaza. He had always said that it was necessary to have settlement outposts in the Jordan River Valley as a defensive plan against Jordan and Iraq—the Eastern Front—but now Saddam was in jail and the Jordanians had a long-standing treaty with Israel. Couldn't those settlements go? I asked Sharon.

"We just don't know," he said. "When you are dealing with security in a tiny country, you have to look to the future, and the Jordan Valley is very important. We don't know how things will develop with Iran or Iraq or Syria. We have to be very careful."

When we spoke, the election was just a few days away. Abbas was performing well, almost transformed. He seemed to be gaining a taste for oratory, and his poll ratings were rising. Sharon's critics were saying that he might have been the only person in the Middle East who missed Arafat, because now he would have to deal with a democratically elected antagonist and negotiating partner.

"As a Jew, the most important thing for me is the historic possibility to secure the Jewish people," Sharon said. "In this part of the world, declarations, promises, proposals, even signatures are one thing. Only acts are serious. It's not a matter of if I trust the Arabs. Only acts can be taken seriously. And they have to dismantle terror organizations, collect their weapons. They have to do it, not promise it."

Sharon said that the disengagement from Gaza would be just a first step in reengaging the Palestinians in a negotiating process, so long as the new head of the Palestinian Authority made a concerted effort to take guns and explosives out of the hands of Hamas, Islamic Jihad, and the Al-Aqsa Martyrs Brigades. "I know Abu Mazen, I know him well," he said. "I've met him here many times. He has to dismantle terror organizations and fight terror. He has to see the Palestinians be fully committed to the cessation of terror. . . . We will be watching what happens."

Sharon relied on bromides, and his attention seemed fixed on the schedule typed out on a sheet of paper before him—the one piece of paper on his desk. But then, just before I left, he stood and, like an expert thespian trying to make a pronouncement seem improvised, the product of passion and sudden thought, he said, "When it comes to security, I will never make compromises. Never! Not as long as I'm here. And I have no plans to leave anytime soon."

The Israeli settlers—more than seven thousand in Gaza, approximately a quarter of a million in the West Bank—do not all share an ideology. Some of the larger, more established settlements around Jerusalem and Tel Aviv resemble bedroom communities in the farthest commuting reaches of Phoenix or Los Angeles. People moved there not for messianic reasons but because the government encouraged them, gave them breaks on housing, on taxes. Some even vote Labor. However, the vast majority of settlers are politically right-wing, and, as in all politics, the most persistently newsworthy are the sanctimonious, the paranoiacs, the cranks, the dangerous. There are plenty of settlers outside Hebron, Nablus, and Jenin who see themselves as soldiers of Greater Israel, soldiers of God—some of the most radical are called the hilltop youth— and Israeli intelligence officials told me they fear that some fanatics might go well beyond civil disobedience in order to put a halt to Sharon's plan to dismantle the Gaza settlements this summer.

In a Knesset committee meeting, Avi Dichter, the head of the Shabak, Israel's equivalent of the FBI, said that a few dozen extremist settlers are likely to spread rumors that Army snipers are going to fire on settlers in order to goad them into firing back and cause an all-out battle. Dichter said that he had to be concerned both about Palestinian militants obtaining anti-aircraft missiles via tunnels dug under the Egyptian border and about Jewish settlers stealing weapons from Israeli military garrisons. "The Gaza Strip could become southern Lebanon," he said.

The principal leadership of the settlers, the Yesha Council, had issued a proclamation calling on supporters in Israel and abroad to gather around the settlers in Gaza and "disobey this Transfer Law and be prepared in large numbers to pay the price of going to prison." The document, written by Pinchas Wallerstein, the head of the Binyamin regional council, and distributed in all the settlements and on the Internet, said that disengagement was "an immoral undertaking." The tone was desperate, self-righteous: "Were Martin Luther King to be alive today to witness the singling out of Jewish residents as Jews for expulsion from their homes, perhaps he might point out that his constituency was similarly singled out to be prevented from being present in schools, restaurants, and, yes, neighborhoods."

One morning, a public-relations executive named Aliza Herbst picked me up at my hotel in Jerusalem in a bulletproof van to take me to see Wallerstein. Herbst is a serious woman in her fifties who, as we drove north into the West Bank, compared her commitment to living in a settlement to the counterculture life she led in the sixties at the University of Wisconsin. "My husband was involved in the environment and was in on the first Earth Day," she said. "That's where the idealism came from." We were driving along the main spine of the West Bank, Route 60, past Arab villages and Jewish settlements, past sections of the wall. The complexity of the geography, its security lines, has been made preposterously complicated by the Israeli government in the past thirty-seven years. We detoured off the main road and up a hill to a small settlement called Migron, a collection of a few dozen trailers surrounded by a fence and barbed wire. It seemed like a dubious place to live, on top of a bare and windy hill, surrounded by nothing but Arab villages and Biblical memories. There were no stores, no theaters—just the trailer homes. Herbst did not see it that way. "It's like summer camp," she said. "What could be bad?"

We arrived in Pesagot, a much larger Jewish settlement that overlooks Ramallah. Wallerstein has his office here. Herbst, who lives in the nearby settlement of Ofra, got out of the van and said that it was clear to her that the Gaza disengagement would lead "inevitably" to the end of Ofra, the end of Pesagot, and she was, in her own way, ready to resist. "Pinchas is saying, 'Wake up! This is really happening,'" she said. "I have a right to be here, just like you have a right to be in New Mexico or Tennessee."

Wallerstein greeted us in his office. He is balding and wears a large knit *kipa*—a variety of skullcap that, in the precise language of Israeli headgear, indicates a religious nationalist—and he walks with a limp, the result of a wound from the 1967 war. Wallerstein showed me a small hole in one of his telephones and another in his window frame—the result, he said, of sniper fire from a nearby Arab village. Wallerstein is one of the founding fathers of the settler movement. A former biology teacher, he moved to Ofra in 1975 and became an officer in the Gush Emunim (Bloc of the Faithful) and later a member of the Yesha Council.

As we spoke, Wallerstein periodically checked his e-mail. Ever since he published his call for passive resistance against the disengagement from Gaza, he has been getting thousands of messages from all over the world, nearly all supportive, and no small number of them calling for sterner measures. He swiveled the computer screen around to let me see a message he'd just called up: "Any method is legitimate to protect against the action that Sharon wants to take."

Wallerstein has known the Prime Minister for decades. They worked together on mapping out new settlements when Sharon was in Begin's Cabinet, but now, even though Wallerstein is careful with his language, it is clear that he feels he has been betrayed. He implied that Sharon had "changed" after the death of his wife, Lily, in 2000, that he was trying to sanitize his historical reputation abroad.

Unlike some of the settlers, Wallerstein said that he did not favor the old absolutist solution to the Palestinian problem—forced transfer of the Arab population to Jordan. But, for him, a two-state solution, whether along the 1967 borders or in the vastly more limited, interim sense propounded by Sharon's allies, was still unthinkable.

I asked him how long he thought the Palestinians would tolerate living in islets of territory surrounded by troops, checkpoints, and Jewish settlements, and whether he imagined a Bantustan arrangement, as in South Africa under apartheid. Wallerstein was not offended by the analogy. "Bantustans? Maybe. If you want to be honest, the problem is not just the Arabs in Judea and Samaria. It's the Arabs throughout the country. The part that is hardest to swallow about the withdrawal from Gaza is that it is not being done for peace. The potential to attack Israel will now increase."

He resented that the settlers were becoming increasingly isolated from the rest of Israel, that now even Sharon's supporters, not just traditional liberals, saw them as obstinate, potentially dangerous, inhabitants of another state, "the Settler state."

"It's easier to paint the world in black-and-white, so it's better if a set-tler has horns growing out of his head and has a knife between his teeth," Wallerstein said. "Otherwise you may have to deal with complicated questions of history and morality. I believe that I am part of the Zionist movement, which began establishing facts on the ground one hundred years ago."

On election day, I went to Gaza. The main entrance into the Strip, the Erez crossing, has been a fairly sleepy scene in recent years. Tens of thousands of Palestinian workers used to cross into Israel every morning and work as farmhands, factory workers, and domestic staff, and then return home in the evening. A crossing often took two or three hours. Unemployment may be as much as seventy percent in Gaza, and the salaries for work in Israel were a relative fortune: twenty to fifty dollars a day. During the second intifada, however, the Israelis virtually cut off this daily migration and decided that they could make do with cheap labor from Southeast Asia.

Even on an easy day, when there have been no bombings, it takes about an hour to pass through all the controls and walk the long outdoor corridor to get to the other side. It is a severe passage: on one side, rich, green farmland and smooth highways and strip malls; on the other, cheap, crowded housing, sewage in the streets, honking and dust, and the ubiquitous posters extolling the martyrdom of teenagers who have been sent into Israel as suicide bombers. Walking along the concrete corridor, I noticed an enormous hole in the wall and the metal roof. "There was a bomber in here last week," someone said.

It was a Sunday. Voters were arriving at polling stations all over Gaza, lining up, marking their ballots, and leaving with purple ink on their thumbs as an indication of having voted. Celebrity observers—Jimmy Carter, Joseph Biden, John Kerry—were in East Jerusalem and the more accessible towns of the West Bank, but there were few complaints.

"This could be a new era," Ziad Abu-Amr, the Palestinian legislator, said. "What's interesting about the way the campaign has gone in the past few weeks is that the front-runner did not take his success for granted. There was real anxiety in the inner circles. Arafat never feared elections; he was never worried about the result and never really both-ered to campaign. Abu Mazen had to become popular in a short period of time. The anxiety in Fatah was whether he could be popular enough."

Political figures like Abu-Amr will play a crucial role in Gaza in the months to come; he has long been a conduit for Fatah to the leadership of Hamas. Until the targeted assassinations of Hamas leaders, among them Sheikh Yassin, in the past two years, the group was tightly organized, using its social-services facilities, its mosques, and its reputation for incorruptibility as effective recruitment tools. Now much of the decision-making has shifted to Khaled Mashal, the Hamas leader in Damascus. Abu-Amr said there was no secrecy surrounding Hamas's decision not to run an opponent against Abbas. "Even if a Hamas candidate won," he said, "he'd either have to negotiate with Israel or declare all-out war with Israel, and Hamas cannot afford that choice." Better to boycott the election and not run the risk of demystifying Hamas.

One of the few senior Hamas leaders left in Gaza, it seemed, was a physician named Mahmoud al-Zahar, whom I'd interviewed before the intifada reached its peak. At that time, Zahar met fairly regularly with journalists, dispensing the usual slogans of Islamist absolutism, conspiracy theories, and threats to the Israeli state. In September 2003, an Israeli F-16 dropped a bomb on his house, killing his eldest son and badly injuring his wife. Zahar, who was not seriously wounded, has been underground ever since.

Some colleagues and I made an appointment to see Zahar at around midnight at the Ramattan television studios in Gaza City. He'd clearly made the calculation that this was one day when the Israelis would leave him alone.

We arrived at the studios and watched on a monitor as Abbas accepted the good news in Ramallah. He had won around sixty-two percent of the vote. "In the name of God," he told his supporters, "this victory is for the soul of Yasir Arafat! . . . It's also a gift for the Palestinian people from Rafah to Jenin. Also for the souls of the martyrs and wounded and the eleven thousand prisoners in Israeli jails! They are all celebrating this victory with you now! . . . Also the Al-Aqsa Martyrs Brigades are welcoming you!"

Down the hall, someone was coughing significantly. "Um . . . Mr. Zahar will see you."

Zahar welcomed us into a dingy studio. He was stouter than I'd remembered, sallow, with dark rings under his eyes. He closed his eyes wearily and nodded by way of greeting and started off by finding fault with the elections, about the fact that the polling day had been extended by two hours to give Abbas better turnout figures. "We were looking for a clean process," he complained.

We could still hear Abbas speaking on the monitor outside.

"Our attitude to Abu Mazen depends first of all on his attitude to the Palestinian factions and the resistance movements," Zahar said. "Disarming the military units in Fatah, Hamas, and Islamic Jihad will create an internal Palestinian military confrontation.

"No one will give him a chance to do that. . . . Hamas will never allow Abu Mazen to take our guns while there is still Israeli aggression. These soldiers are here to protect the Palestinians. If Abu Mazen attacks Hamas and denounces our national rights"—and here his tone grew threatening—"he'll lose a great deal."

In other words, there was only one language that Sharon or any other Israeli understood. "Why did Israel leave southern Lebanon and not the Golan Heights? Because there was effective armed struggle," Zahar said. "Why is Sharon leaving Gaza? Because armed struggle became too costly for the Israelis. . . . We don't trust them. Mahmoud Abbas is going to talk to them. But these people can't be trusted."

All this was to be expected. More interesting was that Hamas, which has always maintained an absolutist position—Israel cannot be permitted on Arab lands—had circulated a document to Fatah saying that it might be prepared to work jointly with Fatah for a two-state solution along the 1967 lines. It was hard to know how seriously to take this development. "If you leave Gaza and stop the aggression, we can give a *hudna,* a long *hudna,*" Zahar said, using the Arabic word for "truce." "The PLO was in a hurry. They recognized Israel without getting anything. They depended on the goodwill of the Israelis. If we got the West Bank, Gaza, and Jerusalem"—meaning East Jerusalem as a capital—"I could see a *hudna* for ten years. Maybe even longer than that. But we are not trusting the Israelis."

I mentioned that Israeli intelligence and some Palestinian commentators were concerned that Hamas might take the most extreme measures if it could not reach an accommodation with the new leader of the Palestinian Authority. Zahar glared and said, "Abu Mazen should have no fear from Hamas. We have a religious faith that does not allow us to kill an innocent man."

Walk around the neighborhoods of Gaza and it is hard to believe that Abbas can stifle terror either quickly or completely—not when a culture of martyrdom and its glorification has taken such root. The Martyrs' Cemetery. Martyr posters. Martyr cards. Martyr T-shirts. Martyr videotapes. One day, I passed by the Maslam Martyr Pharmacy. This distortion of identity is a crisis as great as politics. In the Sheikh Radwan neighborhood, a Hamas stronghold, I spoke to a group of teenagers.

"Do you want to be a martyr?" I asked one.

"God willing," Muhammad Talmas, an eighteen-year-old student, said.

"And, if not that, what?"

"An engineer, maybe."

"Can you be both?"

"Well, look at Ismail Abu Shanab," he said. The boy knew martyrology the way American kids know ballplayers. "He did both. He was killed in a missile attack last year. I want to go to Heaven. The Prophet Muhammad used to say, 'I want to go to Heaven after long work and deeds.' *Inshallah.*"

"What do you think of Abu Mazen?"

"The words of Abu Mazen conflict with the Palestinian national interest. There are thousands of martyrs and prisoners in Israeli jails. The Palestinians should receive a reward on their behalf—all of Palestine."

"No coexistence? No two states?"

"No, no, no," he said. "Never."

The most prominent psychologist in Gaza, Eyad al-Sarraj, told me that if there was ever a settlement between Israel and the Palestinians the culture of martyrdom would dwindle dramatically. "When Sadat came to Israel and laid down his sword, the Israeli psychology changed overnight," Sarraj said. Until then, he said, the young men—and even the young women—of Gaza and the West Bank would seek martyrdom.

"Martyrs are at the level of prophets," Sarraj said. "They are untouchable. I can denounce suicide bombings, which I have many times, but not the martyrs themselves, because they are like saints. If you do that, you will discredit yourself completely. This is why when the stupid Bush said these are not martyrs, they are murderers—as if the only martyrs are Christian. We, too, have our martyrs. . . . He sacrifices himself for the nation. If you want to be a part of this culture, you have to understand this. I don't believe in religion myself, but I cannot say that Muhammad was nothing but a magician or that martyrs are wrong. This disqualifies you from the culture."

In the two weeks that followed the elections, violence certainly did not stop—there were rocket attacks, military reprisals, border incidents. But the incidents were fewer as time passed. Abbas went to Gaza to negotiate a *hudna* with the armed factions. The Israelis and the Palestinians talked about new security arrangements, even about military

withdrawals from the West Bank. The newspapers were filled with speculation about an eventual meeting between Sharon and Abbas. Sharon
spoke of a possible "historic breakthrough." No one spoke much anymore about Arafat, about his last years, about his mysterious end. There
was no longer time for that.

(2005)

•

Later in 2005, Ariel Sharon made good on his promise to evacuate and
close the Israeli settlements in Gaza. Emotional scenes of withdrawal,
which were televised around the clock, riveted the country, but significant opposition to Sharon's policy was limited mainly to the right wing of
the Likud Party.

In November, Sharon calculated that after years of vilification on the
left for his role at Sabra and Shatila and other dark episodes of military
and political history, and distrust among the Likud leadership, he had
now won support of the broad middle of the Israeli electorate. As a
result, he announced that he would leave Likud, create a new centrist
party called Kadima (Forward), and compete under that banner for
another term as Prime Minister. The Palestinian electorate, meanwhile,
was fracturing, as Hamas gained strength and younger factions in Fatah
became increasingly disenchanted with the older guard, including Mahmoud Abbas, for its corruption, mismanagement, and political failures.

Until January 2006, there was every sign that Sharon would win his
reelection and continue on a more or less unilateral path toward ceding a
state to the Palestinians—a distinctly limited state shaped out of Gaza
and contiguous portions of the West Bank, though not the larger, more
established West Bank settlements or, crucially, Jerusalem. Then Sharon
suffered a catastrophic stroke and suddenly the Israeli leadership—and
the Israeli direction—seemed unsure, lacking a central politician with
the capacity to move the country toward even a limited agreement.
Ehud Olmert, Sharon's deputy, would be the first to try.

The Democracy Game:
Hamas Comes to Power
in Palestine

Every Friday, just before midday prayers, thousands of men and women in the West Bank town of Dura stop to gossip and shop in the market stalls that lead to the steps of the Grand Mosque. I visited Dura on the first Friday after Hamas had swept the Palestinian elections. And yet that morning all the talk was of cartoons: a dozen caricatures of the Prophet Muhammad had been published in the Danish daily *Jyllands-Posten*, igniting a worldwide paroxysm of apocalyptic hysteria that brought into use, once more, that *Star Wars*–like phrase "a clash of civilizations." The imam at the Dura Grand Mosque is a man in his late forties named Nayef Rajoub. Although Sheikh Nayef is a leader of Hamas and the top vote-getter in the entire West Bank, his supporters told me that he, too, was focused on the cartoons. He would be speaking that day on the Danish caricatures as a "weapon of the Western Crusaders."

Outside the mosque, I met a group of people standing around a fruit-and-vegetable store run by a man called Eichmann Abu Atwan. I thought I'd misheard his name, but he smiled, showed his identity card, and said, "Eichmann. Like the Nazi." His father had named him during the trial of Adolf Eichmann, in Jerusalem in 1961. "He was an early fighter, killing Israelis in the seventies," Eichmann said proudly. "And my brother was such a fierce fighter that a Syrian paper compared him to Abdel-Aziz al-Rantisi"—one of the founders of Hamas. Eichmann was a supporter of Fatah, the Palestinian nationalist group that Yasir Arafat founded some fifty years ago, and, like everyone else I'd been talking to in the occupied territories, he said that Hamas had won for a variety of reasons: the financial corruption of Fatah and its leadership; the utter failure of the Oslo process; a marked increase in Islamic practice throughout Gaza and the West Bank; Hamas's dual mastery in providing social services for Palestinians and launching armed assaults on the Israelis. "Time has run out for Fatah," Eichmann said.

As the muezzin summoned the people of Dura to the mosque, Nayef's fraternal twin, Yasir, stopped by the store. "Are you all coming to hear the Sheikh?" he said. Like Nayef, Yasir had been affiliated with Hamas from the start, but their older brother, Jibril Rajoub, was one of Arafat's most powerful aides and a Fatah lord. Jibril had run the Preventive Security Service in the West Bank, and he was one of the losers in the elections.

Prayers began at eleven-thirty, and we filed into the mosque and knelt down. The walls were whitewashed. A dozen fluorescent tubes dangled low from the ceiling, giving off a vague yellow light. The room was filled entirely with men, but I was hardly inconspicuous. My translator, an aspiring young journalist from the West Bank named Khaldoun, quickly came to realize that his principal task, after rendering the Sheikh's sermon into English, was to explain to all who inquired (and many did) that the foreign visitor was "not Danish." Al Jazeera and the other Arab-language television stations had broadcast fiery protests throughout Europe, Asia, and the Middle East.

"Danish?" a man asked me.

Khaldoun responded with a prolonged explanation featuring the word "Am-rika," which has not been something to brag about in recent years, but this time it did the trick.

Sheikh Nayef has a graying beard, close-cropped hair, and a tranquil, strangely distant gaze. His posture was as straight as the microphone stand before him. I was told that outside the mosque his personality was shy, even remote—a marked contrast to his worldly and fierce-looking brother Jibril——but he soon rose to a register of high dudgeon in his sermon. The Danish cartoons, the Sheikh said, were reminiscent of the calumnies hurled at the Prophet fourteen hundred years ago. Muhammad "was accused of being a magician, of being insane. The same thing is happening now in Denmark, in France, although many mosques in Europe are spreading his message. . . . What happened in Denmark is an offense against Muhammad and his followers. It is an act of aggression against us and against our feelings."

The Sheikh was not about to get into the origins of the demonstrations, how they had been fanned not only by an imam in Copenhagen and various jihadi groups but also by regimes, like the Saudis', that make a show of their piety in order to placate their Islamist subjects. "That's not my topic today," he said. His theme was power and humiliation, Western offense and Islamic will. The cartoon affair, he said, was yet another episode in the Crusaders' assault on the faith, and the reason for "the Prophet's humiliation is the weakness of our nation." The demonstrations proved that Hamas and the Islamic movement around the world were unimpressed by such "excuses" as freedom of speech and were absolutely determined to reject the pieties of "the heathen."

The Sheikh continued, "The people who bow down to the White House and to the Western way of life must all wake up and realize that this life is not suitable for us. Today we are told to accept our enemies, to give up our principles, to give up resistance, and do the same as the previous government"—the Palestinian Authority under Fatah. "But that is not our model. Our model is the Prophet Muhammad. What did the previous government get from compromise? It got failure, the denial of our rights, a blockade—Arafat was caught in a blockade. We have no partner in Israel. A people with principles will not repeat this failure. If our people repeat this, the next thing will be the Israelis telling us to stop praying, to stop fasting, to change our names, to take off the *hijab*. We will not repeat these mistakes. Palestine is for the Muslims, and no one can give it up. . . . Those who injure God and his Prophet will suffer now and after death."

Dura is a town in the region of Hebron, and Hebron is the largest city in the West Bank. It is also one of the most purely Islamic cities in the occupied territories, and a center of terror. One reason for the extraordinary tension in Hebron, beyond the general privations of the nearly four-decades-long occupation, is the presence, amid a hundred and fifty thousand Palestinians, of five hundred Jewish settlers protected by more than two thousand Israeli troops. On the Jewish holiday of Purim in 1994, a doctor and settler from Brooklyn, Baruch Goldstein, opened fire with an assault rifle on Arabs praying at the Tomb of the Patriarchs, killing twenty-nine and setting off riots and reprisals all over the region. A few years ago, at the height of the Al Aqsa intifada, Jihad, a soccer team sponsored by a local mosque, instituted a rigorous training schedule: the players fasted on Mondays and Thursdays, pledged daily allegiance to Hamas, and practiced nearly every afternoon wearing jerseys bearing a hand brandishing an axe and the inscription "Al Jihad: Prepare for Them." The team's fame relied only secondarily on an impressive record on the field. Eight team members, including the player-coach, carried out suicide bombing operations, one after the other, killing more than twenty people and wounding dozens more. The city exhausted its sense of hope years ago. What now greets every visitor on the road running south from Jerusalem into Hebron is a huge green banner reading, "Welcome to Hamas City!"

Hamas, which was founded in 1987, during the first intifada, and is considered a terrorist organization by Israel, the United States, and the European Union, won seventy-four of the hundred and thirty-two seats in the Palestinian Legislative Council. Fatah won only forty-three. Hamas swept the slate in the Hebron region, taking nine of nine seats. Ever since Arafat signed the Oslo accords, in 1993, and the Palestinian leadership ended its long exile in Tunis to establish the Palestinian Authority in the West Bank and the Gaza Strip, he had used the leaders of Fatah, men like Jibril Rajoub, to make sure that Islamists like Nayef Rajoub did not extend their influence beyond the mosque. Jibril made his bones as a resistance fighter by spending seventeen years of his youth in Israeli prisons—much of that time for throwing a dud grenade at a convoy of Israeli soldiers—but his political prospects in middle age have been dashed. As Preventive Security chief, he jailed members of Hamas and other Islamist groups. Soon it is likely that Hamas will control Preventive Security—its five thousand troops and its arms.

The Rajoub family was conservative and provincial, but not especially religious. Nayef became devout when he studied Islamic law in Jordan. Yasir, who is a director of an Islamic charity that looks after orphans, has been arrested nine times and spent a total of eleven years in Israeli jails. In 1992, he and Nayef, along with more than four hundred other members of Hamas and Islamic Jihad, were forcibly deported by Israel to the mountain village of Marj al-Zahour, in southern Lebanon, where they lived in tents for a year until the government let them go home. The meetings and discussions conducted among the deportees helped form the core of the Islamist leadership that is now coming to power; the Islamists called their Lebanese exile "Ibn Taymiyya University," referring to a medieval Islamic thinker. Seven of the nine Hamas candidates in Hebron had been among the deportees. When I asked Yasir Rajoub about his brother Jibril, he smiled magnanimously and said that the family was close and the brothers' disagreements were "nothing personal."

"Jibril even arrested me and detained me for a month," he said. "I was taken to Jericho," where Preventive Security had its offices and jail cells. "Others were tortured in that jail, but not me—maybe because Jibril is my brother. When the Israelis arrested us, Jibril tried to look after us. He sent money to my family."

After the midday prayers, Sheikh Nayef accepted congratulations for his sermon on the steps of the mosque and in the market stalls. He shook hands, blessed children, and then, because he does not own a car, started looking for a ride home. He invited me along for lunch.

"Jibril is rich, but the Sheikh is poor, a simple man," one of his admirers told me. "He had to seek a loan just to pay the fee to get his name on the election ballot." The Fatah chieftains are known in the territories for skimming aid money and for taking kickbacks on businesses like oil, gas, and concrete. Their opulent houses, on the beach in Gaza, in the hills of the West Bank, mock the crumbling apartment blocks of their subjects.

The Sheikh's modest house squats at the end of a pitted dirt road on the outskirts of Dura. A group of women, including the Sheikh's wife, daughters, and nieces, were in the garage tending a gas stove and stacking loaves of pita; in a cauldron they were boiling hunks of mutton and rice. With some of his children trailing behind him, the Sheikh led his guests—family members, aides, and friends from the mosque—into the house, to a room furnished only with carpets and a floor lamp. A teenage son spread several oilcloths over the floor and another laid out plates and platters of food.

"Go ahead," the Sheikh said. "It's not easy preaching for so long. Let's eat for a while and then we'll talk."

It is an irony of history that the first Islamist party in the Arab world to come to power in democratic elections is based not in Cairo or Amman but, rather, in the territories occupied by the Jewish state. President Hosni Mubarak of Egypt and King Abdullah of Jordan have kept Islamists in their countries at bay by alternating repression, co-option, and limited access to meaningless ballots; Mubarak and Abdullah were just as dismayed as the Israelis to see the rise of Hamas on their borders.

Israel and the United States are already discussing schemes to isolate and destabilize the Palestinian Authority if Hamas refuses to recognize Israel and renounce violence. According to a report by Steven Erlanger in *The New York Times,* the Israelis could cause a financial crisis in the Palestinian territories by refusing to hand over the more than fifty million dollars a month in taxes and customs duties that they collect on behalf of the Palestinian Authority. They could make economic life even more arduous by tightening control on the movement of goods and workers between Israel and the territories. Western governments have said that they, too, could discontinue financial aid. These moves might result in a billion-dollar annual deficit leaving the Palestinian Authority unable to pay its hundred and forty thousand employees, who support more than a third of the Palestinian population. If Hamas decides to rebel rather than yield to outside pressure, that could lead to yet another armed conflict with Israel—a third intifada. The Israelis are gambling that Hamas—which won the elections without a majority of the votes and gained more support for its promises of reform than for its extremist views on Israel—would rather compromise than be forced to choose between poverty and war.

Islamist resistance movements appeared in Palestine well before the creation of Israel. The military battalions of Hamas are named for Izz al-Din al-Qassam, a Syrian-born sheikh who, during the Mandate period, carried out numerous attacks on British and Jewish officials. (He was killed by the British in 1935.) In one sermon he said, "Nothing will save us but our arms."

The Muslim Brotherhood, the root organization of Hamas and of nearly every contemporary Islamist group in the Arab world, was founded in 1928 by a schoolteacher named Hassan al-Banna, who decried both English colonial rule and secular Arab nationalism. For Banna and the Muslim Brothers, the Koran was both spiritual guide and worldly constitution. In the nineteen-sixties, as the Brotherhood gained popularity, the Egyptian ruler Gamal Abdel Nasser cracked down, trying and executing the group's most influential and radical thinker, Sayyid Qutb.

In the same series of arrests, the Egyptian police briefly imprisoned a young Gazan sheikh named Ahmed Yassin. When, following the 1967 Six-Day War, Gaza became Israeli-occupied territory, Sheikh Yassin set up a range of charities and social-service organizations, and took over professional associations and the Islamic University of Gaza, all of which were linked to the authority of the mosques. Because thousands of Palestinians worked each day in Israeli cities like Tel Aviv, Yassin was obsessed with the whore-of-Babylon influence that such places might have on his people. In 1973, he started the Islamic Center, the Al-Mujamma al-Islami, whose aim was to strengthen the authority of Islam over the population.

"In those days, Yassin's concern was men and women swimming together," Emmanuel Sivan, one of Israel's leading scholars of modern Islam, told me. Yassin's emphasis was on *da'wa*—social work and preaching—and he skillfully attracted aid from local donors, the Palestinian diaspora, and other Islamists abroad. The Israeli government, which was pouring its resources into combating Arafat, determined that the Islamists were more of a threat to the PLO than to Israel and so did little to get in Yassin's way. "Israel operated on the simple Western logic of supporting the rival of your enemy," said Shaul Mishal, a professor at Tel Aviv University and the co-author of a scholarly history, *The Palestinian Hamas*. "That strategy did not last long."

By the early eighties, many disaffected young men among the Palestinian Islamists were getting involved in the violent resistance to Israel, which was dominated by PLO fighters. To keep them within the authority of the mosques, Yassin and his associates began importing arms and organizing militias of their own. When, in December 1987, the intifada began—first in the Jabalia refugee camp, in Gaza, then throughout the occupied territories—the Islamists joined the rebellion full force, and Hamas, an acronym for Harakat al-Muqawama al-Islamiyya, the Islamic Resistance Movement, was born. (*Hamas* means "zeal.")

The Hamas charter, a nine-thousand-word document adopted by the leadership in August 1988, remains the group's ideological foundation, melding Islamic fundamentalism with a national movement. From the start, the PLO had included a range of ideologies and tendencies, among them Arab nationalism and Marxism, but Hamas rejected such "foreign" influence. In its charter, historical Palestine—the territory *min al-nahr ila al-bahr*, from the River Jordan to the Mediterranean—is declared part of the Islamic *waqf* ("endowment"), "consecrated for future Muslim generations until Judgment Day," and indivisible. To relinquish any part of the land—in other words, to permit the presence of an alien Jewish state—is forbidden. Hamas "strives to raise the banner of Allah over every inch of Palestine," the charter reads, for, under the Jews, "the state of truth has disappeared and been replaced by the state of evil."

The Hamas charter also reflects an unabashedly anti-Semitic, conspiracy-based view of regional and world history. Article 22 asserts that the Jewish people have "ignited revolutions" throughout the world from 1789 to 1917. Jews triggered the First World War in order to destroy the Islamic caliphate and the Second World War in order to make "huge profits from trading war materiel." In short, "No war broke out anywhere without their fingerprints on it." The Jews also have formed "secret organizations" and "destructive spying" agencies—Freemasons, Rotary Clubs, Lions Clubs, and others—to promote the Zionist project, which "has no limits. . . . After Palestine it will strive to expand from the Nile to the Euphrates." This plan is "outlined in 'The Protocols of the Elders of Zion,' " the tsarist-era forgery of a Jewish plan for world domination.

The charter's view of negotiations and "the so-called peaceful solutions" is unambiguous. "There is no solution to the Palestinian problem except by Jihad. The initiatives, proposals, and international conferences are but a waste of time and sheer futility."

After the first intifada and the advent of the Oslo process, in 1993, Arafat became wary of Hamas and its refusal to accept the peace process, Israel's right to exist, or, above all, his authority in Gaza and the West Bank. According to Mishal's book, Arafat once referred to Hamas as a "Zulu tribe," an allusion to the Inkatha movement, which refused to come under the command of Nelson Mandela and the African National Congress. Arafat also found himself competing with Hamas for money; when he supported Iraq in the Gulf War in 1991, Saudi Arabia, Kuwait, and other states on the Arabian Peninsula began diverting to Hamas funds that had once gone to the PLO. In the early nineteen-nineties, according to Gilles Kepel, the author of *Jihad: The Trail of Political Islam*, Hamas gained adherents from three social classes: impoverished young men, who took part in the armed resistance; the devout middle classes; and Islamist intellectuals in the region and in the West.

Israel and the United States, in the meantime, grew deeply frustrated with Arafat's inability, or unwillingness, to confront Hamas, which had become a pioneer in the art of terror. The first modern suicide bombing was carried out in 1981 against the Iraqi Embassy in Beirut; in 1983, Hezbollah, the Iranian-funded Shiite militia in southern Lebanon, used suicide bombers to attack American and French barracks in Beirut. In 1993, Hamas took it up with terrifying frequency.

After the assassination of Yitzhak Rabin, in 1995, Hamas became perhaps the most important factor in the search for a successor: a series of bombings that it carried out in Israel during the campaign turned Israeli voters toward the right-wing Likud Party and brought Benjamin Netanyahu, who promised no concessions to the Palestinians, to power. Netanyahu declared himself determined to destroy Hamas, but he managed instead to return the favor, ordering an operation that helped its leadership immeasurably.

In 1997, Netanyahu dispatched a team of Mossad agents to Amman to assassinate Khaled Meshal, the chief Hamas leader abroad. Two agents approached Meshal on the street from behind and one pricked his ear with a needle loaded with a deadly nerve toxin. Meshal's bodyguard, however, turned out to be a spectacular athlete and ran down the Israeli agents, first by car and then on foot, beat them, and brought them to a local prison. Once the Israeli agents confessed to the poisoning on videotape, King Hussein, furious that the Mossad had carried out the mission on Jordanian territory long after he had made peace with Israel, called Netanyahu and demanded the antidote to the poison. Netanyahu refused. Only after Hussein appealed to Bill Clinton and the Israeli press began criticizing Netanyahu for ordering such a spectacularly stupid operation did he relent. Meshal survived. Hussein, who had his own Palestinian majority to placate, extracted another concession from Netanyahu: rather than lose the peace with Jordan, the Israeli Prime Minister agreed to release Sheikh Yassin from prison.

For several years, Yassin served as the strategic and spiritual guide for Hamas. Israel maintained that he gave the final assent to terrorist operations. In 2004, during the Al Aqsa intifada and the Israeli attempt to wipe out the Hamas leadership, Yassin was killed in a missile attack. Since then, when I have visited Hamas leaders in Gaza and the Muslim Brotherhood's headquarters in Cairo, I've seen portraits of Yassin in every office. "He is our holy man," Mahmoud al-Zahar, the Hamas leader in Gaza, told me. "He is our greatest martyr."

The principal Hamas leaders—Zahar and Ismail Haniyeh in Gaza, and Musa Abu-Marzuq and Khaled Mashel in Damascus—have never feigned innocence of the attacks committed in their name, but they are fairly schooled in the arts of diplomatic wrangling and media manipulation. Their public language attempts to yoke contradictory goals. Like the leaders of the IRA decades ago, they are trying to enter the realm of politics without relinquishing the perquisites of armed resistance and the purity of ideological rejectionism. They want to maintain the support of their most radical fighters without losing the funding of the European Union. They hint at the possibility of a *hudna*—a prolonged truce—if Israel retreats to the borders that existed before the Six-Day War, but they also reserve the "historical" goal of absolute dominion made plain in their charter.

Sheikh Nayef Rajoub is more typical of the men and women of Hamas who will make up the majority of the next Palestinian legislature. Unlike the Fatah politicians, who have traveled the world, navigated diplomatic receptions, and dealt closely with the Israelis for many years, they are provincial, inexperienced, and leery of the task of governing even a proto-state. Few polls showed that Hamas would win the election, and its leaders were as surprised as Fatah or Israeli intelligence. But now Sheikh Nayef was prepared to be magnanimous toward his more famous older brother.

"In the past, my brother and I had reasons for tension," he said as we ate the last of the mutton. "These days, our relationship is better than ever. We are civilized people, and everyone has his choice, including religion. My choice is Islam and Jibril's choice is something else. I think Jibril did pray for a little while and then he stopped. It's sad for me."

The Sheikh felt that he was part of a "worldwide historical wave." He said that Hamas, after years of keeping its distance from official politics, had decided to "accept the democracy game," and he was sure that if the same opportunity were available elsewhere in the Arab world Islamist parties would prevail. "The failure of all other ideologies is sending Muslims toward Islam, and this is the case in Palestine," he said. "Twenty years ago when I was working in the mosque, around a hundred and fifty, two hundred people came on Friday. Now it's a few thousand. At that time, there was only one mosque in Dura. Now there are twelve." Hamas even won a considerable crossover vote, polling well in cities with sizable Christian populations, such as Ramallah and Bethlehem.

The Sheikh said he knew that, despite the heavy vote for Hamas, the majority of Palestinians tell pollsters that they favor an end to the occupation and a two-state solution. But Hamas, he added, would "never" bow to Israeli, American, European, and even Egyptian demands that it acknowledge the existence of Israel and disarm.

"How can the world want us to recognize the state of Israel when Israel will not give us the right to exist, when it took our land and imposed occupation and does not recognize our rights?" he said. "Resistance for us is a legitimate action. Divine and human laws give us the right to resist."

Hamas has not executed any suicide bombings in the past few months, but the Israelis do not take the lull to reflect a nascent desire for compromise. "The conflict with Israel is not a matter of land," Sheikh Nayef said. "It's a matter of ideology. All the Israeli slogans—the 'chosen people,' the 'promised land'—the basis of their state is religious. But these are religious legends, false stories. God did not give them this land as if Israelis, Jews, are preferred above all other peoples on earth and all other peoples were meant to serve them." The Sheikh went on, "Two hundred years ago in Europe, they were conservative people, but now the fashion world, the media—it's controlled by the Jews. And their people are sexually open. Freud, a Jew, was the one who destroyed morals, and Marx destroyed divine ideologies. If it is not all Jews, well, they were a big part of this. And now it is the Jewish lobby in the United States that is setting policy in the world and causing the United States to wage war all over the world."

One of the biggest financial supporters of Hamas has been the fundamentalist Shiite regime in Tehran, according to Israeli and U.S. intelligence agencies. At a conference in Tehran last October called "A World Without Zionism," Iran's current President, Mahmoud Ahmadinejad, urged the Palestinians to maintain a maximalist position toward Israel. Quoting Ayatollah Khomeini's statement that Israel "must be eliminated from the pages of history," Ahmadinejad instructed the Palestinians never to bow to the demands of diplomacy. They must not recognize Israel—and anyone who does, he declared, "should know that he will burn in the fire of the *Ummah,*" the Islamic nation.

I asked the Sheikh if he agreed with Ahmadinejad's argument, much publicized in recent months, that the Holocaust was a myth and a pretext for the creation of Israel.

The question, the Sheikh said, had direct bearing on his morning homily about the Danish cartoons and the will of the Muslims to resist humiliation: "When Ahmadinejad spoke, everyone in the West condemned him, but why didn't the West say that Ahmadinejad had his right of freedom of speech?" The Sheikh smiled like one who has scored an irrefutable point. "If the issue concerns Jews, it's always anti-Semitism, anti-Semitism, but when it concerns other religions it's a matter of freedom of speech."

But did he agree with the Iranian leader? I asked.

The Sheikh smiled again, this time indulgently.

"If I answer, you'll provide me with a real headache, won't you?" he said. "I don't want to tell you my opinion on this. No doubt, it's too controversial. If I say I agree with Ahmadinejad, Hamas will be added to the list of those who deny the Holocaust. If I don't agree with him, it will provide the Jews with the excuse that, since they suffered a lot in the Second World War, it justifies what they are doing now. What I do know about for sure is the crimes of the Jews in Lebanon and the West Bank and Gaza."

Word came that the Sheikh's brother Jibril was going to visit. Through the window we could see a convoy led by an armored Land Cruiser and a BMW sedan—the rewards of Fatah power—pulling up in front of the house. The Sheikh sighed. He did not seem entirely ready to greet his big brother. To cheer him up I asked him what else he did besides preach and teach the Koran.

"I am also the head of the Hebron Beekeepers Union," he said.

I asked him if he got stung a lot.

The Sheikh rolled his eyes. "Don't ask," he said.

In the mid-nineteen-nineties, Jibril Rajoub, Marwan Barghouti, who led the Fatah militia, and Muhammad Dahlan, the head of security for the Palestinian Authority in the Gaza Strip, were considered potential successors to "the Old Man"—Arafat. Unlike Jibril, his colleagues won seats in the new parliament, despite certain disadvantages: Barghouti is in jail serving five life sentences (plus forty years) for helping to kill four Israelis and a Greek monk; Dahlan is thought to have enriched himself and his extended family outrageously and illegally. Jibril, however, could not overcome the complexities of his history and his personality. During the campaign, his reputation suffered not only because of his arrogance—the swaggering demeanor, the wealth he has allegedly acquired—but also because he had lost touch with his potential voters. Since returning to the West Bank from the PLO's exile in Tunis, he has lived and worked almost entirely in Jericho and Ramallah.

Khalid Amayreh, a journalist in Dura who writes for the Al Jazeera Web site, told me, "Jibril is flamboyant, ostentatious, a self-inflated egomaniac with a sense of megalomania. His tongue often functions much more quickly than his mind. He is no intellectual. As they say, 'Manchester born, Manchester bred, / Strong in the arm, weak in the head.' In his speeches he attacked his opponents hysterically and frantically, calling them all kinds of names. He said, 'I was shooting Israelis when Sheikh Nayef was still playing with little kids.' And he mocked Hamas. It was all a public-relations disaster."

Mocking Hamas when Hamas has been able to build a reputation among Palestinians for grass-roots charity and incorruptibility was a dubious strategy for any Fatah candidate. In Palestinian eyes, Hamas had created a kind of shadow civil society long before it won a reputation for suicide bombings.

One morning, I visited the Islamic Charitable Society, in Hebron, a sprawling facility for several thousand children that includes schools, a medical clinic, and an orphanage. The director, a former marketing manager named Khalil Herbawi, said that the society was funded by various Western non-governmental organizations, by Arab groups, and by private donors. Herbawi's predecessor was in Hamas and had been arrested in 2002 for helping to finance and plan an attack on the nearby settlement of Adora. Herbawi said that he had voted for Hamas in the elections but added, "I am not in Hamas myself." Last September, Israeli troops took over the society's administrative building, confiscating documents, fax machines, printers, and computers and then sealing the doors as if it were a crime scene, an action that outraged Herbawi.

"The Israelis say that we take care of children whose parents martyred themselves," Herbawi said. "But we take all the orphans, the ones whose parents are suicide bombers or who died of cancer or heart attacks. . . . Of the thousand orphans here, only twenty or twenty-one are orphans because of suicide bombing. Another twenty or so are children of collaborators who were killed. So it evens out."

As we looked in on classrooms full of children learning math and science and then looked out from a balcony onto a playground filled with girls, all of them wearing the *hijab,* Herbawi said, "Is this terrorism? Maybe they will arrest me, too."

Such institutions understandably helped make Hamas popular. Gaza and the West Bank are poor, and although in the past decade Western and Arab governments have poured billions of dollars into the accounts of the Palestinian Authority, most Palestinians believe that, thanks to the corruption of Fatah, they have been systematically robbed of much of that aid money. Western intelligence agencies believe that Hamas has used its social institutions for armed operations, indoctrinating children in schools, inciting violence and recruiting cells in mosques, establishing safe houses, and providing funds for weapons and for the families of fighters who have blown themselves up for the cause.

In 1998, Sheikh Yassin said that the political and social branches of Hamas could not be distinguished from the military. "We cannot separate the wing from the body," he said, according to a report by Reuters. "If we do so, the body will not be able to fly. Hamas is one body."

In most Palestinian cities and towns, the elections were so consuming that for weeks campaign placards replaced the usual posters of young men and women hoisting AK-47 rifles in their last moments alive. Democracy obscured the cult of martyrdom. Fatah outspent Hamas and the smaller parties, and the Bush Administration funneled nearly two million dollars through U.S.A.I.D. funding projects in the occupied territories that it hoped would help Fatah's election chances.

Hamas did manage to hire Nashat Aqtash, a professor of media studies at Bir Zeit University, to advise them on public relations. Aqtash told me when I visited him in Ramallah that his job was not as difficult as it seemed to outsiders. "For you, Hamas is suicide bombing and that's it," he said. "But suicide bombing is only a small fraction of what Hamas is for the Palestinian people." Hamas, he insisted, was "all pluses, no minuses." Its image of distributing charity and having borne the brunt of the Al Aqsa intifada and, by contrast, Fatah's almost surreal disorganization was just part of the story. The American contributions backfired. "The Palestinians are stubborn and don't want to be told what to do, least of all by the United States of America," he said.

Hamas ran three television commercials in the last week of the campaign, and none of them called on the familiar imagery of teenage martyrs and declarations of jihad. Aqtash showed me the ads on his computer screen. One ad alternated images of Palestinian children suffering at the hands of Israeli soldiers and the words "Our blood"—in red—"is a fence to protect our holy places." Very soft-soap by Hamas standards. Another featured Ismail Haniyeh, Hamas's lead candidate on the national slate, who is expected to be named Prime Minister. "We will protect the resistance movement until we gain back all the occupied territories," Haniyeh said, speaking almost in a whisper.

Aqtash had counseled Hamas candidates not to talk about killing Israelis and to limit their speeches about taking back all of historical Palestine. "You see," he said proudly, "it is clear that he means the territories occupied in 1967. Only crazy people talk about going beyond the 1967 borders."

If a Hamas-led government was going to attract funds from abroad for the Palestinians, I asked, what was its next public-relations strategy?

Aqtash smiled and reminded me that his contract had run out on Election Day; nevertheless, he offered some final words of advice. "Our rhetoric was ineffective because we used Islamic rhetoric that is understandable to us but incomprehensible, and scary, to you," he said. "At funerals, you would see masked people carrying rifles. In Gaza, this is a cultural thing, trying to show our grief and support to the families. But these images in the West mean 'We will kill you.' We need to organize the Palestinian message to the West and put it in a context that the West can understand. Israelis kill Palestinians, but they also have the talent to explain themselves."

Stout, smiling through a scowl, and sitting in his chair with one arm slung over his seatback like a sultan, Jibril Rajoub instantly became the focal point of his younger brother's living room. A boy appeared balancing a tray holding many glasses of tea. Jibril was served first. Sheikh Nayef began to work his worry beads at a fantastic clip while Jibril talked about devoting himself to the revival of Fatah and trying to coexist with Hamas as a matter of familial duty.

"Having a brother in Hamas is O.K., and I am proud of him," he said. "Sheikh Nayef is a moderate, he's realistic, a pragmatist. He was never an extremist. Politically, in the nineties, there were two different strategies. We in Fatah saw certain things as the rules of the game where negotiations were concerned. But in the past five years the Israelis stopped dealing with the Palestinian Authority as a partner, and the gap between the two Palestinian factions grew smaller. . . . We'll remain in the opposition as an honest partner, and we won't try to undermine Hamas's authority. We wish them success."

Jibril had imprisoned many Hamas activists in his time, but now he acted the part of the defeated opponent graciously offering advice to his successors. "Most people in Hamas are realistic," he said. "I don't think anything will take place on a social level—like forcing women to wear the *hijab*. Hamas has to focus on international legitimacy and assure the international community that an Islamic leadership will contribute to regional stability."

A couple of days later, I visited Jibril at his office in Ramallah. During the Al Aqsa intifada, the Israelis shelled the building, but now it was repaired and filled with aides gossiping about Jibril's future and the coming of Hamas. Jibril gave me a copy of his "autobiography"—a book-length series of interviews about his years in Israeli prisons, his ascension to Arafat's circle, and his contacts with Israeli and American intelligence. The book featured photographs of him as a young man in Israeli custody and also ones of him—older, heavier—with George Tenet, Nelson Mandela, and Israeli officials. Jibril knew that such relationships, a remnant of the Oslo years, were part of what killed his election chances.

"There are all kinds of stories about how close I was to the Americans, the CIA, and all the rest," Jibril said bitterly. "But how close? When I had cancer in 2002, after I left Preventive Security, I was treated first in Egypt, and they urged me to go to the Mayo Clinic, in Minnesota. But I was refused an American visa." He went to England instead. "I never once talked with the Israelis without a green light from Abu Amar," he went on, using Arafat's *nom de guerre*. "And after I met with the Israelis I always reported straight to him."

Jibril had been at Arafat's side, but it had always been a prickly relationship. In Tunis, according to Matt Rees's book *Cain's Field,* Rajoub once refused Arafat's request to drive his future wife, Suha Tawil, to the airport on the ground that he would not "chauffeur a whore." In May 2002, Arafat fired Jibril as the head of Preventive Security after the Israelis demanded that the various Palestinian security agencies be put under Rajoub's control. A month earlier, Israel had attacked Jibril's compound. Jibril and his men had been allowed to escape, but only after giving up the Islamist prisoners in their custody. In 2003, Arafat brought Jibril back into the Palestinian leadership, appointing him national-security adviser. "Our relationship had its ups and downs, which happens in any relationship that goes on for many years," Jibril said. "At a certain point, Arafat felt that I was a threat to his regime, but I was always loyal to him. He was always the symbol of the Palestinian people and contributed to the cause more than anyone else."

After Arafat died, in November 2004, and his heir in Fatah, Mahmoud Abbas, won election as President of the Palestinian Authority, Hamas had an easier time portraying itself as the incorruptible champion of resistance and Fatah as a spent force. Among his doubters, Abbas is considered timid, indecisive, and incapable of extracting anything from the Israelis. Jibril fought with Arafat over many issues, but he said, "If Arafat were still alive, Hamas would never have won. Arafat's loss was a loss for everyone and in every way. He was the only Palestinian leader truly committed to the reconciliation of two peoples. He had the long view."

If Arafat had such a long view, I asked, why did he turn down a deal at Camp David in 2000 that, for all its deficiencies, would have been a far better arrangement than anything contemplated by the Israelis today? Sheikh Nayef had told me that Camp David would have been an "unacceptable betrayal." His brother did not answer directly, but it was clear that his opinion was not the same.

"Excuse me! Why ask this question?" he said. "The Israelis talk of unilateralism now. Camp David is long over. There's no use crying over spilled milk."

The Israelis have begun an election campaign of their own, to choose a successor to Ariel Sharon, who has been in a coma since early January, when he suffered a stroke. And even though they are well aware that Sharon's unilateral withdrawal from Gaza last year has been interpreted by Hamas as a credit to armed resistance, all polls show that the Kadima Party, led by Olmert, Sharon's deputy prime minister, will win. Olmert gave an interview to Israel's Channel 2 making it plain that, like Sharon, he planned to close dozens of smaller settlements on the West Bank but retain the main blocs of Ariel, Gush Etzion, and Ma'ale Adumim. He said that he would also retain "control" of the Jordan Valley and sovereignty over all of Jerusalem. This is less than what Ehud Barak and Bill Clinton proposed to Arafat five years ago, and it came as no surprise that the Hamas leadership dignified Olmert's offer only with mockery. In Cairo, Musa Abu-Marzuq, who once led the Hamas political bureau from northern Virginia, said, "When we restore historical Palestine, the Jews can come live with us. They will then acquire the Palestinian nationality."

In early February, while the Hamas leadership made plans for a new government, the security situation deteriorated. Gaza was turning into a lawless state, with Palestinian militias launching Qassam rockets into Israeli territory and the Israeli Army killing militants, mainly from the air. In Hebron, local Islamists assaulted the headquarters of a European observer team; a dozen Danes on the team had to be escorted out of Hebron by the Israeli Army—precisely the soldiers they had been sent to observe. The same week, the Israelis arrested a group of religious militants who "identify with Hamas" and charged them with killing six Jews in the past year.

In Israel, there was no sense that the rise of Hamas could be dismissed simply as a protest vote. Even a liberal scholar like Emmanuel Sivan, an expert in fundamentalism who has met Sheikh Yassin and other Hamas representatives over the years, told me, "If you are living in Israel it is always good to be anxious. We are a state living on edge." He did say, however, that "the typical American-Jewish oy-vey reaction" was not warranted.

"An Arab friend told me, 'Fatah is the crime and Hamas is the punishment,'" Sivan said. "Three-quarters of the Palestinians want a long-term arrangement with Israel and understand they have got only so far with violence, but they also want the rascals out." The biggest danger facing Israel, he said, was that anarchy would begin to prevail, with uncontrolled militias and criminal gangs causing such a state of unrest that elements from Al Qaeda could exploit the situation and make their way to Gaza and the West Bank.

The Israeli security establishment is particularly worried about the relationship between Hamas and the Islamic regime in Tehran. "I am concerned about Iran's efforts to engulf Israel with Islamist fundamentalist terror groups on the border: with Hezbollah in southern Lebanon, and with Hamas in Gaza and the West Bank," Yuval Steinitz, the chairman of the Defense and Foreign Affairs committee in the Knesset, told me. "If Hamas takes control of the Palestinian armed forces and police, that means it will establish an armed threat right near Jerusalem, Tel Aviv, and Ben-Gurion airport." Avi Dichter, who recently stepped down as the head of Shin Bet, the Israeli FBI, and is now running for a seat in the Knesset, said that while the Israeli military had killed, arrested, or detained dozens of Hamas fighters and leaders during the Al Aqsa intifada, support from Iran, and the new ability to operate in Gaza with less Israeli interference, means that the militias remain a threat. In addition, Fatah's own battalions, which adopted suicide bombing as a tactic in order to keep up with Hamas in the race for street credibility, have not disbanded, despite repeated statements from Abbas decrying violence.

For all the anxiety about Hamas, there remains in Israeli society a broad consensus for a two-state solution—a desire born less of an Oslo-era optimism about an integrated "new Middle East" and more of sheer weariness with occupation and an understanding that to retain the territories is to risk the Zionist idea of maintaining a Jewish majority in a democratic state.

"I don't see any chance of reaching an agreement that you would call real peace between the Israelis and the Palestinians," Shlomo Gazit, a retired, dovish Army general who used to command the West Bank and Gaza, told me. "This is not in the stars for the next hundred years. The Arab world does not accept a foreign people, a foreign religion, in the Middle East. All we can strive for is practical coexistence."

"There is no resolution to this conflict," Yehoshua Porath, a scholar of Middle Eastern history, says. "It is like a person living with a chronic disease for which there is no cure. You take palliatives and partial remedies. You know there is no final cure yet, but you keep investing in the search. Here the final cure is a peace settlement."

In Gaza and the West Bank, the politicians, academics, and activists who were shocked by the Hamas victory have also searched for ways to soften the blow. The most common argument is that Hamas did not win many more votes than Fatah; it took fifty-six per cent of the seats but with only forty-four per cent of the vote. Part of the reason for the landslide is that Fatah ran an inept campaign, often putting forward more than one candidate against a single Hamas candidate, and splitting the vote. Hamas was also the beneficiary of a collective protest against the Palestinian Authority's inability to cope with Sharon and Olmert, and the indignity of occupation. But the idea that Hamas will modify its ideology because it is now faced with the prospect of making good on its promises, of creating jobs and collecting the garbage, of day-to-day governing, does not impress many Palestinian analysts. In Iran, after all, Ahmadinejad came to power not because of his insistence on building a nuclear weapon or his anti-Semitic rhetoric; he, too, won popularity largely on social issues.

Ghassan Khatib, the Palestinian Authority's minister of planning, told me that the Fatah hierarchy is worried that there is a direct relationship between poverty and radical fundamentalism, and if the situation in the territories worsens an even more radical Hamas will take hold.

"The Muslim Brotherhood believes that it is possible to reestablish the Islamic regimes in the Islamic world and reach the point of a single Islamic superpower, as in the old days," Khatib said. "It wants to be a huge modern state and compete with the modern superpowers. But it's a fantasy. You cannot govern by Islam. Islamic ideology is not suitable for that. It has fixed ideas on economics and government that are inflexible and irrelevant for modern times.

"Hamas can moderate in the tactical sense, but not fundamentally. It will play tactics on the question of violence and in its political slogans. What it wants is the freedom to maneuver, to build people into 'real and proper Muslims,' to keep building its base. . . . This is very dangerous for the Palestinians, and they should think about ending this Hamas majority. The Israelis need to take the opportunity to negotiate with Abbas and the peace camp. There are three years until the next Presidential elections. This is the historical window of opportunity. If Hamas wins the Presidency, that will be the end of it."

For the moment, Abbas does have greater power than the legislature. But Hamas has every intention of continuing to play what its leaders call "the democracy game" and winning it outright. One night in Hebron, I dropped by the Hamas headquarters to see Aziz al-Dweik, who will be joining the legislature next month as speaker of parliament.

When he was a young man, Dweik studied in Jordan and then earned a doctorate in urban and regional planning at the University of Pennsylvania. The geography of his life has been varied: he spent eight years in Philadelphia, one year in southern Lebanon with his fellow-Islamists in forced exile, and four in an Israeli prison.

When Dweik returned to Hebron in 1988, he said, "I spoke my mind just as I did in the mosque at the University of Pennsylvania." The Israelis did not appreciate it, jailing him several times for incitement and for membership in Hamas, which had been outlawed by Israel.

I mentioned that *The Jerusalem Post* had published a Hamas poster from the Al Aqsa intifada period that yoked together portraits of Sheikh Yassin, Shamil Basayev, a Chechen rebel leader, and Osama bin Laden. If Hamas was going to present itself as a rational political group, I said, why was it linking itself to Al Qaeda?

"Bin Laden is a fighter for the cause of Islam, and this man has his way of serving his God," Dweik said. "He has offered the West a truce many times, saying that he will put down his arms if the West stops interfering in our affairs. We have no right to hate bin Laden. We respect him. Hiding this fact does not serve the truth."

This was the most arresting aspect of the Hamas leaders; their thinking—their charter, their goals, short-range and long—was unconcealed and calmly provided. While diplomats and journalists sifted through the language looking for shades of meaning, Hamas was politely answering every question. Hamas is focused primarily on the question of Palestine, of forming a government and resisting the Israeli occupation, but it also sees the election as part of a regional phenomenon, a historical tide, which, with time, not only would dislodge a few hundred settlers from Hebron but could cross borders into Egypt, Jordan, and beyond.

"Whenever and wherever people are given the choice, this is what happens," Dweik said. "Secularism is an import. It's not indigenous. Islam is a practical and idealistic way of life. Islam is the religion of God, which God has chosen for the guidance of mankind.

"Please stop asking us to recognize the occupier and not the needs of our own lives. This is slavery, slavery of a kind that did not even happen in Africa or in any other country! The Jews suffered the Holocaust, but it only happened for a short period of time. The Palestinians have been living a whole century in a holocaust. . . . The truth is on our side. The Israelis have the illusion that truth is on their side, but the Koran is the last revelation. The Israelis in this city have to move somewhere else. They have to acknowledge the facts on the ground. The future is ours.

"The situation with the Rajoub brothers, well, you may call it the ongoing conflict between secularism and Islam. The big brother is a secularist and the younger is an Islamist. But the Islamist won in a democratic vote. The two brothers gave you the shape of history—one has prevailed and the other will vanish."

(2006)

Part V

Kid Dynamite Blows Up: Mike Tyson

The conventions of the ring demand that a fighter in training become a monk. For months at a time, he hardens his body on roadwork and beefsteak, and practices an enforced loneliness—even (tradition has it) sexual loneliness—the better to focus the mind on war. Mike Tyson's monastery in the Nevada desert is a mansion next door to Wayne Newton's mansion, and it could be said to lack the usual austerity. There is a chandelier worthy of Cap d'Antibes. There is a painting on silk of Diana Ross. There are books, magazines, a big television, leather couches. But the diversions are not what they could be. When Tyson is not preparing for fights, he keeps lions and tigers around as pets and wrestles with them. "Sometimes I go swimming with the tiger," he told a visitor. "But, personally, I'm a lion man. Lions are very obedient, like dogs." Tyson was keeping his pets elsewhere, though. He has estates in Ohio, in Connecticut, and off a fairway on the Congressional Country Club, in Bethesda, Maryland. The big cats are most often in Ohio. The Nevada mansion is surrounded by life-size statues of warrior heroes whom Tyson has read about and come to revere: Genghis Khan, Toussaint-Louverture, Alexander the Great, Hannibal. "Hannibal was very courageous," Tyson said. "He rode elephants through Cartilage." In a week's time, Tyson himself would be going through cartilage, too.

After spending three years in an Indiana prison for raping a teenager named Desiree Washington, Tyson went back to fighting in 1995. He denied to the end that he had ever raped anyone, but he said he was a better man now. Tyson converted to Islam—indeed, the bumper sticker on his Bentley reads "I ♥ Allah"—and he told his visitors in jail that he had spent his time studying the Koran, Machiavelli, Voltaire, Dumas, the lives of Meyer Lansky and Bugsy Siegel, "and a lot of Communist literature." He ordered up icons for his shoulders, a diptych tattoo: Arthur Ashe on one side, Mao Zedong on the other. He declared himself ready to regain his place in boxing. He would reclaim not only his title but also his image of invincibility. Iron Mike. Kid Dynamite. Once more, he would be the fighter who had expressed only disappointment after a knockout of one Jesse Ferguson, saying, "I wanted to hit him one more time in the nose so that bone could go up into his brain."

But after easily dispatching a selection of unworthies who provided an extended warmup drill worth tens of millions of dollars, Tyson finally met a real fighter, if not a great one, named Evander Holyfield, who backed him down and beat him up. Holyfield took Tyson's title last November, in one of the cleverest displays of boxing guile since February 1964, when Muhammad Ali, then Cassius Clay, stunned another invincible—Tyson's fistic precursor, Sonny Liston. Liston, like Tyson, had grown up in an environment of crime and never left it; Liston had done time for armed robbery, he mugged people, he beat up a cop, he broke heads for the Mob. And, like Tyson, he was considered a killer in the ring, unbeatable. Against Clay, Liston had been favored so strongly that the lead boxing writer for *The New York Times* skipped the fight and left it to a rookie in the office, Robert Lipsyte. But Clay, with his magnificent speed, dodged Liston's plodding bombs and bloodied the big man's eye. Liston quit on his stool, claiming a sore shoulder. Against Holyfield, Tyson had been similarly unmasked. "He's like any bully," said Gil Clancy, one of the game's legendary trainers. "Once Tyson saw his own blood, he backed down." The referee stopped the beating in the eleventh round. When it was over, Tyson was in such a daze that he turned to one of his handlers and asked, "What round did I knock him out in?"

The rematch with Holyfield would be worth thirty million dollars to Tyson, thirty-five million to Holyfield. The fight's promoter, Don King, whose good word, of course, is all one ever needs, promised record receipts for the live gate and pay-per-view television: "A hundred and fifty million, maybe two hundred million. After all, we got three billion people in Red China alone!" Whatever. If Tyson won, he would regain not only his championship but also his place as "the baddest man on the planet." Holyfield would be remembered as a fighter who on a given night had risen above himself and then, in the rematch, fell to earth.

After coming out of jail, Tyson showed signs of domestic stability. In April, he married a doctor named Monica Turner. (Turner's first husband was sentenced to ten years in prison on a cocaine-dealing charge.) Tyson and Turner have one child; another is due this summer. Until now, marriage had been a miserable topic for Tyson. His first wife, the television star Robin Givens, was famously manipulative. She had been a Sarah Lawrence girl and, even in public, treated Tyson with an airy condescension. There were, in some cynical corners, suspicions that Givens had actually married for money. Tyson was not slow to express his annoyance. The former light-heavyweight champion José Torres once asked Tyson what the best blow he had ever thrown was. "Man, I'll never forget that punch," Tyson said. "It was when I fought with Robin in Steve's apartment. She really offended me and I went *bam,* and she flew backward, hitting every fucking wall in the apartment." The marriage ended in divorce.

Unlike Givens, Turner has, for the most part, stayed out of her husband's business affairs and out of camera range, and there have been no reports of fights, physical or otherwise. Turner mainly stayed away from Las Vegas. Tyson's most frequent visitors at his desert house were the members of his entourage, each in his own way a sterling influence: Don King, a former numbers runner from Cleveland who once stomped a man to death in a dispute over six hundred dollars and then became the greatest carnival barker since Barnum; Tyson's co-managers, Rory Holloway, an old friend, and John Horne, a failed standup comic from Albany who specializes in yelling at reporters; Tyson's trainer, Richie Giachetti, a street guy from Cleveland who worked with Larry Holmes; and a self-described "master motivator" named Steve (Crocodile) Fitch, who admits that "in another life" he spent five years in jail for manslaughter. ("But I didn't do it," he told me. "A complete setup.") Crocodile proved to be a prophetic character. During the week leading up to the fight, he could be seen in fatigues and wraparound shades, all the while screaming his suggestive war cries: "It's time for ultimate battle! Ultimate battle! Time to bite! Time to bite!"

. . .

Tyson avoided the press—especially the print media. Horne and Holloway had done a good job of convincing him that the papers were filled with nothing but lies, that the New York reporters on the boxing beat— Michael Katz, of the *Daily News,* Wallace Matthews, of the *Post*—were out to get them. Early in the morning, before the sun was high, Tyson ran along the empty desert roads. Then he sparred in the gym. His workouts were closed. For recreation, he watched one gangster movie after another, sometimes through the night. He is partial to James Cagney, Edward G. Robinson, and John Garfield. He can recite whole scenes of *Raging Bull, On the Waterfront,* and—his favorite—*The Harder They Fall.*

Tyson would have preferred to be alone—or, at least, alone with his entourage and his movies—but Don King knew that in order to rouse pay-per-view orders the goat had to be fed. Tyson would not allow interviews at his house, but five days before the fight he agreed to go out to King's place to meet with a group of writers. And so on an afternoon of long shadows and hundred-degree heat a couple of white vans pulled out of the driveway of the MGM Grand Hotel, away from the new family-friendly downtown, away from the Brooklyn Bridge and the black glass Pyramid of Cheops, away from the palace of the Caesars and the Folies Bergere, out of earshot, finally, of the unending music of the city, the air-conditioned hum and the mad electronic ringing of a thousand acres of slot machines and the slushy spill of silver coins pouring into curved silver trays. Don King does not live on the Strip. He lives out where it is quiet, at the outermost edge of the city, where the desert resumes.

In all honesty, no one would ride to the edge of the desert to talk with Evander Holyfield. No one much cared about Holyfield. He was likable enough. But he was dull copy. He hadn't raped anyone. He hadn't been to jail. He talked about Jesus Christ all the time and literally sang gospel music while hitting the heavy bag. He seemed like a good fellow, but what story did he offer? He talked in the polite clichés of doing my best, having faith in my abilities and in the will of God—but what did he mean? Heavyweight championship fights, from the days of John L. Sullivan onward, are stories, morality plays, and this story, regardless of its end, was all about Tyson. This was a war between middle-class aspiration and ghetto insolence, gospel and rap. Without Tyson there was no sense of danger, no interest, no hundred million dollars.

"People are full of shit. They want to see something dark," Tyson's former trainer Teddy Atlas told me. "People want to feel close to it and in on it, but, of course, only from the distance of their suburban homes. They want to have the benefit of comfort, security, safety, respect, and at the same time the privilege of watching something out of control—even promote it being out of control—as long as we can be secure that we're not accountable for it. With Tyson, the dark thing was always the anticipation that someone was going to get knocked out. The whole Kid Dynamite thing. But we wanted to believe that the monster was also a nice kid. We wanted to believe that Mike Tyson was an American story: the kid who grows up in the horrible ghetto and then converts that dark power into a good cause, into boxing. But then the story takes a turn. The dark side overwhelms him. He's cynical, he's out of control. And now the story is even better. It's like a double feature now, like you're getting *Heidi* and *Godzilla* at the same time."

King's minions wanted the reporters to understand that this was a special invitation—a very rare one, these days. The whole charade seemed absurd to the reporters who had been around boxing for a while. Until not so long ago, fighters before a big bout were available athletes, the least guarded of men. Like sultans, they often used to greet their visitors propped up on a few pillows in bed; reporters would sit perched at the edge of the bed or hard on the floor, notebooks out, ready to catch pearls. Archie Moore, the great light-heavyweight, could unburden himself of a monologue worthy of Molly Bloom or the Duke of Gloucester. Boxers were free of the solemn self-importance of modern athletes in the team sports. They liked having people around. In the moments before fighting for the championship, Floyd Patterson napped in his dressing room, and a few writers were allowed to stay around, close enough to register the movement under the champion's eyelids, the timbre of his snore. Patterson would describe his dreams, the depths of his fear. He talked and talked, one of the great analysands of the prize ring.

Tyson used to be like that. When he was coming up as a fighter, and even as a young champion, he loved to talk to the press, tell his story. He was immensely aware of himself as the star of an ongoing Cagney movie. Some writers even saw a sweetness in him, the yearning for love and a home. Certainly it was a life beyond the imagination of the middle-class reporters who came calling. He was the kid from Amboy Street in Brooklyn's Brownsville, an especially vicious and hopeless delinquent. When he was six, his idea of a prank was to slit his big brother's arm with a razor while he slept. His father was nowhere in evidence, his mother was overwhelmed by poverty. Tyson idolized the pimps and the thieves in the neighborhood, and by the time he was ten he was mugging old ladies and shooting into crowds for kicks. As he told his story, he could sense the titillation in the writer, and more details would pour out: "I'd shoot real close to them, skin them or something, make them take off their pants and then go run in the streets." After he had racked up dozens of arrests and was sent off to reform school, Cus D'Amato, an old and eccentric trainer who had settled upstate, along the Hudson, took him in. D'Amato was a kindly paranoiac. When he was still working out of the Gramercy Gym, in Manhattan, he used to sleep in the back with nothing to keep him company but a shotgun and a dog. To his fighters, he was a kind of Father Divine, at once inspiring and full of righteous gas. He preached the value of terror, the way that all fighters faced fear and the good ones learned to harness it, to make it their friend. He was an ascetic. Money, he said, "was something to throw off the back of trains." Writers loved D'Amato, the way any writer would have loved, say, Moll Flanders had she been presented, whole, in real life, and available for quotation.

Tyson represented D'Amato's last hope—the chance, after Patterson and José Torres, to have a third world champion. As if to satisfy every convention of the boxing movie, D'Amato "adopted" Tyson, became his legal guardian, but he died a year before his "son" won the crown. On winning the title, Tyson wept. If only Cus had seen it, he said, if only Cus were here. It was over the top, even for Hollywood, but not for the conventions of the boxing story.

Tyson was also good copy partly because he was brutal and unabashed about being so. Unlike Ali, whose helium rants usually had more to do with camp comedy or the prophecies of Elijah Muhammad than with the violence of his profession, Tyson was blunt, clinical. He knew he had been trained to hurt other men, and he saw no good reason to deflect attention from that. He was in the beating business and he had never acquired the tact or the reflexes to say he didn't enjoy it. In his comically high voice, he spoke of throwing punches with "bad intentions to vital areas," of blows to the heart, to the kidneys, to the liver, and the pleasure he took in delivering them. He talked of his yearning to break an opponent's eardrum, to shatter his will, to make him "cry like a woman."

At the same time, Tyson was self-aware, almost academic in his regard for boxing. In a time when most baseball players hardly know the name Jackie Robinson, Tyson grew obsessed not just with all the obvious contemporaries and near contemporaries but also with Harry Greb and Kid

Chocolate, with Willie Pep and Stanley Ketchel. The writers ate that up. With boxing under attack as crippling, as atavistic and cruel, his talk made them feel that their subject was important, somehow—not merely a skein of beatings in the parking lots of betting parlors but a matter of aesthetics and history. Tyson spent hundreds of hours watching old fights, and from those films he not only learned the details of his craft but also assumed certain traits of favored precursors. He cut his hair to resemble Jack Dempsey's. He took to wearing bulky button-up sweaters because he had seen such sweaters on some of the old fighters in the old newsreels. And so, while Tyson's story was not Ali's, while he lacked that level of wit, physical improvisation, and epic, his story was a good one, good enough for half a dozen biographies, good enough, certainly, to make him the best-paid athlete in history.

We drove out Flamingo Road, past the plastic-surgery parlors, past all the clip joints and software palaces that look as if they were built last week. We arrived at a "gated community," one of the high-security mansion neighborhoods that you see now in every city where there is sun and money and heightened fear of larceny. We rang the buzzer and the gates swung open. Don King's house is Spanish style, perhaps—a riot of white stucco. There were Range Rovers and BMWs parked outside and an enormous satellite dish parked on the roof. We walked up the front steps and were greeted by a portrait of Don King. The real thing was in the kitchen.

"Welcome! Welcome to my home!" he boomed. King invited us in for an early dinner. He had ordered out from Popeyes.

King is the evil genius of boxing, the latest in a long line. His electrified hair is merely a way to use "personality" to hide his substance. In his way, he is even more powerful than the so-called Octopus Inc., of the nineteen-fifties—James Norris's corrupt International Boxing Club. Tyson, like so many boxers, cannot bear King. He does not especially trust King. But he does business with King, because King is the singular presence in big-time boxing. They make a lot of money together, and so Tyson is as indulgent of King's conniving as King is of Tyson's tantrums. There is no profit in judgment.

In the kitchen, King was telling me that three billion people would watch the fight. The key was penetration, he said—that is, how many people would sign up for the fifty-dollar fee and order the fight on pay-per-view. "If we get ten percent of the universe, then we'll be fine," he added. He never quite explained what that meant. He knew I would not bother to ask. "Mike generates more capital than anyone in the history of the world. Why do they want to destroy him, the goose that laid the golden egg?"

After a long wait, Tyson showed up. He took his place on a white leather couch. As he waited for the first question, he assumed the expression of a man who has eaten a bad egg and is waiting to be sick. One by one the questions came, and Tyson answered them in a way designed to make the questioner feel like an idiot. Yes, he felt good. No, he wouldn't make the same mistakes again against Holyfield. Yes, he expected to win. But, no, it wouldn't change his life if he lost. "The way my deals are set up, I'm pretty much set." At times, he spoke as a man obsessed less with a fight than with the rational distribution of his mutual funds.

To be with Tyson even for just a couple of hours is to witness the power of a ghetto kid's fatalism. He has, his accountants claimed, all he could ever want. He will never—or should never—end up like Joe Louis, coked up on the casino floor, working as a greeter. And yet he is forever saying "My life is over" and "I am taking the blows for my children." He has a boundless sense of self-drama, of the dark future. Even here, surrounded by his co-managers Rory Holloway and John Horne, he said he had no friends, he trusted no one. And who could doubt him?

"We have to trust, but people by nature are not to be trusted," Tyson said. "That's just the way it is. I got a Machiavellian effect as far as that's concerned. I'm not a philosopher, I'm not Machiavelli in that respect, but you can't be a person always willing to do good in an environment where people are always willing to do bad. You know what I mean?

"I have no friends, man. When I got out of prison, all my old friends, they had to go. If you don't have a purpose in my life, man, you have to go. . . . Why would you want someone around in your life if they have no purpose? Just to have a pal or a buddy? I got a wife. My wife can be my pal and buddy. I'm not trying to be cold, but it's something I picked up. . . . If I'm gonna get screwed, I'm not gonna get screwed over by the people that screwed me before. I'm gonna get screwed by the *new* people.

"I've been taken advantage of all my life. I've been used, I've been dehumanized, I've been humiliated, and I've been betrayed. That's basically the outcome of my life, and I'm kind of bitter, kind of angry at certain people about it. . . . Everyone in boxing makes out well except for the fighter. He's the only one who suffers, basically. He's the only one who's on Skid Row. He's the only one who loses his mind. He sometimes goes insane, he sometimes goes on the bottle, because it's a highly intensive, pressure sport, and a lot of people lose it. There's so much you can take and then you break."

In an effort to lighten Tyson's mood, some of the writers started asking about a subject close to his heart: his new family. For a few moments, he was as fuzzy as a character in *thirtysomething.*

"That's all I have, my children," he said. "Wives are known to run off and fall in love with other people, because they are human, even die. But you have to take care of children. . . . The way I see it is that every fight I have is for their future. Every fight. Every fight is a different future for my children." Tyson said that he played games with his kids, ate ice cream with them. "They love *Barney,*" he said. "I *hate Barney.*

"I have a stepdaughter and one day she was crying and she says, 'Mama, Jane don't want to play with me today.' And I burst out, 'She doesn't want to play with you? Then fuck her!' My wife didn't like that too much. But we're different people. She studied psychology and believes in working on a kid's mind. I believe in being strict—if you get out of line, you're getting hit! They're too young for that now, but I'm a strong believer in that. I think kids should learn discipline. If they get out of line, they should learn discipline. At what age? I don't know. Ten years old?

"See, I've been beaten all my life. My kids have parents, one's a doctor, a bright woman, and a father who's a . . . a father who's rich. I had an alcoholic and a pimp for parents. So they're gonna have a great life, if they don't turn out to be bad children. . . . I just don't want them out on the street, because these hustlers, they can be very exciting, people gravitate to them. I survived it, but they may not be lucky enough to survive. All my real friends are in prison or dead. The ones still out are so messed up on drugs they don't know their own name."

It was as if Tyson knew something that no one else knew—not his accountants, not his managers. He was convinced of his own wretched end. Nothing, save the well-being of his kids, would please him. Last summer, Tyson threw himself a million-dollar three-day-long thirtieth-birthday party at his estate in Farmington, Connecticut. There were magnums of Cristal, and cigars rolled specially for the occasion. Tyson handed out BMWs and Range Rovers to six of his flunkies. And yet he had an awful time. "I don't know half the people here," he said as he wandered his many acres. "This isn't what I wanted."

Horne and Holloway may know nothing about boxing, but they have been expert at feeding Tyson's sense of persecution. "Nobody's on our side," Tyson told us as his co-managers nodded like proud puppeteers.

"The courts are against us, the corporations are against us, the news reporters are against us, the papers—your bosses—are against us. We have nobody on our side, and we're still fighting and we're still doing well. If we had you guys on our side, we'd be a phenomenon!"

From the back of the room, King yelled, "If you would just print the truth! You write what people throw out to you as a smoke screen!"

"The fact is, they call us monsters, that we're inhuman, they want people to be afraid of us," Tyson said. (In fact, Tyson has always cultivated that image. He once told his former friend José Torres, "I like to hurt women when I make love to them. I like to hear them scream with pain, to see them bleed. It gives me pleasure.")

"Who do you mean?" one of the reporters said. "Who's calling you monsters?"

"You. Not you individually, but reporters," Tyson said. "They write that we're monsters, that we're hideous, that we commit heinous crimes."

"Let's take the Newfield book, for example," said King, referring to Jack Newfield's scrupulous biography of him. "The Newfield book is all lies, and yet everyone uses it as the defining factor on me! Everything in there is a lie! So a guy who's a good writer knows how to *speculize* and *dramatize* those lies! You know what I mean?"

"They hope it leads to you being incarcerated," said Horne, who was standing at Tyson's shoulder.

"Look," Tyson said. "Don is still a fool to have you over to his house and talk to you. He had to beg me to come over here and talk to you, because of what you guys write about me. The people that know me, love me, they read this. It feels like shit.

"And this guy, knowing you guys ain't gonna give him no justice, he still, stupidly, has you guys in his house talking to you, knowing you'll write it was a good fight and then try to put his ass in jail. They're gonna write some madman tales, how he robbed this guy and killed this other guy. I don't know. I wasn't there when he killed the guy, but, shit, if a guy got killed he was probably doing something he wasn't supposed to be doing. You know what I mean? I'm a strong believer in that. Not in a drive-by shooting, but very few people get killed for no reason, from where I come from."

King was delighted by this moving show of support. "Just watch me prove that he attacked me," he said. "All I want is fair play! I'm still crazy enough to love America!"

We, the Americans, must have been moved to the core. There was a long silence. A European writer shyly turned to Tyson and said, "Mike, with all of that said, why don't you come out more and go on Larry King again, and go on David Letterman and set the record straight?"

Tyson's eyes narrowed. He flapped his hand in disgust. "Ah, fuck y'all. Fuck y'all," he said. "I don't have to suck your dick to justify me being a good guy. Listen, man, I'm a man! I don't go begging someone to love me."

"It's not begging," the European ventured. "It's—"

"Yes, it is!" Tyson said. "You see, O. J. Simpson, he's going around all the time trying to prove his innocence. By court of law, he's innocent. Maybe common sense tells you he's not, but in a court of law he's innocent. I'm not going to go around saying, 'Well, I've done this or this for this organization.' The hell with that, man."

Now Horne started egging Tyson on. "When the intention is to destroy you from the beginning, you can't get no level playing field to set the record straight," Horne said. "Let me say one thing. All of us live different lives. None of y'all have lived the lives that we have. We have different perceptions of things. . . . You guys go into back rooms, you conference about everything, you help each other out, to destroy somebody who is the only reason you are all out here. No other fighter takes you out of the country, no other fighter makes your jobs so interesting."

Finally, Tyson had the presence of mind to wave Horne off, to settle King down. All he really wanted us to know was that he was unknowable. He had probably given more interviews, in his time, than Dora ever gave to Freud, but it didn't matter. "Look," he said. "I'm harder on myself than the goddam reporters. But they don't know me well enough to write what I'm about, that I'm a monster, that I'm this or that. No one knows me. . . . I'd like to be written up like the old-timers. There's no doubt about it, I'm a wild man. I've had my share of the good times. But that's just part of the business, that's just who Mike is. I work hard, I live hard, I play hard, I die hard."

Like mediocre fiction, fights for the heavyweight championship of the world are invariably freighted with the solemnity of deeper meanings. It is not enough that one man shock another's brain and send him reeling. There must be politics, too—or, at least, great lumps of symbol, historical subplots, metaphysical frosting. In team sports—in football, baseball, basketball—there are individual stars, there are rivalries, but, finally, the athletics is the thing. A team athlete's talent is often the mastery of some peculiar and relatively recent invention: kicking a pig's bladder through a set of posts, swinging a stick of polished ash, tossing a ball through an iron hoop. Boxing is ancient, simple, lonely. There is hardly any artifice at all. Padded gloves and the gauze and tape underneath do little to protect the fighters; they merely prevent broken hands, and allow for more punching, more pain. Boxers go into the ring alone, nearly naked, and they succeed or fail on the basis of the most elementary criteria: their ability to give and receive pain, their will to endure their own fear. Since character—the will of a person stretched to extremes—is so obviously at the center of boxing, there is an undeniable urge to know the fighters, to derive some meaning from the conflict of those characters.

John L. Sullivan's triumphs were triumphs of the working class, the immigrant wave, "the people." Joe Louis fought the moral war over German fascism—fascism coming in the bruised and prostrate person of Max Schmeling. Most of all, the fights have come to be parables tinctured with the issues and conflicts of race. Indeed, some of the first boxing matches in America were held on plantations before the Civil War. White slave owners (the promoters) set up fights between their chattel. The slaves were often commanded to fight to the death. Was it such a great leap from there to the MGM Grand? "If [the heavyweights] become champions they begin to have inner lives like Hemingway or Dostoyevsky, Tolstoy or Faulkner, Joyce or Melville or Conrad or Lawrence or Proust," Norman Mailer wrote twenty-six years ago in *Life*.

Dempsey was alone and Tunney could never explain himself and Sharkey could never believe himself nor Schmeling nor Braddock, and Carnera was sad and Baer an indecipherable clown; great heavyweights like Louis had the loneliness of the ages in their silence, and men like Marciano were mystified by a power which seemed to have been granted them. With the advent, however, of the great modern Black heavyweights, Patterson, Liston, then Clay and Frazier, perhaps the loneliness gave way to what it had been protecting itself against—a surrealistic situation unstable beyond belief. Being a Black heavyweight champion in the second half of the twentieth century (with Black revolutions opening all over the world) was now not unlike being Jack Johnson, Malcolm X, and Frank Costello all in one.

Black fighters found themselves fighting intricate wars over racial types, over shifting notions of masculinity, decency, and class. In 1962, with the endorsements of President Kennedy and the National Association for the Advancement of Colored People, Floyd Patterson fought in the name of the black middle class and white liberals against Liston, the gruff ex-con, who represented, as Amiri Baraka (then LeRoi Jones) put it, "the big black Negro in every white man's hallway, waiting to do him in." But Patterson was not physically equal to his preposterous moral task. Liston flattened him in the first round. So shamed was Patterson that he fled Comiskey Park disguised in a fake beard and mustache and drove all night back to New York. He had not merely been defeated. He had let down the race; he had not fulfilled his meaning, his role in the story.

It is hard to imagine today the sense of disappointment in Patterson's loss. A columnist for the *Los Angeles Times* wrote that having Liston as champion "is like finding a live bat on a string under your Christmas tree." Some papers felt free to refer to Liston as a "jungle beast," a "gorilla." Only Murray Kempton, writing in the *Post,* was able to find an arch note of optimism in Liston's ascent. "The Negro heavyweights, as Negroes tend to do, have usually given that sense of being men above their calling," Kempton wrote. "Floyd Patterson sounded like a Freedom Rider. We return to reality with Liston. We have at last a heavyweight champion on the moral level of the men who own him. This is the source of horror which Liston has aroused; he is boxing's perfect symbol. He tells us the truth about it. The heavyweight championship is, after all, a fairly squalid office."

Liston tried desperately to please. He promised to be a good champion, to emulate Joe Louis. He explained that he had been one of twenty-five children in rural Arkansas, that he was illiterate, abused by a violent father. He apologized for his "terrible mistakes." But the country seemed not to accept the apologies; it was hard for whites and blacks alike to countenance a man who, when asked why he would not join in the civil rights marches in the South, had answered, "I ain't got no dog-proof ass." People only laughed when Liston started associating with priests. After Cassius Clay beat Liston in Miami—and then, as Muhammad Ali, beat him again—his story took a tragic course. Liston retired to Las Vegas, where he fought a little, hung out with gangsters like Ash Resnick, and in 1971 died with a needle in his arm. The funeral procession went down the Strip. For a few minutes, people came out of the casinos, squinting in the sun and saying farewell to Liston. The Ink Spots sang "Sunny."

For a long time, especially since coming home from prison, Tyson has seen himself in Liston. Watching films of Liston working out to the old James Brown rendition of "Night Train," he said, was "orgasmic."

"Sonny Liston, I identify with him the most," he said. "That may sound morbid and grim, but I pretty much identify with that life. He wanted people to respect him or love him, but it never happened. You can't make people respect and love you by craving it. You've got to *demand* it.

"People may not have liked him because of his background, but the people who got to know him as an intimate person have a totally different opinion. He had a wife. I'm sure she didn't think he was a piece of garbage. . . . Everyone respected Sonny Liston's ability. The point is respecting him as a man. No one can second-guess my ability, either. But I'm going to be respected. I demand that. You have no choice. You couldn't be in my presence if you didn't."

A few weeks before the fight, I went up to Michigan to see Liston's conqueror. Muhammad Ali lives on a manicured farm in a small town near the Indiana border called Berrien Springs. It was obvious to everyone who saw him tremble as he ignited the Olympic torch in Atlanta that Parkinson's disease has all but silenced Ali and placed a grim mask on what had been the century's most sparkling face. But out of the way of television cameras, which make him nervous and even more rigid than usual, Ali can show delight. He is especially delighted to watch himself when his body was fluid and his voice the most widely recognized in the world. We spent the better part of an afternoon watching videotapes of his fights, the early fights with Liston and then the first bout against Patterson. Ali leaned back and smiled as he watched himself, in black and white, dissect Liston, duck his blows, and sting him with jabs until Liston looked very slow and very sad.

"Ah, Sonny," Ali said. "The big ugly bear!"

Now Liston was quitting. He sat slumped on his stool. Now Ali's younger self was standing at the ropes, hysterical in his triumph, shouting down at the reporters who had dismissed him as a loudmouth and a fake, "Eat your words! Eat your words! I am the greatest!"

"They all thought I'd lose," Ali said. "Thought he'd tear me up."

After a while, I asked Ali about Tyson and whether he compared to Liston.

"Liston was faster than Tyson, but came straight ahead," he said. His voice was whispery, almost all breath.

"Could Tyson have beaten you?" I asked.

"Don't make me laugh," Ali said, and he was laughing. "Tyson don't have it. He don't *have* it." For a second, I wondered what "it" was, but then The Greatest made it clear. He pointed to his head.

About a week later, I took the ferry to Staten Island to visit Teddy Atlas, who had trained Tyson when he was learning to fight in Cus D'Amato's gym. Atlas is one of boxing's most appealing characters, the son of a doctor who used to treat patients in the ghetto for a couple of dollars. He was rebellious, a street kid who learned to box. A knife fight on Rikers Island left him with a scar on his face that runs from his hairline to his jawline. When Atlas was barely twenty, D'Amato taught him how to train fighters and then entrusted him with Tyson. Atlas taught Tyson the catechism according to D'Amato, the peekaboo style of holding the gloves up near the face, the need to overcome the fear inside. During one amateur fight, Tyson told Atlas between rounds that his hand was broken and he couldn't go on, but Atlas knew it was just fear, the fear of disgrace, and he pushed Tyson back out into the ring and to a victory.

Atlas, however, grew disillusioned as he saw D'Amato indulge Tyson in one ugly incident after another. Tyson harassed girls in school, beat other kids up, threatened teachers, and D'Amato nearly always found a way to make it good with the school, with the police. He would have his champion, one way or another. He was not raising a son, after all. He was raising a fighter. But in 1982, when Tyson molested Atlas's adolescent sister-in-law, Atlas lost it. He held a gun to Tyson's head and threatened him. D'Amato never punished Tyson. He did, however, get rid of Atlas.

Tyson's co-manager John Horne had told me that "the only difference between Mike Tyson and Michael Jordan is Mr. and Mrs. Jordan." But Atlas thought that was too simple, too easy on Tyson. When I asked him if he had overreacted when he held the gun to Tyson's head, he said, "This was a kid who did not hesitate to tear out the soul of another human being. He completely violated other people. And then he just moved on.

"Mike is very selfish. He was bred to be selfish. I remember sitting in the kitchen once at Cus's place and there were two plates of spaghetti, one for Mike and one for some other kid, another fighter, who hadn't sat down yet. Tyson went to take the other kid's food, too, and Camille"—D'Amato's companion—"said, 'Mike, no, don't take it.' But Cus said, 'No, go ahead, take it. You're gonna be the next champion of the world.

Eat it.' Tyson was just fifteen or sixteen, and it was the wrong lesson. Listen, there are plenty of kids from Brownsville with that background and some of them are great people, people who find something in themselves to trigger a sense of accountability, the sense that someone else in the universe matters."

Atlas said Tyson was a fighter who depended solely on fast hands and the image of extreme violence. Nearly all his opponents were beaten before they ever got in the ring. Tyson never fought a truly great heavyweight (as Tunney fought Dempsey, as Ali fought Joe Frazier), and on the two occasions when an opponent stood up to him he lost: first to Buster Douglas in Tokyo in 1990, and then to Holyfield last November.

"You can lie to yourself in the ring in a hundred different ways," Atlas said. "You can quit by degrees. You can stop punching, with the idea, crazy as it sounds, that the other guy will stop if you do. Then you can make excuses to yourself, and the people around you will echo the excuses, and everything will seem to be all right. You can even foul and then claim you would have won, given the chance. Remember, this is a kid who used to hide between the walls of condemned buildings to make sure he wouldn't get beaten up. When you live like that, you learn to lie, to coax people that you are the toughest—you learn to scare people, to manipulate them. And when you can't do it you're lost.

"When I see Tyson, I see a guy who's scared, a guy who can't do it on the up and up. In his world, he was never allowed to be scared, or even honest, and so he is neither of those things. He is lost. When Tyson is alone with himself, I don't know if he believes there is one single person around him who is there because of his merits as a person. I don't even know that the women would be around without his ability to raise money. He'd have to show something independent of the ring and of his ability to send people on two-hundred-thousand-dollar shopping sprees."

On the day of the fight, I wandered the Strip. Earlier in the week, the casinos in hotels like the MGM Grand, New York New York, and Excalibur—the new family-friendly places—had been jammed with middle-class parents pushing strollers past the blackjack tables at midnight. Las Vegas is a better deal than Disney World. In Las Vegas, you can get a cheap hotel room, visit the Sphinx (at the Luxor), have your picture taken with a stuffed movie character, induce nausea on the rides, and be in the pool by lunchtime. But at the end of the week (when my room rate shot up from seventy-nine dollars per night to three hundred and ninety-nine) all the strollers were gone. The planes out at McCarran International Airport disgorged high rollers from New York, Tokyo, Taipei, and Beijing, athletes and gang-bangers, movie stars in Armani and hoochie girls in Moschino. The mind reeled—and the neck swiveled—at the effect of health clubs and silicone on the American form at century's end. All that hard work and earnest surgery. From the looks of the women at the luggage belts, there could not have been a single hooker left in the greater Los Angeles area. They had all flown in for the fight.

At the instigation of my friend Michael Wilbon, a sports columnist for *The Washington Post*, I spent the afternoon roaming the most expensive stores in town. Fight day, Wilbon instructed me, is a big shopping day, and many of the key stores—Neiman Marcus, Versace, Escada, Gucci, Armani—signed up extra seamstresses and tailors to get things ready for the evening. You don't buy a three-thousand-dollar suit and then not wear it to the main event. Even if you didn't have tickets—and that meant the vast majority who had "come in for the fight"—you showed up in the casinos looking dowdy at your peril.

At Neiman Marcus, I watched Louis Farrakhan take the Italian boutique by storm. While half a dozen of his bodyguards assumed positions near the ties and the shirt racks, the minister tried on a fine pair of mustard-colored slacks. Zegna is evidently one of his favorite designers. I watched him try on slacks for the better part of half an hour. When I asked one of his guards whether it might be possible to interview him, the guard took off his sunglasses and blinked. I took this to mean no.

The Forum Shops at Caesars Palace proved to be a nice place to hang out, too. The ceilings are painted like a cerulean sky with perfect Biblical clouds, and there is a fountain outside the Versace store that is better than the Trevi Fountain in Rome in that the Las Vegas Rome is air-conditioned.

Versace seemed to be the appointed headquarters of Tyson fans, and even of Tyson himself. Before the first Holyfield fight, the managers shut down the store for Tyson. "He bought real good," a manager told me, but he declined to be more specific. The mythical figure among the boxing writers was that Tyson dropped a hundred and fifty thousand there last time. While I was fingering a blouse worth more than a decent used car, a guy with some major forearms and a purposeful stare came in: Tyson's bodyguard. Even if one did not know him by his face, there were hints: a "Team Tyson" tattoo on his arm and a "Team Tyson Rules" bomber jacket. The manager spotted him and raced over to serve. He actually rubbed his palms. Within seconds, the bodyguard was handed a suit bag. "Mike says thanks," the bodyguard said. He used his phone to order "immediate pickup" and walked out.

The fight crowd was not always thus. In the films of the big fights of the fifties and sixties, you can see that the ringside seats were taken up mainly by boxy white men in boxy blue suits—mobsters, like Blinky Palermo and Frank Carbo, or, on a slightly higher plane, Rat Pack members. When Ali returned from exile in 1971 to fight Jerry Quarry in Atlanta, the fight crowd changed: suddenly, there were blacks at ringside. They held the same reputable and disreputable jobs as their white predecessors, but the plumage was different. The style of the hustler had shifted from Carbo's dour wool (he was known as Mr. Gray) to the iridescent suits of his black inheritors. It was as if a row of sparrows had flown the wire, to be replaced by a flock of cockatoos.

There were still plenty of white big shots around, plenty of pompadours and big-guy rings. One night at dinner at an Italian place, Trevesi, at the MGM Grand, a woman tossed her glass of wine at her big-guy boyfriend. Then she rose from her chair and, after a second of real consideration, took her glass and smashed it over the boyfriend's head. At which point there was blood on the boyfriend's skull and slivers of glass in the capellini of the woman at the next table. That would turn out to be the cleanest blow of the week.

It is customary at a big fight to surround the ring with press people, anonymous high rollers, and, most of all, "luminaries from the world of sports, politics, and the entertainment industry." In the press section, we were handed an alphabetized list of celebrities in attendance: Paul Anka, Patricia Arquette, Stephen Baldwin, Matthew Broderick, Albert Brooks, James Caan, John Cusack, Rodney Dangerfield, Lolita Davidovich, Ellen DeGeneres, Larry Flynt, Michael J. Fox, Cuba Gooding, Jr., etc. This, of course, was "subject to change," the King people warned us.

It is also customary at big fights to come late, to ignore the undercard. But I had seen about as many vermilion leather vests, chartreuse pants, and siliconed bodies as I wanted to see, and headed into the MGM Grand's arena. King had told everyone that the fight was "the greatest boxing event of all time." It was a wonder, then, why he put together one of the grimmest undercards of all time. The highlight was surely the one women's bout, which left the canvas spotted with bloody pools. The woman in the pink shorts, Christy Martin, won the match. She had acquired all the best habits of boxing. She taunted her opponent, Andrea DeShong, at the pre-fight press conference, by saying she was glad DeShong had finally worn a dress. "It's the first time I've seen you look respectable, like a woman," Martin said, thus proving her . . . manhood.

By eight-thirty, the seats were filled and the place buzzed, loud and nervous, a sound peculiar to the mass anticipation of violence, a more manic buzz than at a basketball playoff game or a political convention. Don King opened the proceedings by having the ring announcer tell us that the fight was dedicated to the memory of Dr. Betty Shabazz and to "the many, many innocent victims of crime and violence." We all stood, and the timekeeper sounded the bell ten times, boxing's equivalent of a twenty-one-gun salute.

Tyson, the challenger, came into the arena to the sound of gangsta rap. In the bowels of the arena, he had complained that he could hear Holyfield's music—electric Jesus music—and couldn't Holyfield turn it down? Tyson, as always, wore his warrior look: black trunks, black shoes, no socks. He came surrounded by Giachetti and Horne and Holloway and Crocodile and a dozen other men, all of them strung out on self-importance. They tried very hard to look dangerous.

Then Holyfield, with a far smaller entourage, came down the aisle toward the ring. He wore purple-and-white trunks with the logo "Phil. 4:13" ("I can do all things through Christ which strengtheneth me"). While Tyson assumed his death mask, his intimidator's face, Holyfield was smiling. He mouthed the words to a gospel song that only he could hear. Tyson paced, and Holyfield stood in his corner, satisfied to jiggle the muscles in his arms and legs. One of his seconds massaged the ropes of muscle in his neck.

In the casino, Tyson was the favorite. You had to bet a hundred and eighty dollars on him to win a hundred. Those odds were based almost entirely on Tyson's Kid Dynamite reputation. Holyfield, however, was the pick on press row by a wide margin. And yet we knew why we were here. It was not to listen to Holyfield sing "Nearer My God to Thee."

Mills Lane, a bald and mumbly judge from Reno, was the referee. At the center of the ring, Lane reminded both fighters of their obligations to the law, to boxing, and to the Nevada State Athletic Commission, and both men nodded assent. They would, of course, not dream of trespass. So said their quick nods, the touch of the gloves.

At the opening bell, Tyson came out bobbing and weaving, but with a certain self-conscious air. He had lost the first fight not least because he had forgotten his old defensive moves. For months, Giachetti, his trainer, had been pleading with him to move his head, to jab, to forget about the one-punch knockout. But within half a minute Tyson was back to where he'd been before, throwing one huge hook at a time. Holyfield ducked the hooks easily and then held on, muscling Tyson around the ring. Last time, we had been amazed that Holyfield was stronger than Tyson, that he could push Tyson back on his heels, that he could grab Tyson's left arm in the clinches and save himself untold trauma to the kidneys and the temple. And now it was happening again. All the training, all the instructions were coming to nothing. Tyson could not intimidate Holyfield—he could not, as he had done to so many others before, terrify his man into dropping his guard, into committing a kind of boxing suicide. Holyfield had every intention of winning again, and he took the first round by controlling the pace and scoring big with two left hooks and then a right hand to Tyson's jaw.

Between rounds, as Tyson drank some water and spat in the bucket, Giachetti told him to take his time.

"Jab for the throat!" he said.

Tyson nodded, but who could tell what he was hearing—what inner voice?

In the second round, the pattern was much the same. Holyfield scored left hooks to the meat of Tyson's flank and shoved him around and back toward the ropes. Tyson jabbed occasionally, but more often he threw big, dramatic punches, and Holyfield smothered them, ducked them. Then came the crucial moment of the round—the moment that set off in Tyson some torrent of rage that would, in the end, botch the fight and possibly ruin his career. As the two men wrestled, Holyfield unintentionally rammed his skull into the sharp brow above Tyson's right eye. Within seconds, there were rivulets of blood running down the side of Tyson's face, and in the clinch he looked up at Lane and said, "He butted me." The physical side was bad enough: the gash was sure to bother Tyson throughout the fight. The blood would run in his eyes, and Holyfield, sensing his advantage, would work over the cut—punch at it, grind his head into it in the clinch—and try to win on a technical knockout. What was worse for Tyson was the tremendous fear the butt stirred up in him, the way the blunt pain on his brow summoned up the last fight, his humiliation. Last time, the two men had butted heads inside, two berserk rams, and Tyson had come away the injured one, dazed and bleeding. It was as if his nightmare had come true. It was all happening again. He was in the ring, bleeding, and facing an opponent who would not back down.

Lane warned both men against excessive "roughhousing" (imagine!), but he didn't deduct any penalty points. Now, in the clinch, Tyson grew more desperate. He shoved a forearm into Holyfield's throat. But his punches, his big punches, were still missing, and they were coming in single volleys rather than in combination. Again, Holyfield won the round because of his superior strength, his ability to waltz Tyson around the ring, and the efficiency of his blows. What he threw, for the most part, landed. All three judges scored the first two rounds for Holyfield, ten to nine.

After the bell, a plastic surgeon worked on Tyson's cut.

As the doctor held a compress to Tyson's brow, the fighter jerked back.

"Aaahhh!" Tyson moaned.

"I'm sorry," the doctor said.

Tyson was breathing hard now—harder than he should have been after six minutes in the ring and months of roadwork. He said nothing. He gave no hint to anyone that something was wrong—that something had "snapped," as he put it days later. Tyson got off his stool and waited for the bell. As the two fighters stood facing each other, Holyfield suddenly pointed to his mouth, reminding Tyson that his corner had not put in his mouthpiece. Tyson walked back to Giachetti and opened his jaws; Giachetti put the mouthpiece in.

At the bell for the third round, Tyson stalked forward, and it was clear that he was enraged, desperate to end the fight before his eye failed him. He was relatively controlled at first, throwing his first sharp hooks of the fight. Holyfield was standing up to the blows and was still moving forward, crowding Tyson, but he was suddenly no longer in command. For more than two minutes of fighting, Tyson showed that he was capable of reviving his old style. Now his punches came in combinations. He kept his head moving, side to side, up and down, making it impossible for Holyfield to flick the jab at his gash. In the clinches, however, Holyfield was still in control. He seemed to be telling Tyson that, while he could win the round, he could not win the fight, and Tyson seemed to see the sense in that. And with about forty seconds left in the round, as Holyfield was steering him around the center of the ring, Tyson suddenly spat out his mouthpiece and started gnawing on Holyfield's right ear. For a second, Holyfield seemed not to feel this lunatic attack, but then the sting hit him. He backed away, jumping up and down, pointing to his ear and the blood that now bathed it. At the same time, Tyson turned his head at an angle and spat out a half-inch chunk of ear. Lane called a time-out. Holyfield headed for his corner. Tyson chased him down and shoved him. Holyfield seemed almost to ham it up, to bounce crazily on the ropes, as if to highlight the madness of it all.

Don Turner, Holyfield's trainer, told his man to keep cool, to think about Jesus, just stay calm.

Lane said to a Nevada State Athletic Commission official at ringside that he was ready to disqualify Tyson—and he certainly would have been within his rights to do so—but first he invited the ring doctor, Flip Homansky, onto the canvas to have a look at Holyfield's ear. Homansky gravely inspected the ear and, presumably in the interests of Nevada and boxing's good name, pronounced Holyfield able to continue. Lane went to both corners and explained to the assembled handlers what had happened. He told Giachetti that Tyson "bit him on the ear."

"No, I didn't," Tyson said.

"Bullshit," Lane replied. He had already examined the ear, the teeth marks. "I thought my ear had fallen off!" Holyfield said later. "Blood was all over!" Lane deducted two points from Tyson—one for the bite, one for the shove—and, or so he claimed in a post-fight interview, warned Tyson that if he did it again the fight was over.

The time-out had lasted more than two minutes, long enough for the crowd to see replays of the incident on the big screens around the arena and start booing, enough time for Tyson to decide whether he had "snapped" or would do it again, and more than enough time for the jokes to begin sweeping through the press section: "Tyson's a chomp," "He's Hannibal Lecter," "a lobe blow," "pay per chew," "If you can't beat 'em, eat 'em." There would be a hundred of them.

Finally, Lane cleared the ring and resumed what little was left of the third round. The crowd, which had been fickle, swerving between chants first for Holyfield, then for Tyson, was now greatly affronted. They booed wildly. We were, of course, all prepared to see one fighter deliver a subconcussive blow to the other's brain, but a bite on the ear was beyond imagining. We were offended, disgusted, perhaps even a little thrilled. Boxing is a blood sport. Now there was blood.

Holyfield was intent on following his corner's plea to keep his cool. He marched in and connected with a stiff hook to Tyson's face. His message was delivered thus: you can do what you want, you can foul, you can threaten, you can even quit, but you will not intimidate me.

The fighters clinched again. There were about twenty seconds left in the round. And, incredibly, Tyson once more nuzzled his way into Holyfield's sweaty neck, almost tenderly, purposefully, as if he were snuffling for truffles. He found the left ear and bit. Once more, Holyfield did his jumping dance of rage and pain. The bell sounded.

Tyson's handlers now wore guilty looks; their eyes shifted. They knew what was coming.

Holyfield was not quite so sure. "Put my mouthpiece in," he told his cornermen. "I'm gonna knock him out."

But Lane could not let this go on: "One bite is bad enough. Two bites is the end of the search."

"I had to do some thinking," Lane said, reasonably, later on. "I thought about it and thought about it, and decided it was the right thing to do. Let the chips fall where they may." Tyson was disqualified. Holyfield was declared winner and "still heavyweight champion of the world." Subsequently, Tyson said that he had been forced to retaliate for the butt in the second round. After all, he said righteously, "This is my career. . . . I've got children to raise."

In the mayhem that followed Lane's announcement—Tyson still going berserk in the ring, pushing at the police, and then fans raining down ice cubes and curses as he headed for the locker room—in all that, one bit of business was almost forgotten. A hotel employee named Mitch Libonati found the chunk of ear that belonged to Evander Holyfield. He found it on the ring mat, wrapped it in a rubber glove, and delivered it to the champion's locker room.

"At first, they looked at me like I was pulling a prank, but I told them I had a piece of Evander's ear, and I thought he would want it," Libonati said. "It wasn't really bloody, actually. It was like a piece of sausage."

After leaving the arena and press tent, I walked through the MGM Grand casino toward the elevators. I wanted to drop off some things in my room before heading back out to the Strip. How could you miss the victory parties? But just as I was passing some slot machines I saw a stampede of twenty or thirty people running straight at me. There were screams: "Get down!" and "There's shooting!" and "They got guns!" I had already seen some fistfights between Tyson's fans and Holyfield's fans. It was not beyond reckoning that some of the visitors could be armed. I dived behind a bank of slot machines, feeling at once terrified and ridiculous.

"Keep down!"

"Ya hear the shots!"

People were face down on the carpet, ducking under blackjack tables, roulette tables. And then it was quiet. No shots—not that we could hear, anyway. It seemed safe to walk to the elevators.

But then, as the doors opened, more people started dashing around, ducking behind slot machines and into the elevators. I went up to the fourteenth floor and then went back down in a service elevator. I had to get to the bank of elevators that would get me to the twenty-fifth floor. As I was getting out of the service elevator, Jesse Jackson and a team of police were getting in.

"It's sad. The whole thing is sad," Jackson said. "That's the one word I can think of to describe it. It's a tragedy that no one can explain. As far as Tyson is concerned, I guess the butting triggered something in him. I focus on him and what's going on in his head. And now this. They're out there shooting with Uzis, these bad boys."

It was never entirely clear whether there had been any shooting. I doubt it. But the Nevada Highway Patrol did shut down the Strip from Tropicana Avenue to Koval Lane. No one wanted a repeat of the action after the Tyson-Seldon fight last September, when the rap star Tupac Shakur was shot to death in a car.

The rumors of Uzi fire did little to help the gambling receipts at the MGM Grand, but elsewhere on the Strip the high rollers were happy. We had all been witness to a spectacle—to the unraveling of Mike Tyson. In the days to come, he would apologize. He would reach out "to the medical professionals for help." But who now cared about him? In the ring, at his moment of greatest pressure, he had lost everything: he had proved himself to be what in gentler times would have been called a bum. Biting is certainly not unheard-of in boxing—Holyfield himself once bit Jakey Winters in an amateur bout when he was eighteen—yet Tyson had done it not once but twice, in a championship fight seen by "three billion people," or however many Don King had managed to attract. The abysmal and lonely end that he had seemed to predict for himself had come so soon.

"It's over," he said in the locker room. "I know it's over. My career is over."

No one had envisioned this end more clearly than Tyson himself. On the day before the fight, he had gone out to a cemetery near the airport and laid a bouquet of flowers on the grave of Sonny Liston. The music ahead for Tyson would be not rap but something more mournful. "Someday they're gonna write a blues song just for fighters," his role model, Liston, once said. "It'll be for slow guitar, soft trumpet, and a bell."

(1997)

Cornerman:
Teddy Atlas

Most cornermen have no more to offer a fighter than a bucket to spit in. As they work over their charge—icing his welts, slaking his thirst—they frantically offer up whatever clichés come to mind. There are many. There is the cliché of persistence ("Keep at the jab!"); the cliché of heightened violence ("Bang the liver!"); the cliché of urgent avoidance ("Get off the ropes!"); and, not infrequently, when all else fails, the clichéd assurances of holy accompaniment ("Jesus loves you!"). From the corner toffs of the Regency period to the mobbed-up boyos of the forties and fifties, the trainer is a background figure, the unheeded Polonius. He knows that his pleas and instructions most often go unheard. Fighters, after all, are not modern quarterbacks: they do not wear helmets equipped with radio transmitters; they do not have the benefit of instant, computer-generated analysis in their ears. Finally, a fighter is alone. If his mind is still clear enough, he listens to himself. If not, he listens to instinct and fear.

Over time, however, there have been trainers who, in that frenetic minute between rounds, have been capable of saving a fight or a career, even a life: The Englishman James Figg, the singular master of eighteenth-century fighters. Ray Arcel, Mannie Seamon, and Whitey Bimstein—the great stalwarts of Stillman's Gym, on Eighth Avenue. And, more recently, men like Angelo Dundee and Eddie Futch. When Cassius Clay was blinded in the fourth round of his championship fight with Sonny Liston in 1964 and wanted to quit rather than face the fifth ("I can't see! Cut off the gloves!"), Dundee flooded his eyes with a sponge, and told him to "yardstick" Liston with his jab and wait till his vision cleared. "This is the big one, Daddy!" Dundee told Clay, who was near-hysterical in his protests. "Cut the bullshit! We're not quitting now." Clay knew he could trust Dundee not to send him to harm. His eyes cleared. History, under a new name, soon followed. Eleven years later, in the third Ali-Frazier fight, in Manila—perhaps the fiercest heavyweight title fight of all time—Joe Frazier's cornerman, the sagacious Futch, would not let him into the ring for the fifteenth round. "Sit down," he said quietly. "The fight's over." Frazier's eyes were so swollen that he could no longer see Ali's punches coming, and Futch, as Frazier's proxy, was surrendering. Frazier was not the type to surrender—his style, his ethic, was built around a willingness to absorb punishment in order to get close enough for the knockout blow—but he knew enough to bow to Futch's experience. Futch had in him the experience of death. ("I was there when Davey Moore got killed," Futch once said. "I was there when Talmadge Bussey got killed. I was there when Kid Dynamite got killed.")

These moments of inspiration—of inspired craft or inspired compassion—come rarely. But they happen. Like a healer or a shaman, the trainer is steeped in specialized knowledge. The wisdom of the corner is generally passed down orally, but there are important texts. Professor Michael J. Donovan, a middleweight champion of the mid-nineteenth century and a supreme teacher at the fin de siècle, wrote the definitive guide to the art of preparation, *How to Train for a Fight*. Some of the professor's dicta are dated—"Before beginning real work, say about three days, every man should take mild doses of physic to act on the bowels, liver, and kidneys"—but, in the main, he is our contemporary. His advice on running, sleeping ("He needs ten hours' sleep and rest"), skipping rope, the "punching ball," the avoidance of drafts, and the care of a fighter's hands are part of the common wisdom without which a cornerman must be denied his degree. Donovan, like all the moderns, is an expert in athletic nutrition: "If you desire to increase your weight, drink Guinness' stout instead of Bass's ale." To all this a fighter must pay attention, and yet it is the trainer, as parent, as coddler and scold, who is there to direct the program.

The smartest trainer of the younger generation is a New Yorker in his mid-forties named Teddy Atlas. (Boxing, like baseball, has a genius for the comic-book name: Rocky Kansas, Kid Chocolate, Peppermint Frazer . . . Teddy Atlas.) For boxing, which has always been a sport of the marginals and the last-chancers, Atlas is of unlikely stock. He is a doctor's son. He is also the only doctor's son I know of whose most prominent facial distinguishment is the souvenir of a knife fight, a scar that begins at his hairline, skirts the corner of his left eye, and proceeds longitudinally to below the jaw. Fighting, in the ring and on the street, has provided Atlas with a kind of instant credibility: without his scar and the flattened nose, he might seem a nice-looking guy you'd meet on the ferry to Wall Street; with them, a fighter is forewarned—Do not mess with me. Atlas lives on Staten Island, where he grew up. He has also been housed on Rikers Island. He trained Mike Tyson when Tyson was a teenager; and he trained a heavyweight champion named Michael Moorer, an unsteady fighter of modest skills who never would have won the title without him. Atlas has trained a raft of contenders, but he has walked away from them when they would not listen. He has walked away from a fortune. Atlas, for all his imperfections, is a moralist. This is not an entirely common thing in boxing, now or ever. Atlas admires a code of professionalism. Because he is an honest and direct man in a sport dominated by the treacherous and the sly, he is a favorite of a small and loyal clutch of boxing writers—Ron Borges, of *The Boston Globe*, Mark Kriegel, of the New York *Daily News*, Jack Newfield and Wally Matthews, of the *New York Post*—but, truth be told, he is also acquainted with less elevated sorts, one or two of whom have, at times, been ordered to wear the electronic ankle jewelry issued by the federal judicial system. "I'm not an entirely innocent boy," Atlas says.

Occasionally, Atlas's skills have been recognized beyond the cultish circles of boxing. When the choreographer and modern dancer Twyla Tharp decided, in her early forties, to get in shape and return to the stage, she called on Teddy Atlas. He trained her like a fighter, had her running up flights of stairs, shadowboxing, even sparring, after a fashion. In the ring, Atlas did not hesitate to hit her, not at all hard but enough to remind her to keep moving her head and feet—a creed common to both Nijinsky and Willie Pep. When, later, Tharp performed at the Brooklyn Academy of Music, some members of the audience tossed flowers on the stage; Atlas threw a pair of boxing gloves at his student's feet. Tharp hung up the gloves on the wall of her apartment, on Central Park West. She came to respect the cornerman's art. "In dancing, if you mess up you get embarrassed," she once told a writer for *Ballet News*. "In boxing, if you mess up you die."

Earlier this summer, I drove out to the Rocky Marciano Gym, in Jersey City, where Atlas was training a young light heavyweight, a Kosovar Albanian named Elvir Muriqi. There aren't many gyms left in the metropolitan area. Stillman's and the Times Square Gym are long gone. Gleason's, which used to be near the Garden, moved fifteen years ago to Brooklyn, under the bridge. There's Lou Costello's, in Paterson, the Red Brick, in East Newark, the Kingsway, in Manhattan. The Marciano Gym is not in a particularly elegant neighborhood—it sits squat next to a Punjabi auto-repair garage and near a vacant lot—but it doesn't resemble the rancid hotboxes of yesteryear, either. Trainers of the Stillman's generation would not recognize the Marciano as familiar territory. The first floor is a sleek mirrored room filled with the torture racks of the exercising classes: treadmills, StairMasters, Nautilus machines, free weights. Upstairs is the boxing area, with two rings and, dangling from a complex of exposed beams, a series of heavy bags, speed bags—the usual. It, too, is clean and, suspiciously, odorless. When I arrived, Muriqi, a sturdy but physically unexceptional figure, was loosening up, skipping rope, hitting the heavy bag, snorting all the while. The one familiar and comforting sight in the place was a small group of old-timers who sat on folding chairs and gossiped about a fight card they'd all seen a few nights before at the International Brotherhood of Electrical Workers on Long Island.

Atlas was getting Muriqi ready for a rematch with a Massachusetts fighter named Dan Sheehan. At their first fight, at the Blue Horizon, in Philadelphia, Atlas had worked a kind of double shift, as both cornerman for Muriqi and commentator for ESPN2's *Friday Night Fights*, a regular gig. Muriqi has prospects, but, as Atlas told viewers (during the rounds) and his fighter (between them), his inexperience was showing against Sheehan. Muriqi was holding his own, but, in his frustration, his inability to finish the cloddish yet game Sheehan, he was throwing low blows; with each wince-inducing shot, Atlas betrayed distress.

"He's a little raw, I'm not going to lie to you," Atlas told the viewers. The TV audience could hear Atlas telling Muriqi to "stop the crap." The crowd at the Blue Horizon is a knowledgeable one, even in geopolitical matters, and they were offended.

"You fight like a Serb!" someone shouted.

With just twelve seconds left in the fight, the referee disqualified Muriqi for his fourth low blow. A young fighter with dreams cannot afford such a blemish on his record. Most of Muriqi's cornermen stood around crying or comforting their man. Atlas was unsentimental. With his headset on, he told the viewers, "Right now he's devastated. Now he's got to go back to the gym, enhance his training, or get into another business."

And so here they were, back in the gym. The rematch would take place in a few weeks, in Hyannis, on Cape Cod.

"I got to explain to him that he faltered in the last fight. He wasn't a pro, which is what you strive to become," Atlas told me as we watched Muriqi jump rope. "He wasn't prepared mentally to do the things a pro is prepared to do. It's like a lawyer in a courtroom who comes across an opponent who is tougher than he anticipated, or a doctor who opens a person up and it's worse than he thought. A professional sees what's happening and deals with it. My guy went in there, he was thirteen-and-oh, and thought it was going to be easy, and then he'd give a thirty-second sound bite to ESPN. Well, the other guy didn't want to cooperate, and that bothered his work. Pros don't allow themselves to be bothered from their work."

Atlas has been with fighters at the Garden and in the parking lot of Caesars Palace, in Las Vegas. Why was he bothering with the Kosovo Kid?

Atlas shrugged. He said Muriqi might turn out to have character. "He comes from a place where there's not much, and his father and sister fought for the KLA for freedom. With that kind of pressure around him, maybe it means something," Atlas said. "Whether it's gonna help him transcend himself and be a pro, we'll see."

All good cornermen think of themselves as masters of the psyche. They are Freudians. Atlas is just more so. He is convinced that boxing is, in large measure, psychological, that the loser is the fighter who lies to himself, who finds ways to rationalize his passivity and makes a "silent contract" with his opponent: I won't hurt you if you don't hurt me. They clutch and grab and back up, and while they may think they're being clever they are really signing the contract.

Atlas walked over to Muriqi. He came up close to his man's face, right where he could be seen and heard, and he spoke calmly, sternly.

"Now, look, you've got to be thinking about July seventh," he began.

"You won every round last time, but you didn't do the things you need to be a pro. This is why I hesitate to take guys at this level.

"I might not be too good at other things, but I do know this. I'm going to tell you things that will upset you sometimes, but it will make you better. In your mind, it's easy. What I'm trying to tell you is, it's not. You'll reach the point when it won't be easy. That's what we're preparing for.

"*A pro cannot let go.*" Atlas paused, as if searching Muriqi's eyes for any trace that this was sinking in. "A pro cannot let go. You have to keep from letting yourself do what's easy and just be there. Everything is painful. Everything is painful. There's a difference between making things livable for yourself and doing more. There is pain if you want to be something different: a pro, a champion. And rich."

Muriqi smiled at this last word. Rich. He couldn't help it. Rich is what he wants to be. Atlas stepped away from him for a minute. He thinks hard about these speeches, and he does not mind showing that he is thinking. The fighter can wait. Atlas looked down and scratched his head, very much like a man wondering where he'd parked his car. Muriqi squinted. Then Atlas said, "So what are you going to do in this fight? What do you think?"

Muriqi seemed glad that the lecture was over. He looked eager to get the right answer to Teddy's question.

"Well," he began. "If I have to fight inside—"

"Wrong!" Teddy broke in. "I'm glad I asked. Not 'if.' Never 'if.' If it's 'if,' he gets the jump on you. You fight inside because you want to fight there. Never 'if.' "

After Muriqi finished loosening up, Atlas taped and padded Muriqi's hands and put gloves on him. Atlas himself put on a set of red punching pads, which look like flattened-out catcher's mitts: they catch punches. The two men got in the ring and began a kind of one-sided sparring, in which Atlas kept the mitts moving and Muriqi tried to sharpen his combinations. Fairly often, to keep Muriqi honest, Atlas threw a teasing punch at his face. The choreography was as intricate as anything in the Tharp repertoire. All the while, Atlas barked instructions, tips, warnings.

Between rounds, Atlas gave his fighter water, as if to a baby; there was great solicitude in the way he held up the bottle with one hand and kept a finger under Muriqi's lip, to prevent dribbling. This kind of physical intimacy, this babying, is unique to boxing. Bill Parcells does not water his fullback; Joe Torre does not massage the pitcher.

"Be good at this," Atlas told Muriqi. "Be real good. 'Cause what else you gotta do? You gotta be good at this!"

And then they sparred again, round after round. Soon Atlas's orange

T-shirt was soaked through. He was a junior welterweight when he was a kid. He is neither junior nor welterweight now. And yet it was Muriqi who was breathing most deeply. With each punch, you heard those sharp explosions of breath that fighters make:

Phhh . . . hhh!

Ish! Ish! . . . Ish!

At one point, Atlas whacked Muriqi with a jab, a pedagogical point, and Muriqi backed off. He seemed shy. Atlas told him not to be.

"It's O.K. to be a little scared," he said. "Most people just chase that away so they don't have to think about it. No. Be scared. But do something about it. Make it work for you."

When it was over, there were situps, and a shorter lecture, and Atlas went downstairs to do some work on the treadmill. Before Muriqi went off to the shower, he told me he'd tried hard to get Atlas to train him.

"Teddy's been through everything in life," he said. Muriqi has just a trace of an accent, but it is a little more Bronx than Pristina. "When he was young, he fought, he saw things, he *knows*. Teddy knows what you're thinking. You can't bullshit Teddy. He sees everything."

Teddy Atlas's father, Theodore Atlas, Sr., was the sort of doctor who no longer exists. (Or, if one does, please send along a phone number.) He worked seven days a week, twelve to sixteen hours a day. He made house calls all over Staten Island. At least half his patients paid him only a few dollars or nothing at all. Some paid him with a cake, a Jell-O mold. He helped found Sunnyside Hospital, and when Sunnyside was torn down, in 1962, to make way for the Staten Island Expressway, he helped found Doctors' Hospital. His dedication was absolute. He and his wife, Mary Riley, had five children. Their son Todd was born retarded and suffering from heart problems; he died during heart surgery when he was five years old. On the day of the funeral, Dr. Atlas went to the service and then treated a patient, a sick child.

"My father was the only man I've ever admired, and his strength was his problem," Teddy, Jr., told me one afternoon. We were sitting outside the gym on a curb, enjoying the sun. "My father could not show emotion," he said. "I was so proud of him, even if I didn't know it then. He was the only guy I've ever met—that's of all the pros, the wiseguys, the half-assed wiseguys, the real guys—the only one that I could trust, who never disappointed me, who was always who he said he was without even saying it."

When he was very young, Teddy used to go on house calls with his father. Even in the dead of winter, he'd drive along with him, hoping his father might say something, and then he would wait in the car, in the cold, while his father attended to the sick. His father worked New Year's, Easter, and Christmas if he had to. "His great indulgence was that, once in a while, after working a full day, he'd fly down to Puerto Rico, gamble all night, take a walk in the surf, eat a piece of fresh pineapple, and then fly back for Sunday house calls. He didn't have time for other things. If he would come home from house calls on a Sunday and throw a football with me for ten minutes, it was like a miracle."

After his brother died, Teddy's mother suffered a nervous collapse and the other kids lived with relatives for about a year. Teddy stayed with an uncle who used the neighborhood saloon for day care.

"I measured time at the bar by the number of Cokes and bags of potato chips they'd let me have," Atlas said. The commotion of his childhood, the absolute reserve of his father, he said, left him "a little screwed up." As a teenager, he was about as delinquent a juvenile as it is possible to be. He got into street brawls, he had guns, he robbed gas stations, convenience stores, bars.

"Other people did it to make money," he said. "I wanted to hurt myself to get my father's attention."

Atlas earned his epic scar in a street fight. He and a buddy were driving in the Stapleton neighborhood. Some guys cut them off. They cut *them* off. Everyone pulled over for the rumble.

"I got one guy through a window. I was doing pretty good there for a while! But then one guy hit me with a blackjack. . . . I ran for another guy, but he got out a double-oh-seven, a flick-blade knife. I remember thinking, That's a double-oh-seven. So I knew he had to come next with a downward motion, and I was trying to get close to him. Obviously I was too late. Bad move. I remember holding my face. My hand just went *into* my face. It felt like warm goo. Meanwhile, my friend was on the roof of the car. He was afraid. They thought I was going to die. They took me into a store and laid me out on the floor and covered me with towels. I filled up three or four towels with blood. My guy jumped over the counter, dialed 911, and said a cop had been shot. I remember in the ambulance the cop saying, 'The kid might bleed to death.' We went to Marine Hospital, in the Bailey section. They wheeled me in and all I could do was keep asking them to let my father do it. . . . The last thing I remember thinking about when I went under was my father's schedule. That night he showed up. There was no talking. I had four hundred stitches: two hundred on the inside, two hundred on the outside. He looked over the sutures and that was it."

If Atlas was in the process of breaking his father's heart, his father did all he could to conceal it. During another street fight, someone hit Atlas on the head with a tire iron. With blood all over his shirt, Atlas walked into his father's office. As always, the place was crowded with patients who would have to wait two and three hours to see Dr. Atlas. The nurse rushed to Teddy and led him in to see his father right away.

"But my father just said, 'He'll wait like everyone else,' " Atlas recalled. "When it was my turn to get stitched up, the nurse came in with a syringe full of Novocain. But my father said, 'He doesn't want that. If he's going to live like this, he should know what it feels like.' "

Along with a street friend named Kevin Rooney, Atlas was learning a little boxing. He worked out at the local Police Athletic League. He was a good puncher, with an even better chin. You couldn't knock Teddy out. At the same time, he was running wild. "I was a thief," Atlas said. "The problem was, I wasn't any good at it." One night, Teddy was arrested with a gun in his waistband as he was coming out of a bar that he and his buddies were thinking about robbing. Two days later, as he was awaiting word on that case, he got arrested again. This time, he and his genius friends were holding up a gas station on Forest Avenue.

"We got nothing, but, with the window rolled down, I shot into the air and we took off," Atlas said.

"So we're driving like idiots down the street and a cop car comes up. We'd been doing robberies for hours—bars, gas stations—and still we thought the cops were there by coincidence. So we turn and—boom!— there's a barricade of cop cars: seven of them. I had the gun. The cops had their guns out, and they were screaming at me, 'Don't you fuckin' move or we'll blow your brains out.' And all I kept thinking was Where can I hide the gun? The visor! That's it! The visor! So I start to lift the gun a little toward the visor and they're screaming, 'Put your hand down! Don't move!' None of it seemed real. The gun. The robberies. I was the dangerous one because I had some sense of crazy purpose—to get my father's attention. Finally, I flicked the gun under the seat, and they rushed the car and cuffed us and banged us around a little. We were under arrest."

This was Teddy Atlas's second felony arrest in three days. He was put in a cell on Rikers Island facing up to ten years in prison. Bail was set at forty thousand dollars. His father refused to pay.

On a Saturday evening in June, the night of the Mike Tyson–Lou Savarese fight, I had dinner with Atlas and Jack Newfield at Ballato's, on Houston Street. At dinner, Atlas predicted that Tyson would win in the first round. When I first met Atlas, three years ago, he predicted that Tyson would lose to Evander Holyfield. With Newfield, he had been more specific: Tyson would discover that he could not beat Holyfield right away and before too long he would foul—he would butt or bite Holyfield, anything to end it with a disqualification.

Later, after Tyson had indeed bitten Holyfield twice and lost, Atlas really went on a rant with Ron Borges, the boxing writer for *The Boston Globe:* "I called this one right. Not that I'm no freakin' genius, but I know human nature. I know fighters. I know this particular guy." Atlas could make the claim. He goes back twenty years with Tyson.

Atlas was in Rikers for a few weeks before his father finally did pay the bail (not least because his wife threatened to divorce him if he did not; Dr. Atlas put up his house as collateral). While Teddy awaited trial, Kevin Rooney introduced him to the fight trainer Cus D'Amato, who had led both Floyd Patterson and José Torres to world titles, and Teddy began boxing seriously under D'Amato's tutelage. Atlas avoided prison largely because D'Amato came to the courthouse and told the judge that he had met the young fighter, and that he had "special character." It would be a mistake to put him in jail, he said. D'Amato, an emotionally theatrical man, wept on the witness stand. The judge trusted D'Amato's evaluation and his intuition, and he released Atlas on probation under the condition that he live and work with D'Amato at his house and training camp upstate, in Catskill. Teddy was nineteen; D'Amato was in his late sixties.

D'Amato was by then semi-retired; he was past thinking he'd ever train another champion, but he enjoyed taking in young fighters. He filled them with his cracker-barrel philosophies: that a fighter has to convert his fears into strength, that he cannot afford to lie to himself. He looked a great deal like Rod Steiger, but in the corner he sounded not a little like Burgess Meredith in *Rocky.* At times, D'Amato made his accommodations with the sleazy boxing world, but he also kept clear of men like Frankie Carbo and Blinky Palermo, the mobsters who controlled nearly every champion and contender of their era. Sportswriters loved him. Teddy Atlas came to love him, too. Atlas won a Golden Gloves title, but he would go no further as an athlete; he had a bad back. For some obscure reason, D'Amato saw Atlas as a trainer, a teacher, and put him in charge of the day-to-day training at his gym.

In 1980, Tyson came to Catskill from the Tryon School for Boys, an upstate reform school, and D'Amato gave him to Atlas to train. Tyson was thirteen years old, a hundred and ninety pounds, and soon D'Amato was talking about him as the next heavyweight champion of the world. There is no overstating the emotional bond that grew up between Tyson and Atlas. In Brooklyn, where Tyson lived as a child, and then in reform school, no one had ever paid him much attention, no one had ever cared enough about him to teach him, to put limits on him. After some bouts, Tyson and Atlas would kiss. When Tyson started crying before an amateur fight in Colorado Springs, Atlas knew just the right words to get him into the ring. The job was to harness his ferocity and confine it to the ring and, at the same time, keep together a fragile psyche.

D'Amato liked Atlas. Not only was Atlas taking good care of Tyson, bringing him along, fight by fight; he also saw how dedicated Atlas was to his lesser fighters, how he would drive them every week in a borrowed station wagon to a gym on Westchester Avenue, in the South Bronx, for Saturday-night "smokers," thrown-together amateur bouts, that helped raise their skills, their experience, their self-esteem. The place in the Bronx smelled of sweat and urine and cigar smoke, and at times the referee was drunk, and customers gambled on the fights, but it was worth it: the kids were learning. Sometimes, Atlas had to struggle to get D'Amato to notice.

"Cus would be watching *Barney Miller* and *M°A°S°H* all the time over at the house while I was in the gym till ten every night," Atlas said. "I'd beg him to come. I'd say, 'Cus, fuck *Barney Miller*! Come to the gym! Look at this.' And finally he saw that we had thirty kids and fifteen of them were pretty good. And he said, 'Atlas is a teacher.' And that made me feel really good."

For a while, Atlas saw Cus D'Amato as his surrogate father, a more present and expressive father. In all his years in Catskill, Atlas never got a salary, but still he was convinced that he was getting an invaluable education from a master and, together with D'Amato, building something important. The problem was Tyson. They were splitting over Tyson. As he got older, Tyson developed a sense of invulnerability.

He could do anything. When he got in trouble in school for threatening a teacher or harassing girls (and that was often), Atlas would try to discipline him by suspending him from the gym, but then he would be overruled and undermined by D'Amato. The way Atlas saw it, D'Amato was cutting corners for Tyson, because, above all, he wanted one last champion, one more before he died. Nothing mattered as much, including his principles.

While Atlas was in Catskill, he had married a local girl named Elaine. They moved out of D'Amato's house and were living in a small apartment in town. One day in 1982, Atlas came home and saw Elaine and her eleven-year-old sister sitting at the kitchen table crying. They told Atlas that Tyson, who was then sixteen, had come on to the girl, had touched her, demanded things from her, sexual things. Atlas left the apartment in a rage. He was convinced that Tyson knew exactly what he was doing: by assaulting Teddy's eleven-year-old sister-in-law, he was flaunting his power over the girl and over Atlas.

"This was evil," Atlas told me. "That was taking what no one has a right to take. Sometimes it's better to take someone's life than the life within them."

Atlas went to a friend, a nightclub owner in town. "I knew he had a gun. It was a .38 revolver. I flicked it open, made sure it was loaded, stuck it in my waistband, and left."

In the late afternoon, he worked with his young fighters and then waited around, thinking about what to do. It was getting dark. By chance, a cab pulled up in front of the gym, and Tyson got out.

"I was gonna do whatever I had to do. I was gonna make sure he understood what he'd done, what it meant to people—to real people—and that he would never do it again."

Tyson came toward Atlas, and Atlas grabbed him by the head and pulled him into an alley outside the gym. He drew the gun and jammed it hard into Tyson's ear.

"I said, 'You piece of shit! You piece of shit. Don't you ever put your hands on my family. I will kill you. Do you understand this?' If he would have smiled, if he would have said no, I would have killed him. And I would have lived with that. I'm not saying that's right, but at that time that's what it was for me. When I wasn't sure how to save his life, how to give him a chance, I pulled the gun away from his ear and pulled the trigger. I fired. At that moment, he knew. He got very weak. I could see that in his eyes. That was to let him know this wasn't anything other than what it was. His ear was probably ringing pretty hard and he fell backward a little. . . . Cus had never let Tyson know that the things he was doing to people were real. I was letting him know."

D'Amato's way of solving the problem was to hold on to Tyson and to send an emissary to Atlas with a deal: If Atlas left, he would get five percent of Tyson's earnings for life. Though Atlas could not have known that Tyson would earn tens of millions of dollars, it was clear that he was going to be a heavyweight contender; Atlas refused the deal. Within a week, after going with his kids to the Adirondack Golden Gloves competition, he and Elaine left Catskill and never dealt with D'Amato or Tyson again.

"So now I had my precious apprenticeship, my Harvard degree," Atlas said wryly. "Elaine and I moved into my parents' basement, and I started working with fighters in Brooklyn."

After dinner, Teddy, Jack, and I went to Newfield's place, on Charlton Street, to watch Tyson fight Savarese on television. The pre-fight clips ran through the history: D'Amato died in November 1985; one year later, Tyson became, at twenty, the youngest world heavyweight champion ever, and the most disgraceful—the rape conviction, a prison sentence, the Holyfield "bite fight," the innumerable reports of wife abuse, street fighting. Before the Savarese fight, in Glasgow, Tyson reportedly pushed the promoter around.

Tyson had no problem with Savarese, whose fighting style resembled that of an oak. Atlas's prediction was on the money. Tyson hit Savarese with a left hook, and down he went. Savarese seemed relieved. He was alive, after all. Before it was over, Tyson managed to ignore the referee when he stepped in to separate the two fighters. Tyson felled the referee, too. He was, as usual, out of control. And after the fight—a thirty-eight-second fight—Tyson started ranting about eating his opponents' hearts, about eating their children, and about wanting to demolish the current champion, Lennox Lewis. "I'm Sonny Liston! I'm Jack Dempsey!" he raged on.

"Tyson loves this part," Atlas said. "He may be the best of all time at this part."

The team around Tyson made a fortune. Atlas struggled to pay his bills. In the next ten years, he had some good fighters, some contenders, but a fighter with Tyson's skill does not come around often. In late 1993, a heavyweight contender named Michael Moorer was looking for a trainer. He had exhausted the patience of many trainers already. Moorer was not quite in Tyson's class as a bad actor, nor was he Gentleman Jim. He wore a T-shirt reading "U Have the Right 2 Remain Violent." In high school, he pounded another kid's head—with a hammer, the injured boy's father insisted. His gun collection included Uzis, AK-47s, shotguns, and pistols. His curiosity about physics was unlimited. "I want to break a cheekbone to see what it looks like pushed in," he once announced.

And yet as a fighter Moorer was given to passivity. For all his potential, he seemed to make what both D'Amato and Atlas called the silent contract: the tacit treaty with an opponent to do no great harm.

Teddy's job was to get Moorer ready for the fight of his life, a heavyweight championship bout with Evander Holyfield, in April 1994. (Tyson was in an Indiana prison serving time for the rape of Desiree Washington.) Moorer had heard all about Atlas, about the motivational speeches, the discipline, the code, and he thought he wanted it. But first, it seemed, he had to test both Atlas and himself.

Moorer trained for the Holyfield fight in Palm Springs, California. One night, at around ten, Moorer called Atlas and said, "I ain't running tomorrow."

Atlas smiled. "I had to think, Why would he call and warn me?" he said. "I put on my sneakers and go on over to his room. He pulls open the door a crack—he's got the chain on—and he says, 'What do you want?' I says, 'I came here to read you a fuckin' bedtime story. What do you think I came here for? You're running tomorrow. Open the door.' And he does, and the next thing you know we're going back and forth. We almost get into a fistfight. I tell him, 'You either run or get on a plane and fly home. But you'll have to live with not wanting to fight this fight. You're going to have to live with not being ready to take a heavyweight championship against Evander Holyfield.' We pushed each other. We were chest to chest. All that sharp stuff. He just wanted to see if I'd stand up when there was a risk for me. He was afraid. This was just after Holyfield had beaten Riddick Bowe. He cursed, and we banged a little, and then finally he put his sneakers on and went out and ran into the night! And then the next morning at five he ran again. See, Michael wanted to be the champion of the world, but he didn't know how. And he had to test me, to see if maybe I did. His M.O. had been to quit in training camp. He wanted someone to make him be good, to make him be brave. But no one can make you brave."

The Moorer-Holyfield fight became as freighted with meaning for the trainer as it was for the fighter. A few months before, Theodore Atlas, Sr., died. Teddy buried his father, and he went to the gym that afternoon. "I finally understood things from my father's point of view. My father was not always the best father in the world, but he was the best professional."

At Newfield's, we watched a tape of the Moorer-Holyfield fight.

"You know, I've never seen it since that night," Teddy said. "Michael was filled with self-doubt, and I saw that I had to help him face the fight. I had to validate a lot of things. It was almost as if, well, if we hadn't won, it would be almost as if my father didn't exist."

What followed was not the most remarkable fight anyone had ever seen (at times, the proceedings were as listless as an August afternoon in

Savannah), and yet it was the most inspired moment of training, of coaching, imaginable. Time and again, Moorer would sign on to the silent contract, he would back away, clinch, punch aimlessly, as if he were killing time and waiting for a bus. And every time Moorer reached the critical list, every time he seemed about to check out of the fight, Atlas was in his face, shouting, "Back this guy up and do what we did in training. Otherwise don't come back to this fuckin' corner! Do you hear me!" After one of those harangues, Moorer opened a cut over Holyfield's eye. Then he receded again.

After eight rounds, Moorer was not doing enough to win. He was mainly finding ways not to get hurt. It was the most curious thing: Holyfield was clearly exhausted, in bad form, but Moorer wanted no part of him.

In Holyfield's corner, his trainer was saying things like "Breathe deep" and "Relax" and "Jesus loves you."

Atlas, as the consultants like to say, was more proactive. Before Moorer got back to the corner, Atlas took the stool and sat in it and started screaming, screaming as loud as a man can scream. Moorer, breathing deep, sweat pouring down his face and body, looked down at him, incredulous.

"Do you want me to change places with you? You want me to fight? You want me to change places with you? Listen! This guy is finished." Atlas now got up from the stool. Moorer sat down. Atlas kept at it, but with an actor's modulation, for surely he must have picked up the cadences from *Requiem for a Heavyweight.* He hit every note just right.

"There comes a time in a man's life when he makes a decision to just live, survive—or he wants to win. You're making a decision just to survive. You're doing just enough to keep him off ya and hope he leaves ya alone. You're *lying* to yourself, and I'd be lying to you if I didn't tell you that. And if you don't change you're going to be cryin' tomorrow! Now go out there and back him up and fight a full round."

After every round until the last, the twelfth, Atlas kept beating the same themes:

"You're blowing it! And you're gonna cry afterward because he'll lose the next fight and not this one. This is the fight of your life! This is the rest of your life!"

"Michael, in your mind you are doing your best. But you're not doing your best. Have I ever lied to you?"

Inspired at last, Moorer started hitting. Just in time. He won a split decision and the heavyweight championship—a title that, even if briefly held, guarantees a man tens of millions of dollars. Atlas's achievement was arguably greater than if he had brought Tyson to the title, for Tyson's talent was enormous. Michael Moorer was the least gifted heavyweight champion since Primo Carnera.

In the ring, Moorer went to embrace Atlas, but Teddy somehow could not let up. "You coulda done more, Michael," he said. And then Atlas wandered around, looking for his two young children.

"I felt like I had buried my father, and now I wanted my kids," he said.

Atlas and I were sitting in a pizza place not far from Marciano's Gym, in Jersey City. Things were going all right for him. He drove a red Lexus sports car that Moorer had given him after the title fight. He and Elaine had just built a house. He had his ESPN job and his fighter, Muriqi. But there was no big money. Atlas would have got eight hundred thousand dollars of Moorer's eight million for the Holyfield rematch, but the two men fell out when Moorer considered switching management.

For a while, Moorer was happier with his new trainer, Freddie Roach, because, he said, "Freddie allows me to be me."

When I repeated Moorer's line, Atlas laughed. "My job was *not* to let Michael be Michael," he said. Moorer lost to Holyfield in the rematch, and he has more or less disappeared from the scene.

Moorer used to call Atlas from time to time, usually when he'd been drinking. He made overtures to him to come back. But Atlas refused the pleading. Once, when he was furious with Moorer, he wrote a letter accusing the fighter of betrayal. It began without a salutation: "I won't call you by name. You don't have a name as far as I'm concerned. I am writing this for one reason—so you don't get a free ride thinking and telling yourself lies." At one point, I asked Atlas whether he was being too tough, too unforgiving. After all, he'd been given second and third chances, he'd been forgiven more than once.

Atlas paused awhile, and then he said, "There's a chance you are right. What's the sense of being so strict with other people? But you have to understand my world. I'm not dealing with stockbrokers or doctors. This is a world where if you don't come back in the proper way I can't be a top trainer. There are certain balances, certain codes that have to be answered to and paid for. When I'm in a gym demanding that a person make certain concessions, I have to have a certain landscape to do that in. By giving someone too much room in this world means you lose. Michael called me from a bar drunk, and then he got arrested in Tennessee for driving into a ditch. I told him to remember who he was, that he shouldn't be there, hanging out with those jerkoffs he hangs out with. He told me he loved me, and I said, 'Look Michael, love yourself and get out of there.'

"You see, boxing is a great equalizer. It's a metaphor for a lot of shit. In boxing, you get to see everything. People are exposed. The temptations are big, and they're contained in a small area. And the serpent is always either money or ego. But I can't walk away. I couldn't just quit it all. This is what I do."

A couple of weeks later, I flew up to Hyannis to see Elvir Muriqi's rematch with Dan Sheehan. The fight was part of a Friday night ESPN2 card, and the network was promoting it as "The War at the Shore 3." The arena, the Cape Cod Melody Tent, is the summer venue for a lot of geezer rock bands. Chicago was a sellout.

The dressing rooms were in a shed beyond the tent. When I got there, about a dozen fighters and their trainers, some with family and girlfriends, milled around nervously in a couple of dim rooms. Muriqi tried to nap on a couch, but without much success. All the fighters looked nervous, from the most promising heavyweight to the eternal set-'em-up (one ancient from Panama had a record of 8-42-1). They shadow-boxed, they stood stock still and stared at the wall, they gossiped with one another—no matter what they did, you could tell they were nervous.

Atlas walked in and looked around. "This never changes," he said. "Through the annals of time, this never changes."

I stopped by the other dressing room and saw Muriqi's opponent, Dan Sheehan, a beefy young man with a square jaw. He stood up. His trunks were of red sequin, like Dustin Hoffman's gown in *Tootsie*. Muriqi wore black.

The ESPN producer told the trainers to get their fighters ready at nine; this would be the first televised fight of the night.

As Atlas greased Muriqi's brow, he softly told him, "You know what you got to do. Pressure makes you forget. The pro remembers."

They marched into the tent. About half the seats were filled, mostly with Irish kids from around the state who were there to see their friends. One of them was Dan Sheehan. As soon as the fight began, it was pretty clear that Muriqi should win. His mechanics, which were adequate, were practically balletic compared to Sheehan's. But, round after round, Muriqi let opportunities pass. He would strike once and then step back, as if to admire his handiwork. He would duck a punch but then make nothing of it. In Atlas-ese, he was not doing what needed doing. After every round, Atlas told him these things in his usual terms: "Punch more! Make the choice to punch!" "Stop lying to yourself!"

As Atlas came down the steps with the stool and settled into the pit to watch Muriqi in the fifth, he turned to me and said, "He's making the choice just to get by. He's satisfied, but I can't let him be satisfied. I have to tell him. I gotta be the bad parent."

Muriqi finished well in the sixth, the final round, but he never really hurt Sheehan. This did not promise well for his dreams. He will not be rich, not from boxing.

As we waited in the ring for the decision, Muriqi and Sheehan embraced. Once, twice, three times. Sheehan kissed Muriqi on the brow. Fight fans are often stunned by these shows of affection, but they are genuine; they seem like gestures of mutual relief, like passengers who have just survived a dangerous flight. *We made it.* The ring announcer gave the decision: Muriqi on all three cards. Muriqi went to embrace Atlas, but Atlas, almost imperceptibly, stepped back, patted Muriqi on the shoulder. He was not through teaching, even now.

"You gotta throw more punches," he told him. "You gotta do better now, or you won't later."

The next morning, I flew back to LaGuardia with Atlas, and I asked him why a fighter like Muriqi, with decent skills and the willingness to listen, could not follow up on his corner's repeated instructions.

"It's the pressure, that dome of pressure that the civilian can't quite comprehend," he said. "Nature, everyone's nature, is to avoid what's gonna bring you closer to danger and risk. The reason he didn't throw those extra punches, no matter how much he listened and nodded yes to me, was because he allowed his weaker nature to tell him, 'You don't *have* to do this.' The basis of nature is to survive. What I'm telling him is against nature. I'm telling him how to be a brute and not just survive. A trainer's got to lead a fighter into a dark place, and not too many want to go."

(2000)

Comeback:
Larry Holmes

L ike epic poetry, boxing is a dead art. In both cases, there are modern
practitioners, even interesting ones—James Merrill and Vikram
Seth made passes at the epic; Mike Tyson had his moment a decade
ago—but in both cases the era is one not of bronze but of lead. It is only
in such a fallen age that, in the wake of the great Tyson ear-chomping
episode, the art of boxing would try to redeem itself with the spectacle of
Larry Holmes, age (and waist) forty-seven, versus a young slip of a fellow
named Maurice. Last week's fight took place not in Madison Square
Garden but in its miniature annex, the venue for such parental jungle
missions as *Sesame Street Live.*

In his time, Holmes was a distinguished champion, just one tier below
the empyrean once occupied by his old sparring partner Muhammad
Ali. Above the shoulders, Holmes looks much the same, except that he
now lacks the sense to stay home. His head is tapered like a rocket shell,
making him, at one time anyway, hard to hit. He entered the arena to the
sounds of "Ain't No Stopping Us Now," a tune as foreign to the young as

"*E lucevan le stelle.*" Once inside the ring, Holmes kept his satin robe on for as long as possible, but, like any middle-aged man facing the terrible reckoning of the day at the beach, he soon had to face facts and disrobe. It was instantly apparent that he had been training on doughnuts and naps. Covering the ruins of his bulky musculature was the sort of thick coating of insulation traditionally worn by nineteenth-century bankers and modern television repairmen. He was very fat. The promoters were hoping that Holmes would triumph and then go on to a big-money fight against the other hulking geriatric of the sport, George Foreman, and so they selected an opponent rather the way royal gamekeepers used to select a particularly lame deer for the king's afternoon hunt. Maurice—Maurice Harris, of Newark—is twenty-one and, coming into the fight, boasted a "winning record" most narrowly defined: nine wins, eight losses, and two draws.

From the opening bell onward, Maurice discovered that the old man was very old indeed, and gained confidence. Every time he snapped a jab into Holmes's face, the Holmes family, seated at ringside, would wince as one.

"C'mon, Daddy! Double up!"

Daddy could not double up. He could not have beaten Maurice if he had been handed a baseball bat. The fight went the distance, ten rounds, and one truly feared that Holmes would end up with an attack of angina. His face was a puffy bruise. He couldn't have won more than three rounds. But boxing being boxing, of course, the judges awarded him the fight.

"I wish Daddy would stop," Holmes's daughter, Kandie, said as the family filed toward the locker rooms. The Champ was at his end, and so, too, it seemed, was boxing, though both promised to go on and on.

(1997)

The Moralist:
Lennox Lewis

From distant shores, it is hard to figure out why so few Britons have proved supreme in the prize ring since the passing of the Regency era and the advent of the padded glove. An age of futility has followed William Hazlitt's patriotic contention that "the noble science of boxing is all our own." England has certainly not lost its taste for the fight—there are still would-bes sparring in gyms from Merseyside to Brixton—and yet most of the British moderns, especially the heavyweights, pale, bony men like Henry Cooper, have been notable mainly for a stoutness of soul that is inevitably undermined by a propensity to bleed.

Until now, the last British champion among the heavies was Robert Prometheus Fitzsimmons, who won his title in Carson City, Nevada, in 1897 (a blow to the solar plexus doubled up "Gentleman Jim" Corbett), and lost it two years later to James Jeffries at Coney Island. Fitzsimmons was not a champion of the first rank. Nor was he an impressive specimen. He was spindly, knock-kneed, and rapidly losing his carrot-colored hair. "Stripped for action he looked like an elderly red pelican," wrote the estimable boxing historian O. F. Snelling. To make things worse for loyal Britons, Fitzsimmons was an inconstant national. He and his family had left England for New Zealand when he was nine, and he died, in 1917, in Chicago—a citizen of the United States.

Lennox Lewis, the current heavyweight champion, is a legit Brit. He is thirty-six and was born in England; he spent his childhood in the East End. But the story grows motley from there. Lennox was an adolescent in Kitchener, Ontario, won an Olympic gold medal for Canada, in 1988, and, since his parents are Jamaican, is, by his own description, "part Rasta man." Lewis speaks in what might be called High Plains–Cockney–Bob Marley, an accent rounded off by the influence of the high-rent precincts he now inhabits in Hertfordshire and Miami, to say nothing of the Concorde waiting lounge. Lewis, in other words, is a man of the fluid modern world. This is not something the English customarily appreciate: to leave London and make a success elsewhere is often a mark of betrayal. And yet at Lewis's fights, wherever they may be, his most ardent fans, his most reliable supporters, are British. When Lewis fought Evander Holyfield at the Garden three years ago and the judges robbed him of a decision—they called it, preposterously, a draw after Lennox had pummeled Evander all night—Eighth Avenue was suddenly awash in men in Union Jack T-shirts and Bob Hoskins sharkskins, who improvised pleasantly obscene chants limning their outrage and their undying affection for Lewis.

It is no fault of Lewis's, but the heavyweight championship, like the British throne, is an ever more marginal office. Just as Elizabeth II struggles to dampen the *News of the World* impression of her unruly clan, Lewis has, for years, been haunted by his own tabloid ghost, Mike Tyson. No matter that Tyson has not been himself as an athlete since his incarceration, in the early nineties, for raping a beauty queen in Indianapolis. Somehow the legacy of Tyson's youthful ferocity—his string of one- and two-round knockouts when he was barely out of his teens—coupled with his penchant for theatrically toxic behavior and interviews scripted by a hip-hop Jean Genet, grabbed whatever little cultural fascination was left to the fight game. Lewis was justly convinced that he would not be acknowledged a "supreme sweet scientist" (he loves the Regency terminology) until he had defeated Tyson.

On January 22, the fighters and their myriad seconds gathered at the Hudson Theatre, on West Forty-fourth Street, to announce that the fight would take place in Las Vegas. Unfortunately, Tyson decided to act up, and he walked toward his opponent in what Lewis described to me as "a most provocative fashion." Suddenly, the two fighters and their seconds were on the floor in a tumbling scrum, and somewhere in the pile, unseen by the cameras, Tyson bit Lewis on the thigh, a poetic echo of his double chomp of Evander Holyfield's ear, in 1997. Lewis wisely kept the crescent-shaped wound to himself; to have revealed it before the fight was safely rescheduled would have been to risk a fight he yearned for, to say nothing of a purse of at least seventeen million dollars. Tyson declared himself contrite (he allowed that he was no angel, but no mass murderer, either). Nevada could not bring itself to understand, but Memphis, hungry for spectacle and revenue, was more forgiving. The match was set for June 8.

A few weeks before the fight, I visited Lewis at his training camp in the Poconos. I went twice, first with a passel of other reporters, and a second time alone. At the initial meeting, Lewis decided that he could now confirm the bite without risk of cancellation. "I was surprised he saw my leg as a pork chop," he said, sitting on the edge of the ring mat. Lewis was wearing running clothes, and his dreadlocks were tucked demurely under a Jamaican knit hat. "I went up to my hotel room and got my tetanus shot," he continued. "I didn't say anything, so he couldn't get out of the fight." Lewis passed around a photograph that had been taken of his thigh: a terrible disgrace, we all agreed, as we solemnly passed the forensics from hand to hand. The bite, Lewis declared, "changed the whole thing." He would fight with vengeance, as well as simple victory, in mind. This was hard to believe. Lewis is enormous—six-five, two hundred and forty-odd pounds, and with the musculature of a tight end—and yet neither his fighting style nor his character suggests a tendency to rage. He is laid-back, meticulous in his training habits, a moralist. There is something high-minded about him, at least relative to Tyson. Lewis had been offended not merely by the nibble in New York but also by a meeting with some invited reporters which Tyson had conducted in his training camp in Hawaii just a few days earlier. It had been a vintage Tyson performance, full of contempt for his visitors and fury at the world; there is more nihilism in an hour with Tyson than in a chapter of *The Possessed*.

"I'm just a dark guy from the den of iniquity," Tyson told the gathering. "You guys would rather be with someone else who's equal to your status in life. Tiger Woods, or somebody. I come across as crass, a Neanderthal, a babbling idiot sometimes. I like to show you that person. I like that person. He makes you want to come and listen to me.

"You guys have written so much bad stuff about me I can't remember the last time I fucked a decent woman. I have to go with strippers and hos and bitches because you put that image on me."

Tyson expressed a desire to "kill" Lewis, to "smear his brains" around the ring. He had been disrespected, he said. At Crustacean, a restaurant in Beverly Hills, Tyson's wife at that time had spotted Lewis and told her husband to be gracious, to go over to Lennox and say hello. Tyson agreed reluctantly and approached the champion, but Lewis did not return the greeting. He just stared Tyson down, and Tyson was humiliated. Tyson explained the moment thus: "My wife took my balls from underneath me. She gave this punk-ass motherfucker my nuts."

And on it went. In the absence of a comedian like Muhammad Ali or a wizened don like Archie Moore, Tyson is what passes in the fight game for "colorful." We are asked to understand that he represents a certain racial and hip-hop generational "feeling," yet he rarely betrays a rapper's pleasure in the perquisites he has allowed himself: the fleet of cars, the houses, the racing pigeons, the pet tigers. As the fight approached, loathing and self-loathing defined Tyson's entire sentimental range. "I wish that you guys had children, so I could kick them in the fucking head or stomp on their testicles so you could feel my pain," he said.

When these comments were played back to Lewis in the Poconos, his reaction was wry. "We've heard all these words before—though not the testicle ones, that was new," he said. "This is how he carries on. Life is evolution, and he shows he hasn't graduated. After a while, you have to self-teach. He sounds like a cartoon character when he says those things. He sounds like an ignorant person. Mike Tyson wants to be seen as the baddest man on the planet. But I don't even think he wants to fight, listening to what he's saying. You can't help but feel sorry for him. This is definitely a puppy with some problems."

A few days later, I drove back to Lewis's camp. He and his entourage, led by the trainer Emanuel Steward, a "chief confidant" from Ghana named Prince, and his mother, Violet, were set up in a series of cabins in the town of Scotrun, Pennsylvania, near the Delaware Water Gap. The cabins were part of a modest resort, where the honeymoon suites had heart-shaped tubs and there was archery and miniature golf for the kids and paddleboats on a lake. It was the sort of quiet sylvan outpost that boxers forty or fifty years ago used to favor. Every afternoon, Lewis did his floor work and sparring in a barnlike gym near the lake. His handlers made much of the fact that I was being allowed to watch him spar, as if his fight plan for Tyson could not have been predicted. (Survive Tyson's early charges, fend him off with the long left jab, tire him out, and then finish it.) In the ring, Lewis was dealing with a stumpy Tyson simulacrum named Egerton Marcus, who was fat around the middle but did a decent job of aping Tyson's bobble-head style. Lewis was trim and faster than usual, and he picked apart Marcus, bouncing jab after jab off the brow of his headgear. Lewis grew up idolizing Muhammad Ali and, like dozens of fighters of his generation, took on all of Ali's dubious habits, especially the way he kept his hands low and depended for defense on his ability to fall away from a punch. The imitation is reasonable—Raymond Chandler doing Hemingway—but not the real article, either. Lewis has never had Ali's foot or hand speed or his ability to shift tactics mid-battle. Still, he looked sharp, and it was only his gentlemanly adherence to custom that prevented him from flattening the Tyson doppelgänger before him. After eight rounds of sparring, Lewis climbed out of the ring, smiled at me, and said, "You wouldn't believe we're good friends, would you?"

While I waited for Lewis to shower, I met his mother, a plump, quiet woman in her sixties, who had been present at her son's camp from the start. Lewis has a girlfriend, too, but she was barred from camp. In training, Lewis, unlike Tyson, unlike many of the moderns, practices the Spartan code: work, celibacy, boredom, and games—chess, mainly. The maternal presence provides warmth but a certain added discipline, too. "My mother grounds me," Lewis told me later in the day. "She still tells me to clean up my room."

Violet Lewis grew up poor in Port Antonio, Jamaica, and one of her few pleasures was to watch the rich people on the island, Errol Flynn among them, come and go from their yachts. When Violet was a teenager, her family shipped her off to London, where they thought the economic prospects would be better. In London, she lived in tenement houses and worked as a nurse's aide. She had a boyfriend, a Jamaican auto-plant worker named Carlton Brooks, but, when Violet became pregnant with Lennox, Brooks finally informed her that in fact he had a family back in Jamaica. He could not marry Violet. "I was thinking about it all the time. Should I abort the baby?" she told her son's ghostwriter, Joe Steeples. "The sister at the hospital booked an appointment for me, but I couldn't do it. The sister knew I had a son already, and she said, 'It's going to be even more difficult for you, Vi. It's going to be very hard. Think about it.'" She did, and gave birth to Lennox, already a giant at ten pounds, ten ounces. Years later, in another search for a better job, Violet left Lennox with an aunt in London while she tried to make a go of it in

Kitchener. She found a job in a styrofoam factory—a job that she held for seventeen years, until Lennox became a professional fighter and told her to quit. Lennox was a big athletic kid and a fighter, a hothead, who seemed to be on an errant path, especially during the years that he was separated from his mother. "I think to a degree I had it in me to become a delinquent, but always inside me I was ruled by good ethics and good moral codes," he once said. "When my mother sent for me to join her in Canada"—he was eleven—"I think I was caught at the right time. It was a complete change for me, a change for the better."

Manny Steward was waiting for Lewis to dress. Steward, who runs the Kronk Gym, in Detroit, is preternaturally calm, an abundantly experienced trainer. When Lewis lost in 1994 to a mediocrity named Oliver McCall, he sensibly robbed McCall of his trainer, Steward, and they have worked together ever since. In recent years, the men in Tyson's corner have usually been hysterics of meager knowledge. This, perhaps, was Lewis's most distinct advantage. As we looked out the gym window at a sailboat on the lake, I remarked to Manny that none of the vacationers here seemed to care much that the heavyweight champion was working out. "Well, camps are always a reflection of the fighter," Steward said. "Lennox likes the tranquillity here, the organization. But, you know, Lennox is my twenty-ninth champion—I've been in boxing for fifty years—and he is the biggest party animal of them all. He knows where to go in every city you can imagine. He's better than Leon Spinks, better than anybody. He'll pick me up at three in the morning and start from there. But when we're in training—nothing. He's the consummate professional. If he has a fault, it's that he thinks too much, he's too intelligent. But eventually he snaps out of it. When he gets hit, it kind of stimulates him. And then he responds."

Another Ghanaian in Lewis's camp, a "media man" named Kojo, took me to a cabin across the lake. I played chess there with Prince, who has known Lewis for years.

"Lennox plays all the time," Prince said, "and he always beats me."

"What have we got here?" Lewis said as he came in and settled on a couch. He was relaxed, happy to be finished with his work for the day. He was looking forward to dinner, a game of Ping-Pong, maybe a video. Every day followed the ancient prescription: roadwork before dawn and sparring in the afternoon.

"Boxing is a job. It's my job," he said. "And here I'm like a man who gets up and puts his suit on and goes to work."

Sometimes, Lewis said, he had trouble sleeping, so deep was his obsession with beating Tyson. "I dream about the fight. I think about it all day long and when I go to sleep at night and then in my sleep. I see the fight like a math problem and I have to go out and solve it. How do you solve the problem of this boxer? To me, Mike Tyson is an easy problem. He's one-dimensional. He's going to come straight forward, like a whirlwind, I suppose. I won't have to go looking for him." Lewis said that he and Manny Steward had discussed how to react if Tyson tried to pull something. "I can't play into his madness," he said. "I had a dream that he bit me and I bit him back."

Lewis spotted a magazine tucked under my notebook.

"May I?" he said.

It was an issue of *Sports Illustrated,* which featured a photograph of Tyson on the cover, snarling, and a story that highlighted Tyson's profligacy between 1995 and 1997: $338,858 for "lawn care (Ohio)"; $309,133 for "lawn care (Las Vegas)"; etc.

Lewis glared at the cover.

Then he said, "My friends say, 'Can you believe they're putting Mike Tyson on the cover of *Sports Illustrated?*'" He was sounding more like Lady Astor now. "They focus on the evil and not on the good stuff. No one wants to celebrate the goodness, the gentlemen. Like me. Badness sells in America. I can understand the appeal of looking at train wrecks, but there are people getting killed in the meantime."

Lewis was not entirely censorious. He seemed almost wistful about four days he'd spent sparring in the Catskills with Tyson when they were both teenage prospects.

"In those days, I was just a junior fighter and I still thought of boxing as a sport," he said. "We both needed training, and they got us together. On the first day we were together, he came right at me—I still remember it clearly—and he tried to hurt me. That's what opened me up to the ferocity of boxing, that moment, and I thought, Right! This is how the game goes. And so I adapted. You need certain dramas in your life to wake you up to certain things. Tyson was the drama that opened me to the reality of boxing."

Lewis recalled fondly how the two would go at each other in the ring in the mornings and then hang up a white sheet on a bedroom wall in the evenings and, using a rickety projector, screen hours of old fights: Marciano, Louis, Willie Pep. But that had been a long time ago, before Tyson's rape conviction and the many other assaults on what Lewis called "decent society."

"Boxing's got a bad name, and he is the reason," Lewis said. "When I was coming up in the sport and trying to get sponsorship, they said No, back off, boxers rape people. This is what he created. I'm the knight in shining armor. And you know what else? I'm the hyena killer, the lion on my perch, watching those hyenas bothering my flock. When I'm good and ready, I swoop down and I snap their necks. Then I go back up on my perch and chill."

Forty years ago, when boxing was not the sideshow it is now, Presidents took an interest in matches of any moment, especially when there was a moral stake to be contrived. President Kennedy, in the hope of defending virtue against vice, encouraged Floyd Patterson, who had the endorsement of the NAACP, to defend his heavyweight title against Sonny Liston, an ex-con, who did not. Vice knocked out Virtue in two minutes, six seconds of the first round. In Memphis a few days before the Lewis-Tyson fight, the putative morality play of the event was not the source of much conversation. The question was whether the fight would happen at all. Would Tyson find a way to cancel? Would he bite Lewis? Would he try to break his arm? As a precaution, the two fighters were not to meet before the opening bell: they would have their own press conferences and weigh-ins; yellow-shirted security guards would form a human wall across the ring to keep the two camps apart until the bell.

On the day of the weigh-ins, at the Memphis convention center, I asked one of Tyson's trainers, Stacey McKinley, about the peculiar arrangements. "Lennox is the coward," he said. "He's the one crying that we need separate press conferences, separate flights to Memphis, separation in the ring. He's worried that he might run into Mike at Blockbuster. He's the coward. See, other than Mike, today's fighters are fraudulent. They hold, they hang on waiting for the bell to get some water. Everyone knows that when Mike Tyson fights he gives you a full three minutes. People want to see him. He's the original K.O. artist. Lennox is scared to death. He fights reluctantly. And a great fighter like Mike Tyson can sense that."

The oddsmakers did not. Lennox was favored to win fairly easily. The thinking was simple: in the past decade, Tyson had fought only one top heavyweight, Evander Holyfield—and he had lost twice. Lewis, on the other hand, although he was prone to distraction against inferior fighters, continued to get stronger, sharper, more dominant.

As the fight approached, the customary planeloads of hucksters and hookers arrived in town. (This demographic shift could be accurately observed in the lobby of the Peabody Hotel in the evenings and on Beale Street at midnight.) Memphis is not a fight town. Geoff Calkins, a sports columnist for the *Commercial Appeal,* wrote that until Lewis-Tyson the top bouts in the city included Elvis Presley's 1956 fistfight with a gas-station attendant; the time when Al Green's girlfriend hurled a pot of boiling grits at him while he was in the bath; and Andy Kaufman's Dada pro wrestling match in 1982 with Jerry (the King) Lawler. The biggest crowd for a fight in the city's history assembled on the banks of the Mississippi River in 1862: ten thousand Tennesseans saw the Union Navy rout the Confederate Navy, thereby securing the Memphis depot for the duration of the Civil War. The promoters of Lewis-Tyson were promising closer to fifteen thousand at the Pyramid, but they could not vouchsafe a sellout.

On the night of the fight, the skies above the Pyramid were choked with helicopters. It took a long time to get through the metal detectors and past the professional friskers, though it seemed that the women of uncertain profession, along with their raffish masculine handlers, were accorded more courtesy than the rest of us. There were certifiable celebrity types all around, mainly film stars like Denzel Washington, Morgan Freeman, and Samuel L. Jackson, and a flotilla of NBA players. There was much relief in finding out that one hadn't been given a seat behind Dikembe Mutombo or Magic Johnson. At a quarter past ten, the processionals began. Tyson, as the challenger, was herded to the ring first, skipping along to a rap beat and wearing his usual black Jack Dempsey outfit. Lewis let him linger there for a while, and then the PA system started pumping out Bob Marley's "Crazy Baldheads," and the champion made his entrance. I was sitting with two professorial figures, Michael Eric Dyson, of the University of Pennsylvania, and Stanley Crouch, of the *Daily News,* and both assured me that Tyson still had enough of his old power to win with a single punch (though they did not guarantee it) and that the challenger would have the crowd. I was surprised to hear both opinions. They were right about the crowd. All the cheering was for Tyson. America First prevailed over considerations of character.

At the bell, Tyson reprised his *el toro* routine, charging out at Lewis, snorting all the way, and, for a time, his aggression was rewarded. He landed a couple of rights. Tyson was not hitting Lewis especially well or hard, but Lewis's expression was worrying. He was wide-eyed, nervous, pawing at the air like an upended colt. But then, with a minute left in the round, things began to go as Manny Steward had predicted. Tyson's blows seemed to arouse Lewis: first his concern, then his interest, and, finally, his own keenness. The transformation in Lewis was reminiscent of Wilberforce (Battling) Billson, in P. G. Wodehouse's *He Rather Enjoyed It*:

A moment before the audience had been solidly anti-Billson. Now they were unanimously pro. For these blows, while they appeared to have affected him not at all physically, seemed to have awakened Mr. Billson's better feelings as if somebody had turned on a tap. They had aroused in Mr. Billson's soul that zest for combat which had been so sadly to seek in round one. For an instant after the receipt of that buffet on the ear the Battler stood motionless on his flat feet, apparently in deep thought. Then, with the air of one who has suddenly remembered an important appointment, he plunged forward.

By the second round, the pattern was thoroughly woven: Tyson would charge out to begin the round; Lewis would rebuff him, tie him up, and then commence rapping off his brow the stiffest left jab since Ali's in mid-career. In his prime, Tyson charged up to his opponent's chest and unleashed his blows; now, with Lewis stuffing his maw with jabs, he could not get within hitting range. For the rest of the bout, Tyson wore a permanent wince—the wince from the blow he'd just received and the wince anticipating the next.

"Tyson found it difficult to get to me," Lewis would tell me a few days later. "And it seemed that he burned up all his energy real fast. He exerts himself so much to do simple things and then he's gone. So I was playing the matador and he was the bull, running himself down. In the first round, he was like a whirlwind and I just let the whirlwind play itself out."

With every jab, a nimbus of sweat appeared around Tyson's skull and his head whipped backward on the stem of his neck. By the third round, there was a cut above his right eye and bloody little welts had begun to appear all over. In the third and the fourth, Lewis was utterly confident, cocky even, and he began following the jabs with harder right crosses and uppercuts, blows that would have knocked out nearly anyone else.

The cornermen also reflected the direction of the fight: there was panic and cross talk in Tyson's corner, with two or three people trying to issue orders at once. They had little to offer him other than the imprecations to "get closer" and "use your hands." By contrast, Steward saw it as his job to point out to Lewis just how bad Tyson looked—"You got a dead man in front of you!"—and to encourage him to finish the fight before some *x* factor (a bad decision, a head butt, a bite, something untoward) robbed him of certain victory. Soon, Steward was screaming—"Get this motherfucker outta here!" But Lewis stared vacantly. He was doing what he could. What he did not tell Steward was that in the fourth round he had hurt his right hand punching Tyson on the top of the head.

Rounds five, six, and seven were repetitive in the extreme, with Lewis winning every exchange; he was outpunching Tyson by four to one, according to the higher mathematicians at ringside. In the corner before the eighth round, Tyson's men were tending to his welts and swabbing the blood from his nostrils, and one of the trainers, Ronnie Shields, implored his man to throw punches. But Tyson quietly said, "You've got to stop it."

If it was possible to pity Tyson, now was the time. He plodded out gamely to the center of the ring to receive his final beating. After a little more than a minute, Lewis complied, connecting with a left uppercut and then a right that caused Tyson to genuflect but not quite fall. The referee, Eddie Cotton, who had been as solicitous as a grandfather to Tyson, stepped in and seemed to rule it a knockdown before there actually was one. Tyson soon went back into the fray but he could do nothing but wait for something more final. The blow came with less than a minute left, a quick, unseen right to the jaw, and now Tyson was on the canvas, blacked out, rubbing lightly at the blood under his eyes. Cotton counted to ten and then gently helped Tyson to his corner.

In the ring afterward, Tyson gave his best, and most winning, performance of the night, take it as you will. Gone was the thuggery and the nihilism of Maui. Tyson praised Lewis as unbeatable, a "magnificent" and "prolific" fighter, and he sweetly thanked Lewis for the consideration.

"The payday was wonderful," Tyson went on. "I really appreciate it. And if you would be kind enough, I would really love to do it again. I think I could beat you if we tried one more time." Tyson assured Lewis and anyone willing to believe him that all the talk in Maui had been a con: "Everything I said was in proposition for promoting the fight." When Lewis was given a chance to speak, Tyson made his most meaningful physical gesture of the night. With a look of love in his eyes, he gently wiped some blood off the champion's cheek. The blood, of course, was his own.

"Lennox knows I love him and his mother, too," Tyson said finally, and he kissed Violet to emphasize the point.

Later, in his dressing room, Tyson admitted that he probably had no hope of ever winning against Lewis and would likely drift into "oblivion." His only motivation for taking another such beating would be to work off the millions in debt he owes to the U.S. government; his adviser, Shelly Finkel; to his backer, Showtime; and, presumably, to his lawn- and pet-care proprietors. "If they pay me enough money, I'll fight a lion," he said.

Lewis, his entourage, and his girlfriend left Memphis as soon as they could and spent nearly a week partying in New York. They made the gossip columns with their choice of champagne: Cristal. Lewis stayed at a ten-thousand-dollar-a-night triplex on the highest floors of the Palace Hotel, on Madison Avenue. When I went to visit, he wore a perpetual grin, a gigantic cat who had drunk all the cream in the city. He stretched out on a gold couch and fairly purred.

I couldn't help it. "How does it feel, champ?" I asked.

"Look at me," he said. "I'm at the top of the food chain!" Indeed. Lewis may not rank with the top heavyweights in history—Johnson, Dempsey, Louis, Ali, Marciano—but now he could sensibly argue kinship with the next rung, with Charles, Frazier, Foreman, and Holmes, and there was, for the time being, no one around to touch him.

What little swelling there had been on Lennox's face was now gone, but he could not shake my hand. The fingers and wrist were still swollen. "Manny thought the referee was taking me out of the fight and creating possibilities for Tyson down the line," he said. "So he wanted me to take him out. But I really hurt my hand there in the fourth round, and I couldn't go crazy on him like I wanted."

Lewis is known as a gentleman, but he politely refused to feign friendship with, or even a belief in, the new, gentler version of Tyson. "I guess the way he talked in the ring afterward was admirable, but some people don't believe anything until you show them," he said. "They don't show respect until you beat it into their heads." The champion gave a quick, self-satisfied smile and gestured to his minions: they had a flight to catch for London. There were limits to his grace, after all.

(2002)

Tyson's Corner

It is always perilous to predict the end of anything (ask Francis Fukuyama), but it was surely an adequate sign of boxing's eclipse that, among the fifteen thousand people who paid to see Mike Tyson fight a very tall tomato can named Kevin McBride the other night at the MCI Center, in Washington, many more knew the details of Iron Mike's credit record (more than twelve million in arrears to Internal Revenue) than they did the current and parlous state of the heavyweight division.

As an athlete, Tyson misplaced his dark cloak of invincibility fifteen years ago in Tokyo, when a wan and pillowy pug named Buster Douglas knocked him out. Ever since, the pattern has been the same. Those whom Tyson could intimidate quickly with thudding left hooks and the memory of his criminal reputation were soon safely dispatched, but the game opponents who could brave two or three rounds of the Tysonian whirlwind profited by the desperate rages that inevitably followed: the ear-biting, the head-butting, the attempts to break a limb. Tyson would unravel, fall down, or be disqualified.

And so no one in Washington was paying for athletic display. Tyson was everyone's freak show, a grotesque and guilty entertainment at once violent, unpredictable, haunted, thrilling—but truly dangerous only to himself, to his opponent, and to those who, like Desiree Washington, the beauty queen, ended up testifying in court. People paid to see Mike Tyson, one ex-wife suggested, in the same spirit in which they went to horror movies or rode the roller coaster.

And yet Tyson also provided his audiences and chroniclers with a kind of three-penny Raskolnikov and Bigger Thomas. He asked to be pitied, adored, and despised; above all, he pitied, adored, and despised himself. He reeked authenticity. John McEnroe was outrageous to the extent that the son of a partner at Paul, Weiss, Rifkind, Wharton & Garrison can be outrageous. He never bit Bjorn Borg, never threatened to eat the spawn of Jimmy Connors. Tyson was unschooled in the niceties. He didn't know his father or who he might have been. His mother, Tyson once said, died in a cardboard box, and he was sure he would end up the same way. As a kid, he was a thug, following old ladies into elevators and beating them up and stealing their groceries. When he became champion, his renunciation of poverty was absolute. During one thirty-three-month period in the mid-nineties, he spent $4,477,498 on cars and motorcycles. (Over the years, he owned a red Lamborghini Countach, a Bentley, and a Lamborghini "jeep" that had been built for the Saudi king.) He spent $95,000 a month on jewelry and clothing, $411,777 on pigeons and cats, and an untold amount on pet lions, tigers, and "royal blood" Shar-Peis. When he was not training, he redirected his energies. For one erotic marathon, a satrap lined up twenty-four women for the night. His cultural influences were various. When all the tattooing was complete, his face was that of a Maori warrior; Mao smiled murderously from one biceps, and the pacific tennis ace Arthur Ashe was portrayed on the other. Ashe's widow, Jeanne, once said, "If I could sue a body part, I would."

That was the Tyson that all had come to see in Washington. But he was no Kid Dynamite now. Before the fight, Tyson told McBride that he would "gut him like a fish," but he said it gently and without conviction. All the indulgences are, for the most part, sold off, a memory. He lives now in a brick ranch house in a middle-class neighborhood in Scottsdale, Arizona, with a girlfriend and their two children. He refuses to be a monster. "I don't want to be that guy anymore," he said a few days before the fight.

The fight was the usual chapter in Tyson's late-mannerist phase. He was generous in referring to McBride as a "C fighter." McBride's physique suggested a taste for Guinness and idle afternoons in a lawn chair. And yet, in the first three rounds, he absorbed whatever simulacra of the old power Tyson could project. Tyson would hit him square on the jaw and McBride merely stepped back and blinked a few times, looking more confused than pained. Confused, perhaps, that he was not more in pain than he was. By the fourth round, McBride was emboldened to try some punching of his own, and Tyson was chewing on the thumb of his glove, a sure sign, to experienced observers, that he was tired and looking for a way out. In the corner, Tyson's trainer had only survivalist counsel to offer: "Breathe, Mike, breathe!" And in the sixth Tyson tried everything. He tried to break McBride's arm in the clinch, and, when that led to no conclusive injury, he cocked his head to the right and slammed it leftward into McBride's brow, opening a bloody cut. The referee penalized Tyson two points and gave McBride a moment to clear his head. Defogged and unfazed, McBride bullied Tyson into the ropes and belted him a few times and then, like a man looking for a boost from a friend, pressed down on Tyson's shoulders. Tyson couldn't bear the weight. He slumped to the canvas. And it was there, on his backside, that Tyson (if ensuing vows can be trusted) concluded his career. Once on his stool, he declined a seventh round. He had quit.

In the sweaty aftermath, Tyson was gracious to his opponent and stayed around to browse his own psyche one last time. "I'm a peasant," he said. "At one point, I thought life was about acquiring things. Life is totally about losing everything." Asked what he might do next, Tyson said, "I'm going to look into doing missionary work." Maybe in Africa, maybe Bosnia. He was unsure how he would pay his bills. Maybe he just wouldn't. He was sure, he said, only that the ferocity was gone. "I don't have it in me anymore," he said. "I can't even kill the bugs in my house."

(2005)

ACKNOWLEDGMENTS

I owe an enormous debt to all of my colleagues at *The New Yorker*. Without their indulgence I would not have had the opportunity to report and write for the magazine; and without their help on these pieces—without their counsel, editing, and fact-checking—I'd be in all kinds of trouble. I'd like to thank Dorothy Wickenden, Henry Finder, and Jeffrey Frank, my friend and editor for so many years, for their intelligent and meticulous work on these profiles and essays, and S. I. Newhouse, Jr., for his constant support. Sonny Mehta, Dan Frank, Pamela McCarthy, and Kathy Robbins made this book possible; Brenda Phipps, Beth Johnson, Dana Goodyear, Kate Taylor, and Louisa Thomas helped in a thousand ways; and Lillian Ross provided a title. And, above all, my love and gratitude to my family.